Less managing. More teaching. Greater learning.

 # INSTRUCTORS...

Would you like your **students** to show up for class more **prepared**? *(Let's face it, class is much more fun if everyone is engaged and prepared...)*

Want ready-made application-level **interactive assignments,** student progress reporting, and auto-assignment grading? *(Less time grading means more time teaching...)*

Want an **instant view of student or class performance** relative to learning objectives? *(No more wondering if students understand...)*

Need to **collect data and generate reports** required for administration or accreditation? *(Say goodbye to manually tracking student learning outcomes...)*

Want to **record and post your lectures** for students to view online?

 ## With **McGraw-Hill's *Connect™ Plus Marketing,***

INSTRUCTORS GET:

- Interactive Applications – **book-specific interactive assignments** that require students to APPLY what they've learned.

- Simple **assignment management,** allowing you to spend more time teaching.

- **Auto-graded** assignments, quizzes, and tests.

- **Detailed Visual Reporting** where student and section results can be viewed and analyzed.

- Sophisticated **online testing** capability.

- A **filtering and reporting** function that allows you to easily assign and report on materials that are correlated to accreditation standards, learning outcomes, and Bloom's taxonomy.

- An easy-to-use **lecture capture** tool.

Want an online, **searchable version** of your textbook?

Wish your textbook could be **available online** while you're doing your assignments?

 ## *Connect™ Plus Marketing* eBook

If you choose to use *Connect™ Plus Marketing*, you have an affordable and searchable online version of your book integrated with your other online tools.

Connect™ Plus Marketing eBook offers features like:

- Topic search
- Direct links from assignments
- Adjustable text size
- Jump to page number
- Print by section

 Want to get more **value** from your textbook purchase?

Think learning advertising should be a bit more **interesting**?

 ## Check out the STUDENT RESOURCES section under the *Connect™* Library tab.

Here you'll find a wealth of resources designed to help you achieve your goals in the course. You'll find things like **quizzes, PowerPoints, and Internet activities** to help you study. Every student has different needs, so explore the STUDENT RESOURCES to find the materials best suited to you.

advertising

William F. Arens

David H. Schaefer

Michael F. Weigold

McGraw-Hill
Irwin

advertising

VICE PRESIDENT AND EDITOR-IN-CHIEF **BRENT GORDON**

EDITORIAL DIRECTOR **PAUL DUCHAM**

PUBLISHER **DOUG HUGHES**

EXECUTIVE EDITOR **SANKHA BASU**

EXECUTIVE DIRECTOR OF DEVELOPMENT **ANN TORBERT**

DEVELOPMENT EDITOR **KELLY I. PEKELDER**

EDITORIAL COORDINATOR **ANDREA HEIRENDT**

VICE PRESIDENT AND DIRECTOR OF MARKETING **ROBIN J. ZWETTLER**

MARKETING DIRECTOR **AMEE MOSLEY**

MARKETING MANAGER **KATIE MERGEN**

VICE PRESIDENT OF EDITING, DESIGN, AND PRODUCTION **SESHA BOLISETTY**

PROJECT MANAGER **DANA M. PAULEY**

BUYER II **DEBRA R. SYLVESTER**

SENIOR DESIGNER **MARY KAZAK SANDER**

SENIOR PHOTO RESEARCH COORDINATOR **KERI JOHNSON**

PHOTO RESEARCH COORDINATOR **JOANNE MENNEMEIER**

PHOTO RESEARCHER **JENNIFER BLANKENSHIP**

SENIOR MEDIA PROJECT MANAGER **JENNIFER LOHN**

MEDIA PROJECT MANAGER **JOYCE J. CHAPPETTO**

TYPEFACE **10/12 MINION PRO REGULAR**

COMPOSITOR **APTARA®, INC.**

PRINTER **QUAD/GRAPHICS**

ADVERTISING

Publishing by McGraw-Hill/Irwin, a business unit of The McGraw-Hill Companies, Inc., 1221 Avenue of the Americas, New York, NY, 10020.
Copyright © 2012 by The McGraw-Hill Companies, Inc. All rights reserved. No part of this publication may be reproduced or distributed in any form or by any means, or stored in a database or retrieval system, without the prior written consent of The McGraw-Hill Companies, Inc., including, but not limited to, in any network or other electronic storage or transmission, or broadcast for distance learning.

Some ancillaries, including electronic and print components, may not be available to customers outside the United States.

This Book is printed on acid-free paper.

Printed in the United States of America.

2 3 4 5 6 7 8 9 0 QDB/QDB 1 0 9 8 7 6 5 4 3 2 1

ISBN   978-0-07-802891-5
MHID   0-07-802891-4

Library of Congress Control Number: 2010940142

www.mhhe.com

brief
contents

contents

CHAPTER 5   COMMUNICATION AND CONSUMER BEHAVIOR 122

part five REACHING THE TARGET AUDIENCE 278

advertising

the evolution
of advertising

one

> We just made history. All of this happened because you gave your time, talent and passion. All of this happened because of you. Thanks.

—Barack Obama

Advertising pros pay careful attention to the work of others, and they pay extra attention when ads are inspired and effective. One such campaign ran from the end of 2006 through November 2008. But this campaign was not for a soap brand or some other product; it was for a young candidate who, seemingly coming from nowhere, won election to the highest office in the land.

Barack Obama is a natural leader and an exciting speaker. Even so, when he announced that he would run for president, it took audacity, to borrow from an Obama book title, to believe he would win. Just 46 years old, Obama had only two years of experience in national office. Indeed, he was a long shot even for the nomination of his party.

The Obama team's assessment of his situation in late 2006 revealed it would be an uphill climb. In the Democratic primary, polls gave Hillary Clinton three times as many supporters as Obama.[1] Nationally the story was even bleaker. A survey found a matchup with likely Republican nominee John McCain would give McCain every state but two, Illinois and Hawaii.[2]

The situation analysis also revealed some great opportunities. Understanding those

continued on p. 4

LEARNING OBJECTIVES

LO1 Define advertising and distinguish it from other forms of marketing communications.

LO2 Explain the role advertising plays in business and marketing.

LO3 Illustrate the functions of advertising in a free market economy.

LO4 Discuss how advertising evolved with the history of commerce.

LO5 Describe the impact of advertising on society.

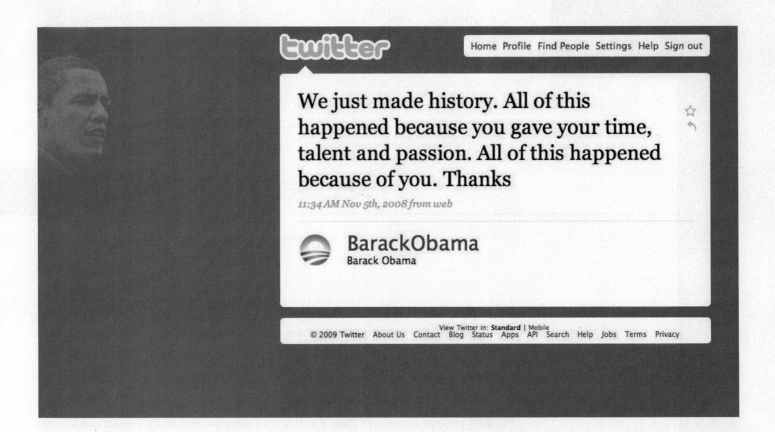

We just made history. All of this happened because you gave your time, talent and passion. All of this happened because of you. Thanks

11:34 AM Nov 5th, 2008 from web

BarackObama
Barack Obama

continued from p. 3

opportunities, and developing a strategy for seizing them, proved central to creating Obama's great ads. Obama's team knew that Hillary Clinton, in addition to being ahead in the polls, was well known. Many of her enthusiastic supporters were excited at the prospect that she would become the first female president. But she also had vulnerabilities, chief among them her vote giving President Bush the authority to go to war in Iraq and her association with her husband's administration eight years earlier.

Obama's team decided that he would be positioned as the candidate of change. Every message coming from the campaign, whether in ads, speeches, Web sites, press releases, posters, bumper stickers, or any other medium, would resonate with that theme. As you'll see later in this book, *positioning* is a term marketers use when they create an image of a product, person, organization, or idea in the minds of a group of people.

Creating a campaign around the core idea of change was brilliant. It turned Obama's outsider status and lack of experience into a plus. And it transformed a seeming strength of Clinton into a liability. Obama's message to an electorate that wanted

fresh approaches was that electing Clinton would bring more of the old ways of governing. Obama's advisors were right. In 2008, voters were more interested in change than experience.

The election pitted Obama against Republican John McCain. Would the "change" message still work against a self-described "maverick," a candidate known for bucking his own party? Obama's advisors thought so. They would neutralize McCain's maverick status by linking him to President Bush. Obama's ads and speeches linking McCain to Bush occurred with such frequency that during the final debate an exasperated McCain cried out: "If you want to run against President Bush, you should have run four years ago."

Obama had a solid core strategy: convince voters that he was the candidate of change. Tactically his campaign also made several smart moves. One tactic was to spend heavily on advertising, in fact a record amount of over $310 million. McCain, less effective at raising money, could only spend $135 million.[3] Spending lots of money was important for Obama since voters were relatively unfamiliar with him. And spend he did, more than any other candidate in history.

Where did the money go? Most was spent on television spots, with only a tiny amount, about $8 million, going to online media.[4] But the money comparisons are misleading because traditional and online media were used for different audiences and purposes. With television, Obama was able to reach large numbers of undecided voters. These individuals are generally politically unengaged, and TV, an intrusive medium, proved an effective way to familiarize such voters with the candidate. Conversely, new media are interactive, people seek out information. So online options, such as search engine ads and social media, were vital for communicating with supporters. But the biggest benefit of online media can be summed up in a single word: money. The campaign raised over $500 million on the Internet, with more than 6 million people sending donations online.

Obama, of course, made history by winning and becoming the first American president of African-American descent. But his campaign made history as well. Future campaigns, both for candidates and for products and services, will learn much from his success.[5] ■

marketing communications
The various efforts and tools companies use to initiate and maintain communication with customers and prospects, including solicitation letters, newspaper ads, event sponsorship, publicity, telemarketing, statement stuffers, and coupons, to mention just a few.

advertising
The structured and composed nonpersonal communication of information, usually paid for and usually persuasive in nature, about products (goods, services, and ideas) by indentified sponsors through various media.

consumers
People who buy products and services for their own, or someone else's, personal use.

various tools is **marketing communications**. And advertising is just one type of marketing communication.

So, then, what is advertising?

At the beginning of the twentieth century, Albert Lasker, generally regarded as the father of modern advertising, defined advertising as "salesmanship in print, driven by a reason why."[6] But that was long before the advent of radio, television, or the Internet. The nature and scope of the business world, and advertising, were quite limited. More than a century later, our planet is a far different place. The nature and needs of business have changed, and so have the concept and practice of advertising.

Definitions of advertising abound. Journalists, for example, might define it as a communication, public relations, or persuasion process; businesspeople see it as a marketing process; economists and sociologists tend to focus on its economic, societal, or ethical significance. And some consumers might define it simply as a nuisance. Each of these perspectives has

[Advertising is salesmanship in print.
—Albert Lasker, 1899]

LO1 Define advertising and distinguish it from other forms of marketing communications.

WHAT IS ADVERTISING?

You are exposed to hundreds and maybe even thousands of commercial messages every day. They may appear in the forms used by the Obama campaign—television commercials, Web sites, and text messages—or in the form of product placements in TV shows, coupons, sales letters, event sponsorships, telemarketing calls, or e-mails. These are just a few of the many communication tools that companies and organizations use to initiate and maintain contact with their customers, clients, and prospects. You may simply refer to them all as "advertising." But, in fact, the correct term for these

some merit, but for now we'll use the following functional definition:

> **Advertising** is the structured and composed nonpersonal communication of information, usually paid for and usually persuasive in nature, about products (goods, services, and ideas) by identified sponsors through various media.

Let's take this definition apart and analyze its components. Advertising is, first of all, a type of *communication*. It is actually a very *structured* form of communication, employing both verbal and nonverbal elements that are *composed* to fill specific space and time formats determined by the sponsor.

Second, advertising is typically directed to groups of people rather than to individuals. It is therefore *nonpersonal,* or *mass communication.* These people could be **consumers**, who buy products for their personal use. Or they might be businesspeople who would buy large quantities of products for resale in their stores.

my ad campaign

Overview [1–A]

Welcome to My Ad Campaign, a new feature of this text. My Ad Campaign should be useful in any of the following situations:

• Your instructor has asked students in your class to work on part or all of an ad campaign, either individually or in groups.
• You are doing an internship and want practical advice on how to help your company advertise.
• You want to try to apply the concepts and ideas that you are reading about in this book in the real world.

Professors approach advertising projects differently. Some assign students to create ads for a real product, although you never actually contact the company that makes the product. Some assign a fictional brand in a real product category. Perhaps your professor has offered your talents to a client, such as a small local business or firm. You may even have to find a client yourself by making inquiries in your community. Finally, your professor may ask you to help a charity or nonprofit with its advertising. No matter which of these things is true, the good news is that developing an advertising campaign follows a similar path. And the My Ad Campaign feature is designed to help you do it well.

Let's begin with a definition. An advertising campaign involves the creation and placement of a series of strategic communications that are unified by an underlying theme or core message. The communications are intended to help promote a brand, product, service, organization, or idea. The messages are typically designed to resonate with a group called a target audience. Campaigns usually have specific objectives, such as increasing product awareness or persuading people to try a service or donate money to a candidate. And to ensure that the target audience receives them, messages appear in various media, such as newspapers, radio commercials, or Web pages. You may not do all of these activities, especially placing ads in real media. But you will get a chance to do some serious thinking, planning, and brainstorming.

We can make our definition of a campaign a bit more concrete by thinking back to the opening vignette of this chapter. President Obama, of course, is not a "product," but for purposes of winning the election his team had to plan their messages as though he was one. Previously we noted that an ad campaign has an underlying theme or core message. In the Obama campaign this theme was "change," specifically that Obama represented change and his opponents did not. Many years ago, a famous advertising professional named David Ogilvy referred to a great campaign's theme as "the big idea." Deciding what the "big idea" is for your brand will be one of the most important decisions you will make. The big idea of "change" proved central to Obama's victories over both Hillary Clinton and John McCain.

Obama's team also did an excellent job of identifying target audiences that should receive campaign messages. Two of the most important audiences were undecided voters and young voters, and the campaign developed specific messages for each. It wanted to persuade undecided voters that they could only change Washington by voting for Obama. For young voters, the objective was different. Young voters already liked Obama and wanted him to win. The campaign's challenge with this group was to get them to register to vote, something young voters had not done in large numbers in previous elections. To do all of this, the campaign used a variety of media, both traditional (TV, radio, print) and new (Facebook, Twitter, MySpace).

Hopefully you've inferred from all of this that advertising is very strategic. Lots of planning takes place long before ads are created. For that reason, while you may be itching to create some advertisements for your client, you have lots of work to do before you begin brainstorming ideas for actual ads. Obama's team was successful not only because they created great ads, but because they understood their candidate, his opponents, the audiences that were important to reach, the media that could be used to reach them, and the objectives that were crucial to success. On a much smaller scale and with far less resources, you face similar challenges. My Ad Campaign is designed to help you to meet that challenge.

In subsequent chapters, we'll help you learn to develop a deeper understanding of your brand or client, develop a plan for marketing and advertising activities, conduct research so that you can better understand your target audience, formulate media strategy, and design effective advertisements. Finally, we'll teach you how to implement evaluation programs to test whether your ads have been successful. By the end of the semester, you won't be a top advertising professional. But you'll have some real experience in the art and science of developing an ad campaign.

The My Ad Campaign topics are listed below. You may find it useful or necessary to jump around as you develop your own campaign.

1. Overview/Tools for Teamwork
2. Your Campaign Assignment
3. Understanding What Your Client Wants
4. Segmenting the Audience
5. Understanding Your Customer and Product
6. Conducting Marketing and Advertising Research
7. Situation Analysis, Objectives, and Budgets
8. The Creative Brief
9. Developing the Creative Product
10. Producing Advertisements
11. Magazine and Newspaper Advertising
12. Television and Radio Advertising
13. Digital Interactive Media
14. Out-of-Home, Direct Mail and Specialty Advertising
15. Developing Media Objectives and Strategies
16. Developing a Plans Book
17. Blogging/The Client Presentation

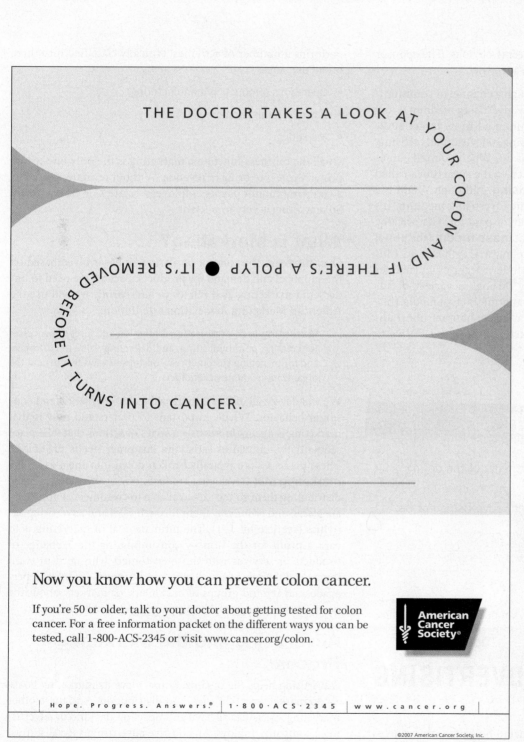

THE DOCTOR TAKES A LOOK AT YOUR COLON AND IF THERE'S A POLYP ● IT'S REMOVED BEFORE IT TURNS INTO CANCER.

Now you know how you can prevent colon cancer.

If you're 50 or older, talk to your doctor about getting tested for colon cancer. For a free information packet on the different ways you can be tested, call 1-800-ACS-2345 or visit www.cancer.org/colon.

American Cancer Society®

Hope. Progress. Answers.® | 1·800·ACS·2345 | www.cancer.org

©2007 American Cancer Society, Inc.

Even nonprofits use advertising to bring in needed revenue.

Most advertising is *paid* for by sponsors. GM, Walmart, the Obama campaign, and your local fitness salon pay the newspaper or the radio or TV station to carry the ads you read, see, and hear. But some sponsors don't have to pay for their ads. The American Red Cross, United Way, and American Cancer Society are among the many national organizations whose **public service announcements (PSAs)** are carried at no charge because of their nonprofit status. Likewise, a poster on a school bulletin board promoting a dance is not paid for, but it is still an ad—a structured, nonpersonal, persuasive communication.

Of course, most advertising is intended to be *persuasive*—to win converts to a product, service, or idea. Some ads, such as legal announcements, are intended merely to inform, not to persuade. But they are still ads because they satisfy all the other requirements of the definition.

In addition to promoting tangible **goods** such as oranges, iPods, and automobiles, advertising helps publicize the intangible **services** of bankers, beauticians, bike repair shops, bill collectors, and Internet providers. Increasingly, advertising is used to advocate a wide variety of **ideas**, whether economic, political, religious, or social. In this book the term **product** encompasses goods, services, and ideas.

medium
An instrument or communications vehicle that carries or helps transfer a message from the sender to the receiver.

word-of-mouth (WOM) advertising
The passing of information, especially product recommendations, by verbal communication, in an informal, unpaid, person-to-person manner, rather than by advertising or other forms of traditional marketing.

mass media
Print or broadcast media that reach very large audiences. Mass media include radio, television, newspapers, magazines, and billboards.

marketing
An organizational function and a set of processes for creating, communicating, and delivering value to customers and for managing customer relationships in ways that benefit the organization and its stakeholders.

marketing mix
Four elements, called the 4Ps (product, price, place, and promotion), that every company has the option of adding, subtracting, or modifying in order to create a desired marketing strategy.

An ad *identifies* its sponsor. This seems obvious. The sponsor wants to be identified, or why pay to advertise?

Finally, advertising reaches us through a channel of communication referred to as a **medium**. An advertising medium is any nonpersonal means used to present an ad to its target audience. Thus, we have radio advertising, television advertising, newspaper ads, Google ads, and so on. When you tell somebody how much you like a product, that's sometimes called **word-of-mouth (WOM) advertising**. Although WOM is a communication medium, it's not an advertising medium. It's not structured, or openly sponsored, or paid for. Historically, advertisers have used the traditional **mass media** (the plural of medium)—radio, TV, newspapers, magazines, and billboards—to send their messages. Modern technology enables advertising to reach us efficiently through a variety of addressable media (like direct mail) and interactive media (like the Internet). Advertisers also use a variety of other nontraditional media such as shopping carts, blimps, and DVDs to find their audience.

check yourself ✓

1. What are the six key components of the definition of advertising?

2. Under what conditions might advertising not be paid for?

LO2 Explain the role advertising plays in business and marketing.

THE ROLE OF ADVERTISING IN BUSINESS

In Chapter 5 we discuss in more detail how advertising helps to inform and persuade consumers, but first let's consider advertising's role in business. Every business organization performs a number of activities, typically classified into three broad divisions:

- Operations (production/manufacturing)
- Finance/administration
- Marketing

Of all the business functions, marketing is the only one whose primary role is to bring in revenue. Without revenue, of course, a company cannot pay its employees' salaries or earn a profit. So marketing is very important.

What Is Marketing?

Over the years, the concept of marketing has evolved based on the supply of and demand for products. Because we need to understand marketing as it relates to *advertising*, we will use the American Marketing Association's definition:

> **Marketing** is an organizational function and a set of processes for creating, communicating, and delivering value to customers and for managing customer relationships in ways that benefit the organization and its stakeholders.[7]

We will devote all of Part 2 to the subject of marketing and consumer behavior. What's important to understand now is that marketing is a *set of processes*—a series of actions that take place sequentially—aimed at satisfying customer needs profitably. These processes are typically broken down into the 4 Ps of the **marketing mix**: developing *products, pricing* them strategically, distributing them so they are available to customers at appropriate *places*, and *promoting* them through sales and advertising activities (see Exhibit 1–1). The ultimate goal of marketing is to earn a profit for the firm by consummating the exchange of products or services with those customers who need or want them. And the role of advertising is to promote—to inform, persuade, and remind groups of customers, or markets, about the need-satisfying value of the company's goods and services.

Advertising and the Marketing Process

Advertising helps the organization achieve its marketing goals. So do market research, sales, and distribution. And these other marketing specialties all have an impact on the kind of advertising a company employs. An effective advertising specialist must have a broad understanding of the whole marketing process in order to know what type of advertising to use in a given situation.

Companies and organizations use many different types of advertising, depending on their particular marketing strategy. The **marketing strategy** will help determine who the targets of advertising should be, in what markets the advertising should appear, and what goals the advertising should accomplish. The **advertising strategy**, in turn, will refine the target audience and define what response the advertiser is seeking—what that audience should notice, think, and feel. We will discuss the development of marketing, advertising, and media strategies later in the text.

But first, we need to understand the economic dimension of advertising and how advertising has evolved as both an economic and a societal tool.

marketing strategy
The statement of how the company is going to accomplish its marketing objectives. The strategy is the total directional thrust of the company, that is, the how-to of the marketing plan, and is determined by the particular blend of the marketing mix elements (the 4Ps), which the company can control.

advertising strategy
The advertising objective declares what the advertiser wants to achieve with respect to consumer awareness, attitude, and preference; the advertising strategy describes how to get there. Advertising strategy consists of two substrategies: the creative strategy and the media strategy.

> # The role of advertising is to promote—to inform, persuade, and remind.

check yourself ✓

1. What is the ultimate goal of marketing?

2. What are the 4 Ps of the marketing mix and under which does advertising fall?

3. What roles does advertising play in helping marketing meet its goals?

LO3 Illustrate the functions of advertising in a free market economy.

ECONOMICS: THE GROWING NEED FOR ADVERTISING

Economics has driven the growth of advertising since its earliest beginnings and has made it one of the hallmarks of the free enterprise system.

Today, business—and advertising—are undergoing dramatic changes. To understand the nature of these changes and why they're taking place, we need to look at how advertising has evolved. We'll explain how the changing economic environment has influenced the evolution of advertising through the centuries. Then, in Chapter 2, we'll look at how advertising influences the economy and society and, as a result, is often an object of controversy and criticism.

Principles of Free Market Economics

Our economy is based on the notion of competition. While there is no such thing as

▼**EXHIBIT 1–1** Advertising is just one of several activities that fall under the promotion component of the marketing mix.

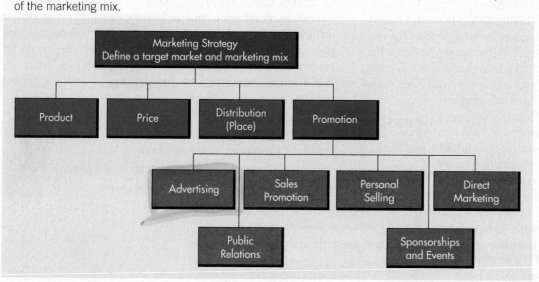

perfect competition, there are four fundamental assumptions of free market economics that a market-driven society strives to achieve:

1. *Self-interest.* People and organizations tend to act in their own self-interest. People are acquisitive and always want more—for less. Therefore, open competition between self-interested sellers advertising to self-interested buyers naturally leads to greater product availability at more competitive prices.

2. *Complete information.* Access by buyers and sellers to all information at all times about what products are available, at what quality, and at what prices, leads to greater competition and lower prices for all. (This is why attorneys are now allowed to advertise.)

3. *Many buyers and sellers.* Having a wide range of sellers ensures that if one company does not meet customer needs, another will capitalize on the situation by producing a more market-responsive product. Similarly, having a wide range of buyers ensures that sellers can find customers who are interested in the unique products they are able to produce at a fair price. (This is why we have antitrust laws.)

4. *Absence of externalities (social costs).* Sometimes the sale or consumption of products may benefit or harm other people who are not involved in the transaction and didn't pay for the product. In these cases, the government may use taxation and/or regulation to compensate for or eliminate the **externalities**. (This is why there are restrictions and requirements placed on tobacco advertisers.)

Now, given these basic assumptions, let's see how advertising fits into the scheme of a free-market economy.

Functions and Effects of Advertising in a Free Economy

For any business, advertising may perform a variety of functions, and, when executed correctly, its effects may be dramatic. To see how this works, let's go back to the beginnings of Coca-Cola, when druggist John Pemberton was still mixing the syrup in his lab.

Pemberton's business partner and bookkeeper, Frank Robinson, suggested the name "Coca-Cola" to identify the two main flavors (coca leaves and kola nuts) and because he thought that "the two Cs would look well in advertising."[8] Robinson wrote down the name in his flowing script, creating a logo that is now instantly recognizable around the world and is one of Coca-Cola's more valued assets. Later, a distinctive bottle shape—purportedly the brainchild of a bored glassblower who based the design on a cacao pod instead of a caca nut, as intended—became the standard throughout the company. The proprietary curvy bottle helped customers differentiate Coca-Cola from other drinks. The creation of the Coca-Cola logo and contour bottle demonstrates one of the most basic functions of **branding** as well as advertising: *to identify products and their source and to differentiate them from others.* (The functions and effects discussed here are listed in Exhibit 1–2.)

Coca-Cola was first served at a small pharmacy in Atlanta in 1886. The word "drink" was added to signs to let people know it was a beverage.

When Pemberton first began selling Coca-Cola at Jacobs' Pharmacy, he needed to let people know what it was—although we associate the word *cola* with a cold, bubbly beverage, the people of Atlanta didn't automatically make the same connection. Therefore, Pemberton and Robinson added the suggestion *drink* before *Coca-Cola* on the signs that they had painted and placed in front of the drugstore.[9] Ads in the *Atlanta Journal* let readers know why they should drink it (because it is "delicious, exhilarating, refreshing and invigorating," it was the perfect

> **EXHIBIT 1–2** Functions and effects of advertising as a marketing tool.
>
> - To identify products and differentiate them from others.
> - To communicate information about the product, its features, and its place of sale.
> - To induce consumers to try new products and to suggest reuse.
> - To stimulate the distribution of a product.
> - To increase product use.
> - To build value, brand preference, and loyalty.
> - To lower the overall cost of sales.

"temperance drink" during Prohibition), how much it cost, and where they could get it. Here is another basic function of advertising: *to communicate information about the product, its features, and its location of sale.*

After Asa Candler gained control of the Coca-Cola Company, he began to develop the market for the drink on a grander scale. With the help of Frank Robinson and a city directory, he mailed thousands of coupons for free drinks to Atlanta residents. Coupons were also handed out on the street and inserted in magazines. To cover the costs of the samples, the company gave free syrup to the soda fountains that offered the beverage. Later, the free sample campaign went along whenever Coca-Cola was introduced in a new market. Candler also distributed promotional items to vendors so that the Coca-Cola logo was visible everywhere both outside and inside the shop. To us, this campaign demonstrates another function of advertising: *to induce consumers to try new products and to suggest reuse.*

Through the early part of the twentieth century, Coca-Cola wasn't the dominant force we know today. Competitors such as Pepsi and the now-defunct Moxie cut into Coca-Cola's market share. Outside forces also threatened the entire industry; sugar rationing during wartimes was especially damaging. Before the United States became involved in World War II, Coca-Cola executives preempted a repeat of the setbacks the company suffered during World War I rationing. They persuaded the government to give troops Coca-Cola instead of alcoholic beverages to boost their morale. The D'Arcy advertising agency gathered endorsements from U.S. officers in training camps to support the company's bid to become an official military supplier—and therefore be exempt from rationing. The War Department agreed to the plan, and Coca-Cola borrowed $5.5 million to establish 64 bottling plants near the front lines. The risky investment had great returns. When the soldiers returned home, a survey showed they preferred Coke by eight to one over Pepsi.[10] Coca-Cola blended patriotism with another of the important functions of advertising: *to increase product use.*

As soft drinks became a staple throughout the U.S., Coca-Cola began campaigns outside the country to affect beverage consumption globally. The first international Coca-Cola bottling plants were established in Canada, Cuba, and Panama in 1906; today the company bottles Coke in more than 200 countries. Coca-Cola franchise bottlers around the world can tweak the recipe to match local tastes. Bottlers and distributors also supplement Coke advertising with their own promotions and sponsorships. Through various activities, Coca-Cola has succeeded in accomplishing yet another function of advertising: *to stimulate the distribution of a product,* in this case, on a global level.

In a free-market economy, when one company starts to make significant profits, other companies immediately jump in to compete. Over the years, to battle the constant competitive threat, Coca-Cola has funded ongoing marketing communications campaigns to accomplish yet another function of advertising: *to build value, brand preference, and loyalty.* Although the taste test wars of the 1980s showed that many people liked the taste of Pepsi better than that of Coke, such blind preference has never knocked Coca-Cola out of the top spot. A century of consistently upbeat marketing communications has made its mark. Coca-Cola advertising, such as its current campaign, "Open Happiness," has always promoted a common voice and a common

For more than 120 years, Coca-Cola has effectively built and maintained strong brand preference and loyalty among its customers. Coke's current campaign, just like all previous campaigns, confirms that drinking Coca-Cola makes our lives happier.

preindustrial age
Period of time between the beginning of written history and roughly the start of the nineteenth century, during which the invention of paper and the printing press and increased literacy gave rise to the first forms of written advertising.

theme: Coca-Cola makes life's relaxing moments even better.

For more than 120 years, the Coca-Cola Company has used a variety of media to communicate this message to diverse audiences. Why? To achieve the most significant function of advertising: *to lower the overall cost of sales.* For the cost of reaching just one prospect through personal selling, companies can reach thousands of people through media advertising. The average cost to make a face-to-face field sales call is about $400. Multiply that $400 by the more than 24 million

THE EVOLUTION OF ADVERTISING AS AN ECONOMIC TOOL

Thousands of years ago, people devoted most of their efforts to meeting basic survival needs: food, clothing, shelter. They lived in small, isolated communities where artisans and farmers bartered products and services among themselves. Distribution

[Advertising contributes to a free economy.]

people who watch a top-rated prime-time TV show, and the cost comes to a mind-boggling $9.6 billion. However, for only $1 million Coca-Cola can buy a 30-second TV commercial during a regular season show of *American Idol* and reach the same 24 million people. Through television, advertisers can talk to a thousand prospects for only $42—about 10 percent of what it costs to talk to a single prospect through personal selling.[11]

Now, considering this brief synopsis of Coca-Cola history, how does Coke's advertising fit with the basic assumptions of a free-market economy? Has Coke's advertising helped make the soft drink available to more people at lower cost? Has it informed them about where they can buy Coke? Has the freedom to advertise contributed to the competitive environment? What externalities might have had a positive or negative impact on the Coca-Cola Company's efforts to market its beverages?

Perhaps you can see from this one example how advertising contributes to a free economy. But if it's so good, then why didn't advertising take off until the twentieth century? (For a time line of advertising history, see Exhibit 1–3.) Why wasn't it developed and used for the last several thousand years of recorded history?

was limited to how far vendors could walk and "advertising" to how loud they could shout. Because goods weren't produced in great quantity, there was no need for advertising to stimulate mass purchases. There were also no mass media available for possible advertisers to use. (See Exhibit 1–3.)

The Preindustrial Age

As markets grew larger and became more complex, the demand for products increased, and the need for advertising slowly developed. At first, merchants hung carved signs in front of their shops so passersby could see what products were being offered. Most people couldn't read, so the signs often used symbols, such as a boot for a cobbler. This period was called the **preindustrial age**, and, for Western civilization, it extended from the beginning of recorded history to roughly the start of the nineteenth century.[12]

During the preindustrial age, several important developments enabled the eventual birth of modern advertising. The

An early form of advertising. Until the advent of public schooling, most people couldn't read—so signs featured symbols of the goods or services for sale, such as the jerkin on this tailor's sign in Williamsburg, Virginia.

check yourself ✓

1. What are the seven functions of advertising as a marketing tool?

2. Provide an example of each function from the history of Coca-Cola.

▼EXHIBIT 1–3 Timetable of advertising history.

3000 BC–AD 1	AD 500–1599	1600–1799	1800–1899
3000 BC Written advertisement offering "Whole gold coin" for runaway slave "Shem."	**1455** First printed Bible.	**1650** First newspaper ad offers reward for stolen horses.	**1841** Volney B. Palmer becomes first "newspaper agent" (advertising agent) in America.
500 BC Political and trade graffiti on Pompeii walls.	**1472** First printed ad in English tacked on London church doors.	**1662** *London Gazette* offers first advertising supplement.	**1844** First magazine ad runs.
AD 1 First uppercase lettering appears on Greek buildings.	**1544** Claude Garamond, first "typefounder," perfects a roman typeface that bears his name and is still used today.	**1704** First ads in America published in the *Boston Newsletter.*	**1869** Francis W. Ayer founds ad agency bearing his father's name, N. W. Ayer & Sons, in Philadelphia. He initiates first "for commission" ad contract (1876), first market survey for an ad (1879), and first on-staff creative services (art in 1890, copywriting in 1892).
		1729 Ben Franklin is first to use "white space" and illustration in ads.	
		1785 Widespread use of advertising and long print runs become possible.	**1888** *Printers' Ink* is first U.S. publication for ad profession.

1900–1919	1920–1939	1940–1959	1960–1969
1900 Psychologists study the attention-getting and persuasive qualities of advertising.	**1920s** Albert Lasker, father of modern advertising, calls advertising "salesmanship in print." First ad testimonials by movie stars appear. Full-color printing is available in magazines.	**1946** America has 12 TV stations broadcasting to the public.	**1960s** Doyle Dane Bernbach's "Think small" ad for American Volkswagen becomes one of the most famous ads of the decade, establishing a strong market position for the smallest European import. The agency's slogan for Avis, "We're only No. 2, so we try harder," is also very successful. New York's Madison Avenue becomes known worldwide as the center of the advertising world and features the best in advertising creativity.
1900 Northwestern University is first to offer advertising as a discipline.	**1922** First radio ad solves radio's need for financing.	**1947** Lanham Trademark Act protects brand names and slogans.	
1903 Scripps-McRae League of Newspapers appoints ad censor, rejects $500,000 in ads in first year.	**1924** N. W. Ayer produces first sponsored radio broadcast, the "Eveready Hour."	**1948** 46 TV stations are operating and 300 others are awaiting FCC approval.	
1905 First national ad plan is for the "Gillette Safety Razor."	**1930** *Advertising Age* magazine is founded.	**1950** First political ads, by Gov. Dewey of New York, appear on TV.	
1911 First "truth in advertising" codes are established by what is now called the American Advertising Federation (AAF).	**1938** Wheeler-Lea amendments to FTC Act of 1938 grant FTC further power to curb false ad practices.	**1950s** David Ogilvy's "Hathaway man" and "Commander Whitehead" become popular ad personae.	

1970–1979	1980–1989	1990–2000	2001–2010
1971 Armed services begin first advertising for the new "all-volunteer" military ("Be all that you can be in the Army").	**1980s** Ad agency megamergers take place worldwide.	**1990s** A recession leads marketers to shift funds from advertising to sales promotion.	**2002** A general economic slump hammers ad spending.
1972 The *Ad Age* article "Positioning: The Battle for Your Mind" by Al Ries and Jack Trout details the strategy of positioning that dominates the 1970s.	**1982** First edition of *Contemporary Advertising* is published.	**1994** Media glut leads to market fragmentation; network TV is no longer sole medium for reaching total marketplace. Ad professions adopt integrated marketing communications (IMC) as the new strategy to build market relationships.	**2005** Online advertisers spend $8.32 billion to reach the 170 million wired U.S. residents.
1973 Oil shortages begin period of "demarketing," ads aimed at slowing demand.	**1984** The Internet (government controlled since 1973) is turned over to the private sector.		**2006** Advertisers begin creating HDTV spots (shooting digitally instead of on analog tape).
1970s (late) Growth in self-indulgence, signified by popularity of self-fulfillment activities, spurs some agencies into making infomercials.	**1986** *Marketing Warfare* by Al Ries and Jack Trout portrays marketing in terms of classic warfare manual written by General Clausewitz in 1831.	**2000** The Internet is the fastest-growing new ad medium since TV, with 400 million users.	**2007** U.S. ad agency revenue surges 8.6% to $31 billion, led by double-digit growth in digital advertising.
			2009 Broad global recession leads to cutbacks in ad expenditures. Two major advertisers, GM and Chrysler, are guided through restructuring after a government takeover.

Chinese invented paper and Europe had its first paper mill by 1275. In the 1440s, Johannes Gutenberg invented the printing press in Germany. The press was not only the most important development in the history of advertising, and indeed communication, but it also revolutionized the way people lived and worked.

The introduction of printing allowed facts to be established, substantiated, recorded, and transported. People no longer had to rely on their memories. Some entrepreneurs bought printing presses, mounted them in wagons, and traveled from town to town, selling printing. This new technology made possible the first formats of advertising—posters, handbills, and signs—and, eventually, the first mass medium—the newspaper. In effect, the cry of the vendor could now be multiplied many times and heard beyond the immediate neighborhood.

In 1472, the first ad in English appeared: a handbill tacked on church doors in London announcing a prayer book for sale. Two hundred years later the first newspaper ad was published, offering a reward for the return of 12 stolen horses. Soon newspapers carried ads for coffee, chocolate, tea, real estate, medicines, and even personal ads. These early ads were still directed to a very limited number of people: the customers of the coffeehouses where most newspapers were read.

By the early 1700s, the world's population had grown to about 600 million people, and some major cities were big enough to support larger volumes of advertising. In fact, the greater volume caused a shift in advertising strategy. Samuel Johnson, the famous English literary figure, observed in 1758 that advertisements were now so numerous that they were "negligently perused" and that it had become necessary to gain attention "by magnificence of promise." This was the beginning of *puffery* in advertising.

In the American colonies, the *Boston Newsletter* began carrying ads in 1704. About 25 years later, Benjamin Franklin, the father of advertising art, made ads more readable by using large headlines and considerable white space. In fact, Franklin was the first American known to use illustrations in ads.

The Industrializing Age

In the mid-1700s, the Industrial Revolution began in England and by the early

It wasn't until 1729 that Ben Franklin, innovator of advertising art, made ads more readable by using larger headlines, changing fonts, and adding art. This 1767 ad announces the availability of Stage Waggons to carry passengers from Powles Hook Ferry to Philadelphia.

1800s it had reached North America. By using machines to mass-produce goods with uniform quality, large companies increased their productivity. For the first time, it cost people less to buy a product than to make it themselves. As people left the farm to work in the city, mass urban markets began to emerge. This further fueled market development and the growth of advertising.

By the mid-1800s, the world's population had doubled to 1.2 billion. Suddenly, producers needed mass consumption to match the high levels of manufactured goods. Breakthroughs in bulk transportation—the railroad and steamship—facilitated the distribution of products beyond a manufacturer's local market. But with the need for mass consumption came the increasing need for mass marketing techniques such as advertising to inform new markets of the availability of products.

During this **industrializing age**, which lasted roughly until the end of World War I (1918), manufacturers were principally concerned with production. The burden of marketing fell on wholesalers. They used advertising primarily as an information vehicle, placing announcements in publications called *price currents* to let retailers know about the sources of supply and shipping schedules for unbranded commodities. Advertising to consumers was the job of the local retailer and the large mail-order catalog companies like Montgomery Ward and Sears Roebuck. Only a few innovative manufacturers foresaw the usefulness of mass media advertising to stimulate consumer demand for their products.

For Americans, the *profession* of advertising began when Volney B. Palmer set up business in Philadelphia in 1841. He contracted with newspapers for large volumes of advertising space at discount rates and then resold the space to advertisers at a higher rate. The advertisers usually prepared the ads themselves.

In 1869, at the ripe old age of 21, Francis Ayer formed an ad agency in Philadelphia and, to make it sound more credible, named it after his father. N. W. Ayer & Sons was the first agency to charge a commission based on the "net cost of space" and the first to conduct a formal market survey. In 1890, Ayer became the first ad agency to operate as agencies do today—planning, creating, and executing complete ad campaigns in exchange for media-paid commissions or fees from advertisers. In 1892, Ayer set up a copy department and hired the first full-time agency copywriter.

The technological advances of the Industrial Revolution enabled great changes in advertising. Photography, introduced in 1839, added credibility and a new world of creativity. Now ads could show products, people, and places as they really were, rather than how an illustrator visualized them.

In the 1840s, some manufacturers began using magazine ads to reach the mass market and stimulate mass consumption. Magazines provided for national advertising and offered the best quality reproduction.

The telegraph, telephone, typewriter, phonograph, and later, motion pictures, all let people communicate as never before. In 1896, when the federal government inaugurated rural free mail delivery, direct-mail advertising and mail-order, selling flourished. Manufacturers now had an ever-increasing variety of products to sell and a new way to deliver their advertisements and products to the public.

Public schooling helped the nation reach an unparalleled 90 percent literacy rate. Manufacturers gained a large reading public that could understand print ads. The United States thus entered the twentieth century as a great industrial state with a national marketing system propelled by advertising. With the end of World War I, the modern period in advertising emerged.

industrializing age
The period of time from the mid-1700s through the end of World War I when manufacturers were principally concerned with production.

industrial age
A historical period covering approximately the first 70 years of the twentieth century. This period was marked by tremendous growth and maturation of the U.S. industrial base. It saw the development of new, often inexpensive brands of the luxury and convenience goods we now classify as consumer packaged goods.

consumer packaged goods
Everyday-use consumer products packaged by manufacturers and sold through retail outlets. Generally these are goods such as food and beverages, health and beauty care, cleaning products, and detergents that get used up and have to be replaced frequently.

The Industrial Age

The **industrial age** started around the turn of the twentieth century and lasted well into the 1970s. It was a period marked by tremendous growth and maturation of the country's industrial base. As U.S. industry met the basic needs of most of the population, commodity markets became saturated. Fresh mass markets then developed for new brands of consumer luxury and convenience goods we refer to as **consumer packaged goods**.

In the early 20th century, the Industrial Revolution was in full force. Factories were producing products like Ford automobiles, not just for Americans, but also for overseas markets, as this ad shows.

In 1890, N. W. Ayer & Sons became the first agency to operate as agencies do today—planning, creating, and executing complete ad campaigns for advertisers. This 1899 Ayer ad for Uneeda biscuits (catch the play on words) was one of a series of popular ads of the times.

During the industrializing age of the nineteenth century, manufacturers changed their focus from a *production* orientation to a *sales* orientation. They dedicated themselves to new product development, strengthened their sales forces, packaged and branded their products, and engaged in heavy national brand advertising. Early brands of this era included Wrigley's spearmint gum, Coca-Cola, Jell-O gelatin, Kellogg's Corn Flakes, and Campbell's soup.

In the 1920s, the United States was rich and powerful. As the war machine returned to peacetime production, society became consumption driven. The era of salesmanship had arrived and its bible was *Scientific Advertising,* written by the legendary copywriter Claude Hopkins at Albert Lasker's agency, Lord & Thomas. Published in 1923, it became a classic and was republished in 1950 and 1980. "Advertising has reached the status of a science," Hopkins proclaimed. "It is based on fixed principles." His principles outlawed humor, style, literary flair, and anything that might detract from his basic copy strategy of a preemptive product claim repeated loudly and often.[13]

Radio was born at about this same time and rapidly became the nation's primary means of mass communication and a powerful new advertising medium. World and national news now arrived direct from the scene, and a whole new array of family entertainment—music, drama, and sports—became possible. Suddenly, national advertisers could quickly reach huge audiences. In fact, the first radio shows were produced by their sponsors' ad agencies.

To differentiate their products from competitors, several manufacturers branded their products and advertised those brands aggressively. Wrigley's has been selling the same product, with the same brand name, for more than a century.

On October 29, 1929, the stock market crashed, the Great Depression began, and advertising expenditures plummeted. In the face of consumer sales resistance and corporate budget cutting, the advertising industry needed to improve its effectiveness. It turned to research. Daniel Starch, A. C. Nielsen, and George Gallup had founded research groups to study consumer attitudes and preferences. By providing information on public opinion, the performance of ad messages, and sales of advertised products, these companies started a whole new business: the marketing research industry.

During this period, each brand sought to sell the public on its own special qualities. Wheaties became the "Breakfast of Champions" not because of its ingredients but because of its advertising. Manufacturers followed this strategy of **product differentiation** vigorously, seeking to portray their brands as different from and better than the competition by offering consumers quality, variety, and convenience.

The greatest expansion of any medium up to that time occurred with the introduction of television in 1941. After World War II, TV advertising grew rapidly, and in time achieved its current status as the largest advertising medium in terms of revenues.

During the postwar prosperity of the late 1940s and early 1950s, consumers tried to climb the social ladder by buying more and more modern products. Advertising entered its golden era. A creative revolution ensued in which ads focused on product features that implied social acceptance, style, luxury, and success. Giants in the field emerged—people such as Leo Burnett, David Ogilvy, and Bill Bernbach, who built their agencies from scratch and forever changed the way advertising was planned and created.[14]

Rosser Reeves of the Ted Bates Agency introduced the idea that every ad must point out the product's USP **(unique selling proposition)**—features that would differentiate it from competitive products. The USP was a logical extension of the Lasker and

Hopkins "reason why" credo. But as the USP was used over and over, consumers started finding it difficult to see what was unique anymore.

Finally, as more and more imitative products showed up in the marketplace, all offering quality, variety, and convenience, the effectiveness of this strategy wore out. Companies turned to a new mantra: **market segmentation**, in which marketers searched for unique groups of people whose needs could be addressed through specialized products. The image era of the 1960s was a natural culmination of the creative revolution. Advertising's emphasis shifted from product features to brand image or personality as advertisers sought to align their brands with profitable market segments. Cadillac, for example, became the worldwide image of luxury, the consummate symbol of success.

While this was all going on in the United States, across the Atlantic a new generation of advertising professionals had graduated from the training grounds of Procter & Gamble (P&G) and Colgate-Palmolive and were now teaching their international clients the secrets of mass marketing.

The Postindustrial Age

Beginning around 1980, the **postindustrial age** has been a period of cataclysmic change. People became truly aware of the sensitive environment in which we live and alarmed by our dependence

> ## What really mattered was how the brand stacked up against the competition in the consumer's mind.

But just as me-too product features killed the product differentiation era, me-too images eventually killed the market segmentation era. With increased competition, a new kind of advertising strategy evolved in the 1970s, where competitors' strengths became just as important as the advertiser's. Jack Trout and Al Ries trumpeted the arrival of the *positioning era* by insisting that what really mattered was how the brand stacked up against the competition in the consumer's mind—how it was positioned.

Positioning proved effective in separating a particular brand from its competitors by associating that brand with a particular set of needs that ranked high on the consumer's priority list. Thus, it became a more effective way to use product differentiation and market segmentation. The most famous American ads of the positioning era were Volkswagen ("Think small"), Avis ("We're #2"), and 7Up ("The uncola"). Product differentiation, market segmentation, and positioning are all very important concepts to understand, so we will discuss them further in Chapter 4.

Will one lead to another and another? You don't have to be an alcoholic to know that the first drink is the easiest to refuse. It's your choice to keep off the hook.

Demarketing is used to dampen demand for products, especially those that create unwanted costs for society. This public service message uses the metaphor of a fish hook to convey the dangerous addictive qualities of alcohol.

on vital natural resources. During the energy shortages of the 1970s and 1980s, a new term, **demarketing**, appeared. Producers of energy started using advertising to *slow* the demand for their products. Ads asked people to refrain from operating washers and dryers during the day when the demand for electricity peaked. In time, demarketing became a more aggressive strategic tool for advertisers to use against competitors, political opponents, and social problems. For example, many organizations today actively seek to demarket the use of tobacco.

The collapse of the Soviet Union ended the Cold War and with it the need for a defense-driven economy. Companies were anxious to develop the untapped markets in the former Warsaw Pact states. To expand their power globally, big multinational companies and their advertising agencies went on a binge, buying other big companies and creating a new word in the financial lexicon: *megamerger*.

By now European and Asian advertising had caught up with the United States. TV was the hot medium, and agencies focused

Think small.

Our little car isn't so much of a novelty any more.
A couple of dozen college kids don't try to squeeze inside it.
The guy at the gas station doesn't ask where the gas goes.
Nobody even stares at our shape.
In fact, some people who drive our little

flivver don't even think that about 27 miles to the gallon is going any great guns.
Or using five pints of oil instead of five quarts.
Or never needing anti-freeze.
Or racking up about 40,000 miles on a set of tires.
That's because once you get used to

some of our economies, you don't even think about them any more.
Except when you squeeze into a small parking spot.
Or renew your small insurance. Or pay a small repair bill. Or trade in your old VW for a new one.
Think it over.

Hailed by Jack Trout and Al Ries as "the most famous ad of the 60s," this Volkswagen ad co-opted the "small" position in consumers' minds, giving VW (www.volkswagen.com) a leadership rank for many years.

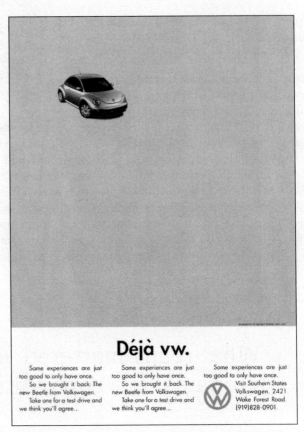

Déjà vw.

Some experiences are just too good to only have once.
So we brought it back. The new Beetle from Volkswagen.
Take one for a test drive and we think you'll agree...

Some experiences are just too good to only have once.
So we brought it back. The new Beetle from Volkswagen.
Take one for a test drive and we think you'll agree...

Some experiences are just too good to only have once.
Visit Southern States Volkswagen. 2421 Wake Forest Road.
(919)828-0901.

In recent years, VW has attempted to recapture the style of its 60s advertising.

on growth, acquisitions, and superior creative executions. For several years, Young & Rubicam in New York and Dentsu in Japan alternated as the largest advertising agency in the world. Then two brothers in London, Charles and Maurice Saatchi, started acquiring agencies globally. In rapid succession, a number of high-profile U.S. agencies disappeared under the Saatchi & Saatchi umbrella. Saatchi & Saatchi was suddenly the largest agency in the world. Then followed more buyouts as the big agencies from Europe, the United States, and Japan emulated the merger mania of their huge multinational clients. Names of agency founders disappeared from the doors, replaced by initials and acronyms: WPP Group, RSCG, TBWA, FCA, DDB Needham, and FCB, to mention just a few.[15]

Then, sparked by unprecedented layoffs in the defense industries, the global economy fell into an economic recession. The mergers temporarily stopped, the business world sucked in its collective belt, and management turned to new theories of Total Quality Management (TQM), reengineering, and downsizing—

> **These newly affluent consumers concerned themselves more with the quality of their lives.**

theories aimed at cutting costs and increasing efficiency. Two related economic factors characterized marketing in this period: (1) the aging of traditional products, with a corresponding growth in competition, and (2) the growing affluence and sophistication of the consuming public, led by the huge baby-boomer generation.[16]

The most important factor was competition, intensified by growing international trade. As high profits lured imitators into the marketplace, each offering the most attractive product features at lower cost, consumers discovered more choices, higher quality, and lower prices.

These newly affluent consumers concerned themselves more with the quality of their lives. With their basic needs met, the baby boomers were interested in saving time and money to spend on products, services, and social causes that represented who they aspired to be.

By the mid-1980s, an avalanche of ads—especially in the toiletry and cosmetics industries—was aimed at the "me" generation ("L'Oreal. Because I'm worth it."). At the same time, the

The recession of the early 90s slammed the advertising industry with over 13,500 layoffs. However, specialists in small, regional creative shops were able to snatch away some large accounts during this period and produce ads for established corporations. This Coca-Cola ad came from the clever minds at Creative Artists Agency in Hollywood (a talent agency).

magazines, and TV networks all lost advertising dollars. About 40 magazines went out of business during the two-year slump.[19]

By the mid-1990s, U.S. marketers had begun shifting dollars back from sales promotion to advertising to rebuild value in their brands. In 1994, ad budgets surged ahead by 8.1 percent to $150 billion nationally. And throughout the rest of the 1990s, ad spending increased about 7 percent every year until the year 2000, when U.S. advertisers spent $247.5 billion, a whopping 11.3 percent increase over the previous year.[20]

But then the bubble burst. In 2001, the combination of a mild recession, the collapse of the stock market, and the bust of the dot-coms all contributed to a record decline in advertising activity. On September 11 of that year, terrorists attacked the United States and suddenly all marketing and advertising seemed to stop—not just in the United States, but also around the world.[21] Spending in the United States declined 6.5 percent to $231 billion, and overseas spending dropped 8.6 percent to $210 billion.[22]

A year later, though, the economy seemed to be turning around and marketers were again starting to spend money on advertising.

nation's largest industrial concerns spent millions of dollars on corporate advertising to extol their social consciousness and good citizenship.

As the U.S. economy slowed, many companies were chasing too few consumer dollars. Clients trimmed their ad budgets,

> [Technology, evolving lifestyles, new fears over security, and the rising cost of reaching consumers had already changed the advertising business forever.]

and many turned to more cost-effective **sales promotion** alternatives, such as coupons, direct mail, and direct marketing to build sales volume. By 1990, advertising had lost 25 percent of its share of the marketing budget to other forms of marketing communications.[17]

As the 1990s unfolded, the traditional advertising industry found itself threatened on all sides and suffering from overpopulation.[18] Clients demanded better results from their promotional dollars; small, imaginative, upstart agencies competed for (and won) some big accounts; TV viewers appeared immune to conventional commercials; and an abundance of new media technologies promised to reinvent advertising. In three short years, the advertising agency business lost over 13,500 jobs. Major clients such as Coca-Cola defected from the big agencies, giving various portions of their business to specialists in small, regional creative shops and media-buying services. But the setback went far beyond the agency business. Throughout the media world, newspapers,

By 2005, U.S. advertising expenditures had reached $264 billion, more than completely recovering from the 2001 decline.[23] But hardly anybody thought the problems were over. Technology, evolving lifestyles, new fears over security, and the rising cost of reaching consumers had already changed the advertising business forever. With the explosion of the Internet, we had entered a new electronic frontier—what Tom Cuniff, VP/ creative director at Lord, Dentsu & Partners, called "the second creative revolution."[24]

The Global Interactive Age: Looking at the Twenty-first Century

The explosion of new technologies in the last decade has affected advertising considerably. With cable TV and satellite receivers, viewers can watch channels devoted to single types of programming, such as straight news, home shopping, sports, or

Tools for Teamwork [1–B]

Advertising agencies look for at least three qualities in the people they hire: talent, knowledge, and the ability to work well with others. If you are working on your campaign in a group, you'll find those qualities—especially the third—to be important as well.

Your campaign assignment may be the first time you've worked on a group project. If so, you'll discover that working in a team is very different from doing a project on your own.

First, you will need to coordinate everything that you do. That means each person must create schedules that accommodate not only his or her own obligations, but those of the group. Second, you will be sharing work. Tools that help you share documents, calendars, and other files will help you produce better work and do it faster. Third, you should consider the importance of leadership in a group. Your group will usually perform better if someone is formally appointed as leader, at least in the sense of organizing meetings, maintaining a calendar, and keeping track of what has to be done. Finally, everyone is accountable. Talk to your professor about whether he or she expects peer evaluations or some other means to assess differences in group member effort and performance.

Many Internet tools are now available to help improve the coordination of teams. Best of all, they are free. The ones I prefer are those created by Google because they are easy to use, powerful, and integrated (both with each other and with mobile devices). If you would prefer not to use a Google product, I've tried to find equivalents where possible.

Staying Connected

E-mail, of course, remains an essential tool. You may have a school e-mail account, but these can be problematic because (1) your in-box space is limited, (2) spam filters in these accounts are often very aggressive (too much useful mail is moved to the spam folder), and (3) they lack many useful tools for organizing and labeling your mail. Gmail (www.gmail.com) is an excellent free mail service that you will most likely never fill up (which means you never have to delete e-mails and your inbox never gets too full). You can use "labels" to quickly identify mail from people in your group. And with "contacts" you can set up groups of e-mail addresses to message easily and quickly. Use "tasks" to create a to-do list right in your e-mail list. These programs also work well with many mobile devices. Microsoft Windows Live Hotmail and Yahoo! Mail offer similar functions (http://mail.live.com and http://mail.yahoo.com).

Creating Documents

Google docs (http://docs.google.com) is a free suite of simple yet powerful document creation tools that includes a word processor, a spreadsheet program, and a presentation creator. What makes the programs special is that you can share some or all of the documents you create with others and edit them simultaneously. So if a group member is working on a creative brief, he or she can share it immediately with everyone else for edits and comments. If you would prefer a non-Google solution, Thinkfree "My Office" is similar to Google docs (www.thinkfree.com).

Staying Organized

Many people find that calendars and to-do lists are essential. Google has an excellent calendar program (www.google.com/calendar) that everyone in the team can edit. You can also sync the calendar with many mobile devices. As I indicated before, Google's "task" program is built into gmail. A very nice program that builds a to-do list function into a calendar is TaskFive (www.taskfive.com).

Conducting Research

Powerful tools for doing research are also available for free on the Web. For secondary research purposes it is great to have a program that allows you to copy and store documents, Web pages, photos, charts, and other kinds of information. Of course, Google has one of these, Google Notebook (www.google.com/notebook). An equally powerful and popular program is Evernote (www.evernote.com). Your group may also find itself collecting primary data. If you need to administer a survey, consider a useful component of Google docs called "forms." With forms you can easily create a Web-based survey and have your data set up in a Google spreadsheet as it comes in. A non-Google program that does the same thing is SurveyMonkey (www.surveymonkey.com).

Working Well and Staying Accountable

Learning to adapt to group projects is not easy for everyone. Knowing what to expect and developing the skills to work well with others is essential. For guidance, consider these thoughts from experts:

- Brian Tracy: http://www.myarticlearchive.com/articles/6/079.htm
- Susan Heathfield: http://humanresources.about.com/od/workrelationships/a/play well.htm
- Stanford University on effective teams: http://www.stanford.edu/class/el40/el40a/effective.html

If you volunteer to be a team leader (or are appointed one), some helpful tips can be found here:

- http://www.cooper.com/journal/2008/11/habits of effective teams.html
- Stephen Covey: http://www.stephencovey.com/blog/?p=6
- Jack Welch, former CEO of GE (this is an hour-long video filmed at the MIT School of Management) http://mitworld.mit.edu/video/260/

If you are doing peer evaluations in your class, your professor will likely have a form that you should use. These types of forms can be found throughout the Web. Some examples include these:

- https://courses.worldcampus.psu.edu/public/faculty/PeerEvalForm.html
- http://www.utexas.edu/courses/kincaid/peerevaltips.html

Television networks are turning to the Internet to market themselves. Episodes of the most popular shows can be viewed online and there's even an app for iPad owners so they can watch their favorite ABC shows anywhere, any time. Of course, you have to watch an advertisement first.

comedy. This shift transformed television from the most widespread of mass media to a more specialized, **narrowcasting** medium.[25] Now small companies and product marketers that appeal to a limited clientele can use TV to reach audiences with select interests.

A concurrent change that didn't please advertisers was the growing presence of VCR and remote controls, which allow viewers to avoid commercials altogether by channel surfing during breaks or zipping through them when watching a previously recorded show. Advertisers and TV executives became even more upset with the introduction of DVRs (**digital video recorders**) like TiVo, which allow viewers to pause, fast-forward, and rewind live TV, store programming, and skip commercials altogether. To its credit, TiVo never promoted the ad-skipping feature to consumers, but it was no secret. Everybody knew.

Ironically, though, within a very short time, TiVo executives were courting marketers and agencies to join its charter advertiser program, which would let viewers opt in to a marketer's "advertainment" show. Best Buy bought in early and so did Sony Pictures, Lexus, Procter & Gamble, and Miller Brewing. One of the major features of TiVo is its ability to target potential customers and measure effectiveness against that target. As *Advertising Age* pointed out, the Holy Grail to advertisers is a one-to-one relationship with consumers, and that becomes increasingly possible with permission-based, opt-in, and two-way interactions with viewers.[26]

Digital technology has also had a huge impact. Personal computers, mobile phones, the Internet, and e-mail give advertisers new media for reaching potential customers. In response to products such as TiVo, and perhaps as a result of the hard lessons learned by the recording industry, which experienced declines in music sales as a result of file-sharing technologies, the broadcast networks realized they would have to adapt to the digital age. In 2006, ABC was the first network to offer hit shows for Internet download just days after the programs aired, posting episodes of popular series such as *Lost* and *Desperate Housewives* on Apple's iTunes Web site. For a couple of bucks consumers could download the shows and watch them commercial free on their computers or iPods. The broadcast networks also developed Web sites for watching streamed versions of the shows with embedded Web-only advertisements. AOL reached into the vault of classic TV series, such as *Kung Fu, Growing Pains,* and *F-Troop,* and made the shows available for free, ad-supported viewing. Clearly, TVs and personal computers are melding into something new, vibrant, and exciting: technologies that make custom entertainment schedules available to viewers when and where they want them. TVs, computers, and network advertising will never be the same. A writer's strike that affected the industry for months in late 2007 and early 2008 was motivated partially by compensation issues surrounding digital entertainment.

What we are witnessing is an interactive revolution. Advertising is evolving into a two-way medium where consumers with PCs, Internet connections, and cable TV can choose the information they access and then spend time researching the product information they

> # AGENCIES NOW HAVE THE OPPORTUNITY TO PROVE ONCE AGAIN THAT ADVERTISING CREATIVITY IS NOT ABOUT WINNING AWARDS BUT ABOUT HELPING MARKETERS *SELL* THINGS.[28]

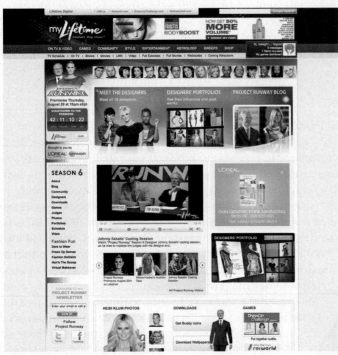

Broadcast networks, such as ABC, allow viewers to watch full episodes of their favorite shows on the Internet, with embedded Web-only advertisements (http://abc.go.com/watch).

In truth, despite strong government intervention on behalf of banks, insurers, and auto manufacturers, capitalism is likely to remain the greatest influence on markets in the United States. Looking ahead, economists are hopeful that the U.S. and global economies will emerge from their difficulties in 2010 or 2011. When America's economy does emerge, it is likely that those companies smart enough to continue their advertising through tough times will reap significant benefits.

Advertising has come a long way from the simple sign on the bootmaker's shop. Today it is a powerful device that announces the availability and location of products, describes their quality and value, imbues brands with personality, and simultaneously defines the personalities of the people who buy them while entertaining us. More than a reflection of society and its desires, advertising can start and end fads, trends, and credos—sometimes all by itself.[29]

The endless search for competitive advantage and efficiency has made advertising's journey in the last 100 plus years fascinating. Now companies are realizing that their most

desire.[27] As we discuss in Chapter 13, this is a revolutionary way for advertisers to reach consumers. Agencies now have the opportunity to prove once again that advertising creativity is not about winning awards but about helping marketers *sell* things.[28]

In September of 2008 the global economy began an economic slowdown. Many companies, faced with declining sales and lower revenue, cut back on advertising expenditures.

Particularly hard hit was the newspaper industry. Several high-profile papers, including the *Christian Science Monitor* and the *Rocky Mountain News,* already weakened by lower ad sales, shut down their presses. Markets, roiled by uncertainty, dropped to levels not seen in decades. Some critics even asked whether capitalism itself was at risk.

New technology has meant new media, manifested largely in the Internet. This has opened new avenues of exposure for advertisers. This Web site for Daum shows that beautiful layout and design is not confined to the traditional medium of print.

Their most important asset is their customer and the relationship they have with that person or organization.

important asset is not capital equipment or their line of products. In the heated competition of the global marketplace, their most important asset is their customer and the relationship they have with that person or organization. Protecting that asset has become the new marketing imperative for the twenty-first century. In an effort to do a better job of *relationship marketing*, companies are now learning that they must be consistent in both what they say and what they do. It's not enough to produce outstanding advertising anymore. They must integrate all their marketing communications with everything else they do, too. That's what *integrated marketing communications* really means. And that will present exciting new challenges to marketing and advertising professionals in the immediate future.

check yourself ✓

1. What are the five identified periods in the history of Western civilization and what key developments characterized each period?

2. Explain how one development during each period impacted the evolution of advertising.

LO5 Describe the impact of advertising on society.

SOCIETY AND ETHICS: THE EFFECTS OF ADVERTISING

Advertising has been a major factor in improving the standard of living in the United States and around the world. By publicizing the material, social, and cultural opportunities of a free enterprise society, advertising has encouraged increased productivity by both management and labor.

With just a small amount of money, for instance, you can buy a car today. It may be secondhand, but from advertising you know it's available. If you earn more money, you can buy a new car or one with more luxury features. You can also make a statement about yourself as an individual with the vehicle you purchase. As with many products, advertising has created a personality for each automobile make and model on the market. As a free individual, you can select the product that best matches your needs and aspirations.

Advertising serves other social needs besides simply stimulating sales. Newspapers, magazines, radio, television, and many Web sites all receive their primary income from advertising. This facilitates freedom of the press and promotes more complete information. Public service announcements also foster growth and understanding of important social issues and causes. The Red Cross, Community Chest, United Way, and other noncommercial organizations receive continuous financial support and volunteer assistance due in large part to the power of advertising.

However, advertising is certainly not without its shortcomings. Since its beginnings, the profession has had to struggle with issues of truthfulness and ethics. In fact, in the early 1900s, the advertising profession was forced to mend its ethical ways. Consumers suffered for years from unsubstantiated product claims, especially for patent medicines and health devices. The simmering resentment finally boiled over into a full-blown consumer movement, which led to government regulation and ultimately to industry efforts at self-regulation.

In 1906 Congress responded to public outrage by passing the Pure Food and Drug Act to protect the public's health and control drug advertising. In 1914, it passed the Federal Trade Commission Act to protect the public from unfair business practices, including misleading and deceptive advertising.

Advertising practitioners themselves formed groups to improve advertising effectiveness and promote professionalism and started vigilance committees to safeguard the integrity of the industry. The Association of National Advertisers (ANA), the American Advertising Federation (AAF), and the Better Business Bureau (BBB) are today's outgrowths of those early groups. These organizations are the result of a fundamental truth: the biggest opponents of unethical advertisers are advertisers who embrace ethical and truthful communication practices.

But in times of economic crisis, false and misleading advertising has invariably reappeared, perhaps out of advertiser desperation. During the Depression years, several best-selling books exposed the advertising industry as an unscrupulous exploiter of consumers.

In a 1962 message to Congress, President Kennedy asserted, "if consumers are offered inferior products, if prices are exorbitant . . . if the consumer is unable to choose on an informed basis, then his dollar is wasted . . . and the national interest suffers." In his Bill for Consumer Rights, Kennedy gave the American consumer four basic rights, including the right "to be protected against fraudulent, deceitful, or grossly misleading information, advertising, labeling, or other practices, and to be given the facts s/he needs to make an informed choice."

In the 1970s, a new American consumer movement grew out of the widespread disillusionment following the Kennedy assassination, the Vietnam War, the Watergate scandals, and the sudden shortage of vital natural resources—all communicated instantly to the world via new satellite technology. These issues fostered cynicism and distrust of the establishment and tradition, and gave rise to a new twist in moral consciousness. On the one hand, people justified their personal irresponsibility and self-indulgence in the name of self-fulfillment. On the other, they attacked corporate America's quest for self-fulfillment (profits) in the name of social accountability.

Today, corporate America has generally cleaned up many of the inequities in advertising. But now attention has shifted to more subtle problems of puffery,

To save the earth, the LORAX shows you
That kids can help and it's easy to do.
Turn off lights, TVs, and things you won't use
Save energy with your computer - set it to snooze.
Get your friends and your family to all do their part
Just look for the ENERGY STAR - the best way to start.
Let's show greedy Once-lers what is right
Against global warming, join EPA in the fight!

JOIN THE LORAX AND EPA IN THE FIGHT AGAINST GLOBAL WARMING.
We can all do our part by making easy changes in our homes, at school, and at work. Learn more at **energystar.gov**.

ENERGY STAR

Dr. Seuss properties TM & © 2009 Dr. Seuss Enterprises, L.P. All Rights Reserved.

These public service announcements, encouraging people to look for Energy Star ratings on appliances, are distributed by the EPA to radio stations with a request to play them on air.

advertising to children, the advertising of legal but unhealthful products, and advertising ethics. We believe ethics in advertising is such an important issue that we have included features on this topic throughout the text.

In short, advertising has had a pronounced effect on society as well as the economy. It has also fostered a host of social attitudes and laws that have dramatically affected advertising itself. We'll take a closer look at these issues in Chapter 2. ■

check yourself ✓

1. What are some of the social needs that are served by advertising in the United States?

2. What are some of advertising's societal shortcomings?

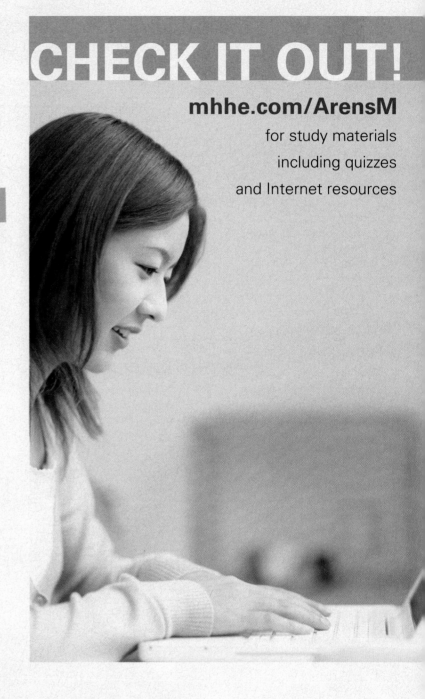

CHECK IT OUT!

mhhe.com/ArensM

for study materials

including quizzes

and Internet resources

chapter two

the economic, social, and regulatory
aspects of advertising

Would you be more likely to buy a watch brand if you knew that Jeff Gordon or Brad Pitt wears it? What if it was the preferred brand of Maria Sharapova or Uma Thurman? Swiss luxury watchmaker TagHeuer must think so, since it pays celebrities to appear in ads. Nike spends millions on endorsement contracts and has long partnered with Michael Jordan, Derek Jeter and Tiger Woods. The athletes agree to wear Nike clothes and use Nike gear during competitions. Many also appear in Nike ads.

Are celebrity endorsements worth the large amounts that companies spend on them? Business professors Jagdish Agrawal and Wagner Kamakura argue that celebrities help to make ads believable, enhance ad recall, increase brand recognition, and ultimately influence consumers to choose an endorsed brand.[1] So it should be no surprise that as many as one of five TV commercials features someone famous.

But what happens when brands are linked with celebrities who attract the wrong kind of attention? It happens all the time. The long list of famous individuals who have lost endorsement deals because of controversy includes Madonna (Pepsi), Ludacris (Pepsi), Jose Canseco (California Egg Commission), Kobe Bryant (McDonald's), Mary Kate Olsen (milk), Eminem (Ford), and Kate Moss (Chanel).

continued on p. 28

LEARNING OBJECTIVES

LO1 Describe the impact of advertising on the economy.

LO2 Examine the validity of the various social criticisms of advertising.

LO3 Explain the difference between social responsibility and ethics in advertising.

LO4 Describe how government agencies regulate advertising to protect both consumers and competitors.

LO5 Discuss the activities of nongovernment organizations in fighting fraudulent and deceptive advertising.

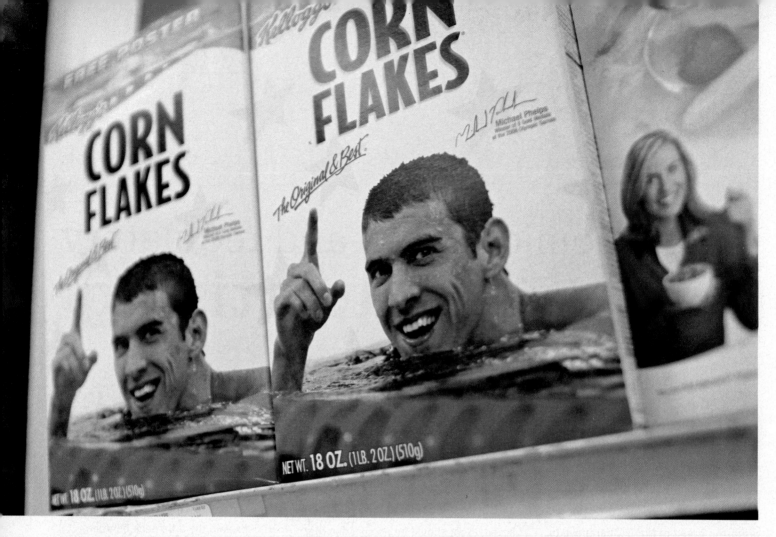

continued from p. 27

For Michael Phelps, controversy erupted almost immediately after his ascent to fame. Phelps was photographed at a college party using a device associated with smoking marijuana. The photo was later distributed to the press and appeared throughout the world. Phelps was not charged with a crime, but he issued a heartfelt apology and took responsibility for his mistake. Even so, some of his sponsors severed their contracts. Others stood by the Olympian, believing his error did not rise to the level of a serious offense. Which companies did the right thing?

One of the biggest sports stories of 2010 concerned the scandal surrounding Tiger Woods and his alleged infidelities. Woods, who, until the scandal broke, earned more from sponsorships and endorsements than any athlete in history, found that some sponsors abandoned him entirely (Gatorade) while others stood by him (Nike). In an unusual move, Nike created an ad that offered a mea culpa of sorts, in which Tiger seemed to received a stern lecture from his decreased father. Was Nike using the spot to acknowledge Tiger's sins? Or merely protecting its most important sports asset? Opinions were mixed.

Companies understand that they take a risk when they associate their brands too closely with a single endorser. Jeremy Mullman, writing for *Advertising Age,* says that Nike has been recently moving toward an "ensemble approach" to endorsements. Translation: Nike uses a pool of athletes to promote its wares rather than one big star. Risk to the brand is reduced, therefore, should any of the athletes stumble. Under Armour, a Nike competitor, uses a similar approach. A company VP notes that Under Armour doesn't "let any one person get bigger than the brand."[2]

Lessons? The same dynamics that can benefit a brand linked to an admired celebrity can damage a brand associated with a controversial one. Mr. Clean, the Maytag Repairman, and the Burger King will never embarrass anyone—these "celebrities" only exist in ads. However, when brands partner with real people, life gets much more complicated. Tiger Woods and Michael Phelps earned big endorsement contracts because of the things they

Views of offensiveness vary a great deal. This ad from Shoebaloo is entitled "Amputee." Do you find the image inspiring or disturbing?

can do as athletes. And yet, in the end, their all too human weaknesses created marketing challenges. The quandaries faced by Woods's and Phelps's sponsors helped reinforce a basic truth: ethics and social responsibility are every company's business. ■

THE MANY CONTROVERSIES ABOUT ADVERTISING

Advertising is a highly visible activity. Companies risk public criticism and attack if their advertising displeases or offends or if their products don't measure up to the advertised promises. Proponents of advertising say it's therefore safer to buy advertised products because, when a company's name and reputation are on the line, it tries harder to fulfill its promises.

Advertising is both applauded and criticized not only for its role in selling products but also for its influence on the economy and on society. For years, critics have denigrated advertising for a wide range of sins—some real, some imagined.

John O'Toole, the late chair of Foote, Cone & Belding and president of the American Association of Advertising Agencies, pointed out that many critics attack advertising because it *isn't something else.*

Advertising isn't journalism, education, or entertainment—although it often performs the tasks of all three—so it shouldn't be judged by those standards. Sponsors advertise because they hope it will help them sell some product, service, or idea.[3]

Notwithstanding O'Toole's articulate defense, many controversies still swirl around the whole field of advertising. Some focus on advertising's *economic* role. For example, how does advertising affect the value of products? Does it cause higher or lower prices? Does it promote competition or discourage it? How does advertising affect overall consumer demand? What effect does it have on consumer choice and on the overall business cycle?

Other controversies focus on the *societal* effects of advertising. For instance, does advertising make us more materialistic? Does it force us to buy things we don't need? Does it reach us subliminally in ways we can't control? How does it affect the art and culture of our society? Does advertising debase our language?

From these controversies, new questions arise regarding the responsibility for and control of advertising. What is the proper role for participants in the marketing process? How much latitude should marketers have in what products they promote and how they advertise them? Do consumers have some responsibility in the process? Finally, what is the proper role of government? What laws should we have to protect consumers? And do laws sometimes go too far and violate the marketer's freedom of speech?

These are important questions, and there are no simple answers. But debate is healthy. This chapter addresses some of the major questions and criticisms about advertising, both the pros and the cons, and delves into the regulatory methods used to remedy advertisers' abuses.

Recall from Chapter 1 the underlying principle of free-market economics—that a society is best served by empowering people to make their own decisions and act as free agents within a system characterized by four fundamental assumptions: *self-interest, many buyers and sellers, complete information,* and *absence of externalities (social costs).*

added value The increase in worth of a product or service as a result of a particular activity. In the context of advertising, the added value is provided by the communication of benefits over and above those offered by the product itself.

This framework, derived from the goal of society to promote behaviors that foster the greatest good for the most people, offers a system of economic activity—free enterprise—that has accomplished that goal better than any other economic system in history. This is why societies around the world are increasingly adopting free enterprise economics.

By using this framework for our discussion of advertising controversies, we have a basis for understanding how advertising may contribute to, or detract from, the basic goal of free enterprise: "the most good for the most people."

LO1 Describe the impact of advertising on the economy.

THE ECONOMIC IMPACT OF ADVERTISING

Advertising accounts for approximately 2 percent of the U.S. gross domestic product (GDP). In relation to the total U.S. economy, this percentage is small. Still the United States has the highest per capita ad spending in the world. As Marcel

▼ **EXHIBIT 2–1** A country's level of ad spending is closely related to its standard of living.

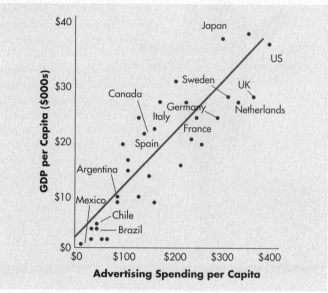

Source: Direct Mail Marketing Trends: United States and Western Europe, Direct Mail Advertising Board, October 1, 2005.

Bleustein-Blanchet, the father of modern French advertising, pointed out, it's no coincidence that the level of advertising investment in a country is directly proportional to its standard of living.[4] Exhibit 2–1 shows the relationship between advertising spending per capita and standard of living (GDP per capita) around the world.

The economic effect of advertising is like the break shot in billiards or pool. The moment a company begins to advertise, it sets off a chain reaction of economic events, as shown in Exhibit 2–2. The extent of the chain reaction, although hard to predict, is related to the force of the shot and the economic environment in which it occurred. Let's consider the economic questions we posed earlier.

Effect on the Value of Products

Why do most people prefer Coca-Cola to some other cola? Why do some people prefer the iPod to some unadvertised brand? Are the advertised products functionally better? Not necessarily. But, in the mind of the consumer, advertising has given these brands **added value**.

▼ **EXHIBIT 2–2** The economic effect of advertising is like the opening break shot in billiards.

Prix bas.

Prix bas tout compris.

DARTY

Does advertising lead to higher prices? Economists believe that ads can actually contribute to lower product prices. This ad for Darty, a French retailer, is designed to attract price-sensitive consumers. "Low price or low price with everything included."

ANTHONY'S PIZZA

6237 Cermak Rd., Berwyn, IL

708 **749-1100**

$3.00 OFF
ON ANY $10.00 or MORE
FOOD or PIZZA Purchase!
You must mention this coupon when ordering.
Not valid with any other coupons,
discounts or offers.
Limit one coupon per order, per customer.
Excluding Tax & Delivery.
EXPIRES MARCH 31, 2006
ANTHONY'S PIZZA • (708) 749-1100

Fast - Hot Delivery Starting at 11:00am

MON - THURS ~
11 AM to 12 Midnight
FRI & SAT ~ 11 AM to 1 AM
SUNDAY ~
11 AM to 12 Midnight

Advertising often makes it possible for small businesses to compete effectively against large corporations. Anthony's Pizza's freedom to advertise allows this neighborhood pizza parlor to compete with the national chains.

Some believe that a product's *image,* created in part by advertising and promotion, is *an inherent feature of the product itself.*[5] While an ad may not address a product's quality directly, the positive image conveyed by advertising may imply quality. By simply making the product better known, advertising can make the product more desirable to the consumer. In this way, advertising adds value to the brand.[6] That's why people pay more for Bufferin than an unadvertised brand displayed right next to it—even though all buffered aspirin, by law, is functionally the same.[7] Advertising also adds value to a brand by educating customers about new uses for a product. Kleenex was originally advertised as a makeup remover, later as a disposable handkerchief. Arm & Hammer baking soda experienced a surge in sales when it was advertised as a refrigerator deodorant.

In a free market system, consumers can choose the values they want in the products they buy. If low price is important, they can buy an inexpensive economy car. If status and luxury are important, they can buy a fancy sedan or racy sports

> " It's no coincidence that the level of advertising investment in a country is directly proportional to its standard of living.[4] "

car. Many of our wants are emotional, social, or psychological rather than functional. One way we communicate who we are (or want to be) is through the products we purchase and display. By associating the product with some desirable image, advertising offers people the opportunity to satisfy those psychic or symbolic wants and needs.

In terms of our economic framework, by adding value to products, advertising contributes to self-interest—for both the consumer and the advertiser. It also contributes to the number of sellers. That increases competition, which also serves the consumer's self-interest.

Effect on Prices

If advertising adds value to products, it follows that advertising also adds cost, right? And if companies stopped all that expensive advertising, products would cost less, right?

Not necessarily.

Some advertised products do cost more than unadvertised products, but the opposite is also true. Both the Federal Trade Commission and the Supreme Court have ruled that by encouraging competition, advertising has the effect of keeping prices down. This again serves the consumer's self-interest.

Sweeping statements about advertising's positive or negative effect on prices are likely to be too simplistic. We can make some important points, though.

- As a cost of doing business, advertising is indeed paid for by the consumer who buys the product. In most product categories, though, the amount spent on advertising is very small compared with the total cost of the product.

- Advertising often enables manufacturers to engage in mass production, which in turn lowers the unit cost of products. These savings can then be passed on to consumers in the form of lower prices.

- In regulated industries (agriculture, utilities), advertising has historically had no effect on prices. When industries are deregulated, advertising has affected price—usually downward, but not always.

- In retailing, price is prominent in many ads, so advertising tends to hold prices down. On the other hand, national manufacturers use advertising to stress features that make their brands better; in these cases advertising tends to support higher prices.

Effect on Competition

Some believe advertising restricts competition because small companies or industry newcomers can't compete with the immense advertising budgets of large firms.

Intense competition does tend to reduce the number of businesses in an industry. However, firms eliminated by competition

The famous "Got Milk?" campaign promotes primary rather than selective demand because it promotes consumption of milk in general, rather than a specific brand of milk.

may be those that served customers least effectively. In other cases, competition is reduced because of mergers and acquisitions.

High costs may inhibit the entry of new competitors in industries that spend heavily on advertising. In some markets, the original brands probably benefit greatly from this barrier. However, the investments needed for plants, machinery, and labor are of far greater significance. These are typically greater barriers to entry than advertising.

Advertising by big companies often has only a limited effect on small businesses because a single advertiser is rarely large enough to dominate the whole country. Regional oil companies, for example, compete very successfully with national oil companies on the local level. In fact, the freedom to advertise encourages more sellers to enter the market. And we've all seen nonadvertised store brands of food compete very effectively with nationally advertised brands on the same grocery shelves.

Effect on Consumers and Businesses

The question of advertising's effect on total consumer demand is extremely complex. Numerous studies show that promotional activity does affect aggregate consumption, but they disagree as to the extent of its influence. For example, the demand for flat-panel TVs, cellular phones, and laptop computers expanded at a tremendous rate, thanks in part to advertising but more to favorable market conditions. At the same time, advertising hasn't reversed declining sales of such items as hats, fur coats, and manual typewriters.

Advertising can help get new products off the ground by giving people more "complete information," thereby stimulating **primary demand**—demand for the entire product class. In declining markets, when the only information people want is price information, advertising can influence **selective demand**—demand for a particular brand. But the only effect it will have on primary demand is to slow the rate of decline. In growing markets, advertisers generally compete for shares of that growth. In mature, static, or declining markets, they compete for each other's shares.

Manufacturers who want to beat the competition need to make their product different. For example, look at the long list of car models, sizes, colors, and features designed to attract different buyers. The freedom to advertise encourages businesses to create new brands and improve old ones. When one brand reaches market dominance, smaller brands may disappear for a time. But the moment a better product comes along and is advertised skillfully, the dominant brand loses out to the newer, better product. Once again, the freedom to advertise promotes the existence of more sellers, and that gives consumers wider choices.

Historically, when business cycles dip, companies cut advertising expenditures. That may help short-term profits, but studies prove that businesses that continue to invest in advertising during a recession are better able to protect, and sometimes build, market shares.[8] However, no study has shown that if everybody just kept advertising, a recessionary cycle would turn around. We conclude that when business cycles are up, advertising contributes to the increase. When business cycles are down, advertising may act as a stabilizing force by encouraging buyers to continue buying.

The Abundance Principle: The Economic Impact of Advertising in Perspective

To individual businesses such as Apple, the local car dealer, and the convenience store on the corner, advertising pays back

Advertising stimulates a healthy economy. It also helps create financially healthy consumers who are more informed, better educated, and more demanding. Consumers today insist that manufacturers be held accountable for their advertising. This has led to an unprecedented level of social criticism and legal regulation, the subject of our next sections.

check yourself ✓

1. Why do you think countries with higher advertising spending per capita tend to have a higher standard of living?

2. Explain the effect that advertising has on brands, prices, competition, and primary and selective demand.

3. What beneficial roles does advertising play in a healthy economy?

> [Advertising helps create financially healthy consumers who are more informed, better educated, and more demanding.]

more than it costs. If advertising didn't pay, no one would use it. But advertising costs less for the consumer than most people think. The cost of a bottle of Coke includes about a penny for advertising. And the $20,000 price tag on a new car usually includes a manufacturer's advertising cost of less than $400.

To the broader economy, the importance of advertising is best demonstrated by the **abundance principle**. This states that in an economy that produces more goods and services than can be consumed, advertising serves two important purposes: It keeps consumers informed of their alternatives (*complete information*), and it allows companies to compete more effectively for consumer dollars (*self-interest*). In North America alone, the U.S. and Canadian economies produce an enormous selection of products. Most supermarkets carry more than 30,000 different items. Each automaker markets dozens of models. This competition generally results in more and better products at similar or lower prices.

Advertising stimulates competition (*many buyers and sellers*). In countries where consumers have money to spend after their physical needs are satisfied, advertising also stimulates innovation and new products. However, no amount of advertising can achieve long-term acceptance for products that people don't want. Despite massive advertising expenditures, fewer than a dozen of the 50 best-known cars developed in the twentieth century are still sold today.

L02 Examine the validity of the various social criticisms of advertising.

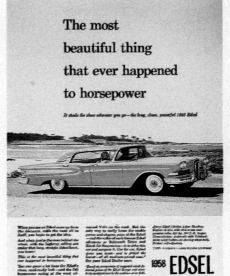

The most beautiful thing that ever happened to horsepower

1958 EDSEL

Despite extensive advertising efforts, some products, like the Edsel automobile, will fail simply because they do not meet the expectations of customers at that particular time. Many of the best-known cars developed in the twentieth century are no longer sold today. Ironically, the Edsel has since become a pricy collector's item for automobile aficionados.

THE SOCIAL IMPACT OF ADVERTISING

Because it's so visible, advertising gets criticized frequently, for both what it is and what it isn't. Many of the criticisms focus on the *style* of advertising, saying it's deceptive or manipulative. Other criticisms focus on the *social* or *environmental impact* of advertising. Let's look at some of these common criticisms of advertising, debunk some misconceptions, and examine the problems that do exist.

Deception in Advertising

One of the most common criticisms of advertising style is that it is so frequently deceptive. If a product does not live up to its ads, dissatisfaction occurs—something that is as harmful to the advertiser as to the buyer.

For advertising to be effective, consumers must have confidence in it. So deception not only detracts from the complete information principle of free enterprise but also risks being self-defeating. Even meaningless (but legal) puffery might be

Daffy's (*www.daffys.com*) *uses tongue-in-cheek humor to take a stand against advertising puffery—inflated promises and claims often accompanied by inflated prices. Daffy's beckons smart consumers to shop where they can find the same quality goods with "no bull" price tags.*

> "Advertising, by its very nature, is *not* complete information. It is biased in favor of the advertiser."

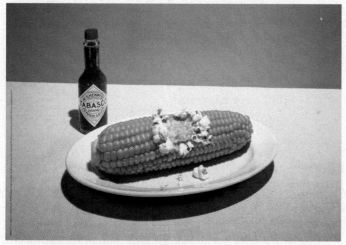

Puffery is rarely so literal as it is in this German advertisement for Tabasco hot sauce. Although the peppery condiment won't actually cause corn kernels to pop off the cob, such puffery is not illegal because it is so unbelievable.

taken literally and therefore mislead. **Puffery** refers to exaggerated, often subjective claims that can't necessarily be proven true or false, such as "the best" or "the only way to fly."

Under current advertising law, the only product claims—explicit or implied—that are considered deceptive are those that are *factually false* or convey a false impression and therefore have the potential to deceive or mislead reasonable people.[9] But puffery is excluded from this requirement because regulators maintain that reasonable people don't believe it anyway.

Of course, advertising, by its very nature, is *not* complete information. It is biased in favor of the advertiser and the brand. People expect advertisers to be proud of their products and probably don't mind if they puff them a little. But when advertisers cross the line and create false expectations, people begin to object. One problem is the difficulty of seeing the line, which may be drawn differently by different people. Papa John's Pizza no doubt thought it was just puffing when it advertised "Better ingredients. Better pizza." Pizza

Truth in Advertising: Fluffing and Puffing

In advertising, puffery means exaggerated commendation, or hype. The term comes from the Old English word *pyffan,* meaning "to blow in short gusts" or "to inflate; make proud or conceited." Puffery surely predates recorded history.

The Nature of Puffery

Regardless of its long heritage and current widespread use, we should question puffery's role in advertising. Puffery erodes advertising's credibility as a trustworthy messenger by lowering the public's belief in the advertising they see. People begin to question those who support and create such advertising—the advertisers, ad professionals, and ultimately the media that run such ads.

Defining Puffery

Regardless of the criticisms, puffery remains legal. And in the United States, it's relatively well defined by law.

The Federal Trade Commission, in the late 1950s, confirmed, "Puffery does not embrace misstatements of material facts."

Puffery's legal definition establishes that the characteristics puffed must, in fact, exist. The challenge is defining where puffing crosses over from exaggeration into falsehood and then to deception. Exaggeration is often the starting point of falsehood, but falsehood is not necessarily harmful or injurious—in fact, it may be playful and creative. Deception, however, is potentially injurious to consumers and is therefore illegal.

Take, for example, the case with Papa John's International, which invested millions of dollars over the years in its "Better ingredients, Better pizza" advertising campaign. The vague and subjective claim might be considered puffery. But when it named its rival Pizza Hut in ads, the issue changed from mere puffery to comparison. And comparison advertising requires convincing substantiation; otherwise it may be considered deceptive.

In 1998, Pizza Hut filed a lawsuit in Dallas federal court against Papa John's, alleging that its campaign was "false, misleading, and deceptive." A Texas jury ruled in favor of Pizza Hut, charging that Papa John's "Better ingredients, Better pizza" campaign constituted deceptive advertising. Pizza Hut was awarded $467,619.75. Papa John's was ordered to remove its slogan from ads, pizza boxes, restaurant signage, and delivery trucks.

Later, the decision was reversed by the District Court of Appeals after Papa John's removed the references to Pizza Hut. But the point had still been made: Advertisers have to be careful about the puffery claims they make—they no longer have free rein. Marketers need to be able to substantiate any claims that they make. An indirect comparison, or even the appearance of one, could render them liable.

The Use of Puffery

Common usage portrays puffery as praise for the item to be sold using subjective opinions, superlatives, exaggerations, and vagueness, and generally stating no specific facts.

Puffery often takes the form of "nonproduct facts," information not specifically about the product and therefore not directly testable as true or false. Nonproduct facts are typically about consumers: their personalities, lifestyles, fears, anxieties. An example was the Army's positioning message, "Be all that you can be in the Army" (1981–2001). The claim relied on the potential for what could happen to the ad's readers while they were in the Army. It didn't actually promise any specific benefits such as improved physical fitness or more education. Thus, regardless of what actually happened to readers who joined up, the claim was neither true nor false about the Army.

Puffery can also be "artful display," the visual presentation of a product. Although not well defined by law, visual exaggeration is ever present in ads to enhance moods, excite viewers, and more. The existence of professional models, for example, suggests that some individuals are more visually attractive than others. This factor makes them appealing. But does their appearance in an ad imply that owning the product will make the buyer more physically attractive?

Judging Puffery

We live in exciting times. Populations are more literate, satellites and the Internet keep the world informed instantly, and modern technology speeds up the way we live and play. And part of the glitz of our modern life is puffery, adding pizzazz and stimulating our dreams.

But who should protect consumers from puffery, especially when puffery crosses the line and becomes injurious? Who should evaluate puffery's ethics? The courts may, but only when a consumer challenges an advertiser. The actions and attitudes of the advertising profession can make a huge difference.

CHAPTER 2 | The Economic, Social, and Regulatory Aspects of Advertising 35

Hut saw it differently, though, and sued Papa John's for deceptive advertising. A U.S. District judge agreed and awarded Pizza Hut close to half a million dollars in damages. The judge then ordered Papa John's to stop using its "Better ingredients" slogan.[10] This decision was later overturned on appeal, but the case still goes to show that there are limits on what an advertiser can safely puff. For more on this story and on puffery, see "Ethical Issues: Truth in Advertising: Fluffing and Puffing" on page 35.

The Subliminal Advertising Myth

Wilson Bryan Key promotes the notion that, to seduce consumers, advertisers intentionally create ads with sexual messages hidden in the illustrations. He calls this **subliminal advertising**. His premise is that by embedding dirty words in the ice cubes in a liquor ad, for instance, advertisers can make us want to buy the product. Many academic studies have debunked this theory.[11] In fact, to date no study has proved that such embedding exists or that it would have any effect if it did exist.[12]

The nerve that Key has been able to touch, though, is important. The widespread fear is that advertisers are messing with our heads—manipulating us—without our consent, into buying things we don't want or need. This gets to the heart of the *complete information* principle because the criticism suggests that advertising does not give consumers information but rather manipulates us through brainwashing. Consumers are, therefore, like captured prey, helpless in the jaws of marketing predators.

If you think about all the products you buy, how many involve a choice between different brands and different models? And how many involve a decision based on price or convenience? Probably most. So how many of your purchases can you trace to having been helplessly manipulated? Probably none. You receive information from many different sources: friends and relatives, store displays, ads, packaging, and retail store clerks. At some point, you make a decision. In many cases, your decision is *not* to buy at all—to wait for either more information or more money. As always, the customer, acting in his or her own self-interest, makes the decision.

Advertising and Our Value System

An argument, often voiced by critics, is that advertising degrades people's value systems by promoting a hedonistic, materialistic way of life. Advertising, they say, encourages us to buy more cars, iPods, clothing, and junk we don't need. It is destroying the essence of our "citizen democracy," replacing it with a self-oriented consumer democracy.[13]

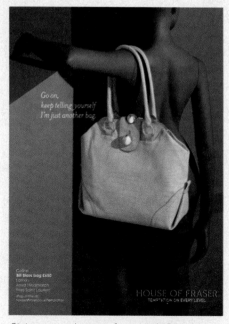

Status comes in many forms and often vivid imagery can be quite inviting to prospective buyers. This ad for House of Fraser contrasts the beautiful white Bill Blass handbag with a dark background and challenges the reader to "keep telling yourself I'm just another bag."

This manipulation works because ads play on our emotions and promise greater status, social acceptance, and sex appeal. They cause people to take up harmful habits, make poor kids buy $170 sneakers, and tempt ordinary people to buy useless products in the vain attempt to emulate celebrity endorsers.[14] Again, critics claim advertising is so powerful consumers are helpless to defend themselves against it.

Others believe this argument exaggerates the power of advertising. They note that most Americans express a healthy skepticism toward it. One study showed that only 17 percent of U.S. consumers see advertising as a source of information to help them decide what to buy.[15] Perhaps that's why more advertised products fail than succeed in the marketplace.

Still, there's no question that advertisers do indeed spend millions trying to convince people their products will make them sexier, healthier, and more successful. The very amount of advertising we witness every day seems to suggest that every problem we have can be solved by the purchase of some product.

The Proliferation of Advertising

One of the most common environmental complaints about advertising is that there's just too much of it. In the United States alone, the average person may be exposed to 500 to 1,000 commercial messages a day. With so many products competing for attention (more than 30,000 in the average supermarket), advertisers themselves worry about the negative impact of excessive advertising. According to Nielsen, ad clutter is still on the rise. In 2005, the amount of nonprogram time ranged from a low of 16 minutes per hour in prime time to nearly 21 minutes per hour in daytime, a daypart that is particularly important to advertisers.[16] Popular shows are the most cluttered: *Desperate Housewives* had nearly 17 minutes per hour.[17] The networks add to the problem themselves by jamming every possible moment with promotions for their shows. Too much advertising is annoying not only for consumers, but for the advertisers themselves—the more commercials that hit the consumer's brain, the less effective paid advertising is. Conscious of this, Clear Channel—the largest radio group in the United States, with over 1,200 stations, introduced the "Less Is More" program in 2004. When fully implemented the program (now called "Better Radio") will cut advertising by 20 percent. Reduced inventory allowed Clear Channel to raise the price of its scarcer spots. Listeners have responded positively; in 2005, Clear Channel's share had increased in 18 of its 25 largest markets.

While the clutter problem is irksome to viewers and advertisers alike, most people tolerate it as the price for free TV, freedom of the press, and a high standard of living. However, with the proliferation of new media choices, this externality is only likely to get worse. Virtually every popular Web site is cluttered with advertising banners, and our e-mail boxes are flooded with advertising messages on a daily basis. While the Federal Communications Commission exercises no jurisdiction over the Internet, it did consider reinstating commercial time limits on television. But, as of now, the only limits currently in force relate to TV programming aimed at children 12 and under—advertising may not exceed 10.5 minutes per hour on weekends and 12 minutes per hour on weekdays.[18]

Stereotypes in Advertising

Advertising has long been criticized for insensitivity to minorities, women, immigrants, the disabled, the elderly, and other groups.[19] Marketing and advertising practitioners sometimes lose touch with the very people they are trying to reach. This is one reason the discipline of *account planning* (discussed in Chapter 6) is growing so rapidly.

In recent years, national advertisers have become more sensitive to the concerns of minorities and women. Latinos, African Americans, Asians, Native Americans, and others are now usually portrayed favorably in ads, not only because of pressure from watchdog groups, but also because it's just good business; these consumers represent sizable target markets. Marilyn Kern-Foxworth, a Texas A&M professor and an expert on minorities in advertising, points out that positive role portrayal in some mainstream ads has had a positive effect on the self-esteem of African American youth.[20] This positive trend has accelerated with the emergence of many ad agencies that specialize in reaching minority markets.

In national advertising, the image of women is also changing from their historic depiction as either subservient housewives or sex objects. This may be partially due to the increasing number of women in managerial and executive positions with both advertisers and agencies. In 2007, about 59 percent of all women were in the workforce, with more than 48 million of them in managerial and professional careers.[21] Advertisers want to reach, not offend, this sizable market of upwardly mobile consumers. Some agencies now retain feminist consultants to review ads that may risk offending women.[22] In 2003, Ann Fudge was named CEO of Young and Rubicam and became the first African-American woman to head a major U.S. advertising agency. *Forbes* named Fudge one of the 100 most powerful women in America in 2004. And in 2007, Nancy Hill became the first female head of the American Association of Advertising Agencies (AAAA).

However, problems still exist, especially in local and regional advertising and in certain product categories such as beer and sports promotions. Many advertisers are just not aware of the

Critics have long complained about the way some ads depict women as sex objects.

externalities that their ads can create, and they may perpetuate male and female stereotypes without even realizing it.[23]

Other advertisers resort to **stereotypes** for convenience. A stereotype is a generalization about a group. Some critics believe ads stereotype women as homemakers or elderly people as weak and frail. And the underrepresentation of minorities in mainstream ads, both local and national, still smacks of tokenism. Observers hope that with increasing numbers of women and minorities joining the ranks of marketing and advertising professionals, and with continuing academic studies of minority and sex-role stereotyping, greater attention will be focused on these issues.

Offensive Advertising

Offensiveness is another style argument that also speaks to externalities. Many parents, for instance, were incensed at Abercrombie & Fitch's ads because they perceived them as pornographic, thereby causing a social cost that extended beyond the limited scope of merely selling clothes. The fact is, people just don't want their children exposed to messages that they deem immoral, offensive, or strictly adult-oriented.[24]

Taste, however, is highly subjective: What is bad taste to some is perfectly acceptable to others. And tastes change. What is considered offensive today may not be so tomorrow. People were outraged when the first ad for underarm deodorant appeared in a 1927 *Ladies Home Journal;* today no one questions such ads.

Grooming, fashion, and personal hygiene products often use partial nudity in their ads. Where nudity is relevant to the product, people are less likely to regard it as offensive—except when the advertising is targeting kids. In many European countries, in fact, nudity in commercials is commonplace. Even the usually staid Brits are starting to see women's breasts in TV commercials and posters.[25]

Some consumers get so offended by both advertising and TV programming that they boycott sponsors' products.[26] Of course, they also have the option to just change the channel. Both of these are effective strategies for consumers because, ultimately, the marketplace has veto power. If ads don't pull in the audience, the campaign will falter and die.[27]

The Social Impact of Advertising in Perspective

Marketing professionals say advertising encourages the development and speeds the acceptance of new products and technologies. It fosters employment. It gives consumers and business

La Chica Que Siempre Llega Tarde.

El ION Red Line De Saturn Con 205 Caballos De Fuerza.

Pensar primero en la gente también significa ayudarle a llegar a tiempo. Con su motor superpotente de 205 caballos de fuerza, suspensión deportiva y rines metálicos de 17", el ION™ Red Line cupé puede hacerte llegar mucho más temprano. Más información en Saturn.com

La gente primero.

With tightening markets, advertisers must double their efforts to maintain or expand market share. One way is to expand into minority communities, which have enormous buying power and offer a significant amount of market share. Minorities are now portrayed more favorably in ads, not only because of societal pressure, but because it's good for business.

[Ultimately, the marketplace has veto power. If ads don't pull in the audience, the campaign will falter and die.[27]]

customers a wider variety of choices. By encouraging mass production, it helps keep prices down. And it stimulates healthy competition between producers, which benefits all buyers.[28] Advertising, they point out, also promotes a higher standard of living; it pays for most of our news media and subsidizes the arts; it supports freedom of the press; and it provides a means to disseminate public information about important health and social issues. These benefits, they believe, are important.

Critics might agree with some of these points but certainly not all of them. For example, critics charge that rather than supporting a free press, advertising actually interferes with it. The media, they say, pander to national advertisers to attract the big ad dollars. In the process, they modify their editorial content to suit marketers and shirk their primary journalistic responsibility of presenting news in the public interest.[29]

In summary, we can conclude that while advertising may legitimately be criticized for offering less-than-complete information and, in some instances, for creating unwanted problems, it should also be applauded when it contributes to the benefits of a free economy. In most cases, by being a rich information source (albeit not complete), advertising contributes

check yourself ✓

1. Describe six common criticisms of advertising and discuss how you might refute them.

Without advertising, public service organizations would be unable to reach a mass audience to educate people about important health and social issues. Here, the Ad Council promotes the benefits of losing weight.

what society views as best for the welfare of people in general or for a specific community of people. Together, ethics and social responsibility can be seen as the moral obligation of advertisers not to violate our basic economic assumptions, even when there is no legal obligation.

Advertisers' Social Responsibility

Advertising plays an important role in developed countries. It influences a society's stability and growth. It helps secure large armies, creates entertainment events attracting hundreds of thousands of fans, and often affects the outcome of political elections. Such power places a burden of responsibility on those who sponsor, buy, create, produce, and sell advertising to maintain ethical standards that support the society and contribute to the economic system.

In the United States, for example, the advertising industry is part of a large business community. Like any good neighbor, it has responsibilities: to keep its property clean, participate in civic events, support local enterprises, and improve the community. U.S. advertising professionals meet these challenges by forming local advertising clubs, the American Advertising Federation (AAF), the American Association of Advertising Agencies (AAAA), and the Ad Council. These organizations provide thousands of hours and millions of dollars' worth of *pro bono* (free) work to charitable organizations and public agencies. They also provide scholarships and internships, contributions that serve the whole society. As we discuss later, they even regulate themselves fairly effectively.

to the existence of many buyers and sellers and, therefore, to the self-interest of both consumers and marketers.

L03 Explain the difference between social responsibility and ethics in advertising.

SOCIAL RESPONSIBILITY AND ADVERTISING ETHICS

Numerous laws determine what advertisers can and cannot do, but they also allow a significant amount of leeway. That's where ethics and social responsibility come into play. An advertiser can act unethically or irresponsibly without breaking any laws. As advertising professor Ivan Preston says, ethics begin where the law ends.[30]

Ethical advertising means doing what the advertiser and the advertiser's peers believe is morally right in a given situation. **Social responsibility** means doing

Today's consumer is more sophisticated than ever about social issues like environmentalism. Leclerc addresses the issue of "plastic bag pollution" in a beautifully produced campaign, where it tells customers "No, Leclerc does not really want to be seen everywhere." Other ads in the series say, "There are some places we don't want to see our name," and "Some advertising we'll pass up willingly."

Ethics of Advertising

Philosophies of ethics span the centuries since Socrates. We can hardly do them justice here. But for practical purposes, let's consider three levels of ethical responsibility and apply them to advertising.

On one level, ethics comprise two interrelated components: the traditional actions taken by people in a society or community and the philosophical rules that society establishes to justify such past actions and decree future actions. These components create the primary rules of ethical behavior in the society and enable us to measure how far an individual or company (or advertiser) strays from the norm. Here, the individual's rights are subject to the standards of what is customary (and therefore proper) for the group.

Every individual also faces a second set of ethical issues: the attitudes, feelings, and beliefs that add up to a personal value system. When these two systems conflict, should the individual act on personal beliefs or on the obligation to serve society? When people cannot resolve an ethical dilemma, they must redefine the issue in dispute. Thus, the third level of ethics concerns singular ethical concepts such as good, bad, right, wrong, duty, integrity, and truth. Are these concepts absolute, universal, and binding? Or are they relative, dependent on situations and consequences? People may differ in their answers.

Most advertisers today strive to maintain fair ethical standards and practice socially responsible advertising. Ad agencies rarely force employees to work on accounts they morally oppose. Once a free-swinging, unchecked business, advertising is today a closely scrutinized and heavily regulated profession. Advertising's past shortcomings have resulted in laws, regulations, and regulatory bodies. Consumer groups, governments, special-interest groups, and even other advertisers now review, control, and modify advertising in order to create more *complete information* and reduce unwanted *externalities*.

Your Campaign Assignment

You will be working on an advertising/IMC campaign, or part of one, this semester. Few things are more important for you when preparing for a semester-long project than understanding the final product that is expected of you. It is only when you know what is expected at the end that you can plan what happens in between.

What You May Be Working On
Different classes have different projects, but it is likely that you will work on one or more of the following for a brand, service, or firm:

- A campaign audit.
- A research report.
- A marketing or IMC plan, including a SWOT analysis.
- An advertising or IMC budget.
- A media plan.
- A creative brief or creative platform.
- A plans book.

Below we explain each of these in turn and give you guidance about where you can find information in this text and on the Internet.

Campaign Audit
Many classes begin by having teams audit the plans books from prior semesters. This accomplishes several things. First, it gives you an idea about what you will be doing all semester. Second, it introduces you to the importance of seeing how research, strategy, planning, budgeting, and creativity all flow together. If you don't have access to the work of other students, why not look over the work of the very best? Visit the Effie Award Web site (http://www.effie.org/winners/search), where you can find great ads and a lot of background information about the campaigns.

Research Report
You may be asked to conduct formative research for the brand. This may include secondary research, useful for gathering information for your IMC plan; qualitative primary research, in which you conduct a focus group or series of depth interviews; and quantitative research, in which you administer a survey. You'll find a lot of information in Chapter 6 about these activities. Your school might have a Web page devoted to secondary marketing research. Google also

1. Provide examples of actions that advertisers or their agencies might take that would demonstrate social responsibility and ethical behavior.

LO4 Describe how government agencies regulate advertising to protect both consumers and competitors.

CURRENT REGULATORY ISSUES AFFECTING U.S. ADVERTISERS

Federal and state courts have made many significant rulings pertaining to advertising issues. The most important of these concern First Amendment rights and privacy rights. We'll review these, while paying special attention to controversies surrounding tobacco advertising and advertising to children.

Freedom of Commercial Speech

The Supreme Court historically distinguishes between "speech" and "commercial speech" (speech that promotes a commercial transaction). But decisions over the last two decades suggest that truthful commercial speech is also entitled to significant, if not full, protection under the First Amendment.

The trend started in 1976 when the Supreme Court held in *Virginia State Board of Pharmacy v. Virginia Citizens Consumer Council* that ads enjoy protection under the First Amendment as commercial speech.[31] The next year the Court declared that the ban by state bar associations on attorney advertising also violated the First Amendment. Now a third of all lawyers advertise, and a few states even permit client testimonials. In 1980 the Court used *Central Hudson Gas v. Public Service Commission* to test whether specific examples of commercial speech can be regulated.[32] The *Central Hudson* test includes the following four parts:

1. *Does the commercial speech at issue concern a lawful activity?* The ad in question must be for a legal product and must be free of misleading claims.

2. *Will the restriction of commercial speech serve the asserted government interest substantially?* The government must prove that the absence of regulation would have a substantial negative effect.

3. *Does the regulation directly advance the government interest asserted?* The government must be able to establish conclusively that regulating advertising would be effective in furthering the government's interest.

4. *Is the restriction no more than necessary to further the interest asserted?* The government would have to establish that there are no other means to accomplish the same end without restricting free speech.[33]

In 1982, the Supreme Court upheld an FTC order allowing physicians and dentists to advertise. Since then, advertising for medical and dental services has skyrocketed.

In 1993, the Supreme Court gave the advertising industry its biggest win in years. It said the Cincinnati City Council violated

---

provides a useful directory here: http://directory.google.com/Top/Business/Marketing_and_Advertising/

Marketing or IMC Plan

Many classes require that you create a marketing or IMC plan. We've included lots of information in this text to help. Be sure to read Chapter 7 carefully, as it is your guide to the art and science of planning. Then, to make things more concrete, search for examples of "advertising plan outlines" on the Web. Your instructor may have his or her own outline; if so, use that.

Media Plan

A media plan shows the specific allocations of the budget to different media and promotional activities. It will also specify what vehicles will be used for the campaign, as well as when and how often the ads will run. You will most likely want to use a spreadsheet to show the calendar. We have a sample media plan flowchart in Chapter 15.

The Creative Brief

The creative brief is a fairly short document that is used to inform and guide the people who create the ads. It contains information that has

been distilled from some of the documents that we've just reviewed, such as the IMC plan. There are as many different outlines for creative briefs as there are ad agencies, but in many instances the differences are superficial. Chapter 8 provides some examples of a creative brief and shows you the elements of a message strategy. For examples of creative briefs, visit the following sites:

- Emily Cohen: http://www.emilycohen.com/creativebriefs.pdf
- SmileyCat blog (for a brief written for a Web campaign): http://www.smileycat.com/miaow/archives/000226.php

The Plans Book

If you are doing a plans book it means you are doing almost everything we've reviewed to this point. A typical plans book will include research findings, an IMC plan, a creative brief, media plans, and, in many cases, mock-ups of real ads. But it puts these things together in a seamless, integrated way, so that the reader has a clear understanding of the entire arc of a planned campaign. In many plans books there will also be a section on campaign evaluation (ways of assessing the campaign).

The Importance of Good Legal Counsel in Advertising [2–A]

For many years, Jack Russell had dreamed of this opportunity—opening a members-only club for young people who were not yet old enough to drink. He could already taste the success that was about to be his—money, fame, and fortune were all within his reach. He took every avenue possible to promote the new, exclusive club. He ran ads in local entertainment magazines and community newspapers. Local rock radio stations, though, were the mainstay—shouting out the good news for kids all over town, complete with a phone number and address for sending in their charter membership fees. Jack's wonderful idea was about to take flight. But then the local district attorney ripped the magic carpet out from underneath him. You see, Jack Russell was selling memberships to a club that had not opened yet. In fact, he hadn't even signed the lease on the proposed premises. To the DA, it smelled of scam. He figured Jack was taking money from kids for something that didn't exist. The DA charged him with false advertising—and fraud. When Jack answered his ringing doorbell, two uniformed officers were standing there. They handcuffed him, gave him a ride downtown, and threw him in jail. If Jack had just passed his ads by a communications lawyer, he could have avoided a very embarrassing and expensive nightmare. And he'd be a free man.

Ethical and legal problems with advertising seem to pop up constantly. Not only government officials but also competitors and consumer rights groups scrutinize ads carefully—either for their own self-interest or to protect the rights of consumers. As a result, every agency and advertiser needs to have a strong understanding of the laws that govern advertising. They also need to retain the services of a good law firm that specializes in advertising and communications law.

One such firm is Reed Smith's Advertising, Technology, and Media Group. With 77 communications law specialists spread among its 18 offices, Reed Smith is well situated to counsel advertisers throughout the United States, United Kingdom, and Europe. Its clients come from all levels of the industry—from blue chip advertisers (such as Merck, Pfizer, Sony, and Lancôme) to ad agencies (such as Worldwide Partners, Inc.) to advertising associations (such as the Association of National Advertisers and the Advertising Research Foundation).

Reed Smith routinely provides its clients with a wide array of services: checking advertising copy for legal acceptability; reviewing conventional and online promotional concepts involving sweepstakes, games, and contests; researching comparative advertising and copyright violations; and representing clients before federal and state regulatory bodies and courts. The firm also helps clients in their relationships with media, Internet service providers, talent, and performers' unions.

The chair of the firm's advertising, technology, and media group, Douglas J. Wood, is the author of *Please Be Ad-Vised* (ANA, 2004), a comprehensive reference written for advertising and marketing professionals.

Reed Smith also publishes a free e-mail newsletter and a sophisticated Web site, both under the name of *Adlaw by Request*, which provide clients and prospects with summaries and analyses of new and proposed legislation affecting advertising. The Web site (adlaw.com) offers a wide array of regularly updated resources, including downloadable contract forms, sample legal documents, and articles on the legal complexities of all types of advertising and marketing communications.

Applying the Breaks

1. Go to adlaw.com and explore the Web site. Click on the "In the Courts" tab and read about current advertising-related legal cases. Pick one that interests you, read it, and then write a brief report including the title of the case, the names of the parties involved, the issues at stake, and a summary of the decision that was handed down if there has been a judgment.

2. Click on the "ARB Knowledge Base" tab and then the " Adlaw Resources" link on the left. Select one of the checklists from the list of resources. Read and analyze the checklist, making note of which items seem to be common sense, which ones you'd never before considered, and which ones are too densely "legalese" for you to understand. Present the checklist and your analysis to your study group or class.

3. What ethical, social, or legal issues do you think will be addressed in the next 10 years relative to advertising and the Internet?

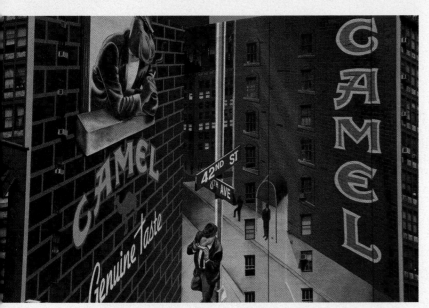

Joe Camel appeared in R.J. Reynolds' Camel advertising beginning in 1988. He became a well-known character among children, but R.J. Reynolds denied that Joe Camel was ever targeted at the youth market. In 1997, under pressure from various public-interest groups, R.J. Reynolds replaced Joe Camel with a more traditional, four-legged dromedary.

the First Amendment when it banned racks of advertising brochures from city streets for "aesthetic and safety reasons" while permitting newspaper vending machines.[34]

The issue of freedom of commercial speech is far from settled. Allowing greater freedom of commercial speech enhances the "government interests" of many buyers and sellers and complete information. But the additional interest of reducing externalities creates heated controversies surrounding issues like tobacco and alcohol advertising and advertising to children. These will likely continue for years to come.

Tobacco Advertising

While tobacco is a legal product, the harm created by smoking ends up killing or disabling more than half a million people annually and costing taxpayers billions of dollars every year in health costs—a major externality. To recover these costs, a number of states' attorneys general sued the tobacco industry. In 1998, they reached a historic settlement. It imposed limits on brand-name promotion at events with young attendees, banned the use of cartoon characters (like Joe Camel) in cigarette ads, and created a fund of over $200 billion to be used by the various signatory states. Today, state budgets rely heavily on the money secured in the settlement.[35]

privacy rights
Of or pertaining to an individual's right to prohibit personal information from being divulged to the public.

Advertising to Children

Advertising to children presents different challenges. Kids are not sophisticated consumers. Their perceptions of self, time, and money are immature. As a result, they know very little about their desires, needs, and preferences—or how to use economic resources rationally to satisfy them. And the nature of child-oriented advertising can lead to false beliefs or highly improbable product expectations.

More and more children are becoming the sole decision makers about the products they consume. To protect them, and their parents, both critics and defenders agree that advertisers should not intentionally deceive children. The central issue is how far advertisers should go to ensure that children are not misled.

To promote responsible children's advertising and to respond to public concerns, the Council of Better Business Bureaus established the *Children's Advertising Review Unit (CARU)*. The basic activity of CARU is the review and evaluation of child-directed advertising in all media. When children's advertising is found to be misleading, inaccurate, or inconsistent with the *Guidelines,* CARU seeks changes through voluntary cooperation of the advertisers.[36] For an overview of the basic principles underlying CARU's *Guidelines,* see Exhibit 2–3.

In the developed world, other countries are far more strict than the United States about advertising to children. Sweden and Norway, for example, do not permit any television advertising to be directed toward children under 12, and no advertisements at all are allowed during children's programs. While the highest level of advertising to children is in Australia (an average of 34 ads per hour), that country allows no ads on programs aimed at preschool children.[37]

Consumer Privacy

The second major regulatory issue facing advertisers is privacy. With the increased use of wireless handheld devices, cell phones, and the Internet, all of which can be used for advertising, the issue of **privacy rights** is in the news. The issue deals with people's right to protect their personal information. As we shall see in Chapter 13, privacy is an ethical issue as well as a legal one. It's also a practical issue: Prospective customers

The following Core Principles apply to all practices covered by the self-regulatory program.

1. Advertisers have special responsibilities when advertising to children or collecting data from children online. They should take into account the limited knowledge, experience, sophistication, and maturity of the audience to which the message is directed. They should recognize that younger children have a limited capacity to evaluate the credibility of information, may not understand the persuasive intent of advertising, and may not even understand that they are being subjected to advertising.

2. Advertising should be neither deceptive nor unfair, as these terms are applied under the Federal Trade Commission Act, to the children to whom it is directed.

3. Advertisers should have adequate substantiation for objective advertising claims, as those claims are reasonably interpreted by the children to whom they are directed.

4. Advertising should not stimulate children's unreasonable expectations about product quality or performance.

5. Products and content inappropriate for children should not be advertised directly to them.

6. Advertisers should avoid social stereotyping and appeals to prejudice, and are encouraged to incorporate minority and other groups in advertisements and to present positive role models whenever possible.

7. Advertisers are encouraged to capitalize on the potential of advertising to serve an educational role and influence positive personal qualities and behaviors in children (e.g., being honest and respectful of others, taking safety precautions, engaging in physical activity).

8. Although there are many influences that affect a child's personal and social development, it remains the prime responsibility of the parents to provide guidance for children. Advertisers should contribute to this parent-child relationship in a constructive manner.

Source: Reprinted with permission of Children's Advertising Review Unit.

who find pop-up ads, telemarketing calls, and e-mail spam annoying and intrusive aren't likely to buy the offending company's products.

Internet users worry about people they don't know, and even businesses they do know, getting personal information about them. And their concern is not without merit. Many Web sites create profiles of their visitors to get data such as e-mail addresses, clothing sizes, or favorite books. Some sites also track

Children are not sophisticated consumers and can easily be misled by advertising that makes unrealistic promises. This advertisement for Gatorade Kids might suggest to children that a sweet, flavored sports drink will give them extraordinary strength (or that they should punch someone).

users' surfing habits, usually without their knowledge, to better target ads for products.

To create these user profiles, Web sites use tiny software programs, called **cookies**, that keep a log of where people click, allowing sites to track customers' Web-surfing habits. The cookies are placed on people's computers when they first visit a site or use some feature like a personalized news service or a shopping cart.[38]

Internet companies argue that such tracking is not personal; it's typically performed anonymously and helps them customize content to match users' interests.[39] However, Double-Click, a leading provider of marketing tools for Web advertisers, direct marketers, and Web publishers, has acquired Abacus Direct, a direct mail company with an extensive offline database of retail and catalog purchasers. This potentially enables DoubleClick to combine online profiles with offline names, addresses, demographic information, and purchasing data.[40]

One survey revealed that only 27 percent of Internet users accept the industry's claim that tracking is helpful. Somewhat more than half, 54 percent, consider it harmful, and 11 percent believe that it both helps and hurts. A large majority of those surveyed, 87 percent, believe sites should ask permission before collecting personal information.[41]

Fortunately, consumers are not completely helpless. They can disable the cookies on their computers. But this may limit their Internet access because some Web sites *require* that cookies be accepted. Internet surfers also have the option to "opt in." This feature allows users to set the terms under which they give personal information.[42] Also available is the "opt-out" feature, which

Controlling How You Share

Facebook is about sharing. Our privacy controls give you the power to decide what and how much you share. Learn how to manage who can see your information on and off Facebook. See what's new

Read our privacy policy

Privacy Controls

Edit your privacy settings

The settings you choose control which people and applications can see your information. You can share your information with friends, friends of friends or everyone, and we offer presets to help you do that. Or, if you prefer, you can customize your settings.

In 2009, Facebook, the Internet's second largest Web site, came under assault for the amount of personal information it disclosed to third parties. The 50 privacy settings spanning seven pages was considered an onerous task for users seeking to limit disclosure. Facebook responded by reducing this to 15 settings, but many critics of the social networking site are not satisfied that Facebook truly respects the privacy of its users.

allows visitors to specifically inform the site not to gather information by clicking on a button.[43]

Responding to consumer concerns, the Federal Trade Commission together with the Network Advertising Initiative (an organization comprised of leading Internet advertising networks, including AdKnowledge, 24/7, Ad Force, and DoubleClick)

- *Enforcement,* a requirement that all industry members subject themselves to monitoring by an independent third party to ensure compliance with the Fair Information Practice Principles.[44]

Naturally Internet companies would prefer to avoid government intervention and the layers of laws and regulations that would bring. So it's in everybody's interest for self-regulation to work.

> ## Prospective customers who find pop-up ads, telemarketing calls, and e-mail spam annoying and intrusive aren't likely to buy the offending company's products.

has created a framework for self-regulation of online profiling. The "Fair Information Practice Principles" consist of five core elements:

- *Notice,* which requires that the Web site clearly post its privacy policy.

- *Choice,* which relates to consumers' level of control over being profiled and how their information is used.

- *Access,* the ability for consumers to access information collected about them and make amendments to it.

- *Security,* which requires that network advertisers make reasonable efforts to protect the data they collect from loss, misuse, or improper access.

FEDERAL REGULATION OF ADVERTISING IN THE UNITED STATES

The U.S. government imposes strict controls on advertisers through laws, regulations, and judicial interpretations. Among the many federal agencies and departments that regulate advertising are the Federal Trade Commission, the Food and Drug Administration, the Federal Communications Commission, the Patent and Trademark Office, and the Library of Congress. Because their jurisdictions often overlap, advertisers may sometimes have difficulty complying with their regulations.

The U.S. Federal Trade Commission

The *Federal Trade Commission (FTC)* is the major regulator of advertising for products sold in interstate commerce. Established by an act of Congress, the FTC is charged with ensuring "that the nation's markets function competitively, and are vigorous, efficient, and free of undue restrictions."[45] The commission enforces a variety of federal antitrust and consumer protection laws and works to regulate the marketplace by eliminating acts or practices that are deceptive or unfair. In other words, it is the FTC's responsibility to maintain the existence of *many sellers* in the marketplace, strive to provide more *complete information* to consumers, and keep the marketing process as free of *externalities* as possible.

The FTC's job is complicated by the fact that the definitions of deceptive and unfair are controversial.

Defining Deception The FTC defines **deceptive advertising** as any ad that contains a misrepresentation, omission, or any other practice that can mislead a significant number of reasonable consumers to their detriment. Proof that consumers were deceived is not required, and the representation may be either expressed or implied. The issue is whether the ad conveys a false impression—even if it is literally true.[46]

Take the case of the FTC against Office Depot, Buy.com, and Value America. According to the FTC, the companies engaged in deceptive practices in advertising "free" and "low-cost" personal computer (PC) systems because they failed to adequately disclose the true costs and important restrictions on the offers. The low cost of the PCs was tied to rebates that were conditioned on the purchase of long-term Internet service contracts.[47] Commercial Break 2–B lists some common deceptive practices that have been found illegal by the courts.

Defining Unfairness According to FTC policy, some ads that are not deceptive may still be considered unfair to consumers. **Unfair advertising** occurs when a consumer is "unjustifiably injured" or there is a "violation of public policy" (such as other government statutes). In other words, unfair advertising is due to the inadequacy of *complete information* or some other *externality*. For example, practices considered unfair are claims made without prior substantiation, claims that exploit vulnerable groups such as children and the elderly, and cases where the consumer cannot make a valid choice because the advertiser leaves out important information about the product or competitors mentioned in the ad.[48]

In one case, the FTC found that an automaker's failure to warn of a safety problem was not deceptive but was unfair. Advertising organizations have argued that the word "unfair" is so vague it can mean whatever any given individual wants it to. They have lobbied Congress to eliminate the FTC's power to prosecute on unfairness grounds, and Congress did pass a compromise bill requiring the

When planning to advertise overseas, companies must be very cautious about the do's and don'ts of other countries. Typically, they retain the services of attorneys familiar with local laws. Many international law firms have Web sites that can be quickly located on the Internet. Hall Dickler, a law firm which specializes in advertising and marketing, refers its clients to GALA (www.gala-marketlaw.com), an international network of lawyers to which it belongs.

The courts have held that these acts constitute unfair or deceptive trade practices and are therefore illegal.

False Promises

Making an advertising promise that cannot be kept, such as "restores youth" or "prevents cancer." When Listerine claimed to prevent or reduce the impact of colds and sore throats, the FTC banned the campaign and required the company to run millions of dollars' worth of corrective ads.

Incomplete Description

Stating some but not all of a product's contents, such as advertising a "solid oak" desk without mentioning that only the top is solid oak and the rest is pine.

False and Misleading Comparisons

Making false comparisons, either explicitly or by implication, such as "Like Tylenol, Advil doesn't upset my stomach." That implies that Advil is equal in avoiding stomach upset, though in truth Tylenol is better. To some people, Advil's claim might even suggest that Tylenol upsets the stomach, which is also false.

Bait-and-Switch Offers

Advertising an item at an unusually low price to bring people into the store and then "switching" them to a higher-priced model by claiming that the advertised product is out of stock or poorly made.

Visual Distortions and False Demonstrations

Using trick photography or computer manipulation to enhance a product's appearance—for example, a TV commercial for a "giant steak" dinner special showing the steak on a miniature plate that makes it look extra large. In one classic case, General Motors and its window supplier, Libby Owens-Ford, rigged a demonstration to show how clear their windows were. The GM cars were photographed with the windows down, the competitor's car with the windows up—and Vaseline smeared on them.

False Testimonials

Implying that a product is endorsed by a celebrity or authority who is not a bona fide user, or implying that endorsers have expertise that in fact they don't.

Partial Disclosure

Stating certain facts about the advertised product but omitting other material information. An example is claiming, "Kraft's Singles processed cheese slices are made from five ounces of milk," which give Singles more calcium than the imitators' products without mentioning that processing loses about two ounces of the milk.

Small-Print Qualifications

Making a statement in large print, such as Beneficial's "Instant Tax Refund," only to qualify or retract it in obscure, small, or unreadable type elsewhere in the ad: "If you qualify for one of our loans." To the FTC, if readers don't see the qualification, it's not there.

Applying the Breaks
Referring to the acts described above, describe or provide examples of unfair or deceptive practices you have seen in advertising.

FTC to show that (1) an alleged unfair practice involves substantial, unavoidable injury to consumers; (2) the injury is not reasonably avoidable by consumers themselves; and (3) the injury is not outweighed by benefits to consumers or competition.[49] This legislation suggests that in the future the FTC will have to balance on a far narrower beam in its effort to regulate unfairness.[50]

Comparative Advertising

Advertisers use **comparative advertising** to claim superiority to competitors in some aspect. In the United States, such ads are legal (and encouraged by the FTC) so long as the comparison is truthful. In fact, the FTC cracked down on the Arizona Automobile Dealers Association for restricting truthful, nondeceptive comparative price advertising among its members.[51]

> **Any advertiser that misrepresents its own or another firm's goods, services, or activities is vulnerable to a civil action.**

Under current law, any advertiser that misrepresents its own or another firm's goods, services, or activities is vulnerable to a civil action. In addition to being truthful, comparative ads must compare on some objectively measurable characteristic. And the greatest scrutiny must be given to the substantiation. Given the potential for sizable damages—up to millions of dollars—for faulty comparative advertising, the greatest care must be exercised in this area.[52]

Investigating Suspected Violations

If it receives complaints from consumers, competitors, or its own staff members who monitor ads, the FTC may decide to investigate an advertiser. The agency has broad powers to pursue suspected violators and demand information

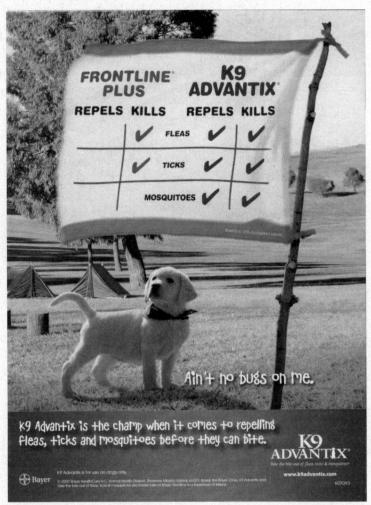

The purpose of comparative ads is to demonstrate the superiority of one product over another. K9 Advantix makes a clear case for its advantages versus a competitor's. And its brand name reinforces that superiority claim.

Remedies for Unfair or Deceptive Advertising

When the FTC determines that an ad is deceptive or unfair, it may take three courses of action: negotiate with the advertiser for a *consent decree,* issue a *cease-and-desist order,* and/or require *corrective advertising.*

A **consent decree** is a document the advertiser signs agreeing to stop the objectionable advertising without admitting any wrongdoing.

If an advertiser won't sign a consent decree, the FTC may issue a **cease-and-desist order** prohibiting further use of the ad. Advertisers who violate either a consent decree or a cease-and-desist order can be fined up to $11,000 per showing of the offending ad.

The FTC may also require **corrective advertising** for some period of time to explain and correct offending ads. In 1999 the FTC ruled that pharmaceutical giant Novartis advertised without substantiation that its Doan's Pills brand was more effective against back pain than its rivals. Because the deceptive advertising had gone on for more than nine years, the FTC ordered Novartis to run $8 million worth of corrective advertising. The advertising was to include the statement: "Although Doan's is an effective pain reliever, there is no evidence that Doan's is more effective than other pain relievers for back pain." They also ordered Doan's to place the statement on their packaging for a year.[55]

from them. Typically, the FTC looks for three kinds of information: *substantiation, endorsements,* and *affirmative disclosures.*

If a suspected violator cites survey findings or scientific studies, the FTC may ask for **substantiation**. Advertisers are expected to have supporting data before running an ad, although the FTC sometimes allows postclaim evidence.

The FTC also scrutinizes ads that contain questionable **endorsements** or **testimonials**. If a noncelebrity endorser is paid, the ad must disclose this onscreen.[53] The endorsers may not make claims the advertiser can't substantiate. Further, celebrity endorsers must actually use the product or service (if portrayed), and they can be held personally liable if they misrepresent it.[54]

Advertisers must make **affirmative disclosure** of their product's limitations or deficiencies: for example, EPA mileage ratings for cars, pesticide warnings, and statements that saccharin may be hazardous to one's health.

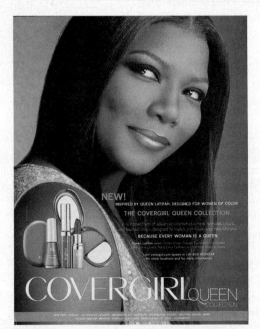

Advertising law requires that celebrity endorsers actually use the product. For example, this ad for Cover Girl makeup (www.covergirl.com) features the actress Queen Latifah. Because the implication is that Cover Girl helps her to "look younger," she would have to be an actual user of the product.

substantiation
Evidence that backs up cited survey finding or scientific studies that the FTC may request from a suspected advertising violator.

endorsements
The use of satisfied customers and celebrities to endorse a product in advertising.

testimonials
The use of satisfied customers and celebrities to endorse a product in advertising.

affirmative disclosure
Advertisers must make known their product's limitations or deficiencies.

consent decree
A document advertisers sign, without admitting any wrongdoing, in which they agree to stop objectionable advertising.

cease-and-desist order May be issued by the FTC if an advertiser won't sign a consent decree; prohibits further use of an ad.

corrective advertising May be required by the FTC for a period of time to explain and correct offending ads.

Nutritional Labeling and Education Act (NLEA) A 1994 congressional law setting stringent legal definitions for terms such as *fresh, light, low fat,* and *reduced calorie;* setting standard serving sizes; and requiring labels to show food value for one serving alongside the total recommended daily value as established by the National Research Council.

The Food and Drug Administration (FDA)

The *Food and Drug Administration (FDA)* is authorized by Congress to enforce the Federal Food, Drug, and Cosmetic Act and several other health laws. The agency monitors the manufacture, import, transport, storage, and sale of over $1 trillion worth of products annually, which accounts for 9 cents of every dollar spent each year by American consumers.[56] And it does so at a cost to taxpayers of about $3 per person.[57]

It's the FDA's job to see that the food we eat is safe, the cosmetics we use won't hurt us, and the medicines and therapeutic devices we buy are safe and effective. The FDA requires manufacturers to disclose all ingredients on product labels, in in-store product advertising, and in product literature. The label must accurately state the weight or volume of the contents. Labels on therapeutic devices must give clear instructions for use. The FDA can require warning statements on packages of hazardous products. It regulates "cents off" and other promotions on package labels and has jurisdiction over the use of words such as "giant" or "family" to describe package sizes.

When consumer-oriented drug ads became common in the mid-1980s, the FDA ruled that any ad for a brand-name drug must include all the information from the package insert.[58] That meant advertisers had to run lengthy commercials or use minuscule type in print ads. In 1997, the FDA changed that rule, allowing pharmaceutical companies to advertise their drugs on broadcast media as long as they mentioned any important possible side effects and directed people to their print ads, their Internet sites, or consumers' own doctors for more information.[59] With that ruling, prescription drug advertising soared on television and radio, tripling over the next five years. It's estimated that in 2005, pharmaceutical companies spent some $4 billion in direct-to-consumer advertising.[60] Although the FDA is responsible for ensuring that these ads are fair and accurate, the agency is so understaffed that many questionable and, unfortunately, deceptive or misleading ads do get through. However, any time the FDA has sent a letter to marketers citing false advertising claims, the companies have stopped running the misleading ads.[61]

The **Nutritional Labeling and Education Act (NLEA)**, which went into effect in 1994, gave the FDA additional muscle by setting stringent legal definitions for terms such as *fresh,*

light, low fat, and *reduced calories.* It also sets standard serving sizes and requires labels to show food value for one serving alongside the total recommended daily value as established by the National Research Council.[62]

The first time the FDA took severe action against a prominent marketer over a labeling dispute, it seized 2,400 cases of Procter & Gamble's Citrus Hill Fresh Choice orange juice. Fresh Choice was made from concentrate, not fresh-squeezed juice as P&G claimed.[63] Due to increased FDA scrutiny, many advertisers are now more cautious about their health and nutritional claims.

The Federal Communications Commission (FCC)

The seven-member *Federal Communications Commission (FCC)* is an independent federal agency with jurisdiction over the radio, television, telephone, satellite and cable TV industries, and the Internet. Its control over broadcast advertising stems from its authority to license broadcasters (or take away their licenses). The FCC can restrict both the products advertised and the content of ads. For example, the FCC required stations to run commercials about the harmful effects of smoking even before Congress banned cigarette advertising on TV and radio.

In the 1980s, the FCC decided there were enough buyers and sellers that marketplace forces could adequately control broadcast media, so it deregulated both radio and TV stations. The FCC no longer limits commercial time or requires stations to maintain detailed program and commercial logs.

The 1992 Cable Television Consumer Protection and Competition Act gave the FCC additional teeth. It placed new controls on the cable TV industry to encourage a more service-oriented attitude and to improve the balance between

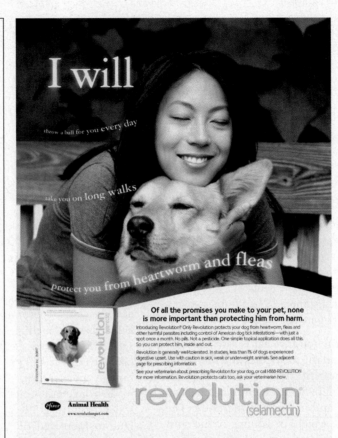

To provide consumers with more complete information, the U.S. Food and Drug Administration regulates the content of pharmaceutical ads. It used to require that advertisers include all the information from the package insert in their TV ads. This necessitated lengthy commercials with minuscule copy. In 1997, the rule was changed, allowing pharmaceutical companies to advertise on TV and radio as long as they mentioned any important side effects and directed consumers to other sources for further information, such as their magazine ads or their Web site. Notice how this magazine ad for Animal Health's Revolution (*www.revolutionpet.com*) complies with the FDA's disclosure requirements.

rates and escalating ad revenues.[64] The FCC can set subscriber rates for cable TV, so subscription revenues should slow while advertising rates rise.

The FCC's visibility as an arbiter of broadcast decency increased immediately following Janet Jackson's "wardrobe malfunction," which exposed the singer's breast during the 2004 Super Bowl halftime show. A record 500,000 complaints were registered with the FCC. According to FCC rules, over-the-air television channels cannot air "obscene" material at any time. The FCC defines obscene material as describing sexual conduct "in a patently offensive way" and lacking "serious literary, artistic, political or scientific value." The FCC later levied a fine of $550,000 for the Super Bowl incident. The FCC's fine was voided by the United States Court of Appeals in 2008 but the Supreme Court sent the case back to the Court of Appeals for reconsideration in 2009.

The Patent and Trademark Office and the Library of Congress

A basic role of government is to promote and protect the economic well-being (*self-interest*) of its citizens. One way the U.S. government does this is by registering and protecting its citizens' **intellectual property**.[65]

Through the issuance of **patents**, the government provides incentives to invent, invest in, and disclose new technology worldwide. By registering trademarks and copyrights, the government helps businesses protect their investments, promote their goods and services, and safeguard consumers against confusion and deception in the marketplace (*complete information*).

A trademark such as Coca-Cola, AT&T, or Levi's is a valuable asset. According to the Lanham Trademark Act (1947), a **trademark** is "any word, name, symbol, or device or any combination thereof adopted and used by a manufacturer or

> ## A trademark such as Coca-Cola, AT&T, or Levi's is a valuable asset.

Coca-Cola's trademark varies from country to country. But the overall look is retained through use of similar letterforms and style, even with different alphabets.

1. Arabic   5. Spanish
2. French   6. Chinese
3. Japanese 7. Hebrew
4. Thai   8. Polish

merchant to identify his goods and distinguish them from those manufactured or sold by others."

Patents and trademarks are registered with and protected by the *U.S. Patent and Trademark Office.* Ownership of a trademark may be designated in advertising or on a label, package, or letterhead by the word *Registered,* the symbol®, or the symbol™. If someone persists in using a trademark owned by another or one confusingly similar to another's mark, the trademark owner can ask for a court order and sue for trademark infringement.

The Library of Congress protects all copyrighted material, including advertising, in the United States. A **copyright** is a form of protection provided to the authors of "original works of authorship," including literary, dramatic, musical, artistic, and certain other "intellectual works."[66] A copyright issued to an individual grants the exclusive right to print, publish, or reproduce the protected material for the life of the copyright owner plus 70 years. If it is the work of corporate authorship, the term is the shorter of 95 years from publication or 120 years from creation.

STATE AND LOCAL REGULATION

Advertisers are also subject to state or local laws. Since the U.S. federal deregulation trend of the 1980s, state and local governments have taken a far more active role.

State legislation governing advertising is often based on the truth-in-advertising model statute developed in 1911 by *Printer's Ink,* for many years the major trade publication of the industry. The statute holds that any maker of an ad found to contain "untrue, deceptive, or misleading" material is guilty of a misdemeanor. Today most states enforce laws patterned after this statute.

All states also have "little FTC acts," consumer protection laws that govern unfair and deceptive business practices. States can investigate and prosecute cases, and individual consumers can bring civil suits against businesses. To increase their clout, some states team up on legal actions—for example, to challenge deceptive ad promotions in the airline, rental car, and food-making industries. As one observer pointed out, "Many of the food manufacturers could litigate some of the smaller states into the ground, but they might not be willing to fight it out against 10 states simultaneously."[67]

Different states have different regulations governing what can be advertised. Some states prohibit advertising for certain types of wine and liquor, and most states restrict the use of state flags in advertising.

broadcast standards department
A department at a TV network that reviews all programs and commercials to be broadcast to see that they meet all applicable standards.

This can present a major problem to national marketers. And in some cases, it actually hurts consumers. For example, many companies trying to conduct environmentally responsible marketing programs feel stymied by the different state laws governing packaging materials and recycling.[68]

Many cities and counties also have consumer protection agencies to enforce laws regulating local advertising practices. The chief function of these agencies is to protect local consumers against unfair and misleading practices by area merchants.

In a case against Los Angeles–based Closet Factory, Inc., the DA collected $40,000 in fines to settle a false advertising suit. The company was charged with running newspaper ads that gave consumers a false sense of urgency regarding "sales" that actually never end. This type of advertising, known as a *continuous sale,* violates the state's Business and Professions Code. Since the sale is never really over, the sale price becomes the regular price.[69]

check yourself ✓

1. Describe an action that has been taken by a government agency to restrict the activities of advertisers.

2. What is an example of an Internet-related privacy concern?

L05 Discuss the activities of nongovernment organizations in fighting fraudulent and deceptive advertising.

NONGOVERNMENT REGULATION

Nongovernment organizations also issue advertising guidelines (see Exhibit 2–4). In fact, advertisers face considerable regulation by business-monitoring organizations, related trade associations, the media, consumer groups, and advertising agencies themselves.

The Better Business Bureau (BBB)

The largest of the U.S. business-monitoring organizations is the *Better Business Bureau (BBB),* established in 1916. Funded by dues from more than 100,000 member companies, it operates primarily at the local level to protect consumers against fraudulent and deceptive advertising and sales practices. When local bureaus contact violators and ask them to revise their advertising, most comply.

The BBB's files on violators are open to the public. Records of violators who do not comply are sent to appropriate government agencies for further action. The BBB often works with local law enforcement agencies to prosecute advertisers guilty of fraud and misrepresentation. Each year, the BBB investigates thousands of ads for possible violations of truth and accuracy.

The National Advertising Review Council (NARC)

The *National Advertising Review Council (NARC)* was established in 1971. Its primary purpose is to promote and enforce standards

▼ **EXHIBIT 2–4** American Association of Advertising Agencies policy statement and guidelines for comparative advertising.

The Board of Directors of the American Association of Advertising Agencies recognizes that when used truthfully and fairly, comparative advertising provides the consumer with needed and useful information.

However, extreme caution should be exercised. The use of comparative advertising, by its very nature, can distort facts and, by implication, convey to the consumer information that misrepresents the truth.

Therefore, the Board believes that comparative advertising should follow certain guidelines:

1. The intent and connotation of the ad should be to inform and never to discredit or unfairly attack competitors, competing products, or services.

2. When a competitive product is named, it should be one that exists in the marketplace as significant competition.

3. The competition should be fairly and properly identified but never in a manner or tone of voice that degrades the competitive product or service.

4. The advertising should compare related or similar properties or ingredients of the product, dimension to dimension, feature to feature.

5. The identification should be for honest comparison purposes and not simply to upgrade by association.

6. If a competitive test is conducted, it should be done by an objective testing source, preferably an independent one, so that there will be no doubt as to the veracity of the test.

7. In all cases the test should be supportive of all claims made in the advertising that are based on the test.

8. The advertising should never use partial results or stress insignificant differences to cause the consumer to draw an improper conclusion.

9. The property being compared should be significant in terms of value or usefulness of the product to the consumer.

10. Comparatives delivered through the use of testimonials should not imply that the testimonial is more than one individual's thought unless that individual represents a sample of the majority viewpoint.

Source: Copyright © 2009 American Association of Advertising Agencies. Reprinted with permission.

of truth, accuracy, taste, morality, and social responsibility in advertising. NARC is one of the most comprehensive and effective mechanisms for regulating American advertising. A U.S. district court judge noted in a 1985 case that its "speed, informality, and modest cost," as well as its expertise, give NARC special advantages over the court system in resolving advertising disputes.[70]

The NARC has two operating arms: the *National Advertising Division (NAD)* of the Council of Better Business Bureaus and the *National Advertising Review Board (NARB)*. The NAD monitors advertising practices and reviews complaints about advertising from consumers and consumer groups, brand competitors, local Better Business Bureaus, trade associations, and others. The appeals board for NAD decisions is the NARB, which consists of a chairperson and 70 volunteer members (40 national advertisers, 20 agency representatives, and 10 laypeople).

The case of the leather flight jacket shows how well the NAD process works. Neil Cooper LLC is a company that manufactures a leather jacket. In its print ads it claims that its A-2 leather flight jackets are the "official battle gear of U.S. Air Force Pilots." Avirex, Ltd., a competing company, complained to the NAD since the A-2 jacket currently being purchased by the Department of Defense and worn by U.S. pilots is the jacket manufactured by them, not Neil Cooper. Neil Cooper explained that, while it was not the current supplier, many pilots continued to buy from Neil Cooper directly because they preferred that product. Notwithstanding, the NAD sided with Avirex and recommended that Neil Cooper qualify its claims to make it clear that it is selling a reproduction of an authentic A-2 flight jacket rather than the current official jacket of the U.S. Air Force. Neil Cooper agreed.[71]

Regulation by the Media

Almost all media companies review ads and reject material they regard as objectionable, even if it isn't deceptive.

Television Of all media, the TV networks conduct the strictest review. Advertisers must submit all commercials intended for a network or affiliated station to its **broadcast standards department**. Many commercials (in script or storyboard form) are returned with suggestions for changes or greater substantiation. Some ads are rejected outright if they violate network policies.

The five major U.S. broadcast networks base their policies on the original National Association of Broadcasters Television Code. But network policies vary enough that it's difficult to prepare universally acceptable commercials. Cable networks and local stations tend to be much less stringent.

To help consumers make informed decisions, *Good Housekeeping* magazine tests the products in its ads and provides a seal of approval to those advertisers, such as Heat-N-Glo, who substantiate their claims. This gives the consumer a more authoritative voice to listen to when trying to decide on purchases.

Radio The U.S. radio networks, unlike TV networks, supply only a small percentage of their affiliates' programming, so they have little or no say in what their affiliates advertise. A radio station is also less likely to return a script or tape for changes.

Some stations, such as KLBJ in Austin, Texas, look mainly at whether the advertising is illegal, unethical, or immoral.[72] They don't want spots to offend listeners or detract from the rest of the programming.

Every radio station typically has its own unwritten guidelines. KDWB, a Minneapolis/St. Paul station with a large teenage audience, turned down a psychic who wanted to buy advertising time but did allow condom and other contraceptive ads.[73] KSDO in San Diego, a station with a business and information format, won't air commercials for X-rated movies or topless bars.[74]

Magazines National magazines monitor all advertising, especially by new advertisers and for new products. Newer publications eager to sell space may not be so vigilant, but established magazines, such as *Time* and *Newsweek*, are highly scrupulous. Many magazines will not accept advertising for certain types of products. The *New Yorker* won't run discount retail store advertising or ads for feminine hygiene or self-medication products. *Reader's Digest* won't accept tobacco ads.

Some magazines test every product before accepting the advertising. *Good Housekeeping* rejects ads if its tests don't substantiate the advertiser's claims. Products that pass are allowed to feature the Good Housekeeping "Seal of Approval," and the magazine will stand behind those products.

Newspapers Newspapers also monitor and review advertising. Larger newspapers have clearance staffs who read every ad submitted; most smaller newspapers rely on the advertising manager, sales personnel, or proofreaders.

The advertising policies set forth in *Newspaper Rates & Data* specify, "No objectionable medical, personal, matrimonial, clairvoyant, or palmistry advertising accepted; no stock promotion or financial advertising, other than those securities of known value." Another rule prohibits ads that might easily be mistaken for regular reading material unless they feature the word *advertisement*.

One problem advertisers face is that newspapers' codes are far from uniform. Handgun ads may be prohibited by one newspaper, accepted by another if the guns are antique, and permitted by a third as long as the guns aren't automatic.

Regulation by Consumer Groups

Starting in the 1960s, the consumer movement became increasingly active in fighting fraudulent and deceptive advertising.

consumerism
Social action designed to dramatize the rights of the buying public.

consumer advocate
An individual or group that actively works to protect consumer rights, often by investigating advertising complaints received from the public and those that grow out of their own research.

Consumers demanded that products perform as advertised and that more product information be provided for people to compare and make better buying decisions. The consumer movement gave rise to **consumerism,** social action to dramatize the rights of the buying public.

Consumer advocate groups investigate advertising complaints received from the public and those that grow out of their own research. If a complaint is warranted, they ask the advertiser to halt the objectionable ad or practice. If the advertiser does not comply, they release publicity or criticism about the offense to the media and submit complaints with substantiating evidence to appropriate government agencies for further action. In some instances, they file a lawsuit to obtain a cease-and-desist order, a fine, or other penalty against the violator.

Today, with so many special-interest advocacy groups, even the most responsible advertisers feel challenged. To attract attention, advertising must be creative and stand out from competing noise. Yet advertisers fear attention from activists. Calvin Klein ads were attacked by the Boycott Anorexic Marketing group. A Nike ad starring Porky Pig was protested by the National Stuttering Project in San Francisco. An animated public service spot from Aetna Insurance drew complaints from a witches' rights group.[75]

When the protests start, the ads usually get pulled. As Shelly Garcia noted in *Adweek,* "The way things are these days, nothing motivates middle managers like the need to avoid attention. She lamented the fact that "there are fewer and fewer opportunities to have any fun in advertising."[76]

> Nothing motivates middle managers like the need to avoid attention.

Self-Regulation by Advertisers and Ad Agencies

Advertisers also regulate themselves. They have to. In today's competitive marketplace, consumer confidence is essential. Most large advertisers gather strong data to substantiate their claims. They maintain careful systems of advertising review to ensure that ads meet both their own standards and industry, media, and legal requirements. Ad agencies also monitor their own practices. Professional advertising associations oversee members' activities to prevent problems that might trigger government intervention.

Agencies can be held legally liable for fraudulent or misleading advertising claims. For this reason, most major advertising agencies have an in-house legal counsel and regularly submit their ads for review. If any aspect of the advertising is challenged, the agency asks its client to review the advertising and either confirm claims as truthful or replace unverified material.

Several associations monitor industrywide advertising practices. The *American Association of Advertising Agencies (AAAA),* an association of the largest advertising agencies throughout the United States, controls agency practices by denying membership to any agency judged unethical. The *American Advertising Federation (AAF)* helped to establish the FTC, and its early vigilance committees were the forerunners of the Better Business Bureau. The *AAF Advertising Principles of American Business,* adopted in 1984, define standards for truthful and responsible advertising (see Exhibit 2–5). The *Association of National Advertisers (ANA)* comprises 370 major manufacturing and service companies that are clients of member agencies of the AAAA. These companies pledge to uphold the ANA code of advertising ethics.

▼**EXHIBIT 2–5** Advertising Principles of American Business of the American Advertising Federation (AAF).

1. *Truth.* Advertising shall tell the truth, and shall reveal significant facts, the omission of which would mislead the public.

2. *Substantiation.* Advertising claims shall be substantiated by evidence in possession of the advertiser and the advertising agency prior to making such claims.

3. *Comparisons.* Advertising shall refrain from making false, misleading, or unsubstantiated statements or claims about a competitor or his products or services.

4. *Bait advertising.* Advertising shall not offer products or services for sale unless such offer constitutes a bona fide effort to sell the advertised products or services and is not a device to switch consumers to other goods or services, usually higher priced.

5. *Guarantees and warranties.* Advertising of guarantees and warranties shall be explicit, with sufficient information to apprise consumers of their principal terms and limitations or, when space or time restrictions preclude such disclosures, the advertisement shall clearly reveal where the full text of the guarantee or warranty can be examined before purchase.

6. *Price claims.* Advertising shall avoid price claims that are false or misleading, or savings claims that do not offer provable savings.

7. *Testimonials.* Advertising containing testimonials shall be limited to those of competent witnesses who are reflecting a real and honest opinion or experience.

8. *Taste and decency.* Advertising shall be free of statements, illustrations, or implications that are offensive to good taste or public decency.

GOVERNMENT RESTRAINTS ON INTERNATIONAL ADVERTISERS

Now that advertising has become global, many campaigns use similar themes and even the same ads across frontiers. But foreign governments often regulate advertising considerably more than the United States. And while Europe has moved toward uniformity in marketing activities, the laws governing advertising remain largely national.[77] So advertisers need to keep up with the changing legal environments of the countries in which they advertise.

Some governments not only regulate what ads say, show, or do; they often impose severe restrictions or outright bans on advertising specific products. The Swedes ban advertising to children on television. The Greeks ban toy advertising before 10:00 p.m. Throughout Europe, broadcast advertising for tobacco products is prohibited, and liquor ads are sharply restricted, especially in France.[78]

Many countries prohibit puffery superlatives. In Germany, for example, advertisers may use only scientifically provable superlatives. McCann-Erickson once had to retranslate the old Coca-Cola slogan, "Refreshes you best," because it implied a leadership position that was unprovable. The agency substituted "Refreshes you right" in Germany.

Many European countries also ban coupons, premiums, free tie-in offers, and the like. Companies may advertise price cuts only during "official sales periods," and advertisers often need government approval before publishing a sale ad. Across Europe, advertising on television must be clearly recognizable and kept separate from other programming. Paid *product placements* in programs, therefore, are typically prohibited.[79] In international advertising, the only way to navigate the morass of potential legal problems is to retain lawyers who specialize in advertising law.

check yourself ✓

1. Why do advertisers and ad agencies work so diligently to regulate their own activities?

THE ETHICAL AND LEGAL ASPECTS OF ADVERTISING IN PERSPECTIVE

Unquestionably, advertising offers considerable benefits to marketers and consumers alike. However, there's also no disputing that advertising has been and still is too often misused.

As *Adweek* editor Andrew Jaffe says, the industry should do all it can to "raise its standards and try to drive out that which is misleading, untruthful, or downright tasteless and irresponsible." Otherwise, he warns, the pressure to regulate even more will become overwhelming.[80]

Advertising apologists point out that of all the advertising reviewed by the Federal Trade Commission in a typical year, 97 percent is found to be satisfactory.[81] In the end, advertisers and consumers need to work together to ensure that advertising is used intelligently, ethically, and responsibly for the benefit of all. ■

the business of
advertising

chapter three

Bestselling author Thomas Friedman once wrote that "No two countries that both had McDonald's had fought a war against each other since each got its McDonald's." Friedman's point was that economic development and international trade reduce conflict. Still, who can rule out the possibility that international harmony grows in direct proportion to the availability of Happy Meals?

The foods you can get at McDonald's are the same as those sold in thousands of competing restaurants and chains. Its menu item ingredients—ground beef, French fries, and more recently, salads and yogurt—are widely available. And indeed, there are plenty of competitors out there. But none are so successful. What is McDonald's secret?

One could start with the company's dedication to offering value: a tasty, inexpensive meal served quickly.

But it's hard to avoid the conclusion that advertising is part of the equation as well. Throughout its history, McDonald's has spent billions on advertising, both in the United States and around the world.

continued on p. 58

LEARNING OBJECTIVES

LO1 List the various groups in the advertising business and explain their relationship to one another.

LO2 Discuss the differences between local, national, and transnational advertisers.

LO3 Explain how advertisers organize themselves to manage their advertising both here and abroad.

LO4 Define the main types of advertising agencies.

LO5 Explain the range of tasks people perform in an ad agency and an in-house advertising department.

LO6 Discuss how agencies get new clients and how they make money.

continued from p. 57

And that investment has paid dividends by helping to make the McDonald's brand one of the most valuable in the world.

The slogans are part of advertising lore. "You deserve a break today." "Two all beef patties, special sauce, lettuce, cheese, pickles, onions, on a sesame seed bun." "Have you had your break today?" And, of course, the current global campaign, "I'm lovin it!" The ads made the Golden Arches a part of the world's shared culture.

Let's look at how McDonald's uses integrated marketing communications (IMC), including advertising, to maintain its status as the biggest prepared-food seller in the world.

McDonald's has franchises in over 100 countries. But the essence of the McDonald's brand always shines through. Customers can always expect to encounter the arches, American fast-food items, and fast, friendly service. Employees dress in colorful, clean uniforms.

The unified brand message is reinforced with advertising. McDonald's campaign runs globally, so customers everywhere hear the familiar, "bah, bah, bah, bah, bah," followed by "I'm lovin' it" (naturally translated into the native language).

Another secret to the company's success is its willingness to customize its offerings to suit local preferences. So, for example, McDonald's does not serve pork in predominantly Muslim countries (and it refers to hamburgers as "beefburgers)." In countries where meat is not a big part of the regular diet (such as India), the company offers "veggie burgers." Even in the United States, menu items and food preparation adapt to local preferences.

This willingness to suit local tastes while remaining true to the McDonald's brand is also reflected in the company's advertising. McDonald's allocates a substantial portion of its advertising budget to cooperative efforts with franchises. Franchise groups make their own decisions about ad agencies and campaign themes.

Even at the national level, McDonald's often runs several campaigns simultaneously. For example, in addition to the "I'm lovin it" ads, the company runs ads promoting specific menu items, such as its premium salad offerings. Other spots target carefully selected markets, such as Hispanics, African Americans, working moms, or kids.

With its dominance of the fast-food landscape, what could possibly be left for McDonald's to conquer?

The answer may be found in McDonald's newest effort: promoting its line of premium coffees. The success of Starbucks did not escape the food giant's attention. So in 2008 McDonald's tested coffee bars where customers could get not only premium coffees, but cappuccinos, mochas, and lattes. Critics immediately claimed that nobody would go to "Mickey D's" for good coffee. But the McDonald's initiative has been a resounding success as coffee sales are up 40 percent. The company has now rolled out coffee bars nationwide and added over a billion dollars in sales.

Why should anyone be surprised? In tough times people want value, and McDonald's has shown time and again that a great brand and great advertising are an unbeatable combination. ■

LO1 List the various groups in the advertising business and explain their relationships to one another.

THE ADVERTISING INDUSTRY

The range of work performed by advertising people goes far beyond what we see daily on TV. Moreover, many people and organizations besides those usually thought of as advertising folks are involved in advertising and IMC. That's because every successful company needs to communicate with customers.

The Organizations in Advertising

The advertising business has has four distinct groups. The two main ones are the *advertisers* and the *agencies*. The **advertisers** (or *clients*) are companies—like Honda, Coca-Cola, or the local

advertisers Companies that sponsor advertising for themselves and their products.

advertising agencies Independent organizations of creative people and businesspeople that specialize in developing and preparing advertising plans, advertisements, and other promotional tools for advertisers. The agencies also arrange for or contract for purchases of space and time in various media.

suppliers People and organizations that assist both advertisers and agencies in the preparation of advertising materials, such as photography, illustration, printing, and production.

media A plural form of *medium*, referring to communications vehicles paid to present an advertisement to their target audience. Most often used to refer to radio and television networks, stations that have new reporters, and publications that carry news and advertising.

shoe store—that pay to advertise themselves and their products. Advertisers range in size from small independent businesses to huge multinational firms, and in type from service organizations to industrial manufacturers to local charities. The second group, **advertising agencies**, helps advertisers to plan, create, and prepare IMC campaigns.

A third group, the **suppliers**, includes the photographers, illustrators, printers, digital service bureaus, video production houses, Web developers, and others who assist advertisers and agencies in preparing advertising materials. Suppliers also include consultants, research firms, and professional services. The fourth group, the **media**, sells time (on radio and TV) and space (in print, outdoor) or both (digital media) for delivering the advertiser's message to the target audience.

The People in Advertising

When people think of advertising they imagine the copywriters and art directors who work for ad agencies. But most people in advertising are actually employed by advertisers rather than by agencies. Companies usually have an advertising department, even if it's just one person.

In addition, many other people work for the suppliers and the media. They're in advertising, too. The fact is, advertising is a very broad field that employs a wide variety of people.

In this chapter, we'll see what all these people do at the various places where they work. In the process, we'll get a good understanding of how the advertising industry operates both in the United States and abroad.

check yourself ✓

1. What are the four distinct groups the ad business has evolved into?

2. What is the difference between an advertiser and an advertising agency?

THE ADVERTISERS (CLIENTS)

While most companies have some sort of advertising department, its importance depends on the company's size, industry, and advertising budget, as well as on the role of advertising in the company's marketing mix and the involvement of top management.

To get a sense of the diversity of companies that advertise, we'll look first at local advertisers to see how they operate. Then, we'll examine regional and national advertisers. Finally we'll look at the companies that market their products in foreign countries.

L02 Discuss the differences between local, national, and transnational advertisers.

Local Advertising: Where the Action Is

When Ralph Rubio opened his first Mexican restaurant, he offered an unusual specialty: fish tacos. At the time, very few other Mexican eateries offered fish tacos. So Rubio found fish tacos hard to sell, even with his secret batter recipe. The first month's sales at the restaurant averaged only $163 a day.

Rubio started using small newspaper ads with coupons to lure courageous customers. It worked. As business picked up, he expanded his advertising to radio and TV, targeting his market with ads on Hispanic stations (whose listeners knew what fish tacos were). And he went after younger, venturesome customers ages 18 to 34 by advertising at local movie theaters. Business picked up some more. Rubio soon opened another restaurant, and then another.

With each new opening, Rubio distributed direct-mail flyers in the area and took free samples to nearby stores. Working with an artist, he created a cartoon character named Pesky Pescado based on the fish taco. He purchased a 15-foot inflatable Pesky to display at his restaurants. Employee T-shirts sported Pesky's picture, and Rubio sold Pesky T-shirts and sweatshirts to enthusiastic patrons. He also offered bumper stickers and antenna balls to add some fun to his promotions. To further integrate his activities, Rubio took an active part in community

local advertising
Advertising by businesses within a city or county directed toward customers within the same geographical area.

advertising manager The person that performs all the administrative, planning, budgeting, and coordinating functions. They may lay out ads, write ad copy, and select the media.

[Local advertising is critically important because most consumer sales are made (or lost) locally.]

affairs, including tie-ins with a blood bank, a literacy program, and fund-raising activities for both a Tijuana medical clinic and a local university's athletic program.

As the popularity of the fish taco grew, so did Rubio's revenues, doubling every year for the first five years. He trademarked the phrase "Rubio's, Home of the Fish Taco," and a local restaurant critic, commenting on things San Diegans couldn't do without, called fish tacos "the food San Diegans would miss the most." Today, Rubio's Fresh Mexican Grill has over 180 restaurants in five states. And they still make great fish tacos.[1]

Every year, advertisers spend billions of dollars in the United States. Almost half of that is spent on **local advertising** by local businesses targeting customers in their geographic area.

Local advertising is sometimes called *retail advertising* because so much is placed by retail stores. But retail advertising isn't always local; Sears and JCPenney advertise nationally. And many businesses besides retail stores use local advertising: banks, movie theaters, auto mechanics, plumbers, radio and TV stations, local politicians, and McDonald's franchises, to name a few.

Local advertising is critically important because most consumer sales are made (or lost) locally. McDonald's may spend billions advertising worldwide, but if it doesn't make a strong effort locally, the dollars may be wasted. When it comes to making the sale and dealing with customers, local advertising is where the action is—where relationships often start and truly develop.

Types of Local Advertisers

There are four main types of local advertisers.

- Dealers or local franchisees of national companies (Honda, McDonald's, Mail Boxes Etc., H&R Block).

- Stores that sell a variety of branded merchandise (convenience, grocery, and department stores).

- Specialty businesses and services (banks, restaurants, music stores, remodeling contractors, florists, hair salons, attorneys, accountants).

- Governmental and nonprofit organizations (municipalities, utility companies, charities, arts organizations, political candidates).

A small, local business—say, a hardware, clothing, or electronics store—may have just one person in charge of advertising.

Many local advertisements are for retail stores that sell a variety of branded merchandise or for specialty businesses. This ad for Loehmann's Plaza promotes the shopping center, anchored by Loehmann's (*www.loehmanns.com*), as well as all of the individual stores and restaurants that serve the local community.

That person, the **advertising manager,** performs all the administrative, planning, budgeting, and coordinating functions. He or she may lay out ads, write ad copy, and select the media. A manager with some artistic talent may even design the ads and produce them on a computer.

Chain stores often maintain an advertising department to handle production, media placement, and marketing support services. A typical small advertiser structure is shown in Exhibit 3–1.

Types of Local Advertising

Most local ads are product, institutional, or classified advertising. Each serves a different purpose.

▼**EXHIBIT 3–1** Typical department structure for small advertisers with high volumes of work, such as grocery store chains.

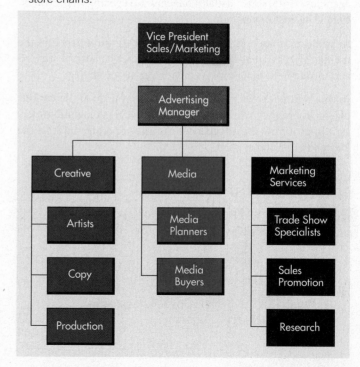

product advertising
Advertising intended to promote goods and services; also a functional classification of advertising.

sale advertising
A type of retail advertising designed to stimulate the movement of particular merchandise or generally increase store traffic by placing the emphasis on special reduced prices.

institutional advertising A type of advertising that attempts to obtain favorable attention for the business as a whole, not for a specific product or service the store or business sells. The effects of institutional advertising are intended to be long term rather than short range.

classified advertising Used to locate and recruit new employees, offer services, or sell or lease new and used merchandise.

Product advertising promotes a specific product or service and stimulates short-term action while building awareness of the business. To stimulate sales of merchandise or increase store traffic, local merchants frequently use **sale advertising**, placing items on sale and offering two-for-one specials or other deals.

Institutional advertising attempts to create a favorable long-term perception of the business as a whole, not just of a particular product or service. Many businesses use institutional advertising to promote an idea about the company and build long-term goodwill. It makes the public aware of what the business stands for and attempts to build reputation and image.

Advertisers use **classified advertising** for a variety of reasons: to locate and recruit new employees, offer services (such as those of an employment agency or business opportunity

Understanding Your Client [3–A]

Obtaining a clear understanding of what your client wants from you and what you are prepared to do for your client is essential for a mutually satisfying relationship. From your end it is vital that you be clear about the finished product. In many classes this might be a plans book, which contains research, an advertising plan, a media plan, and even some creative plans. In other classes you might not provide all of that. In either case, make sure your client knows what to expect. If previous classes have done campaign work for other clients, you might wish to show your client that work.

As important as it is that your client understand you, it is equally crucial that you understand your client's expectations. Recognize that some clients may not have a clear set of expectations at first; these may in fact evolve over time. Even in this instance, asking the right questions can get your client thinking about what they hope advertising will do for them.

Below you will find some questions that might prove useful for getting to know your client better. Dr. Debbie Treise, who regularly teaches advertising campaigns at the University of Florida, uses this form. Sending it to the client in advance of a meeting can make your first interaction more useful and informative.

1. Provide a complete description of your product/service:
   What is its current position?
   What is the brand personality as you perceive it?
   Does it need changing?
   Are there seasonal trends for your product?
   Would you be willing to share annual sales trend information?
2. Do you have information on your company to share? Your mission statement? How would you describe the culture of your organization?

3. Do you have a definite target market in mind? Are you targeting consumers, groups, businesses or some combination?
4. Is the market local? Regional? National? International?
5. Would you be willing to share:
   Information on your competition?
   Information on your market?
   Information on market trends? Legal trends?
   Advertising that your competition has used?
   Previous advertising efforts you have undertaken?
6. What is the time period of this campaign? Do you have definite start and stop dates in mind?
7. What is the budget?
8. Do you have any specifications on the budget breakdown in terms of promotion versus advertising? Any other specifications?
9. What are your marketing objectives for this campaign?
10. Please list your advertising/communications objectives for this campaign (that is, to increase knowledge, change attitudes, elicit a specific behavior).
11. Are there media that you would like us to be sure to consider?
12. Are there media that you would prefer we not recommend?
13. Do you have a current, active Web site? If so, what is its primary purpose? Who accesses it?
14. Do you have any specifications on creative executions? Are you looking to continue current efforts or to come up with something completely different?
15. Are there any current clients/consumers that we could contact?
16. Are there potential clients/customers that we could contact?
17. Who is the individual in your organization we should contact when we have questions? What is the best time to contact this person? How does he or she prefer to be contacted (e-mail, phone, fax)?

integrated marketing communications (IMC) The process of building and reinforcing mutually profitable relationships with employees, customers, other stakeholders, and the general public by developing and coordinating a strategic communications program that enables them to make constructive contact with the company/brand through a variety of media.

cooperative (co-op) advertising The sharing of advertising costs by the manufacturer and the distributor or retailer. The manufacturer may repay 50 or 100 percent of the dealer's advertising costs or some other amount based on sales.

broker), or sell or lease new and used merchandise (such as cars, real estate, and office equipment).

Local Advertisers and IMC

When Ralph Rubio built his restaurant business, his promotional activities involved a lot more than just running ads. In fact, he did everything he could to build relationships with his customers and to promote word-of-mouth. That meant using publicity, sales promotion, and direct response as well as media advertising—all integrated with consistently good food, reasonable prices, and excellent service. This combination constitutes **integrated marketing communications (IMC)**—joining together in a consistent manner every element that communicates with customers including the actual delivery of the product or service.

Creating Local Advertising

Cal Worthington first pitched his car dealership on Los Angeles TV stations in 1951 and 56 years later, he's still at it. He sponsors third-rate movies on latenight and Saturday afternoon TV. In his zany ads, he often appears in cowboy garb with a variety of domesticated wild animals, all introduced as "my dog Spot" (www.mydogspot.com).

The principles for developing good local advertising are really no different than the general principles presented throughout this book. However, given limited budgets and the need to see immediate results, local advertisers have to make every word and every dollar count. To direct and control the creative aspects of their ads and commercials and ensure consistency, local advertisers should adhere to a list of creative do's and don'ts. (See My Ad Campaign 3–B, "Creating Local Advertising," on page 65.)

Local advertisers rely on several sources for creative help, including reps from the local media, local ad agencies, freelancers and consultants, creative boutiques, syndicated art services, and the cooperative advertising programs of wholesalers, manufacturers, and trade associations. McDonald's offers its franchise owners considerable help in designing IMC messages.

Cooperative Advertising

Wholesalers and manufacturers often provide local advertisers with ready-made advertising materials and cooperative advertising programs where the costs are shared.

Cooperative (co-op) advertising has two key purposes: to build the manufacturer's brand image and to help distributors, dealers, or retailers increase sales.[2] Every year, national manufacturers give local retailers more than $20 billion for co-op projects. Newspapers, television, and radio are the favored media of co-op spending.[3] Walmart alone benefits from almost $100 million in vendor funding for ads.[4] Exhibit 3–2

In addition to its national campaigns, individual McDonald's franchises also engage in local advertising. One purpose of local ads is to recruit new employees.

Manufacturers, such as Hoover (www.hoover.com), provide retailers with advertising materials and co-op dollars to encourage dealers like Sears (www.sears.com) to promote the manufacturer's products. If these products are not promoted at the local level, the manufacturer's national advertising efforts will be less effective.

regional advertisers
Companies that operate in one part of the country and market exclusively to that region.

national advertisers
Companies that advertise in several geographic regions or throughout the country.

▼**EXHIBIT 3–2** The importance of co-op advertising dollars.

Store	Co-op Dollars as a Percentage of Total Ad Budget
Appliance dealers	80%
Food stores	75
Drugstores	70
Department stores	50
Shoe stores	50
Clothing stores	35
Furniture stores	30
Household goods	30
Jewelers	30
Discount stores	20

demonstrates how important co-op advertising dollars are for certain retail businesses. (Commercial Break 3–A provides questions to consider when contemplating co-op advertising.)

Regional and National Advertisers

Some companies operate in one part of the country—in one or several states—and market exclusively within that region. These are referred to as **regional advertisers**. Typical examples include regional grocery and department store chains, governmental bodies (such as state lotteries), franchise groups (such as the Southern California Honda dealers), and statewide or multistate banks (Bank of America).

Other companies sell in several regions or throughout the country and are called **national advertisers**. These include consumer packaged-goods manufacturers (such as Procter & Gamble and Johnson & Johnson), national airlines (Delta, American), media and entertainment companies (Disney, Time Warner), electronics manufacturers (Apple, Hewlett-Packard),

The Co-op Marriage [3–A]

On the surface, cooperative advertising seems like a great arrangement for retailers. A manufacturer supplies advertising materials (saving the retailer production costs) and pays a percentage of the media cost. The retailer drops in the store's logo, arranges for the ad to run, and collects the co-op dollars from the manufacturer. The small retail business can stretch its ad budget and associate its business with a nationally advertised product. The retailer receives professionally prepared ads and acquires greater leverage with the local media that carry the co-op ads.

But as with any marriage, there is give and take.

A retailer may have to sell a lot of merchandise to qualify for significant co-op funds. More often, the retailer and manufacturer have different advertising objectives and different ideas about how the ads should be executed.

The manufacturer often wants total control. The manufacturer expects co-op ads to tie in with its national advertising promotions. It wants the right product advertised at the right time. Manufacturers prepare guideline pamphlets specifying when and where the ads should appear, what form they should take, and what uses of the name and logo are not allowed.

Retailers have their own ideas about which products to feature. They're more concerned with daily volume and with projecting an image of value and variety. An appliance store might prefer to advertise inexpensive TVs even though the manufacturer wants to emphasize its top-of-the-line models.

Manufacturers worry that retailers will place the product in a cluttered, ugly ad or next to inferior products; that the ad will run in inappropriate publications; and that it will not run at the best time. Retailers counter that they know the local market better. In short, manufacturers think they don't have enough control; retailers think the manufacturers have too much.

A retailer contemplating co-op funds should consider the following questions:

• What requirements must be met in order for ads to qualify for co-op money?
• What percentage is paid by each party?
• When can ads be run?
• What media can be used?
    • Are there special provisions for message content?
    • What documentation is required for reimbursement?
    • How does each party benefit?
    • Do cooperative ads obscure the retailer's image?

Applying the Breaks

1. Look through today's edition of a daily paper in your city. Identify two ads that can qualify as co-op. Do the ads fit both the store's image and the manufacturer's image? Explain.

2. A store may develop its own ad and drop in the manufacturer's logo or it may take an ad created by the manufacturer and simply add the store's location. Which do your two ads do?

▼**EXHIBIT 3–3** Top 10 advertisers in the United States ranked by total U.S. advertising.

				Percent Allocated to:					
Rank	Marketer	Total U.S. Spending 2008 (000, 000)	% Change from 2007	Magazine	Newspaper	Outdoor	TV	Radio	Web
1	Procter & Gamble	4838.1	−6.6%	19.8%	3.9%	0.0%	44.5%	0.4%	1.0%
2	Verizon Communications	3700.0	9.5	2.9	18.4	2.3	31.5	5.6	3.9
3	AT&T	3073.0	−10.4	1.8	9.4	2.1	43.3	5.7	2.3
4	General Motors Corp.	2901.1	−5.2	15.4	11.1	0.8	40.6	2.6	6.5
5	Johnson & Johnson	2529.2	5.0	15.8	1.9	0.2	35.7	0.8	1.8
6	Unilever	2422.6	0.2	9.0	1.2	0.1	19.8	0.3	0.7
7	Walt Disney Co.	2217.6	11.0	8.9	6.5	2.0	30.3	4.0	4.9
8	Time Warner	2207.7	−19.9	10.4	9.2	2.3	31.3	2.2	3.5
9	General Electric Co.	2019.3	12.7	6.8	8.5	2.2	33.3	5.7	2.6
10	Sears Holdings Corp.	1864.9	−4.7	3.2	10.3	0.0	23.2	1.9	0.9

Source: Bradley Johnson, "Spending Fell (only) 2.7% in '08," *Advertising Age,* June 22, 2009, pp. 1, 12.

and many restaurant chains such as McDonald's. These firms also make up the membership of the *Association of National Advertisers (ANA),* which includes the largest advertisers in the country (see Exhibit 3–3).

How National and Local Advertisers Differ The basic principles of advertising are the same in both local and national advertising. However, local advertisers have special challenges stemming from the day-to-day realities of running a small business (see Exhibit 3–4).

Focus. National companies are concerned about building their *brands,* so their advertising tends to focus on the competitive features of one brand over another. Local merchants or dealers often carry hundreds of different brands, so they focus on attracting customers to a particular *location*—their place of business.

Big companies battle for *market share* against a few competitors, and every share point is worth millions of dollars. Local advertisers compete with many companies, so their focus is on gross sales or *volume:* 60 cars a month, five new insurance policies a week, 55 oil changes a day.

> "National advertisers plan strategically . . . Local advertisers think tactically."

▼**EXHIBIT 3–4** Differences between local and national advertisers.

	National	Local
Focus	Brand	Location
	Market share	Volume
	Strategies	Tactics
	Markets	Customers
Time	Long-term campaigns	Short-term ads
Resources	$5–$10 million+	Less than $1 million
	Many specialists	A few generalists

National advertisers plan *strategically* to launch, build, and sustain brands. Local advertisers think *tactically.* Will a new $15,000 sign bring more people into the store? Should we stay open Labor Day? Can we attract more lunchtime customers by reducing our prices or by offering free refills on soft drinks?

The relationship with the customer may be the greatest difference between national and local advertisers. National advertisers' marketing executives rarely see their customers; instead, they traditionally think of them in terms of segments, niches, or target *markets.* They design their strategies and campaigns to appeal to these large groups.

But local advertisers deal with individual *customers* every day. The local advertiser gets regular feedback on the company's advertising, prices, product performance, customer service, store decor, and the new sign out front.

Time orientation. National companies think long term. They develop five-year strategic plans and budget for annual advertising campaigns. Local advertisers worry that this week's ad didn't *pull* (a term rarely used by national marketers) as well as last week's; a New York advertiser may have months to develop a network TV campaign; the little market on Main Street may have to churn out a new newspaper ad every week.

Resources. Finally, national advertisers have more resources—both money and people. The national advertiser has millions of dollars and an army of *specialists* dedicated to the successful marketing of its brands. The local advertiser may have a small staff of *generalists* or just one person—the owner—to market the business. So the local entrepreneur has to know about every facet of IMC.

LO3 Explain how advertisers organize themselves to manage their advertising both here and abroad.

How Large Companies Manage Their Advertising

In large companies, many people are involved in advertising. Company owners and top corporate executives make key advertising decisions; sales and marketing personnel often assist in the creative process, help choose the ad agency, and evaluate proposed ad programs; artists and writers produce ads,

Creating Local Advertising [3–B]

Is your client a local business or service? Use these time-tested practices to guide your thinking about how local advertising can help.

• *Stand out from the competition.* Make your ads easily recognizable. Ads with unusual art, layout, and typefaces have higher readership. Make the ads distinctive but keep their appearance consistent.

• *Use a simple layout.* The layout should carry the reader's eye through the message easily and in proper sequence from headline to illustration to explanatory copy to price to store name. Avoid too many typefaces.

• *Use a dominant element.* A large picture or headline ensures quick visibility. Photos of real people and action pictures win more readership, as do photos of local people or places. Color attracts more readers.

• *Stress the benefits.* Present the emotional reason to buy or the tangible performance element customers seek.

• *Make the headline count.* Use a compelling headline to feature the main benefit.

• *Watch your language.* Make your writing style active, lively, and involving. Make the readers feel they already own the product. Avoid negativism and profanity.

• *Let white space work for you.* White space focuses the reader's attention and makes the headline and illustration stand out.

• *Make the copy complete.* Emphasize the benefits most appealing to customers.

• *Make your visual powerful and eye-catching.* Focus on the benefit. The main visual is often more important than the headline. Photos work better than artwork.

• *Specify branded merchandise.* If the item is a known brand, say so.

• *Include related items.* Make two sales instead of one by offering related items along with a featured one.

• *Urge readers to buy now.* Ask for the sale. Stimulate prompt action by using "limited supply" or "this week only."

• *Don't forget the business name and address.* Check every ad to be certain the business name, address, phone number, and hours are included.

• *Don't be too clever.* Many people distrust or misunderstand cleverness.

• *Don't use unusual or difficult words.* Everyone understands simple language. Use it.

• *Don't generalize.* Be specific. Shoppers want all the facts before they buy.

• *Don't make excessive claims.* Advertisers lose customers when they make claims they can't back up.

• *Plan ad size carefully.* Attention usually increases with size.

• *Consider your target customers.* People notice ads more if they are directed at their own gender or age group.

• *Use tie-ins* with local or special news events.

brochures, and other materials; product engineers and designers give input to the creative process and provide information about competitive products; administrators evaluate the cost of ad campaigns and help plan budgets; and clerical staff coordinate various promotional activities, including advertising.

A large company's advertising department may employ many people, led by an advertising manager who reports to a marketing director or marketing services manager. The exact department structure can vary. Most large advertisers tend to use some mix of two basic management structures: *centralized* and *decentralized*.

Centralized organization. Some companies are concerned with cost efficiency and continuity in their communications programs. Thus, many embrace the **centralized advertising department** because it gives the greatest control and offers both efficiency and continuity across divisional boundaries. In centralized

Large agencies working on national campaigns often blend advertising and sales promotion efforts. This ad for McDonald's is an example.

departments, an advertising manager typically reports to a marketing vice president. The advertising department may be organized in any of five ways:

- By product or brand.
- By subfunction of advertising (copy, art, print production, media buying).
- By end user (consumer advertising, trade advertising).
- By media (radio, TV, Web, outdoor).
- By geography (western advertising, eastern advertising, international advertising).

General Mills's, for example, is one of the nation's largest advertisers. It operates a vast advertising and marketing services department with some 350 employees. It spends nearly $1 billion annually in media advertising and other promotional activities.[5]

General Mills's Marketing Services is really many departments within a department. Its centralized structure (see Exhibit 3–5), enables it to administer, plan, and coordinate the promotion of more than 60 brands. It also supervises outside ad agencies and operates its own in-house agency for new or smaller brands.

Organized around functional specialties (market research, media, graphics), Marketing Services helps General Mills' **brand managers** consolidate expenditures for maximum efficiency. Of course, even a traditional company like General

▼ **EXHIBIT 3–5** General Mills has a centralized advertising department like this model.

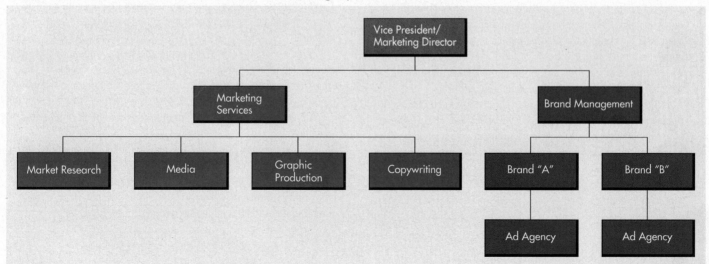

Mills has to engage consumers in new and exciting ways. The company is investing heavily in blogs, Facebook, and iPhone apps. Digital efforts and campaigns that target fast-growing minority segments are a particular priority.[6]

Decentralized organization.

As some companies become larger, diversify their product line, acquire subsidiaries, and establish divisions in different regions or even different countries, a centralized advertising department often becomes impractical.

In a **decentralized system**, the company sets up separate ad departments for different divisions, subsidiaries, regions, brands, or other categories that suit the company's needs. The general manager of each division or brand is responsible for that group's advertising. A brand manager, who oversees each individual brand, typically works under a marketing manager. This system gives significant authority to the individuals responsible for each brand.

For large companies with many divisions, decentralized advertising is more flexible. Campaigns and media schedules can be adjusted faster. New approaches and creative ideas can be introduced more easily, and sales results can be measured independently of other divisions. In effect, each division has its own marketing department, with the marketing manager reporting to the division head (see Exhibit 3–6).

A drawback, though, is that decentralized departments often concentrate on their own budgets, problems, and promotions rather than the good of the whole company. Across divisions, ads may lack uniformity, diminishing the power of repetitive corporate advertising. Rivalry among brand managers may even escalate into unhealthy competition.

Transnational Advertisers

Companies advertising abroad typically face markets with different value systems, environments, and languages. Their customers have different purchasing abilities, habits, and motivations. Media customary to U.S. and Canadian advertisers may be unavailable or ineffective. The companies will therefore likely need different advertising strategies. But they face a more basic problem: How should they manage and produce the advertising? Should their U.S. agency or in-house advertising department do it? Should they use a foreign agency or set up a local advertising department?

Procter & Gamble is a $79 billion company that sells more than 300 consumer brands in over 180 countries. These brands include such market leaders as Tide, Ivory soap, Pampers, Folgers, Pringles, and Crest toothpaste.[7]

P&G is one of the biggest and most influential consumer advertisers in the world; its expenditures worldwide exceed $9.5 billion in 2010.[8] Each overseas division is set up almost like a

▼**EXHIBIT 3–6** In a decentralized structure, each division has its own marketing department.

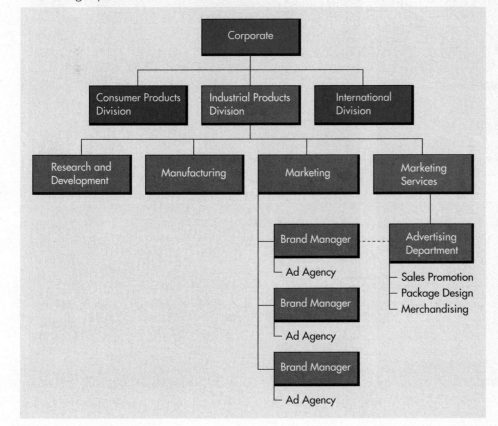

COMPANIES DO A LOT OF RESEARCH BEFORE ATTEMPTING A GLOBAL ADVERTISING STRATEGY.

separate company with its own research and development department, manufacturing plant, sales force, and finance and accounting staff. Each division also has an advertising department to help coordinate programs across brands within that division.

As companies continue to grow and prosper around the world, they may invest directly in many countries. True **multinational corporations** strive for full, integrated participation in world markets.[9] Foreign sales often grow faster than domestic sales. In 2002 global, U.S.-based companies derived about 33 percent of all sales from other countries. By 2007 global customers accounted for almost half of all sales.[10]

Multinationals that use a *standardized approach* to marketing and advertising in all countries are considered **global marketers**, and they create global brands. Their assumption is that the way the product is used and the needs it satisfies are universal.[11]

McDonald's "I'm lovin' it," campaign, first begun in 2003, runs in all 118 countries where the company sells food.[12] Other global advertisers include Coca-Cola, Ford, Apple, GE, and L'Oreal.[13]

Companies do a lot of research before attempting a global advertising strategy. So much depends on the product and where they try to sell it. A "no" answer to any of the following questions means the attempt will probably fail.

1. *Has each country's market for the product developed in the same way?* A Ford is a Ford in most markets. On the other hand, many Europeans use clotheslines, so they don't need fabric softeners for dryers.

2. *Are the targets similar in different nations?* Japanese consumers like jeans, running shoes, and game consoles. The same is true for consumers in Europe and the United States. But they might not share a liking for certain foods or other fashions.

In Canada, all packages and labels must be printed in both English and French, and most major companies also run their ads in both languages. The layout of the French version of this HP (www.hp.com) ad is modified to accommodate the slightly longer text.

This ad for McDonald's helps to celebrate an Islamic observance. Sensitivity to the infinite diversity of worldwide cultures and beliefs is important for a global advertiser's success.

3. *Do consumers share the same wants and needs?* Breakfast in Brazil is usually a cup of coffee. Kellogg's Corn Flakes won't be served the same way as in the United States, where people commonly eat cereal for breakfast.[14]

Advertisers who cannot answer "yes" to the above questions will often take a *localized approach* to international marketing and advertising. They will consider differences in product use, economic development, media options, local laws, technology, and customs. The outcome will often be the adaptation of products, packages, and advertising campaigns to suit each market.

The secret to success in global advertising may be knowing how to tap into basic human emotions and uncover universal appeals that don't depend solely on language. In addition, social media can help global advertisers capitalize on the universal appeal of word-of-mouth.[15]

Media Around the World

In the United States, if you want to promote a soft drink as a youthful, fun refresher, you might use television. In some parts of Europe, Asia, South America, and Africa you may not be able to. Around the world, broadcast media are sometimes owned and controlled by the government, and many governments do not allow commercial advertising. In Egypt, one creative medium used by Coca-Cola and others is the fleet of boats plying the Nile with corporate logos emblazoned on their sails.[16]

Where TV ownership is high, it cuts across the spectrum of income groups. In less-developed countries, though, TV sets may be found only among upper-income groups. This means advertisers may need a different media mix in foreign markets.

Virtually every country has access to radio, television, newspapers, magazines, outdoor media, and direct mail. However, the legalities of different media forms vary from country to country. Generally, the media available to the international advertiser can be categorized as either *international* or *foreign media,* depending on the audience they serve.

International Media In the past, **international media**— which serve several countries, usually without any change in content—have been limited to newspapers and magazines. Several large American publishers such as Time, McGraw-Hill, and Scientific American circulate international editions of their magazines abroad. Usually written in English, they tend to be read by well-educated, upper-income consumers and are therefore good vehicles for advertising high-end, brand-name products. *Reader's Digest,* on the other hand, is distributed to 126 foreign countries and printed in the local language of each. Today, television is also becoming a viable international medium. We are beginning to see the emergence of *global media vehicles,* such as MTV.

Foreign Media Advertisers use **foreign media**—the local media of each country—for large campaigns targeted to consumers or businesses within a single country. Because foreign media cater to their own national audience, advertisers must produce their ads in the language of each country. In countries such as Belgium and Switzerland, with more than one official language, ads are produced in each language.

Unlike the United States, most countries have strong national newspapers that are good vehicles for national campaigns. Advertisers also get broad penetration of lower-income markets through radio, which enjoys almost universal ownership. And cinema advertising is a good alternative to TV in markets with low TV penetration or restricted use of commercial TV.

check yourself ✓

1. What factors determine the type of organizational structure that advertisers use?

2. What additional challenges are faced by companies that advertise internationally?

3. What determines whether a multinational advertiser is a global marketer or not?

The Role of the Advertising Agency

The American Association of Advertising Agencies (AAAA) defines an **advertising agency** as an independent organization of creative people and businesspeople who specialize in developing and preparing marketing and advertising plans, advertisements, and other promotional tools. Agencies also purchase advertising space and time in various media on behalf of different advertisers (clients) to find customers for their goods and services.[17]

This definition offers clues to why so many advertisers hire ad agencies. First, an agency like Leo Burnett is *independent*. The agency isn't owned by the advertiser, the media, or the suppliers, so it can bring an outside, objective viewpoint to the advertiser's business—a position the advertiser can never attain.

Second, like all agencies, Leo Burnett employs a combination of *businesspeople* and *creative people,* including administrators, accountants, marketing executives, researchers, market and media analysts, writers, and artists. They have day-to-day contact with outside professional suppliers who create illustrations, take photos, retouch art, shoot commercials, record sound, and print brochures.

> [Agencies don't work for the media or the suppliers. Their moral, ethical, financial, and legal obligation is to their clients.]

THE ADVERTISING AGENCY

Why does a company such as McDonald's hire ad agencies in the first place? Couldn't it save money by hiring its own staff and creating its own ads? How does an advertising agency, such as Leo Burnett, one of McDonald's agencies, win such a large account? Must an agency's accounts be that big for it to make money? This section sheds some light on these issues and gives a clearer understanding of what agencies do and why so many advertisers use agencies.

LO4 Define the main types of advertising agencies.

The agency provides yet another service by researching, negotiating, arranging, and contracting for commercial space and time with different print, electronic, and digital media. Because of its *media expertise,* Burnett saves its clients time and money.

Agencies don't work for the media or the suppliers. Their moral, ethical, financial, and legal obligation is to their clients. Just as a well-run business seeks professional help from attorneys, accountants, bankers, or management specialists, advertisers use agencies out of *self-interest,* because the agencies can create more effective advertising and select more effective media than the advertisers can themselves. Today, almost all sizable advertisers rely on an ad agency.

Finally, a good agency serves its clients' needs because of its daily exposure to a broad spectrum of marketing situations and problems both here and abroad. As technology has enabled companies to work across borders with relative ease, the advertising business has boomed worldwide. Most large U.S. agencies maintain offices abroad.

Types of Agencies

Advertising agencies are typically classified by their geographic scope, the range of services they offer, and the type of business they handle.

Geographic Scope

Every community of any size has reputable **local agencies** that offer expert assistance to local advertisers. Unfortunately, local advertisers use ad agencies less extensively than do national advertisers. Many local advertisers simply don't spend enough money on advertising to warrant hiring an agency. And some large agencies don't accept local advertisers because their budgets are too small.

Every major city has numerous ad agencies that can produce and place the quality of advertising suitable for national campaigns. **Regional** and **national agencies** typically participate in either the 4As (American Association of Advertising Agencies) or some similar trade group such as the Western States Advertising Agency Association (WSAAA). The *Standard Directory of Advertising Agencies* (the Red Book) lists these agencies geographically, so they're easy to find.[18]

The largest national agencies are also **international agencies**. That is, they have offices or affiliates in major communications centers around the world and can help their clients market internationally or globally as the case may be. Likewise, many foreign-based agencies have offices and affiliates in the United States. For example, the largest advertising agency organization in the world today, WPP Group, is based in London. But it owns several top U.S. agencies, including Ogilvy & Mather and J. Walter Thompson.

Range of Services

The modern **full-service advertising agency** supplies both advertising and nonadvertising services in all areas of communications and promotion. *Advertising services* include planning, creating, and producing ads; performing research; and selecting media. *Nonadvertising services* run the gamut from packaging to public relations to producing sales promotion materials, annual reports, and trade-show exhibits. With the trend toward IMC, many of the largest agencies today are in the forefront of *interactive media.*[19]

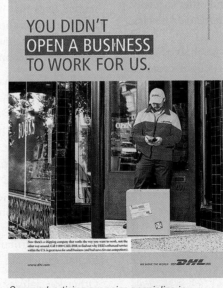

YOU DIDN'T **OPEN A BUSINESS** TO WORK FOR US.

Some advertising agencies specialize in business-to-business advertising. In this ad, DHL (www.dhl.com) is promoting its shipping services to small businesses.

Full-service agencies may specialize in certain kinds of clients. Most, though, can be classified as either *general consumer agencies* or *business-to-business agencies.*

General consumer agencies. A **general consumer agency** represents the widest variety of accounts, but it concentrates on *consumer accounts*—companies that make goods purchased chiefly by consumers (soaps, cereals, cars, pet foods, toiletries). Most of the ads are placed in consumer media (TV, radio, magazines, and so on) that pay a *commission* to the agency. General agencies often derive much of their income from these commissions.

General agencies include the international superagency groups headquartered in communication capitals such as New York, London, Paris, and Tokyo, as well as many other large firms in Chicago, Los Angeles, Minneapolis, Montreal, and Toronto. A few of the better-known names in North America are McCann-Erickson; Ogilvy & Mather; Draft FCB; Grey Advertising; BBDO; DDB Needham; Y & R; and Cossette Communication Group (Canada). But general agencies also include the thousands of smaller *entrepreneurial agencies* located in every major city across the country (Martin Agency, Richmond, Virginia; RPA, Los Angeles; MMB, Boston; and Wieden & Kennedy, Portland, Oregon).

Profit margins in entrepreneurial agencies are often slimmer, but these shops are typically more responsive to the smaller clients they serve. They offer the hands-on involvement of the firm's principals, and their work is frequently startling in its creativity. For these reasons, many large agencies are spinning off smaller subsidiaries. Gotham Advertising, for example, is a hot creative shop in New York that was spun off by the Interpublic Group of Companies to do work for a variety of clients its bigger sister agencies couldn't serve.[20] Some entrepreneurial agencies, such as Zubi Advertising in Coral Gables, Florida, carve a niche for themselves by serving particular market segments.

Business-to-business agencies. A **business-to-business agency** represents clients that market products to other businesses. Examples are electronic components for computer manufacturers, equipment used in oil and gas refineries, and MRI equipment for radiology. High-tech advertising requires some technical knowledge and the ability to translate that knowledge into precise and persuasive communications. While you may be a customer for McDonald's food, the company is itself a customer, and thus an advertising target, for suppliers of soft drinks, eggs, beef, chicken, lettuce, bread, napkins, employee uniforms, and so on.

Most business-to-business advertising is placed in trade magazines or other business publications. These media are commissionable, but their circulation is smaller, so their rates are far lower than those of consumer media. Because commissions usually don't cover the cost of the agency's services, business agencies typically charge their clients service fees. They can be expensive, especially for small advertisers, but failure to obtain a business agency's expertise may carry an even higher price in lost marketing opportunities.

Specialized Service Agencies

Many agencies assist their clients with a variety of limited services. There has been a continuing trend towards specialization, giving impetus to many of the small agencies called *creative boutiques* and other specialty businesses such as *media-buying services* and *interactive agencies*.

Creative boutiques. Some talented artists—such as graphic designers and copywriters—have set up their own creative services, or **creative boutiques**. They work for advertisers and occasionally subcontract to ad agencies. Their mission is

The Internet offers advertisers yet another medium for building brands. An interactive agency helped the advertiser create its Web messages.

to develop exciting creative concepts and produce fresh, distinctive advertising messages. In the 1990s, Creative Artists Agency (CAA), a Hollywood talent agency, caused a stir on Madison Avenue (the collective term for New York agencies) by taking on the role of a creative boutique, using its pool of actors, directors, and cinematographers to create a series of commercials for Coca-Cola. McCann-Erickson Worldwide remained Coke's *agency of record,* but the majority of the creative work came from CAA. Since then, Coke has allowed numerous other smaller shops to work on its account.[21]

Advertising effectiveness depends on originality in concept, design, and writing. However, while boutiques may be economical, they usually don't provide the research, marketing, sales expertise, or deep customer service that full-service agencies offer. Thus, boutiques tend to be limited to the role of creative suppliers.

Media-buying services. Some years ago, a few experienced agency media people started setting up organizations to purchase and package radio and TV time. The largest **media-buying service** (or *media agency*) is Initiative Media. Based in Los Angeles, it is owned by the Interpublic Group, has 99 offices in 58 countries around the world, and places more than $20 billion worth of advertising annually for a wide variety of clients from AOL and Tommy Hilfiger to Home Depot.[22]

Media time and space is perishable. A 60-second radio spot at 8 p.m. can't be sold later. So radio and TV stations presell as much time as possible and discount their rates for large buys. Media-buying services negotiate a special discount with the media and then sell the time or space to agencies or advertisers.

Media-buying firms provide customers (both clients and agencies) with a detailed analysis of the media buy. Once the media package is sold, the buying service orders spots, verifies performance, sees that stations "make good" for any missed spots, and even pays the media bills. Compensation methods vary. Some services charge a set fee; others get a percentage of what they sell or how much they save the client.

Media agencies have experienced so much growth in the last decade that they have become major players on the advertising stage. We'll discuss them in greater detail in Chapter 15, "Media Planning and Buying."

Interactive agencies. A heightened interest in IMC and digital advertising has led to a new breed of specialist—the **interactive agency**. Agency.com and Tribal DDB are some of the many firms that have sprung up within the last few years with specialized experience in designing Web pages and creating fun, involving, information-rich, online advertising. The biggest digital agencies in 2008 included Havas and Aegis.[23]

Other specialists, such as *direct-response* and *sales promotion agencies,* are also growing in response to client demands for greater expertise and accountability as advertisers add new marketing approaches.

check yourself ✓

1. Why do so many advertisers hire ad agencies?

2. What are the main types of advertising agencies?

L05 Explain the range of tasks people perform in an ad agency and an in-house advertising department.

WHAT PEOPLE IN AN AGENCY DO

An agency's purpose is to interpret to the public, or to desired segments of the public, information about a legally marketed product or service. How does it do this? First, it studies the client's product to determine its strengths and weaknesses. Next, it analyzes the product's present and potential market. Then, using its knowledge of product distribution and media alternatives, the agency formulates a plan to carry the advertiser's message to consumers or businesses. Finally the agency writes, designs, and produces ads; contracts for media space and time; verifies media insertions; and bills for services and media used.

The agency also works with the client's marketing staff to enhance the advertising's impact through package design, sales research and training, and the production of sales literature and displays. To understand these functions, consider the people who were involved, directly and indirectly, in the creation, production, and supervision of McDonald's advertising.

Account Management The **account executives (AEs)** at Leo Burnett are the liaison between the agency and the client. Large agencies have many account executives, who report to **management** (or **account**) **supervisors**. They

> To succeed today, an AE needs to be more of a strategist than an advocate.

in turn report to the agency's director of account (or client) services.

Deena Di Stefano is McDonald's account executive at Burnett. Like many AE's, she can find herself often caught in the middle of the fray, as she is responsible for formulating and executing advertising plans (discussed in Chapter 7), mustering the agency's services, representing the client's point of view to the agency, and the agency's point of view to the client. To succeed today, an AE needs to be more of a strategist than an advocate. She must be well versed in an extraordinary range of media and demonstrate how her agency's creative work satisfies both her client's marketing needs and the market's product needs. That means she must be enterprising and courageous, demanding yet tactful, artistic and articulate, meticulous, forgiving, perceptive, persuasive, ethical, and discreet—all at once. And she must always deliver the work on time and within budget.

Research and Account Planning Clients and agencies must give their creatives (artists and copywriters) a wealth of product, market, and competitive information because, at its core, advertising is based on information. Therefore, before creating any advertising, agencies research the uses and advantages of the product, analyze current and potential customers, and try to determine what will influence them to buy. After the ads are placed, agencies use more research to investigate how the campaign fared. Chapter 6 discusses some of the many types of research ad agencies conduct.

Account planning is a hybrid discipline that uses research to bridge the gap between account management and creatives. The account planner also defends the consumer's point of view and the creative strategy in the debate between the agency's creative team and the client.

Account planners study consumer needs and desires through a variety of methods. They help the creative team translate their findings into imaginative, successful campaigns. Not attached to either account management or creative, the account planner balances both elements to make sure the research is reflected in the ads.[24] More about this in Chapter 6.

When McDonald's wanted to attract kids to its Kiddie Crew Workshop in the Philippines, DDB account planner Lester Obice helped to guide the creative team to a brilliant execution that merged images of McDonald's fries and yellow crayons. See their effort at http://www.bored panda.com/31-creative-ads-from-mcdonalds-are-you-loving-it/

Media Planning and Buying

Ad agencies perform a variety of media services for their clients: research, negotiating, scheduling, buying, and verifying. **Media planning** is critical, because the only way advertisers can communicate is through some medium. We discuss media planning extensively in Chapter 15, but for now it's important to understand that changes over the last decade have made the media function even more important.

With the unprecedented fragmentation of audiences from the explosion of new media options and the trend toward IMC and relationship marketing, the media task has taken on added significance. Tightening budgets demand ingenious thinking, tough negotiating, and careful attention to detail. Media planners must understand how advertising works in coordination with other marketing communication tools and come up with creative media solutions to tough marketing challenges. Today, many products owe their success more to creative media planning and buying than to clever ads.

Creative Concepts

Most ads rely heavily on **copy**, the words that make up the headline and message. The people who create these words, **copywriters**, must condense all that can be said about a product into a few pertinent, succinct points.

Ads also use nonverbal communication. That is the job of the **art directors**, graphic designers, and production artists, who determine how an ad's verbal and visual symbols will fit together. (The creative process is discussed in Part 4.) A copywriter and an art director work as a creative team under a **creative director**. Each team is usually assigned a particular client's business.

One award-winning ad for McDonald's focuses on the Ronald McDonald House charity. Entitled "First Step," the ad tells the story of a young toddler whose medical care was made more affordable by the company. The beautiful spot was developed by an experienced DDB Chicago team, including creative director Bill Cimino, copywriter Geoff McCartney, and art director Gordon West.

Advertising Production: Print and Broadcast

An ad approved by the client is then turned over to the agency's print production manager or broadcast producers.

For print ads, the **production department** buys type, photos, illustrations, and other components and works with printers, engravers, and other suppliers. For a broadcast commercial, production people work from an approved script or storyboard. Actors, camera operators, and production specialists (studios, directors, editors) help to produce a commercial on audiotape (for radio) or on film or videotape (for TV). The "First Step" commercial described above was helmed by a famous commercial director named Joe Pytka and was filmed at Pytka's studio.

But production work is not just limited to ads and commercials. Dealer kits and direct mailings are just two examples of other materials that may be created as part of a campaign.

Traffic Management

One of the greatest sins in an ad agency is a missed deadline. If an agency misses a deadline for a monthly magazine for example, the agency will have to wait another month before they can run the ad, much to the client's displeasure.

The agency **traffic department** coordinates all phases of production and makes sure everything is completed and approved before client and/or media deadlines. Traffic is often the first stop for entry-level college graduates and an excellent place to learn about agency operations.

Additional Services

The growth of IMC has caused many agencies to employ specialists who provide services besides advertising. Larger agencies may have a fully staffed **sales promotion department** to produce dealer ads, window posters, point-of-purchase displays, and dealer sales material. Or, depending on the nature and needs of their clients, they may employ public relations people and direct marketing specialists, Web page designers, home economics experts, or package designers.

Agency Administration

In small agencies, administrative functions may be handled by the firm's principals. Large agencies often have departments for accounting, human resources, data processing, purchasing, financial analysis, legal issues, and insurance.

Warm, orange-glazed chicken.

Red peppers, crisp snow peas and edamame.

Sweet Mandarin oranges.

Toasted almonds.

THERE'S A NEW WAY TO COOL DOWN AFTER EXERCISE.

new asian salad

i'm lovin' it®

Some McDonald's advertising is devoted to specific menu items. These ads give existing customers a reason to visit the restaurant chain more often, and may attract new customers who are unaware of the variety of offerings at McDonald's.

Thanks to modern telecommunications, clients and agencies can locate themselves almost anywhere. Today, virtual manufacturers work out of seaside resorts and their agencies can operate the same way—tied to their researchers, creatives, media departments, and suppliers by phones, fax machines, personal digital assistants, and high-speed Internet connections.

How Agencies Are Structured

An ad agency organizes its functions, operations, and personnel according to the types of accounts it serves, its size, and its geographic scope.

The owner or general manager usually supervises daily business operations, client services, and new-business development. Account executives (AEs) generally handle day-to-day client contact. In smaller agencies, AEs may also do some creative work. Artwork may be produced by an art director or purchased from an independent studio or freelance designer. Most agencies

have production and traffic departments or an employee who fulfills these functions. They may have a media buyer, but in very small agencies account executives also purchase media time and space. Exhibit 3–7 shows how a typical advertising agency might be organized.

Medium and large agencies are usually structured in a *departmental* or *group system*. In the **departmental system**, the agency organizes its various functions—account services, creative services, marketing services, and administration—into separate departments.

▼**EXHIBIT 3–7** Typical departmental advertising agency organization.

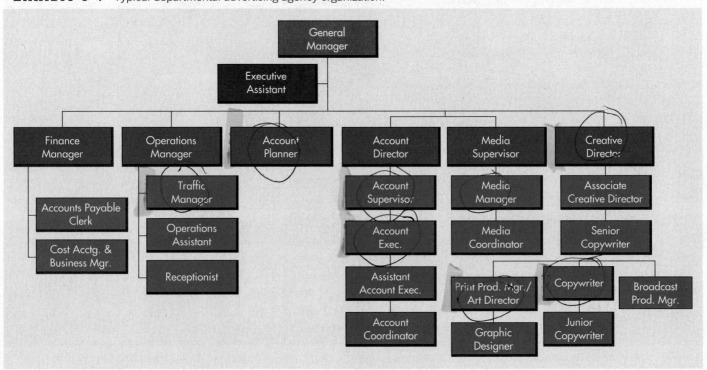

departmental system The organization of an ad agency into departments based on function: account services, creative services, marketing services, and administration.

group system System in which an ad agency is divided into a number of little agencies or groups, each composed of an account supervisor, account executives, copywriters, art directors, a media director, and any other specialists required to meet the needs of the particular clients being served by the group.

media commission Compensation paid by a medium to recognized advertising agencies, traditionally 15 percent (16⅔ percent for outdoor), for advertising placed with it.

markup A source of agency income gained by adding some amount to a supplier's bill, usually 17.65 percent.

fee-commission combination A pricing system in which an advertising agency charges the client a basic monthly fee for its services and also retains any media commissions earned.

straight-fee A method of compensation for ad agency services in which a straight fee, or *retainer*, is based on a cost-plus-fixed-fees formula. Under this system, the agency estimates the amount of personnel time required by the client, determines the cost of that personnel, and multiplies by some factor.

In the **group system**, the agency is divided into a number of "little" agencies or groups. Each group may serve one large account or, in some cases, three or four smaller ones. An account manager heads each group's staff of account executives, copywriters, art directors, a media director, and any other necessary specialists. A very large agency may have dozens of groups with separate production and traffic units.

check yourself ✓

1. In what ways does the role of an account planner differ from that of an account executive?

2. What do people in an ad agency do?

L06 Discuss how agencies get new clients and how they make money.

How Agencies Are Compensated

To survive, agencies must make a profit. But recent trends in the business—mergers of superagencies, shifts in emphasis from advertising to sales promotion and direct marketing, increased production costs, and the fragmentation of media vehicles—have all cut into agency profits.[25] Moreover, different clients demand different services, forcing agencies to develop various compensation methods. Still, there are really only three ways for agencies to make money: *media commissions, markups,* and *fees* or *retainers.*

Media Commissions As we saw in Chapter 1, when ad agencies first came on the scene more than 100 years ago, they were really space brokers, or reps, for the newspapers. Because they saved the media much of the expense of sales and collections, the media allowed the agencies to retain a 15 percent **media commission** on the space or time they purchased on behalf of their clients. That started a tradition that endures to this day, although it is now changing rapidly. Let's see how it works.

Say a national rate-card price for a full-page color magazine ad is $100,000. The magazine bills the agency, and the agency in turn bills the client for the $100,000. The client pays that amount to the agency, and the agency sends $85,000 to the magazine,

keeping its 15 percent commission ($15,000). For large accounts, the agency typically provides extensive services (creative, media, accounting, and account management) for this commission. With dwindling profits, though, and clients negotiating smaller commissions, many agencies now must charge a fee for services that used to be included for free. After years of dwindling commissions, agencies are now starting to demand better compensation.[26]

Markups In the process of creating an ad, the agency normally buys a variety of services or materials from outside suppliers—for example, photos and illustrations. The agency pays the supplier's charge and then adds a **markup** to the client's bill, typically 17.65 percent of the invoice (which becomes 15 percent of the new total).

For example, a markup of 17.65 percent on an $8,500 photography bill yields a $1,500 profit. When billing the client, the agency adds the $1,500 to the $8,500 for a new total of $10,000. When the client pays the bill, the agency keeps the $1,500 (15 percent of the total) and sends $8,500 to the photographer.

$$\$8,500 \times 17.65\% = \$1,500$$
$$\$8,500 + \$1,500 = \$10,000$$
$$\$10,000 \times 15\% = \$1,500$$

Some media—local newspapers, for example—allow a commission on the higher rates they charge national advertisers but not on the lower rates they charge local advertisers. So, to get their commission, local agencies have to use the markup formula above.

Fees Clients today expect agencies to solve problems rather than just place ads, so fees are becoming more common. In fact, one study shows that only about one-third of national advertisers still rely on the traditional 15 percent commission system. An equal number now use some fee-based system. The rest use some modified commission or incentive system.[27]

There are two pricing methods in the fee system. With the **fee-commission combination**, the agency charges a basic monthly fee for all its services to the client and retains any media commissions earned. In the **straight-fee** or

Outdoor posters were turned into large interactive push puzzles that consumers could solve in order to "sort your head out".

This was done to promote McDonald's Large Coffee for only 1 Euro.

McDonald's uses the creative talent of its partner agencies to develop clever executions like this interactive out-of-home ad.

retainer method, agencies charge for all their services, either by the hour or by the month, and return any media commissions earned to the client. This latter method addresses a common objection to the commission system, namely that commissions lead agencies to recommend more media spending, rather than looking for ways to spend the client's money more efficiently. The fee method also addresses the fact that many clients are now using media buying services to purchase space and time.

Accountability is a major issue in client/agency relationships. With a new type of agency compensation, the **incentive system** (sometimes called *pay-for-performance*), the agency earns more if the campaign attains specific, agreed-upon goals. DDB Needham, for example, offers its clients a "guaranteed results" program. If a campaign is successful, the agency earns more; if it fails, the agency earns less. Kraft General Foods rewards its agencies based on their performance. An A grade gets an extra 3 percent commission; C grades are put on review.[28]

The In-House Agency

Some companies set up a wholly owned **in-house agency** (or *house agency*) to save money and tighten control over their advertising. The in-house agency may do all the work of an independent full-service agency, including creative tasks, production, media placement, publicity, and sales promotion.

Advertisers with in-house agencies hope to save money by cutting overhead, keeping the media commission, and avoiding markups on outside purchases. Small, local advertisers in particular seek this goal.

Advertisers also expect more attention and faster turnaround from their house agencies, which know the company's products and markets better and can focus all their resources to meet its deadlines. Management is often more involved in the advertising when it's done by company people, especially in "single-business" companies. And some in-house advertising is outstanding, especially in the fashion field.

Just as you may like some ads better than others, advertisers sometimes choose an agency based on the quality of their work for other clients. Any advertiser who encountered this creative out-of-home ad (the billboard actually has plants growing on its surface to highlight McDonald's salads), might be tempted to hire the agency that created it.

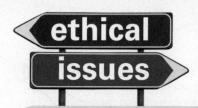

Is Ronald McDonald Bad for Kids? Are Parents?

Deborah Lapidus has found the "person" responsible for the childhood obesity epidemic that is sweeping the United States. While the culprit can often be found visiting children's hospitals and performing at other charity events, Lapidus is unmoved. She wants him gone for good, or, in her words, "retired." Anyone interested in joining Ms. Lapidus's quest should be on the lookout for an easily recognized, flamboyantly dressed individual with flaming red hair and a bright round nose. Because Deborah Lapidus wants to retire Ronald McDonald.[i]

To make her point, in 2010 she traveled all the way to Oak Brook, Illinois, the location of McDonald's annual meeting, to protest Ronald's prominence in the company's advertising. Her trip was funded by her 30,000-member advocacy group, named "Corporate Accountability." Corporate Accountability wants Ronald gone.

Does McDonald's market to children? The evidence is pretty compelling. Like any smart family-oriented eatery, McDonald's knows that kids exercise enormous influence in family dining decisions. In response, it has created Happy Meals and playgrounds that make its restaurants fun places for kids to eat and play (and for Mom and Dad to relax). And, of course, kids love Ronald, one of the world's most recognized brand symbols.

And it is undeniable that America has a health problem, and food is a big part of it. Obama Secretary of Health and Human Services Kathleen Sebelius suggests that one in three kids in the U.S. is overweight, a number that has grown 400 percent in just 20 years. Sebelius recently urged the U.S. Conference of Mayors to join a program initiated by First Lady Michelle Obama called "Let's Move," aimed at encouraging healthier lifestyles among children.[ii]

So the problem that Lapidus is calling attention to is real. What is in question is her proposed solution. Will retiring Ronald make America's children skinnier?

Interestingly, McDonald's may be way ahead of Lapidus. The company has developed a broader line of healthy menus for its Happy Meals, ones that include fresh fruits and veggies. Playgrounds are slowly being phased out at McDonald's in favor of coffee bars. Ads that feature Ronald are difficult to find anymore, part of a recent trend towards reducing McDonald's ads that target children. In fact, while the company's overall ad spending in the first quarter of 2010 was up 30 percent from 2009, ads directed at kids were down 23 percent.[iii]

So McDonald's seems to be doing its part. Lapidus should be thrilled.

But one commentator, Courier News writer Julia Doyle, thinks Lapidus has missed the real source of childhood obesity: moms and dads.[iv]

If our kids are fat, it automatically has to be because there's a goofy, smiley-faced clown telling them to eat cheeseburgers and French fries, right? It can't possibly have anything to do with Mom or Dad stopping for fried chicken, tacos or burgers every night rather than cooking a healthy dinner when they get home. And if our kids are fat, it has everything to do with the pizza, chicken fingers and hot dogs served in their school cafeterias and nothing to do with the fact that their parents can't be bothered to pack them a healthy lunch to take to school each day. I think it's high time these so-called watchdog groups get off their high horses and stop blaming corporate America for everything they think is wrong with us.

The ethical issues here are complex. Is it right for McDonald's, or any company, to advertise to children? Is it morally acceptable for a fast-food chain to feature playgrounds and brand symbols that kids find appealing? Would these activities be more ethically permissible if the company exclusively sold healthy food? Can the obesity problem affecting American children (and adults) be blamed on a single company? McDonald's has been using Ronald in its ads since the 1960s, a time when children were generally fitter and slimmer than they are today. So how can he be the root cause, or even a significant factor, of the problem? What about Doyle's points regarding the role of parents, both as role models for good eating and as gatekeepers for the types of foods their children eat? Does she have a fair point or not? America's children have a health problem. How significant is advertising as a cause?

[i] http://www.metrowestdailynews.com/opinion/x1218688656/Chesto-Boston-group-pushes-for-Ronald-McDonalds-retirement
[ii] http://www.google.com/hostednews/ap/article/ALeqM5h_6x0AU_CynNNRPSPbTlu_pPzemgD9G9EGE80
[iii] http://www.chicagobusiness.com/cgi-bin/article.pl?articleId=33474
[iv] http://www.suburbanchicagonews.com/couriernews/news/talk/2311466,3_1_EL25_02TALK_S1-100525.article

But usually companies sacrifice more than they gain. In-house flexibility is often won at the expense of creativity. Outside agencies typically offer greater experience, versatility, and a larger talent pool. In-house agencies have difficulty attracting and keeping the best creative people, who tend to prefer the variety and challenges offered by independent agencies.

The biggest risk for in-house agencies may be a loss of objectivity. In the shadow of internal politics, linear-thinking policymakers, and criticism from management, ads may become bland and self-serving, rather than imaginative messages relevant to customers. In advertising, that's the kiss of death.

THE CLIENT/AGENCY RELATIONSHIP

Many factors affect the success of a company's advertising program, but one of the most important is the relationship between the advertiser and its agency.

How Agencies Get Clients

To succeed, advertising agencies need clients. New clients come from personal contact with top management, referrals from satisfied clients or advertising consultants, publicity on recent successful campaigns, trade advertising, direct-mail solicitation, or an agency's general reputation.[29] The three most successful ways to develop new business are having clients who strongly champion the agency, having superior presentation skills, and cultivating a personal relationship with a network of top executives.

Referrals Most good agencies get clients by referral—from existing clients, friends, review consultants, or even other agencies. The head of one company asks another who's doing her ads, and the next week the agency gets a call. If a prospective client presents a conflict of interest with an existing client, the agency may decline the business and refer the prospect to another agency.[30]

Independent *agency review consultants* often help arrange marriages between agencies and clients. In fact, independent advisors were involved in many important account shuffles on Madison Avenue: Domino's Pizza, DirecTV, Burger King, Compaq computers, and Monster.com, to name just a few.[31]

Sales reps for media and suppliers frequently refer local advertisers to an agency they know. So it's important for agencies to maintain good relations with the media, suppliers, other agencies, and, of course, their existing clients.

Some companies such as Benetton (*www.benetton.com*) prefer to create ads using their own in-house agencies. Advertisers may hope to save money and gain more attention by using their house agencies, but they can lose the greater experience, objectivity, and talent of an outside agency.

Some advertisers ask for or imply that they want a **speculative presentation**, meaning they want to see what the agency intends to do for them before they sign on. But most agencies prefer to build their presentations around the work they've already done, to demonstrate their capabilities without giving away ideas for a new campaign. Invariably, the larger the prospective client, the bigger the presentation. Some agencies now spend upwards of $500,000 to stage a new business presentation.

The presentation process also allows the agency and the advertiser to get to know each other before they agree to work together. Advertising is a people business, so human qualities—mutual regard, trust, and communication—play an important role.

Networking and Community Relations Agencies frequently find that the best source of new business is the people their employees know socially in the community. Some agencies work *pro bono* (for free) for charities or nonprofit organizations. Matt Freeman, the young CEO of Tribal DDB, McDonald's digital agency, volunteers for the Ad Council and a hunger charity. Leo Burnett is a partner with Global Giving, an organization that matches donors with good causes.

Soliciting and Advertising for New Business Lesser-known agencies must be more aggressive. An agency may solicit new business by advertising, writing letters, making cold calls, or following up leads from sources in the business. An agency principal usually takes the responsibility for soliciting new business.

Today, more agencies are advertising themselves. Many agencies submit their best ads to competitions around the world to win awards and gain publicity and professional respect for their creative excellence.[32]

> Most good agencies get clients by referral—from existing clients, friends, review consultants, or even other agencies.

Presentations An advertiser may ask an agency to make a presentation (a pitch)—anything from a simple discussion of the agency's philosophy, experience, personnel, and track record to a full-blown audiovisual presentation of a proposed campaign. Successful agencies, therefore, need excellent presentation skills.

Factors Affecting the Client/Agency Relationship

Many forces influence the client/agency relationship. Generally they can be grouped into the four Cs: *chemistry, communication, conduct,* and *changes.*

The most critical factor is the personal *chemistry* between the client and people in the agency.[33] Agencies are very conscious of this factor and wine and dine their clients in hopes of improving relations. Smart clients do the same.

Poor *communication,* a problem often cited by both agencies and advertisers, leads to misunderstandings about objectives, strategies, roles, and expectations—and to poor advertising. Constant, open communication and an explicit agreement on mutual contribution for mutual gain are key to a good relationship.[34]

Dissatisfaction with agency *conduct,* or performance, is the most commonly cited reason for agency switches in every country.[35] The service the agency gave two years ago may not be valued by the client in the same way today.[36] Or perhaps the agency doesn't understand the client's marketing problems. And clients change, too. Does the client give the agency timely, accurate information? Does it appreciate good work, or does it treat the agency like a vendor?[37]

Changes occur in every relationship. Unfortunately, some of them damage the agency/client partnership. The client's

Agency Review [3–C]

What will your client look for in your agency team? This agency review should give you an idea. To use this scale, an advertiser would rate each agency on a scale from 1 (strongly negative) to 10 (strongly positive).

General Information
____ Size compatible with our needs.
____ Strength of management.
____ Financial stability.
____ Compatibility with other clients.
____ Range of services.
____ Cost of services; billing policies.

Marketing Information
____ Ability to offer marketing counsel.
____ Understanding of the markets we serve.
____ Experience dealing in our market.
____ Success record; case histories.

Creative Abilities
____ Well-thought-out creativity; relevance to strategy.
____ Art strength.
____ Copy strength.
____ Overall creative quality.
____ Effectiveness compared to work of competitors.

Production
____ Faithfulness to creative concept and execution.
____ Diligence to schedules and budgets.
____ Ability to control outside services.

Media
____ Existence and soundness of media research.
____ Effective and efficient media strategy.
____ Ability to achieve objectives within budget.
____ Strength at negotiating and executing schedules.

Personality
____ Overall personality, philosophy, or position.
____ Compatibility with client staff and management.
____ Willingness to assign top people to account.
____ Ability to articulate rationale behind work.

References
____ Rating by current clients.
____ Rating by past clients.
____ Rating by media and financial sources.

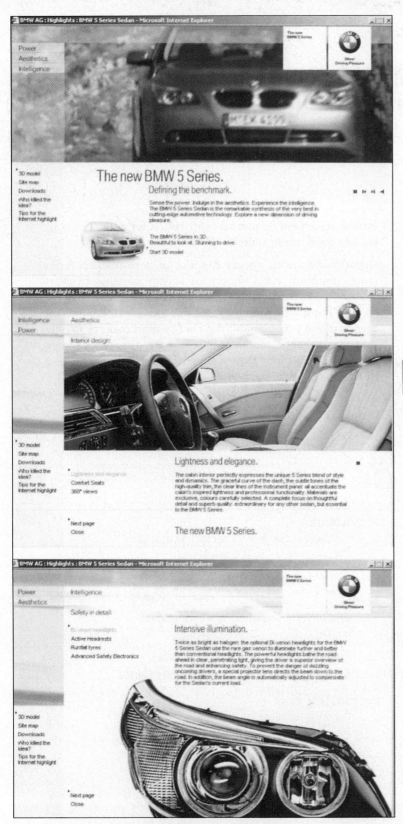

As the Internet continues to grow at an alarming speed, so does the demand for Web design houses that understand both the intricacies of programming languages and the various elements of good Web design. This Web site for the BMW 5 Series sedan (www.bmw.com/5series) uses streaming multimedia technologies to provide rich content. At the same time, its elegance and crisp design complement the vehicle's handsome shape.

market position or policies may change, or new management may arrive. Agencies may lose key staff people. Client conflicts may arise if one agency buys another that handles competing accounts. Legally, an ad agency cannot represent a client's competition without the client's consent.[38] Saatchi & Saatchi was forced to resign Helene Curtis under pressure from Saatchi's biggest client, Procter & Gamble.[39]

Perhaps the best way to improve understanding between clients and agencies would be to have staff members change places for a while. A Foote, Cone & Belding account executive did just that with great success, filling in temporarily as marketing manager at Levi's Jeans for Women. It gave her a whole new perspective on her agency job and the daily challenges faced by her client.[40]

check yourself ✓

1. How have accountability concerns affected agency compensation?

2. What do you think is the best way to compensate an agency? Explain your answer.

3. What are the most important things an advertiser should consider when selecting an agency?

THE SUPPLIERS IN ADVERTISING

The people and organizations that provide specialized services to the advertising business are called **suppliers**. Without their services it would be impossible to produce the billions of dollars' worth of advertising placed every year. Important suppliers include *art studios and Web design houses, printers, film and video production houses,* and *research companies.*

Art Studios and Web Designers

Art studios design and produce artwork and illustrations for advertisements. They may supplement the work of an agency's art department or even take its place for small agencies. Art studios are usually small with as few as three or four employees. Some, though, are large enough to employ several art directors, graphic designers, layout artists, production artists, and sales reps.

Most studios are owned and managed by a graphic designer or illustrator, who calls on agencies and advertising managers to sell the studio's services, takes projects back to the office to be produced, and then delivers them for the client's approval. The work is time-consuming and requires a talent for organization and management as well as a core competency in art direction and computer graphics.

Similar to art studios, **Web design houses** employ specialists who understand the intricacies of Internet programming languages and can design ads and Web pages that are both effective and cost efficient.

Printers and Related Specialists

The printers who produce brochures, stationery, business cards, sales promotion materials, and point-of-purchase displays are vital to the advertising business. Ranging from small instant-print shops to large offset operations, **printers** employ or contract with highly trained specialists who prepare artwork for reproduction, operate digital scanning machines to make color separations and plates, operate presses and collating machines, and run binderies. Their sales reps must be highly skilled, and they often earn very large commissions.

Film and Video Houses

Few agencies have in-house TV production capabilities. Small agencies often work with local TV stations to produce commercials. But the large agencies normally work with independent **production houses** that specialize in film or video production or both. We discuss production in Chapter 10.

Research Companies

Advertisers are concerned about the attitudes of their customers, the size of potential markets, and the acceptability of their products. Agencies want to know what advertising approaches to use, which concepts communicate most efficiently, and how effective past campaigns have been.

The media are concerned with the reading and viewing habits of their audiences, the desired markets of their advertiser-customers, and public perceptions toward their own particular medium.

Research, therefore, is closely allied to advertising and an important tool for marketing professionals. But most firms do not maintain a fully staffed research department. Instead, they use independent **research suppliers** or consultants. Research firms come in all sizes and specialties, and they employ statisticians, field interviewers, and computer programmers, as well as analysts with degrees in psychology, sociology, and marketing. We discuss research in Chapter 6.

THE MEDIA OF ADVERTISING

The *medium* that carries the advertiser's message is the vital connection between the company that manufactures a product or offers a service and the customer who may wish to buy it. Although the plural term **media** commonly describes channels of mass communication such as television, radio, newspapers, and magazines, it also refers to other communications vehicles such as direct mail, out-of-home media (transit, billboards, etc.), specialized media (aerial/blimps, inflatables), specialty advertising items (imprinted coffee mugs, balloons), and new communication technologies such as digital media, interactive TV, and satellite networks. (Exhibit 3–8 shows the largest U.S. media companies.)

It is important to understand the various media, their role in the advertising business, and the significance of current media trends. For a person seeking a career in advertising, the media may offer the first door to employment, and for many they have provided great financial rewards.

We classify advertising media into six major categories: print, electronic, digital interactive, out-of-home, direct mail, and other media. Due to recent media trends, there is some overlap. These media categories are discussed in Chapters 11–14.

Newspapers			Broadcast Television		
1. Gannett Co.	$4.6	−7.6%	1. CBS Corp.	6.2	1.9
2. Tribune Co.	3.6	−8.8	2. Walt Disney Co.	5.3	−0.2
3. The New York Times Co.	2.8	−11.2	3. NBC Universal	5.0	−20.4
4. McClatchy Co.	2.2	−8.1	4. News Corp.	4.9	1.3
5. Advance Publications	2.1	−4.9	5. Univision Communications	1.5	−1.4
Magazines			**Cable Networks**		
1. Advance Publications	3.9	10.0	1. Walt Disney Co.	7.8	13.2
2. Time Warner	3.6	−0.9	2. Time Warner	7.2	4.6
3. Hearst Corp.	2.4	7.3	3. Viacom	5.9	7.5
4. Meredith Corp.	0.9	−2.4	4. News Corp.	4.2	17.7
5. McGraw-Hill Cos.	0.9	5.7	5. NBC Universal	3.4	10.5

Top Three Search Engines (percent of searches and percent change from 2007 to 2008)		
1. Google sites	63%	6.5%
2. Yahoo! sites	19.6	0.0
3. MSN/Windows Live	8.3	−3.0

Source: "Top Companies by Medium," *Advertising Age,* December 29, 2008, p. 42.

CURRENT TRENDS

The ad agency business continues to go through many transitions. We mention just a few of the most important ones here: *industry consolidation,* the *decline of the commission system, changes resulting from new media,* and *the economic downturn that began in 2008.*

In the 1990s a consolidation left most of the famous agencies from decades earlier merged, dissolved, or absorbed, so that advertising was dominated by four enormous conglomerates. These were Omnicom and the Interpublic Group, both headquartered in New York; Publicis, based in Paris; and London's WPP Group. Together these companies account for over half of all advertising spending in the world. Structurally, the conglomerates act as giant holding companies for an assortment of agencies that specialize in different promotional activities (advertising, public relations, sales promotion, direct-response, media buying, etc.) and audiences (general consumer, B2B, minorities, etc.).

Why did this consolidation happen? One important factor is globalization and the emergence of global brands. The conglomerates can offer big advertisers services in markets around the world and in whatever promotional channels such clients might require. A second factor is the decline in importance of traditional media and the growing interest in IMC. Profitable agencies have found they need to offer a menu of services rather than rely on income from only one part of the promotional mix. Third, the conglomerates can save their clients money, both because they have substantial power in negotiating favorable media rates for their clients and because they've reached new heights in efficiency by reducing administrative overhead and expenses.

> " . . . another industry trend has been the slow death of the commission system. "

But bigger is not always better, and in recent years the ad industry has witnessed a countervailing trend toward small specialty shops and boutiques. This is because some advertisers are not happy with the quality of the creative work that comes out of the conglomerate agencies. They also question whether the giants have too much power over media spending. And clients have sometimes been hesitant to give their account to an agency within a conglomerate where a separate agency serves a competitor.

As noted earlier, another industry trend has been the slow death of the commission system. While still used, a number of

Ways to Be a Better Client [3–D]

These are some ideas your client may wish to keep in mind as they think about working with you.

Relationships
- *Cultivate honesty.* Be truthful in your meetings and in your ads.
- *Be enthusiastic.* When you like the ads, let the agency know.
- *Be frank when you don't like the advertising.* Always cite a reason when turning down an idea.
- *Be human.* React like a person, not a corporation. Laugh at funny ads even if they don't work.
- *Be willing to admit you're unsure.* Don't be pressured. Let your agency know when you need time.
- *Allow the agency to feel responsible.* Tell the agency what you feel is wrong, not how to fix it.
- *Care about being a client.* Creative people work best for clients they like.

Management
- *Don't insulate your top managers from creative people.* Agency creatives work best when objectives come from the top, not filtered through layers.
- *Set objectives.* For timely and quality service from your agency, establish and openly share your marketing objectives.
- *Switch people, not agencies.* When problems arise, agencies often prefer to bring in fresh talent rather than lose you as a client.
- *Be sure the agency makes a profit on your account.* Demanding more services from your agency than fees or commissions can cover hurts relationships.

Production
- *Avoid nitpicking last-minute changes.* Perfection is important, but waiting until the last moment to make minor changes can damage the client/agency relationship. Agencies see such behavior as indecisive and/or arrogant and lose respect for the client.
- *Be aware of the cost of changes (both time and money).* The cost of making major changes at the production stage may be five times greater than in the earlier stages.
- *Don't change concepts during the production stage.* Late changes can inadvertently alter product positioning and image.

Media
- *Understand the economics (and economies) of media.* Be prepared to deal with costs per thousand (CPMs), costs per ratings point (CPP), and other key elements of media planning and buying so that you can evaluate and appreciate your agency's media strategy.
- *Understand the importance of lead time.* Early buys can eliminate late fees, earn discounts, make you eligible for special promotions, strengthen your agency's buying position, and reduce anxiety.
- *Avoid interfering with the agency's media relationship.* The stronger your agency's buying position, the greater the discounts available to you. Refrain from cutting deals with media reps directly and plan media use well in advance.
- *Avoid media arrogance ("they need us").* Some media will deal with clients, and some won't. Misinterpret this relationship and you may either pay more than you should or be too late to get into a medium you need.
- *Avoid insularity.* Be willing to let your mind travel beyond your immediate environment and lifestyle.
- *Suggest work sessions.* Set up informal give-and-take sessions with creatives and strategists.
- *Keep the creative people involved in your business.* Agency creatives do their best work for you when they're in tune with the ups and downs of your business.

Research
- *Share information.* Pool information to create new and bigger opportunities.
- *Involve the agency in research projects.* An agency's creative talent gets its best ideas from knowledge of your environment.

Creative
- *Learn the fine art of conducting the creative meeting.* Deal with the important issues first: strategy, consumer benefits, and reasons why.
- *Look for the big idea.* Concentrate on positioning strategy and brand personality. Don't allow a single ad—no matter how brilliant—to change the positioning or personality of the product.
- *Insist on creative discipline.* The creative process stimulates concepts and actions. Discipline helps keep focus on those that count the most.
- *Don't be afraid to ask for great advertising.* Agencies prefer the high road, but as the client you must be willing to accompany them. If the agency slips, be strong and ask it to try again.

NO CHANGE WROUGHT BY THE NEW MEDIA IS OF GREATER IMPORTANCE THAN AUDIENCE EMPOWERMENT.

influential advertisers no longer pay commissions and instead insist on an incentive approach. From the perspective of many clients, commissions have at least two significant problems: First, they provide a powerful incentive for agencies to select media that are expensive and commissionable (like television) instead of media that might be more likely to reach and persuade consumers. Second, commissions encourage agencies to focus on the ad budget rather than on strategy and ideas. Pat Fallon and Fred Senn of Fallon Worldwide have suggested that some agencies have fallen into the trap of thinking that advertisers should "outspend rather than outthink" competitors. They argue that agencies can better serve their clients by focusing on "creative leverage," not "media leverage."[41]

Throughout its history, advertising has experienced dramatic changes in the face of new media technologies. This is just as true today. Among the important trends here are the growth of media options, the empowerment of consumers as content creators, and reorganization in the ranks of media companies as new upstarts replace established firms in importance.

Media options are exploding with technologies such as video on demand, the Internet, computer games, smart phones, PDAs, iPods, GPS systems, and so on. Even older technologies like radio and television are experiencing rapid change (digital cable, interactive TV, satellite radio). These technologies present real opportunities, but also significant challenges, to the knowledge and skills of people who work in agency media and creative departments.

No change wrought by the new media is of greater importance than audience empower-

ment. The days of expecting media consumers to follow the dictates of content creators, whether they be newspapers, television networks, or magazines, are over. Today people watch what they want, when they want, and expect it for free. Web site Hulu fits this trend perfectly. Many of the most popular Web sites offer seemingly infinite content created by and for ordinary users. Older consumers may still watch network TV, but younger ones are often found elsewhere. These young consumers frequent popular Web sites like Facebook, MySpace, and Digg where there is little difference between those who create the content and those who consume it. Agencies know how important these sites are to many consumers, and they have responded by trying to create "viral" ads that social site users can find and recommend to friends. This may or may not ultimately prove effective. But for the foreseeable future the consumer is in charge as never before.

New media are reorganizing the players on the media side of the equation. Web sites such as YouTube, Facebook, MySpace, and Google, created by young programmers with small budgets, show how successful small, nimble, and talented entrepreneurs can be. Many of the big media companies, some of whom have failed miserably to generate Internet profits, have tried buying some of the upstarts (Rupert Murdoch owns MySpace, for example). But no one believes that the pace of change in new media will abate any time soon.

Finally, the entire advertising industry has been affected by the economic downturn that started in 2008 and was still affecting Americans and much of Europe in 2011. The downturn has transformed entire industries (such as the U.S. auto industry) and even led to some grumbling about capitalism, the engine of American prosperity for much of the twentieth century. To make matters worse, an oil-spill disaster in the Gulf of Mexico caused many to question the business practices of large companies. History says that when companies face a recession they cut back on marketing. And despite a few exceptions, this decline has been no different. Having to do more with less, the agency landscape has been changed, perhaps forever. ■

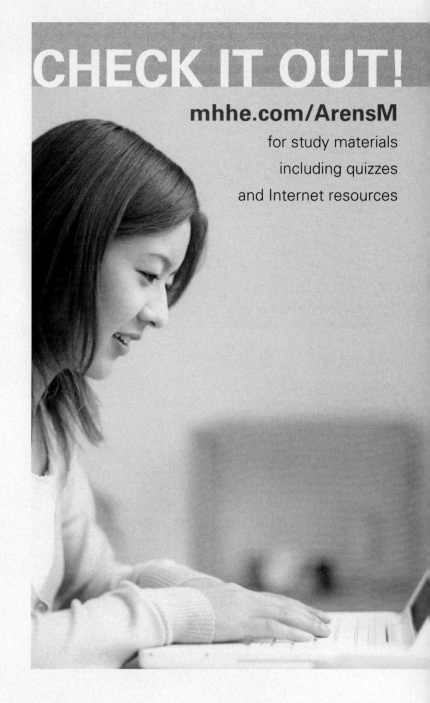

CHECK IT OUT!

mhhe.com/ArensM

for study materials

including quizzes

and Internet resources

four

segmentation, targeting, and the marketing mix

Differentiation between automobiles used to be as clear as price, performance, and size. However, more recently, increased product offerings have blurred those lines as automakers added products across price points and genres. Nowadays, one can buy a Mercedes-Benz for under $30,000 or a Chevrolet for much more. For an automotive brand, success is determined by how quickly one can establish a well-defined identity, stick with it, and convey it to the public. With the success of low-volume niche brands, such as the MINI, mass-market models must learn to live with diminished sales expectations in fragmented markets. The new approach requires pitching targeted models to a certain buyer and relying less on the mass-market models.[1]

Aiming its sights on increasing its global market share and surpassing GM as the world's biggest automaker, Toyota turned its focus to the coveted 18- to 25-year-olds worldwide who will dominate global car sales by 2020. However, its first attempt to connect with generation Y was a flop. The imagery and the cars that Toyota initially pitched to young buyers never meshed with consumer demand. Facing declining sales to the under-25 demographic,[2] a 63 million–strong consumer base in the United States alone, Toyota knew it had to do something drastic.

continued on p. 90

LEARNING OBJECTIVES

LO1 Explain the role of advertising in facilitating satisfying exchanges.

LO2 Illustrate the various methods advertisers use to segment and aggregate consumer and business markets.

LO3 Discuss how defining a target market enhances a product's marketing strategy.

LO4 Describe the elements of the marketing mix and the role advertising plays in each element of the mix.

continued from p. 89

A newly formed team, led by Brian Bolain, identified the need for a major shift in strategy. The Toyota name alone was not enough of a draw for these young consumers; they needed a more emotional appeal, and advertising and marketing alone would never be as important as the product or cars themselves. What Toyota needed was a new brand complete with radically designed new cars.

On a nearly parallel path, Tetsuya Tada, a chief engineer at Toyota, was presenting his new-car design proposal to Toyota's executive committee members. His presentation: a seven-minute music video, featuring thumping techno, gritty urban scenes, and images of a boxy, low-slung vehicle that resembled a baby Chevy Astro van. This concept car, dubbed bB, would later become the full production model known at launch as the xB. The presentation left Toyota Chairman Hiroshi Okuda nearly speechless; all he could say was "I can't offer any relevant input; this is a vehicle design and concept that is clearly not for anyone in this room."[3]

On a trip to Japan to plead his case about Toyota's need for a new brand and new cars, Bolain met Tada. To Bolain the bB was just weird enough to attract attention and seemed like the perfect car to launch under a new brand in the United States. Once Bolain and team got the go-ahead, they turned their attention to marketing to what was becoming a very fickle target.[4] The general consensus was that they don't want to be marketed to. For help, Bolain turned to Attik, a little-known graphic design shop. Attik launched the Scion brand based on a personalization strategy it developed through Taxi, its in-house research operation. Taxi relied on a group of trend-watching youth who communicate primarily via e-mail and are compensated through perks such as concert admission or products.

One of their findings was that, with every purchase, young consumers look to make a personal statement. With that nugget Attik focused on the personalization of vehicles, touting its more than 40 accessories, ranging from 18-inch racing wheels to illuminated cup holders. The guerilla-marketing launch efforts delivered on that theme with lines such as "No Clone Zone," "Rage Against Beige" and "Ban Normality" with the payoff of "What Moves You."[5]

This gave Toyota the emotional connection it was looking for and helped the company beat its initial sales target of 100,000 cars sold by nearly 50 percent.[6] ▪

LO1 Explain the role of advertising in facilitating satisfying exchanges.

THE LARGER MARKETING CONTEXT OF ADVERTISING

All advertisers face the challenge of how to present their products, services, and ideas effectively through the media to buyers. To do this, they must comprehend the important relationship between the product and the marketplace. That relationship is the focus of marketing.

Unfortunately, marketing's role is often misunderstood and occasionally overlooked. For example, everybody knows that a business can't survive without proper financing, and, without production, there are no products to sell. But how does a company know *what* products or services to produce? Or *where* to distribute them, or through *what* channels? That's where marketing comes in.

A company prospers only if it can attract and keep customers who are willing to pay for the firm's goods and services. This means a company must be able to locate prospective customers—where they live, work, and play—and then understand their needs, wants, and desires; create products and services that satisfy such desires better than the products of competitors; and finally communicate that information in a powerful, clear, and compelling way. This chapter will help you better understand advertising's role in that process.

Customer Needs and Product Utility

As we discussed in Chapter 1, marketing is a set of processes for creating, communicating, and delivering value to customers. The ultimate purpose of marketing is to *create exchanges that satisfy the perceived needs and wants of individuals and organizations.*

The Honda Element (www.honda.com) was designed to provide form utility—to meet the functional needs of its target market. This print ad clearly communicates the Element's utility.

Superior quality will not close a sale by itself. Marketing people must make the product available and promote its advantages, whether it's a graphite tennis racket, a high-performance sports car, or even the prompt, friendly service of a bank.

A key fact in any product's success is that it must satisfy consumers' *needs*. The capability to satisfy those needs is called *utility*. Five types of functional utility are important to consumers: form, task, possession, time, and place. A product may provide psychic utility as well as functional utility.

Companies create *form utility* whenever they produce a tangible good, such as a bicycle. They provide *task utility* by performing a task for others. However, merely producing a bicycle—or repairing it—doesn't guarantee consumer satisfaction. Consumers must want the bicycle or require the repair, or no need is satisfied and no utility occurs. Thus, marketing decisions should guide the production side of business too.

Even when a company provides form or task utility, marketers must consider how consumers can take possession of the product. This includes distribution, pricing strategies, shelf availability, purchase agreements, and delivery. Money is typically exchanged for possession utility. An antique bicycle on display, but not for sale, lacks *possession utility* because the customer cannot purchase it.

Providing the consumer with the product when he or she wants it is known as *time utility*. Having an ample supply of jam, cars, or bank tellers on hand when the consumer has the need is thus another marketing requirement.

Place utility—having the product available where the customer can get it—is also vital to business success. Customers won't travel very far out of their way to get bicycles or cars. They're even less likely to travel long distances for everyday needs. That's why banks have so many branches. And that's why 24-hour convenience markets, which sell gasoline and basic food items, are so popular.

Finally, consumers gain *psychic utility* when a product offers symbolic or psychological need satisfaction, such as status or sex appeal. Psychic utility is usually achieved through product promotion (advertising) and may fulfill esteem and self-actualization needs.

Whether it be psychic utility or the functional utilities of form, task, possession, time, and place, product utility is an essential component of marketing success.

Applying the Breaks

Select an ad from a weekly magazine and describe in detail what utilities it speaks to: psychic utility and/or the functional utilities of form, task, possession, time, and place.

[A company prospers only if it can attract and keep customers.]

One of the important elements of that definition is the special relationship between a customer's needs and a product's need-satisfying potential. This is known as the product's *utility*. **Utility** is the product's ability to satisfy both functional needs and symbolic (or psychological) wants.[7] One of the primary roles of advertising is to communicate this utility. Thus, some ads promote how well a product works (function); others tout glamour, sex appeal, or status (symbolism). Commercial Break 4–A discusses the important relationship between needs and utility.

Companies use marketing research to discover the needs and wants that exist in the marketplace. The goal is to use this information for product shaping—designing products, through manufacturing, packaging, or advertising, to satisfy more fully the customers' needs and wants.

To woo Gen Xers and Echo Boomers (the children of baby boomers), for example, Ford Motor Company developed Focus—a low-priced sporty compact car. Optional extras included a sports rack and an unconventional, removable pet holder with a foldable dish, designed to keep Rover from sliding around on the seat. The company also gave buyers the choice of flowers or swirls on the outside and fleece, jersey, or neoprene on the seats. Ford's marketers uncovered their customers' needs and wants and developed a product to satisfy them.

Businesspeople all too often give the marketing process short shrift. Some companies introduce a product without a clear idea of its utility to the customer, hoping that poorly conceived advertising will somehow magically move the product off the shelf.

Exchanges: The Purpose of Marketing and Advertising

Any transaction in which a person or organization trades something of value with someone else is an **exchange**. We all engage in exchanges. It's a natural part of our human self-interest. Buyers do it to acquire more things and better their situation. Sellers do it to grow their business and make a profit.

Marketing facilitates these exchanges, thus increasing our potential for satisfaction. How does it do this? In a variety of ways: by developing goods and services we might want; by pricing them attractively; by distributing them to convenient locations; and by informing us about them through advertising and other communication tools. By providing information, advertising makes people aware of the availability of products and of the selection alternatives among different brands. Advertising communicates product features and benefits, price options, and locations where the product can be purchased. In the case of direct marketing, advertising may even close the sale.

Even after an exchange occurs, *satisfaction* remains an issue. Satisfaction must occur every time customers use the product, or people won't think they got a fair exchange. Satisfaction leads to more exchanges: Satisfied customers repurchase; and satisfied customers tell their friends. Positive word of mouth creates even more sales and contributes to a good reputation. And while word of mouth has always been important, it is crucial in the new age of social media such as Facebook. Thus, while satisfaction is the goal of the customer, it must also be the fundamental goal of any sophisticated marketer.

Advertising *reinforces* satisfaction by reminding customers why they bought the product, helping them defend the purchase against skeptical friends and associates, and enabling them to persuade other prospects to buy it.

Thus, we can think of marketing as the process companies use to make a profit by identifying and satisfying their customers' needs and desires. This chapter defines and outlines marketing issues to clarify advertising's proper role in the marketing function. As we shall see, the relationship between advertising and marketing is critical.

LO2 Illustrate the various methods advertisers use to segment and aggregate consumer and business markets.

THE MARKET SEGMENTATION PROCESS

Marketing and advertising people constantly scan the marketplace to see how consumers and businesses might be better satisfied. The process of market segmentation involves two steps: *identifying groups of people* (or organizations) with certain shared needs and characteristics and *aggregating* (combining) these groups into larger market segments according to their interest in the product's utility. This process should result in market segments large enough to target and reachable through a suitable mix of marketing activities—including advertising.

Markets often consist of many segments. A company may differentiate its products and marketing strategy for every segment, or concentrate its marketing activities on only one or a few segments. Either task is far from simple. Toyota worked to rebuild its brand by targeting a broad segment with the Scion brand: 63 million generation Ys. Toyota also has two other brands, Toyota and Lexus, that it uses to differentiate products by segment. Catering to all these needs on a global level requires a sophisticated marketing and communications system. In this chapter, we look first at how marketers identify and categorize *consumer markets* and second at the techniques they

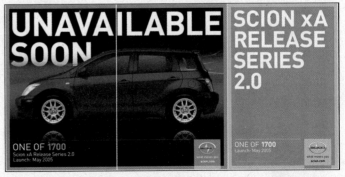

Scion's target market values individuality. This ad, which emphasizes the limited availability of the Scion xA, is designed to appeal to a desire for uniqueness.

Toyota's decision to target 18- to 25-year-old drivers had important implications for many strategic advertising decisions, including those related to media and creativity.

use to segment *business markets*. Then we discuss various strategic options companies use, including advertising, to match their products with markets and create profitable exchanges.

Types of Markets

A firm's marketing activities are always aimed at a particular segment of the population—its **target market**. Likewise, advertising is aimed at a particular group called the **target audience**. When we see an ad that doesn't appeal to us, it may be because the ad is not aimed at any of the groups we belong to. For example, a TV commercial for denture cream isn't meant to appeal to youngsters. They're not part of either the target market or the target audience. There are two main types of target markets, consumers and businesses.

Consumer Markets Most of the advertising we see daily in the mass media—TV, radio, newspapers, and magazines—falls under the broad category of consumer advertising. Usually sponsored by the producer (or manufacturer) of the product or service, these ads are typically directed at consumers, people who buy the product for their own or someone else's personal use. The consumer market is huge, spending close to $9.7 trillion every year on products and services in the United States alone.[8]

In the end, customers are people. So advertising professionals must understand how people act and think—and why they buy what they buy. This requires great skill. In fact, this area of study is the province of another specialty in marketing, consumer behavior, a topic we'll discuss in Chapter 5.

Business Markets Companies use business advertising to reach people who buy goods and services for resale, for use in their own business, or for manufacturing other products. It tends to appear in specialized business publications or professional journals, in direct-mail pieces sent to businesses, or in trade shows. Since business advertising (also called business-to-

business, or B2B, advertising) rarely uses consumer mass media, it is typically invisible to consumers. However, some business-to-business ads, by firms such as computer manufacturers or overnight parcel shippers, do appear on TV and in consumer magazines.

In addition to general business advertising, there are three specialized types of business advertising: trade, professional, and agricultural. Companies aim trade advertising at resellers (wholesalers, dealers, and retailers) to obtain greater distribution of their products. For example, Sunkist places trade advertising in publications such as *Progressive Grocer* to develop more grocery outlets and to increase sales to existing outlets. Advertising aimed at teachers, accountants, doctors, dentists, architects, engineers, lawyers, and the like is called professional advertising and typically appears in official publications of professional societies (such as the *Archives of Ophthalmology*). Companies use agricultural (or farm) advertising to promote products and services used in agriculture to farmers and others employed in agribusiness. FMC Corp., for example, might advertise its plant nutrition products to citrus growers in *Farm Journal Magazine*.

Business customers are often very knowledgeable and sophisticated, and they may require extensive technical information before buying. So people who work in business-to-business advertising often need more specialized product knowledge and experience than their consumer advertising colleagues.

Segmenting the Consumer Market: Finding the Right Niche

The concept of *shared characteristics* is critical to market segmentation. Marketing and advertising people know that, based on their needs, wants, and mental files, consumers leave "footprints in the sand"—the telltale signs of where they live and work, what they buy, and how they spend their leisure time. By following these footprints, marketers can locate and define groups of consumers with similar needs and wants, create messages for them, and know how and where to send those messages. The goal is to find that particular niche (or space) in the market where the advertiser's product or service will fit.

Marketers group these shared characteristics into categories (*behavioristic, geographic, demographic,* and *psychographic*) to identify and segment consumer markets (see Exhibit 4–1). The marketer's purpose is twofold: first, to identify people who are likely to be responsive; and second, to develop rich descriptions of them in order to better understand them, create marketing mixes for them, and reach them with meaningful advertising or other communications.

Behavioristic Segmentation One of the best ways to segment markets is to group consumers by purchase behavior. This is called **behavioristic segmentation.** Behavioral segments are determined by many variables, but the most important are *user status, usage rate, purchase occasion,* and *benefits*

> ## The goal is to find that particular niche in the market where the advertiser's product or service will fit.

▼**EXHIBIT 4–1** Methods for segmenting consumer markets.

Variables	Typical Breakdowns	Variables	Typical Breakdowns
Geographic		**Demographic**	
Region	Pacific; Mountain; West North Central; West South Central; East North Central; East South Central; South Atlantic; Middle Atlantic; New England	Age	Under 6, 6–11, 12–19, 20–34, 35–49, 50–64, 65+
County size	A, B, C, D	Gender	Male, female
Climate	Dry, humid, rain, snow	Family size	1–2, 3–4, 5+
City or SMSA size	Under 5,000; 5,000–19,999; 20,000–49,999; 50,000–99,999; 100,000–249,000; 250,000–499,999; 500,000–999,999; 1,000,000–3,999,999; 4,000,000 or over	Family life cycle	Young, single; young, married, no children; young, married, youngest child under 6; young, married, youngest child 6 or over; young, unmarried, with children; older, married, with children; older, unmarried, with children; older, married, no children under 18; older, single; other
Density	Urban, suburban, rural		
Behavioristic		Income	Under $10,000; $10,000–20,000; $20,000–30,000; $30,000–40,000; $40,000–60,000; $60,000–100,000; $100,000–150,000; $150,000 and over
Purchase occasion	Regular occasion, special occasion		
Benefits sought	Economy, convenience, prestige		
User status	Nonuser, ex-user, potential user, first-time user, regular user		
Usage rate	Light user, medium user, heavy user	Occupation	Professional and technical; managers, officials, and proprietors; clerical, sales; craftspeople, supervisors; operatives; farmers; retired; students; homemakers; unemployed
Loyalty status	None, medium, strong, absolute		
Readiness stage	Unaware, aware, informed, interested, desirous, intending to buy		
Marketing-factor sensitivity	Quality, price, service, advertising, sales promotion	Education	Grade school or less; some high school; high school graduates; some college; college graduates
Psychographic		Religion	Catholic, Protestant, Jewish, other
Societal divisions	Upper crust, movers and shakers, successful singles, Social Security, middle of the road, metro-ethnic mix	Race	White, Black, Asian
		Nationality	American, British, French, German, Scandinavian, Italian, Latin American, Middle Eastern, Japanese
Lifestyle	Strivers, achievers, actualizers		
Personality	Compulsive, gregarious, authoritarian, ambitious		

BEHAVIORAL SEGMENTATION TELLS US WHO OUR CUSTOMERS ARE NOW, WHEN AND WHY THEY BUY, AND HOW MUCH THEY CONSUME.

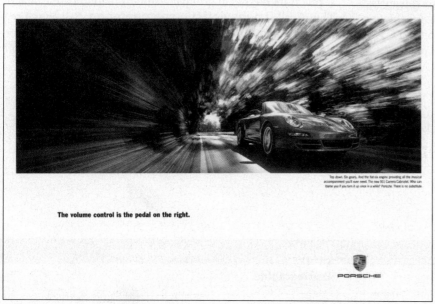

The volume control is the pedal on the right.

PORSCHE

Behavioristic segmentation is one of the best ways to organize consumer markets. Purchase behavior variables, such as the benefits sought by the consumer, determine how the segments are defined. In this ad, Porsche (www.porsche.com) appeals to performance enthusiasts for whom speed is everything.

sought. These categories tell us who our customers are now, when and why they buy, and how much they consume.

User-status variables. Many markets can be segmented by the **user status** of prospective customers. Researchers Stephan and Tannenholz have identified six categories of consumers based on user status.

Sole users are the most brand loyal and require the least amount of advertising and promotion. *Semisole* users typically use Brand A but have an alternate selection if it is not available or if the alternate is promoted with a discount. *Discount users* are the semisole users of competing Brand B. They don't buy Brand A at full price but perceive it well enough to buy it at a discount. *Aware nontriers* use competitive products in the category but haven't taken a liking to Brand A. A different advertising message could help, but these people rarely offer much potential. *Trial/rejectors* bought Brand A's advertising message, but didn't

CRATE AND BARREL
NOW SELLS FURNITURE.

Crate&Barrel

The expanded Dallas Crate and Barrel opens Thursday, October 9, on the corner of Knox Street and McKinney.

While Crate and Barrel (www.crateandbarrel.com) is better known for its extensive kitchenware, it uses its strong brand name to promote its furniture. For sole users, this ad reinforces the brand, and for repertoire users—those most likely to alternate between brands they believe to be equally superior—it enhances brand perception.

like the product. More advertising won't help; only a reformulation of Brand A will bring them back. *Repertoire users* perceive two or more brands to have superior attributes and will buy at full price. They are the primary brand switchers and respond to persuasive advertising based on their fluctuating wants and desires. Therefore, they should be a primary target for brand advertising.[9]

Usage-rate variables. It's usually easier to get a heavy user to increase usage than a light user. In **volume segmentation**, marketers measure people's **usage rates** to define consumers as light, medium, or heavy users of products (see Exhibit 4–2). Often, 20 percent of the population consumes 80 percent of the product. Marketers want to define that 20 percent and aim their advertising at them. Hardee's, a fast-food hamburger chain owned by CKE Restaurants, Inc., even has a pet name for its prized 17- to 34-year-old male market segment: the HFFU (pronounced who-foo). According to Andrew Puzder, CKE's CEO, "That's the 'heavy fast-food user,' someone who eats there four or five times a week. . . . It is the sweet spot of the industry and what appeals to him is drippy, messy burgers. He is not interested in little 99-cent burgers or low-carb anything."[10]

By finding common characteristics among heavy users of their products, marketers can define product differences and focus ad campaigns more effectively. For example, independent businesspeople who travel at their own expense, the group that Fallon Worldwide describes as "road warriors," are heavy users of budget hotel chains, with some spending over a hundred nights a year on the road. In creating a campaign that targeted this group for Holiday Inn Express, Fallon also discovered that road warriors make their travel plans at the beginning of the week and like to watch ESPN, CNN, and the Weather Channel. Such knowledge was vital in helping Fallon media people schedule messages when and where the target audience would be most responsive.

user status Six categories into which consumers can be placed, which reflect varying degrees of loyalty to certain brands and products. The categories are *sole users, semisole users, discount users, aware nontriers, trial/rejectors,* and *repertoire users.*

volume segmentation Defining consumers as light, medium, or heavy users of products.

usage rates The extent to which consumers use a product: light, medium, or heavy.

purchase occasion A method of segmenting markets on the basis of *when* consumers buy and use a good or service.

benefits The particular product attributes offered to customers, such as high quality, low price, status, speed, sex appeal, good taste, and so on.

benefit segmentation Method of segmenting consumers based on the benefits being sought.

geographic segmentation A method of segmenting markets by geographic regions based on the shared characteristics, needs, or wants of people within a region.

▼ **EXHIBIT 4–2** Usage rates vary for different products.

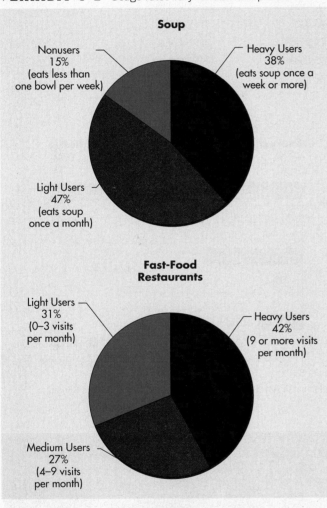

Soup

Nonusers 15% (eats less than one bowl per week)

Heavy Users 38% (eats soup once a week or more)

Light Users 47% (eats soup once a month)

Fast-Food Restaurants

Light Users 31% (0–3 visits per month)

Heavy Users 42% (9 or more visits per month)

Medium Users 27% (4–9 visits per month)

Marketers of one product sometimes find that their customers are also heavy users of other products and can define target markets in terms of the usage rates of the other products. For example, upper-income households are overrepresented among buyers of Infinitis, Samsung mobile phones, Starbucks coffee, and Tom's of Maine toothpaste. Conversely, low-income households are more likely to buy Kias, prepaid mobile phones, and Pepsodent toothpaste.[11]

Purchase-occasion variables. Buyers can also be distinguished by when they buy or use a product or service—the **purchase occasion**. Air travelers, for example, may fly for business or vacation so one airline might promote business travel while another promotes tourism. The purchase occasion might be affected by frequency of need (regular or occasional), a fad (candy, computer games), or seasons (water skis, raincoats). The Japan Weather Association tracked buying patterns on 20,000 items and correlated them to the outside temperature. Not surprisingly, when the temperature goes up, people buy more sunshades, air conditioners, watermelons, and swimwear. When there's a chill in the air, sales of suits, sweaters, and heaters take off.[12] A marketer who discovers common purchase occasions for a group has a potential target segment and can better determine when to run specials and when to promote certain product categories.

Benefits-sought variables. Consumers seek various **benefits** in the products they buy—high quality, low price, status, sex appeal, good taste, health-conscious. Hardee's customers may value the size and taste of Thickburgers, or they may prefer the low-carb, bunless chicken sandwich that has only half the fat. In addition to tangible benefits, consumers are motivated by *symbolism*—what the brand name means to them, to their friends, or to some social reference group. **Benefit segmentation** is the prime objective of many consumer attitude studies and the basis for many successful ad campaigns.

Some product categories are characterized by substantial *brand switching* from one purchase occasion to the next. Researchers have determined that switching occurs in response to different *need states* that consumers may experience from one occasion to another.

Using behavioristic segmentation, we can accomplish the first step of identifying likely prospects for our marketing and advertising efforts. The next step in developing rich profiles of these customers makes use of geographic, demographic, and psychographic characteristics.

Geographic Segmentation

One simple way to define markets is by using **geographic segmentation**. People in one region of the country (or the world) have needs, wants, and purchasing habits that differ from those in other regions. People in Sun Belt states, for example, buy more suntan lotion. Canadians

demographic segmentation Based on a population's statistical characteristics such as sex, age, ethnicity, education, occupation, income, or other quantifiable factors.

geodemographic segmentation Combining demographics with geographic segmentation to select target markets in advertising.

▼**EXHIBIT 4–3** Projected U.S. Hispanic population and Hispanic media ad spending growth rates.

Year	Hispanic	Total U.S.	Hisp. % Total
2000	35,621,721	282,124,631	12.6
2005	41,800,971	295,507,134	14.1
2010	47,755,585	308,935,581	15.5
2015	53,647,237	322,365,787	16.6
2020	59,755,555	335,804,546	17.8
2025	66,190,911	349,439,199	18.9
2030	73,055,166	363,584,435	20.1
2035	80,242,372	377,886,238	21.2
2040	87,584,907	391,945,658	22.3
2045	95,025,560	405,862,392	23.4
2050	102,559,846	419,853,587	24.4

Source: U.S. Census Bureau.

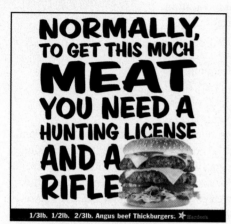

This Hardee's ad is clearly using behavioristic segmentation. Marketing of the Thickburger is directed at heavy users who seek the benefit of large, meaty burgers.

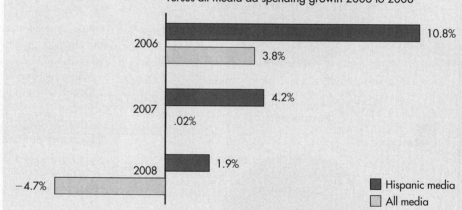

Advertising and Marketing
Hispanic Media Ad Spending Growth Rates
Versus all media ad spending growth 2006 to 2008

2006 — 10.8%
2006 — 3.8%

2007 — 4.2%
2007 — .02%

2008 — 1.9%
2008 — −4.7%

■ Hispanic media
□ All media

Source: Hispanic Fact Pack, Supplement to *Advertising Age*, 2009 Edition, from U.S. Census Bureau.

buy special equipment for dealing with snow and ice—products many Floridians have never seen in stores.

When marketers analyze geographic data, they study sales by region, country size, city size, specific locations, and types of stores. Many products sell well in urban areas but poorly in suburban or rural ones, and vice versa. As we'll see in Chapter 15, this type of information is critical in developing advertising media schedules because, with limited budgets, marketers want to advertise in areas where their sales potential is best.

Even in local markets, geographic segmentation is important. For example, a local progressive politician might send a mailer only to precincts where voters typically support liberal causes, and a local retail store rarely draws customers from outside a fairly limited *trading area*.

Demographic Segmentation
Demographic segmentation is a way to define groups by their statistical characteristics: sex, age, ethnicity, education, occupation, income, and other quantifiable factors. For example, research shows that people who identify themselves as "strongly Hispanic" tend to be very loyal to certain brands. And, as Exhibit 4–3 reveals, the number of Americans with Hispanic ancestry is expected to grow at a rate much faster than the overall population well into

This Levi's ad promotes the more relaxed fit of the Silver Tab line of jeans, targeted to those who seek comfortable clothing.

Brand Niching May Cause Brand Switching

this century. This has meant a surge in advertising dollars allocated to Hispanic media. Many blue-chip advertisers, such as Procter & Gamble, AT&T, McDonald's, and General Motors, now aim a significant portion of their advertising specifically at this trillion dollar market.

Demographics are often combined with geographic segmentation to select target markets for advertising. This is called **geodemographic segmentation**. JCPenney, for example, discovered that its Sandra Salcedo line of clothing for Hispanic women sold well in Texas and Northern California stores but not in heavily Mexican-American Los Angeles, where urban influences hold greater sway. In other words, people's lives are influenced by their environment as well as by their ethnicity.[13]

As people grow older, their responsibilities and incomes change, and so do their interests in various product categories (see Exhibit 4–4). The auto industry didn't forget that over half of America's consumers are now young adults. In fact, as the opening vignette discussed, the 63 million children of baby boomers are now potential car buyers. To reach out to this group, Toyota promoted its Yaris sedan with a campaign that includes a mobile phone series, a profile page on MySpace.com, and skits featuring the Yaris on the TV show *MADtv*.[14] Similarly, Ford targeted 25- to 35-year-olds with a series of "rockumentary" films about its Fusion sedan. The films, which featured the Norwegian rock group Hurra Torpedo, are available online and represent an attempt by the automaker to reach younger consumers.[15]

Demographic segmentation has long been understood in the fast-food industry. Once stigmatized as unsanitary meat fit only for poor people, chains like White Castle and McDonald's used advertising to change the hamburger's image, fashioning it into the national cuisine by the 1950s.[16] Now, children are McDonald's primary target consumers. Decades of ads for Happy Meals have made an impression. Among fictional characters, Ronald McDonald's cultural penetration is surpassed only by Santa Claus: 96 percent of schoolchildren in the United States can identify the yellow-jumpsuited clown.[17] Against this giant's brand value and advertising expenditures, competitors have returned to the hamburger's traditional consumer, the young male. In the segment where McDonald's is slightly weaker, Hardee's intends to be strong.

psychographic segmentation Method of defining consumer markets based on psychological variables including values, attitudes, personality, and lifestyle.

psychographics The grouping of consumers into market segments on the basis of psychological makeup—values, attitudes, personality, and lifestyle.

primary motivation The pattern of attitudes and activities that help people reinforce, sustain, or modify their social and self-image. An understanding of the primary motivation of individuals helps advertisers promote and sell goods and services.

resources A term in the Values and Lifestyles (VALS) typology relating to the range of psychological, physical, demographic, and material capacities that consumers can draw upon. The resource axis includes education, income, self-confidence, health, eagerness to buy, and energy level.

▼**EXHIBIT 4–4** Heavy usage patterns of various age groups.

Age	Name of Age Group	Merchandise Purchased
0–5	Young children	Baby food, toys, nursery furniture, children's wear
6–19	Schoolchildren and teenagers	Clothing, sporting goods, tapes and CDs, school supplies, fast food, soft drinks, candy, cosmetics, movies
20–34	Young adults	Cars, furniture, housing, food and beer, clothing, diamonds, home entertainment equipment, recreational equipment, purchases for younger age segments
35–49	Younger middle-aged	Larger homes, better cars, second cars, new furniture, computers, recreational equipment, jewelry, clothing, food and wine
50–64	Older middle-aged	Recreational items, purchases for young marrieds and infants, travel
65 and over	Senior adults	Medical services, travel, pharmaceuticals, purchases for younger age groups

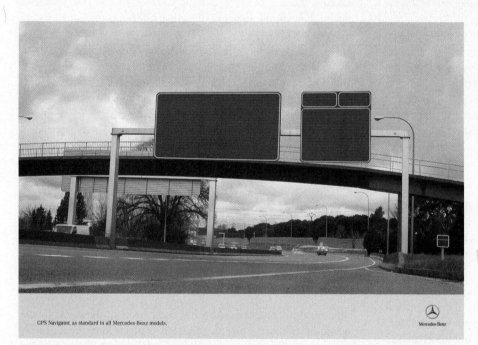

GPS Navigator, as standard in all Mercedes-Benz models.

Mercedes-Benz

Changing demographics in many international markets open up new opportunities for advertisers. In Spain, the growing upper middle class and the availability of good expressways enable Mercedes-Benz (www.mercedesbenz.com) to promote its navigation system in this very creative ad.

In international markets, the demographics of many populations are changing rapidly. From India to Brazil to Poland, middle-class life is becoming available to more people in former Third World countries. This emerging middle class has an apparently insatiable appetite for consumer goods—everything from color TVs and MP3 players to video cameras, cars, and refrigerators.[18] In India, for example, the average salary increased 14 percent in 2005. Spending habits have shifted from buying necessities to purchasing lifestyle products. China has emerged as one of the world's fastest-growing advertising markets as companies try to reach that country's increasingly wealthy consumers. According to CTR Market Research, China now ranks third (with the United Kingdom and Germany) after the United States and Japan in the global advertising market, with annual spending reaching $43 billion in 2007.[19]

Geographic and demographic data provide information about markets but little about the psychology of individuals. People in the same demographic or geographic segment may have widely differing product preferences and TV viewing habits. Rarely can demographic criteria alone predict purchase behavior.[20] That's why marketers developed the study of *psychographics.*

Psychographic Segmentation For certain products, appeals to emotions and cultural values may be persuasive. So some advertisers use **psychographic segmentation** to define consumer markets. With **psychographics**, marketers group people by their values, attitudes, personality, and lifestyle. Psychographics enables marketers to view people as individuals with feelings and inclinations. Then, they can classify people according to what they feel, what they believe, the way they live, and the products, services, and media they use.[21]

Perhaps the best-known psychographic classification system is VALS™, a product of Strategic Business Insights (SBI), a

Ads for Adidas (www.adidas.com) capture the attitude and lifestyle of its target market—young people around the world who like to make their own fashion statement. Segmentation along psychographic lines is difficult because it is not easily quantifiable. Nevertheless, lifestyle advertisements play a critical role in marketing products that involve feelings, personalities, values, and attitudes.

▼ **EXHIBIT 4–5** The VALS™ (www.strategicbusinessinsights. com/VALS) classification system places consumers with abundant resources—psychological, physical, and material means and capacities—near the top of the chart and those with minimal resources near the bottom. The chart segments consumers by their basis for decision making: ideals, achievement, or self-expression. The boxes intersect to indicate that some categories may be considered together. For instance, a marketer may categorize Thinkers and Believers together.

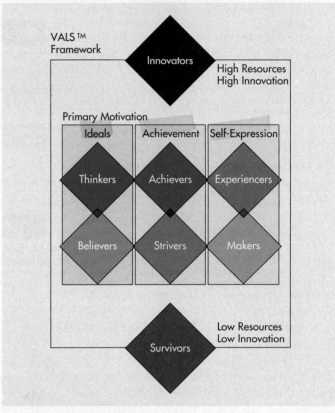

spinout of SRI International. VALS assigns consumers to one of eight groups based on two dimensions: **primary motivation** and **resources**. According to SBI, individuals are primarily motivated to buy by one of three things: ideals (or basic principles), achievement (tangible markers of success or accomplishment), or self-expression (a desire for experiences or to take risks). In addition, people possess varying levels of resources, which include money, education, or self-confidence. Those with the fewest resources are placed near the bottom of the VALS typology, while those with the most are at the top (see Exhibit 4–5).[22]

According to SBI, the purpose of VALS is to help marketers identify whom to target, uncover what the target group buys and does, locate where concentrations of the target group live, identify how best to communicate with them, and gain insight into why the target group behaves the way it does. The system has been applied to a variety of areas: new product development and design, target marketing, product positioning, advertising message development, and media planning, to name a few.[23] In one case, for example, a

Psychographics enables marketers to view people as individuals with feelings and inclinations.

foreign car manufacturer used VALS to reposition its sports utility vehicle after its award-winning but ineffective television campaign failed to result in higher sales. Using VALS, the company targeted a new "rebellious" consumer group with a new campaign using a "breaking the rules" theme. Nothing changed but the advertising. But sales increased 60 percent in six months.[24]

Several other classification systems have been developed to help marketers in the U.S. and worldwide target consumers based on their values, motivations, and lifestyles. These psychographic segmentation schemes include ValueScope from Roper Starch Worldwide, BehaviorGraphics from Experian Simmons, and MindBase, a product offered by Yankelovich Partners. The MindBase consumer groups are described in Exhibit 4–6.

How might marketers use psychographic segmentation schemes such as these? Recall our discussion about product

Who Are the MindBase Segments?

I am Expressive
my motto is *Carpe Diem.*

I live life to the fullest and I'm not afraid to express my personality. I'm active and engaged and I embody a true "live in the now" attitude with a firm belief that the future is limitless and that I can be or do anything I put my mind to.

I am Driven
my motto is *Nothing Ventured, Nothing Gained*

I'm ambitious with a drive to succeed both personally and professionally. I think of myself as self-possessed and resourceful, and I'm determined to show the world I'm on top of my game in all I do, from career ambitions to family, home, and my social life.

I am At Capacity
my motto is *Time Is of the Essence*

My life is very busy and I'm looking for control and simplification. I am a demanding and vocal consumer, and I'm looking for convenience, respect, and a helping hand so I can devote more of my time to the important things in life.

I am Rock Steady
my motto is *Do the Right Thing*

I think of myself as a positive individual. I draw energy from my home and family. I'm dedicated to living an upstanding life and I listen to my own instincts in terms of making thoughtful decisions in my personal life and in the marketplace.

I am Down to Earth
my motto is *Ease on Down the Road*

I'm cruising down life's path at my own pace, seeking satisfaction where I can. I'm looking to enhance my life, stretch myself to try new things and treat myself through novel experiences and products along the way.

I am Sophisticated
my motto is *Sense and Sensibility*

I am intelligent and upstanding, and I have an affinity for the finer things in life. I also have high expectations both for myself and for the companies to which I give my business. I am dedicated to doing a stellar job at work but I balance my career dedication with a passion for enriching experiences.

I Measure Twice
my motto is *An Ounce of Prevention*

I'm a mature individual and I like to think of myself on a life path to actualization and fulfillment. I live a healthy, active life. I'm dedicated to ensuring that my future is both secure and highly rewarding and vitalized.

I am Devoted
my motto is *Home Is Where the Heart Is*

I'm traditional and rooted in the comforts of home. Some would say my beliefs are conventional, but they make sense to me. I'm spiritual and content with my life. I like things the way they have always been and I don't need novelty for novelty's sake or newfangled technology.

Source: Copyright © Yankelovich, Inc.

utility. We argued that people often buy products in an effort to satisfy functional needs and psychological wants. Psychographic tools like VALS attempt to group people in terms of shared needs and wants. Advocates of this approach believe that doing so provides both a more precise way of target marketing and a deeper understanding of what the target market is like. As an example, consider a company that markets high-end motorcycles. A demographic profile of the company's target market might suggest that prospects are males between the ages of 30 and 50. A psychographic profile could extend this analysis by noting that the best prospects are experiencers: men motivated by self-expressive needs who also have sufficient resources to buy an expensive bike. Understanding the motivations of experiencers not only helps the company realize they are a good target market; it also suggests benefits of the product that the marketer should advertise. VALS is thus very useful in a variety of areas, including new product development and design, target marketing, product positioning, advertising message development, and media planning.

An influential book, *The Tipping Point* by cultural observer Malcolm Gladwell, suggests another reason why advertisers may wish to psychologically segment consumers: identifying those who are important social influences on others. Gladwell argues that certain types of people are involved in creating what he calls *social epidemics,* typified by the almost overnight increase in the popularity of a product, fashion, or idea. Gladwell believes that social epidemics are traceable to the actions of three types of people, which he labels *Connectors, Mavens,* and *Salesmen.* Connectors are people with very wide social circles; they have the ability to bridge different social groups that would not ordinarily interact with each other. Mavens are people who spend the time and energy accumulating knowledge that most people simply can't be bothered to find out for themselves. Connectors and Mavens are sources of information about new products, trends, and ideas, but the job of persuading people to embrace these things falls to Salesmen. Salesmen are people whom most individuals find credible, trustworthy, and authoritative. Gladwell's analysis suggests that relatively small groups of people are very influential in affecting the consumption habits of much larger segments of society.[25]

Limitations of Consumer Segmentation Methods
Advocates of psychographic systems claim they help address the emotional factors that motivate consumers. However, for some products psychographics may offer little real value—especially since it oversimplifies consumer personalities and

purchase behavior. Some typologies, such as VALS, are also criticized for being too complicated.[26]

Still, it's important for marketers to monitor and understand their customers. It helps them select target markets, create ads that match the attributes and image of their products with the types of consumers who use them, develop effective media plans, and allocate their advertising dollars wisely.

Segmenting Business and Government Markets: Understanding Organizational Buying Behavior

Business markets (or industrial markets) include manufacturers, government agencies, wholesalers, retailers, banks, and institutions that buy goods and services to help them operate. These products may include raw materials, electronic components, mechanical parts, office equipment, vehicles, or services used in conducting their businesses. Many business marketers sell to resellers, such as retailers that resell to consumers. For example, much of Hardee's food is supplied by Siméus Foods International, a processing, production, and distribution conglomerate. Siméus's two plants produce and freeze menu items, such as hamburger and chicken patties, to the specifications of customers like Hardee's and Denny's. The end product is resold by Hardee's with no mention of Siméus. Hardee's reselling contract with Coca-Cola, however, is a much more visible *brand partnership;* Coke products are often featured in Hardee's advertising.

Identifying target markets of prospective business customers is just as complex as identifying consumer markets. Many of the variables used to identify consumer markets can also be used for business markets—for example, geography and behavior (purchase occasion, benefits sought, user status, and usage rate).

Business markets also have special characteristics. They employ professional buyers and use systematic purchasing procedures. They may be concentrated geographically. And in any single market there may be only a small number of buyers.

Business Purchasing Procedures

When businesspeople evaluate new products, they use a process far more complex and rigid than the consumer purchase process we will describe in Chapter 5. Business marketers must design their advertising programs with this in mind.

Large firms have purchasing departments that act as professional buyers. They evaluate the need for products, analyze proposed purchases, weigh competitive bids, seek approvals from users and managers, make requisitions, place orders, and supervise all product purchasing. This structured purchase decision process implies a rational approach. Research, however, shows that professional buyers often exhibit a willingness to pay a substantial premium for their favorite brand. This is especially true for buyers concerned about the negative conse-

quences of a product failure. In other words, buyers perceive well-known brands as a way to reduce risk. (FedEx addresses the fears of freight service buyers in its advertising when it promises to deliver overnight.) Buyers' feelings about brands also tend to transfer from one product category to another, even when the products are very different (e.g., from fax machines to CDs).[27] This suggests that advertising may play a larger role in business-to-business marketing than previously thought.

Making a sale in business markets may take weeks, months, or even years, especially to government agencies. Purchase decisions often depend on factors besides price or quality, among them product demonstrations, delivery time, terms of sale, and dependability. Marketers often emphasize these issues in advertising and promotional appeals.

Before deciding on a target market, business marketers should consider how the purchase decision process works in various segments. New companies, for instance, may want to target smaller

Although business purchases are often made according to a company's well-defined needs and policies, the actual purchasers are people who might be persuaded by traditional forms of product branding. For this reason, business-to-business advertising for AIG SunAmerica (www.sunamerica.com) places emphasis on establishing and reinforcing the SunAmerica name.

firms where the purchase decision can be made quickly. Or they may use commissioned reps to call on the larger prospects that require more time. These decisions will dictate where advertising should be placed.

Industrial Classification System

Industrial customers need different products, depending on their business. For example, apparel manufacturers such as Levi's are the main customers for buttons and zippers. Marketing managers need to focus their sales and advertising efforts on those firms that are in the right business for their products.[28] The U.S. Census Bureau classifies all U.S. businesses—and collects and publishes industry statistics on them—using the **North American Industry Classification System (NAICS) codes**. Because the system was developed in cooperation with Canada and Mexico, consistency throughout North America is guaranteed.

▼**EXHIBIT 4–7** NAICS hierarchy and codes. A business marketer selling goods or services to firms in the paging industry can use the NAICS codes to locate prospective companies in directories or in subscription databases.

Level	Code	Sector
Sector	51	Information
Subsector	513	Broadcasting and telecommunications
Industry group	5133	Telecommunications
Industry	51332	Wireless telecommunications carriers (except satellite)
U.S. industry	513321	Paging

Market Concentration

Many countries' markets for industrial goods are concentrated in one region or several metropolitan areas. In the United States, for example, the industrial market is heavily concentrated in the Midwest, the South, and California (see Exhibit 4–8). Market concentration reduces the number of geographic targets for an advertiser.

Buyers perceive well-known brands as a way to reduce risk.

NAICS organizes industries into 20 broad sectors such as mining, manufacturing, wholesale trade, and information. These are then subdivided into four hierarchical levels of classification, including sectors, subsectors, industry groups, industries, and finally 1,170 distinct U.S. industries. (See Exhibit 4–7 for a breakdown of NAICS codes in the information and wireless telecommunications industry.) The Census Bureau uses NAICS to offer marketers an abundance of information, such as the number of firms, sales volumes, and number of employees by geographic area. Thus, the NAICS codes help companies segment markets and do research, and advertisers can even obtain lists of companies in particular NAICS divisions for direct mailings.[29]

▼**EXHIBIT 4–8** The states in this map are represented in proportion to the value of their manufactured products.

my ad campaign

Moreover, business marketers deal with fewer buyers than consumer marketers. Less than 7 percent of U.S. manufacturing establishments employ nearly 75 percent of all production workers and account for almost 80 percent of all manufacturing dollars.[30] Customer size is a critical issue for market segmentation. A firm may concentrate its marketing and advertising efforts on a few large customers, many smaller ones, or both.

Levi Strauss markets through three channels: independent department stores; specialty stores (such as Urban Outfitters);

Segmenting the Audience [4]

What is the target market for your product? The answer to this question is rarely simple; thus your choices again will require the application of strategic thinking. To make the decision you will need to gather as much information from your client and from secondary sources as you can, focusing on the product's market, users, and the competition. The information you gather about the consumer in the My Ad Campaign from Chapter 6 will be important as well. And in some instances it may make sense to conduct primary research with current customers or with individuals who use competing products.

You may have the opportunity to offer counsel to your client about whether it is pursuing the right target market. Check to be sure before offering such advice; some clients may not wish to receive it. If the client is interested, consider whether there are underserved segments that offer sales or profit potential. For example, if your client is a local pizzeria located near campus, it may be focusing on attracting students. This is to be expected since students normally represent a sizeable market in any college town. In addition, your client is doubtless using the timeworn strategy of attracting hungry, cash-strapped undergrads with messages that emphasize low prices, large servings, and coupons. But while students may represent a large market for pizza, there are probably dozens of other food businesses competing for this segment. If so, it might be smarter to refocus on a smaller but underserved segment, especially one that offers great profit potential. If your town lacks an upscale pizzeria that serves specialty pies, the client might be better served by improving its offerings and dining facility, raising prices, and promoting to non-students who would be willing to pay more for quality pizzas.

Of course, to evaluate opportunities in a market you will need to segment. Many advertisers find that it makes sense to segment on the basis of standard demographic characteristics such as age, gender, ethnicity, location, social class, or income level. Dividing your market according to product loyalty or product usage levels is also worth strongly considering. Understanding your market with respect to psychographics and lifestyles can be incredibly valuable, especially later when you begin to develop your creative brief. Such data can be more difficult to obtain however.

Defining the Target Market

	Your Client's Customers	The Competition's Customers	Nonusers
Demographics			
Age			
Gender			
Ethnicity/race			
Location/region			
Social class			
Income			
Education			
Behaviors			
Product usage (light, medium, heavy)			
Brand loyalty (loyal, switchers)			
Psychographics			
Principle-oriented			
Status-oriented			
Action-oriented			
Benefits Sought			
Low price			
Quality			

primary demand trend The projection of future consumer demand for a product category, based on past demand and other market influences.

target marketing The process by which an advertiser focuses its marketing efforts on a target market.

target market The market segment or group within the market segment toward which all marketing activities will be directed.

and chain stores (such as Walmart and JCPenney). Its top 100 accounts provide 80 percent of the company's annual sales and are made through 13,000 retail outlets. Its remaining accounts (20 percent of sales) represent another 13,000 stores. Major accounts are served by sales reps from Levi's various divisions, smaller accounts by telemarketers and companywide sales reps. Bartle Bogle Hegarty creates and coordinates advertising for most Levi Strauss divisions in the United States.

Business marketers can also segment by end users. For example, a firm may develop software for one industry, such as banking, or for general use in a variety of industries. That decision, of course, affects advertising media decisions.

Aggregating Market Segments

Once marketers identify and locate broad markets with shared characteristics (behavioristic, geographic, demographic, or psychographic), they can proceed to the second step in the market segmentation process. This involves (1) selecting groups that have a mutual interest in the product's utility and (2) reorganizing and aggregating (combining) them into larger market segments based on their potential for sales and profit.

Levi's has introduced several product lines in an effort to satisfy the needs and wants of different consumer segments. In this seemingly simple ad, the style of slim jeans is communicated to a younger, more contemporary market segment.

Let's take a look at how this process might work for Levi Strauss & Co. in the U.S. market.

First, the company's management needs to know the **primary demand trend** of the total U.S. market for pants. This is the market potential for jeans and casual pants in various market areas across the country. To do this it uses a variety of *marketing research techniques* (discussed in Chapter 6). Then management must identify the needs, wants, and shared characteristics of the various groups within the casual apparel marketplace who live near the company's retail outlets. It may use the services of a large marketing information company such as Claritas, which collects data on purchasing behaviors and creates profiles of geographic markets across the country.

The company finds many prospective customers throughout the United States: students, blue-collar workers, young singles, professionals, homemakers, and so on. It then measures and analyzes households in each major retail area by demographic, lifestyle, and purchasing characteristics, sorts them into 66 geodemographic segments, and labels them with terms such as those in Exhibit 4–9: Big City Blues, Movers & Shakers, Country Squires, Pools & Patios, and the like. All of these people have apparel needs and many may be interested in the style, cachet, and durability of the Levi's brand.

Selecting Groups Interested in Product Utility

Levi Strauss next selects groups that would like and be able to afford the benefits of Levi's apparel—suitability for work or play, comfort, style, reasonable cost, durability, and so on. Groups interested in all these features make up the total possible market for Levi's clothes.

Part of the challenge of market segmentation is estimating the profits the company might realize if it (1) aims at the whole market or (2) caters only to specific segments. Apparel is a highly competitive market, but 10 percent of 1,000 is always larger than 90 percent of 100. So for a company such as Levi Strauss, the target market must be a large mass market or it won't be profitable.[31]

Combining Groups to Build Target Market Segments

The company needs to find groups that are relatively homogeneous (similar) and offer good profit potential. Market data turn up many demographic and lifestyle groups, including middle-aged couples, seniors, and ethnically diverse young singles, as well as groups labeled New Empty Nest, Park Bench Seniors, and Low Rise Living, respectively. These groups, each constituting just over 1 percent of consumer households, have minimal retail or credit activity, and they are thus not prime targets for premium-branded department store products.

Other segments offer greater potential—young to middle-aged households with medium to high incomes and average to high retail activity. These include groups like Movers & Shakers, Bohemian Mix, and Home Sweet Home, each constituting nearly 2 percent of all households. By combining these groups with

Dominant PRIZMne Cluster by ZIP Code

- 03 - Movers & Shakers
- 05 - Country Squires
- 09 - Big Fish, Small Pond
- 10 - Second City Elite
- 11 - God's Country
- 15 - Pools & Patios
- 19 - Home Sweet Home
- 20 - Fast-Track Families
- 23 - Greenbelt Sports
- 25 - Country Casuals
- 27 - Middleburg Manager
- 30 - Suburban Sprawl
- 33 - Big Sky Families
- 36 - Blue-Chip Blues
- 37 - Mayberry-ville
- 39 - Domestic Duos
- 44 - New Beginnings
- 46 - Old Glories
- 49 - American Classics
- 51 - Shotguns & Pickups
- 52 - Suburban Pioneers
- 53 - Mobility Blues
- 54 - Multi-Culti Mosaic
- 59 - Urban Elders
- 61 - City Roots
- 65 - Big City Blues

2 miles

the young professionals in the Young Influentials and New Beginnings segments, Levi Strauss can target young to middle-aged people on their way up. Nationally, that amounts to nearly 20 million households. That's not everybody, but it's a large and potentially very profitable mass-market segment. These prospects might like the style and comfort of Levi's 550s as well as the tradition of a brand they know and trust. Levi's can expect that a well-conceived campaign will appeal to their particular needs, wants, and self-images.

check yourself ✓

1. What is the marketer's goal in segmenting markets?

2. What characteristics are used in psychographic segmentation?

3. Why do marketers aggregate market segments?

L03 Discuss how defining a target market enhances a product's marketing strategy.

THE TARGET MARKETING PROCESS

Once the market segmentation process is complete, a company can proceed to the **target marketing** process. This will determine the content, look, and feel of its advertising.

Target Market Selection

The first step in target marketing is to assess which of the newly created segments offer the greatest profit potential and which can be most successfully penetrated. The company designates one or more segments as a **target market**—those consumers the company wishes to appeal to, design products for, and tailor its marketing activities toward.[32] It may designate another set of segments as a secondary target market and aim some of its resources at it.

Let's look at the most likely target market for loose-fitting jeans: young to middle-aged customers with moderate to high income and education who like the style, comfort, and fashion of Levi's apparel. This group represents a large percentage of the apparel market, and if won, will generate substantial profits. Levi's offers what these prospects need and want: the style and fashion of the jeans they grew up with, updated to be more comfortable for the adult body.

But the middle-class, comfort-oriented segment is not enough for Levi's to be profitable, so it also caters to at least two other important market segments. In response to the enormous number of consumers who shop at giant, low-cost retailers like Walmart and Target, Levi's has developed a value-priced line, Levi's Signature. The Signature collection appeals to budget-conscious families with children such as Family Thrifts and Big Sky Families. And at the top end, Levi's met the needs of young, twenty-something, image-conscious consumers with its Warhol Factory X Levi's jeans. This line retailed for $250 and was sold at high-end retailers such as Nordstrom's.

Understanding the Product Element: Starbucks Coffee [4–B]

America's java giant began as the seed of an idea by a man with a dream whose tender care and commitment eventually built the familiar coffee empire of today. While on a trip to Italy in 1983, Howard Schultz discovered and fell in love with the coffee bars of Milan and Verona. They were a combination of coffee and community. He was sure Americans would love this concept.

At the time, Starbucks (www.starbucks.com) was a little 11-store chain of roasted coffee stores in Seattle. Schultz was in charge of marketing. He pitched the coffee bar concept to the company's management but received only a lukewarm response. They didn't want to be in the restaurant business. Howard held on to his vision, though. Leaving Starbucks in 1987, he launched a handful of coffee bars on his own and named them Il Giornale. Two years later, with some investor backing, his demonstrated success enabled him to acquire Starbucks. Today, he is chairman and chief global strategist of a publicly traded company that boasts more than 16,000 retail locations in 50 countries. Serving tens of millions of Americans each week, Starbucks has definitely become a household name.

To Schultz, the most important component for success is consistent product quality. "Our long-range goal is to be nothing less than the most recognized and respected brand of coffee in the world," Schultz says.

Thanks to management's demand for consistency, a double-tall latte tastes the same in New York as it does in Seattle; and your perfectly pulled espresso won't sit for more than 10 seconds before being poured into your cup. This attention to detail has earned Starbucks its place in the premium coffee category.

Of course a good product is best prepared and served by skilled, happy employees. And that also adds to an organization's profitability. Ranked by *Fortune* as one of the "100 Best Companies to Work for in 2010" poll, Starbucks's management believes that if it takes care of its workers, they in turn will take care of the public. Employees who work at least 20 hours a week receive full benefits, with dental and extended health care, including eyeglass and contact lens prescriptions—after only 90 days with the company. Starbucks even offers these benefits to the same-sex partners of employees. To further ensure consistent product quality, Starbucks has implemented procedures for monitoring the working conditions of the overseas producers who supply materials to the company.

Today, the coffee market is quite competitive, but Starbucks retains its leading position by continually introducing new products. With PepsiCo, Starbucks formed a partnership to produce its Frappuccino beverage in 1995. In 1996, Starbucks entered into a joint venture with Dreyers Grand Ice Cream to market "Starbucks Coffee Ice Cream." In 1998 and 1999, Starbucks strengthened its presence within the tea segment by introducing a mixture of tea, fruit juice, and ice called Tiazzi, and it aquired Tazo, a Portland, Oregon–based tea company. In 2002, a bottled espresso drink dubbed the DoubleShot joined the long line of creative products. And in 2009, VIA Ready Brew instant coffee joined the portfolio of products. If you're drinking a coffee or tea beverage these days, Starbucks may well have created it—even if you purchased it elsewhere.

Applying the Breaks

A basic rule of advertising is that the most ingenious campaign in the world cannot save a bad product. Think of a brand in the marketplace that you consider successful and analyze which product elements make it profitable and unique. Are there any similarities to the elements that made Starbucks successful? If so, what?

> The target market is those consumers the company wishes to appeal to, design products for, and tailor its marketing activities toward.

The Marketing Mix: A Strategy for Matching Products to Markets

Once a company defines its target market, it knows exactly where to focus its attention and resources. Marketers and advertisers generally try to shape their basic product into a total **product concept**: the consumer's perception of a product or service as a bundle of utilitarian and symbolic values that satisfy functional, social, psychological, and other wants and needs. Companies have many strategic options they can employ to enhance this product/service concept and effect marketing exchanges (make sales). The company can design special features for its target market (such as certain colors or special sizes). It can establish proper pricing. And it can determine the criteria for locating stores or dealers and prepare the most convincing advertising messages.

Marketers categorize these options under four headings: (1) *product*, (2) *price*, (3) *distribution*, and (4) *communication*.[33] The way the marketer mixes and blends these different elements creates the company's marketing strategy—often called the **marketing mix**. For convenience, marketing educator E. Jerome McCarthy developed a mnemonic device to help recall these four functions: *product, price, place*, and *promotion*—or the **four Ps (4Ps)**.[34]

The 4Ps are a simple way to remember the basic elements of the marketing mix. But within each element are many marketing activities a company can use to fine-tune its product concept and improve sales. Advertising, for example, is one instrument of the communication (promotion) element. The remainder of this chapter focuses on the relationship between advertising and the other elements of the marketing mix.

LO4 Describe the elements of the marketing mix and the role advertising plays in each element of the mix.

ADVERTISING AND THE PRODUCT ELEMENT

In developing a marketing mix, marketers generally start with the **product element**. Major activities typically include the way the product is designed and classified, positioned, branded, and packaged. Each of these affects the way the product is advertised.

Product Life Cycles

Marketers theorize that just as humans pass through stages in life from infancy to death, products (and especially product categories) also pass through a **product life cycle** (see Exhibit 4–10).[35] A product's position in the life cycle influences the target market selected and the marketing mix used. There are four major stages in the product life cycle: *introduction, growth, maturity,* and *decline*.

When a company introduces a new product category, nobody knows about it. Through market segmentation, the company will try to identify those prospects who are known to be

▼**EXHIBIT 4–10** A product's life cycle curve may vary, depending on the product category, but almost every product or service passes through these stages. Marketing objectives and strategies change as the product proceeds from one stage to the next.

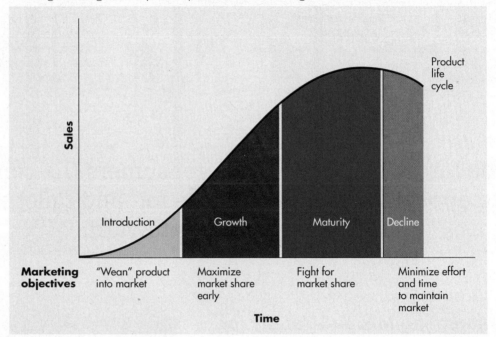

| Marketing objectives | "Wean" product into market | Maximize market share early | Fight for market share | Minimize effort and time to maintain market |

early adopters—willing to try new things—and begin promoting the new category directly to them. The idea is to stimulate **primary demand**—consumer demand for the whole product category, not just the company's own brand.

During the **introductory phase** of any new product category, the company incurs considerable costs for educating customers, building widespread dealer distribution, and encouraging demand. It must advertise heavily at this stage to establish a position as a market leader and to gain a large share of market before the growth stage begins.

When cell phones were introduced in the late 1980s, advertisers had to first create enough consumer demand to pull the product through the channels of distribution (called **pull strategy**). Advertising educated consumers about the new product and its category, explained what cellular phones are, how they work, and the rewards of owning one. Promotional efforts aimed at retailers (called **push strategy**) encouraged distributors and dealers to stock, display, and advertise the new products.

When sales volume begins to rise rapidly, the product enters the **growth stage**. This period is characterized by rapid *market expansion* as more and more customers, stimulated by mass advertising and word-of-mouth, make their first, second, and third purchases. Competitors jump into the market, but the company that established the early leadership position usually reaps the biggest rewards. As a percentage of total sales, advertising expenditures should decrease, and individual firms will realize their first substantial profits.

During the early 1990s, the demand for cell phones exploded, and category sales quadrupled every year. Many competitors suddenly appeared. With increased production and competition, prices started to fall, which brought even more consumers into the market. By 2007, 80 percent of all U.S. families owned cell phones.[36]

In the **maturity stage**, the marketplace becomes saturated with competing products and the number of new customers dwindles, so industry sales reach a plateau. Competition intensifies and profits diminish. Companies increase their promotional

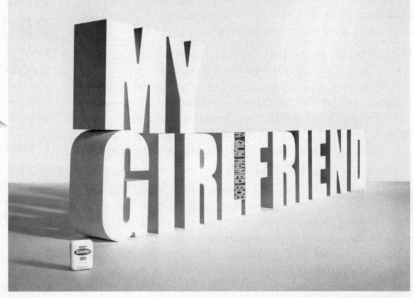

Glide dental floss exists in a mature product category. To differentiate itself from competing floss products, the brand emphasizes its smoothness and ease of use in tight spaces between teeth.

push strategy
Marketing, advertising, and sales promotion activities aimed at getting products into the dealer pipeline and accelerating sales by offering inducements to dealers, retailers, and salespeople.

growth stage The period in a product life cycle that is marked by market expansion as more and more customers make their first purchases while others are already making their second and third purchases.

maturity stage That point in the product life cycle when the market has become saturated with products, the number of new customers has dwindled, and competition is most intense.

selective demand Consumer demand for the particular advantages of one brand over another.

decline stage The stage in the product life cycle when sales begin to decline due to obsolescence, new technology, or changing consumer tastes.

efforts but emphasize **selective demand** to impress customers with the subtle advantages of their particular brand. At this stage, companies can increase sales only at the expense of competitors. The strategies of market segmentation, product positioning, and price promotion become more important during this shakeout period as weak companies fall by the wayside and those remaining fight for market share.

By the mid-1990s, for example, cellular phones that once sold for $1,500 were suddenly advertised regularly for $100 to $200. Ads emphasized features and low prices, and the product became a staple of discount merchandisers. Today, of course, one can get a cell phone for free, just by signing up for the service.[37]

Late in the maturity stage, companies may have to scramble to extend the product's life cycle. Without innovation or marketing support, name brands eventually see their sales erode. If the advertised brand has no perceived advantage, people will buy whatever's cheapest or most convenient. Professor Brian Wansink, who directs the Brand Lab at the University of Illinois Urbana–Champaign, suggests that the reason many old brands die is less for life cycle reasons and more for marketing neglect. He points out that aging brands often pack plenty of brand equity. The challenge for marketers is to determine which brands can be revitalized and then decide how to do it. With today's high price tag on introducing new products (often $100 million or more), revitalization should be the strategy of choice whenever possible. Marketers may try to find new users for the brand, develop new uses for the product, change the size of packages, design new labels, improve quality, or use promotions to increase frequency of use.[38] One such revitalization effort in the portable computer category may be Apple's new iPad, which is attracting attention for its multiple uses, including reading books, viewing photos, watching movies, playing music, and surfing the Web on a touch screen for under $500.

If they're not revitalized, products will finally enter the **decline stage** because of obsolescence, new technology, or changing consumer tastes. At this point, companies may cease all promotion and phase the products out quickly, as in the case of record turntables and albums, or let them fade slowly away with minimal advertising.

Product Classifications

The way a company classifies its product is important in defining both the product concept and the marketing mix. As Exhibit 4–11

▼**EXHIBIT 4–11** Product classifications.

By Market	By Rate of Consumption and Tangibility	By Purchasing Habits	By Physical Description
Consumer goods Products and services we use in our daily lives (food, clothing, furniture, cars).	**Durable goods** Tangible products that are long-lasting and infrequently replaced (cars, trucks, refrigerators, furniture).	**Convenience goods** Purchases made frequently with a minimum of effort (cigarettes, food, newspapers).	**Packaged goods** Cereals, hair tonics, and so forth.
Industrial goods Products used by companies for the purpose of producing other products (raw materials, agricultural commodities, machinery, tools, equipment).	**Nondurable goods** Tangible products that may be consumed in one or a few uses and usually need to be replaced at regular intervals (food, soap, gasoline, oil).	**Shopping goods** Infrequently purchased items for which greater time is spent comparing price, quality, style, warranty (furniture, cars, clothing, tires).	**Hard goods** Furniture, appliances. **Soft goods** Clothing, bedding.
	Services Activities, benefits, or satisfaction offered for sale (travel, haircuts, legal and medical services, massages).	**Specialty goods** Products with such unique characteristics that consumers will make special efforts to purchase them even if they're more expensive (fancy photographic equipment, special women's fashions, stereo components).	**Services** Intangible products.
		Unsought goods Products that potential customers don't yet want (insurance, encyclopedias) or don't know they can buy (new products), so they don't search them out.	

Product Positioning

Once an advertising person understands the product's stage in the life cycle, how it's classified, and how it's currently perceived by the marketplace, the first strategic decision can be made: how to **position** the product. The basic goal of positioning strategy is to own a word that establishes the product in the prospect's mind. Levi's owns "jeans" (or at least they did for a long time). BMW owns "performance." Maytag owns "reliability." And Volvo owns "safety." By developing a unique position for the brand in the consumer's mind, the marketer helps the consumer remember the brand and what it stands for.

Product Differentiation

Product differentiation creates a product difference that appeals to the preferences of a distinct market segment. In advertising, nothing is more important than being able to tell prospects truthfully that your product is different. Unfortunately, in response to increased competitive pressures, burgeoning innovation and technology, and various constraints on distribution, new-product development cycles have shortened dramatically. As a result, many brand managers find themselves launching new products that are "only 85 percent there." So it's not surprising that many "new" products fail to impress consumers. (See Exhibit 4–12.)

Differences between products that are readily apparent to the consumer are called **perceptible differences**. Snapple, for example, received its initial impetus because of its unique ingredients and taste, and the company now spends millions of dollars annually to advertise this difference to consumers nationwide.[39] **Hidden differences** are not so readily apparent. Trident gum may look and taste the same as other brands, but it is differentiated by the use of artificial sweeteners. While hidden differences can enhance a product's desirability, advertising is usually needed to let consumers know about them.

For many product classes, such as aspirin, salt, gasoline, packaged foods, liquor, and financial services, advertising can create

At a time when sport utility vehicles were so popular that competing companies all seemed to be offering the same benefits, Jeep (www.jeep.com) positioned itself as the "only one" to go anywhere on the planet. Positioning is important in tight markets to help differentiate similar products.

shows, there are many ways to classify tangible goods: by markets, by the purchasing habits of buyers, by the consumption rate or degree of tangibility, or by physical attributes.

▼ **EXHIBIT 4–12** What's new? Not much. Consumers didn't think these products were as new as they claimed to be, as indicated by the grades awarded.

Product	New and Different	Purchase Probability	Price/Value	Overall Grade
Airwick Botanicals	F	A	A	B
Mr. Clean Glass & Surface Cleaner	F	A	A	B
Spic & Span with Bleach	F	A	B	B
Aspirin-Free Bayer Select	F	B	B	C
Sugar Twin Plus low-calorie sweetener	F	B	A	C
Lady Power Clear Roll-On antiperspirant	F	B	A	C

Most of us might stick a thermometer in our mouths when we come down with a fever, but the Braun Thermoscan (www.braun.com) isn't just any thermometer. The company's product concept, using the ear rather than the mouth, differentiates its thermometer as one that is gentle yet effective for the temperament of children.

> Nothing is more important than being able to tell prospects truthfully that your product is different.

induced differences. Banks, brokerage houses, and insurance companies, for example, which offer virtually identical financial products and services, use advertising and promotion to differentiate themselves. However, few have yet discovered the image asset of **branding** as used by the national packaged-goods marketers. That is created through the accumulation of consistent advertising campaigns, favorable publicity, special-event sponsorship, and good word-of-mouth.[40]

Product Branding

The fundamental differentiating device for all products is the **brand**—that combination of name, words, symbols, or design that identifies the product and its source and distinguishes it from competing products. Without brands, consumers couldn't tell one product from another, and advertising them would be nearly impossible.

A manufacturer may establish an **individual brand** for each product it makes.

Chanel is one of the top perfume brands in the world. To reinforce its image of luxury and glamor, Chanel ads feature stars such as Nicole Kidman and Keira Knightley.

Unilever, for example, markets its toothpastes under the individual brand names Aim, Pepsodent, and Close-Up. Such companies designate a distinct target market for each product and develop a separate personality and image for each brand. However, this strategy is very costly.

On the other hand, a company might use a **family brand** and market different products under the same umbrella name. When Heinz promotes its ketchup, it hopes to help its relishes too. This decision may be cost effective, but one weak product in a line can hurt the whole family.

Because it is so expensive for manufacturers to market **national brands** (also called *manufacturer's brands*), some companies use a *private-labeling* strategy. They manufacture the product and sell it to resellers (distributors or dealers) who put their own brand name on the product. **Private labels** are typically sold at lower prices in big retail stores and include such

> # "Advertising is much more effective if it exploits the brand's positioning.

familiar names as Kenmore, Craftsman, and DieHard (Sears), Kirkland (Costco), 365 (Whole Foods), Lucerne (Safeway), and Sam's Choice (Walmart). They now account for almost 22 percent of the grocery items purchased.[41] The responsibility for creating brand image and familiarity with private label brands rests with the distributor or retailer, who is also the principal benefactor if the brand is successful. Recent trends have moved toward premium private labels, such as President's Choice, which has enjoyed immense success. These products feature better packaging, superior quality, and a higher price, often comparable to national brands.

Branding decisions are critical because the brands a company owns may be its most important capital asset. Imagine the value of owning a brand name such as Coca-Cola, Nike, Porsche, or Levi's. *BusinessWeek*'s annual brand-value report ranks Coca-Cola as the most valuable brand in the world, followed by Microsoft, IBM, GE, Nokia, and Toyota (see Exhibit 4–13).[42] Some companies pay a substantial fee for the right to use another company's brand name. Thus, we have **licensed brands** such as Sunkist vitamins, Coca-Cola clothing, Porsche sunglasses, and Mickey Mouse watches. Starbucks's rising status as a brand is discussed in Commercial Break 4–B.

Product packaging is important around the globe. Kern's uses colorful, attention-grabbing labels to increase sales of its Nectar line and reinforce its familiar brand name.

The Role of Branding

For consumers, brands offer instant recognition and identification. They also promise consistent, reliable standards of

quality, taste, size, or even psychological satisfaction, which adds value to the product for both the consumer and the manufacturer. In a survey conducted by TWICE/Campaigners, 44 percent of consumers ranked brand name as the most important factor when making a major electronics purchase. Price, by the way, ranked second.[43]

Brands must be built on differences in images, meanings, and associations. It's up to manufacturers to differentiate their products clearly and deliver value competitively. The product has to taste better, or get clothes cleaner, or be more environmentally friendly.[44] Advertising for an established brand, particularly a well-differentiated one, is much more effective if it exploits the brand's positioning.[45] Ideally, when consumers see a brand on the shelf, they instantly comprehend the brand's promise and have confidence in its quality. Of course, they must be familiar with and believe in the brand's promise (a function of advertising effectiveness). The goal is *brand loyalty*—because it serves both the consumer and the advertiser. For the consumer, it reduces shopping time. For the advertiser, it builds **brand equity**, the totality of what consumers, distributors, dealers—even competitors—feel and think about the brand over an extended period of time. In short, it's the value of the brand's assets.

High brand equity offers a host of blessings to a marketer: customer loyalty, price inelasticity, long-term profits. A loyal customer can be nine times as profitable as a disloyal one.[46] But building brand equity requires time and money. Brand value and preference drive market share, but share points and brand loyalty are usually won by the advertisers who spend the most. Charlotte Beers, the former head of J. Walter Thompson, believes companies must maintain consistency in their message by integrating all their marketing communications— from packaging and advertising to sales promotion and publicity—to maintain and reinforce the brand's personality and avoid mistakes such as changing the distinctive color of a Ryder rental truck.[47]

Product Packaging

The product's package is a component of the product element that can determine the outcome of retail shelf competition. In fact, packaging may be a particular brand's one differential advantage—and it's the marketer's last chance to communicate at the point of sale. Package designers (who sometimes work in

▼ **EXHIBIT 4–13** World's most valuable brands.

Rank	Brand	2007 Brand Value (in Billions)
1	Coca-Cola	$65.3
2	Microsoft	58.7
3	IBM	57.0
4	GE	51.5
5	Nokia	33.7
6	Toyota	32.0
7	Intel	30.9
8	McDonald's	29.4
9	Disney	29.1
10	Mercedes-Benz	23.6

Source: Reprinted from *BusinessWeek* by special permission. Copyright © 2007 by The McGraw-Hill Companies, Inc.

Consumers frequently associate higher prices with higher quality. Volvo (www.volvo.com) capitalizes on this by reinforcing that the safety value of its automobiles is worth a higher cost.

agencies) must make the package exciting, appealing, and at the same time functional. The four considerations in package design are *identification; containment, protection, and convenience; consumer appeal;* and *economy*. These functions may even become **copy points**—copywriting themes—in the product's advertising.

ADVERTISING AND THE PRICE ELEMENT

As we all know, the **price element** of the marketing mix influences consumer perceptions of a brand. Companies that don't compete on price typically use image advertising to create a particular perception of the company or personality for the brand. Companies that are more price-competitive may regularly use sale advertising, clearance advertising, or loss-leader advertising.

Key Factors Influencing Price

Companies typically set their prices based on market demand for the product, costs of production and distribution, competition, and corporate objectives. Interestingly, though, a company often has relatively few options for determining its price strategy, depending on the desired product concept.

Marketers believe that consumers are often less concerned with a product's actual price than with its perceived price relative to competitors. Many premium-priced brands, such as L'Oréal, are touted for the very fact that they cost more. Setting a high price to make a product seem more valuable is an example of **psychological pricing**. Image advertising may be used to justify the higher price. The important thing is that the price be consistent with the brand image; you can't charge a Rolex price for a Timex watch. And similarly, the brand's advertising must be consistent with its pricing strategy.

ADVERTISING AND THE DISTRIBUTION (PLACE) ELEMENT

Before the first ad can be created, the **place**, or **distribution**, **element** must be decided. It is important for marketers to understand that the method of distribution, like the price, must be consistent with the brand's image. People will not pay Nordstrom prices at Target. To understand Starbucks's distribution strategy, see Commercial Break 4–C.

Companies use two basic methods of distribution: *direct* or *indirect*.

Direct Distribution

When companies sell directly to end users or consumers, they use **direct distribution**. Avon, for example, employs sales

network marketing
A method of direct distribution in which individuals act as independent distributors for a manufacturer or private-label marketer.

reseller Businesses that buy products from manufacturers or wholesalers and then resell the merchandise to consumers or other buyers; also called *middlemen.* The most common examples of resellers are retail stores and catalog retailers.

distribution channel The network of all the firms and individuals that take title, or assist in taking title, to the product as it moves from the producer to the consumer.

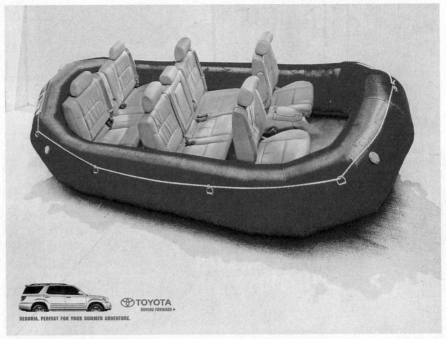

Toyota dealers, like dealers for many other auto manufacturers, share the cost of their advertising through regional cooperatives. For example, the 165 dealerships that fall under the Southeast Toyota Distributors (*www.jmfamily.com/SET/default.htm*) umbrella would have split the expenses for this print ad.

reps who sell directly to consumers. Medical equipment suppliers and insurance companies often sell and distribute their products and services directly to customers without the use of wholesalers or retailers. In these cases, the advertising burden is carried entirely by the manufacturer.

One of the fastest-growing methods of direct distribution today is **network marketing** (also called *multilevel marketing*), in which individuals act as independent distributors for a manufacturer or private-label marketer. These people sign up friends and relatives to consume the company's products and recruit others to join. Through a gradual, word-of-mouth process, they form a "buying club" of independent distributors who buy the products wholesale direct from the company, use them, and tout them to more and more friends and acquaintances.

The Internet may be the ultimate direct distribution vehicle. As we will discuss in Chapter 13, Web sites allow marketers like Dell computers to make direct contact with

their customers, develop interactive relationships, and consummate the sale of their products or services, all at a lower cost than any other method. The Internet is not appropriate for the distribution of all products, but its acceptance is rapidly spreading.

Indirect Distribution

Manufacturers usually don't sell directly to end users or consumers. Most companies market their products through a *distribution channel* that includes a network of *resellers.* A **reseller** (also called a *middleman*) is a business firm that operates between the producer and the consumer or industrial purchaser. It deals in trade rather than production.[48] Resellers include both wholesalers and retailers, as well as manufacturers' representatives, brokers, jobbers, and distributors. A **distribution channel** comprises all the firms and individuals that take responsibility for the product as it moves from the producer to the consumer.

The advertising a company uses depends on the product's method of distribution. Much of the advertising we see is not prepared or paid for by the manufacturer, but by the distributor or retailer.

An important part of the marketing strategy is determining the amount of coverage necessary for a product. Procter & Gamble, for example, distributes Crest toothpaste to virtually every supermarket and discount, drug, and variety store. Other products might need only one dealer for every 50,000 people. Consumer goods manufacturers traditionally use one of three distribution strategies: *intensive*, *selective*, or *exclusive*.

Intensive Distribution Soft drinks, candy, Timex watches, and other convenience goods are available at every possible location because of **intensive distribution**. In fact, consumers can buy them with a minimum of effort. The profit on each unit is usually very low, but the volume of sales is high. The sales burden is usually carried by the manufacturer's national advertising. Ads in trade magazines *push* the product into the retail "pipeline," and in mass media they stimulate consumers to *pull* the products through the pipeline. As a manufacturer modifies its strategy to more push or more pull, special promotions may be directed at the trade or at consumers to build brand volume.

Selective Distribution By limiting the number of outlets through **selective distribution**, manufacturers can cut their distribution and promotion costs. Many hardware tools are sold

Starbucks and the Place Element [4–C]

The *place* (or distribution) element of marketing strategy is always integral to successful business. You may have the most wonderful product in the world—but potential customers won't buy it if they can't find it.

Starbucks is a phenomenon that changed the way people view coffee. This can be explained, in large part, by the creative use of the place element. You'll notice that Starbucks cafés are found in high-traffic, high-visibility locations in each of their market areas. In some markets, Starbucks seems to appear on virtually every street corner. Although the average consumer may find this excessive, Starbucks actually picks and plans each retail location with great care.

To a company like Starbucks, street space is the same as shelf space. In this sense, buying out existing coffeehouses is the same as Coca-Cola buying shelf space in supermarkets. Starbucks's management believes that chain expansion is as much a part of the company's success as is its coffee bar and customer service concepts. Since its opening, stores have sprouted up in virtually every major city across the globe, and Starbucks has no intention of stopping. Opening stores at a rate of three to four per day, Starbucks has more than 16,000 stores worldwide.

Aside from its store locations, Starbucks's unique coffee blends are now found in selected airlines, restaurants, hotels, and supermarkets. Additional venues include a mail-order business, a coast-to-coast alliance with Barnes & Noble bookstores, partnerships with major grocery chains, distribution to the Washington State Ferry system, Holland America Line–Westours cruises, Safeco Field in Seattle, Hyatt Hotels, and Chicago's Wrigley Field.

commercial break

Starbucks is also joining the Internet craze. Starting in 2001, Starbucks began a campaign to integrate high-speed wireless Internet access terminals at some stores. With thousands of stores currently up and running with Internet access, customers are now able to browse the Net, send e-mails, and drink their coffee all at the same time.

Obviously, Starbucks intends to fully saturate every coffee market. When consumers go shopping for groceries, they aren't likely to make a separate trip to Starbucks for coffee. So Starbucks now competes directly with other specialty coffees sold in supermarkets. In 1998 Kraft Foods signed on with Starbucks and agreed to distribute and market Starbucks coffee beans in more than 25,000 grocery stores in the United States. Kraft is the largest packaged-food company in North America. This collaboration is a major stepping-stone in surpassing Folgers as the leading coffee brand in the United States. Other placement strategies include the incorporation of Starbucks's latest product, the DoubleShot, into supermarkets. By partnering with PepsiCo in developing and implementing the new drink, Starbucks can take advantage of PepsiCo's vast network of distribution channels and place its product almost anywhere, bringing the company one step closer to its original dream—"Planet Starbucks."

Applying the Breaks
Take the product you used in Commercial Break 4–B and compare the distribution principles used by Starbucks with your product. In addition, think about the factors that should be considered when placing your product or service in other venues. How does it compare with Starbucks?

cooperative (co-op) advertising The sharing of advertising costs by the manufacturer and the distributor or retailer. The manufacturer may repay 50 or 100 percent of the dealer's advertising costs or some other amount based on sales.

exclusive distribution The strategy of limiting the number of wholesalers or retailers who can sell a product in order to gain a prestige image, maintain premium prices, or protect other dealers in a geographic region.

selectively through home-improvement centers and hardware stores. Automobile manufacturers limit the number of dealers that can sell their cars in each market. Levi Strauss sells through better department and chain stores. Manufacturers may use national advertising, but the sales burden is normally carried by the retailer. The manufacturer may share part of the retailer's advertising costs through a **cooperative advertising** program, as we discussed in Chapter 3. For example, a Levi's retailer may receive substantial allowances from the manufacturer for advertising Levi's clothing in its local area. In return, the retailer agrees to advertise and display the clothing prominently.

Exclusive Distribution Some manufacturers grant **exclusive distribution** rights to a wholesaler or retailer in one geographic region. For example, a small city is not likely to have more than one Jaguar dealer. This is also common in high fashion, major appliances, and furniture lines. What is lost in market coverage is often gained in the ability to maintain a prestige image and premium prices. Exclusive distribution agreements also force manufacturers and retailers to cooperate closely in advertising and promotion programs.

Vertical Marketing Systems: The Growth of Franchising

To be efficient, members of a distribution channel need to cooperate closely with one another. This need gave rise to the **vertical marketing system (VMS)**, a centrally programmed and managed distribution system that supplies or otherwise serves a group of stores or other businesses.

There are many types of vertical marketing systems. ACE Hardware is an example of a **retail cooperative**. For the last quarter century, the greatest growth has been in **franchising**—such as McDonald's or Mailboxes Etc.—in which retail dealers (or *franchisees*) pay a fee to operate under the guidelines and direction of the parent company or manufacturer (the *franchisor*). It's now estimated that 50 percent of all retail sales in the United States are made

through franchise outlets,[49] although there are only 1,500 registered franchisors throughout the United States and Canada, compared to some 1.5 million retail businesses in the United States alone.[50]

Franchising and other vertical marketing systems offer both manufacturers and retailers numerous advantages, not the least of which are centralized coordination of marketing efforts and substantial savings and continuity in advertising. Perhaps most important is consumer recognition: The moment a new McDonald's opens, the franchisee has instant customers. Moreover, a single newspaper ad can promote all of a chain's retailers in a particular trading area.

Many marketers find that franchising is the best way to introduce their services into global markets. Subway sandwich shops, for example, is one of the fastest-growing franchise operations in the world with a total of more than 33,000 stores in 92 countries.[51]

ADVERTISING AND THE PROMOTION (COMMUNICATION) ELEMENT

Once it determines product, price, and distribution, a company is ready to plan its marketing communications, of which advertising is just one component. The **promotion**, or **communication**, **element** includes all marketing-related communications between the seller and the buyer. (See Commercial Break 4–D.)

Marketing communications (often called *marcom*) refers to all the planned messages that companies and organizations create and disseminate to support their marketing objectives and strategies. In addition to advertising, major marketing communication tools include *personal selling, sales promotion, direct marketing,* and *public relations activities*. The extent to which an organization uses any or all of these tools again depends on its marketing needs.

Each marketing communication tool offers particular opportunities and benefits to the marketer. In Chapters 16 and 17 we will discuss how these tools can best be integrated into the *marketing mix*. Since advertising people are frequently called on to solve a variety of marketing problems, it is critical that they understand how to

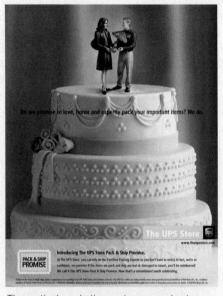

The vertical marketing system gave rise to a number of successful business plans, like franchising, in which franchisees pay a fee and operate under the guidelines of a parent company. For instance, the nearly 4,400 The UPS Store locations are franchised and provide greater access to UPS shipping services in addition to packing services and supplies, copying, digital printing, and more.

vertical marketing system (VMS) A centrally programmed and managed system that supplies or otherwise serves a group of stores or other businesses.

retail cooperative A group of independent retailers who establish a central buying organization to acquire discounts from manufacturers and gain economies from joint advertising and promotion efforts.

franchising A type of vertical marketing system in which dealers pay a fee to operate under the guidelines and direction of the parent company or manufacturer.

promotion (communication) element Includes all market-related communications between the seller and the buyer.

marketing communications The various efforts and tools companies use to initiate and maintain communication with customers and prospects, including solicitation letters, newspaper ads, event sponsorships, publicity, telemarketing, statement stuffers, and coupons.

Price and Promotion [4-D]

Starbucks classifies its product as "gourmet" coffee—in other words, it's positioned as a premium product. This suggests that it probably costs more than the typical coffee in the supermarket. However, since Starbucks targets a younger demographic of 20- to 49-year-olds, it must still be careful about how much it charges. Currently, regular brewed coffee at Starbucks costs $1.55, but the most expensive beverage runs approximately $5.00. Whole-bean coffee ranges from $9.95 to $16.50 per pound. Overall, Starbucks coffee may be a bit pricier, but it offers a higher-quality product and tries to add value through superior employee service.

To promote awareness, many new companies dedicate enormous budgets to advertising. However, this is not always necessary. Starbucks certainly never dreamed it could establish the degree of brand loyalty that it did in such a short time. But it managed to do so with only a minimal amount of advertising. It wasn't that the company didn't believe in advertising; it just didn't think it could afford to advertise. So Starbucks focused on creating product value and giving better service.

Initially, the only promotional elements the company used were public relations and some small sales promotions. These were designed to create initial awareness and interest in its gourmet coffees. As interest and awareness have grown, so have promotional activities. Among the new campaigns was the "Matches Made over Coffee" contest. To strengthen its brand and celebrate coffeehouse romances, Starbucks devised a competition in which the winner with the most "creative, romantic, and coffee-rich, true love story" would receive an all-expense-paid trip for two to Vienna, Austria.

To demonstrate its social concern, Starbucks also ventured into philanthropic activities. In fact, it is now the largest corporate sponsor of CARE, an international relief and development organization that aids the very communities from which the company buys its coffee.

With the coffee culture trend growing, increased competition was a given, forcing Starbucks to spend more on advertising to maintain its market share. Initially,

Starbucks spent $17.8 million on a direct-response campaign. It also sold merchandise such as mugs, coffee grinders, espresso machines, and gourmet food bearing the Starbucks logo via catalog and the Internet. While Starbucks continued its public relations involvement with communities, it recognized the growing need to invest in mass-media advertising. Its first major campaign began in 1997, under the creative design of Goodby, Silverstein & Partners, to promote its new Frappuccino beverage. Three television and three radio spots were created for the campaign, focusing on the jingle "Starbucks, purveyors of coffee, tea, and sanity." In the fall of 1997, though, Starbucks changed agencies and hired BBDO West, claiming that Goodby hadn't yet found the right "creative voice" for Starbucks. Since then, Starbucks has utilized the creative input of numerous top agencies, including Fallon as well as Saatchi & Saatchi.

The current focus of Starbucks's advertising is split between individual promotions for its wide array of products, including the "What Stirs You?" tagline for the "Toffee Nut Latte," as well as more cause-related marketing programs that focus on philanthropic endeavors abroad. In an ad that ran in *The New York Times,* Starbucks conveyed its charitable efforts in coffee-producing countries through an ad that began "Every sip is born out of respect" and concluded with the tagline "We're always serving more than coffee." As more corporations such as Starbucks spread to a global level, many experts believe we are likely to see more such cause-related advertisements in the future, as these companies attempt to maintain a positive image around the world.

Applying the Breaks

When constructing the marketing mix for your chosen product or service (refer to Commercial Breaks 4–B and 4–C), consider these last two elements: price and promotion. At what level should you price your product and why? What media should you use to advertise your product or service, and why? Do you think that Starbucks should advertise in more traditional mass media or continue to focus on public relations efforts?

IT IS CRITICAL THAT ADVERTISING PEOPLE UNDERSTAND HOW TO INTEGRATE THE WHOLE MIX OF COMMUNICATIONS TECHNIQUES. "

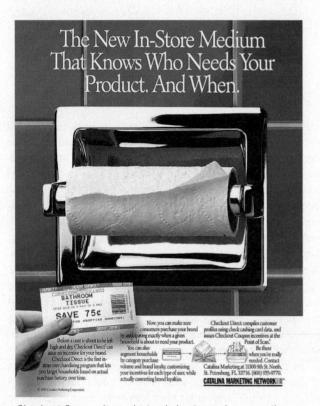

Checkout Coupon is an electronic in-store sales promotion that delivers incentives to shoppers at the checkout counter, based on what they buy. Catalina Marketing Network (www. catalinamarketing.com) helps the retailer coordinate the campaigns with tie-in of the coupons to in-store posters, shelf-talkers, savings on related store products, and newspaper ads.

integrate the whole mix of communications techniques.

For creating brand awareness, familiarity, and image, as well as for reinforcing prior purchase decisions, advertising is usually the marcom

tool of choice. Certain products lend themselves to advertising so much that it plays the dominant communications role. The following factors are particularly important for advertising success:

- Strong primary demand trend.
- Chance for significant product differentiation.
- Hidden qualities highly important to consumers.
- Opportunity to use strong emotional appeals.
- Substantial sums available to support advertising.

Where these conditions exist, companies spend large amounts on advertising, and the ratio of advertising to sales dollars is often quite high. For completely undifferentiated products, such as sugar, salt, and other raw materials or commodities, advertising is usually less important and the other marketing mix elements play a more significant role.

THE MARKETING MIX IN PERSPECTIVE

With the target market designated and the elements of the marketing mix determined, the company has a complete product concept and a strategic basis for marketing to that target. Now it can formalize its strategies and tactics in a written marketing and advertising plan. As part of the planning process, companies use marketing and advertising research. We will discuss this in Chapter 6 before dealing with the formal planning process in Chapter 7. But first we'll examine the process of human communication and some theories of consumer behavior. ■

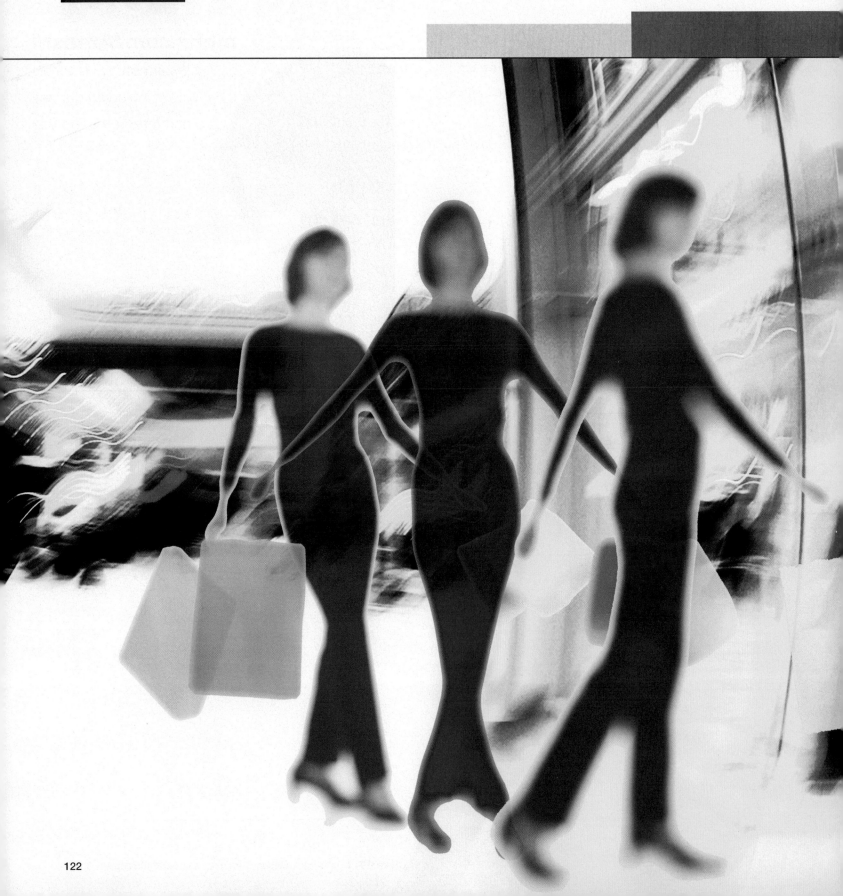

chapter five

communication and
consumer behavior

What is a great ad?[1] It could be argued that a campaign that can turn an unknown actor into an overnight sensation qualifies as great. From 1997 to 2003, Taco Bell's "spokesman" was perhaps America's favorite advertising icon. Although technically, this celebrity was not a man. Or a woman either. It was a small dog whose catchphrase, "Yo quiero Taco Bell!" became an instant classic. The dog was so popular that many were stunned when the restaurant chain discontinued the campaign and severed its relationship with the agency that created it.

Does liking an ad translate into liking the advertised product? In academic jargon, the issue is whether a favorable attitude towards an ad creates a favorable attitude towards the brand.[2] In many cases, the research literature suggests that the answer is yes.[3]

But the situation is complicated, because consumers tend to like the ads for their preferred brands. This relationship gets it backwards: attitude towards the brand creates attitude towards the ad.

And confusing matters even more, sometimes we love ads that fail to arouse interest in the advertised product. The Taco Bell Chihuahua was a case in point. People did love the ad. But those positive emotions failed to generate consumer interest in eating at Taco Bell.[4]

The history of advertising is sprinkled with cases in which agencies did a better job of creating love for the ad than love for the brand. Case in point: the first Internet superstar was a sock puppet created as the advertising mascot for Pets.com. People liked the puppet, but the company went under fairly quickly when sales failed to materialize. An Alka-Seltzer spot from the

continued on p. 124

LEARNING OBJECTIVES

LO1 Explain how advertising differs from the basic communication process.

LO2 Outline the consumer perception process and explain why advertising people say "perception is everything."

LO3 Explain how a consumer's level of involvement with a product influences the decision-making process and the advertising approach.

LO4 Describe the fundamental motives behind consumer purchases.

LO5 Discuss the various influences on consumer behavior.

MCCANN-ERICKSON, THE AD AGENCY FOR COCA-COLA AND MASTERCARD, SAYS THAT ADVERTISING IS "TRUTH WELL TOLD."

continued from p. 123

early 1970s created another phrase that entered the popular jargon, "Mamma mia, that's-a *spicy meat ball-a!*" This "ad within an ad" spot featured an actor appearing to flub takes for a fictitious brand of meatballs. His increasing heartburn was finally alleviated by Alka-Seltzer. Despite the ad's popularity, the spot stopped running after sales remained flat.[5] And America's favorite campaign from 1990 featured the newly introduced "Energizer Bunny." An *Ad Age* survey confirmed that consumers loved the ads. But research suggested that viewers were confused as to whether the pink toy was a symbol of Energizer or rival Duracell, so liking again failed to translate into sales.[6]

All of which suggests that creating great advertising involves more than creating likable advertising. Certainly from an advertiser's perspective, a truly great ad is one that engages consumers with the featured brand. Taco Bell is not in the business of selling Chihuahuas. It sells Mexican-themed fast food. The Taco Bell ads that run today may not feature a cute dog. But they do give consumers a "reason-why" they should consider Taco Bell restaurants when they are looking for an inexpensive break from the hamburgers.

In the end, it is not that difficult to excite people about a cute dog, a funny puppet, or a feisty plush toy. Exciting people about fast food, pet supplies, or batteries? That is great advertising. ■

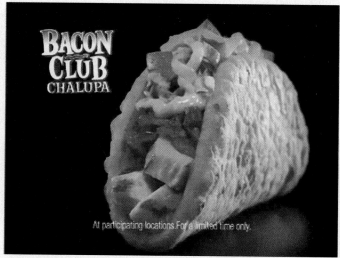

COMMUNICATION: WHAT MAKES ADVERTISING UNIQUE

In the last chapter, we learned that communication is a key element of the marketing mix. However, for communication to be effective, the marketer must construct a message that is meaningful to consumers and that will elicit the desired behavior.

In Chapter 1, we defined advertising as "the structured and composed nonpersonal communication of information." Advertising is a special kind of communication. McCann-Erickson, the ad agency for Coca-Cola and MasterCard, says that advertising is "Truth well told." This means that ethical advertisers and their agencies work as a team to discover the best methods possible to tell their story truthfully and creatively. To succeed, they must understand the elements of the advertising communication process, which is derived from the basic human communication process.

LO1 Explain how advertising differs from the basic communication process.

The Human Communication Process

From our first cry at birth, survival depends on our ability to inform others or persuade them to take action. As we develop, we learn to listen and respond to others' messages. The traditional model in Exhibit 5–1 summarizes the series of events that take place when people share ideas in informal oral communication. The process begins when one party, the source, formulates an idea, encodes it as a message, and sends it via some channel to another party, the receiver. The receiver must decode the message in order to understand it. To respond, the receiver formulates a new idea, encodes it, and then sends the new message back through some channel. A message that acknowledges or responds to the original message constitutes feedback, which also affects the encoding of a new message.[7] And, of course, all this takes place in an environment characterized by noise—the distracting cacophony of many other messages being sent at the same time by other sources.

Applying the Communication Process to Advertising

Applying this model to advertising, we could say that the source is the sponsor, the message is the ad, the channel is the medium, the receiver is the consumer or prospect, and the noise is the din of competing ads and other messages. A good deal of advertising today is a one-way process, with the message moving from the sponsor to the consumer. However, interactive forms of marketing—personal selling, telemarketing, digital advertising—let consumers participate in the communication by extracting the information they need, manipulating what they see and hear, and responding in real time.

The Source The ultimate **source** of a marketing message is the organization that has information it wishes to share with others. However, within the context of an advertisement, a real or imaginary spokesperson actually lends voice or tone to the communication. Because the receiver's perception of the source influences the effectiveness of the communication, the spokesperson must appear to be knowledgeable, trustworthy, and relevant to the audience.

▼**EXHIBIT 5–1** The human communication process.

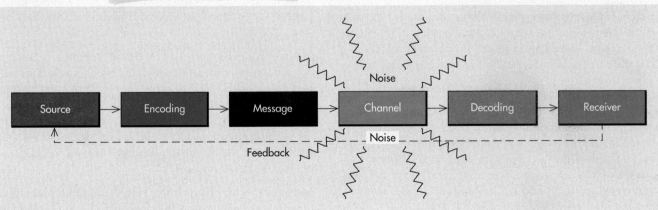

The Message The information contained in a **message** must be **encoded** so that the receiver understands what is being communicated. This involves using words or symbols that are familiar to the intended audience. Depending on the medium used, the message may be verbal or nonverbal. **Semiotics** is the study of how humans use words, gestures, signs, and symbols to convey feelings, thoughts, ideas, and ideologies.[8] For example, the cowboy in the Marlboro advertisements symbolizes ruggedness and individualism. The Energizer bunny communicates reliability and persistence.

The Channel The **channel** is the means by which the encoded message travels from the source to the receiver. Communications channels can be categorized as personal or nonpersonal. **Personal channels**, such as personal selling, involve direct contact between

A deep discussion about youth, beauty, and water.

evian your natural source of youth

Symbols are often used in advertising to encode messages. In this ad, Evian (www.evian.com) uses a flower to symbolize water's ability to restore, revitalize, replenish, and hydrate. Evian would like you to think of its spring water as a beauty product.

of the receivers are also very important, and the sponsor may know little or nothing about them. We'll see later in this chapter that attitudes, perceptions, personality, self-concept, and culture are just some of the many influences that affect the way people receive and respond to messages and how they behave as consumers.

Complicating this problem is the fact that the sponsor's advertising message must compete with hundreds of other commercial and noncommercial messages every day. This is referred to as **noise**. So the sender doesn't know how the message is received, or even if it is received, unless a consumer acknowledges it.

Feedback and Interactivity That's why **feedback** is so important. It completes the cycle, verifying that the message was received. Feedback employs the sender-message-receiver

> With interactive media such as the Internet, consumers can give instantaneous, real-time feedback.

the parties. **Nonpersonal channels** of communication are those that rule out interpersonal contact between the sender and the receiver. Mass communications, such as television, newspapers, magazines, radio, and billboards, are sent to many individuals at one time.

The Receiver The **receiver** is usually the consumer who receives the advertiser's message. The advertiser must always be concerned about how the consumer will **decode**, or interpret, a message. The last thing an advertiser wants is to be misunderstood. Unfortunately, message interpretation is only partially determined by the words and symbols in the ad. The advertising medium may have an effect as well. As Marshall McLuhan said, "The medium is the message." The unique characteristics

pattern, except that it is directed from the receiver back to the source.

In advertising, feedback can take many forms: redeemed coupons, phone inquiries, visits to a store, requests for more information, increased sales, responses to a survey, e-mail inquiries, or clicks on a banner ad. Dramatically low responses to an ad indicate a break in the communication process. Questions arise: Is the product wrong for the market? Is the message unclear? Are we using the right media? Without feedback, these questions cannot be answered.

In the past, the consumer's feedback used different channels than the original message. But now, thanks again to technology, the audiences of advertising are no longer just passive receivers

nonpersonal channels Means of communication that don't involve interpersonal contact between the sender and the receiver. Examples would include advertising, publicity, and sales promotion.

receiver In oral communication, this party decodes the message to understand it.

decode To interpret a message by the receiver.

noise The sender's advertising message competing daily with hundreds of other commercial and noncommercial messages.

feedback A message that acknowledges or responds to an initial message.

interactive media Media such as the Internet and interactive television that permit consumers to give instantaneous, real-time feedback on the same channel used by the original message sender.

consumer behavior The activities, actions, and influences of people who purchase and use goods and services to satisfy their personal or household needs and wants.

consumer decision process The series of steps a consumer goes through in deciding to make a purchase.

of impersonal mass messages. They are now active decision makers who can control what communications they receive and choose the information they want about a particular product. With **interactive media** such as the Internet, they can give instantaneous, real-time feedback on the same channel used by the original message sender.

CONSUMER BEHAVIOR: THE KEY TO ADVERTISING STRATEGY

Effective communication happens when the marketer selects a relevant source, develops an appropriate message, encodes it correctly, and then finds a suitable medium that will best reach the target audience. All of these steps rely upon the marketer knowing the receiver of the message and understanding how that individual might respond.

Take a look at your friends in class, or the people you work with. How well do you know them? Could you describe their lifestyles and the kinds of products they prefer? Do they typically eat out or cook for themselves? Do they ski? Play tennis? If so, what brands of equipment do they buy? Do you know which radio stations they listen to? What TV programs they watch? What Web sites they visit? If you were Sony's advertising manager and wanted to advertise a new Blue-ray player to these people, what type of appeal would you use? What media would you use to reach them?

The Importance of Knowing the Consumer

Advertisers spend a lot of money to keep individuals and groups of individuals (markets) interested in their products. To succeed, they need to understand what makes potential customers behave the way they do. The advertiser's goal is to get enough relevant market data to develop accurate profiles of buyers—to find the common ground (and symbols) for communication. This involves the study of **consumer behavior**: the mental and emotional processes and the physical activities of people who purchase and use goods and services to satisfy particular needs and wants.[9]

The Consumer Decision Process: An Overview

Social scientists have many theories of consumer behavior to explain the process of making a purchase decision. Let's look at this information from the viewpoint of the advertiser.

Advertising's primary mission is to reach prospective customers and influence their awareness, attitudes, and buying behavior. To succeed, an advertiser must make the marketing communications process work very effectively.

The moment we receive an advertising message, our mental computer runs a rapid evaluation called the **consumer decision process**. The conceptual model in Exhibit 5–2 presents the basic steps we go through in making a purchase decision. As you can see, the full process involves a rather lengthy sequence of activities: *problem recognition* (which may occur as a result of seeing an ad), *information search, evaluation and selection* of alternative brands, *store choice and purchase,* and finally *postpurchase behavior.* For simple, habitual, everyday purchases

DON'T BE SURPRISED IF THE MISSUS STARTS REFERRING TO YOU AS HER

PERSONAL MECHANICAL BULL

KEMO SABE

ASPEN | VAIL

personal processes
The three internal, human operations—perception, learning, and motivation— that govern the way consumers discern raw data (stimuli) and translate them into feelings, thoughts, beliefs, and actions.

interpersonal influences Social influences on the consumer decision-making process, including family, society, and cultural environment.

nonpersonal influences Factors influencing the consumer decision-making process that are often out of the consumer's control, such as time, place, and environment.

evaluation of alternatives Choosing among brands, sizes, styles, and colors.

postpurchase evaluation Determining whether a purchase has been a satisfactory or unsatisfactory one.

▼**EXHIBIT 5–2** The basic consumer decision process is a set of steps that the consumer experiences during and after the purchase. Advertising and other influences can affect the consumer's attitude at any point in this process.

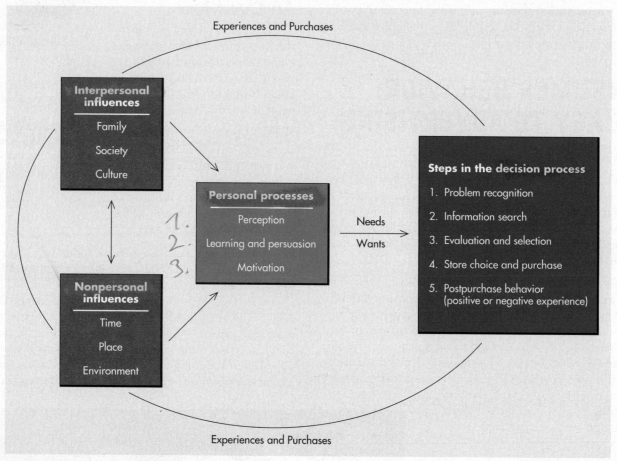

with low levels of involvement, the decision-making process is typically very abbreviated. But in those situations where we are highly involved in the purchase, it's not at all unusual for us to substantially extend the decision process.

Whether the process is limited or extended, though, numerous sociological and psychological factors invariably play a role in the way we behave. These include a series of personal subprocesses that are themselves shaped by various influences.

The three **personal processes** govern the way we discern raw data (stimuli) and translate them into feelings, thoughts, beliefs, and actions. The personal processes are the *perception,* the *learning and persuasion,* and the *motivation* processes.

Second, our mental processes and behavior are affected by two sets of influences. **Interpersonal influences** include

our *family, society,* and *culture.* **Nonpersonal influences**— factors often outside the consumer's control—include *time, place,* and *environment.* These influences further affect the personal processes of perception, learning, and motivation.

After dealing with these processes and influences, we face the pivotal decision: to buy or not to buy. But taking that final step typically requires yet another process, the **evaluation of alternatives**, in which we choose brands, sizes, styles, and colors. If we do decide to buy, our **postpurchase evaluation** will influence our subsequent purchases.

Like the communications process, the decision process is circular in nature. What we learn from one experience influences our behavior the next time. The advertiser who understands this process can develop messages more likely to reach and make sense to consumers.

perception Our
personalized way of sensing
and comprehending stimuli.

If they find MonsterMalt satisfying, they likely will continue to purchase it. These three personal processes of consumer behavior—perception, learning and persuasion, and motivation—are extremely important to advertisers. By studying these, advertisers can better evaluate how their messages are perceived.

LO2 Outline the consumer perception process and explain why advertising people say "perception is everything."

check yourself ✓

1. What is meant by noise and how might it affect an advertiser's efforts?
2. What are the key differences between human communication and advertising communication?

PERSONAL PROCESSES IN CONSUMER BEHAVIOR

Assume you are the advertising manager preparing to launch a new high-tech, vitamin-laden beverage brand for athletes and sports participants. We'll call it MonsterMalt. What's your first objective?

The first task in promoting any new product is to create awareness *(perception)* that the product exists. The second is to provide enough compelling information *(learning and persuasion)* about the product for prospective customers to become interested and make an informed decision. Finally, you want your advertising to stimulate customers' desire *(motivation)* to satisfy their needs and wants by trying the product.

The Consumer Perception Process

Perception is everything. It guides all our activities from the people we associate with to the products we buy. How a consumer perceives each of the different brands in a category determines which ones he or she uses.[10] The perception challenge, therefore, is the first and greatest hurdle advertisers must cross. Some marketers spend millions of dollars on national advertising, sales promotion, point-of-purchase displays, and other marketing communications only to discover that many consumers don't remember the product or the promotion. The average adult may be exposed to thousands of ads each day but notices only a handful and remembers even fewer.[11] How does this happen? The answer lies in the principle of perception.

We use the term **perception** to refer to the personalized way we sense, interpret, and comprehend various *stimuli*. This definition suggests there are several key elements to the consumer perception process, as shown in Exhibit 5–3.

> # The perception challenge is the first and greatest hurdle advertisers must cross.

▼ **EXHIBIT 5–3** The model of the consumer perception process portrays how consumers perceive, accept, and remember an ad or other stimulus to buy.

Physical data (stimuli)	Physiological screens (sensory)	Psychological screens (emotional)	Cognition (awareness)	Mental files (memory)
• Ad/commercial • Promotion • News item • Product/store • Price tag • Conversation	• Sight • Hearing • Touch • Taste • Smell	• Personality • Self-concept • Attitudes • Beliefs • Habits	Awareness Nonawareness	• Information • Needs • Wants

Feedback

Stimulus

A **stimulus** is physical information we receive through our senses. When we look at a new car, we receive a number of stimuli. We might note the color of the paint, the smell of the leather, the purr of the engine. When we look at a theater ad in the newspaper, we see a collection of type, art, and photography arranged in a way that we interpret as an ad. That's the stimulus. So, for our purposes, assume that a stimulus is any ad, commercial, or promotion that we see.

Advertising stimuli can appear in a variety of forms: a window display at a local department store, the brightly colored labels on cans of Campbell's tomato soup, or even the red price tag on a pair of skis at the Sport Chalet. These objects are all physical in nature; they stimulate our senses (with varying degrees of intensity) in ways that can be measured.

Perceptual Screens

The second key element in perception is the personalized way of sensing and interpreting the stimulus data. Before any data can be perceived, they must first penetrate a set of **perceptual screens**, the subconscious filters that shield us from unwanted messages. There are two types of screens, *physiological* and *psychological*.

The **physiological screens** comprise the five senses: sight, hearing, touch, taste, and smell. They detect incoming data and measure the dimension and intensity of the physical stimuli. A sight-impaired person can't read an ad in *Sports Illustrated*. And if the type in a movie ad is too small for the average reader, it won't be read, and perception will suffer. Similarly, if the music in a TV commercial for a furniture store is not complementary to the message, the viewer may tune out, change channels, or even turn off the TV. The advertiser's

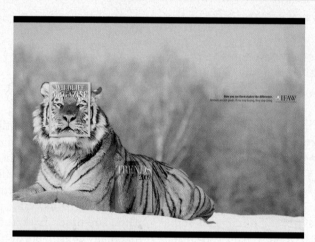

Screens are barriers that ads must penetrate. This is acknowledged in this ad for the IFAW, which suggests that how you see the Tiger depends on the screen you are looking through.

Advertisers frequently capitalize on consumers' concepts of themselves to generate attention and interest in a particular product. This ad takes the next step: It shows consumers that they can temporarily identify with their wilder sides by renting a Harley-Davidson (www. harleydavidson.com).

message is effectively screened out when the viewer can't interpret it; perception does not occur, and the furniture goes unsold.[12]

We are limited not only by the physical capacity of our senses but also by our feelings and interests. Each consumer uses **psychological screens** to evaluate, filter, and personalize information according to subjective emotional standards. These screens evaluate data based on *innate factors,* such as the consumer's personality and instinctive human needs, and *learned factors,* such as self-concept, interests, attitudes, beliefs, past experiences, and lifestyle. They help consumers summarize unwieldy or complex data.

After extensive consumer research, Bally's Health & Tennis determined that the perfectly chiseled body, glorified by earlier health club advertising and exemplified by buff Hollywood stars, was no longer penetrating the psychological screens of its 4.5 million members. That premise no longer fit their **self-concept** (the image we have of who we are and who we want to be). In a major strategy shift, Bally's refocused its advertising on customers such as Beth from Costa Mesa, California, who is seen rock climbing in a TV commercial while telling viewers, "I think I climb because I'm afraid of heights. . . . There is nothing better than being able to conquer that fear. That's why I work out at Bally's, so I can do more on the rocks." The tagline: "If you can get here [Bally's], you can get there [a mountaintop]."

As this example shows, advertisers face a major problem dealing with consumers' perceptual screens. As overcommunicated consumers, we unconsciously screen out or modify many of the sensations that bombard us, rejecting those that conflict with our experiences, needs, desires, attitudes, and beliefs.[13] We simply focus on some things and ignore others. This is called **selective perception**. Hence, Olympus may run a series of outstanding ads for its new digital camera in the daily newspaper, but they won't penetrate the psychological screens of consumers who don't need or want a new camera. Later these people probably won't even remember seeing the ads.

Cognition
The third key element in perception is **cognition**: comprehending the stimulus. Once we detect the stimulus and allow it through our perceptual screens, we have the opportunity to understand and accept it. Now perception can occur, and the stimulus reaches the consumer's reality zone.

But each of us has his or her own reality. For example, you may consider the tacos advertised by Taco Bell to be "Mexican" food. That perception is your reality. But someone from Mexico might tell you that a fast-food taco bears little resemblance to an authentic Mexican taco. That person's reality, based on another perception, is considerably different. As much as possible, advertisers seek commonly shared perceptions of reality as a basis for their advertising messages.

Mental Files
The mind is like a memory bank, and the stored memories in our minds are called the **mental files** (or perceptual files). Just as stimuli bombard our senses, information crowds our mental files in today's overcommunicative society. To cope with the complexity of stimuli such as advertising, we rank products and other data in our files by importance, price,

perceptions can rarely be changed through advertising alone.[15] But once a new perception does enter our mental files, the information alters the database on which our psychological screens feed.

Because perceptual screens are such a major challenge to advertisers, it's important to understand what's in the consumer's mental files and, if possible, modify them in favor of the advertiser's product. That brings us to the second process in consumer behavior: *learning and persuasion.*

LO3 Explain how a consumer's level of involvement with a product influences the decision-making process and the advertising approach.

> As overcommunicated consumers, we unconsciously screen out or modify many of the sensations that bombard us.

quality, features, or a host of other descriptors. Consumers can rarely hold more than seven brand names in any one file—more often only one or two. The remainder either get discarded to some other file category or rejected altogether.[14] How many brands of running shoes can you quickly name, for example?

Because of our limited memory, we resist opening new mental files, and we avoid accepting new information inconsistent with what is already filed. Experiences consumers have using a brand help to solidify their perceptions of it. These fixed

Learning, Persuasion, and the Role of Involvement in the Ways that Consumers Process Information

By definition, **learning** is a relatively permanent change in thought process or behavior that occurs as a result of experience. Like perception, learning works off the mental files and at the same time contributes to them. Learning produces our habits and skills. It also contributes to the development of interests, attitudes, beliefs, preferences, prejudices, emotions, and standards of conduct—all of which affect our perceptual screens and our purchase decisions.

Theories of Learning

There are numerous theories of learning, but advertisers classify most into two broad categories—*cognitive theory* and *conditioning theory*—depending on the level of consumer involvement (high or low) required to make a purchase. **Cognitive theory** views learning as a mental process of memory, thinking, and the rational application of knowledge to practical problems. This theory may be an accurate description of how we learn from the experience of others, such as our parents, and how we evaluate a complex purchase such as insurance, stocks and bonds, or business products. **Conditioning theory**—also called **stimulus-response theory**—treats learning as a trial-and-error process. Some stimulus (perhaps an ad) triggers the consumer's need or want, and this in turn creates the drive to respond. If the consumer's response reduces the drive, then satisfaction occurs, and the response is rewarded or reinforced. And that produces repeat behavior the next time the drive is aroused, demonstrating that learning has taken place. Exhibit 5–4 shows simple diagrams of these two theories.

What determines which type of process, conditioning or cognitive, consumers are likely to use when learning information? **Consumer involvement** appears to play an important role. Involvement refers to how important or relevant a decision is to a consumer. More important and personally relevant decisions result in greater involvement.

Conditioning theory is more applicable to the simple, basic, low involvement purchases consumers make every day, such as soap, cereal, toothpaste, and paper towels. And it is here that reinforcement advertising plays its most important role—along with superior product performance and good service. If learning is reinforced enough and repeat behavior is produced, a purchasing habit may result. Cognitive theories seem most applicable in highly involving situations, as when a consumer buys a car or an expensive TV.

Learning and persuasion are closely linked. **Persuasion** occurs when the change in belief, attitude, or behavioral intention is caused by promotion communication (such as advertising or personal selling).[16] Naturally, advertisers are very interested in persuasion and how it takes place.

The Elaboration Likelihood Model

Researchers have identified *central* and *peripheral routes to persuasion*. As with learning theory, each depends on the consumer's level of

▼ **EXHIBIT 5–4** Cognitive theory views learning as a mental process; conditioning theory treats learning as a trial-and-error process.

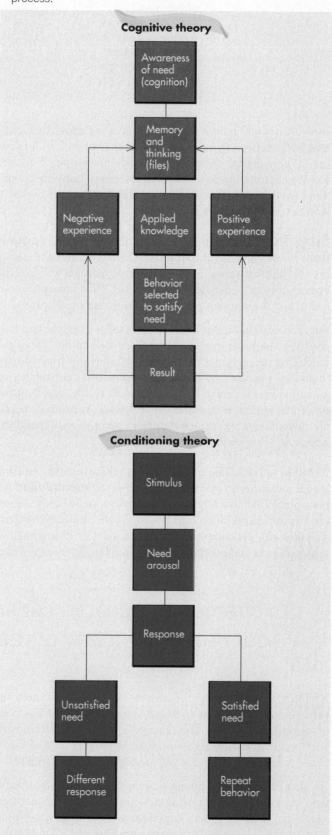

Cognitive theory

- Awareness of need (cognition)
- Memory and thinking (files)
- Negative experience
- Applied knowledge
- Positive experience
- Behavior selected to satisfy need
- Result

Conditioning theory

- Stimulus
- Need arousal
- Response
- Unsatisfied need
- Satisfied need
- Different response
- Repeat behavior

▼ **EXHIBIT 5–5** The Elaboration Likelihood Model.

involvement with the product and the message. When the consumer's level of involvement is higher, the central route to persuasion is more likely. On the other hand, the peripheral route to persuasion predominates when consumer involvement is low.[17]

We can see how this works by looking at the **Elaboration Likelihood Model** in Exhibit 5–5. In the **central route to persuasion**, consumers have a higher level of involvement with the product or the message, so they are motivated to pay attention to the central, product-related information, such as product attributes and benefits or demonstrations of positive functional or psychological consequences. Because of their high involvement, they tend to learn cognitively and comprehend the ad-delivered information at deeper, more elaborate levels. This can lead to product beliefs, positive brand attitudes, and purchase intention.[18]

Suppose you are in the market for a significant purchase, say, a new camera or a computer. Because the purchase is relatively expensive, your level of involvement is higher. Perhaps you ask for advice from some friends or family members. You may shop different stores to compare models and prices. And you probably read ads for these products thoroughly to understand the variety of product features and benefits. That's central processing. And in that situation, a well-written, informative ad that provides compelling reasons to buy can be very persuasive.

The **peripheral route to persuasion** is very different. It's more like stimulus-response learning. People who are not in the market for a product typically have low involvement with the product message. They have little or no reason to pay attention to it or to comprehend the central information of the ad. As a result, direct persuasion is also low, and consumers form few if any brand beliefs, attitudes, or purchase intentions. However, these consumers might attend to some peripheral aspects—attractive sources, up-tempo music, exciting editing—for their entertainment value. And whatever they feel or think about these peripheral, nonproduct aspects might integrate into a positive attitude toward the ad. At some later date, if a purchase occasion does arise and the consumer needs to make some brand evaluation, these ad-related meanings could be activated to form some brand attitude or purchase intention.

Because very few people are actually in the market at any given time, most mass media advertising receives peripheral processing. We all know that most of the ads we see have little

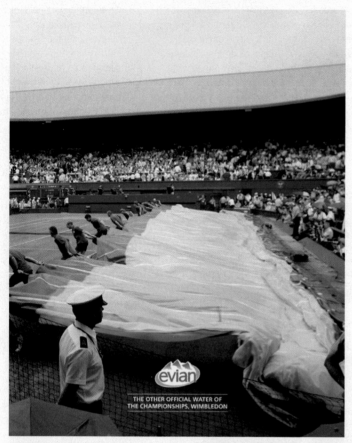

Evian relies on a humorous image and an association with Wimbledon in this clever attempt to persuade via the peripheral route.

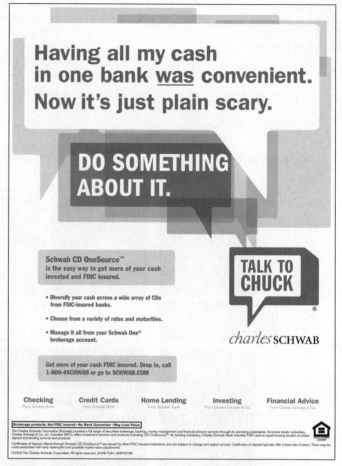

For the high-involvement consumer, information is everything. Schwab offers useful facts to its prospects because strong arguments are important in central route processing.

relevance to our immediate goals or needs, so we are not motivated to think about them. Our involvement is very low. That's why we also have very little recall of ads we saw yesterday. In cases where there is little product differentiation, advertisers may actually *want* us to engage in peripheral processing. Their ads focus more on image or entertainment than product features.

But when a product has a distinct advantage, the advertiser's goal should be to encourage central route processing by increasing consumers' involvement with the message. This is where we see a lot of comparative advertising.[19]

One key to learning and persuasion is repetition. Just as a student prepares for an exam by repeating key information to memorize it, an advertiser must repeat key information to prospective and current customers so they remember the product's name and its benefits. Repeat messages penetrate customers' perceptual screens by rekindling memories of information from prior ads. The repetition achieved by

"Because very few people are actually in the market at any given time, most mass media advertising receives peripheral processing."

Pet.com's high level of advertising spending was intended to firmly plant the company's name and benefits in prospective customers' mental files.

Learning Produces Attitudes and Interest An **attitude** is our evaluation of some idea or object. An important advertising objective is developing messages that foster positive consumer attitudes.

In Japan, for instance, dishwashers are not a common household appliance. Not only is there very little space for them; Japanese housewives feel guilty about using the labor-saving device. As a result, dishwasher manufacturers have had to change attitudes by designing smaller, space-saving machines and then promoting them using good hygiene themes rather than convenience appeals.[20]

For mature brands in categories with familiar, frequently purchased products, *brand interest* is even more critical for motivating action. **Brand interest** is an individual's

Brand loyalty and interest are two important components of marketing automobiles. Mini USA (www.miniusa.com) has successfully maintained an image of fun and cleverness, as demonstrated by this installation in Toronto's Union Station.

openness or curiosity about a brand.[21] Enjoyable, entertaining advertising can enhance interest in the brand and reduce the variety-seeking tendencies of consumers who become bored with using the same old product.[22]

Learning Leads to Habits and Brand Loyalty

Attitude is the mental side and *habit* the behavioral side of the same coin. **Habit**—the acquired behavior pattern that becomes nearly or completely involuntary—is the natural extension of learning. We really are creatures of habit.

Most consumer behavior is habitual for three reasons: It's safe, simple, and essential. First, regardless of how we learned to make our purchase decision (through either central or peripheral route processing), if we discover a quality product, brand, or service, we feel *safe* repurchasing it through habit.

Second, habit is *simple*. To consider alternatives we must evaluate, compare, and then decide. This is difficult and time-consuming. Habits allow us to skip those steps.

Finally, because habit is both safe and easy, we rely on it for daily living. Imagine rethinking every purchase decision you make. It would be virtually impossible, not to mention impractical. So it's really *essential* to use habit in our lives.

The major objective of all brand marketers is to produce *brand loyalty*, a direct result of the habit of repurchasing and the reinforcement of continuous advertising. **Brand loyalty** is the consumer's conscious or unconscious decision, expressed through intention or behavior, to repurchase a brand continually.[23] It occurs because the consumer *perceives* that the brand offers the right product features, image, quality, or relationship at the right price.

In the quest for brand loyalty, advertisers have three aims related to habits:

1. *Breaking habits.* Get consumers to unlearn an existing purchase habit and try something new. Advertisers frequently offer incentives to lure customers away from old brands or stores. Or they may use comparative advertising to demonstrate their product's superiority. As Pets.com discovered, it is very difficult to get consumers to change their habits. Even coupons and discounts couldn't lure customers from their traditional pet products suppliers.

2. *Acquiring habits.* Teach consumers to repurchase their brand or repatronize their establishment. To get you started, Columbia House advertises free CDs when you sign up, tied to a contract to purchase more later on.

3. *Reinforcing habits.* Remind current customers of the value of their original purchase and encourage them to continue purchasing. Many magazines, for example, offer special renewal rates to their regular subscribers. Hotels offer loyalty programs and airlines award frequent flier miles for the same reason.

Developing brand loyalty is much more difficult today due to consumers' increased sophistication and the legions of habit-breaking activities of competitive advertisers.[24] Only recently have advertisers come to realize that their years of habit-breaking activities have undermined their own *habit-building* objectives. In the quest for instant results, they shifted much of their advertising budgets to sales promotions (deals, coupons, price cuts). But advertising, unlike sales promotion, is an integral part of what makes a brand salable. It's advertising that reinforces brand loyalty and maintains market share.[25] We revisit this topic in our discussion of sales promotion in Chapter 16.

motivation The underlying drives that stem from the conscious or unconscious needs of the consumer and contribute to the individual consumer's purchasing actions.

informational motives The negatively originated motives, such as problem removal or problem avoidance, that are the most common energizers of consumer behavior.

needs The basic, often instinctive, human forces that motivate us to do something.

wants Needs learned during a person's lifetime.

hierarchy of needs Maslow's theory that the lower biological or survival needs are dominant in human behavior and must be satisfied before higher, socially acquired needs become meaningful.

negatively originated motives Consumer purchase and usage based on problem removal or problem avoidance. To relieve such feelings, consumers actively seek a new or replacement product.

Learning Defines Needs and Wants

The learning process is both immediate and long term. The moment we file a perception, some learning takes place. When we see a succulent food ad, we may suddenly feel hungry; we *need* food. As we collate the information in our mental files, comparing new perceptions with old ones, further learning takes place. The need may become a *want*. This leads to the next personal process, motivation.

check yourself ✓

1. What is the difference between the central route and the peripheral route to persuasion?

2. What is the difference between the cognitive theory and the conditioning theory of learning?

3. What is the role of involvement in learning and persuasion?

LO4 Describe the fundamental motives behind consumer purchases.

The Consumer Motivation Process

Motivation refers to the underlying forces (or motives) that contribute to our actions. These motives stem from the conscious or unconscious goal of satisfying our needs and wants. **Needs** are the basic, often instinctive, human forces that motivate us to do something. **Wants** are "needs" that we learn during our lifetime.[26]

Motivation cannot be observed directly. When we see people eat, we assume they are hungry, but we may be wrong. People eat for a variety of reasons besides hunger: They want to be sociable, it's time to eat, or maybe they're nervous or bored.

People are usually motivated by the benefit of satisfying some combination of needs, which may be conscious or unconscious, functional or psychological. *Motivation research* offers insights into the underlying reasons for certain observed consumer behavior. The reasons *(motives)* some people stop shopping at Ralph's Supermarket and switch to Vons may be that the Vons market is closer to home, it has a wider selection of fresh produce, and (most likely) they see other people like themselves shopping at Vons. Any or all of these factors might make a shopper switch even if prices are lower at Ralph's. It's possible that Pets.com did not provide sufficient motives for pet owners to change their behavior.

To better understand what motivates people, Abraham Maslow developed the classic model shown in Exhibit 5–6 called the **hierarchy of needs**. Maslow maintained that the lower, physiological and safety needs dominate human behavior and must be satisfied before the higher, socially acquired needs (or wants) become meaningful. The highest need, self-actualization, is the culmination of fulfilling all the lower needs and realizing one's true potential.

The promise of satisfying a certain level of need is the basic promotional appeal for many ads. In such affluent societies as the United States, Canada, Western Europe, and Japan, most individuals take for granted the satisfaction of their

▼**EXHIBIT 5–6** The hierarchy of needs suggests that people meet their needs according to priorities. Physiological and safety needs carry the greatest priority. In advertising, the message must match the need of the market or the ad will fail. Advertisers use marketing research to understand the need levels of their markets and use this information in determining the marketing mix.

Need	Product	Promotional appeal
Self-actualization	Golf lessons	"Realize your full potential"
Esteem	Luxury car	"The pursuit of perfection"
Social	Jewelry	"Show her you care"
Safety	Tires	"Bounces off hazards"
Physiological	Breakfast cereal	"The natural energy source"

WE ALL HAVE NEEDS AND WANTS, BUT WE ARE FREQUENTLY UNAWARE OF THEM. "

physiological needs. So advertising campaigns often portray the fulfillment of social, esteem, and self-actualization needs, and many offer the reward of satisfaction through personal achievement.

In focus groups for Nabisco Snack-Wells, for example, it became apparent that middle-aged women today have a high sense of self-worth. Wellness, to them, is no longer about looking good in a bathing suit, but rather celebrating what they do well. The advertiser wondered if it could use women's positive attitude about themselves to change their attitude toward the concept of snacking. Nabisco's agency, Foote, Cone & Belding, capitalized on the idea in a new campaign aimed at boosting women's self-esteem. The message: "Snacking is not about 'filling' yourself, but 'fulfilling' yourself."[27]

We all have needs and wants, but we are frequently unaware of them. Before the advent of the desktop computer, people were completely unaware of any need for it. But the moment a consumer consciously recognizes a product-related want or need, a dynamic process begins. The consumer first evaluates the need and either accepts it as worthy of action or rejects it. Acceptance converts satisfaction of the need into a goal, which creates the motivation to reach a particular result. In contrast, rejection removes the necessity for action and thereby eliminates the goal and the motivation to buy.

Modern researchers translated Maslow's theory about needs and motives into more strategic concepts for use by marketers and advertisers. Rossiter and Percy, for example, identify eight fundamental purchase and usage motives (see Exhibit 5–7). They refer to the first five as *negatively originated (informational) motives* and the last three as *positively originated (transformational) motives.*[28]

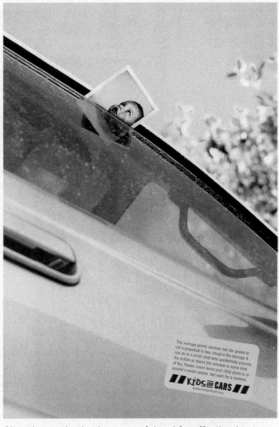

Negative motivation is a powerful tool for affecting human behavior. This ad for Kids and Cars speaks to the potential danger of power windows and attempts to scare readers into adopting safe habits around children.

Negatively Originated (Informational) Motives The most common energizers of consumer behavior are the **negatively originated motives**, such as problem removal or problem avoidance. Whenever we run out of something, for instance, we experience a negative mental state. To relieve those feelings, we actively seek a new or replacement product. Thus, we are temporarily motivated until the time we make the purchase. Then, if the purchase is satisfactory, the drive or motivation is reduced.

These are also called **informational motives** because the consumer actively seeks information to reduce the negative mental state. In fact, Rossiter and Percy point out, these could also be called "relief" motives because consumers work to find relief from a problem.

Positively Originated (Transformational) Motives From time to time, we all want to indulge ourselves by buying some brand or product that promises some benefit

▼ **EXHIBIT 5–7** Rossiter and Percy's eight fundamental purchase and usage motives.

Negatively Originated (Informational) Motives
1. Problem removal
2. Problem avoidance
3. Incomplete satisfaction
4. Mixed approach–avoidance
5. Normal depletion

Positively Originated (Transformational) Motives
6. Sensory gratification
7. Intellectual stimulation or mastery
8. Social approval

or reward. With the **positively originated motives**, a positive bonus is promised rather than the removal or reduction of some negative situation. The goal is to use positive reinforcement to increase the consumer's motivation and to energize the consumer's investigation or search for the new product.

The three positively originated motives—sensory gratification, intellectual stimulation, and social approval—are also called **transformational motives** because the consumer expects to be transformed in a sensory, intellectual, or social sense. They could also be called "reward" motives because the transformation is a rewarding state.[29]

For some consumers, the purchase of a particular product (say, a new suit) might represent a negatively originated motive (they don't really want to spend the money on it, but they have to have it for work). But for other consumers, it might be positively originated (they love to shop for new clothes). This suggests two distinct target markets that advertisers must understand and that may call for completely different advertising strategies.

Before creating messages, advertisers must carefully consider the goals that lead to consumer motivations. Denny's Restaurants would make a costly mistake if its ads portrayed the reward of a romantic interlude if the real motive of most Denny's customers is simply to satisfy their need to reduce hunger with a filling, low-priced meal.

The issues of high-involvement and low-involvement products and informational and transformational motives are so important that we will revisit them in Chapter 7 when we discuss the development of marketing and advertising plans.

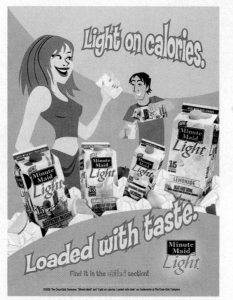

Ads that make use of positively originated motives promise to reward consumers in some way. This Minute Maid Light ad (www.minutemaid.com) addresses two positively originated motives—sensory gratification and social approval—by promising the consumer both great taste and an attractive figure.

L05 Discuss the various influences on consumer behavior.

INTERPERSONAL INFLUENCES ON CONSUMER BEHAVIOR

For advertisers, it's not enough just to know the *personal* processes of perception, learning and persuasion, and motivation. Important **interpersonal influences** affect—sometimes even dominate—these processes. They also serve as guidelines for consumer behavior. These influences can best be categorized as the *family,* the *society,* and the *cultural environment* of the consumer.

Family Influence

From an early age, family communication affects our socialization as consumers—our attitudes toward many products and our purchasing habits. This influence is usually strong and long-lasting. A child who learns that the "right" headache relief is Bayer aspirin and the "right" name for appliances is General Electric has a well-developed adult purchasing behavior.

From 1970 to 1990, married couple households with children declined sharply—from 40 to 26 percent of all households. Since 1990, that decline has been slower—to 22 percent in 2006. Still, this suggests that family influence has greatly diminished in the United States over the last 35 years as working parents take a less active role in raising their children and youngsters look outside the family for social values.[30] As this happens, the influence of the social and cultural environments intensifies.

Societal Influence

The community we live in exerts a strong influence on all of us. When we affiliate with a particular societal division or identify with some reference group or value the ideas of certain opinion leaders, it affects our views on life, our perceptual screens, and eventually the products we buy.

Societal Divisions: The Group We Belong To

Sociologists traditionally divided societies into **social classes**: upper, upper-middle, lower-middle, and so on. They believed that people in the same social class tended to have similar attitudes, status symbols, and spending patterns.

But today this doesn't apply to most developed countries. U.S. society, especially, is extremely fluid and mobile—physically,

Often purchases are made by a group rather than an individual. In many families, everyone must be happy with a brand, a fact acknowledged by Brazilian retailer BH in this ad.

anymore. From the advertiser's point of view, social class seldom represents a functional or operational set of values.

To deal with these often bewildering changes, marketers seek new ways to classify societal divisions and new strategies for advertising to them. We discussed some of these in Chapter 4. Exhibit 5–8 outlines some of the classifications marketers use to describe society today: for example, Upper Crust; Brite Lites, Li'l City; Young Influentials; and Urban Achievers. People in the same group tend to have similar patterns of behavior and product usage.

Reference Groups: The People We Relate To

Most of us care how we appear to people whose opinions we value. We may even pattern our behavior after members of some groups we affiliate with. This is the significance of **reference groups**—people we try to emulate or whose approval

> # Americans, regardless of their social class, believe strongly in getting ahead, being better than their peers, and winning greater admiration and self-esteem.

socially, and economically. Americans, regardless of their social class, believe strongly in getting ahead, being better than their peers, and winning greater admiration and self-esteem.

Because of this mobility, dramatic increases in immigration, and the high divorce rate, social-class boundaries have become quite muddled. Single parents, stockbrokers, immigrant shopkeepers, retired blue-collar workers, and bankers all see themselves as part of the great middle class. So "middle class" doesn't mean anything

concerns us. Reference groups can be personal (family, friends, co-workers) or impersonal (political parties, religious denominations, professional associations). A special reference group, our peers, exerts tremendous influence on what we believe and how we behave. They determine which brands are cool and which are not.[31] To win acceptance by our peers (fellow students, co-workers, colleagues), we may purchase a certain style or brand of clothing, choose a particular place to live, and acquire behavioral habits that will earn their approval.

Upper Crust	Blue-Chip Blues
The nation's most exclusive address. Upper Crust is the wealthiest lifestyle in America—a haven for empty-nesting couples over 55 years old. No segment has a higher concentration of residents earning over $200,000 a year or possessing a postgraduate degree. And none has a more opulent standard of living.	Blue-Chip Blues is known as a comfortable lifestyle for young, sprawling families with well-paying blue collar jobs. (Ethnically diverse—with a significant presence of Hispanics and African Americans—the segment's aging neighborhoods feature compact, modestly priced homes surrounded by commercial centers that cater to child-filled households.

Brite Lites, Li'l City	Old Glories
Not all of America's chic sophisticates live in major metros. Brite Lights, Li'l City is a group of well-off, middle-aged couples settled in the nation's satellite cities. Residents of these typical DINK [double income, no kids] households have college educations, well-paying business and professional careers, and swank homes filled with the latest technology.	Old Glories are the nation's downscale suburban retirees. Americans aging in place in older apartment complexes. These racially mixed households often contain widows and widowers living on fixed incomes, and they tend to lead home-centered lifestyles. They're among the nation's most ardent television fans, watching game shows, soaps, talk shows, and newsmagazines at high rates.

Young Influentials	City Startups
Once known as the home of the nation's yuppies, Young Infuentials reflects the fading glow of acquisitive yuppiedom. Today, the segment is a common address for young middle-class singles and couples who are more preoccupied with balancing work and leisure pursuits. Having recently left college dorms, they now live in apartment complexes surrounded by ball fields, health clubs, and casual dining restaurants.	In City Startups, young, multi-ethnic singles have settled in neighborhoods filled with cheap apartments and a commercial base of cafés, bars, laundromats, and clubs cafés cater to twenty-somethings. One of the youngest segments in America—with 10 times as many college students as the national average—these neighborhoods feature low incomes and high concentrations of Hispanics and African Americans.

Urban Achievers	Low-Rise Living
Concentrated in the nation's port cities, Urban Achievers is often the first stop for up-and-coming immigrants from Asia, South America, and Europe. These young singles and couples are typically college educated and ethnically diverse; about a third are foreign-born, and even more speak a language other than English.	The most economically challenged urban segment, Low-Rise Living is known as a transient world for young, ethnically diverse singles and single parents. Home values are low—about half the national average—and even then less than a quarter of residents can afford to own real estate. Typically, the commercial base of Mom-and-Pop stores is struggling and in need of a renaissance.

Often an individual is influenced in opposite directions by two reference groups and must choose between them. For example, a college student might feel pressure from some friends to join a Greek house and from others to live independently off campus. In ads targeted to students, a local apartment complex might tap the appeal of reference groups by showing students splashing in the complex's pool.

Opinion Leaders: The People We Trust

An **opinion leader** is some person or organization whose beliefs or attitudes are respected by people who share an interest in some specific activity. All fields (sports, religion, fashion, politics) have opinion leaders. An opinion leader may be some expert we find credible. We reason, "If Picabo Street thinks Marker makes the best ski bindings, then it must be so. She knows more about the sport than I do." Thus, the purchasing habits and testimonials of opinion leaders are important to advertisers.

When choosing an opinion leader as a spokesperson for a company or product, advertisers must understand the company's target market thoroughly. Even if executives in the company do

not relate to the spokesperson, they must follow market tastes and interests. A spokesperson out of sync with the market undermines his or her credibility—and the company's. On the other hand, an internal person such as Dave Thomas, the founder of Wendy's, might turn out to be a highly credible spokesperson without the risks associated with outside celebrities and athletes.[32]

Of course, using a superstar spokesperson such as Tiger Woods is extremely expensive. It is estimated that Mr. Woods's annual endorsement income exceeds $100 million. In comparison, Woods earned just under $12 million from his golf victories.[33]

Cultural and Subcultural Influence

Culture has a tenacious influence on consumers. **Culture** refers to the whole set of meanings, beliefs, attitudes, and ways of doing things that are shared by some homogeneous social group and typically handed down from generation to generation.[34] Americans love hot dogs, peanut butter, corn on the cob,

WE ARE ALL WITNESSES.

Believe at nikebasketball.com

Reference groups are those individuals or groups whose opinions matter to us. Sports stars are often role models for fans, which makes superstar LeBron James worth every penny that Nike pays him.

The United States, in particular, is a great melting pot of minority subcultures. A **subculture** is a segment within a culture that shares a set of meanings, values, or activities that differ in certain respects from those of the overall culture.[37] According to the U.S. Census, 38 million African Americans, 43 million Hispanics, and 13 million Asians live in the United States (plus an unknown number of undocumented foreign nationals). These three minority groups alone account for more than 31 percent of the American population, projected to grow to 35 percent by 2015.[38] Canada has two major subcultures, anglophones and francophones, based on language (English and French), plus a mosaic of many other cultures based on ethnic and national origins.

and apple pie. Canada, Russia, Germany—every country has its own favorite specialties. And advertisers find it much easier to work with these tastes than try to change them.

Global marketers are especially concerned with the purchase environment. Of all business functions, marketing activities are the most susceptible to cultural error.[35]

When creating ads for foreign consumption, marketers must consider many environmental factors: cultural trends, social norms, changing fads, market dynamics, product needs, and media channels.[36]

In countries where people earn little income, demand for expensive products is low. So the creative strategy of an automobile advertiser might be to target the small group of wealthy, upper-class consumers. In a country with a large middle class, the same advertiser might be better off mass-marketing the car and positioning it as a middle-class product.

The United States and Canada embrace many subcultures, some of them quite large. They may be based on race, national origin, religion, language, or geographic proximity. The advertiser must understand these subcultures, for differences among them may affect responses to both products and advertising messages.

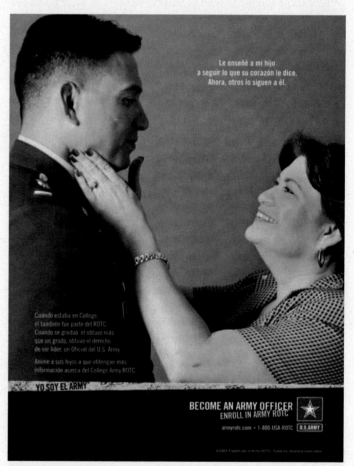

Le enseñé a mi hijo a seguir lo que su corazón le dice. Ahora, otros lo siguen a él.

Cuando estaba en College, él también fue parte del ROTC. Cuando se graduó, él obtuvo más que un grado, obtuvo el derecho de ser líder, un Oficial del U.S. Army. Anime a sus hijos a que obtengan más información acerca del College Army ROTC.

YO SOY EL ARMY

BECOME AN ARMY OFFICER
ENROLL IN ARMY ROTC
armyrotc.com • 1-800-USA-ROTC **U.S.ARMY**

Advertisers realize that English speakers are not the only market in the United States. Subcultures exist and offer enormous markets for the culturally savvy. Here, the U.S. Army (www.goarmy.com) suggests to the Spanish-speaking audience that the soldier pictured followed his heart, and now "others follow it."

evoked set The particular group of alternative goods or services a consumer considers when making a buying decision.

evaluative criteria The standards a consumer uses for judging the features and benefits of alternative products.

products, and household furnishings, to name a few. As we saw in Chapter 3, many ad agencies now specialize in minority markets as more advertisers realize that tailoring their appeals to minorities makes good business sense. Recognizing the rapid growth of the Hispanic population, for example, Procter & Gamble spends $170 million per year to understand and tap this market. Other major marketers that develop messages specifically for Hispanic consumers include Ford Motor Co., AT&T, and Sears Roebuck.[39]

Subcultures tend to transfer their beliefs and values from generation to generation. Racial, religious, and ethnic backgrounds affect consumers' preferences for styles of dress, food, beverages, transportation, personal care

The social environments in countries from Italy to Indonesia, from Sweden to Surinam are also based on language, culture,

ethical issues

Is It Marketing or Is It Exploitation?

Commercial sponsorship is one way to help fund primary and secondary schools. San Francisco–based School Properties, Inc., offers various sponsorship programs—including licensing school names and mascots, fund-raising catalogs, and affinity credit cards—to national and regional marketers. They test products and hold focus groups at schools, display banners at events, and use former student athletes for company appearances. School Properties, aware that budget cuts jeopardize extracurricular school activities, feel this program is a natural outgrowth of existing athletic and special-event sponsorships. Supporters feel it will help mobilize resources for schools, but opponents say that school funding is the government's problem and commercial product logos don't belong in education. Others wonder if this allows advertisers to take unfair advantage of captive kids.

The ethical dilemma concerns promoting products for advantage or profit at the unreasonable expense of the customer. Commercial products work only if they meet consumer needs, and advertising must appeal to those needs. But what happens if advertisers overstep a need, in a crisis situation, for example, and edge into exploitation?

Look at the public concern about the commercialization of children. In response to complaints about Saturday morning advertising to kids, broadcasters of children's TV are now banned from advertising toys during shows that feature those toys and they must clearly separate commercials from the program by announcing commercial breaks. In a different arena, most baby formula companies don't yet advertise directly to consumers because many doctors think breast-feeding is preferable to using formula. The companies don't want to be accused of exploitation; instead, they market their products through health care professionals, hospitals, and new-mother clubs.

Drastic changes in particular market segments may make new fields fertile for exploitation. For example, the emerging Third World middle class seems to have an insatiable appetite for buying things. While tradition and culture play a big role in what people buy and why, the evolving role of women, a burgeoning youth culture, and a middle class with higher expectations and more money than ever before make whole groups of consumers ripe for new products.

Some critics believe China is especially vulnerable to exploitation. A couple living in a cramped Beijing apartment may have a $270 refrigerator, a $700 foreign-made color TV, a telephone that came with a $600 installation charge, a $600 Panasonic VCR, a $1,200 Toshiba air conditioner, and a $1,200 piano—all purchased on a salary of $300 a month. In Mexico, companies pitch credit cards to people earning as little as $650 a month. The National Association of Credit Card Holders estimates 5 million Mexicans carry credit cards, but 1 million of them can't pay their bills. In the United States, the elderly and mentally incapacitated are targeted and exploited by sweepstakes promoters, misleading them into believing they've won contest monies and prizes. The elderly are bilked out of thousands of dollars in fees and merchandise they don't need and can't afford. State lotteries also prey on the hopes of the poor in their advertising, underplaying the long odds of winning significant prizes and exploiting gambling addictions.

Critics say that companies act irresponsibly when they target these groups for marketing and advertising activities because the average consumer can't afford the products being advertised.

However, researchers have investigated how advertising messages influence people to act. One finding, known as the third-person effect, holds that people generally believe others are more influenced by the media than they are. Perhaps the critics need to consider this. While they themselves can resist advertising appeals, they seem to believe the average consumer lacks their sophistication. So where do you draw the line between what is ethical (marketing) and what is not (exploitation)?

Questions
1. Do you think playing on people's desire for material possessions has a place in advertising? When does this become exploitation?
2. Is it the advertiser's responsibility to determine whether prospective customers can afford a product or service? Why or why not?
3. Are marketers enhancing the quality of life in developing countries, or are they exploiting vulnerable consumers? Is this an example of the third-person effect?

> The United States is a melting pot of subcultures, segments within a culture that share sets of meanings, values, or activities that differ from those of the overall culture.

literacy rate, religion, and lifestyle. Advertisers who market products globally can't ignore these distinctions.

In North America, advertising encourages us to keep our mouths clean, our breath fresh, and our teeth scrubbed. But people in some southern European countries consider it vain and improper to overindulge in toiletries. Consumers in the Netherlands and the United Kingdom use three times as much toothpaste as those in Spain and Greece. To communicate effectively with Spanish consumers, who view toothpaste as a cosmetic product, advertisers use chic, creative executions rather than dry, therapeutic pitches.[40]

Clearly, many interpersonal factors influence consumers. They have an important effect on our mental files, screens, and subsequent purchase decisions. Awareness of these interpersonal influences helps marketers, both domestic and international, create the strategies on which much advertising is based.

check yourself ✓

1. What is a reference group and why is it important?

2. What is culture? How does it differ from a subculture?

THE PURCHASE DECISION AND POSTPURCHASE EVALUATION

Now that we understand the elements in the consumer purchase decision process, let's examine how it might work in a typical situation. A hypothetical consumer named Chris is thinking about buying an MP3 player.

Chris is enrolled at a state university and financed in part by a small scholarship. He also has a part-time job but must act conservatively when it comes to spending money because tuition, books, and other expenses are costly.

One day, thumbing through a consumer electronics magazine, Chris sees an exciting ad for a new, top-of-the-line MP3 player. A beautiful photograph shows the product's modern, yet understated design. The ad copy highlights the player's special features. They exude high-tech class—it's

just the right style. The ad's signature: "Exclusively at Tech Depot."

In a split second Chris leaps from perception to motivation. Got to have it! He is highly involved and he wants this personal reward for all his hard work.

The next day Chris visits Tech Depot. While looking for the advertised MP3 player, he encounters a variety of alternative styles and models by well-known manufacturers.

The ad has already done its work; the purchase decision process is well under way. At the point of making a purchase decision, though, consumers typically search, consider, and compare alternative brands.

Consumers evaluate selection alternatives (called the **evoked set**). To do this, they establish **evaluative criteria**, the standards they use to judge the features and benefits of alternative products. Not all brands make it to the evoked set. In fact, based on their mental files, most consumers usually consider only four or five brands—which presents a real challenge to advertisers. If none of

People will go to great lengths to avoid cognitive dissonance. For example, if someone just spent a lot of money for a new mattress from Tempur-Pedic (www.tempurpedic.com), they are more likely to be interested in ads like this one that reinforce their decision.

When Polaroid needed to capture the attention of photo enthusiasts, it turned to the creatives at Leonard/Monahan to design a series of ads that would exhibit the advantages of the instant film over other photo products. The first challenge for the creative design team was to break through the consumers' resistance, the subtle barrier that begins with perceptual screens. Second, the team had to present a picture as being worth a thousand words while avoiding clichés.

The advertisement's headline—"The victim refuses to speak. The pictures refuse to keep quiet."—commands your attention and expresses the big idea with urgency. The ad's black-and-white visual of a battered victim suggests the subject's grave nature while allowing the color Polaroids to jump out, emoting a raw portrayal of reality. The ad becomes credible by demonstrating the benefits of Polaroid photos and how effectively they can be used (to investigate, prosecute, and win). The tagline, "Instant evidence," sums up the product's features and helps the prospective consumer recall the product's benefits.

Applying the Breaks

Choose an ad from a popular magazine and explain how the visuals, the words, and the overall design of the ad accomplish the following tasks. Provide specific details to support your answers.

The victim refuses to speak. The pictures refuse to keep quiet. Too often, victims are unwilling to testify. But pictures don't need courage and they don't heal or change their stories. With Polaroid instant film and cameras, investigators can document abuse and use it to prosecute, even without the victim's testimony. And they win. Call 1-800-662-8337, ext. 916 to order a Spectra Law Enforcement Kit or a product catalog. **Instant evidence. Polaroid**

1. Penetrate consumers' perceptual screens.
2. Address consumers' existing mental files.
3. Stimulate consumer learning.
4. Persuade via the central or peripheral route.
5. Stimulate consumer needs and wants to achieve motivation and action.

---

the alternatives meets the evaluative criteria, the consumer may reject the purchase entirely or postpone the decision.

Chris finally finds the advertised MP3 player. But it looks less stylish on the shelf than it did in the ad. Two other good players are also displayed; both are attractive, both expensive. While trying out the devices, Chris considers other unique qualities of style and design. "This one may be a little too bulky." "This one would fit in my pocket." "This one would be okay for relaxing, but I'm not sure about using it when I'm jogging."

Using central route processing, Chris compares the MP3 players, considering their style, technology, possible advantages, and price (the models are all within $50 of each other). The advertised player really is the best buy and would be the most satisfying. None of Chris's friends has one like it. The purchase decision is complete when Chris writes out a check for the MP3 player.

On the way home, the postpurchase evaluation begins. Chris suddenly envisions some friends' possible negative reactions to the purchase. Maybe it wasn't wise to spend so much money on a top-of-the-line MP3

player. Perhaps his friends made better choices. Chris starts to worry—and to plan.

"It's really a great player. It's excellent quality and worth the money. I'll get a lot of use out of it."

A key feature of the postpurchase evaluation is *cognitive dissonance*. The theory of **cognitive dissonance** holds that people strive to justify their behavior by reducing the dissonance, or inconsistency, between their cognitions (their perceptions or beliefs) and reality.[41] In fact, research shows that, to combat dissonance, consumers are more likely to read ads for brands they've already purchased than for new products or competing brands.[42]

Back at the dorm, Chris puts the magazine on the desk with a Post-it note marking the ad (for his roommate to discover). Then he phones a friend and describes the purchase, emphasizing its technology, its great design, the enjoyment it will bring, and how expensive it was.

During the postpurchase period, the consumer may enjoy the satisfaction of the purchase and thereby receive reinforcement for the decision. Or the purchase may turn out to be unsatisfactory for some reason. In either case, feedback from the postpurchase evaluation updates the consumer's mental files, affecting perceptions of the brand and similar purchase decisions in the future.

This story is common for a high-involvement purchase decision. Of course, if Chris's decision had merely involved the purchase of a pack of gum, the process would have been significantly simpler.

Chris may typify a particular group of consumers, and that is important to marketers. As we saw in Chapter 4, marketers are interested in defining target markets and developing effective marketing strategies for groups of consumers who share similar characteristics, needs, motives, and buying habits.

cognitive dissonance The theory that people try to justify their behavior by reducing the degree to which their impressions or beliefs are inconsistent with one another.

FCB grid A two-dimensional model that categorizes consumer products into four quadrants based on "high involvement" or "low involvement," and "think" or "feel." By positioning brands in the grid, an agency can determine the type of advertising that would be most appropriate.

Kim-Lord grid A variation of the FCB grid, which allows for the fact that the level of consumer involvement in a product does not have to be high "think" and low "feel" (or vice versa) but can be high (or low) in both categories.

DIFFERENT RESPONSES FROM DIFFERENT PRODUCTS

In the 1980s, Richard Vaughn at Foote, Cone & Belding took the fact that different kinds of products typically evoke different *levels* of consumer involvement (either high or low) and different *types* of involvement, either *cognitive* (think) or *affective* (feel) and concluded therefore that different products called for different kinds of advertising. He created a two-dimensional model known as the **FCB grid**, which categorized consumer products into four quadrants based on "high involvement" or "low involvement," and "think" or "feel." By positioning brands in the grid based on the degree and type of involvement consumers brought to the purchase decision, the agency could determine which type of advertising would be most appropriate.

As shown in Exhibit 5–9, a product's location on the grid also indicates how the product is purchased and how advertising copy should be written (more emotional or more rational).[43] High involvement/thinking products lend themselves to logical explanations and consumers will probably follow the traditional learn-feel-do model. At the other extreme, high involvement/feeling products are more likely to stress emotional motives and consumers may follow a feel-learn-do sequence. In the case of low involvement products, which are associated with routinized or impulse purchase behavior, *learning* and *feeling* may not occur until after *doing*. In such cases, simply gaining exposure or awareness may be the primary advertising objective.

More recently, Kim and Lord recognized that people can be both cognitively and affectively involved at the same time. So they developed a variation of the FCB grid, shown in Exhibit 5–10. The **Kim-Lord grid** also

▼**EXHIBIT 5–9**   The Foote, Cone & Belding (FCB) grid.

	Thinking	Feeling
High involvement	**1. Informative (thinker)** Car-house-furnishing-new products model: Learn-feel-do (economic?) **Possible implications** Test: Recall Diagnostics Media: Long copy format Reflective vehicles Creative: Specific information Demonstration	**2. Affective (feeler)** Jewelry-cosmetics-fashion apparel-motorcycles model: Feel-learn-do (psychological?) **Possible implications** Test: Attitude change Emotional arousal Media: Large space Image specials Creative: Executional Impact
Low involvement	**3. Habit formation (doer)** Food-household items model: Do-learn-feel (responsive?) **Possible implications** Test: Sales Media: Small space ads 10-second I.D.s Radio; POS Creative: Reminder	**4. Self-satisfaction (reactor)** Cigarettes-liquor-candy model: Do-feel-learn (social?) **Possible implications** Test: Sales Media: Billboards Newspapers POS Creative: Attention

Understanding What Consumers Look For in a Product [5]

Your client's hope is that you can offer helpful advice on creating promotional messages that will get people to do something. In most cases, that something will be buying the client's product or using the service. If your client is a nonprofit, it might involve donating time and/or money.

This seems like common sense, but in fact persuading people to do something they are not already doing can be quite difficult. To help you organize your approach, it may be useful to review what marketing and psychology scholars have learned about consumers and how they are persuaded.

Your challenge at this point in the campaign is to understand the consumer and to get a sense of how the product or service your client offers relates to the consumer's life. Doing this well will require at least two things: a complete understanding of the product and its possible benefits, and a thorough understanding of the consumer.

Maslow's hierarchy of needs suggests that individuals have a range of needs they seek to satisfy in life.

Here is Maslow's hierarchy and some examples that involve food. Consider whether your client's product or service might have benefits that relate to one or more needs:

Need	Examples Involving Food
Self-actualization	Culinary arts degree
Esteem	Cooking lessons
Social	What everyone is eating
Safety	Healthful, organic foods
Physiological	Something that satisfies your hunger

Informational motives involve eliminating a problem, whereas transformational motives involve getting a reward. Consider the possible informational and transformational motives that exist in your consumers that might be addressed by your product.

Informational Motives	
Motive	**Solution**
Problem removal	"Eliminates your headache fast"
Problem avoidance	"Stay out in the sun—you're protected"
Incomplete satisfaction	"The diet drink that doesn't taste like a diet drink"
Mixed approach-avoidance	"Pain-free dental care"
Normal depletion	"Last gas station for 20 miles"

Transformational Motives	
Sensory gratification	"These headphones sound like you are at the show"
Intellectual stimulation	"Hours of fun with challenging puzzles"
Social approval	"Your spouse will love the way you look"

The Foote, Cone, & Belding grid was developed to classify how consumers learn about different types of products. Although it was originally designed with the idea that different products would fit in different quadrants, some believe that the quadrants can also be used to classify competing brands within a product category (for example, luxury brands versus discount brands). Where would you place your client's brand? What does that suggest for how you might persuade consumers?

The following guides can help you determine where your client's brand belongs in the FCB grid:

Involvement

1. Is the decision to buy or use the product an important one or an unimportant one?
2. Does the consumer stand to lose a great deal or very little if he/she chooses the wrong brand?
3. Does the decision require a great deal of consideration or very little?

Think versus Feel

Think

1. The decision is based on objective criteria.
2. The decision is based primarily on factual information.

Feel

1. The decision is based on a feeling.
2. The decision is closely related to the consumer's personality.
3. The decision is based on the senses (taste, touch, etc.).

FCB Grid

	Think	Feel
High Involvement	I. Informative Learn—Feel—Do (products: major purchases such as insurance, appliances, computers) Strategy: Follow steps of the creative pyramid, beginning with awareness.	II. Affective Feel—Learn—Do (products: expensive car, jewelry, high end apparel) Strategy: Focus on self-esteem and ego benefits of product purchases.
Low Involvement	III. Habitual Do—Learn—Feel (products: car fuel, detergents, razor) Strategy: Focus on offering samples and creating habits in consumer purchasing.	IV. Satisfaction Do—Feel—Learn (products: experiential products such as beer, chewing gum, greeting cards, pizza) Strategy: Focus on social factors and peer use of the product.

▼ **EXHIBIT 5–10** The Kim-Lord grid.

Affective involvement (Feel)

	Low	High
High (Cognitive involvement (Think))	College • • Video camera • Motor oil	• Car • Shampoo Skin lotion
Low	• Laundry detergent • Paper towels	Greeting card • • Pizza • Bread

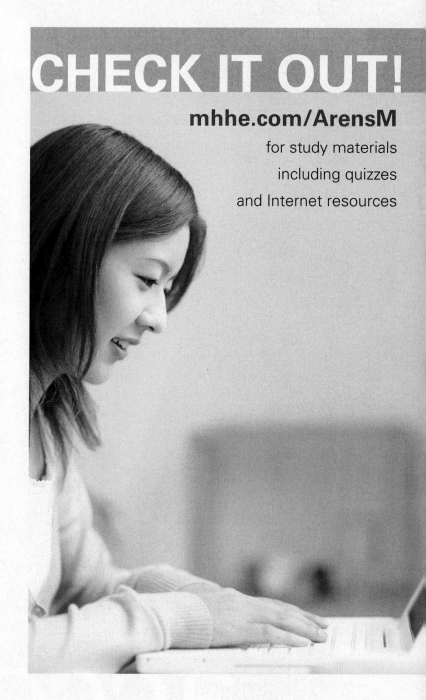

depicts the degree and the kind of involvement a consumer brings to the purchase decision for different products. Some purchases, like cars, require a high degree of personal involvement on both the cognitive and affective levels.[44] For others, like detergent, involvement is low on both axes. Sometimes a marketer uses an advertising strategy aimed at shifting the product to higher involvement on either axis. ■

account
planning and research

Limited-service hotels have proven increasingly effective in capturing business from the nearly two and a half million travelers seeking a room each night in America. By sacrificing some luxuries common to bigger hotels, travelers typically get a clean room, breakfast, and a lower bill at chains such as Hampton Inn, Courtyard by Marriott, and, as of 1997, Holiday Inn Express. Fallon Worldwide, headquartered in Minneapolis, initially appeared to be a long shot to become the advertising agency of record for the new chain because Fallon already serviced its sister chain, Holiday Inn. But the agency convinced its client that because "it knew the territory," it could do the job better than anyone else.

continued on p. 150

LEARNING OBJECTIVES

LO1 Describe the role of account planners in advertising agencies.

LO2 Discuss how research can help advertisers select target markets, media vehicles, and advertising messages.

LO3 Explain the basic steps in the marketing research process.

LO4 Explain the common methods used in qualitative and quantitative research.

LO5 Evaluate the challenges of pretesting and posttesting advertising.

LO6 Identify issues that can affect the accuracy and usability of quantitative research.

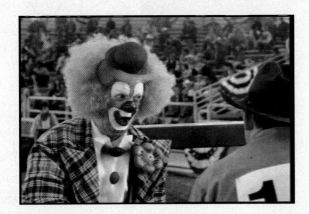

continued from p. 149

To ensure that Express did not *cannibalize* (take) customers from its sister hotel, the agency focused its efforts on a completely different target audience from that of Holiday Inn, a group known as *road warriors.* Road warriors are independent businesspeople who spend as many as a hundred nights or more per year on the road. Predominantly male, road warriors usually foot their own travel bills. Initial discussions with this target made it clear that Holiday Inn Express had a good opportunity because warriors believed that competitor hotel chains were ignoring them.

Fallon knew that creating effective messages for warriors meant account planners and creatives would have to deeply understand their audience, in terms not just of their hotel preferences but also their personalities and lifestyles. So the planners paired up with some warriors and ventured out on the road. As summarized in Pat Fallon and Fred Senn's book, *Juicing the Orange,* "Our planners videotaped the road warriors while they drove cross-country. We talked to them about their work, their families, and their daily experiences. One account planner barreled down Highway 70 with a guy who was like John Candy's character in the movie *Planes, Trains and Automobiles.*"[1]

Based on its research, Fallon renamed the category *drive-ups* because members of the group often selected a hotel at the end of the day with no advance reservation. Psychologically, these individuals wanted a hotel that provided the basics, afforded them control, and showed them respect. As Fallon and Senn

noted, drive-ups "had dreams and aspirations, but doing the work itself was the emotional reward. They were working hard and working smart and that was going to be their ticket to success."[2]

The research also revealed that drive-ups found it deeply rewarding to save on their travel budgets by forgoing unneeded luxuries, and the good feelings from making the "smart choice" remained with the customers long after they had checked out of the hotel. Fallon captured the emotional benefits of Holiday Inn Express with the simple slogan "Stay Smart." Ads developed for the campaign were funny, unexpected, and centered on the theme of how staying at a Holiday Inn Express was proof that the traveler was smart (see these ads and others by Fallon at www.juicingtheorange.com). In the commercial pictured above, a clown gives professional advice to a nervous rodeo rider who gratefully proclaims, "You rodeo clowns are a lifesaver!" The clown explains that he's actually with a birthday party in the stands, but stresses that he "stayed at a Holiday Inn Express last night."

Posttesting research showed that the ads increased brand awareness by 40 percent, and Holiday Inn Express became the fastest-growing hotel in its category. Moreover, the chain achieved $1 billion in sales a year earlier than expected. Attitudinal research showed that Holiday Inn Express easily beat industry averages for key image considerations that drive hotel business such as "good hotel for the money" and "good hotel for business travelers." And much of this success could be attributed to gaining a clear understanding of the target consumer through research. ■

LO1 Describe the role of account planners in advertising agencies.

THE ACCOUNT PLANNER AS CONSUMER ADVOCATE

Jeff Goodby, cochairman at Goodby, Silverstein & Partners, is famous for award-winning television ads including the Budweiser Lizards and the Got Milk? campaign. He believes that everything an agency does should be geared toward getting into people's heads to figure out what they currently think and understand how best to influence them.[3]

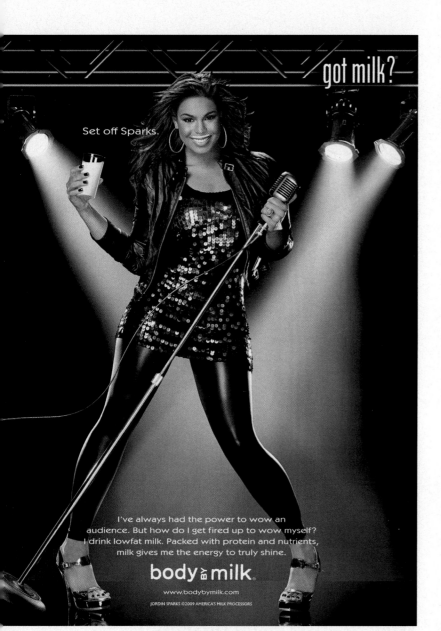

Set off Sparks.

got milk?

I've always had the power to wow an audience. But how do I get fired up to wow myself? I drink lowfat milk. Packed with protein and nutrients, milk gives me the energy to truly shine.

body BY milk

www.bodybymilk.com

JORDIN SPARKS ©2009 AMERICA'S MILK PROCESSORS

The success of "Got Milk?" and many other notable campaigns is often attributed to the ability of account planners to get into the heads of their prospects. This approach enables brands to develop meaningful relationships with their customers.

account planner
The individual at an advertising agency primarily responsible for account planning.

Boase Massimi Pollitt is considered by some to be the "father" of account planning. He described planners as "the architects and guardians of their clients' brands, the detectives who uncovered long-hidden clues in the data and gently coerced consumers into revealing their inner secrets. . . ."[4]

By putting the consumer, instead of the advertiser, at the center of the process, account planning changes the task from simply creating an advertisement to nurturing a relationship between consumer and brand. That requires tremendous understanding, intuition, and insight. But when performed properly, planning provides that mystical leap into the future—the brilliant, simplifying insight that lights the client's and the creative's way. Interestingly, the U.S. agencies that have adopted account planning in the last decade are the very ones now considered to be the hottest shops. They're performing the best work, getting the biggest accounts, and winning all the awards.

In large agencies, account planners work side-by-side with account managers. They share a common goal but with different orientations. Where the account planner brings a research perspective and represents the consumer, the account manager brings more of a business perspective and represents the client. In smaller agencies without account planning departments, the consumer's advocate would typically be someone from account management.

Whoever plays this role is responsible for ensuring that the advertising strategy and executions are relevant to the target audience. The account planner is responsible for injecting a wealth of information into the planning process, monitoring the creative development, and testing the finished product to determine if it has achieved its goal of communicating with the intended audience.

Jon Steel summarizes the account planner's mission as follows: "They need to be able to take information of all sorts, shuffle it around, and rearrange it in new patterns until something inter-

[The advertiser must understand what is happening in the consumers' heads.]

This task is shared by many individuals during the process of planning advertising, but has, in recent years, been focused on the **account planner**, described in Chapter 3. The account planner's primary role is to represent the consumer in this process. The late Stanley Pollitt of the London agency

esting emerges."[5] One does not necessarily need to conduct research to get that information. Some questions can be answered without research, or the answers may have been uncovered in previous explorations. But in all cases, the advertiser must understand what is happening in consumers' heads.

In this chapter we will examine various types of research and the role that research plays in the development of advertising.

LO2 Discuss how research can help advertisers select target markets, media vehicles, and advertising messages.

THE NEED FOR RESEARCH IN MARKETING AND ADVERTISING

Every year companies spend millions of dollars creating ads and promotions that they hope their customers and prospects will notice and relate to. Then they spend millions more placing their communications in print and electronic media, hoping their customers will see and hear them and eventually respond.

Advertising is expensive. In the United States the cost of airing a single 30-second commercial on prime-time network TV averages around $100,000.[6] Likewise, a single, full-page color ad in a national magazine can cost over $250,000.[7] That's too much money to risk unless advertisers have very good information about who their customers are, what they want and like, where they spend their media time, and whether the ads are effective. And that's why advertisers need research. Research provides the information that drives marketing and advertising decision making. Without that information, advertisers are forced to use intuition or guesswork. In today's fast-changing, highly competitive, global economy, that invites failure.

What Is Marketing Research?

To help managers make marketing decisions, companies develop systematic procedures for gathering, recording, and analyzing new information. This is called **marketing research**. Marketing research does a number of things: It helps identify consumer needs and market segments; it provides the information necessary for developing new products and devising marketing strategies; and it enables managers to assess the effectiveness of marketing programs and promotional activities.

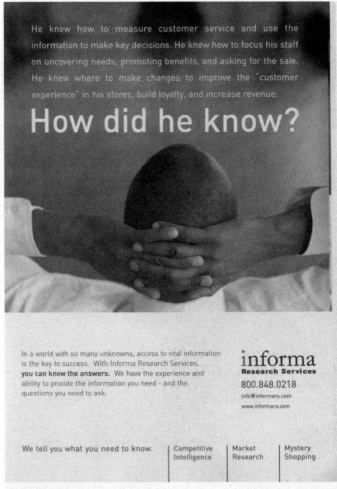

He knew how to measure customer service and use the information to make key decisions. He knew how to focus his staff on uncovering needs, promoting benefits, and asking for the sale. He knew where to make changes to improve the "customer experience" in his stores, build loyalty, and increase revenue.

How did he know?

In a world with so many unknowns, access to vital information is the key to success. With Informa Research Services, **you can know the answers.** We have the experience and ability to provide the information you need – and the questions you need to ask.

informa Research Services
800.848.0218
info@informars.com
www.informars.com

We tell you what you need to know. | Competitive Intelligence | Market Research | Mystery Shopping

Marketing research is the important process of gathering, recording, and analyzing information about customers and prospects. Companies such as Informa Research Services (www.informars.com) collect data for their clients and provide critical insights into the markets they serve.

What Is Advertising Research?

Before developing any advertising campaign, a company needs to know how people perceive its products, how they view the competition, what brand or company image would be most credible, and what ads offer the greatest appeal. To get this information, companies use *advertising research*. While marketing research provides the information necessary to make marketing decisions, **advertising research** uncovers the information needed for making advertising decisions. By definition, it is the systematic gathering and analysis of information to help develop or evaluate advertising strategies, individual ads, and entire campaigns.

Fallon's research suggested that drive-ups emotionally benefited from the smart choice of using Holiday Inn Express instead of more expensive hotels. The agency's creatives used these findings to develop funny and unexpected commercials. In the one depicted here, a woman confronted by an enormous bear is offered helpful advice from a man. When someone asks if he is a park ranger, the man replies that he is not, but he did stay the night before at a Holiday Inn Express.

marketing research The systematic gathering, recording, and analysis of information to help managers make marketing decisions.

advertising research The systematic gathering and analysis of information specifically to facilitate the development or evaluation of advertising strategies, ads and commercials, and media campaigns.

In this chapter, we consider the importance of information gathering to the development of advertising plans and strategies; we look at how companies use research to test the effectiveness of ads before and after they run; and we explore a number of specific research techniques.

Applying Research to Advertising Decision Making

Advertising research serves various purposes, most of which can be grouped into four categories: *strategy research, creative concept research, pretesting,* and *posttesting.*

1. *Advertising strategy research.* Used to help define the product concept or to assist in the selection of target markets, advertising messages, or media vehicles.

2. *Creative concept research.* Measures the target audience's acceptance of different creative ideas at the concept stage.

3. *Pretesting of ads.* Used to uncover and diagnose possible communication problems before a campaign begins.

4. *Posttesting of ads.* Enables marketers to evaluate a campaign after it runs.

As Exhibit 6–1 shows, marketers use the different categories of advertising research at different stages of ad or campaign development. The techniques they use at each stage also vary considerably. We'll examine each of these categories briefly before moving on to discuss the research process.

Advertising Strategy Research

As we will discuss in the next chapter, an advertising strategy is comprised of the *creative strategy* and the *media strategy.* Developing these strategies requires a clear understanding of

▼ **EXHIBIT 6–1** Categories of research in advertising development.

	Advertising Strategy Research	Creative Concept Research	Pretesting	Posttesting
Timing	Before creative work begins	Before agency production begins	Before finished artwork and photography	After campaign has run
Research problem	Product concept definition Target audience selection Media selection Message-element selection	Concept testing Name testing Slogan testing	Print testing TV storyboard pretesting Radio commercial pretesting	Advertising effectiveness Consumer attitude change Sales increases
Techniques	Consumer attitude and usage studies Media studies Qualitative interviews	Free-association tests Qualitative interviews Statement-comparison tests	Consumer juries Matched samples Portfolio tests Storyboard test Mechanical devices Psychological rating scales	Aided recall Unaided recall Attitude tests Inquiry tests Sales tests

STRATEGY RESEARCH IS ESSENTIAL TO DEVELOP A BLUEPRINT FOR CREATIVES TO FOLLOW.

the *product concept,* the *target audience,* the *media* alternatives, and possible *message elements.* To gain this understanding, companies use **advertising strategy research**.

Product Concept As we saw at the beginning of this chapter, advertisers need to know how consumers perceive their brands. They also want to know what qualities lead to initial purchases and, eventually, to brand loyalty.

Using this information, they try to establish a unique *product concept* for their brand—that bundle of values we discussed in Chapter 4 that encompasses both utilitarian and symbolic benefits to the consumer.

From its research, Fallon knew that drive-ups were interested in the kind of value that a stay at a Holiday Inn Express afforded. They also knew that value translated emotionally as feeling good about being "smart" by saving money by forgoing unnecessary luxuries.[8]

It's this kind of information that can lead to an effective positioning strategy for the brand. Advertising can shape and magnify a brand's position and image over time. In fact, this is one of the most important strategic benefits of advertising. But to use media advertising effectively, strategy research is essential to develop a blueprint for creatives to follow.[9]

Advertising works differently for different product categories and, often, even for different brands within a category. This means that each brand must develop a template for the creative based on an understanding of its particular consumers' wants, needs, and motivations. Only if this is done correctly over time (say, one to two years), can brand equity be built.[10]

To determine how brands are built and how they derive their strength, the Young & Rubicam ad agency developed a model called the BrandAsset Valuator. It measures brands in terms of differentiation, relevance, esteem, and familiarity, in that order. According to Y&R's theory, a brand must first develop differentiation—it must offer something unique and different—to survive. Second, it must be perceived by the target market as relevant to their needs and wants. Finally, it needs to build stature through esteem and knowledge. Once all these steps are accomplished, a brand achieves leadership status.

Following Y&R's lead, other agencies have developed their own brand equity studies. In 1998, WPP Group introduced a research tool titled "BRANDZ." Then, in 2000, DDB Worldwide introduced "Brand Capital," and Leo Burnett unveiled its brand of research dubbed "Brand Stock." All of these are aimed at understanding how consumers connect with brands before spending millions on advertising.[11]

Target Audience Selection We pointed out in Chapter 4 that no market includes everybody. Therefore, one of the

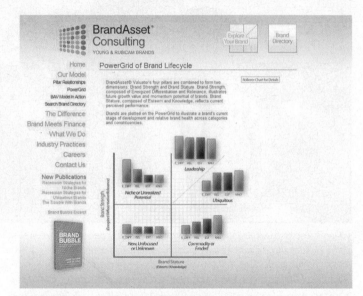

Young & Rubicam's BrandAsset® Valuator is a model to statistically ascertain how brands are built and the assets from which they derive their market strength. BrandAsset® Valuator has to date surveyed more than 800,000 consumers about 40,000 brands. Data has been collected since 1993.

major purposes of research is to develop a rich profile of the brand's target markets and audiences. The marketer will want to know which customers are the primary users of the product category and will study them carefully to understand their demographics, geographics, psychographics, and purchase behavior. If the target audience is accurately defined, the advertising will be delivered to the most prospects with the least waste.

In the case of Holiday Inn Express, Fallon believed it was important to find a target audience who would be heavy users of hotels but who would be unlikely to stay at its sister brand, Holiday Inn. Drive-ups, consisting of independent-minded male businesspeople, typically working in small companies or for themselves, fit the bill perfectly. As heavy users of hotels, they represented a highly profitable market segment. And because drive-ups believed that no hotel brand was particularly interested in them, Fallon could design ads that targeted their needs and concerns.

Media Selection To develop media strategies, select media vehicles, and evaluate their results, advertisers use a subset of advertising research called **media research**. Agencies subscribe to syndicated research services (such as Nielsen, Arbitron, Experian Simmons, or Standard Rate & Data Service) that monitor and publish information on the reach and effectiveness of media vehicles—radio, TV, newspapers, and so on—in every major geographic market in the United States and Canada. (We'll discuss these further in Chapter 8 and in Part Five.)

For Holiday Inn Express, Fallon researched the media habits of drive-ups and discovered that this group tended to watch cable

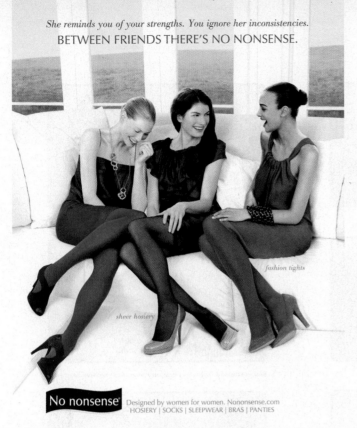

She reminds you of your strengths. You ignore her inconsistencies.
BETWEEN FRIENDS THERE'S NO NONSENSE.

fashion tights

sheer hosiery

No nonsense Designed by women for women. Nononsense.com
HOSIERY | SOCKS | SLEEPWEAR | BRAS | PANTIES

No Nonsense (www.nononsense.com) identified the special relationship between girlfriends to be an important source of product information. This insight was translated into an advertising campaign.

likes and dislikes in relation to brands and products. Kraft Foods, for example, was looking for ways to dissuade moms from switching to less-expensive brands of processed cheese. While its Kraft Singles brand dominated the processed cheese slices category, it was concerned that the brand wasn't keeping up with overall growth in the market.

Working with several research companies and its ad agency, J. Walter Thompson, the company conducted a series of qualitative consumer attitude studies to figure out how women, particularly mothers, felt about Kraft Singles, with the hope of discovering possible advertising themes. The mothers said they felt good giving their kids Kraft Singles because of the brand's nutritional value. But there was a catch—they also said they'd switch to a competitive product if it were cheaper. Fortunately, a phone survey provided some clues for solving the problem. Among those polled, 78 percent considered the brand an extra source of calcium for their kids. And 84 percent of women with kids under 12 said they'd be motivated to buy the brand because of that added benefit.[12]

From this information, the agency used concept testing to determine which message elements might prove most successful.

> **If the target audience is accurately defined, the advertising will be delivered to the most prospects with the least waste.**

fare focused on news and sports, including such networks as ESPN, CNN, and the Weather Channel. Research also suggested that the target audience formulated travel plans early in the week, so Fallon ran the ads only on Sunday and Monday nights. While the overall ad budget was comparatively small, the concentration of ads on two evenings using a small number of networks gave the campaign a larger presence on those occasions when drive-ups would actually be watching TV and thinking about travel. In addition, because the campaign was so fresh and unusual, it got an additional boost from unpaid references to the "No, but I did stay at a Holiday Inn Express last night" slogan on ESPN, *Late Night with David Letterman,* NPR, and the *Washington Post.*

Message Element Selection

Companies hope to find promising advertising messages by studying consumers'

Creative Concept Research

Once it develops an advertising strategy, the company (or its agency) will begin developing creative concepts for the advertising. Here again, research is helpful in determining which concepts to use.

From all their studies, Kraft researchers came up with two message elements that might keep mothers from defecting to competitive brands. First, show how much kids like Kraft Singles, and second, emphasize the fact that the brand provides the calcium kids need. J. Walter Thompson prepared two rough TV spots and then conducted focus groups of mothers to get their reaction. With a discussion leader moderating the conversation, each group viewed the commercials. The groups' reactions were measured, taped, and observed by JWT and Kraft staff behind a one-way mirror. Immediately, problems surfaced. The idea that

pretesting Testing the effectiveness of an advertisement for gaps or flaws in message content before recommending it to clients, often conducted through focus groups.

posttesting Testing the effectiveness of an advertisement after it has been run.

marketing information system (MIS) A set of procedures for generating an orderly flow of pertinent information for use in making marketing decisions.

informal research The second step in the research process, designed to explore a problem by reviewing secondary data and interviewing a few key people with the most information to share.

MED: on Edmund as he looks bored with his breakfast

TIGHT: on Edmund's suprise as cereal hovers towards him

Buzzing! Shot of Cereal in the air

MED: of Edmund looking at the cereal being poured into a breakfast bowl

TIGHT: on Cereal and bee.

Good Flakes: Great cereal, Good for you!

HIVE   HIVE

Advertisers can avoid mistakes and save money on production by testing creative concepts in animatic form. Animatics are illustrated by hand and then computer animated. This animatic was created by the Hive (www.hivedoes.com).

kids love the taste of Kraft Singles just didn't come across strongly enough. And the statement that Kraft provides calcium wasn't persuasive. Moms said, "Of course it has calcium, it's cheese." The agency had to find a newsier way to communicate the information.

Tweaking the commercials, JWT came up with a new spot showing youngsters gobbling gooey grilled-cheese sandwiches while a voice-over announcer stated that two out of five kids don't get enough calcium. More focus groups ensued. Now the mothers agreed that the shots of kids devouring sandwiches communicated the great-taste theme, but some moms thought the two-out-of-five statement played too much on their guilt.

To soften the message, the agency switched to a female announcer and then brought in the Dairy Fairy, a character from an earlier campaign, to lighten the whole tone of the spot. This seemed to work better, so the agency proceeded to copy test a finished ad.

Pretesting and Posttesting

Advertising is one of the largest costs in a company's marketing budget. No wonder its effectiveness is a major concern!

Companies want to know what they are getting for their money—and whether their advertising is working. And they'd like some assurance before their ads run.

Kraft was no exception. Millward Brown Research performed a number of copy tests to see how the agency's latest spot would perform. The tests showed that the spot performed significantly better than the norm on key measures such as branding and persuasion. Following the copy tests, the company aired "The Calcium They Need" commercial in five test markets to see how it would affect sales. They quickly achieved a 10 percent increase in sales in those markets. Based on such a strong showing, Kraft rolled the campaign out nationally in 1999 and sales took off, growing 11.8 percent.[13]

The campaign was so successful that in 2000, the Advertising Research Foundation named Kraft and J. Walter Thompson finalists for its prestigious David Ogilvy Research Award, given to the most effective ad campaign guided by research.

The Purpose of Testing Ads
To increase the likelihood of preparing the most effective advertising messages, companies use **pretesting**. Some agencies, like DDB Needham, pretest all ad copy for communication gaps or flaws in

Crispin Porter + Bogusky used hidden cameras to capture the reactions of real Burger King customers who were told that the Whopper sandwich had been "discontinued." Research showed the ads were better recalled than any other ever tested.

STEPS IN THE RESEARCH PROCESS

Now that we understand the various types of decision-related information that marketers seek, let's explore how they gather this information by looking at the overall research process and some of the specific techniques they use.

There are five basic steps in the research process (see Exhibit 6–2):

1. Situation analysis and problem definition.

2. Informal (exploratory) research.

3. Construction of research objectives.

message content before recommending it to clients.[14] When companies don't pretest their ads, they may encounter a surprising reaction from the marketplace. Schering Canada received a torrent of complaint letters from customers who said they didn't like its commercial introducing the antihistamine Claritin to the over-the-counter market in Canada. Most negative responses, though, are more subtle: Consumers simply turn the page or change the channel, and sales mysteriously suffer. This is why it's also important to evaluate the effectiveness of an ad or campaign *after* it runs. **Posttesting** (also called *ad tracking*) provides the advertiser with useful guidelines for future advertising. We'll discuss methods for testing ads later in this chapter.

4. Formal research.

5. Interpretation and reporting of findings.

Step 1: Analyzing the Situation and Defining the Problem

The first step in the marketing research process is to *analyze the situation* and *define the problem.* Many large firms have in-house research departments. Often the marketing department also maintains a **marketing information system (MIS)**—a sophisticated set of procedures designed to generate a continuous, orderly flow of information for use in making marketing decisions. These systems ensure that managers get the information they need when they need it.[15]

Most smaller firms don't have dedicated research departments, and their methods for obtaining marketing information are frequently inadequate. These firms often find the problem-definition step difficult and time-consuming. Yet good research on the wrong problem is a waste of effort.

Step 2: Conducting Informal (Exploratory) Research

The second step in the process is to use **informal research** (or exploratory research) to learn more about the market, the

check yourself ✓

1. What are some things that might be tested with creative concept research?

2. Why do companies pretest their advertising?

▼**EXHIBIT 6–2** The marketing research process begins with evaluation of the company's situation and definition of the problem.

competition, and the business environment, and to better define the problem. Researchers may discuss the problem with wholesalers, distributors, or retailers outside the firm; with informed sources inside the firm; with customers; or even with competitors. They look for whoever has the most information to offer.

There are two types of research data: *primary* and *secondary*. Information collected from the marketplace about a specific problem is called **primary data**; acquiring it is typically expensive and time-consuming. So during the exploratory stage, researchers frequently use **secondary data**—information previously collected or published, usually for some other purpose, by the firm or by some other organization. This information is readily available, either internally or externally, and can be gathered more quickly and inexpensively than primary data.

Assembling Internal Secondary Data Company records are often a valuable source of secondary information. Useful internal data include product shipment figures, billings, warranty-card records, advertising expenditures, sales expenses, customer correspondence, and records of meetings with sales staffs.

A well-developed marketing information system can help researchers analyze sales data, review past tracking studies, and examine previous marketing research data. This information might point the way toward an interesting headline or positioning statement such as Motrin's "Medicine with Muscle."

Sources of External Secondary Data Much information is available, sometimes at little or no cost, from the government, market research companies, trade associations, various trade publications, or computerized databases. Most large companies subscribe to any of a number of syndicated research reports about their particular industry. For example, as the advertising manager for a large nutritional company introducing a new line of vitamins, you might need to know the current demand for vitamins and food supplements, the number of competitors in the marketplace, the amount of advertising each is doing, and the challenges and opportunities the industry faces.

In the United States, frequently used sources of secondary data include:

- Library reference materials (*Business Periodicals Index* for business magazines, *Reader's Guide to Periodical Literature*

for consumer magazines, *Public Information Service Bulletin*, the *New York Times Index*, and the *World Almanac and Book of Facts*).

- Government publications (*Statistical Abstract of the United States*).

- Trade association publications (annual fact books containing data gathered by various industry groups listed in the *Directory of National Trade Associations*).

- Research organizations and their publications or syndicated information (literature from university bureaus of business research, ACNielsen Store Audit, NPD Consumer Tracking, Experian Simmons's Multi-Media Engagement Study, IRI's Consumer Network, and Standard Rate & Data Service).

- Consumer/business publications (*BusinessWeek, Forbes, Fortune, American Demographics, Advertising Age, Prevention*, and thousands more).

- Computer database services (Dialog Information Service, ProQuest, Lexis-Nexis, and Dow Jones Newswires).

- Internet search engines (Bing, Ask, Google, Yahoo!, Dogpile, and others).

It's important to understand that secondary data carry some potential problems. Information may be out of date and therefore obsolete. Much of it is not relevant to the problem at hand. Some information from purported research is just wrong, so the findings are invalid. In other cases, the source may be unreliable. Finally, there is now so much information available (thanks to the Internet) that it's just overwhelming; it's extremely time-consuming to wade through it all.

> "Good research on the wrong problem is a waste of effort."

Step 3: Establishing Research Objectives

Once the exploratory research phase is completed, the company may discover it needs additional information that it can get only from doing primary research. As was the case for Holiday Inn Express, it may want to identify exactly who its customers are and clarify their perceptions of the company and the competition. To do so, the company must first establish *specific research objectives*.

A concise written statement of the research problem and objectives should be formulated at the beginning of any research project. A company must be clear about what decisions it has to make that the research results will guide. Once it knows the application, it can set down clear, specific research objectives.[16] For example, a department store, noticing that it is losing market share, might write its problem statement and research objectives as follows:

Market Share

Our company's sales, while still increasing, seem to have lost momentum and are not producing the profit our shareholders expect. In the last year, our market share declined 3 percentage points. Our studies indicate we are losing sales to other department stores in the same malls and that customers are confused about our position in the market. We need to make decisions about how we position ourselves for the future.

Research Objectives

We must answer the following questions: (1) Who are our customers? (2) Who are the customers of other department stores? (3) What do these customers like and dislike about us and about our competitors? (4) How are we currently perceived? and (5) What do we have to do to clarify and improve that perception?

This statement of the problem is specific and measurable, the decision point is clear, and the questions are related and relevant. The research results should provide the information that management needs to decide on a new positioning strategy for the company. The positioning strategy facilitates the development of marketing and advertising plans that will set the company's course for years to come.

check yourself ✓

1. What is the difference between primary and secondary data?

2. What is the purpose of a "control group" when conducting research?

Research [6–A]

Research is a complicated aspect of preparing a campaign, and without at least one course in advertising research you may find it tough going. However, without research you will find it difficult to make some of the tough creative and strategic decisions that lie ahead. Even without an extensive research background, you can do some secondary and qualitative research that can result in better choices for your campaign.

Secondary Research

Secondary research involves obtaining information from existing sources, including your client. Be sure to obtain all that you can, with the understanding that information shared by your client is valuable and that most clients will insist on strict confidentiality. Breaking a confidentiality agreement is a very serious transgression and should not happen under any circumstances, whether deliberately or through neglect.

For more information, access the secondary research tutorial, http://www.knowthis.com/tutorials/principles-of-marketing/finding-secondary-research.htm.

Qualitative Research

You can also plan some qualitative research studies. Two of the most common are focus groups and observational research. In a focus group, you bring together a collection of carefully chosen participants (users of your brand, users of competing brands, etc.) and lead a group discussion that has the potential to offer strategic insights.

Qualitative Research: Focus Groups

For a tutorial on using focus groups, see www.cse.lehigh.edu/~glennb/mm/FocusGroups.htm. Tips for using focus groups can be found at http://www.groupsplus.com/pages/mn091498.htm.

Observational Research

Observational research techniques involve monitoring the consumer in his or her native environment (the mall, a restaurant, a skateboard park, etc.). The goal is to see how the consumer behaves in a natural setting. Careful attention is ordinarily paid to language, dress, interactions, symbols, and style.

See the observational research tutorial at http://writing.colostate.edu/guides/research/observe/index.cfm. Tips for observational research can be found at http://www.quirks.com/articles/a1997/19971208.aspx?searchID=625728.

Quantitative Research

Your project may also involve administering a survey. Google Forms, introduced in the My Ad Campaign from Chapter 1, may be useful for creating an online survey that is easy and inexpensive to administer. The hard part is writing a good survey instrument and then choosing data analysis techniques that will provide you and your client with useful information. Some Web tutorials are listed below:

Surveys

Writing good questions: http://www.accesswave.ca/~infopoll/tips.htm.

Response options: http://dataguru.org/ref/survey/responseoptions.asp.

Data Analysis Using Excel

http://www.ncsu.edu/labwrite/res/gt/gt-menu.html.

formal research
Collecting primary data directly from the marketplace using qualitative or quantitative methods.

in-depth interview
An intensive interview technique that uses carefully planned but loosely structured questions to probe respondents' deeper feelings.

qualitative research
Research that tries to determine market variables according to unquantifiable criteria such as attitudes, beliefs, and lifestyle.

quantitative research Research that tries to determine market variables according to reliable, hard statistics about specific market conditions or situations.

projective techniques In marketing research, asking indirect questions or otherwise involving consumers in a situation where they can express feelings about the problem or product. The purpose is to get an understanding of people's underlying or subconscious feelings, attitudes, opinions, needs, and motives.

intensive techniques Qualitative research aimed at probing the deepest feelings, attitudes, and beliefs of respondents through direct questioning. Typical methods include in-depth interviews and focus groups.

L04 Explain the common methods used in qualitative and quantitative research.

Step 4: Conducting Formal Research

When a company wants to collect primary data directly from the marketplace about a specific problem or issue, it uses **formal research**. There are two types of formal research: qualitative and quantitative.

To get a general impression of the market, the consumer, or the product, advertisers typically start with **qualitative research**. This enables researchers to gain insight into both the population whose opinion will be sampled and the subject matter itself. Then, to get hard numbers about specific marketing situations, they may perform a survey or use some other form of **quantitative research**. Sophisticated agencies use a balance of both qualitative and quantitative methods, understanding the limits of each and how they work together.[17] (See Exhibit 6–3.)

In this section we'll discuss the basic methods advertisers use for conducting qualitative and quantitative research and then we'll look at how they apply these techniques to testing ads.

Basic Methods of Qualitative Research To get people to share their thoughts and feelings, researchers use qualitative research that elicits in-depth, open-ended responses rather than yes or no answers. Some marketers refer to this as *motivation research*. Unfortunately, no matter how skillfully posed, some questions are uncomfortable for consumers to answer. When asked why they bought a particular status car, for instance, consumers might reply that it handles well or is economical or dependable, but they rarely admit that it makes them feel important. The methods used in qualitative research are usually either *projective* or *intensive techniques*.

Projective techniques. Advertisers use **projective techniques** to understand people's underlying or subconscious feelings, attitudes, interests, opinions, needs, and motives. By asking indirect questions (such as "What kind of people do you think shop here?"), the researcher tries to involve consumers in a situation where they can express feelings about the problem or product.

Projective techniques were adapted for marketing research after their use by psychologists in clinical diagnosis. But such techniques require the skill of highly experienced researchers.

▼**EXHIBIT 6–3** Differences between qualitative and quantitative research.

	Qualitative	Quantitative
Main techniques for gathering data	Focus groups and in-depth interviews.	Surveys and scientific samples.
Kinds of questions asked	Why? Through what thought process? In what way? In connection with what other behavior or thoughts?	How many? How much?
Role of interviewer	Critical: interviewer must think on feet and frame questions and probes in response to whatever respondents say. A highly trained professional is advisable.	Important, but interviewers need only be able to read scripts. They should not improvise. Minimally trained, responsible employees are suitable.
Questions asked	Questions vary in order and phrasing from group to group and interview to interview. New questions are added, old ones dropped.	Should be exactly the same for each interview. Order and phrasing of questions carefully controlled.
Number of interviews	Fewer interviews tending to last a longer time.	Many interviews in order to give a projectable scientific sample.
Kinds of findings	Develop hypotheses, gain insights, explore language options, refine concepts, flesh out numerical data, provide diagnostics on advertising copy.	Test hypotheses, prioritize factors, provide data for mathematical modeling and projections.

A focus group is an intensive research technique used to evaluate the effectiveness of the various elements of a sponsor's ad or advertising campaign. Focus groups are especially effective used in conjunction with market surveys.

Intensive techniques. **Intensive techniques**, such as in-depth interviews, also require great care to administer properly. In the **in-depth interview**, carefully planned but loosely structured questions help the interviewer probe respondents' deeper feelings. The big pharmaceutical company Schering, for example, uses in-depth interviews with physicians to find out what attributes doctors consider most important in the drugs they prescribe and to identify which brands the doctors associate with different attributes.[18] While in-depth interviews help reveal individual motivations, they are also expensive and time-consuming, and skilled interviewers are in short supply.

One of the most common intensive research techniques is the **focus group**, in which the company invites six or more people typical of the target market to a group session to discuss the product, the service, or the marketing situation. The session may last an hour or more. A trained moderator guides the often freewheeling discussion, and the group interaction reveals the participants' true feelings or behavior toward the product. Focus-group meetings are usually recorded and often viewed or videotaped from behind a one-way mirror.

Focus groups don't represent a valid sample of the population, but the participants' responses are useful for several purposes. They can provide input about the viability of prospective spokespeople, determine the effectiveness of visuals, concepts, and strategies, and identify elements in ads that are unclear or claims that don't seem plausible. As in the case of Kraft, focus groups can be particularly useful in gaining a deeper understanding of particular market segments. Focus groups are best used in conjunction with surveys. In fact, focus-group responses often help marketers design questions for a formal survey[19] or, following a survey, focus groups can put flesh on the skeleton of raw data.[20]

Ethnographic research (or ethnography) is an intensive research technique that has been gaining in popularity among advertisers. Ethnographic information was collected by Fallon's planners on behalf of Holiday Inn Express when they accompanied the road warriors on their cross-country adventures. Ethnography involves trying to understand behavior and culture by going out and talking to people wherever they are, while they're doing whatever it is they do. It means entering someone's world for a while, be it a couple of hours or a couple of days.[21] This process can be very labor-intensive and therefore costly and may require long periods of time in the field. Ethnographers must be very skilled in their art and often have specialized training in social science fields such as anthropology.

Basic Methods of Quantitative Research
Advertisers use quantitative research to gain reliable, hard statistics about specific market conditions or situations. There are three basic research methods used to collect quantitative data: *observation, experiment,* and *survey.*

Observation. In the **observation method**, researchers monitor people's actions. They may count the traffic that passes by a billboard, measure a TV audience through instruments hooked to television sets, or study consumer reactions to products displayed in the supermarket. Most observation method research is performed by large, independent marketing research companies, such as Nielsen, Symphony IRI, and GfK NOP, whose clients subscribe to their various services.

Technology has greatly facilitated the observation method. One example is the **Universal Product Code (UPC)** label, an identifying series of vertical bars with a 12-digit number that adorns every consumer packaged good. By reading the codes with optical scanners, researchers can tell which products are selling and how well. The UPC label not only increases speed and accuracy at the checkout counter; it also enables timely inventory control and gives stores and manufacturers accurate point-of-purchase data sensitive to the impact of price, in-store promotion, couponing, and advertising.

For example, Nielsen ScanTrack provides data on packaged-goods sales, market shares, and retail prices from more than 350,000 stores across 30 countries. A companion service,

focus group A qualitative method of research in which four or more people, typical of the target market, are invited to a group session to discuss the product, the service, or the marketing situation for an hour or more.

ethnographic research (ethnography) An intensive research technique that has been gaining in popularity among advertisers. It involves trying to understand behavior and culture by going out and talking to people wherever they are, while they're doing whatever it is they do.

observation method A method of research used when researchers actually monitor people's actions.

Universal Product Code (UPC) An identifying series of vertical bars with a 12-digit number that adorns every consumer packaged good.

This video frame from Envirosell shows how the company uses security-type cameras to observe in-store consumer shopping habits.

not receive the altered stimulus. This type of research is used primarily for new product and new campaign introductions. As we saw in the Kraft story, marketers go to an isolated geographic area, called a **test market**, and introduce the product in that area alone or test a new ad campaign or promotion before a *national rollout*. For example, a new campaign might run in one geographic area but not another. Sales in the two areas are then compared to determine the campaign's effectiveness. However, researchers must use strict controls so the variable that causes the effect can be accurately determined. Because it's hard to control every marketing variable, this method is difficult to use and quite expensive.

Survey. The most common method of gathering primary quantitative research data is the **survey**, in which the researcher gains information on attitudes, opinions, or motivations by questioning current or prospective customers (political polls are a common type of survey). Surveys can be conducted by personal interview, telephone, mail, or on the Internet. Each has distinct advantages and disadvantages (see Exhibit 6–4).

Homescan, uses in-home bar-code scanners to collect data on consumer purchases and shopping patterns from more than 250,000 households in 27 countries.[22] As a result, marketers suddenly have reliable data on the effectiveness of the tools they use to influence consumers. With that information, they can develop empirical models to evaluate alternative marketing plans, media vehicles, and promotional campaigns.[23] In one case, for instance, data might indicate that a 40-cent coupon for toothpaste would create $150,000 in profits but a 50-cent coupon on the same item would create a $300,000 loss.

Video cameras have also affected observation techniques. Envirosell, a New York–based research company, uses security-type cameras to capture consumer in-store shopping habits. To determine the effectiveness of packaging and displays, the company analyzes how much time people spend with an item and how they read the label.[24]

Experiment. To measure actual cause-and-effect relationships, researchers use the **experimental method**. An experiment is a scientific investigation in which a researcher alters the stimulus received by a *test group* and compares the results with that of a *control group* that did

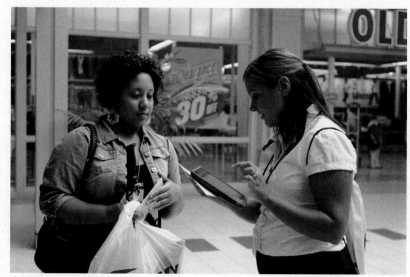

Researchers often collect information on attitudes, opinions, or motivations by conducting surveys of current or prospective customers. A common technique is the mall intercept, in which an interviewer at a shopping mall intercepts a sample of those passing by to ask if they would be willing to participate in a brief research study.

▼ **EXHIBIT 6–4** Comparison of data collection methods.

	Data Collection Method			
	Personal Interview	Telephone	Mail	Internet
Data collection costs	High	Medium	Low	Low
Data collection time required	Medium	Low	High	Medium
Sample size for a given budget	Small	Medium	Large	Large
Data quantity per respondent	High	Medium	Low	Low
Reaches widely dispersed sample	No	Maybe	Maybe	Yes
Interaction with respondents	High	High	None	Medium
Degree of interviewer bias	High	Medium	None	None
Severity of nonresponse bias	Low	Low	High	Medium
Presentation of visual stimuli	Yes	No	Maybe	Yes
Field worker training required	Yes	Yes	No	No

check yourself ✓

1. What are some benefits of qualitative research?

2. Why would an advertiser use quantitative research?

L05 Evaluate the challenges of pretesting and posttesting advertising.

Basic Methods for Testing Ads

Although there is no infallible way to predict advertising success or failure, pretesting and posttesting can give an advertiser useful insights if properly applied.

Pretesting methods. Advertisers often pretest ads for likability and comprehension by using a variety of qualitative and quantitative techniques.

For example, when pretesting print ads, advertisers often ask direct questions: What does the advertising say to you? Does the advertising tell you anything new or different about the company? If so, what? Does the advertising reflect activities you would like to participate in? Is the advertising believable? What effect does it have on your perception of the merchandise offered? Do you like the ads?

Through **direct questioning**, researchers can elicit a full range of responses from people and thereby infer how well advertising messages convey key copy points. Direct questioning is especially effective for testing alternative ads in the early stages of development, when respondents' reactions and input can best be acted on.

GfK Custom Research, ® Starch Advertising Research
Cosmopolitan Magazine-November 2007
eStarch Readership Report

Garnier Fructis Advertisement

Noted	85%
Associated	84%
Read Some	69%
Read Most	30%
Brand Disposition	85% (top three score)

Starch Readership Reports (www.gfkamerica.com) posttests magazine ad effectiveness by interviewing readers. The summary tab at the top of this ad indicates that 85 percent of women readers noted the ad; 84 percent associated the ad with the advertiser (Garnier); and 30 percent read most of the copy.

> ## Some creative people mistrust ad testing; they believe it stifles creativity.

There are numerous techniques for pretesting print ads, including *focus groups, order-of-merit tests, paired comparisons, portfolio tests, mock magazines, perceptual meaning studies,* and *direct-mail tests.* (See My Ad Campaign 6–B "Methods for Pretesting Ads.")

Several methods are used specifically to pretest radio and TV commercials. In **central location tests**, respondents are shown test commercials, usually in shopping centers, and questions are asked before and after exposure. In **clutter tests**, test commercials are shown with non-competing control commercials to determine their effectiveness, measure comprehension and attitude shifts, and detect weaknesses.

The challenge of pretesting. There is no best way to pretest advertising variables. Different methods test different aspects, and each has its own advantages and disadvantages—a formidable challenge for the advertiser.

Pretesting helps distinguish strong ads from weak ones. But since the test occurs in an artificial setting, respondents may assume the role of expert or critic and give answers that don't reflect their real buying behavior. They may invent opinions to satisfy the interviewer, or be reluctant to admit they are influenced, or vote for the ads they think they *should* like. This is why some creative people mistrust ad testing; they believe it stifles creativity.

Methods for Pretesting Ads [6–B]

Advertisers rarely trust intuition alone when evaluating their creative work. There is simply too much on the line. Pretesting is what occurs when advertisers test prototypes of their ads before they are run in the mass media. Below is a comprehensive list of ways that real agencies and advertisers test their work. You don't have the resources to do many of them. But you can use some of these methods to test your creative ideas with a small sample drawn from your target audience. Doing so will give you added ammunition for persuading your client that you've developed a strong strategy for his or her brand.

Print Advertising

- **Direct questioning.** Asks specific questions about ads. Often used to test alternative ads in early stages of development.
- **Focus group.** A moderated but freewheeling discussion and interview conducted with six or more people.
- **Order-of-merit test.** Respondents see two or more ads and arrange them in rank order.
- **Paired comparison method.** Respondents compare each ad in a group.
- **Portfolio test.** One group sees a portfolio of test ads interspersed among other ads and editorial matter. Another group sees the portfolio without the test ads.
- **Mock magazine.** Test ads are "stripped into" a magazine, which is left with respondents for a specified time. (Also used as a post-testing technique.)
- **Perceptual meaning study.** Respondents see ads in timed exposures.
- **Direct mail test.** Two or more alternative ads are mailed to different prospects on a mailing list to test which ad generates the largest volume of orders.

Broadcast Advertising

- **Central location projection test.** Respondents see test commercial films in a central location such as a shopping center.
- **Trailer test.** Respondents see TV commercials in trailers at shopping centers and receive coupons for the advertised products; a matched sample of consumers just gets the coupons. Researchers measure the difference in coupon redemption.
- **Theater test.** Electronic equipment enables respondents to indicate what they like and dislike as they view TV commercials in a theater setting.
- **Live telecast test.** Test commercials are shown on closed-circuit or cable TV. Respondents are interviewed by phone, or sales audits are conducted at stores in the viewing areas.
- **Sales experiment.** Alternative commercials run in two or more market areas.

Physiological Testing

- **Pupilometric device.** Dilation of the subject's pupils is measured, presumably to indicate the subject's level of interest.
- **Eye movement camera.** The route the subject's eyes traveled is superimposed over an ad to show the areas that attracted and held attention.
- **Galvanometer.** Measures subject's sweat gland activity with a mild electrical current; presumably the more tension an ad creates, the more effective it is likely to be.
- **Voice pitch analysis.** A consumer's response is taped, and a computer is used to measure changes in voice pitch caused by emotional responses.
- **Brain pattern analysis.** A scanner monitors the reaction of the subject's brain.

central location tests A type of pretest in which videotapes of test commercials are shown to respondents on a one-to-one basis, usually in shopping center locations.

clutter tests Method of pretesting in which commercials are grouped with noncompetitive control commercials and shown to prospective customers to measure their effectiveness in gaining attention, increasing brand awareness and comprehension, and causing attitude shifts.

attitude tests A type of posttest that usually seeks to measure the effectiveness of an advertising campaign in creating a favorable image for a company, its brand, or its products.

recall tests Posttesting methods used to determine the extent to which an advertisement and its message have been noticed, read, or watched.

inquiry tests A form of test in which consumer responses to an ad for information or free samples are tabulated.

Despite these challenges, the issue comes down to dollars. Small advertisers rarely pretest, but their risk isn't as great, either. When advertisers risk millions of dollars on a new campaign, they *must* pretest to be sure the ad or commercial is interesting, believable, likable, memorable, and persuasive—and reinforces the brand image.

Posttesting methods. Posttesting can be more costly and time-consuming than pretesting, but it can test finished ads under actual market conditions. As we saw with Kraft, some advertisers benefit from pretesting and posttesting by running ads in select test markets before launching a campaign nationwide.

As in pretesting, advertisers use both quantitative and qualitative methods in posttesting. Most posttesting techniques fall into five broad categories: *aided recall, unaided recall, attitude tests, inquiry tests,* and *sales tests.* (See My Ad Campaign 6–B "Methods for Posttesting Ads.")

Some advertisers use **attitude tests** to measure a campaign's effectiveness in creating a favorable image for a company, its brand, or its products. Presumably, favorable changes in attitude predispose consumers to buy the company's product.

Nielsen IAG measures which commercials viewers recalled or found most persuasive last night. The company provides these advertising performance measurement services to such clients as American Express, Toyota, and Verizon. The firm monitors the effectiveness of television commercials, product placement campaigns, and commercial sponsorships by conducting more than 100,000 surveys daily about the programs the consumers watched the night before.[25]

The challenge of posttesting. Each posttesting method has limitations. **Recall tests** reveal the effectiveness of ad components, such as size, color, or themes. But they measure what respondents noticed and remembered, *not* whether they actually intend to buy the product.

For measuring sales effectiveness, attitude tests are often better than recall tests. An attitude change relates more closely to product purchase, and a measured change in attitude gives management more confidence to make informed decisions about advertising plans.

By using **inquiry tests**—in which consumers respond to an ad for information or free samples—researchers can test an ad's attention-getting value, readability, and understandability. These tests also permit fairly good control of the variables that motivate reader action, particularly if a *split-run* test is used (split runs are covered in Chapter 11). Unfortunately, inquiries may not reflect a sincere interest in a product, and responses may take months to receive.

Methods for Posttesting Ads [6–C]

Posttesting involves assessing the impact of a campaign after the ads have run. It is an important way that advertisers judge whether their messages have helped them to achieve their advertising objectives (see Chapter 8). You will most likely not do posttesting for your client. However it is good practice for you to propose HOW the client might posttest your ads. This is material that you can incorporate in your campaigns book. Be sure to reference your advertising objectives when you propose a posttesting technique.

• **Aided recall (recognition–readership).** To jog their memories, respondents are shown certain ads and then asked whether their previous exposure was through reading, viewing, or listening.

• **Unaided recall.** Respondents are asked, without prompting, whether they saw or heard advertising messages.

• **Attitude tests.** Direct questions, semantic differential tests, or unstructured questions measure changes in respondents' attitudes after a campaign.

• **Inquiry tests.** Additional product information, product samples, or premiums are given to readers or viewers of an ad; ads generating the most responses are presumed to be the most effective.

• **Sales tests.** Measures of past sales compare advertising efforts with sales. Controlled experiments test different media in different markets. Consumer purchase tests measure retail sales from a given campaign. Store inventory audits measure retailers' stocks before and after a campaign.

sales tests A useful measure of advertising effectiveness when advertising is the dominant element, or the only variable, in the company's marketing plan. Sales tests are more suited for gauging the effectiveness of campaigns than of individual ads or components of ads.

validity An important characteristic of a research test. For a test to be valid, it must reflect the true status of the market.

reliability An important characteristic of research test results. For a test to be reliable, it must be repeatable, producing the same result each time it is administered.

universe An entire target population.

sample A portion of the population selected by market researchers to represent the appropriate targeted population. Also, a free trial of a product.

Learning that the wash mitt usually given to customers with the purchase of a new Beetle convertible wasn't earning them particularly high marks, Volkswagen (www.vw.com) contacted Arnold Worldwide to come up with a better idea. Arnold decided to create a guidebook to the many things that new owners could see and do in a convertible and included a star chart and wild birdseed with the book.

When advertising is the dominant element or the only variable in the company's marketing plan, **sales tests** are a useful measure of advertising effectiveness. However, many other variables can affect sales (competitors' activities, the season of the year, and even the weather). Sales response may not be immediate, and sales tests, particularly field studies, are often costly and time-consuming. For consumer packaged goods, though, the cost of sales tests has been greatly reduced thanks to grocery store scanners.

Step 5: Interpreting and Reporting the Findings

The final step in the research process involves interpreting and reporting the data. Research is very costly (see Exhibit 6–5), and its main purpose is to help solve problems. The final report must make the findings clear to the company's managers and relevant to their needs.

Tables and graphs are helpful, but they must be explained in words management can understand. Technical jargon (such as "multivariate analysis of variance model") should be avoided, and descriptions of the methodology, statistical analysis, and raw data should be confined to an appendix. The report should state the problem and research objective, summarize the findings, and draw conclusions. The researcher should make recommendations for management action, and the report should be discussed in a formal presentation to allow management feedback and questions and to highlight important points.

check yourself ✓

1. What information might be collected when pre-testing an advertisement?

2. What is the value in knowing if advertising changed a consumer's attitude?

LO6 Identify issues that can affect the accuracy and usability of quantitative research.

IMPORTANT ISSUES IN ADVERTISING RESEARCH

When marketers conduct primary research, there is always one legitimate concern—the accuracy of the findings. This is especially true when conducting formal quantitative research and when doing research in international markets.

Type of Research	Features	Cost	Cost per Respondent	Factors That Can Affect Quality and Costs
Telephone and mail surveys	400 20-minute interviews, with report	$16,000 to $18,000	$40 to $45	Response rates Interview time Incidence of qualified respondents Level of analysis required in the report
E-mail surveys	400 surveys, with report	$3,000 to $5,000	$8 to $16	Extent population can be reached via e-mail Response rates Level of analysis required in the report
Focus group	2 groups with 10 respondents each, with report	$8,000 to $12,000	$400 to $600	Cost of focus group facilities Moderator costs Respondent costs

Sources: WestGroup Research, "Research Fundamentals: Estimating Telephone Survey Research Costs," http://www.westgroupresearch.com/research/phonecosts. html, accessed October 14, 2006; MC Squared Consulting, "Market Research," http://smallbusiness.yahoo.com/r-article-a-2188-m-6-sc-41-holding_a_focus_group_ on_a_budget-i?aid=2188&mcid=6&scid=41&holding_a_focus_group_on_a_budget=i, accessed October 14, 2006; "Survey's Buyers Guide," http://Smallbusiness. yahoo.com/r-article-a-2040-m-6-sc-41-surveys_buyers_guide-i.

Considerations in Conducting Formal Quantitative Research

Quantitative research requires formal design and rigorous standards for collecting and tabulating data to ensure its accuracy and usability. When conducting formal research, advertisers must consider certain issues carefully, especially whether the research is *valid* and *reliable*.

Validity and Reliability

Assume you want to determine a market's attitude toward a proposed new toy. The market consists of 10 million individuals. You show a prototype of the toy to five people and four say they like it (an 80 percent favorable attitude). Is that test valid? Hardly. For a test to have **validity**, *results must be free of bias and reflect the true status of the market*.[26] Five people aren't enough for a minimum sample, and the fact that *you* showed a prototype of *your* toy to these people would probably bias their response.

Moreover, if you repeated the test with five more people, you might get an entirely different response. So your test also lacks **reliability**. For a test to be reliable, it must be *repeatable*—it must produce approximately the same result each time it is administered (see Exhibit 6–6).

Validity and reliability depend on several key elements: the sampling methods, the survey questionnaire design, and the data tabulation and analysis methods.

Sampling Methods

When a company wants to know what consumers think, it typically can't ask everybody. But its research should as nearly as possible reflect the **universe** (the entire target population) of prospective customers. Researchers therefore select from that population a **sample** that they expect will represent the population's characteristics. To accomplish this, they must decide whom to survey, how many to survey, and how to choose the respondents.

A sample must be large enough to achieve precision and stability. The larger the sample, the more reliable the results. However, reliability can be obtained with even very small samples, a fraction of 1 percent of the population, if the sample is drawn correctly. There are two types of samples: probability samples and nonprobability samples.

▼ **EXHIBIT 6–6** The reliability/validity diagram. Using the analogy of a dartboard, the bull's-eye is the actual value of some measure within a population. The top row shows high reliability (repeatability) because the darts are closely clustered. When reliability drops, the darts land more randomly and spread across a wider area, as in both examples in the bottom row. We got different results each time. The left column demonstrates high validity because in both examples the darts center around the bull's-eye. The right column represents low validity because bias in the testing process drew all the darts to one side; we were measuring the wrong thing. The upper-left quadrant reflects the truest picture of the data.

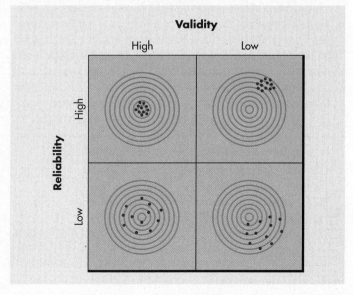

The greatest accuracy is gained from **probability samples** (sometimes referred to as *random samples*) because everyone in the universe has a quantifiable chance of being selected.[27] For example, a researcher who wants to know a community's opinion on an issue could select members of the community at random. But this method has its challenges. Every unit (person) must be known, listed, and numbered so each can be given an equal chance of being selected, an often prohibitively expensive and sometimes impossible task, especially with customers of nationally distributed products.

Instead, researchers often use **nonprobability samples** because they're easier, less expensive, and less time-consuming than probability samples. Sometimes referred to as *convenience samples,* respondents are selected on the basis of their availability (e.g., because they volunteered). Nonprobability samples don't give every unit in the universe an equal chance of being included, so there's no guarantee the sample is representative. As a result, researchers can't be confident in the validity of the responses.[28] However, most marketing and advertising research only needs approximate measures

of the data. For example, the nonprobability method of interviewing shoppers in malls may be sufficient to determine the shopping preferences, image perceptions, and attitudes of target customers.

How Questionnaires Are Designed Constructing a good questionnaire requires considerable expertise. Much bias in research is blamed on poorly designed questionnaires. Typical problems include asking the wrong types of questions, asking too many questions, using the wrong form of a question (which makes it difficult to answer or tabulate), and using a poor choice of words. Exhibit 6–7 shows some typical questions that might be used in a survey for a retail store.

Consider the simple question: "What kind of soap do you use?" The respondent doesn't know what *soap* means. Hand soap, shampoo, laundry detergent, or dishwashing soap? Does *kind* mean brand, size, or type? Finally, what constitutes *use?* What a person buys (perhaps for someone else) or uses personally—or for what purpose? In fact, one person probably uses several different kinds of soap, depending on the occasion. It's impossible to answer this question accurately. Worse, if the consumer does answer it, the researcher doesn't know what the answer means and will likely draw an

Developing an Effective Questionnaire [6–D]

In many years of teaching an advertising research class, I have always told students that the hardest thing they will do is write a good survey. When they hear this students are often skeptical, after all, many of them are good writers. But writing a survey is surprisingly tough if you've never done it before. The key is to write questions and statements that get to the heart of your objectives. Every survey item must be relevant, clear, and useful. Don't waste your respondents' time (or your own) with items that hold little potential for helping you better serve your client. Here are some tips for writing items that can help you make better decisions:

• **List specific research objectives.** Don't spend money collecting irrelevant data.

• **Write short questionnaires.** Don't tax the respondent's patience; you may get careless or flip answers.

• **State questions clearly** so there is no chance for misunderstanding. Avoid generalities and ambiguities.

• **Write a rough draft first,** then polish it.

• **Use a short opening statement.** Include the interviewer's name, the name of the organization, and the purpose of the questionnaire.

• **Put the respondent at ease** by opening with one or two inoffensive, easily answered questions.

• **Structure questions so they flow logically.** Ask general questions before more detailed ones.

• **Avoid questions that suggest an answer or could be considered leading.** They bias the results.

• **Include a few questions that cross-check earlier answers.** This helps ensure validity.

• **Put the demographic questions (age, income, education) and any other personal questions at the end of the questionnaire.**

• **Pretest the questionnaire** with 20 to 30 people to be sure they interpret the questions correctly and that it covers all the information sought.

▼**EXHIBIT 6–7** A personal questionnaire like this helps determine shoppers' feelings toward a chain of stores, its merchandise, and its advertising.

1. Do you intend to shop at _(Store name)_ between now and Sunday?
Yes 1   No   2   (If no, skip to question 5)

2. Do you intend to buy something in particular or just to browse?
Buy 1   Browse 2

3. Have you seen any of the items you intend to buy advertised by _(Store name)_?
Yes 1   (continue)   No   2   (skip to question 5)

4. Where did you see these items advertised? Was it in a _(Store name)_ advertising insert included with your newspaper, a _(Store name)_ flyer you received in the mail, the pages of the newspaper itself, on TV, or somewhere else?
☐ Insert in newspaper   ☐ On TV
☐ Flyer in mail   ☐ Somewhere else (specify) _____
☐ Pages of newspaper   ☐ Don't recall

5. Please rate the _(Store name)_ advertising insert on the attributes listed below. Place an X in the box at the position that best reflects your opinion of how the insert rates on each attribute. Placing an X in the middle box usually means you are neutral. The closer you place the X to the left or right phrase or word, the more you believe it describes the _(Store name)_ insert.

Looks cheap								Looks expensive
Unskillful								Cleverly done
Unappealing								Appealing
Does not show clothing in an attractive manner	1	2	3	4	5	6	7	Shows clothing in an attractive manner

6. Please indicate all of the different types of people listed below you feel this _(Store name)_ advertising insert is appealing to.

☐ Young people   ☐ Quality-conscious people
☐ Bargain hunters   ☐ Low-income people
☐ Conservative dressers   ☐ Budget watchers
☐ Fashion-conscious people ☐ Older people
☐ Rich people   ☐ Middle-income people
☐ Professionals   ☐ Blue-collar people
☐ High-income people   ☐ Women
☐ Men   ☐ Office workers
☐ Someone like me   ☐ Smart dressers
☐ Career-oriented women   ☐ Other (specify) _____

incorrect conclusion. For these reasons, questionnaires *must* be pretested. (See My Ad Campaign 6–C, "Developing an Effective Questionnaire.")

Effective survey questions have three important attributes: *focus, brevity,* and *clarity.* They focus on the topic of the survey. They are as brief as possible. And they are expressed simply and clearly.[29]

The four most common types of questions are *open-ended, dichotomous, multiple choice,* and *scale.* But there are many ways to ask questions within these four types. In Exhibit 6–8, for example, more choices could be added to the multiple-choice format. Neutral responses (the middle choice) could be removed from the scale question so the respondent must answer either positively or negatively. And there is obvious bias in the dichotomous question.

▼**EXHIBIT 6–8** Different ways to phrase research questions.

Type	Questions
Open-ended	How would you describe (_Store name_) advertising?
Dichotomous	Do you think (_Store name_) advertising is old-fashioned? _____ Yes _____ No
Multiple choice	What description best fits your opinion of (_Store name_) advertising? _____ Modern _____ Unconvincing _____ Well done _____ Old-fashioned _____ Believable
Scale	Please indicate on the scale how you rate the quality of (_Store name_) advertising. _____ _____ _____ _____ _____ _____ _____ _____ 1 2 3 4 5 Poor Excellent

Questions should elicit a response that is both accurate and useful. By testing questionnaires on a small subsample, researchers can detect any confusion, bias, or ambiguities and make revisions.

Data Tabulation and Analysis
Collected data must be validated, edited, coded, and tabulated. Answers must be checked to eliminate errors or inconsistencies. For example, one person might answer two years, while another says 24 months; such responses must be changed to the same units for correct tabulation. Some questionnaires may be rejected because respondents' answers indicate they misunderstood the questions. Finally, the data must be tabulated and summarized, usually by computer.

Many researchers want *cross-tabulations* (for example, product use by age group or education). Software programs such as SPSS® and MINITAB® Statistical Software make it possible for small advertisers as well as large corporations to tabulate data on a personal computer and apply advanced statistical techniques.[30] Many cross-tabulations are possible, but researchers must use skill and imagination to select only those that show meaningful and significant relationships.

Collecting Primary Data in International Markets

International marketers face a number of challenges when they collect primary data. For one thing, research overseas is often more expensive than domestic research. Many marketers are surprised to learn that research in five countries costs five times as much as research in one country; there are no economies of scale.[31]

But advertisers must determine whether their messages will work in foreign markets. (Maxwell House, for example, had to change its "great American coffee" campaign when it discovered that Germans have little respect for U.S. coffee.)

Advertisers need more than just facts about a country's culture. They need to understand and appreciate the nuances of its cultural traits and habits, a difficult task for people who don't live there or speak the language. Knowledgeable international advertisers such as Colgate-Palmolive work in partnership with their local offices and use local bilingual marketing people when conducting primary research abroad.[32]

For years, Mattel tried unsuccessfully to market the Barbie doll in Japan. It finally sold the manufacturing license to a Japanese company, Takara, which did its own research. Takara found that most Japanese girls and their parents thought Barbie's breasts were too big and her legs too long. It modified the doll accordingly, changed the blue eyes to brown, and sold 2 million dolls in two years.

Conducting original research abroad can be fraught with problems. First, the researcher must use the local language, and translating questionnaires can be tricky. Second, many cultures view strangers suspiciously and don't wish to talk about their personal lives. U.S. companies found that mail surveys and phone interviews don't work in Japan; they have to use expensive, time-consuming personal interviews.[33]

Marketers are often surprised by some of the differences they encounter when trying to conduct international research. Lead times to begin projects are typically longer, with the Far East being particularly troublesome. Groups can take twice as long to set up overseas. The structures differ too. Focus groups, for instance, rarely use more than 4 to 6 people rather than the 8 to 10 typical of the United States. Screening requirements for participants abroad are typically less rigid, and foreign moderators tend to be much less structured than their U.S. counterparts. Finally, the facilities don't usually have all the amenities of U.S. offices, but the costs are frequently twice as high in Europe and three times as high in Asia.[34]

Despite these problems—or perhaps because of them—it's important for global advertisers to perform research. Competent researchers are available in all developed countries, and major international research firms have local offices in most developing countries.

Today, nearly three-quarters of market research firms use the Internet to conduct some form of market research.[35] With the global adoption of the Internet, experts anticipate further cuts in costs and time for getting valuable customer input for marketing and advertising decision making. ■

This example from Procter & Gamble's Bonux detergent campaign in Lebanon illustrates some of the difficulties inherent in international advertising. Lebanese housewives take great pride in clean washing, so much so that they even brag about laundry secrets and hang their laundry on balconies to be seen by neighbors. Bonux created the "housewives moment of fame" campaign and bought advertising space on the roofs of buses so the ads could be seen from balconies. Radio spots featured interviews with housewives riding the buses. The campaign raised awareness 85 percent, and increased market share by 20 percent.

marketing, advertising, and IMC planning

Nearly 70 years ago, Ally and Barney Hartman of Knoxville, Tennessee, decided to make their own mixer. The brothers cooked up a 7-Up-type brew and tested it on their families and friends. They seemed to like it, so they started bottling the concoction and distributing it to the locals. In 1946, they designed a paper label for their beverage featuring a hillbilly toting a gun and a signature that read "By Barney and Ollie." In honor of the mountain moonshine famous in Tennessee, they named their drink "Mountain Dew."

Over the course of time, the brand grew. The gun-toting Willy the Hillbilly and their apt slogan, "Ya-hoo Mountain Dew," helped make it a regional player. In 1964, PepsiCo bought the brand and, for some years, continued using the old advertising approach. But as sales flattened, Pepsi decided a new direction was called for.

In 1973 Pepsi repositioned and relaunched Mountain Dew. No longer would it be a hillbilly mixer. Rather, the Dew would be cast as a high-energy, youth-oriented, flavored soft drink. New

continued on p. 174

LEANING OBJECTIVES

LO1 Explain the role and importance of a marketing plan.

LO2 Explain the difference between objectives, strategies, and tactics in marketing and advertising plans.

LO3 What makes IMC planning different from traditional methods?

LO4 Explain how to establish specific, realistic, and measurable advertising objectives.

LO5 Explain how advertising budgets are determined.

Shaking the can only makes the Dew™ angry.

continued from p. 173

ads created by BBDO New York featured active young people enjoying outdoor activities to the theme "Hello Sunshine, Hello Mountain Dew." By 1978, the action-oriented approach sent Dew sales over the 100-million-case mark. In the 1980s they added high-octane sports and adventure to the advertising.[1] Then, in 1985, Mountain Dew went nationwide.

Since that time, Mountain Dew has set a standard of how to remain true to its own definition of exuberance across a variety of marketing platforms. "We have a great unity of message and purpose that has been consistent over time about what we are and what we aren't," says Scott Moffitt, director of marketing for Mountain Dew.[2] "The brand is all about exhilaration and energy, and you see that in all that we do, from advertising and community to grass-roots programs and our sports-minded focus. We have a very crystal clear, vivid positioning."

The positioning concept has allowed Mountain Dew to reach consumers in diverse venues—from skateboarding parks to mainstream extravaganzas such as the Super Bowl. Marketing across such a broad spectrum from grass-roots to grandiose advertising events is known within PepsiCo as "mass intimacy." One Pepsi-Cola executive puts it this way: "It's our way of saying we haven't sold out."[3]

Given the great success of BBDO's Dew campaign, the challenge became staying power throughout the 2000s. Young consumers are notoriously fickle and perpetually ready to try something new. One innovative tactic included developing a snowboarding documentary that made only brief references to the brand. The decision to finance a film, which carried a cost close to that of a traditional 30-second TV spot, may have resulted from recognition by the advertiser that its target audience watches less TV than other groups and often see TV commercials as manipulative.[4]

In the mid-2000s, when some soda drinkers turned to noncarbonated alternatives, Mountain Dew experienced a volume increase of nearly 2 percent and the diet version surged nearly 8 percent. The same period saw volume sales of Coke Classic and Pepsi-Cola drop 2 percent and 3 percent, respectively.

Will the Dew success story continue? Cie Nicholson, Mountain Dew's marketing director, believes it can. Nicholson says, "Our position on Mountain Dew is one of the most solid in the industry. I would argue it's one of the best-positioned brands across all brands even outside our category. So we will continue doing what we do."[5]

LO1   Explain the role and importance of a marketing plan.

THE MARKETING PLAN

The successful campaigns created by ad agency BBDO for Mountain Dew demonstrate that business success depends on marketing and advertising planning and advertising creativity.

The Importance of Marketing Planning

Since marketing drives a company's income, the marketing plan may well be its most important document.

The **marketing plan** assembles relevant facts about the organization, its markets, products, services, customers, competition, and so on. It forces all departments to focus on the customer. Finally, it lists goals and objectives for specified periods of time and lays out the precise strategies and tactics to achieve them.

The written marketing plan must reflect the goals of top management and be consistent with the company's mission and capabilities. Depending on its scope, the plan may be long and complex or, in the case of a small firm, very brief. Formal marketing plans are reviewed and revised yearly, but planning is not a one-time event; it's an ongoing activity.

The Effect of the Marketing Plan on IMC

The marketing plan has a profound effect on an organization's marketing communications. It helps managers analyze and improve all company operations, including marketing and advertising programs. It defines the role of advertising in the marketing mix. It enables better implementation, control, and continuity of advertising programs, and it ensures the most efficient allocation of IMC dollars.

Companies have a choice in how they plan. Most still use the traditional top-down planning model; some use a bottom-up model; and now, increasingly, companies are starting to use an IMC model. Let's look at each.

check yourself ✓

1. What is a marketing plan and why is it a company's most important document?

2. How does the marketing plan affect IMC efforts?

L02 Explain the difference between objectives, strategies, and tactics in marketing and advertising plans.

Top-Down Marketing Plans

The traditional **top-down marketing** plan is still quite common. As Exhibit 7–1 shows, the top-down plan has four main

▼**EXHIBIT 7–1** Traditional top-down marketing plan.

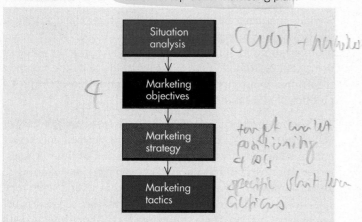

elements: *situation analysis, marketing objectives, marketing strategy,* and *marketing tactics* (or *action programs*). Large companies with extensive marketing plans sometimes include additional sections.

Situation Analysis The **situation analysis** section is a *factual* statement of the organization's current situation and how it got there. It presents all the relevant facts about the company's history, growth, products and services, sales volume, share of market, competitive status, markets served, distribution systems, past advertising programs, marketing research studies, and other pertinent information. A situation analysis is more than a presentation of facts, however. Good marketing plans provide the context for factual information. For example, Diet Mountain Dew's sales growth of 8 percent in 2005 is put into a context when the marketing plan notes that overall sales of carbonated beverages declined that year.

Planners draw attention to the most important aspects of a brand's situation through a SWOT analysis. The **SWOT analysis** uses the facts contained in the situation analysis to point out strengths, weaknesses, opportunities, and threats for the brand. Strengths and weaknesses represent company capabilities, while opportunities and threats represent environmental factors. One obvious strength for Mountain Dew is its well-defined, attractive brand image as a high-energy, full-flavored, carbonated beverage. A possible weakness could be the brand's age. An opportunity for Mountain Dew might be the increased interest in energy drinks. Since Mountain Dew is a highly caffeinated beverage, it stands to profit from such a trend. Threats to Mountain Dew might include rising prices for commodities used to make the product (sugar, flavorings) or distribute the product (fuel) that would force Mountain Dew to raise prices to remain profitable.

Other threats might be changes in the consumption behaviors of its target markets (some of the fastest growing soft-drinks today are vitamin-infused beverages such as Pepsi's Tava).[6]

Marketing Objectives The advertiser's next step is to determine specific marketing objectives. These must consider the amount of money the company has to invest in marketing and production, its knowledge of the marketplace, and the competitive environment.

marketing plan
The plan that directs the company's marketing effort.

top-down marketing The traditional planning process with four main elements: situation analysis, marketing objectives, marketing strategy, and tactics or action programs.

situation analysis
A factual statement of the organization's current situation and how it got there.

SWOT analysis
After assessing a companies situation, the writer of a marketing plan prepares an analysis that identifies the brand's or product's strengths, weaknesses, opportunities, and threats.

3 steps

" Need-satisfying objectives help shift management's perspective from producing products to satisfying needs. "

For example, based on its knowledge about Mountain Dew drinkers, the company decided in 2009 to communicate directly with its user base on the Internet as a way of developing new flavors and brand extensions.[7]

CLIMB ABOARD THE OFFICIAL AIRLINE OF BETTER.

Virgin america

FLY WITH WI-FI, MOVIES, AND FOOD ON DEMAND ALL FOR A RADICALLY LOW FARE.
SAN FRANCISCO • LOS ANGELES • NEW YORK • BOSTON • WASHINGTON, D.C. • SEATTLE • LAS VEGAS • ORANGE COUNTY • SAN DIEGO

Need-satisfying objectives address the real value that a product or service delivers to its customers. Virgin America distinguishes itself from competing airlines by promising better and friendlier service. This promise is attractive to customers unhappy with the frequently stressful experience of flying.

Marketing objectives follow logically from a review of the company's current situation, management's prediction of future trends, and the hierarchy of company objectives. For example, **corporate objectives** are stated in terms of profit or return on investment, or net worth, earnings ratios, growth, or corporate reputation. **Marketing objectives**, which derive from corporate objectives, should relate to the needs of target markets as well as to specific sales goals. These may be referred to as general *need-satisfying objectives* and specific *sales-target objectives*.

To shift management's view of the organization from a producer of products to a satisfier of customers' needs, companies set **need-satisfying objectives**. These have a couple of important purposes. First, they enable the firm to view its business broadly. For example, Revlon founder Charles Revson once said a cosmetics company's product is hope, not lipstick. An insurance company sells financial security, not policies. Mountain Dew executive Cie Nicholson describes her brand as "a high energy drink for people with a zest for life." The beverage's unusual color and taste, its relatively high caffeine level, and its outstanding IMC appeals, all of which emphasize a nonconformist's view of life, mesh seamlessly with what Dew consumers want from a beverage.

Second, by setting need-satisfying objectives, managers must see through the customer's eyes. They have to ask "What are we planning to do for the customer?" and "What is the value of that to our customer?" One of the best ways to define a market is to think about customer needs first and then identify the products that meet those needs.[8]

The second kind of marketing objective is the **sales-target objective**. This is a specific, quantitative, realistic marketing goal to be achieved within a specified period of time. A sales-target objective could be phrased as "What are we planning to do for ourselves?" They may be expressed in several ways: total sales volume; sales volume by product, market segment, customer type; market share in total or by product line; growth rate of sales volume in total or by product line; and gross profit in total or by product line. Mountain Dew, for example, uses a number of measures for its sales-target objectives: case volume, share of market, growth, and/or share of growth.

Marketing Strategy The **marketing strategy** describes how the company plans to meet its marketing objectives (see Commercial Break 7–A, "The Strategies of Marketing Warfare").

"Developing and following a strategy is what keeps you and everybody else on the same course so that you can maximize the effectiveness of your marketing."[9]

Marketing strategy typically involves three steps: (1) defining the particular target markets; (2) determining the strategic positioning; and (3) developing an appropriate marketing mix for each target market. A company's marketing strategy has a dramatic impact on its advertising. It determines the role and amount of advertising in the marketing mix, its creative thrust, and the media to be employed.

my ad campaign

Developing the Situation Analysis [7–A]

In previous chapters you've honed your understanding of the consumer, segmented the audience, and conducted research. It is time to pull all of this information together and create an assessment of your client's current situation. Marketers call such an assessment a situation analysis. Use the list below to organize your analysis.

The Industry
- **Companies in industry:** Dollar sales, strengths.
- **Growth patterns within industry:** Primary demand curve, per capita consumption, growth potential.
- **History of industry:** Technological advances, trends.
- **Characteristics of industry:** Distribution patterns, industry control, promotional activity, geographic characteristics, profit patterns.

The Company
- **The company story:** History, size, growth, profitability, scope of business, competence, reputation, strengths, weaknesses.

The Product or Service
- **The product story:** Development, quality, design, description, packaging, price structure, uses, reputation, strengths, weaknesses.
- **Product sales features:** Exclusive, nonexclusive differentiating qualities, competitive position.
- **Product research:** Technological breakthroughs, improvements planned.

Sale History
- **Sales and sales costs:** By product, model, sales districts.
- **Profit history.**

Share of Market
- **Sales history industrywide:** Share of market in dollars and units.
- **Market potential:** Industry trends, company trends, demand trends.

The Market
- **Who and where is the market:** How was market segmented, how can it be segmented, what are consumer needs, attitudes, and characteristics? How, why, when, where do consumers buy?

- **Past advertising appeals:** Successful or unsuccessful.
- **Who are our customers:** Past and future? What characteristics do they have in common? What do they like about our product? What don't they like?

Distribution
- **History and evaluation:** How and where product is distributed, current trend.
- **Company's relationship:** With the distribution channel and its attitudes toward product/company.
- **Past policies:** Trade advertising, deals, co-op programs.
- **Status:** Trade literature, dealer promotions, point-of-purchase displays.

Pricing Policies
- **Price history:** Trends, relationship to needs of buyers, competitive price situation.
- **Past price objectives:** Management attitudes, buyer attitudes, channel attitudes.

Competition
- **Who is the competition:** Primary, secondary, share of market, products, services, goals, attitudes. What is competition's growth history and size?
- **Strengths and competition:** Sales features, product quality, size. Weaknesses of competition.
- **Marketing activities of competition:** Advertising, promotion, distribution, sales force. Estimated budget.

Promotion
- **Successes and failures:** Past promotion policy, sales force, advertising, publicity.
- **Promotion expenditures:** History, budget emphasis, relation to competition, trend.
- **Advertising programs:** Review of strategies, themes, campaigns.
- **Sales force:** Size, scope, ability, cost/sale.

Selecting the target market. In top-down marketing, the first step in strategy development is to define and select the target market, using the processes of market segmentation and research discussed in Chapters 4 and 6.

When General Motors introduced its new Saturn SC1 model, for instance, it defined its target market as "college-educated import owners and intenders"—highly educated young adults (18 to 34) considering their first or second car purchase. They typically drive a Honda Civic, Toyota Corolla, or Nissan 240SX.

Similarly, Mountain Dew defines its target market as active, young people in their teens as well as young adults 20 to 39 years old. In addition, the brand aims a significant portion of its marketing activities at urban youth, especially African Americans and Latinos.[10]

To Mountain Dew, its prototypical consumer is an 18-year-old, street-smart, male teen.[11]

Positioning the product. Famed researcher and copywriter David Ogilvy said one of the first decisions in advertising is also the most important: how to position the product. **Positioning** refers to the place a brand occupies competitively in the minds of consumers. Every product has some position—whether intended or not—even if the position is "nowhere." Positions are based on consumer perceptions, which may or may not reflect reality. Strong brands have a clear, often unique position in the target market. Ogilvy & Mather, for example, differentiated Dove soap in 1957 by positioning it as a complexion bar for women with dry skin. Now, a half-century later, Dove is still the beauty bar with one-fourth moisturizing cream and is consistently the number one brand, with a 24 percent share of the multibillion-dollar bar soap market, nearly double the share of its closest competitor.

Positions are always available in a market. The big mistake many companies make is not staking out any position. They can't be everything; but they don't want to be nothing.[12] A company might pick a position similar to a competitor's and fight for the same customers. Or it might find a position not held by a competitor—a niche in the market—and

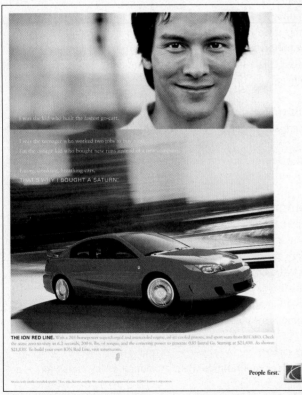

The photography and the copy in this print ad communicate that General Motors has a clear definition of the target market for its Saturn Ion Red Line. The 18- to 34-year-old male pictured in the ad grew up "eating, drinking, breathing cars."

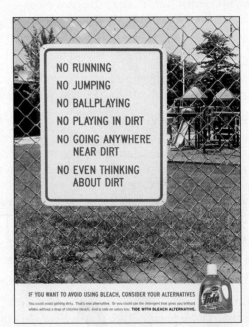

Positioning helps differentiate products from the competition. In the crowded detergent category, Procter & Gamble has clearly positioned this Tide product as an alternative to using bleach. When a consumer wants to get clothes white without bleach, this is the product that should come to mind.

Jack Trout and Al Ries's *Marketing Warfare* is based on the classic book of military strategy, *On War,* written by Prussian general Carl von Clausewitz and published in 1832. The book outlines the principles behind all successful wars, and two simple ideas dominate: *force* and *the superiority of the defense.*

The Strategic Square

How do the principles of warfare apply to marketing? It comes down to the "strategic square":

Out of every 100 companies:
One should play defense.
Two should play offense.
Three should flank.
And 94 should be guerrillas.

Defensive Warfare

Datril opened its war on Tylenol with a price attack. Johnson & Johnson immediately cut Tylenol's price, even before Datril started its price advertising. Result: It repelled the Datril attacks and inflicted heavy losses on the Bristol-Myers entry.

Here are the rules for defensive marketing warfare:

1. Participate only if you are a market leader.
2. Introduce new products and services before the competition does.
3. Block strong competitive moves by copying them rapidly.

Offensive Warfare

Colgate had a strong number one position in toothpaste. But rival Procter & Gamble knew a thing or two about Carl von Clausewitz.

P&G launched Crest toothpaste with not only a massive $20 million advertising budget, but also the American Dental Association "seal of approval." Crest went over the top to become the best-selling toothpaste in the country.

But overtaking the leader is not that common. Most companies are happy if they can establish a profitable number two position.

The rules for waging offensive marketing warfare are:

1. Consider the strength of the leader's position.

2. Launch the attack on as narrow a front as possible, preferably with single products.
3. Launch the attack at the leader's weakest position.

Flanking Warfare

The third type of marketing warfare is where the action is for many companies. In practice, it means launching products where there is no competition. Unilever introduced Mentadent, the first baking soda/peroxide toothpaste, which became a very successful brand.

Here are the principles of flanking marketing warfare:

1. Make good flanking moves into uncontested areas.
2. Use surprise. Too much research often wastes precious time.
3. Keep up the pursuit; too many companies quit after they're ahead.

Guerrilla Warfare

Most of America's companies should be waging guerrilla warfare. The key to success in guerrilla wars is flexibility. A guerrilla should abandon any product or market if the tide of battle changes.

Here are the principles of guerrilla marketing warfare:

1. Find a market segment small enough to defend.
2. No matter how successful you become, never act like the leader.
3. Be prepared to "bug out" at a moment's notice.

Bottom Up

Trout and Ries's later book, *Bottom-Up Marketing* (discussed later in this chapter), continues the military analogy.

"Deep penetration on a narrow front is the key to winning a marketing war," they say. By this they mean that smaller companies should keep their product narrowly focused on a single concept. Many companies spread their forces over too wide a front. In fact, most large corporations today expend significant resources fending off focused attacks by smaller companies.

Applying the Breaks

Think of a successful product and explain its success in terms of marketing warfare. Then select a new or less successful product and explain how it might use marketing warfare strategy to achieve greatness.

---

fill it quickly, perhaps through product differentiation or market segmentation.

One scholar proposes seven distinct approaches to developing a positioning strategy:

1. *Product attribute*—setting the brand apart by stressing a particular product feature important to consumers.

2. *Price/quality*—positioning on the basis of price or quality.

> "Every product has some position—whether intended or not."

3. *Use/application*—positioning on the basis of how a product is used (e.g., Arm & Hammer).

4. *Product class*—positioning the brand against other products that, while not the same, offer the same class of benefits.

5. *Product user*—positioning against the particular group who uses the product.

6. *Product competitor*—positioning against competitors (e.g., Avis/Hertz), using the strength of the competitor's position to help define the subject brand.

7. *Cultural symbol*—positioning apart from competitors through the creation or use of some recognized symbol or icon.[13]

We would add an eighth approach: *By category*—positioning by defining or redefining a business category. A simple way for a company to get the number one position is to invent a new product category.

Xerox, for example, was originally known as *the* copier company, but with increased competition, the copier market became glutted, so Xerox tried to reposition itself as a problem solver. Now calling itself "The Document Company," it offers to use technology to find ways for everyone in an organization to manage and share useful information. But what it has really done is create a new business category occupied by one company: Xerox.[14]

With all its high energy and exhilaration, "youth" is not only the positioning of Mountain Dew; it's the heartbeat of the brand.[15] PepsiCo defines the Dew positioning this way:

> To 18-year-old males who embrace excitement, adventure, and fun, Mountain Dew is the great-tasting soft drink that exhilarates like no other because it is energizing, thirst quenching, and has a unique citrus flavor.

Often, a product's positioning can be discerned from its advertising tagline— *BMW, the ultimate driving machine; Nobody doesn't like Sara Lee; You're in good hands with Allstate; Do the Dew.*

Determining the marketing mix. The next step in developing the marketing strategy is determining a cost-effective marketing mix for *each* target market. The mix blends the various marketing elements the company controls: *product, price, distribution,* and *communications.*

Mountain Dew is blessed with a broad marketing toolbox to draw upon. First, it offers consumers an energizing, thirst-quenching soft-drink *product* with a unique citrus flavor and an image of

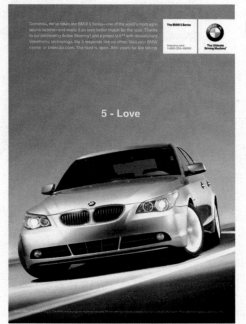

5 - Love

Strong brands have a clear and consistent positioning, often evident in their advertising taglines. BMW (www.bmw.com) has been advertised as "The Ultimate Driving Machine" since 1973.

youthful exuberance, exhilaration, and adventure. To build *distribution,* it uses a variety of promotions to the trade that enable grocers and other resellers to increase both volume and profits. While its *price* is competitive with other soft drinks, Mountain Dew promotes itself aggressively with free samples, premiums, and prizes at various street and sporting events—which effectively lowers the price to consumers.

Finally, Mountain Dew uses an integrated *communications* program that includes advertising on the Internet; sports and event sponsorships; appearances at grass-roots geographical events; plus a host of public relations activities—all designed to develop and promote the distinct Mountain Dew personality.

Companies have many marketing strategy options. They might increase distribution, initiate new uses for a product, change a product line, develop entirely new markets, or lower prices. Each option emphasizes one or more marketing mix elements. The choice depends on the product's target market, its position in the market, and its stage in the **product life cycle**, the progression of growth and decline through which a successful product typically moves.

Marketing Tactics (Action Programs) A company's objectives indicate where it wants to go; the strategy indicates the intended route; and the **tactics** (or *action programs*) determine the specific short-term actions to be taken, internally and externally, by whom, and when. In 2009–2010, Mountain Dew blazed new trails with exciting tactics that included a "Dewmocracy" campaign in which consumers chose three new flavors to be distributed nationwide. Fans voted online to choose their favorite, which became a permanent flavor of Dew. Advertising campaigns live in the world of marketing tactics. These tactics are the key to *bottom-up marketing.*

Bottom-Up Marketing: How Small Companies Plan

In small companies, everybody is both player and coach, and the day-to-day details seem to come first, leaving little or no time for formal planning. However, there is a solution to this dilemma: **bottom-up marketing** (see Exhibit 7–2).

Trout and Ries think an excellent way for a company to develop a competitive advantage is to focus on an ingenious tactic first and then develop that tactic into a strategy. By reversing the normal process, advertisers sometimes make important discoveries.[16] Vicks developed an effective liquid cold remedy but discovered that it put people to sleep. Rather than throw out the research, Vicks positioned the formula as a nighttime cold remedy. NyQuil went on to become the most successful new product in Vicks's history.

The *tactic* is a singular, competitive technique. By planning from the bottom up, entrepreneurs can find unique tactics to exploit. But caution is required. Advertisers should find just *one* tactic, not two or three. The advertiser can then focus all elements of the marketing mix on this single-minded tactic. The tactic becomes the nail, and the strategy is the hammer that drives it home.

The artful combination of tactic and strategy creates a position in the consumer's mind. When Tom Monaghan thought of the tactic of delivering pizza to customers' homes, he focused his whole strategy on that singular idea. He ended up making a fortune and marketing history with Domino's Pizza.

Managers of small companies have an advantage here. Surrounded by the details of the business, they are more likely to discover a good tactic that can be developed into a powerful strategy. However, that's not to say that a large company cannot profit from bottom-up marketing. Many have, like 3M with its Post-it notes.

THE IMPORTANCE OF RELATIONSHIP MARKETING

Most marketers know that the key to building brand equity in the twenty-first century is to develop interdependent, mutually satisfying relationships with customers.

A market-driven firm's overriding purpose is to create happy, loyal customers. Customers, not products, are the lifeblood of the business.[17] This realization has moved firms away from simple *transactional marketing* to **relationship marketing**—creating, maintaining, and enhancing long-term relationships with customers and other stakeholders that result in exchanges of information and other things of mutual value.[18]

Today's affluent, sophisticated consumers can choose from a wide variety of products and services offered by producers located around the world. As a result, the customer relationship—in which the sale is only the beginning—is the key strategic resource of the successful twenty-first-century business.[19] As one commentator notes: "The new *market-driven conception* of marketing will focus on *managing strategic partnerships* and positioning the firm between vendors and customers in the value chain with the aim of delivering *superior value* to the customer."[20]

We define **value** as the ratio of *perceived benefits* to the price of the product.[21]

The Importance of Relationships

To succeed, companies must focus on managing loyalty among customers and **stakeholders** (employees, centers

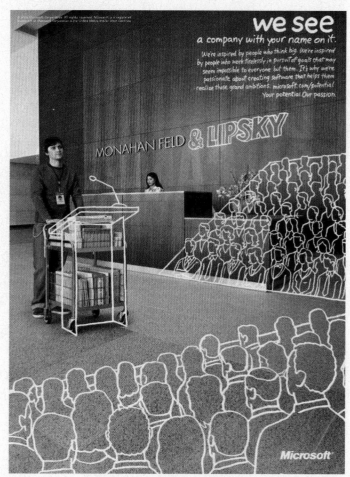

Microsoft (*www.microsoft.com*) understands the lifetime value of a customer. This ad suggests that Microsoft wants to help its software users develop their potential. By nurturing relationships early in individuals' careers, Microsoft is likely to retain their business for years to come.

A War of Comparisons

Which brand of cola tastes best, Coke or Pepsi? In the 1980s, each company advertised that its brand was preferred in blind taste tests. And which company, Pizza Hut or Papa John's, has the best ingredients? Not surprisingly, both thought their own brands did, and they said so in ads.

Comparative advertising, a technique where one company explicitly compares its brand to another in an effort to gain a competitive edge, was actually endorsed by the Federal Trade Commission in the 1970s "as a means of improving competition." Since its inception into the advertising world, comparative advertising has turned out to be a bit of a double-edged sword.

Ideally, comparative advertising should provide consumers with more information about competing products, thereby allowing them to make better-informed purchase decisions. However, research indicates that direct product comparisons often create greater awareness for the lesser-known brand, and that has been directly linked to a decline in sales for the more established brand, since at the point of purchase the consumer often confuses the two.

When taken too far, comparative advertising can be illegal. If an ad's comparisons are shown to be false, deceptive, or deliberately misleading, the campaign may result in litigation. Even ads that are literally correct can be found liable. According to one court, "innuendo, indirect intimations, and ambiguous suggestions" can unjustly injure a competitor. McNeil Consumer Products's Extra-Strength Tylenol, for example, successfully sued American Home Products's Maximum Strength Anacin even though Anacin's ad was literally true. Anacin had implied superiority over Tylenol when in fact both products contain the same amount of pain reliever.

A further complication arises when advertisers manipulate comparisons to cast a more favorable light on their products. In Australia, Duracell ran an ad showing a bunny powered by a Duracell battery outracing one powered by an Energizer battery. What Duracell neglected to mention in the ad was that it was comparing its top-of-the-line alkaline battery to one of Energizer's midrange carbon zinc batteries—apples and oranges in the world of batteries. Energizer took the unfair comparison to court, and Duracell

had to add clarifying text to its ad before it could put it back on the air.

Papa John's attacks Pizza Hut, Visa attacks American Express, and Jack in the Box and Burger King taunt McDonald's. Name-calling, finger pointing, and insulting the competition are all contemporary weapons used in the marketing wars waged between virtually identical brands, which are desperate to stand apart from the competition.

Some researchers estimate that 40 percent of all advertising in the United States is now comparative, whereas in most of the world it is either illegal or strictly regulated.

To keep comparison battles from getting out of hand, numerous groups, including the American Association of Advertising Agencies, the National Association of Broadcasters, and the FTC, issued guidelines for comparative advertising that are often stricter than current laws. TV network NBC, for example, insists that "advertisers shall refrain from discrediting, disparaging, or unfairly attacking competitors, competing products, or other industries."

This is a good step, but the legal language governing comparisons is vague, allowing for a blurry line between healthy one-upmanship and illegal behavior. As competition continues to increase, and ethical and legal guidelines remain ambiguous, the public will no doubt continue to be bombarded by comparative ads. The responsibility, therefore, will continue to fall on consumers to sift through the ads and differentiate fact from fiction.

Questions

1. How do you feel about ads that compare the features and benefits of competitive products and services? Do you believe they are unethical even if the comparisons are honest? Should they be allowed? Why or why not?
2. Select a comparative ad and study the copy. What points of comparison does the ad make? Are the points made honestly and directly, or are they masked by innuendo and implication? Is the ad literally true but still potentially misleading? Do you feel the ad is ethical or not?

---

of influence, stockholders, the financial community, and the press).[22] This is important for a number of reasons:

1. *The cost of lost customers.* No amount of advertising is likely to win back a customer lost from shoddy products or poor service. The real profit lost is the **lifetime customer value (LCV)** of a customer to a firm. For example, the average customer of one major transportation firm represented a lifetime value of $40,000. The company had 64,000 accounts and lost 5 percent of them due to poor service. That amounted to an unnecessary loss of $128 million in revenue and $12 million in profits![23] Moreover, negative word of mouth can have a terrible snowballing effect. Imagine if one lost customer influ-

ences only one other customer to not patronize the business. That immediately doubles the LCV loss. Negative word of mouth is why bad movies disappear so quickly from theaters.

2. *The cost of acquiring new customers.* Defensive marketing typically costs less than offensive marketing because it is hard to lure satisfied customers away from competitors.[24] The fragmentation of media audiences and the resistance of sophisticated consumers to advertising messages make it increasingly difficult to succeed merely by stepping up the advertising volume.[25] In fact, it costs five to eight times as much in marketing, advertising, and promotion to acquire a new customer as it does to keep an existing one.[26]

3. *The value of loyal customers.* Direct-response expert Lester Wunderman says that 90 percent of a manufacturer's profit comes from repeat purchasers; only 10 percent comes from trial or sporadic purchasers.[27] Reducing customer defections by even 5 percent can improve profit potential by 25 to 85 percent.[28] And long-term customers are more willing to pay premium prices, make referrals, increase their annual buying, and demand less hand-holding.[29]

So a company's first market should always be its current customers. In the past, most marketing and advertising effort focused on *presale* activities aimed at acquiring new customers. Now sophisticated marketers shift more of their resources to *postsale* activities, making customer retention their first priority. They have discovered an important benefit of focusing on relationships: increasing retention and optimizing lifetime customer value.[30]

Levels of Relationships

Kotler and Armstrong distinguish five levels of relationships that can be formed between a company and its various stakeholders, depending on their mutual needs:

- *Basic transactional relationship.* The company sells the product but does not follow up in any way (Target).

- *Reactive relationship.* The company sells the product

and encourages customers to call if they encounter any problems (Men's Wearhouse).

- *Accountable relationship.* The company phones customers shortly after the sale to check whether the product meets expectations and asks for product improvement suggestions and any specific disappointments. This information helps the company to continuously improve its offering (Acura dealers).

- *Proactive relationship.* The company contacts customers from time to time with suggestions about improved product use or helpful new products (Apple).

- *Partnership.* The company works continuously with customers (and other stakeholders) to discover ways to deliver better value (Nordstrom's Personal Shopper).[31]

Different stakeholders require different types of relationships. The relationship a company seeks with a customer will rarely be the same as it seeks with the press. However, there is often significant overlap in stakeholder roles. An employee may also be a customer and own stock in the company. Knowing intimately the customers and stakeholders is critical to the success of relationship marketing.

The number of stakeholders is also important. The more there are, the more difficult it can be to develop an extensive personal relationship with each. Moreover, some customers may not want anything more than a transactional relationship.[32] Most people wouldn't want a phone call from Oscar Mayer asking if the hot dogs tasted good or from Gillette asking about the smoothness of their last shave. However, when some Toyota models were

The SWOT Analysis [7–B]

Your situation analysis lays the factual groundwork. Now use this groundwork to recognize weaknesses and threats and to take advantage of strengths and opportunities. Use the grid below to organize your analysis.

	Facilitators of Success	Barriers to Success
Internal factors (brand or company attributes)	Strengths	Weaknesses
External factors (legal, competitive, societal, cultural factors)	Opportunities	Threats

Examples (using a fictitious American automobile company)

- Strengths: Made in the USA, classic heritage, improved reliability, new environmentally friendly models ready for production.
- Weaknesses: More expensive to manufacture than many imports in the same class, inefficient distribution network, smaller ad budget than the competition, high levels of unsold inventory.
- Opportunities: Cultural shift to more environmentally friendly products, weak dollar makes imports more expensive.
- Threats: Americans' concerns about U.S. auto industry, economic recession.

Profit margins

	High	Medium	Low
Many	Accountable	Reactive	Basic
Medium	Proactive	Accountable	Basic
Few	Partnership	Accountable	Reactive

Number of customers

USING IMC TO MAKE RELATIONSHIPS WORK

This interest in relationship marketing coincided with the interest in *integrated marketing communications* (IMC). In fact, according to Northwestern professor Don Schultz, IMC is what makes relationship marketing possible.[35]

IMC: The Concept and the Process

Technology allows marketers to adopt flexible manufacturing, customizing products for different markets. Being "market driven" means bundling services together with products to create a "unique product experience." It means companies and customers working together to find solutions.[36]

The counterpart to flexible manufacturing is flexible marketing—and integrated marketing communications—to reach customers at different levels in new and better ways.

accused of dangerous defects in 2010, the company contacted each existing car owner with a letter explaining the situation and telling the owner what, if anything, Toyota should do to ensure the car's safety. Toyota knew that some customers were likely to believe their relationship with the brand had been violated. Clearly, therefore, brand relationships can be psychological or symbolic as well as personal, and they can be created by brand promotion, publicity, and advertising as well as by people.

Mountain Dew considers that an important aspect of its brand relationship with its customers involves the "Dew-x-perience." Using guerilla-marketing tactics to reach out to urban youth, it employs a variety of hip-hop and Latin recording artists in various "street marketing" efforts to distribute bottles of Dew. It also sponsors extreme athletes and appears at sporting events such as the Gravity Games and ESPN's X Games with vans full of merchandise and giveaways.[33]

The final consideration is the profit margin. High-profit product or service categories make deeper, personal relationships more desirable (see Exhibit 7–3). Low profit margins per customer suggest that the marketer should pursue basic transactional relationships augmented by brand image advertising.[34]

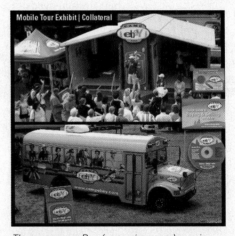

The company eBay (www.ebay.com) was in search of an integrated promotion to stimulate activity during the summer season when people traditionally spend more time outdoors and away from their computers. The promotion featured a Camp eBay bus touring at concerts and venues all across the country. Camp eBay was also featured at Loews theaters and Baskin-Robbins. Camp eBay campers could win prizes by unscrambling online messages with their very own Camp eBay decoder card. Nearly 300,000 people registered for Camp eBay and made over 80,000 purchases.

check yourself ✓

1. What is the difference between an objective, a strategy, and a tactic?

2. What distinguishes a need-satisfying objective and sales-target objective?

3. How can small companies use bottom-up marketing to become big companies?

IMC is both a concept and a process. The *concept* of integration is *wholeness*. Achieving this wholeness in communications creates **synergy**—the principal benefit of IMC—because each product message reinforces the others for greater effect.[37]

For example, when a Mountain Dew grocer runs an **endcap promotion** (a special display at the end of an aisle) alone, it might generate a 10 percent increase in volume. If he runs an ad for Dew with a coupon, that might deliver a 15 percent increase. But running both together might grow volume by 35 percent. That's synergy—the whole is greater than the sum of its parts.

Tom Duncan, IMC expert, points out that IMC is also a *process* in which communication becomes the driving, integrating force in the marketing mix and throughout the organization.

The Evolution of the IMC Concept

Glen Nowack and Joe Phelps, advertising professors from the Universities of Georgia and Alabama, argue that IMC has developed as a consequence of several important trends, including escalating media costs, splintering consumer markets, and skepticism about traditional mass media advertising. These have led marketers to question the wisdom of creating walls between disciplines such as public relations, direct-response advertising, and sales promotion.[38]

Many companies initially took a narrow, *inside-out* view of IMC. They saw it as a way to coordinate and manage their marketing communications (advertising, sales promotion, public relations, personal selling, and direct marketing) to

asset is not their products or their factories or even their employees, but their customers.[40] Defined broadly:

> **Integrated marketing communications** is the process of building and reinforcing mutually profitable relationships with employees, customers, other stakeholders, and the general public by developing and coordinating a strategic communications program that enables them to have a constructive encounter with the company/brand through a variety of media or other contacts.

Whether a company employs the narrow view or the broad view depends to a great extent on its corporate culture. Some companies enjoyed rapid growth and strong customer relationships because they intuitively integrated and focused all corporate and marketing activities. Apple, Honda, Nike, and Banana Republic are just a few. Consider the success for Nike+, a social networking Web site where runners can meet and share observations with other runners.

synergy An effect achieved when the sum of the parts is greater than that expected from simply adding together the individual components.

endcap promotion A merchandising method that uses special displays on shelving at the end of aisles in a store.

Integrated marketing communications The process of building and reinforcing mutually profitable relationships with employees, customers, other stakeholders, and the general public by developing and coordinating a strategic communications program that enables them to make consecutive contact with the company/brand through a variety of media.

> ## IMC seeks to create a wholeness in communications, which in turn results in a synergy among product messages. Each communication element reinforces the other for greater effect.

give the audience a consistent message about the company.[39] The coordination of these communications elements is certainly important and we will examine them more closely in Chapters 16 and 17.

But a broader, more sophisticated, *outside-in* perspective of IMC sees customers as partners in an ongoing relationship, recognizes the terminology they use, acknowledges the importance of the whole communications system, and accepts the many ways they come into contact with the company or the brand. Companies committed to IMC realize their biggest

How the Customer Sees Marketing Communications

To truly understand IMC, we have to look through the customer's eyes. In one study, consumers identified 102 different media as "advertising"—everything from TV to shopping bags to sponsored community events.[41] Customers also develop perceptions of the company or brand through a variety of other sources: news reports, word of mouth, gossip, experts' opinions, financial reports, and even the CEO's personality.

All these communications or brand contacts, sponsored or not, create an *integrated product* in the consumer's mind.[42] In other words, customers automatically integrate all the brand-related messages that emanate from the company or some other source. The way they integrate those messages determines their perception of the company. IMC gives companies a better opportunity to manage or influence those perceptions and create a superior relationship with those stakeholders.

The Four Sources of Brand Messages
The company that embraces IMC accepts the idea that *everything we do (and don't do) sends a message.* That is to say, every corporate activity has a message component. Duncan categorized four types of company/brand-related messages stakeholders receive: *planned, product, service,* and *unplanned.* Each of these influences a stakeholder's relationship decision, so marketers must know where these messages originate, what effect they have, and the costs to influence or control them.

1. **Planned messages**. These are the traditional marketing communication messages—advertising, sales promotions, personal selling, merchandising materials, publicity releases, event sponsorships. These often have the *least* impact because they are seen as self-serving. Planned messages should be coordinated to work toward a predetermined set of communications objectives. This is the most fundamental aspect of (inside-out) IMC.

2. **Product messages**. In IMC theory, every element of the marketing mix (not just promotion) sends a message. Messages from the product, price, or distribution elements are typically referred to as product messages. For example, customers and other stakeholders receive one product message from a $2,500 Rolex watch and a totally different one from a $30 Timex. Product messages also include packaging, which communicates a lot about the product through the use of color, type fonts, imagery, design, and layout.

Product messages have great impact. When a product (or service) performs well, the customer infers a positive message that reinforces the purchase decision. However, a gap between the product's performance and advertised promises is likely to convey a negative message. Managers must realize that all marketing mix decisions are also communication decisions.

3. **Service messages**. Many messages result from employee interactions with customers. In many organizations, customer service people are supervised by operations, not marketing. Yet the service messages they send have greater marketing impact than the planned messages. With IMC, marketing people work with operations to minimize negative messages and maximize positive ones.

4. **Unplanned messages**. Companies have little or no control over the unplanned messages that emanate from employee

IMC is about more than communicating with customers, it is about engaging them and building relationships. Mountain Dew engages its users at its "Dewmocracy" Web site, where it allows them to vote on new products, colors, packaging, and even advertising campaigns.

▼**EXHIBIT 7–4** The integration triangle.

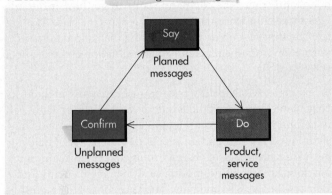

gossip, unsought news stories, comments by the trade or competitors, word-of-mouth rumors, or major disasters. When Walmart created a Facebook page, many of the initial fans criticized the company's policies. Unplanned messages may affect customers' attitudes dramatically, but they can sometimes be anticipated and influenced, especially by managers experienced in the online world.[43]

The Integration Triangle

The integration triangle is a simple illustration of how perceptions are created from the various brand message sources (see Exhibit 7–4). Planned messages are *say* messages, what companies say about themselves. Product and service messages are *do* messages because they represent what a company does. Unplanned messages are *confirm* messages because that's what others say and confirm (or not) about what the company says and does. Constructive integration occurs when a brand does what its maker says it will do and then others confirm that it delivers on its promises.[44]

The Dimensions of IMC

To maximize the synergy benefits of IMC, Duncan suggests three dimensions to an organization's integration process. It should first ensure consistent positioning, then facilitate interactions between the company and its customers or other stakeholders, and finally actively incorporate a socially responsible mission into the organization's relationships with its stakeholders.

Duncan's IMC model shows that cross-functional planning and monitoring of IMC activities results in an enhanced relationship with customers and other stakeholders, which leads to stakeholder loyalty and ultimately to greater brand equity.[45]

The interest in IMC is global.[46] The $88 billion Swiss company Nestlé, for example, uses a variety of IMC strategies, such as building highway rest stops for feeding and changing babies, designed to establish deep, caring relationships between families and the Nestlé Baby Foods division in France.[47]

In short, IMC offers accountability by maximizing resources and linking communications activities directly to organizational goals and the resulting bottom line.[48]

The IMC Approach to Marketing and Advertising Planning

For many companies, IMC is now the standard approach to planning marketing and communications activities. Marketing and communications planning are done together. Using the outside-in process, the IMC approach starts with the customer. Marketers determine which media customers use, the relevance of their message to the customers, and when customers and prospects are most *receptive* to the message. They begin with the customer and work back to the brand.[49]

Marketers now have a wealth of information at their fingertips. With supermarket scanner data, for instance, packaged-goods marketers can (1) identify specific users of products and services; (2) measure their actual purchase behavior and relate it to specific brand and product categories; (3) measure the impact of various advertising and marketing communications activities and determine their value in influencing the actual purchase; and (4) capture and evaluate this information over time.[50] The Internet is another place that marketers can glean a wealth of information about their customers. The Web is so important to Mountain Dew that as of 2010 it has moved all of its advertising efforts there.

A database of customer behavior can be the basis for planning future marketing and communications activities, especially if the database contains information on customer demographics, psychographics, purchase data, and attitudes.

Starting the planning process with a database forces the company to focus on the consumer, or prospect, not on sales or profit goals. Communications objectives and strategies are established for making contact with the consumer and influencing his or her attitudes, beliefs, and purchase behavior. The

> ## The company that embraces IMC accepts the premise that "Everything we do sends a message."

marketer then decides what other elements of the marketing mix (product, price, distribution) can be used to further encourage the desired behavior. Finally, the planner determines what communications tactics to use—media advertising, direct marketing, publicity, sales promotion, special events. All forms of marketing are thus turned into communication, and all forms of communication into marketing.[51]

The Importance of IMC to Advertising

Because customers see all sponsored communications as advertising, advertising people (account managers, creatives, media planners) must grow beyond their traditional specialty to become enlightened generalists, familiar with and able to integrate all types of marketing communications.

In a survey of 122 *Fortune* 500 marketing, advertising, and communications executives, most indicated a general understanding of IMC and agreed that synergy is the key benefit of integrated marketing.[52] However, the study also showed that confusion remains among professionals concerning IMC use. This suggests that many practitioners today still lack the broad knowledge required to develop, supervise, and execute full IMC programs.[53]

THE ADVERTISING PLAN

The **advertising plan** is a natural outgrowth of the marketing plan and is prepared in much the same way. It picks up where the marketing plan leaves off, building on the goals that have been established for the advertising program. Those goals are translated into specific advertising objectives, from which creative and media strategies are developed. The advertising plan typically also incorporates the rationale for a proposed budget and a plan for conducting research.

check yourself ✓

1. What is synergy and how is it created by IMC?

2. What factors do Phelps and Nowack suggest have led to the development of IMC?

3. What are the four types of brand messages identified by Duncan?

Reviewing the Marketing Plan

The advertising manager first reviews the marketing plan to understand where the company wants to go, how it intends to get there, and what role advertising plays in the marketing mix. The first section of the advertising plan should organize information from the marketing plan's situation analysis into a SWOT analysis.

For example, McDonald's restaurants' *strengths* include its strong name identity and thousands of retail locations. However, the company's *weaknesses* include a menu loaded with unhealthy food choices and an image to match. McDonald's is now taking advantage of an *opportunity* to capitalize on nutritious food trends by promoting healthier menu items and a fresh, new image. The company's upscale coffees distinguish it from its fast-food competitors and enable it to draw traffic from Starbucks. In doing so, it is combating *threats* from competitive restaurants and posting impressive sales gains.

L04 Explain how to establish specific, realistic, and measurable advertising objectives.

Setting Advertising Objectives

Based on the marketing plan, the advertising manager determines what tasks advertising must take on. What strengths and opportunities can be leveraged? What weaknesses and threats need to be addressed? Unfortunately, some corporate executives (and advertising managers) state vague goals for advertising, like "increase sales and maximize profits by creating a favorable impression of the product in the marketplace." When this happens, no one understands what the advertising is intended to do, how much it will cost, or how to measure the results. Advertising objectives should be specific, realistic, and measurable.

Understanding What Advertising Can Do Most advertising programs encourage prospects to take some action. However, it is unrealistic to assign advertising the whole responsibility for achieving sales. Sales goals are marketing objectives, not advertising objectives. Before an advertiser can persuade customers to buy, it must inform, persuade, or remind its intended audience about the product or service. A simple adage to remember when setting objectives is "Marketing sells, advertising tells." In other words, advertising objectives should be related to communication outcomes.

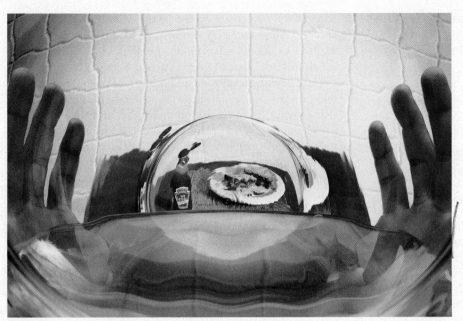

Advertising cannot be assigned full responsibility for a product's success or failure. In 2003, Heinz (www.heinz.com) launched a major ad campaign to introduce new varieties, like its hot ketchup. This campaign, from Leo Burnett's Lisbon office, attracted critical acclaim and earned a Cannes Bronze Lion, but could not sustain interest in specialty condiments.

The Advertising Pyramid: A Guide to Setting Objectives

Suppose you're advertising a new brand in a new product category, but you're not sure what kind of results to expect. The pyramid in Exhibit 7–5 shows some of the tasks advertising can perform. Obviously, before your product is introduced, prospective customers are completely unaware of it. Your first communication objective therefore is to create *awareness*—to acquaint people with the company, product, service, and/or brand.

The next task might be to develop *comprehension*—to communicate enough information about the product that some percentage of the aware group will understand the product's purpose, image, or position, and perhaps some of its features.

Next, you need to communicate enough information to develop *conviction*—to persuade a certain number of people to actually believe in the product's value. Once convinced, some people may be moved to *desire* the product. Finally, some percentage of those who desire the product will take *action*. They may request additional information, send in a coupon, visit a store, or actually buy the product.

The pyramid works in three dimensions: time, dollars, and people. Advertising results may take time, especially if the product is expensive or not purchased regularly. Over time, as a company continues advertising, the number of people who become aware of the product increases. As more people comprehend the benefits of the product, believe in it, and desire it, more will take the final action of buying it.

Let's apply these principles to a hypothetical case. Suppose you are in charge of advertising for the new "Lightning Bug," a hybrid car built by Volkswagen that runs on both gasoline and

▼**EXHIBIT 7–5** The advertising pyramid depicts the progression of advertising effects on mass audiences—especially for new products. The initial message promotes *awareness* of the product to a large audience (the base of the pyramid). But only a percentage of this large group will *comprehend* the product's benefits. Of that group, even fewer will go on to feel *conviction* about, then *desire* for the product. In the end, compared with the number of people aware of the product, the number of people who take *action* is usually quite small.

Not every ad follows the learn-feel-do approach. This ad for Citi invites readers to feel-learn-do with an evocative story about what Citi credit can provide.

electricity. Your initial advertising objectives for this fictional car might read as follows:

1. Within two years, communicate the existence of the Lightning Bug to half of the more than 500,000 people who annually buy imported economy cars.

2. Get two-thirds of this "aware" group to comprehend that the Lightning Bug is a superior economy car with many design, safety, and environmentally friendly features; that it is a brand-new nameplate backed with unmatched service, quality, and value; and that it is sold only through dedicated Volkswagen dealers.

3. Convince two-thirds of the "comprehending" group that the Lightning Bug is a high-quality car, reliable, economical, and fun to drive.

4. Stimulate desire within two-thirds of the "convinced" group for a test drive.

5. Motivate two-thirds of the "desire" group to take action and visit a retailer for a test drive.

These advertising objectives are specific as to time and degree and are quantified like marketing objectives. Theoretically, at the end of the first year, a consumer study could determine how many people are aware of the Lightning Bug, how many people understand the car's features, and so on, thus measuring the program's effectiveness.

Volkswagen's advertising may accomplish the objectives of creating awareness, comprehension, conviction, desire, and action. But once the customer is in the store, it's the retailer's responsibility to close the sale with effective selling and service.

With the advent of integrated marketing communications, we can look at the pyramid in another way. By using a variety of marketing communication tools and a wide menu of traditional and nontraditional media, we can accomplish the communication objectives suggested by the pyramid in a more efficient manner. For instance, for creating sheer awareness for the new Lightning Bug as well as brand image for the car and the company, an intensive program of public relations activities supported by

mass media advertising would be the communication tools of choice. Comprehension, interest, and credibility can be augmented by media advertising, press publicity, direct-mail brochures, and special events such as a sports car show. Desire can be enhanced by a combination of the buzz created by good reviews in car enthusiast magazines, plus media advertising, beautiful brochure photography, and the excitement generated by a sales promotion (such as a sweepstakes). Finally, action can be stimulated by direct-mail solicitation, sales promotion, a Web site where interested buyers can customize their cars, and the attentive service of a retail salesperson in an attractive showroom. Following the sale, media advertising should continue to reinforce the purchase decision. But at the same time, outbound telemarketing calls from the retailer can be used to thank the customer, solicit feedback on that customer's experience, and offer any needed assistance. This acknowledges that the sale was just the beginning of a valuable relationship.

The Old Model versus the New The advertising pyramid represents the *learn-feel-do* model of advertising effects. That is, it assumes that people rationally consider a prospective purchase, and once they feel good about it, they act. The theory is that advertising affects attitude, and attitude leads to behavior. That may be true for certain expensive, high-involvement products that require a lot of consideration. But

There are many ways to deliver a message besides using traditional media. In keeping with its theme of fun and adventure, Mountain Dew traveled around the country in a colorful subway car that was packed with all kinds of treats and memorabilia given away at key events.

> # WHEN MARKETERS ESTABLISH A RELATIONSHIP WITH CUSTOMERS, THE MODEL IS NO LONGER A PYRAMID BUT A CIRCLE. BY STARTING WITH THE CUSTOMER AND INTEGRATING MARKETING COMMUNICATIONS, COMPANIES HOPE TO ACHIEVE LASTING LOYALTY FROM GOOD PROSPECTS.

other purchases may follow a different pattern. For example, impulse purchases at the checkout counter may involve a *do-feel-learn* model, in which behavior leads to attitude which leads to knowledge. Other purchases may follow some other pattern. Thus, there are many marketing considerations when advertising objectives are being set, and they must be thought out carefully.

The advertising pyramid also reflects the traditional mass-marketing monologue. The advertiser talks and the customer listens.[54] But today, as the IMC model shows, many marketers have databases of information on their customers—about where they live, what they buy, and what they like and dislike. When marketers can have a dialogue and establish a relationship, the model is no longer a pyramid but a circle (see Exhibit 7–6). Consumers and business customers can send messages back to the marketer in the form of coupons, phone calls, surveys, and database information on purchases. With interactive media, the responses are in real time. This feedback can help the marketer's product, service, and messages evolve.[55] And reinforcement advertising, designed to build brand loyalty, will remind people of their successful experience with the product and suggest reuse.

By starting with the customer and then integrating all aspects of their marketing communications—package and store design, personal selling, advertising, public relations, special events, and sales promotions—companies hope to achieve lasting loyalty from *good* prospects, not just prospects.[56]

check yourself ✓

1. What are the limits on what advertising can do and how do these affect setting ad objectives?

2. What is the advertising pyramid?

3. How does setting objectives under an IMC approach differ from that under the advertising pyramid?

▼ **EXHIBIT 7–6** Messages go to the customer through advertising and other communication channels. Messages come back via direct response, surveys, and a purchase behavior database. The marketer's message should evolve based on this feedback.

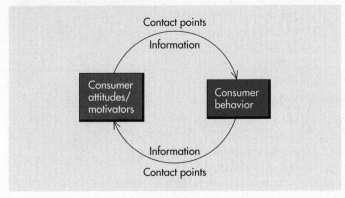

Determining the Advertising Strategy

The advertising *objective* declares what the advertiser wants to achieve with respect to consumer awareness, attitude, and preference; the advertising *strategy* describes how to get there. **Advertising strategy** consists of two substrategies: the creative strategy and the media strategy.

The **creative strategy** is a guide for those developing the advertising. At a minimum, the creative strategy defines the *target audience,* restates the *objective* of the advertising, specifies the key *benefits* to be communicated, and offers *support* for those

my ad campaign

benefits. We discuss the development of the creative strategy in Chapter 8.

The **media strategy** provides direction to the media planners.

It defines the communication objectives that must be achieved and then describes how these will be accomplished through the use of media vehicles. The media planning process is covered in Chapter 15.

Developing Advertising Objectives [7–C]

For the next big sets of decisions you will make, both media and creative, it will be essential that you specify what advertising and other promotions should *do*. Use the checklist below to focus your thinking on your advertising objectives.

Does the advertising aim at immediate sales? If so, objectives might be:

____ Perform the complete selling function.
____ Close sales to prospects already partly sold.
____ Announce a special reason for buying now (price, premium, and so forth).
____ Remind people to buy.
____ Tie in with special buying event.
____ Stimulate impulse sales.

Does the advertising aim at near-term sales? If so, objectives might be:

____ Create awareness.
____ Enhance brand image.
____ Implant information or attitude.
____ Combat or offset competitive claims.
____ Correct false impressions, misinformation.
____ Build familiarity and easy recognition.

Does the advertising aim at building a "long-range consumer franchise"? If so, objectives might be:

____ Build confidence in company and brand.
____ Build customer demand.
____ Select preferred distributors and dealers.
____ Secure universal distribution.
____ Establish a "reputation platform" for launching new brands or product lines.
____ Establish brand recognition and acceptance.

Does the advertising aim at helping to increase sales? If so, objectives would be:

____ Hold present customers.
____ Convert other users to advertiser's brand.
____ Cause people to specify advertiser's brand.
____ Convert nonusers to users.
____ Make steady customers out of occasional ones.
____ Advertise new uses.
____ Persuade customers to buy larger sizes or multiple units.

____ Remind users to buy.
____ Encourage greater frequency or quantity of use.

Does the advertising aim at some specific step that leads to a sale? If so, objectives might be:

____ Persuade prospect to write for descriptive literature, return a coupon, enter a contest.
____ Persuade prospect to visit a showroom, ask for a demonstration.
____ Induce prospect to sample the product (trial offer).

How important are supplementary benefits of advertising? Objectives would be:

____ Help salespeople open new accounts.
____ Help salespeople get larger orders from wholesalers and retailers.
____ Help salespeople get preferred display space.
____ Give salespeople an entrée.
____ Build morale of sales force.
____ Impress the trade.

Should the advertising impart information needed to consummate sales and build customer satisfaction? If so, objectives may be to use:

____ "Where to buy it" advertising.
____ "How to use it" advertising.
____ New models, features, package.
____ New prices.
____ Special terms, trade-in offers, and so forth.
____ New policies (such as guarantees).

Should advertising build confidence and goodwill for the corporation? Targets may include:

____ Customers and potential customers.
____ The trade (distributors, dealers, retail people).
____ Employees and potential employees.
____ The financial community.
____ The public at large.

What kind of images does the company wish to build?

____ Product quality, dependability.
____ Service.
____ Family resemblance of diversified products.
____ Corporate citizenship.
____ Growth, progressiveness, technical leadership.

The creative strategy represents what a company wants to communicate about its product. The benefit communicated by the Seattle Chocolate Company (www.seattlechocolate.com) is that its candies provide sweet tooth decadence and gratification to consumers willing to indulge themselves for a moment. It accomplishes this through tongue-in-cheek humor by parodying the nutritional facts label on other food products.

L05 Explain how advertising budgets are determined.

Allocating Funds for Advertising

Accountants and the Internal Revenue Service consider advertising a current business expense. Consequently, many executives treat advertising as a budget item to be trimmed or eliminated like other expense items when sales are either very high or very low. This is understandable but extremely shortsighted.

The cost of a new factory or warehouse is an investment in the company's future ability to produce and distribute products. Similarly, advertising—as one element of the communication mix—is an investment in future sales. While advertising is often used to stimulate immediate sales, its greatest power is in its cumulative, long-range, reinforcement effect.[57]

Advertising builds consumer preference and promotes goodwill. This, in turn, enhances the reputation and value of the company name and brand. And it encourages customers to make repeat purchases.

media strategy A document that helps media planners determine how messages will be delivered to consumers. It defines the target audience, the communication objectives that must be achieved, and the characteristics of the media that will be used for delivery of the messages.

So while advertising is a current expense for accounting purposes, it is also a long-term investment. For management to see advertising as an investment, however, it must understand how advertising relates to sales and profits.

The Relationship of Advertising to Sales and Profits

Many variables, both internal and external, influence the effectiveness of a company's marketing and advertising efforts. Methods to measure the relationships between advertising and sales and between sales and profits are far from perfect. However, substantial research does support the following principles:

- In consumer goods marketing, increases in market share are closely related to increases in the marketing budget. And market share is a prime indicator of profitability.[58]

- Sales normally increase with additional advertising. At some point, however, the rate of return flattens and then declines. (See Commercial Break 7–B, "The Economic Effect of Advertising on Sales.")

- Sales response to advertising may build over time, but the durability of advertising is brief, so a consistent investment is important.

- There are minimum levels below which advertising expenditures have no effect on sales.

- There will be some sales even if there is no advertising.

- There are saturation limits above which no amount of advertising can increase sales.

To management, these facts might mean: Spend more until it stops working. In reality, the issue isn't that simple. Advertising isn't the only marketing activity that affects sales. A change in market share may occur because of quality perceptions, word of mouth, the introduction of new products, competitive trade promotion, the opening of more attractive outlets, better personal selling, or seasonal changes in the business cycle.

Furthermore, most companies don't have a clear-cut way to determine the relationship between advertising and sales and profit. What if the company sells a variety of products? Which advertising contributes to which sales?

One thing remains clear. Because the response to advertising occurs over time, advertising should be viewed as a long-term investment in future profits. Like all expenditures, advertising should be evaluated for wastefulness. But historically, companies that make advertising the scapegoat during tough times end up losing substantial market share before the economy starts growing again.[59]

The corollary is also true. Sustained ad spending during

As a rule, the level of sales of a product is proportional to the level of advertising expenditure—that is, within reasonable limits, the more you spend the more you sell (assuming the advertising program is effective). Yet, even the most enthusiastic ad agency will admit, reluctantly, that it is possible to spend too much.

Ideally, managers would like to know how much more they will be able to sell per additional dollar of advertising and when additional advertising dollars cease being effective. They would like to have a graph or a statistical equation describing the relationship between advertising and sales.

In our illustration, most of the curve goes uphill as we move to the right (it has a positive slope). This means that additional advertising will continue to bring in business until (at a budget of *x* million dollars) people become so saturated by the message that it begins to repel them and turn them away from the product.

Even if the saturation level cannot be reached within the range of expenditures the firm can afford, the curve is likely to level off, becoming flatter and flatter as the amount spent on advertising becomes greater and greater and saturation is approached. The point at which the

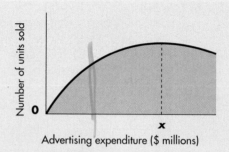

Advertising expenditure ($ millions)

curve begins to flatten is the point at which returns from advertising begin to diminish. When the total advertising budget is small, even a $1 addition to the campaign may bring in as much as $10 in new sales. But when the market approaches saturation, each additional dollar may contribute less than a dollar in new sales, if any at all.

Applying the Breaks

What other factors might influence the level of sales of a product? Why might it be difficult to clearly establish a relationship between advertising levels and sales results?

Advertising isn't the only marketing activity that affects sales. Many other factors can play a role as well.

difficult times protects, and in some cases even increases, market share and builds brands. During the last global recession, the leading European marketers recognized this fact, and fewer than 40 percent of the top spenders in Italy, Austria, Germany, France, and Spain cut their budgets.[60]

Methods of Allocating Funds

Most business executives will spend more money on advertising as long as they are assured it will mean more profit. But how much is too much is hard to predict when advertising budgets are being developed.

Companies use several methods to determine how much to spend on advertising, including the *percentage-of-sales, percentage-of-profit, unit-of-sale, competitive-parity, share-of-market,* and *objective/task methods.*

No technique is appropriate for all situations. The three methods discussed here are commonly used for setting national advertising budgets. However, local retailers can use them too.

Percentage-of-Sales Method The **percentage-of-sales method** is one of the most popular techniques for setting advertising budgets. It may be based on a percentage of last year's sales, anticipated sales for next year, or a combination of the two. Businesspeople like this method because it is the simplest, it doesn't cost them anything, it is related to revenue, and it is considered safe. The problem is knowing what percentage to use. As Exhibit 7–7 shows, even leaders in the same industry use different percentages. Across industries, they range from just 1.5 percent to more than 22 percent.

2008 Rank	Marketer	Total U.S. Ad Spending (billions)	% Change 2007
1	Procter & Gamble Co.	$4.80	−6.6
2	Verizon Communications	3.70	9.5
3	AT&T	3.10	−10.4
4	General Motors Corp.	2.90	−5.2
5	Johnson & Johnson	2.50	5.0
6	Unilever	2.40	0.2
7	Walt Disney Co.	2.20	11.0
8	Time Warner	2.20	−19.9
9	General Electric Co.	2.00	12.7
10	Sears Holdings Corp.	1.90	−4.7

Source: "100 Leading National Advertisers" *Advertising Age* 2009 edition index.

percentage-of-sales method
A method of advertising budget allocation based on a percentage of the previous year's sales, the anticipated sales for the next year, or a combination of the two.

Usually the percentage is based on an industry average or on company experience. Unfortunately, it is too often determined arbitrarily. An industry average assumes that every company in the industry has similar objectives and faces the same marketing challenges. Using company experience assumes that the market is static, which is rarely the case.

However, when applied against a forecast of future sales, this method often works well. It assumes that a certain number of dollars is needed to sell a certain number of units. If the advertiser knows what that relationship is, the correlation between advertising and sales should remain reasonably constant, assuming the market is stable and competitors' advertising remains unchanged.

The greatest shortcoming of the percentage-of-sales method is that it violates a basic marketing principle. Marketing activities

my ad campaign

Ways to Set Advertising Budgets [7–D]

How much should you recommend that your client spend on advertising and promotions? Here is a list of ways companies set their marketing budgets.

- **Percentage of sales.** Advertising budget is determined by allocating a percentage of last year's sales, anticipated sales for next year, or a combination of the two. The percentage is usually based on an industry average, company experience, or an arbitrary figure.
- **Percentage of profit.** Percentage is applied to profit, either past years' or anticipated.
- **Unit of sale.** Also called the *case-rate method*. A specific dollar amount is set for each box, case, barrel, or carton produced. Used primarily in assessing members of horizontal co-ops or trade associations.
- **Competitive parity.** Also called the *self-defense method*. Allocates dollars according to the amounts spent by major competitors.

- **Share of market/share of voice.** Allocates dollars by maintaining a percentage share of total industry advertising comparable to or somewhat ahead of desired share of market. Often used for new product introductions.
- **Objective/task.** Also referred to as the *budget buildup method*, this method has three steps: defining objectives, determining strategy, and estimating the cost to execute that strategy.
- **Empirical research.** Companies determine the most efficient level by running experimental tests in different markets with different budgets.
- **Quantitative mathematical models.** Computer-based programs developed by major advertisers and agencies rely on input of sophisticated data, history, and assumptions.
- **All available funds.** Go-for-broke technique generally used by small firms with limited capital, trying to introduce new products or services.

share-of-market/ share-of-voice method A method of allocating advertising funds based on determining the firm's goals for a certain share of the market and then applying a slightly higher percentage of industry advertising dollars to the firm's budget.

objective/task method A method of determining advertising allocations, also referred to as the *budget-buildup method,* that defines objectives and how advertising is to be used to accomplish them. It has three steps: defining the objectives, determining strategy, and estimating the cost.

are supposed to *stimulate* demand and thus sales, not occur as a *result* of sales. If advertising only increases when sales increase and declines when sales decline, an opportunity is lost that might encourage an opposite move.

Share-of-Market/Share-of-Voice Method

In markets with similar products, a high correlation usually exists between a company's share of the market and its share of industry advertising.

The **share-of-market/share-of-voice method** is a bold attempt to link advertising dollars with sales objectives.[61] It holds that a company's best chance of maintaining its share of market is to keep its share of advertising (voice) comparable to its market share. For example, if Mountain Dew has an 8 percent share of the soft-drink market it should spend roughly 8 percent of the soft-drink industry's advertising dollars.

of their marketing budgets on consumer and trade promotion rather than consumer advertising.[63] Companies must be aware of *all* their competitors' marketing activities, not just advertising.

Objective/Task Method

The **objective/task method**, also known as the *budget buildup method,* is used by the majority of major national advertisers in the United States. It considers advertising to be a marketing tool to help generate sales.

The task method has three steps: defining objectives, determining strategy, and estimating cost. After setting specific, quantitative marketing objectives, the advertiser develops programs to attain them. If the objective is to increase the sales of cases of coffee by 10 percent, the advertiser determines which advertising approach will work best, how often ads must run, and which media to use. The estimated cost of the program becomes the basis for the advertising budget. Of course, the company's financial position is always a consideration. If the cost is too high, objectives may have to be scaled back. If results are better or worse than anticipated after the campaign runs, the next budget may need revision.

The task method forces companies to think in terms of accomplishing goals. Its effectiveness is most apparent when the results

> ## The objective/task budgeting method is used by the majority of major national advertisers. It treats advertising as a marketing tool for generating sales.

The share-of-market/share-of-voice method is commonly used for new product introductions.[62] According to this formula, when a new brand is introduced, the advertising budget for the first two years should be about one and one-half times the brand's targeted share of the market in two years. This means that if the company's two-year sales goal is 10 percent of the market, it should spend about 15 percent of total industry advertising during the first two years.

One hazard of this method is the tendency to oversimplify. Maintaining the targeted percentage of media exposure usually isn't enough to accomplish the desired results. The top national packaged-goods marketers still spend 25 to 30 percent

of particular ads or campaigns can be readily measured. The task method is adaptable to changing market conditions and can be easily revised.

However, it is often difficult to determine in advance the amount of money needed to reach a specific goal. Techniques for measuring advertising effectiveness still have many weaknesses.

The Bottom Line

The principal job of advertising is to influence perception by informing, persuading, and reminding. Advertising *affects* sales, but it is just one of many influences on consumer perception. Advertising managers must keep this in mind when preparing their plans and budgets. ■

check yourself ✓

1. What types of companies tend to use the percentage-of sales method to set an ad budget? Why?

2. How might a packaged-foods manufacturer use the share-of-market/share-of-voice method to introduce a new product?

CHECK IT OUT!

mhhe.com/ArensM

for study materials

including quizzes

and Internet resources

eight

creating ads:
strategy and process

Walmart has changed the retail world. The company's success, a result of its relentless focus on offering a broad selection of goods at low prices, has made it the largest public company by annual revenue in the world.

For stores that compete with Walmart (and in this day and age, that is most stores), finding the right strategy for success is an ongoing challenge.

Some do so by focusing on a single product category, like clothes, electronics, pet supplies, or toys, and presenting a broader selection within that category.

An even riskier strategy is going head-to-head, as Kmart, Sears, Montgomery Ward, and others have learned the hard way. But standing tall among the scattered ruins of Walmart's direct competitors is one company that has seemingly found a way to prosper. And that is Target.

Target's origins date to 1962 when the Dayton Company opened the first Target store in a Minneapolis suburb.[1]

Today the company runs nearly 1,700 stores throughout the United States and is fifth in overall revenue among U.S. retailers. Not bad for an organization whose greatest expansion occurred during the same years that Walmart conquered the world.

Why has Target succeeded where other retail giants have not? In part by being one of the greatest practioners of positioning, a concept we introduced in Chapter 7. Everyone knows that Walmart is synonymous with the concept of a "big box store." To the individual who is looking to save money but finds Walmart's offerings just a bit ordinary, Target proudly proclaims "Expect more, pay less."

continued on p. 200

LEARNING OBJECTIVES

LO1 Identify the members of the creative team and their primary responsibilities.

LO2 What makes great advertising?

LO3 Explain the role of the creative strategy and its principal elements.

LO4 How does creativity enhance advertising?

LO5 Define the four roles people play at different stages of the creative process.

advertising as well and helps to tie the many executions together.

Target spends nearly four times as much on its advertising as a percentage of sales than does Walmart.[4] Its ads are fun and quirky, in direct contrast to Walmart's more conservative, "hard-sell," approach. Target ads are softer, focusing on lifestyle themes that suggest ways that products sold at Target help the shopper become more of an individual.

The recession of 2009 hit most retailers hard, including Target. While Walmart has continued to enjoy steady growth, Target's sales were flat.

Some suggest the problem has been a recent shift. Rather than emphasize the "expect more," part of the equation, recent Target ads have focused on "pay less." It is hard to argue with a focus on low prices in a recession. The problem for Target is that Walmart owns the low price proposition. And during tough economic times, that position is a good place to be. So is Target right in emphasizing that as well? Or should the company be staying with its "expect more" proposition? Only time will tell. ■

continued from p. 199

The slogan says it all. You'll save money at Target (compared to many retailers) and you'll have more fun shopping (compared to Walmart). The promise of a better shopping experience (the "expect more" part of the equation) has been the key. As retailer trade journalist Jeff Arlen asks, "Without Andy Warhol, could Target Stores exist as it is today? Have CEO Bob Ulrich and his team of retailing alchemists learned the secret of turning the mundane into the sublime?[2]

Start with the merchandise. Lots of the things you find at Target you can find at Walmart as well, but Target displays them with more style and space. And some things you can't get at Walmart, or anywhere else—in-house lines like Xhilaration and Cherokee, and specially produced products from Mossimo and Michael Graves.[3]

Then, there is the red. Lots of red. As Michael Francis, senior VP of marketing at the retailer notes, "Trust us, red does go with everything." The strategy at Target is to "own red," that is, have the consumer associate the color with the brand.

One means for communicating that Target owns red is through its retail stores. But the color plays a prominent role in Target

---

LO1 Identify the members of the creative team and their primary responsibilities.

THE CREATIVE TEAM: ORIGINATORS OF ADVERTISING CREATIVITY

In Chapter 5 we discussed the communication process, in which a source encodes a message that is sent through a channel to be decoded by a receiver. In advertising, the *encoding* of messages—the conversion of mental concepts into symbols—is the responsibility of the creative team.

copywriter Person who creates the words and concepts for ads and commercials.

art director Along with graphic designers and production artists, determines how the ad's verbal and visual symbols will fit together.

creative director Head of a creative team of agency copywriters and artists. He or she is ultimately responsible for the creative product— the form the final ad takes.

creatives The people who work in the creative department, regardless of the specialty.

Each member of the creative team plays an essential role. The team's **copywriter** develops the *verbal* message, the copy (words) within the ad. The copywriter typically works with an **art director** who is responsible for the *nonverbal* aspect of the message, the design, which determines the look and feel of the ad. Together, they work under the supervision of a **creative director** (typically, a former copywriter or art director), who is ultimately responsible for the creative product— the form the final ad takes. As a group, the people who work in the creative department are generally referred to as **creatives**, regardless of their specialty.

This chapter focuses on the creative process: where it comes from, how it's developed, and how it relates to a company's marketing and advertising strategy. But to get a proper perspective on creativity, we need to understand the characteristics of great advertising. What is it? Where does it come from?

Bright colorful images, geometric shapes, and strong contrasts in both copy and graphics draw attention to Target messages and help brand the retailer as an "upscale" discount store.

check yourself ✓

1. What does a copywriter do? What does an art director do?

2. Who is ultimately responsible for the creative product?

L02 What makes great advertising?

CREATING GREAT ADVERTISING

We've all seen ads we like. But what do we mean when we say an ad is great?

If we look at some of the classic ads in history, we may get a clue: Volkswagen's famous "Think small" ad; DeBeers's "A diamond is forever" line; Clairol's "Does she or doesn't she?"; Nike's "Just do it"; the Army's "Be all you can be"; and Coca-Cola's "The real thing." What do these campaigns have in common that have made them universally considered great?

This is a very important question, since a lot of research indicates that "ad liking" has a tremendous impact on "ad success." But is a likable ad the same as a great ad?

[Great ads have certain things in common: audience resonance and strategic relevance.]

informational ads
Promising benefits that will offer relief from an undesirable situation or condition. Informational ads tend to address *negatively originated purchase motives,* such as problem removal or avoidance, in an attempt to provide solutions to those problems.

transformational ads Promising benefits that will reward consumers. Transformational ads tend to address *positively originated purchase motives,* such as sensory gratification, intellectual stimulation, or social approval, in an attempt to make people feel happier.

One way that Target communicates about its extraordinary shopping experience is through the use of extraordinary ads.

Whether the "ad" is a billboard, a page in a magazine, a TV or radio spot, or a hot new Web site, great ads have certain things in common. We can lump most of these characteristics into two dimensions of greatness: *audience resonance* and *strategic relevance.*[5]

The Resonance Dimension

To resonate means to echo, reverberate, or vibrate. It also means to boom, ring, or chime. And that's what a great ad does with the audience. It rings their chimes. It echoes in their ears. It reverberates. It *resonates.*

Why? Because of the boom factor.

When a cannon goes "boom," it gets your attention—right now! The same is true with an ad. It's the surprise element—the

Target counts on its ad campaigns to resonate with consumers. Because they do, the company can turn a simple set of stairs into a reminder about the popular retailer.

"aha," or the "wow." But in advertising, it not only gets your attention, it catches your imagination. In this sense it's like great art. It invites you to stop and think about the message.

Look at the Target ad, juxtaposing the image of fashion with people suspended in air. The ad is unusual, even for Target, so we stop to examine it more closely. And as we do so, the colors and the familiar logo convey exactly where we can buy the fashions if they strike our fancy. The ad resonates.

Other ads may resonate for different reasons. In some of the classic campaigns we just mentioned, it's simply the headline that resonates—so much so that it becomes a part of our daily language. Other memorable classics include California Milk Processors's "Got Milk?," and iPhone's "There's an app for that."

Recall from Chapter 5 our discussion of consumer motives. *Negatively originated motives,* such as problem avoidance or problem removal, provide the foundation for many great ads. These resonate with the audience by being highly **informational**, by offering relief from some real or perceived problem (FedEx's "When it absolutely, positively has to be there overnight"). Other motives are *positively originated* as consumers seek pleasant experiences, intellectual stimulation, or social approval. Here, ads may achieve greatness by being **transformational**, using positive reinforcement to offer a reward ("Be all you can be").

Unfortunately, most ads, whether they're informational or transformational, fail to resonate with the audience. Why? Because they lack a "big idea" or they fall down in the *execution.* The copy may be uninspiring, the visual may be less than attractive, or the production techniques used may be low quality. From the consumer's point of view, these ads are just a waste of time, and from the client's point of view, a waste of money. In fact, for them the greatness of the advertising is in the "bang per buck." Great ads give sponsors much more advertising effectiveness per dollar spent. Given this reality, isn't it amazing how much money is invested in ads that are simply not great?

The Relevance Dimension

The second dimension of great advertising is strategic relevance. An ad may get you to think, but what does it get you to think about? A classic example is the old Alka-Seltzer ad "I can't believe I ate the whole thing." It captured everyone's imagination, but it reinforced the wrong feeling—the feeling of the problem (overeating) rather than the solution (Alka-Seltzer). The agency lost the account.

While the text and the visual carry the ad message, behind the creative team's choice of tone, words, and ideas lies an advertising strategy. When the ad is completed, it must be relevant to the sponsor's strategy, or it will fail—even if it resonates with the audience. In other words, it may be great *entertainment,* but not great *advertising.* Great advertising always has a strategic mission to fulfill. In fact, strategy is at the root of all great creative work.

advertising *strategy* then describes a means to achieve that objective through the development of advertising executions and media plans. The *creative strategy* is the component of the advertising strategy that guides those responsible for developing creative advertising.

To be sure that everyone has the same understanding of the task at hand, account managers (or, in larger agencies, account planners) develop a brief statement summarizing the agreed-upon objectives and strategies. Many individuals from both the client and agency—including representatives from creative, media, and research—should have input into this document. The agency and client team should sign off on

> ## An ad may get you to think, but what does it get you to think about?

check yourself ✓

1. What does it mean for advertising to resonate? What causes an ad to resonate?

2. In addition to resonance, what other dimension is important for advertising greatness?

LO3 Explain the role of the creative strategy and its principal elements.

FORMULATING CREATIVE STRATEGY: THE KEY TO GREAT ADVERTISING

Recall from Chapter 7 that the purpose of the advertising *objective* is to state what the advertiser wants to achieve with respect to consumer awareness, attitude, and preference. The

the finished document before the creative process commences. This **creative strategy** serves as the creative team's guide for writing and producing the advertising. In some agencies this document may be referred to as a *creative brief,* a *work plan,* a *copy strategy,* or a *copy platform.*

Target ads are quirky and creative. But the nonverbal elements of color and the familiar logo make them instantly recognizable.

problem the advertising must solve What you want the advertising to do. The specific challenge that marketing communications must overcome to meet the marketing objectives.

advertising objective A specific communication task an advertising campaign should accomplish for a specific target audience.

target audience The specific group of individuals to whom the advertising message is directed.

Writing the Creative Strategy

Regardless of the name, the creative strategy is a simple written statement of the most important issues to consider in the development of an ad or campaign. It usually includes the following elements:

- The basic problem the advertising must address.
- The objective of the advertising.
- A definition of the target audience.
  - The key benefits to communicate.
    - Support for those benefits.
    - The brand's personality.
    - Any special requirements.

Let's look at the creative strategy Target and its agencies developed. We'll then see how they translated that into a mes-

sage strategy and a big idea and, finally, into effective ads.

- What is the **problem the advertising must solve**? Consumers may not be aware that they will save money AND enjoy shopping at Target. Consumers may also be unaware of the unique products that can only be found at Target. *This information often comes straight from the marketing plan's situation analysis.*

- What is the *objective of the advertising?* Target wants consumers to know that it has higher quality offerings and a more attractive shopping environment than its competitors. The **advertising objective** is initially spelled out in the marketing plan.

- What is Target's **target audience**? Target focuses on value-conscious shoppers, usually adults ages 25–49 with families, who seek products that are nicer than those typically found at deep-discount stores. These shoppers are not poor, but they do look to save money (Target reports that the median household income of its shoppers, or "guests," as the company calls them, is $60,000). This group is Target's *primary market*—that's who the company sells to. So Target definitely wants them to see its advertising. Because Target offers both value and a sense of style, 18- to 25-year-olds are another important market. While this group as a whole may not spend as much as the primary market, they act as *centers of influence* (or *key influentials*). This group is a *secondary target audience* for the advertising.

The Creative Brief [8]

Every agency has a slightly different twist on a creative brief. In Chapter 10 we outline the components of most briefs this way:

- Who (the prospect).
- Why (specific wants or needs the ad should appeal to).
- What (are the product features that can satisfy consumer needs?).
- Where and when (will the messages be transmitted?).
- Style, approach, tone.

We also describe the creative brief that Leo Burnett uses for P&G. It is even simpler:

- An objective statement (what are you trying to do?).
- A support statement (the evidence that backs up the promised benefit).
- A tone or brand character statement (emotional descriptions of the advertising strategy).

Finally, for a more in-depth treatment of the structure and functions of the brief, visit Ogilvy.com (http://www.ogilvy.com/viewpoint/view_ko.php?id=36254&iMagaId=4). Here is a summary of their beliefs about a creative brief:

1. What are the communications objectives?
2. What should consumers do differently? Why?

3. How will messages affect consumer beliefs and actions?
4. How are our competitors advertising? How can we make our ads different?
5. Who is the target audience and what is their shared need that the brand can fulfill?
6. Demographics of the audience, but even more importantly, shared attitudes.
7. The brand
   - How does the brand address the shared need?
   - How should the brand experience (as defined by both planned and unplanned messages) be defined?
   - What is the proposition (or benefit)?
   - What evidence gives people a reason to believe the proposition?
   - What is the personality of the brand?
   - How can the mood or tone of the ads be matched to the personality of the brand?

The Ogilvy site is filled with a lot more useful information, including suggestions for maximizing the likelihood that the brief will spark a big idea. Check it out.

- What is Target's *key benefit*? This is summarized nicely in the company's slogan, "Expect more, pay less." In other words, better quality, low prices. The **benefit statement** is the heart of the creative strategy. It is very important to make it as succinct and single-minded as possible. Complex benefit statements can lead to creative executions that promise everything and focus on nothing.

- How is that benefit *supported*? Target's ads provide price information, although not in the "hard sell" approach that Walmart favors. The "expect more" part of the equation is supported with beautiful, stylish, and unexpected ad executions, as many of the featured ads in this chapter demonstrate. The **support statement** should provide information about the product or service that will convince the target audience that the key benefit is true.

- What is the **brand personality**? Target wants its stores to be known for their quality, sophistication, beauty, and value. The creatives will consider this statement when they develop the message strategy.

- Are there any **special requirements**? The company Target allocates ad dollars to television ads, out-of-home magazines, and newspaper inserts. It has different audience objectives for each medium. But certain creative elements, such as the color red and the large "bulls-eye" logo, tie all of the ads together. It is important for the creatives to understand budget and media constraints before they begin.

vast selection of products that are practical, attractive, and fun.

2. *A support statement.* A brief description of the evidence that backs up the product promise; the reason for the benefit. For example:

   Support is found in two types of ads that Target regularly runs. Newspaper ads, including weekly inserts, demonstrate to consumers the low prices of the products sold at Target. Television ads emphasize the quality and value of the everyday products found at Target. Both TV and newspaper ads should do more than focus on the product alone, rather they should help to demonstrate that the products sold at Target make life easier and better.

3. *A tone or brand character statement.* A brief statement of either the advertising's tone or the long-term character of the brand. Tone statements are emotional descriptions of the advertising strategy. Brand character statements are descriptions of the enduring values of the brand. A tone statement might be phrased:

   The tone of Target ads should convey a spirit of optimism and energy. The ads should suggest that Target understands the consumer and the challenges she faces in her life. They should suggest that shopping at Target is fun and that choosing Target as a retailer is a sign of both sensibility (low prices) and sophistication (better offerings).

> The creative strategy identifies the benefits to be presented to consumers, but it doesn't cover execution. How the benefits will be presented is the creative team's job.

The creative strategy identifies the benefits to be presented to consumers, but it doesn't cover execution. How the benefits will be presented is the creative team's job.

Procter & Gamble and Leo Burnett use a simple creative strategy with only three parts:[6]

1. *An objective statement.* A specific, concise description of what the advertising is supposed to accomplish or what problem it is supposed to solve. The objective statement also includes the name of the brand and a brief, specific description of the target consumer. For example:

   Advertising will convince value-conscious consumers that Target stores offer them a way to save money on their everyday purchases. In addition, Target offers a

On the other hand, a brand character statement might be phrased:

   Target offers consumers the selection and value typical of a mass merchandiser in a setting that has the elegance and flair of a department store.

The delivery of the creative strategy to the creative department concludes the process of developing an advertising strategy. It also marks the beginning of the next step: the **creative process**, in which the creative team develops a *message strategy* and begins the search for the *big idea*. After writing the first ad, the copywriter should review the creative strategy to confirm that the ad is "on strategy." If it isn't, the team must start again.

Ads like this one communicate a great deal with little copy. How does Target use design to imply great selection with this out-of-home ad?

Elements of Message Strategy

From the information given by the account team (in the creative strategy) and any additional research it may perform, the creative team develops the message strategy. This may actually occur before, during, or after the creative process of searching for the big idea.

The **message strategy** is a simple description and explanation of an ad campaign's overall creative approach—the main idea, details about how the idea will be executed, and a rationale. The message strategy has three components:

- *Verbal.* Guidelines for what the advertising should say; considerations that affect the choice of words; and the relationship of the copy approach to the medium (or media) that will carry the message.

- *Nonverbal.* Overall nature of the ad's graphics; any visuals that must be used; and the relationship of the graphics to the media in which the ad will appear.

- *Technical.* Preferred execution approach and mechanical outcome, including budget and scheduling limitations (often governed by the media involved); also any **mandatories**—specific requirements for every ad, such as addresses, logos, and slogans.

The verbal elements are the starting point for many advertising campaigns. However, because all these elements of the message strategy intertwine, they typically evolve simultaneously. Language affects imagery, and vice versa.

The message strategy helps the creative team sell the ad or the campaign concept to the account managers and helps the managers explain and defend the creative work to the client. Of course, the message strategy must fit to the creative strategy or it will probably be rejected.

In the development of the message strategy, certain basic questions need to be answered: How is the market segmented? How will the product be positioned? Who are the best prospects for the product? Is the target audience different from the target market? What is the key consumer benefit? What is the product's (or company's) current image? What is the product's unique advantage?[7] At this point, research data are important. Research helps the creative team answer these questions and support their proposed approach.

check yourself ✓

1. What are the important parts of the creative strategy (or creative brief)?

2. What is the message strategy? What are its important parts?

LO4 How does creativity enhance advertising?

HOW CREATIVITY ENHANCES ADVERTISING

The powerful use of imagery, copy, and even humor in Target campaigns demonstrates how creativity enhances advertising. But what exactly is creativity? What is the role of creativity in advertising? And where does creativity come from?

What Is Creativity?

To create means to originate, to conceive a thing or idea that did not exist before. Typically, though, **creativity** involves combining two or more previously unconnected objects or ideas into something new. As Voltaire said, "Originality is nothing but judicious imitation."

Many people think creativity springs directly from human intuition. But as we'll see in this chapter, the creative process is actually a step-by-step procedure that can be learned and used to generate original ideas.

The Role of Creativity in Advertising

Advertisers often select an agency specifically for its creative style and its reputation for coming up with original concepts. While creativity is important to advertising's basic mission of informing, persuading, and reminding, it is vital to achieving the boom factor.

Creativity Helps Advertising Inform Advertising's responsibility to inform is greatly enhanced by creativity. Good creative work makes advertising more *vivid,* a quality that many researchers believe attracts attention, maintains interest, and stimulates consumers' thinking.[8] A common technique is to use plays on words and verbal or visual metaphors, such as "Put a tiger in your tank," "Fly the friendly skies," or "Own a piece of the rock." The metaphor describes one concept in terms of another, helping the reader or viewer learn about the product.[9]

Other creative techniques can also improve an ad's ability to inform. For example, visual cues such as lighting, pose of the model, setting, and clothing style can instantly signal viewers nonverbally whether a fashion ad reflects a romantic adventure or a sporting event.[10]

Creativity Helps Advertising Persuade The ancients created legends and myths about gods and heroes—symbols for humankind's hopes and fears—to affect human behavior and thought. To motivate people to some action or attitude, advertising copywriters have created new myths and heroes, like the Jolly Green Giant, the Geico gecko, and the Energizer Bunny. A creative story or persona can establish a unique identity for the product in the collective mindset, a key factor in helping a product beat the competition.[11]

To be persuasive, an ad's verbal message must be reinforced by the creative use of nonverbal message elements. Artists use these elements (color, layout, and illustration, for example) to increase vividness. Research suggests that, in print media, *information graphics* (colorful explanatory charts, tables, and the like) can raise readers' perception of quality.[12] Artwork can also stimulate emotions. Color, for example, often motivates consumers, depending on their cultural background and personal experiences (see Commercial Break 8, "The Psychological Impact of Color").

Creativity Helps Advertising Remind Imagine using the same invitation to ask people to try your product again and again, year after year. Your invitation would become stale and tiresome. Only creativity can transform your boring reminders into interesting, entertaining advertisements. Nike is proof. Several commercials in a Nike campaign never mentioned the company name or even spelled it on the screen. The ads told stories. And the only on-screen cue identifying the sponsor was the single, elongated "swoosh" logo inscribed on the final scene. A Nike spokesperson said the ads weren't risky "given the context that the Nike logo is so well known."[13] We are entertained daily by creative ads—for soft drinks, snacks, and cereals—whose primary mission is simply to remind us to indulge again.

Creativity Puts the "Boom" in Advertising Successful comedy also has a boom factor—the punchline. It's that precise moment when the joke culminates in a clever play on words or turn of meaning, when the audience suddenly gets it and laughs out loud.

Good punchlines come from taking an everyday situation, looking at it creatively, adding a bit of exaggeration, and then delivering it as a surprise. Great advertising often does the same thing.

When a group of friends greet each other with wagging tongues and an exaggerated "Whassup?" while "watching the game and having a Bud," the audience is completely caught off guard and roars with laughter. Boom!

Metaphors help readers understand the intended message. Leo Burnett, the ad legend who created the Jolly Green Giant, believed strongly in brand icons. Target does as well.

National origin or culture can play a role in color preferences. For example, people from warmer climates, apparently, are most responsive to warm colors—red, yellow, and orange. These colors tend to stimulate, excite, and create an active response. Certain color combinations have ethnic connotations. Metallic golds with reds, for example, are associated with China. Turquoise and beige are associated with the Indian tribes of the American Southwest.

Colors can also convey lifestyle preferences. Vivid primary colors (red, blue, yellow) juxtaposed with white stripes exude decisiveness and are often used in sporting events as team colors. Thus, they are associated with a sporting lifestyle.

The colors we experience during the four seasons often serve as guides for combining colors and for guessing the temperaments of individuals who dress themselves or decorate their houses in specific seasonal colors. Spring colors such as yellows, greens, and light blues, for example, suggest a fresh, exuberant character. Winter colors such as dark blues, deep violets, and black are associated with cool, chilly attitudes.

Because we usually feel refreshed from sleeping, we associate the colors of the morning—emerald green, raspberry, and pale yellow—with energy. And because the mellow colors of sunset predominate when we're usually home relaxing after work, we may associate sunset colors—peach, turquoise, and red-orange—with relaxation and reflective moods.

Some colors are ambiguous. Violet and leaf-green fall on the line between warm and cool. They can be either, depending on the shade.

Here are some more observations:

Red
Symbol of blood and fire. Second to blue as people's favorite color but more versatile, the hottest color with the highest "action quotient." Appropriate for soups, frozen foods, and meats (Campbell's, Ore-Ida). Conveys strong masculine appeal, so is often used for shaving cream containers.

Brown
Another masculine color, associated with earth, woods, mellowness, age, warmth, comfort. Used to sell anything, even cosmetics (Revlon's Braggi).

Yellow
High impact to catch consumer's eye, particularly when used with black. Good for corn, lemons, or suntan products.

Green
Symbol of health and freshness; popular for mint products and soft drinks (7Up).

Blue
Coldest color with most appeal; effective for frozen foods (ice impression); if used with lighter tints becomes "sweet" (Yoplait yogurt, Lowenbrau beer, Wondra flour).

Black
Conveys sophistication and high-end merchandise, and is used to stimulate the purchase of expensive products. Good as background and contrast for other colors.

Orange
Most "edible" color, especially in brown-tinged shades; evokes autumn and good things to eat.

Applying the Breaks
Explain the moods or feelings that are stimulated by two color ads or packages illustrated in this text.

In advertising, though, the boom doesn't always have to be funny. It may come from the sudden understanding of an unexpected double-meaning, as in the case of Target ads. Or from the gentle emotional tug of a Hallmark Cards commercial. Or the breathtaking beauty of a magnificent nature photograph for Timberland shoes. In a business-to-business situation, it may come from the sudden recognition of how a new high-tech product can improve workplace productivity. In short, the boom factor may come from many sources. But it always requires creativity.

Understanding Creative Thinking

Some people may have more of it than others, but creativity lives within us all. Human creativity, developed over millions of years, enabled our ancestors to survive. Without creativity we wouldn't have discovered how to harness fire, domesticate animals, irrigate fields, or manufacture tools. As individuals, we use our natural creativity every time we select an outfit to wear, style our hair, contrive an excuse, decorate our home, cook a meal, or persuade a friend to do us a favor.

Fact-Based versus Value-Based Thinking Most theories of thinking fit into two general categories: value-based or fact-based. Let's examine these styles of thinking more closely.

People whose preferred style of thinking is **fact-based** tend to fragment concepts into components and to analyze situations to discover the one best solution. Although fact-based people can be creative, they tend to be linear thinkers and prefer to have facts and figures—hard data—they can analyze and control. They are not comfortable with ambiguous situations. They like logic, structure, and efficiency.[14]

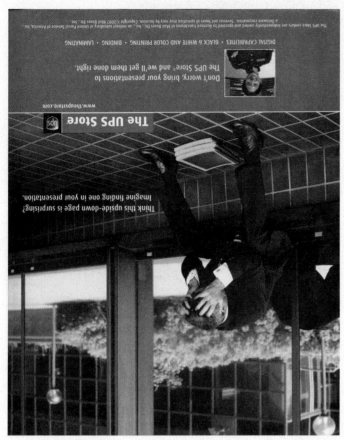

Fact-based thinking can also be creative. The UPS Store (www. theupsstore.com) printed this fact-based ad upside-down to attract the reader's attention and to play on the fear that this could happen in an important presentation. The UPS Store promises to get your presentations done right.

In contrast, **value-based** thinkers make decisions based on intuition, values, and moral codes. They are better able to embrace change, conflict, and paradox. This style fundamentally relies on melding concepts together. Value-based thinkers, for example, attempt to integrate the divergent ideas of a group into an arrangement that lets everyone win. They are good at using their imagination to produce a flow of new ideas and synthesizing existing concepts to create something new.[15]

How Styles of Thinking Affect Creativity If the creative team prefers a value-based thinking style, it tends to produce ads such as those in The UPS Store and Target campaigns—soft, subtle, intuitive, metaphorical. That's fine if the client also prefers that style of thinking.

On the other hand, clients who prefer a fact-based style often seek agencies that produce practical, hard-edged work characterized by simple, straightforward layouts, rational appeals, and lots of data. A fact-based client may even find a value-based campaign to be unsettling.

The creative team needs to understand the campaign's target audience. In some market segments (high-tech, for example) customers may favor one style of thinking over another. And that should dictate which approach to use.

As we shall see in the next section, the best art directors and copywriters use both styles to accomplish their task. In the creative process, they need to use their imagination (value-based thinking) to develop a variety of concepts. But to select the best alternative and get the job done, they often resort to the fact-based style.

Value-based thinking guides the creation of many Target spots. The messages are emotional and avoid specific product facts.

check yourself ✓

1. What is creativity?

2. How does advertising help advertising inform? Persuade? Remind?

3. What is the "boom" factor in advertising?

L05 Define the four roles people play at different stages of the creative process.

THE CREATIVE PROCESS

The creative process is the step-by-step procedure used to discover original ideas and reorganize existing concepts in new ways. By following it, people can improve their ability to unearth possibilities, cross-associate concepts, and select winning ideas.

Over the years, many notions of the creative process have been proposed. Although most are similar, each format has unique merits. Creativity consultant Roger von Oech developed a four-step creative model used today by many *Fortune* 100 companies. It offers flexibility for fact-based and value-based thinkers alike. Von Oech describes four distinct, albeit imaginary, roles that every art director and copywriter has to personally take on at some point in the creative process:[16]

Creative juxtaposition is an essential ingredient for Target advertising.

1. *The Explorer* searches for new information, paying attention to unusual patterns.

2. *The Artist* experiments and plays with a variety of approaches, looking for an original idea.

3. *The Judge* evaluates the results of experimentation and decides which approach is most practical.

4. *The Warrior* overcomes excuses, idea killers, setbacks, and obstacles to bring a creative concept to realization.

THE EXPLORER ROLE: GATHERING INFORMATION

Copywriters and art directors thrive on the challenge of creating **advertising messages**—the encoding process. But first they need the raw materials for ideas: facts, experiences, history, knowledge, feelings.

Taking on the role of the **Explorer**, creatives examine the information they have. They review the creative strategy and the marketing and advertising plan; they study the market, the product, and the competition. They may seek additional input from the agency's account managers and from people on the client side (sales, marketing, product, or research managers).

When the creative team developed ads for Target, they first assumed the Explorer role. They spoke with the company about its products, its marketing history, its competitors, and the competitors' advertising. They reviewed all appropriate sources of advertising for retail stores and studied the company's marketing environment.

Develop an Insight Outlook

In advertising, it's important that when creatives play the Explorer role, they get off the beaten path to look in new and uncommon places for information—to discover new ideas and to identify unusual patterns. One important source of inspiration is the consumer herself. Target's agency creatives spent hours watching women shop at Target stores.

Von Oech suggests adopting an "insight outlook" (a conviction that good information is available and that you have the skills to find and use it). If you're curious and poke around in new areas, you'll improve your chances of discovering new ideas.

Ideas are everywhere: a museum, an art gallery, a hardware store, an airport. The more diverse the sources, the greater your chance of uncovering an original concept.

Know the Objective

Philosopher John Dewey said, "A problem well-stated is a problem half-solved." This is why the creative strategy is so important. It helps define what the creatives are looking for. The creatives typically start working on the message strategy during the Explorer stage because it, too, helps them define what they're looking for.

Brainstorm

As Explorers, the art director and copywriter look first for lots of ideas. One technique is **brainstorming**, a process in which two or more people team up to generate new ideas. A brainstorming session is often a source of sudden inspiration. To succeed, it must follow a couple of rules: All ideas are above

THE ARTIST ROLE: DEVELOPING AND IMPLEMENTING THE BIG IDEA

The next step in the creative process, playing the Artist's role, is both tough and long, but it's also rewarding. The **Artist** must actually accomplish two major tasks: searching for the big idea and then implementing it.

Task 1: Develop the Big Idea

The first task for Artists is the long, sometimes tedious process of reviewing all the information they gathered when they played the Explorer role, analyzing the problem, and searching for a key verbal or visual concept to communicate what needs to be said.

> " If you are curious and poke around in new areas, you'll improve your chances of discovering new ideas. Ideas are everywhere. "

criticism (no idea is "wrong"), and all ideas are written down for later review. The goal is to record any inspiration that comes to mind, a process that psychologists call *free association,* allowing each new idea an opportunity to stimulate another.

Von Oech suggests other techniques for Explorers: Leave your own turf (look in outside fields and industries for ideas that could be transferred); shift your focus (pay attention to a variety of information); look at the big picture (stand back and see what it all means); don't overlook the obvious (the best ideas are right in front of your nose); don't be afraid to stray (you might find something you weren't looking for); and stake your claim to new territory (write down any new ideas or they will be lost).

To keep their creative juices flowing, most copywriters and art directors maintain an extensive library of advertising award books and trade magazines. Many also keep a file of ads that they like.

Some images make the point so well they require no words. This ad for Globetrotter outdoor gear connects the idea of giant seals snug in their skins with campers snug in their sleeping bags. It's amazing how much they look alike. There's a big idea here.

It also means creating a mental picture of the ad or commercial before any copy is written or artwork begun. This step (also called **visualization** or *conceptualization*) is the most important in creating the advertisement. It's where the search for the **big idea**—that flash of insight—takes place. The big idea is a bold, creative initiative that builds on the strategy, joins the product benefit with consumer desire in a fresh, involving way, brings the subject to life, and makes the audience stop, look, and listen.[17]

What's the difference between a strategy and a big idea? A strategy describes the direction the message should take. A big idea gives it life. For example, the creative strategy proposed earlier for the Target campaign contained a strategic brand character statement:

> Target offers consumers the selection and value typical of a mass merchandiser in a setting that has the elegance and flair of a department store.

Target could have used that strategy statement as a headline. But it would have been dreadfully dull. It lacks what a big idea headline delivers: a set of multiple meanings that create interest, memorability, and, in some cases, drama. Note the short, punchy headline that Target chose to convey the same strategic concept: Expect more. Pay less.

John O'Toole said, "While strategy requires deduction, a big idea requires inspiration."[18] The big idea in advertising is almost invariably expressed through a combination of art and copy. Target's approach is to use short but witty copy, beautiful photography, and the immediately recognizable red "target" logo to visually communicate the essence of the brand. Target could save money and use much less creativity in its advertising. Rather than using striking, colorful graphics and layouts, Target's campaigns could emphasize facts and information. But this approach would reduce the boom factor and would end up ignored by the target audience.

Transforming a Concept: Do Something to It

Creative ideas come from manipulating and transforming resources. Von Oech points out that when we adopt the Artist role, we have to do something to the materials we collected

as Explorers to give them value. That means asking lots of questions: What if I added this? Or took that away? Or looked at it backward? Or compared it with something else? The Artist has to change patterns and experiment with various approaches.

At this point in the creative process, a good Artist may employ a variety of strategies for transforming things. Von Oech suggests several techniques for manipulating ideas:[19]

1. *Adapt.* Change contexts. Think what else the product might be besides the obvious. A Campbell's Soup ad showed a steaming bowl of tomato soup with a bold headline underneath: "HEALTH INSURANCE."

2. *Imagine.* Ask what if. Let your imagination fly. What if people could do their chores in their sleep? What if animals drank in saloons? Clyde's Bar in Georgetown actually used that idea. The ad showed a beautifully illustrated elephant and donkey dressed in business suits and seated at a table toasting one another. The headline: "Clyde's. The People's Choice."

3. *Reverse.* Look at it backward. Sometimes the opposite of what you expect has great impact and memorability. A cosmetics company ran an ad for its moisturizing cream under the line: "Introduce your husband to a younger woman." A vintage Volkswagen ad used "Ugly is only skin deep."

Target's newspaper inserts focus more on price. But that doesn't mean they sacrifice creativity or beauty.

Parody is often used to modify concepts and to create a humorous appeal to audiences. Here, the Axe brand of men's cologne places a viagra pill on top of an oyster to suggest how much of an aphrodisiac it is.

7. *Parody.* Fool around. Have some fun. Tell some jokes—especially when you're under pressure. There is a close relationship between the ha-ha experience of humor and the aha! experience of creative discovery. Humor stretches our thinking and, used in good taste, makes for some great advertising. A classical radio station ran a newspaper ad: "Handel with care." And speaking of classics, Fila USA got a rave review from *Advertising Age* for its "bizarre, absolutely hilarious, and totally cool" spot of a praying mantis racing up a leaf stem in Fila sneakers to escape his murderous mate.[20]

4. *Connect.* Join two unrelated ideas together. Ask yourself: What ideas can I connect to my concept? A Target ad showed the rear view of a high-fashion-type model clad only with a backpack and a lampshade—the latter wrapped around her middle like a miniskirt. Next to the Target logo the ad said simply "fashion and housewares." To get people to send for its catalog, Royal Caribbean Cruises ran an ad that showed the catalog cover under the simple headline "Sail by Mail."

5. *Compare.* Take one idea and use it to describe another. Ever notice how bankers talk like plumbers? "Flood the market, laundered money, liquid assets, cash flow, take a bath, float a loan." The English language is awash in metaphors because they help people understand. Jack in the Box advertised its onion rings by picturing them on a billboard and inviting motorists to "Drive thru for a ring job." An elegant magazine ad for the Parker Premier fountain pen used this sterling metaphor: "It's wrought from pure silver and writes like pure silk."

6. *Eliminate.* Subtract something. Or break the rules. In advertising, there's little virtue in doing things the way they've always been done. Seven-Up became famous by advertising what it wasn't ("the Uncola") and thereby positioned itself as a refreshing alternative. To introduce its new models one year, Volkswagen used a series of humorous teaser ads that didn't show any cars. In one, a shaggy dog sat patiently in front of a fan. He was presumably replicating what dogs do in cars, sticking their heads out the window to catch the breeze. The only difference was he was doing it indoors.

Blocks to Creativity Everybody experiences times when the creative juices just won't flow. There are many causes: information overload, mental or physical fatigue, stress, fear, insecurity. Often, though, the problem is simply the style of thinking being used.

In the Explorer stage, when creatives study reams of marketing data, the facts and figures on sales and market share may put them in a fact-based frame of mind. But to create effectively, they need to shift gears to a value-based style of thinking.

Creative blocking may occur when people in the agency start "thinking like the client," especially if the client is a fact-based thinker. This can also be hazardous to the agency's creative reputation and is one reason agencies sometimes resign accounts over "creative differences."

Creative fatigue can also happen when an agency has served an account for a long time and all the fresh ideas have been worked and reworked. It can be difficult to avoid fatigue when a client has rejected a series of concepts; the inspiration is lost and the creatives start trying to force ideas. If this becomes chronic, the only solutions may be to appoint an entirely new creative team or resign the account.

Incubating a Concept: Do Nothing to It When the brain is overloaded with information about a problem, creatives sometimes find it's best to just walk away from it for a while, do something else, and let the unconscious mind mull it over. This approach yields several benefits. First, it puts the problem back into perspective. It also rests the brain, lets the problem incubate in the subconscious, and enables better ideas to percolate to the top. When they return to the task, the creatives frequently discover a whole new set of assumptions.

Target uses dual images that appear to be reverse images of one another. This is similar to a suggestion by creativity guru Roger von Oech.

also shapes the style and choice of photography and illustration. An intimate style uses soft focus and close views, a documentary style portrays the scene without pictorial enhancements, and a dramatic style features unusual angles or blurred action images.

In short, if *copy* is the verbal language of an ad, *art* is the body language. TV uses both sight and sound to involve viewers. Radio commercials use sound to create mental *pictures*. The particular blend of writing, visuals, and sounds makes up an ad's expressive character. So while the quality may vary, every ad uses art.

In advertising, balance, proportion, and movement are guides for uniting words, images, type, sounds, and colors into a single communication so they relate to and enhance each other. We'll discuss more of these concepts in Chapter 9, "Creative Execution: Art and Copy."

Task 2: Implement the Big Idea

Once the creatives latch onto the big idea, they must next focus on how to implement it. This is where the real art of advertising comes in—writing the exact words, designing the precise layout. To have a sense of how advertising creatives do that, we need to understand what art is in advertising, how artistic elements and tools are selected and used, and the difference between good art and bad art.

In advertising, art shapes the message into a complete communication that appeals to the senses as well as the mind. So while **art direction** refers to the act or process of managing the visual presentation of the commercial or ad, the term **art** actually refers to the whole presentation—visual and verbal. For example, the artful selection of words not only communicates information but also stimulates positive feelings for the product. An artfully designed typeface not only makes reading easier; it also evokes a mood. By creatively arranging format elements—surrounding the text with lines, boxes, and colors, and relating them to one another in proportion—the art director can further enhance the ad's message. Art

The Creative Pyramid: A Guide to Formulating Copy and Art

The **creative pyramid** is a model that can guide the creative team as it converts the advertising strategy and the big idea into the actual physical ad or commercial. The cognitive theory of how people learn new information uses a simple five-step structure (the first pyramid in Exhibit 8–1).

▼**EXHIBIT 8–1** The advertising pyramid, discussed in Chapter 7, reflects how people learn new information. Each level of that pyramid can be related to a role that creativity must play. The creative pyramid thus translates advertising objectives into copywriting objectives.

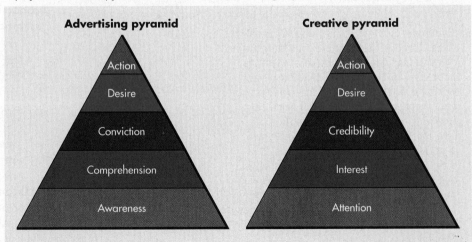

The purpose of much advertising copy and design is to either persuade prospective customers to take some action to satisfy a need or want or to remind them to take the action again. In a new-product situation, people may first need to be made aware of the problem or, if the problem is obvious, that a solution exists. For a frequently purchased product, the advertiser simply has to remind people of the solution close to the purchase occasion. In either case, the advertiser's first job is to get the prospect's *attention*. The second step is to stimulate the prospect's *interest*—in either the message or the product itself. Next, it's important, especially for new products, to build *credibility* for the product claims. Then the ad can focus on generating

art direction
The act or process of managing the visual presentation of an ad or commercial.

art The whole visual presentation of a commercial or advertisement—the body language of an ad. Art also refers to the style of photography or illustration employed, the way color is used, and the arrangement of elements in an ad so that they relate to one another in size and proportion.

creative pyramid
A five-step model to help the creative team convert advertising strategy and the big idea into the actual physical ad or commercial. The five elements are: attention, interest, credibility, desire, and action.

desire and finally on stimulating *action*. These five elements (the second pyramid in Exhibit 8–1) should be addressed in just about every ad or commercial. We'll deal with each step briefly.

> To keep the prospect involved, the copywriter can answer a question asked in the attention step or add facts that relate to the headline.

This ad for a casino is likely to be very successful at the attention stage of the creative pyramid.

Attention For an ad or commercial to be effective it must break through consumers' physiological screens to create the kind of attention that leads to perception. *Attention,* therefore, is the first objective of any ad and the foundation of the creative pyramid. The Artist may spend as much time and energy figuring out how to express the big idea in an interesting, attention-getting way as searching for the big idea itself.

The attention step is critically important to triggering the ad's boom factor. Print ads often use the headline as the major attention-getting device. Usually designed to appear in the largest and boldest type in the ad, the headline is often the strongest focal point. Many other devices also help gain attention. In print media, they may include dynamic visuals, unusual layouts, vibrant color, or dominant ad size. In electronic media, they may include sound effects, music, animation, or unusual visual techniques.

The attention-getting device should create drama, power, impact, and intensity. It must also be appropriate, relating to the product, the tone of the ad, and the needs or interests of the intended audience. This is especially true in business-to-business advertising, where rational appeals and fact-based thinking dominate.

Interest The second step in the creative pyramid, *interest,* is also extremely important. It carries the prospective customer— now paying attention—to the body of the ad. The ad must keep the prospect excited or involved as the information becomes more detailed. To do this, the copywriter may answer a question asked in the attention step or add facts that relate to the

Does Sex Appeal?

It's one of the more blatant uses of sex in advertising in recent memory: a billboard features a young woman, holding a grease gun cartridge in each hand, and leaning over to exhibit an ample amount of cleavage. The headline reads "This is Debbie. She wants you to have this pair in your car." The ad is for auto parts, but the implication seems to be that if you buy this manufacturer's auto parts, you'll get Debbie or someone like Debbie in the bargain. Nothing in the ad says so explicitly, but the innuendo is all that's required to capture the viewer's attention.

Advertisers frequently use the power of suggestion to imply sex, encouraging viewers to come to their own conclusions. However, advertisers who run such risqué ads must contend with the critics and with the often tricky legal distinction between obscenity and indecency. Obscenity is illegal and carries criminal charges, whereas indecency does not. To be considered obscene, an ad must meet three conditions: it appeals to prurient interests, it is patently offensive, and it lacks any redeeming social value.

In general, most ads with sexual appeals don't meet the criteria for obscenity, but they may still be considered indecent, since indecency is in the eyes of the beholder. If enough people believe sexually oriented material is indecent, then "community standards" reflect this belief. In such cases, citizen pressure groups, along with media organizations and local courts, can enforce community standards by disallowing advertising that offends those standards.

Consider Abercrombie & Fitch. The clothing retailer sparked controversy at a mall in Omaha when its window posters featured a topless model covering her breasts with her hands. A Christian group, Family First, quickly objected, claiming that Abercrombie's posters created a "sexualized walkway." Family First began pressuring shoppers and other retailers in the mall to object to the photographs, and within nine days the window displays were changed.

Were the posters obscene or indecent? Advertisers like A&F, who continue to strive for the "sexy" appeal, are beginning to find it increasingly difficult to draw the line between simple sex appeal and unethical exploitation.

There is no easy solution to this dilemma, especially since research shows that sexual appeals can be very effective when sexuality relates to the product. However, when it doesn't, it can distract audiences from the main message and severely demean the advertiser in the consumer's eyes. Many argue that sexually oriented advertising is not only a distraction, but also a source of negative *externalities*—the social costs to consumers outside the target market, such as children who might be indirectly affected.

Advertisers must examine, on a case-by-case basis, at what point sexual appeals become unethical and therefore counterproductive. In one case, an executive on the Valvoline advertising account justified using "girlie calendars" for mechanics by noting that "the calendar may offend some groups—but they aren't our customers."

Miller Lite's "Catfight" campaign raised a few eyebrows. The campaign appeared to signal the company's return to "beer and babes" ads, depicting women as sexual objects. In the commercial, two women in a restaurant begin the classic "tastes great/less filling" debate over Miller Lite. The debate quickly turns into a full-fledged catfight, with the two women stripped down to their bras and panties, splashing around in an adjacent fountain. Moments later, we see the two buxom brawlers going at it in a soggy cement pit. The ad cuts to a bar. It turns out the fight was only the fantasy of two guys in a bar who were dreaming of the perfect beer commercial, much to the shock and disgust of their girlfriends, who were with them at the time.

So what does any of this have to do with selling beer? Hillary Chura, who covers the beer industry for *Advertising Age,* explains that ads such as the "Catfight" commercial are "aspirational." After watching these two beautiful women wrestle around for 30 seconds, Miller wants guys to say, "Hey, if I drink Miller Genuine Draft, I'll get those hot women." And Miller wants women to think "If I drink this beer, I'll look like those women."

But what is the social cost of these unrealistic "aspirations"? In a society rife with confidence-related disorders, should advertisers exploit consumer insecurities in an effort to sell more of their product? At what point do advertisers need to accept some ethical responsibility for the interests of the society to which they owe their existence?

Unfortunately, this debate over sex in advertising may actually be fueling advertisers' desire to continue using blatant sex appeals. The "Catfight" campaign sparked nationwide attention on talk radio, CNN's *Crossfire,* in *USA Today,* and in other media outlets. Similarly, Abercrombie & Fitch's quarterly catalog of scantily clad models makes national headlines with every issue. Controversy equals publicity. Publicity stimulates interest. And interest spawns sales.

In short, sex, and the controversy surrounding it, sells. Until this changes, industry or government policymakers will certainly continue to encounter difficulties in treating advertising sex in a way satisfactory to everyone.

Questions

1. Explain why you believe that sexual appeals in advertising do or do not have "redeeming value."
2. Even if sexual appeals are considered okay by the audiences that are directly targeted, what responsibility does the advertiser have for any effect on indirect targets, such as adults who are offended or children? How can advertisers protect themselves from this problem?
3. Is it acceptable for advertisers to exploit consumer insecurities in an effort to sell more of their product? Should advertisers accept some ethical responsibility for creating unrealistic "aspirations" and intensifying confidence-related disorders?

headline. To maintain audience interest, the tone and language should be compatible with the target market's attitude. As we discussed earlier, the successful ad resonates.

The writer and designer must lead prospects from one step to the next. Research shows that people read what interests them and ignore what doesn't, so the writer must maintain prospects' interest at all times.[21] One way to do so is to sneak through prospects' psychological screens by talking about their problems, their needs, and how the product or service will address them. Copywriters use the word *you* a lot.

There are many effective ways to stimulate interest: a dramatic situation, a story, cartoons, charts. In radio, copywriters use sound effects or catchy dialogue. Television frequently uses quick cuts to maintain interest. We discuss some of these techniques in Chapter 10, "Producing Ads."

Credibility   The third step in the creative pyramid is to establish *credibility* for the product or service. Customers are sophisticated and skeptical. They want claims to be supported by facts. Comparison ads can build credibility, but they must be relevant to customers' needs—and fair.

Well-known presenters may lend credibility to commercials. For example, actor Justin Long effectively represents Macs with his personable, low-key, and slightly bemused style.

Advertisers often show independent test results to back up product claims. To work, such "proofs" must be valid, not just statistical manipulation. Advertisers and agencies must remember that many consumers have extensive product knowledge, even in specialized areas. And customers who believe, rightly or wrongly, that they have been misled rarely come back.

Desire   In the *desire* step, the writer encourages prospects to imagine themselves enjoying the benefits of the product or service.

In print ads, copywriters use phrases like "Picture yourself" or "Imagine." In TV, the main character pulls a sparkling clean T-shirt from the washer, smiles, and says "Yeah!" In radio, the announcer says, "You'll look your best."

In print advertising, the desire step is one of the most difficult to write (which may be why some copywriters omit it). In TV, the desire step can simply show the implied consumer experiencing the benefit of the product. Ever notice how advertisers almost invariably show the happy life that awaits their product's user?

Action   The final step up the creative pyramid is *action*. The goal here is to motivate people to do something—send in a coupon, call the number on the screen, visit the store—or at least to agree with the advertiser.

The call to action may be explicit— "Order now"—or implicit—"Fly the friendly skies." Designers cue customers to take action by placing dotted lines around coupons to suggest cutting and by highlighting the company's telephone number or Web address with large type or a bright color.

This block of the pyramid reaches the smallest audience but those with the most to gain from the product's utility. So the last step is often the easiest. If the copy is clear about what readers need to do and asks or even nudges them to act, chances are they will.

With today's technology, it's important to not only ask people to act but to make it easy for them to do so, through either a toll-free phone number or an attractive Web site. In relationship marketing, the ad enables people to self-select being interested in a relationship. Then the marketer can use more efficient one-on-one media to deepen the relationship.

THE JUDGE ROLE: DECISION TIME

The next role in the creative process is the **Judge**. This is when the creatives evaluate the quality of their big ideas and decide whether to implement, modify, or discard them.[22]

The Judge's role is delicate. On the one hand, the creatives must be self-critical enough to ensure that when it's time to play the Warrior they will have an idea worth fighting for. On the other hand, they need to avoid stifling the imagination of their internal Artist. It's easier to be critical than to explore, conceptualize, or defend. But the Judge's purpose is to help produce good ideas, not to revel in criticism. Von Oech suggests focusing first on the positive, interesting aspects of a new idea. The negatives will come soon enough.

When playing the Judge, creatives need to ask certain questions: Is this idea an aha! or an uh-oh? (What was my initial reaction?) What's wrong with this idea? (And what's right with it?) What if it fails? (Is it worth the risk?) What is my cultural bias? (Does the audience have the same bias?) What's clouding my thinking? (Am I wearing blinders?)

Risk is an important consideration. When the advertising scores a hit, everybody's happy, sales go up, people get raises, and occasionally there's even positive publicity. But when a campaign flops, all hell breaks loose, especially on high-profile accounts. Sales may flatten or even decline, competitors gain a couple of points in market share, distributors and dealers complain, and the phone rings incessantly with calls from angry clients. Perhaps worst of all is the ridicule in the trade press. This is not good for either the agency's stock or the client's. And it's how agencies get replaced. So the Judge's role is vital.

If the Artist-as-Judge does a good job, the next role in the creative process, the Warrior, is easier to perform.

3. *Polished presentation.* The presentation must be prepared and rehearsed; it should use compelling visuals and emotional appeals.

4. *Structural persuasion.* The presentation should be well structured, since clients value organized thinking. The opening is crucial because it sets the tone.

5. *Solve the problem.* Clients have needs, and they frequently report to big shots who ask tough questions about the advertising. Solve the client's problem and you'll sell the big idea—and do it with style.

THE WARRIOR ROLE: OVERCOMING SETBACKS AND OBSTACLES

In the final step of the creative process, the **Warrior** wins territory for big new ideas in a world resistant to change. The Warrior carries the concept into action. This means getting the big idea approved, produced, and placed in the media.

For clients, recognizing a big idea and evaluating it are almost as difficult as creating one. When the agency presents the concepts, the client is suddenly in the role of the Judge, without having gone through the other roles first. David Ogilvy recommended that clients ask themselves five questions: Did it make me gasp when I first saw it? Do I wish I had thought of it myself? Is it unique? Does it fit the strategy to perfection? Could it be used for 30 years?[24]

> ## To get the big idea approved, the Warrior has to battle people within the agency and often the client, too.

To get the big idea approved, the Warrior has to battle people within the agency and often the client, too. So part of the Warrior's role is turning the agency account team into allies for the presentation to the client. At this point, it's imperative that the creatives have a completed message strategy document to support their rationale for the copy, art, and production elements in the concept they're presenting. And the message strategy had better mesh with the creative strategy, or the valiant Warrior will likely face a wide moat with no drawbridge.

Part of the Warrior's task may be to help the account managers present the campaign to the client. Bruce Bendinger says, "How well you *sell* ideas is as important as how good those ideas are." To give a presentation maximum selling power, he suggests five key components:[23]

1. *Strategic precision.* The selling idea must be *on strategy*. The presenting team must be able to prove it, and the strategy should be discussed first, before the big selling idea is presented.

2. *Savvy psychology.* The presentation, like the advertising, should be receiver-driven. The idea has to meet the client's needs, thinking style, and personality.

As Ogilvy pointed out, campaigns that run five years or more are the superstars: Dove soap (one-quarter cleansing cream), Ivory soap (99 and 44/100 percent pure), Perdue chickens ("It takes a tough man to make a tender chicken"), the U.S. Army ("Be all you can be"). Some of these campaigns are still running today, and some have run for as long as 30 years. Those are big ideas!

When the client approves the campaign, the creative's role as a Warrior is only half over. Now the campaign has to be executed. The Warrior will shepherd it through the intricate details of design and production to ensure that it is completed, faithful to the concept, on time, under budget, and of the highest quality possible. At the same time, the creatives revert to their Artist roles to finalize the design and copy and produce the ads.

The next step in the process, therefore, is to implement the big idea, to produce the ads for print and electronic media—the subject of our next two chapters. ■

1. What is the role of the Explorer? The Artist?

2. What are blocks to creativity and how can the creative person deal with a block?

3. What are the steps of the creative pyramid and what role does creativity play in each?

4. What obstacles does the Warrior prepare to do battle with?

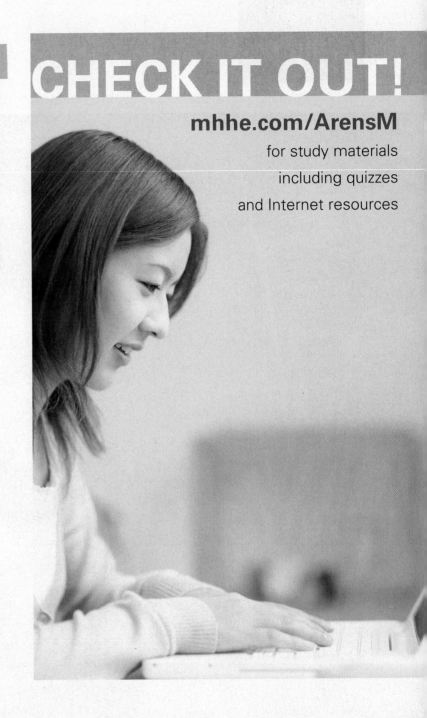

CHECK IT OUT!

mhhe.com/ArensM

for study materials

including quizzes

and Internet resources

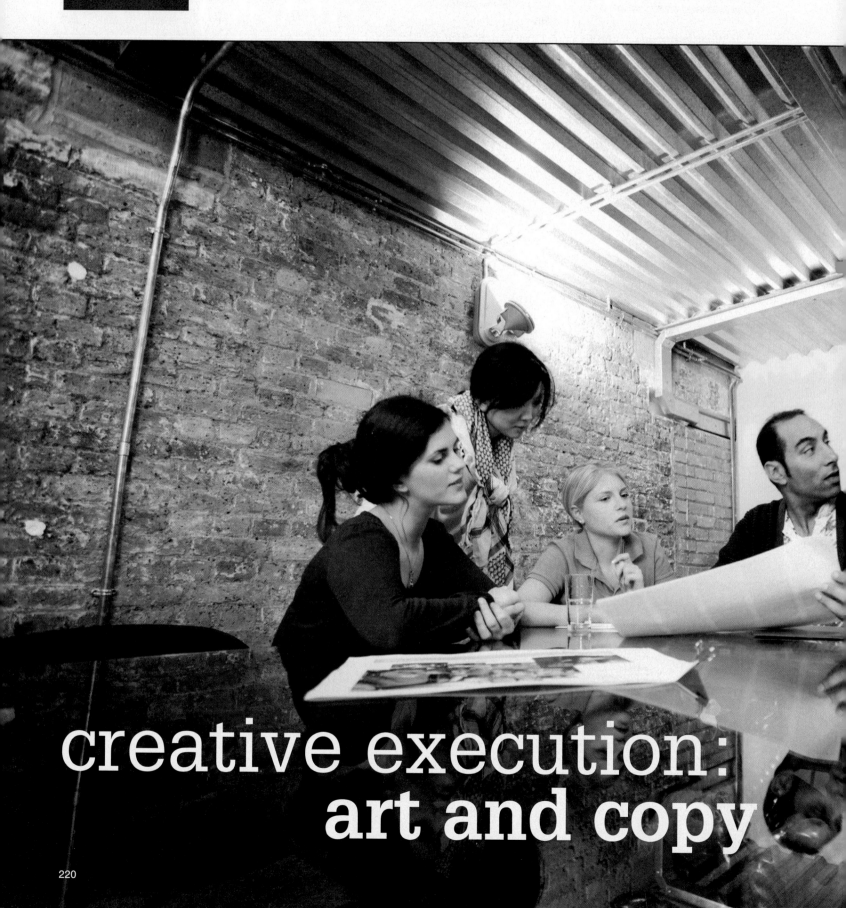

creative execution:
art and copy

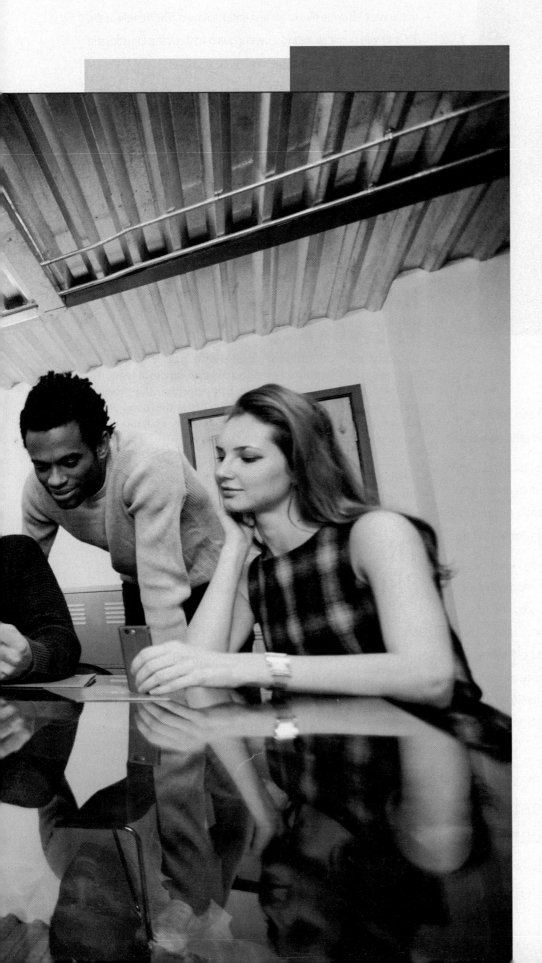

Philips, a Dutch electronics manufacturer, makes premium brands of HDTVs, including its newest model, the Cinema 21:9. The 21:9 is named after its aspect ratio, 21 units of width for 9 units of height. By contrast, a typical HDTV is 16:9.

So who needs the extra width? Anyone who watches movies on their TVs. A 16:9 TV shrinks the height of the video. That permits the entire shot to be viewed, but at a price—dark bars showing above and below the action. With the Philips 21:9, there are no dark bars, just beautiful high definition video.

Philips assigned the account to Tribal DDB. Tribal's solution involved some unusual creative leaps, a partnership with a music video director, dozens of cops and clowns, and a big win at Cannes.[1]

Tribal DDB decided it would not advertise on television, but rather on the Web. But how could Philips attract visitors to

continued on p. 222

LEANING OBJECTIVES

LO1 Describe the factors involved in creating print ads.

LO2 Explain the types of copy and how great copy is created in print ads.

LO3 Outline how great copy is created in electronic ads.

LO4 Discuss the role of art in electronic ads.

LO5 Review the unique requirements in writing for the Web.

of the year." But the film is not just entertainment. The benefit of the TV is driven home by letting viewers compare how the film looks in the traditional 16:9 aspect and in glorious 21:9.[4]

While "Carousel" is a great ad, is it hyperbole to call it groundbreaking? Actually no. For one thing, it was honored with a Cannes Grand Prix, making it the most honored ad of 2009. Even more impressive, it is the first "film" winner to run solely on the Web. Cannes has never before awarded its top prize to an ad that appeared only on the Web. It seems the times they are a changing.[5] ■

DELIVERING ON THE BIG IDEA: THE VISUAL AND THE VERBAL

As "Carousel" demonstrates, what's shown is just as important as what's said. The nonverbal aspect of an ad carries at least half the burden of communication. It helps position the product and create personality for the brand. It creates the mood of the ad, determining the way it *feels* to the audience. That mood flavors the verbal message, embodied in the *copy*.

In this chapter, we discuss how advertising concepts are executed from the standpoints of both art and copy. We examine the visual and the verbal details, first of print advertising and then of electronic and digital media.

THE ART OF CREATING PRINT ADVERTISING

LO1   Describe the factors involved in creating print ads.

Designing the Print Ad

The term **design** refers to how the art director, graphic artist, or graphic designer chooses and structures the artistic elements of an ad. A designer sets a style—the manner in which a thought or image is expressed—by choosing artistic elements and blending them in a unique way.

In general, clean lines, formally composed photographs, and sparse copy give an ad the breathing room needed to draw the reader's eye from one element to the next. Sufficient *white space* gives an ad unity and balance in spite of a diversity of elements.

continued from p. 221

its site? On the Internet, people have to want to see your ad. To attract attention you have to give consumers something special.

Tribal brought in a digital production company, Stink Digital, and a Swedish director, Adam Berg, and asked them to do a digital film that would showcase the cinema experience of the 21:9. The film would have to be good, so good it would generate buzz and drive traffic to the site.

The result was "Carousel," a stunning, wordless, motionless loop of video that clocks in at (not coincidentally) 2 minutes and 19 seconds. The creative idea? Imagine dozens of clowns, after a bank robbery goes wrong, flee to a nearby hospital where they engage in a fight to the death with equal numbers of police officers.[2] To appreciate "Carousel" you have to see it for yourself, which you can do at: http://labs.tribalddb.nl/Cinema219/?ls=gb_en.

Filming took place in an abandoned school in Prague. The entire shoot was completed in two days, with Czech stunt actors and dancers filling in all of the roles.[3]

The film was great, and so was the buzz. Ashton Kutcher glowingly twittered about it and Kanye West labeled it the "hands down video

> " The nonverbal aspect of an ad carries at least half the burden of communication. "

A number of designers, working under the art director, may produce initial layouts of the ad concept. In collaboration with copywriters, these artists call on their expertise in graphic design (including photography, typography, and illustration) to create the most effective ad or brochure.

The Use of Layouts

A **layout** is an overall orderly arrangement of all the format elements of an ad: visual(s), headline, subheads, body copy, slogan, seal, logo, and signature. The layout serves several purposes. First, it helps both the agency and the client develop and evaluate, in advance, how the ad will look and feel. It gives the client (usually not an artist) a tangible item to correct, change, comment on, and approve.

Second, the layout helps the creative team develop the ad's psychological elements: the nonverbal and symbolic components. Sophisticated advertisers want their advertising to do more than

design Visual pattern or composition of artistic elements chosen and structured by the graphic artist.

layout An orderly formation of all the parts of an advertisement.

just bring in store traffic. They want their ads to create personality for the product and to build the brand's equity with the consumer. To do this, the "look" of the ad should elicit an image or mood that reflects and enhances both the advertiser and the product.

Third, once the best design is chosen, the layout serves as a blueprint. It shows the size and placement of each element. Once the production manager knows the dimensions of the ad, the number of photos, the amount of typesetting, and the use of art elements such as color and illustrations, he or she can determine production costs (see Commercial Break 9–A, "The Role of the Advertising Artist").

The Role of the Advertising Artist [9–A]

All the people employed in commercial art are called artists, but they may perform very different tasks. Some can't even draw well; instead, they're trained for different artistic specialties.

Art Directors

Art directors are responsible for the visual presentation of the ad. Along with a copywriter, they develop the initial concept. They may do initial sketches or layouts, but after that they may not touch the ad again. Their primary responsibility is to supervise the ad's progress to completion.

The best art directors are good at presenting ideas in both words and pictures. They are usually experienced graphic designers with a good understanding of consumers. They may have a large or small staff, depending on the organization. Or they may be *freelancers* (independent contractors) and do most of the work themselves.

Graphic Designers

Graphic designers (or artists) are precision specialists preoccupied with shape and form. In advertising they arrange the various graphic elements (type, illustrations, photos, white space) in the most attractive and effective way possible. While they may work on ads, they often design and produce collateral materials, such as posters, brochures, and annual reports.

In an agency, the art director often acts as the designer. Sometimes, however, a separate designer is used to offer a unique talent to a particular ad.

Illustrators

Illustrators paint or draw the visuals in an ad. They frequently specialize in one type of illustrating, such as automotive, fashion, or furniture. Very few agencies or advertisers retain full-time illustrators; most freelance.

Typically, agencies hire different illustrators for different jobs, depending on an ad's particular needs, look, and feel.

Photographers

Like the illustrator, the advertising photographer creates a nonverbal expression that reinforces the verbal message. Photographers use the tools of photography—cameras, lenses, and lights—to create images. They select interesting angles, arrange subjects in new ways, carefully control the lighting, and use many other techniques to enhance the subject's image quality. Many photographers specialize—in cars, celebrities, fashion, food, equipment, or architecture. Agencies and advertisers rarely employ staff photographers. They generally hire freelancers by the hour or pay a fee for the assignment. Photographers also sell stock photography, which is photos on file from prior shootings.

Production Artists

Production (or pasteup) artists assemble the various elements of an ad and put them together the way the art director or designer indicates. Good production artists are fast, precise, and knowledgeable about the whole production process. Production artists are highly computer literate; they use a variety of software programs for pagemaking, drawing, painting, and photo scanning. Most designers and art directors start their careers as production artists and work their way up. It's difficult work, but it is also important, for this is where an ad actually comes together in its finished form.

Applying the Breaks

Select a print ad from any chapter. Explain which types of advertising artists were probably involved in its creation and what the responsibility of each artist was.

The slogan for the popular video game Medal of Honor is "real as life." How do the ads use the nonverbal element to convey that benefit?

my ad campaign

Advertising Design and Production: The Creative and Approval Process

The design process is both a creative and an approval process. In the creative phase, the designer uses thumbnails, roughs, dummies, and comprehensives (comps) to establish the ad's look and feel. Then in the *prepress* (or *production art*) phase, the artist prepares a mechanical: the final artwork with the actual type in place along with all the visuals the printer or the media will need to reproduce the ad. In Chapter 10, "Producing Ads," we'll see how this design process works to produce a finished ad.

Product Facts for Creatives [9–A]

Art directors and copywriters must have a thorough understanding of the brand to create advertising that resonates. Make sure your creatives have the information that will help them write copy that sizzles and create layouts that stop consumers dead in their tracks.

- **Proprietary information**
  Product's trade name.
  Trademark.
  Product symbol.
  Other copyrighted or patented information.

- **History**
  When was the product created or invented?
  Who introduced it?
  Has it had other names?
  Have there been product changes?
  Is there any "romance" to it?

- **Research**
  Are research results available?
  What research about the product does the supplier have?
  Which research will be most useful for each medium?

- **Life cycle**
  What is the product's life or use span?
  What stage is it in now and what style of copy should be used for that stage?
  What stages are competitors in?

- **Market position**
  What is the product's share of the total market?
  Does its market share suggest a positioning strategy?
  What position does the company wish to occupy?

- **Competitive information**
  Who are the product's competitors?
  Does the product have any advantages over them?
  Does it have any disadvantages?
  Are they all about the same?
  Do rival products present problems that this one solves?

- **Product image**
  How do people view the product?
  What do they like about it?
  What do they dislike about it?
  Is it a luxury?
  Is it a necessity?
  Is it a habit?
  Is it self-indulgent?
  Do people have to have it but wish they didn't?

- **Customer use**
  How is the product used?
  Are there other possible uses?
  How frequently is it bought?
  What type of person uses the product?

thumbnail A rough, rapidly produced pencil sketch that is used for trying out ideas.

rough Pencil sketch of a proposed design or layout.

dummy A three-dimensional, hand-made layout of a brochure or other multipage advertising piece put together, page for page, just like the finished product will eventually appear.

comprehensive layout (comp) A facsimile of a finished ad with copy set in type and pasted into position along with proposed illustrations. The "comp" is prepared so the advertiser can gauge the effect of the final ad.

The approval process takes place at each step along the way. At any point in the design and production process, the ad—or the ad concept—may be altered or even canceled.

Thumbnail Sketches

The thumbnail sketch, or **thumbnail**, is a very small (about three-by-four inch), rough, rapidly produced drawing that the artist uses to visualize layout approaches without wasting time on details. Thumbnails are very basic. Blocks of straight or squiggly lines indicate text placement, and boxes show placement of visuals. The best sketches are then developed further.

Rough Layout

In a **rough**, the artist draws to the actual size of the ad. Headlines and subheads suggest the final type style, illustrations and photos are sketched in, and body copy may be simulated with lines or random gibberish *(greek)*. The agency may present roughs to clients, particularly cost-conscious ones, for approval. Several examples of rough layouts are presented in Commercial Break 9–B, "The Art Director's Guide to Layout Styles."

Dummy

A **dummy** presents the handheld look and feel of brochures, multipage materials, or point-of-purchase displays. The artist assembles the dummy by hand, using color markers and computer proofs, mounting them on sturdy paper, and then cutting and folding them to size. A dummy for a brochure, for example, is put together, page by page, to look exactly like the finished product.

Comprehensive and Mechanical

The **comprehensive layout**, or **comp**, is a highly refined facsimile of the finished ad. A comp is generally quite elaborate, with colored photos, the final type styles and sizes, subvisuals, and a glossy spray coat. Copy for the comp is usually typeset on a computer

Why is the product bought?
  Personal use.
  Gift.
  Work.
What type of person uses the product most (heavy user)?
How much does the heavy user buy?
Where do the best customers live?
• **Performance**
What does the product do?
What might it be expected to do that it does not?
How does it work?
How is it made or produced?
What's in it?
  Raw materials.
  Special ingredients.
  Preservatives.
  Chemicals.
  Nutrients.
• **What are its physical characteristics?**
Smell.
Appearance.
Color.
Texture.
Taste.
Others.

• **Effectiveness**
Is there proof the product has been tested and works well?
Do any government or other regulations need to be mentioned or observed?
How does it work compared to its competitors?
• **Manufacturing**
How is the product made?
How long does it take?
How many steps are in the process?
How many people are involved in making it?
Are any special machines used?
Where is it made?
• **Distribution**
How widely is the product distributed?
Are there exclusive sellers?
Is there a ready supply or a limited amount?
Is it available for a short season?
What channels of distribution must be reached?
• **Packaging**
Unit size or sizes offered.
Package shape.
Package design.
  Styling.
  Color.
Special protection for product.
A carrier for product.
Package label.

Thumbnail sketches are usually the first step in the advertising design process. They allow designers to quickly evaluate several layout options for further development. Rough lines and boxes are used to represent copy and graphics.

Ads that employ a poster-style format often test well. A key element of this layout is a compelling visual.

and positioned with the visuals, and the ad is printed as a full-color proof. At this stage, all visuals should be final. A very few advertisers still make traditional **mechanicals**, where type and line art are pasted in place on a piece of white art board (called a **pasteup**). Printers refer to the mechanical or pasteup as **camera-ready art** because they photograph it using a large production camera.

At any time during the design process—until the printing press lays ink on paper—changes can be made on the art. However, the expense may grow tenfold with each step from roughs to mechanicals to printing.

Approval The work of the copywriter and art director is always subject to approval. The larger the agency and the larger the client, the more formidable this process becomes. A new ad concept is first approved by the agency's creative director. Then the account management team reviews it. Next, the client's product managers and marketing staff review it, often changing a word or two or sometimes rejecting the whole approach. Both the agency's and client's legal departments scrutinize the copy

and art for potential problems. Finally, the company's top executives review the final concept and text.

The biggest challenge in approval is keeping reviewers from corrupting the style of the ad. The creative team works hard to achieve a cohesive style. Then a group of nonwriters and nonartists has the opportunity to change it all. Maintaining artistic purity is extremely difficult and requires patience, flexibility, maturity, and persuasive powers to explain why artistic choices were made.

Effect of Computers on Graphic Design

By using graphics or imaging programs on computers, today's graphic artist or designer can do much of the work previously performed by hand. On the screen, the artist can see an entire page layout, complete with illustrations and photos, and easily

> " The work of the copywriter and art director is always subject to approval. The larger the agency and the larger the client, the more formidable this process becomes. "

alter any of them in a few minutes. Before computers, designing a variety of layouts could take days, and final art was not as detailed or complete as designs created today on the computer.

Small systems are ideal for computer design, and sophisticated graphics software is now available for pagemaking *(InDesign),* painting and drawing *(CorelDRAW* and *Adobe Illustrator),* and image manipulation *(Corel Paintshop Photo Pro* and *Adobe Photoshop).* For word processing the most popular programs include *Microsoft Word* and *Google Docs.* Their moderate cost makes such software accessible to freelancers, small businesses, and agency creative departments. Today's graphic artist, illustrator, and retoucher must be computer literate in addition to having a thorough knowledge of aesthetics, rendering, and design.[6]

Principles of Design: Which Design Formats Work Best

Ads must be designed to attract customers and do it fast. Typically, the advertiser has only a second or two to grab the reader's attention. Indeed, studies of ad penetration suggest large numbers of people simply ignore ads.[7] They also show virtually no relationship between how much the advertiser spends and how well the ad is recalled. But the quality of the advertising is important. Good design not only commands attention but holds it. Good design also communicates information completely, quickly, and in a way that is easy to understand.[8]

Advertisers use many different types of layouts (see Commercial Break 9–B, "The Art Director's Guide to Layout Styles"). Traditionally, the ads that score the highest recall employ a standard, **poster-style format** (also called a **picture-window layout** and **Ayer No. 1** in the trade) with a single, dominant visual that typically occupies 60 to 70 percent of the ad's total area.[9] In fact, some research shows that ads scoring in the top third for stopping power devote an average of 82 percent of their space to the visual.[10] Next in ranking are ads that have one large picture and two smaller ones. The visuals are intended to stop the reader and arouse interest, so their content must be interesting.

As we discuss in the next section, headlines also stop the reader and may actually contribute more to long-term memory than the visual.[11] As a design element, the total headline area should normally fill only 10 to 15 percent of the ad, so the type need not be particularly large. Headlines may appear above or below the visual, depending on the situation. However, when the headline appears below the illustration, the ad typically gains about 10 percent more readership.[12] This is probably because the eye tends to follow a Z pattern as it scans down the page. It sees the picture first, then the headline, then the body copy and the signature. Ads that don't interrupt this natural flow seem to score higher.

Research also shows that readership can drop considerably if ads have more than 50 words. So to attract a large number of readers, copy blocks should be kept to less than 20 percent of the ad. However, with many high-involvement products, the more you tell, the more you sell. If communicating detailed information is the objective, then informative body copy becomes important. And long copy works when it's appropriate—when the advertiser is more interested in quality of readership than quantity.[13]

Breaking through the clutter requires fresh approaches. How does the art and copy of this Dove ad challenge your expectations?

(continued on p. 231)

Art directors use many different types of layouts. Creating an ad for the fictitious Imperial Cruise Lines, Tom Michael, the president and creative director of Market Design (Encinitas, California), first prepared several rough layouts using a variety of different styles and headlines to see which ideas would work best.

Note how the copy in each ad is indicated by lines of recurring gibberish. Art directors frequently represent layout text with such incoherent ramblings, referred to in the business as "greek." This saves time, but provides a graphic representation of the actual copy.

Applying the Breaks

Study the different layouts and discuss the advantages and disadvantages of each. Which approach would you recommend for Imperial Cruise Lines? Why? What additional layout or copy ideas can you come up with?

Poster-style layout—"Warm up to the beauty of Alaska."
Also called a picture-window layout, note how the single, large visual occupies about two-thirds of the ad. The headline and copy may appear above or below the "window."

Mondrian grid layout—"Alaska: The last frontier for family fun."
Named after Dutch painter Piet Mondrian, the Mondrian layout uses a series of vertical and horizontal lines, rectangles, and squares within a predetermined grid to give geometric proportion to the ad.

Circus layout—"Picture Yourself Here."
Filled with multiple illustrations, oversize type, reverse blocks, tilts, or other elements to bring the ad alive and make it fun and interesting.

Picture frame layout—"Guaranteed to disrupt your biological clock."
The copy is surrounded by the visual. Or, in some cases, the visual may be surrounded by the copy.

Copy-heavy layout—"Get rocked to sleep on our water bed."
When you have a lot to say and visuals won't say it, use text. But be sure the headlines and subheads make it interesting. In this case, the heavy copy actually frames the headline and visual to add visual interest. However, the headline could just as well have run above or below the copy.

Montage layout—"Open all night. Loitering encouraged."
Similar to the circus layout, the montage brings multiple illustrations together and arranges them by superimposing or overlapping to make a single composition.

Combo layout—"Warm up to Alaska."
Creativity often involves combining two or more unrelated elements to make a new element. The same is true in design. To make an ad more interesting or contemporary, the art director may combine two or more layout types to make a combo layout. This ad, for instance, starts out with a grid layout, but in the center of the grid note how the copy surrounds the headline and logo as in a frame layout.

(continued from p. 227)

Finally, most people who read ads want to know who placed the ad. Company signatures or logos need not be large or occupy more than 5 to 10 percent of the area. For best results, they should be placed in the lower right-hand corner or across the bottom of the ad.

Advertising author Roy Paul Nelson points out that the principles of design are to the layout artist what the rules of grammar are to the writer. The basic rules include the following:

- A design in balance.

- Space within the ad that is broken up into pleasing proportions.

- A directional pattern that is evident so the reader knows in what sequence to read.

- A force that holds the ad together and gives it unity.

- One element, or one part of the ad, that has enough emphasis to dominate all others.[14]

The Use of Visuals in Print Advertising

The artists who paint, sketch, and draw in advertising are called **illustrators**. The artists who produce pictures with a camera are **photographers**.

illustrators The artists who paint, sketch, or draw the pictures we see in advertising.

photographers The artists who use cameras to create visuals for advertisements.

visuals All of the picture elements that are placed into an advertisement.

Together they are responsible for all the **visuals**, or pictures, we see in advertising.

Purpose of the Visual When confronted with a print ad, most prospects spot the picture first, then read the headline, and then peruse the body copy, in that order. Since the visual carries so much responsibility for an ad's success, it should be designed with several goals in mind. Some of the most obvious follow:

- Capture the reader's attention.

- Clarify claims made by the copy.

- Identify the subject of the ad.

- Show the product actually being used.

- Qualify readers by stopping those who are legitimate prospects.

- Convince the reader of the truth of copy claims.

- Arouse the reader's interest in the headline.

- Emphasize the product's unique features.

- Create a favorable impression of the product or advertiser.

- Provide continuity for the campaign by using a unified visual technique in each ad.[15]

Creating Great Headlines and Copy [9–B]

George Felton, in his book *Advertising Concept and Copy*, offers the following suggestions for aspiring copywriters:

Headlines

- "Achieve synergy, not redundancy." The headlines and artwork should work together to create an idea, but not be completely redundant.
- "Let the consumer do some of the work." Avoid ads that insult the audience's intelligence.
- "Combine overstatement and understatement." If the visual is BIG, make the headline small. And vice versa.
- "Emphasize one idea per ad." If you have several ideas, show how they are linked to make them one.

Copy

Freelance copywriter John Kuraoka offers some excellent advice for new copywriters at http://www.kuraoka.com/how-to-write-better-ads.html.

Here are summaries of his recommendations for your visuals:

- Capture the reader's attention.
- Clarify copy claims.
- Let the reader know the ad is directed at him or her.
- Show the product in use.
- Offer evidence for copy claims.
- Emphasize the product's unique features or benefits.
- Unify the different ads in the campaign.

Determining the Chief Focus for Visuals Selecting the focus for advertising visuals is a major step in the creative process. It often determines how well the big idea is executed. Print advertising uses many standard subjects for ad visuals, including

1. *The package containing the product.* Especially important for packaged goods, it helps the consumer identify the product on the grocery shelf.

2. *The product alone.* This usually does not work well for non-packaged goods.

3. *The product in use.* Automobile ads typically show a car in use while talking about its ride, luxury, handling, or economy. Cosmetics ads usually show the product in use with a close-up photo of a beautiful woman or a virile man.

4. *How to use the product.* Recipe ads featuring a new way to use food products have historically pulled very high readership scores.

5. *Product features.* Computer software ads frequently show the monitor screen so the prospect can see how the software features are displayed.

6. *Comparison of products.* The advertiser shows its product next to a competitor's and compares important features.

7. *User benefit.* It's often difficult to illustrate intangible user benefits. However, marketers know that the best way to get customers' attention is to show how the product will benefit them, so it's worth the extra creative effort.

8. *Humor.* If used well, a humorous visual can make an entertaining and lasting impression. But it can also destroy credibility if used inappropriately.

9. *Testimonial.* Before-and-after endorsements are very effective for weight-loss products, skin care lotions, and body-building courses.

10. *Negative appeal.* Sometimes visuals point out what happens if you don't use the product. If done well, that can spark interest.

Selecting the Visual The kind of picture used is often determined during the conceptualization process. But frequently the visual is not determined until the art director or designer actually lays out the ad.

Selecting an appropriate photo or visual is a difficult creative task. Art directors deal with several basic issues. For example, not every ad needs a visual to communicate effectively. Some all-type ads are quite compelling. If the art director determines that a visual is required, how many should there be: one, two, or more? Should the visual be black-and-white or color? These may be budgetary decisions.

The art director must then decide the subject of the picture. Should it be one of the standard subjects listed earlier? Or something else altogether? And how relevant is that subject to the advertiser's creative strategy? The art director also has to decide how the visual should be created. Should it be a hand-rendered illustration? A photograph? What about a computer-generated illustration?

Finally, the art director has to know what technical and/or budgetary issues must be considered. With so many options, selecting visuals is obviously no simple task. In Chapter 10, we'll see how all these decisions come together in the process of producing the final ad.

LO2 Explain the types of copy and how great copy is created in print ads.

PRODUCING GREAT COPY IN PRINT ADVERTISING

Now that we understand the objectives and format elements of good design, let's examine some basic copywriting formats to see how art and copy are linked.

In print advertising, the key format elements are the *visual(s)*, *headlines*, *subheads*, *body copy*, *slogans*, *logos*, and *signatures*. As Exhibit 9–1 on page 235 shows, copywriters can correlate the visual

> Selecting the focus for advertising visuals is a major step in the creative process. It often determines how well the big idea is executed.

my ad campaign

and headline to the *attention* step of the creative pyramid (discussed in Chapter 8). The *interest* step typically corresponds to the sub-head and the first paragraph of body copy. Body copy handles *credibility* and *desire*, and the *action* step takes place with the logo, slogan, and signature block. We'll discuss these elements first and then look at the formats for radio and television commercials.

Headlines

The **headline** contains the words in the leading position in the advertisement—the words that will be read first and are situated

Design Principles [9–C]

Make sure your layout follows these rules of thumb for creating attractive, informative ads.

Balance

The **optical center** is the reference point that determines the layout's balance. The optical center is about one-eighth of a page above the physical center of the page. Balance is achieved through the arrangement of elements on the page—the left side of the optical center versus the right, above the optical center versus below.

_____ **Formal balance.** Perfect symmetry is the key to formal balance: matched elements on either side of a line dissecting the ad have equal optical weight. This technique strikes a dignified, stable, conservative image.

_____ **Informal balance.** A visually balanced ad has elements of different size, shape, color intensity, or darkness at different distances from the optical center. Like a teeter-totter, an object of greater optical weight near the center can be balanced by an object of less weight farther from the center. Many ads use informal balance to make the ad more interesting, imaginative, and exciting.

Movement

Movement is the principle of design that causes the audience to read the material in the desired sequence. It can be achieved through a variety of techniques.

_____ People or animals can be positioned so that their eyes direct the reader's eyes to the next important element.

_____ Devices such as pointing fingers, boxes, lines, or arrows (or moving the actors or the camera or changing scenes) direct attention from element to element.

_____ Design can take advantage of readers' natural tendency to start at the top left corner of the page and proceed in a Z motion to the lower right.

_____ Comic-strip sequence and pictures with captions force the reader to start at the beginning and follow the sequence in order to grasp the message.

_____ Use of white space and color emphasizes a body of type or an illustration. Eyes will go from a dark element to a light one, or from color to noncolor.

_____ Size itself attracts attention because readers are drawn to the biggest and most dominant element on the page, then to smaller elements.

Proportion

_____ Elements should be accorded space based on their importance to the entire ad. Attention-getting elements are usually given more space. Avoid the monotony of giving equal amounts of space to each element.

White Space (Isolation)

_____ White space is the part of the ad not occupied by other elements (note that white space may be some color other than white). White space helps focus attention on an isolated element—it makes the copy appear to be in a spotlight. White space is an important contributor to the ad's overall image.

Contrast

_____ An effective way of drawing attention to a particular element is to use contrast in color, size, or style; for example, a reverse ad (white letters against a dark background) or a black-and-white ad with a red border.

Clarity and Simplicity

_____ Any elements that can be eliminated without damaging the overall effect should be cut. Too many type styles; type that is too small; too many reverses, illustrations, or boxed items; and unnecessary copy make for an overly complex layout and an ad that is hard to read.

Unity

_____ Unity means that an ad's many different elements must relate to one another in such a way that the ad gives a singular, harmonious impression. Balance, movement, proportion, contrast, and color may all contribute to unity of design. Many other techniques can be used: type styles from the same family, borders around ads to hold elements together, overlapping one picture or element on another, judicious use of white space, and graphic tools such as boxes, arrows, or tints.

Continuity

_____ Continuity is the relationship of one ad to the rest of the campaign. This is achieved by using the same design format, style, and tone; the same spokesperson; or the same graphic element, logo, cartoon character, or catchy slogan.

Imitation, Plagiarism, or Flattery?

When two companies run strikingly similar ads, is it imitation, plagiarism, or coincidence? In December 1999, two beverage companies began running television commercials that closely resembled each other. The commercials, for Michelob Light beer and Colombian coffee, were set in supermarkets and shared the same plot: grocery baggers manhandle products until the item being advertised comes down the conveyer belt. For both Michelob Light and Colombian, the bagger wraps the advertiser's package in bubble wrap and carefully gives it to the buyers.

Advertisers and the media commonly point to "coincidence." Bob Garfield, ad critic for *Advertising Age,* said, "It's seldom plagiarism, especially if the ads are appearing simultaneously." Both of the agencies representing Michelob Light beer and Colombian coffee agree. Peter le Comte, president of DDB Worldwide Marketing, said, "We have written it off as an incident of coincidence. Besides, I don't think we share the same consumers. They will run their commercial and we will run ours."

Stephen Bergerson, an attorney specializing in advertising and promotion law at Fredrikson & Byron, Minneapolis, is skeptical. "When you get four or five words that are so specific, simultaneously used by people in the same category, the nose starts to quiver." But Ron Redfern, senior vice president of sales and marketing for the Orange County Register, calls it "coincidental invention. It's like the automobile being invented in France and in the United States within weeks of each other."

Some advertisers try to ignore the problem by convincing themselves that being copied is actually good. Hugh Thrasher, executive VP of marketing for Motel 6 ("We'll leave the light on for you"), says of his often-imitated Tom Bodett commercials: "We think these copycat ads just remind people of the originality of our concept." Nancy Shalek, president of L.A.'s Shalek Agency, maintains that only the best ads are imitated: "If you haven't been ripped off, you're really in trouble."

But Ellen Kozak, a Milwaukee copyright and publishing lawyer, warns against this form of flattery. "There's a fine line between the kind of borrowing that constitutes an admiring bow to a classic work and the kind that's really the theft of another writer's efforts."

Unfortunately, plagiarism is difficult to prove, as long as you make a few changes. There is no set number of words that make up a plagiarized effort. And plagiarism covers not only words but ideas, plots, and characters. In 1996, Kendall-Jackson Winery filed a suit against E&J Gallo Winery, charging that Gallo's Turning Leaf Vineyards brand and labeling infringed on Kendall-Jackson's Colored Leaf trademark. A jury determined there was no infringement and that judgment was affirmed on appeal. It seems that grape-leaf designs have become generic emblems for wine.

The crux of the problem may be that imitation is an accepted part of the business, at least unofficially. Clients tend to avoid the debate, perhaps because they're more comfortable with well-worn ideas than with bold, original concepts. Many art directors and writers collect competitive ads for inspiration. And advertising is such a highly collaborative process that it's often difficult to determine each individual's creative contribution. With personal responsibility so unclear, ignoring professional ethics is relatively easy.

But every so often, someone creates an ad that moves beyond the gray zone of imitation into outright plagiarism. In July 2000, Anheuser-Busch asked Heiser Automotive Group to drop its TV spots with animated frogs croaking, "Buy . . . Hei . . . ser." Heiser had manipulated its "Be Wiser . . . Buy Heiser" slogan to imitate the Budweiser frogs without permission from Anheuser-Busch.

"There are very few original ideas," according to Philip Circus, an advertising law consultant to the Newspaper Society in London. "Plagiarism is the name of the game in advertising. It's about recycling ideas in a useful way."

That's why some industry leaders are passionate about the need for personal ethics. Jim Golden, executive producer of DMH MacGuffin, says, "All we have in this business are creativity and ideas. The moment someone infringes on that, they're reaching into the very core of the business and ripping it out." Ultimately, advertisers must stop "borrowing" ideas from each other and demand greater creativity from themselves.

Questions

1. Some art directors claim that "coincidental invention" explains why many ads look the same. Do you think that's really possible?
2. Who wins and who loses when advertising is imitated? Do you believe that it's actually an advantage to be copied?
3. What would you do if a client asked you to copy an ad that was already running? Is it acceptable to plagiarize advertising ideas, as long as they are recycled "in a useful way"?
4. Is plagiarism justified by the contention that "there are very few original ideas"?

---

to draw the most attention. That's why headlines usually appear in larger type than other parts of the ad.

Role of Headlines Effective headlines attract attention, engage the audience, explain the visual, lead the audience into the body of the ad, and present the key benefit.

Headlines should engage the reader—fast—and give a reason to read the rest of the ad. If the headline lacks immediacy, prospects move on and pass the ad's message by.[16]

Ideally, headlines communicate the complete selling idea. Research suggests that three to five times as many people read the headline as read the body copy. So if the ad doesn't sell in the

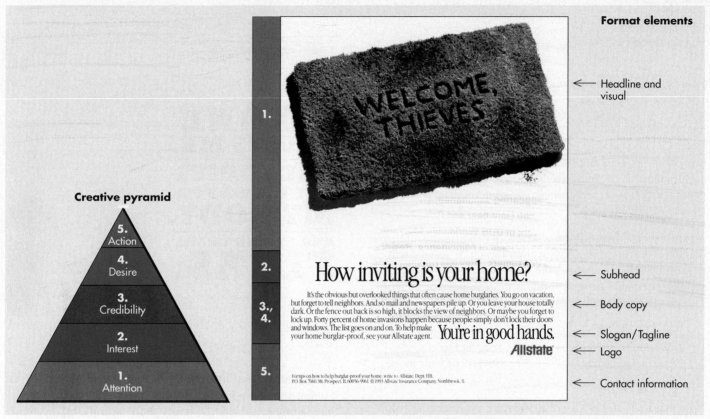

headline, the advertiser is wasting money.[17] Nike uses beautiful magazine and outdoor ads featuring just an athlete, the logo, and the memorable headline: "Just do it." Working off the visual, the headline creates the mood and tells the reader, through implication, to take action—buy Nike.

The traditional notion is that short headlines with one line are best but a second line is acceptable. Many experts believe that headlines with 10 words or less gain greater readership.[18] In one study of more than 2,000 ads, most headlines averaged eight words in length.[19] Conversely, David Ogilvy said the best headline he ever wrote contained 18 words—and became a classic: "At 60 miles an hour, the loudest noise in the new Rolls-Royce comes from the electric clock."[20]

Headlines should offer a benefit that is apparent to the reader and easy to grasp. For example: "When it absolutely, positively has to be there overnight" (FedEx) or "Folds flat for easy storage" (Honda Civic Wagon).[21]

Finally, headlines should present *product news.* Consumers look for new products, new uses for old products, or improvements on old products. If they haven't been overused in a category, "power" words that suggest newness can increase readership and improve the boom factor of an ad. They should be employed whenever honestly applicable.[22] Examples include *free, now, amazing, suddenly, announcing, introducing, it's here, improved, at last, revolutionary, just arrived, new,* and *important development.*

> " Headlines should engage the reader—fast—and give a reason to read the rest of the ad. If the headline lacks immediacy, prospects move on and pass the ad's message by. "

Types of Headlines Copywriters use many variations of headlines depending on the advertising strategy. Typically, they use the headline that presents the big idea most successfully. Headlines may be classified by the type of information they carry: *benefit, news/information, provocative, question,* and *command.*

Advertisers use **benefit headlines** to promise the audience that experiencing the utility of the product or service will be rewarding. Benefit headlines shouldn't be too cute or clever, just simple statements of the product's most important benefit.[23] Two good examples are

Gore-Tex® Fabrics
Keep you warm and dry.   and
Regardless of what falls
Out of the sky.

Speak a foreign
language in
30 days or your money
back.

Note that both of these headlines focus on the benefit of using the product, not the features of the product itself.[24]

The **news/information headline** announces news or promises information. Sea World began its TV announcement of a new baby whale with the headline "It's a girl." The information must be believable, though. A claim that a razor "shaves 200% smoother" probably isn't.[25]

Copywriters use **provocative headlines** to provoke the reader's curiosity—to stimulate questions and thoughts. For example: "Betcha can't eat just one" (Lay's Potato Chips). To learn more, the reader must read the body copy. The danger, of course, is that the reader won't read on. To avoid this, the creative team designs visuals to clarify the message or provide some story appeal.

A **question headline** asks a question, encouraging readers to search for the answer in the body of the ad. An ad for 4 Day Tire Stores asked: "What makes our tire customers smarter & richer than others?" A good question headline piques the reader's curiosity and imagination.

A provocative headline provokes the reader's curiosity and stimulates questions.

A **command headline** orders the reader to do something, so it might seem negative. But readers pay attention to such headlines. Sprite soft-drink ads target youth with the hip headline: "Obey your thirst." Some command headlines make a request: "Please don't squeeze the Charmin" (bathroom tissue).

Subheads

The **subhead** is an additional smaller headline that may appear above the headline or below it. Subheads above the headline are called **kickers** (or *overlines*), while those below the headline are called *underlines*. Subheads may also appear in body copy.

Subheads are usually set smaller than the headline but larger than the body copy or text. Subheads generally appear in **boldface** (heavier) or *italic* (slanted) type or a different color. Like a headline, the subhead transmits key sales points fast. But it usually carries less important information than the headline. Subheads are important for two reasons: Most people read only the headline and subheads, and subheads usually best support the interest step.

Subheads are longer and more like sentences than headlines. They serve as

Benefit headlines offer a reward to the reader. They should be straightforward and preferably include the name of the product that's providing the benefit.

boldface Heavier type.

italic A style of printing type with letters that generally slant to the right.

body copy The text of an advertisement that tells the complete story and attempts to close the sale. It is a logical continuation of the headline and subheads and is usually set in a smaller type size than headlines or subheads.

text What tells the whole story and attempts to close the sale.

straight-sell copy A type of body copy in which the text immediately explains or develops the headline and visual in a straightforward attempt to sell the product.

stepping-stones from the headline to the body copy, telegraphing what's to come.[26] And they help guide readers to get the information they are looking for in an ad.

Body Copy

The advertiser tells the complete sales story in the **body copy**, or **text**. The body copy comprises the interest, credibility, desire, and often even the action steps. It is a logical continuation of the headline and subheads, set in smaller type. Body copy covers the features, benefits, and utility of the product or service.

The body copy is typically read by only 1 out of 10 readers, so the writer must speak to the reader's self-interest, explaining how the product or service satisfies the customer's need.[27] The best ads focus on one big idea or one clear benefit. Copywriters often read their copy aloud to hear how it sounds, even if it's intended for print media. The ear is a powerful copywriting tool.[28]

Body Copy Styles Experienced copywriters look for the technique

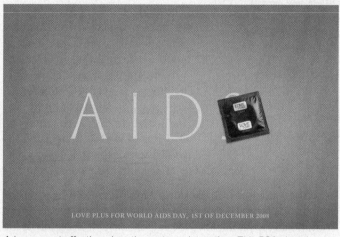

Ads are most effective when the parts work together. This PSA cleverly integrates art and copy in a way that memorably communicates the health message that condoms can help prevent AIDS.

and style with the greatest sales appeal for the idea being presented. Common copy styles include *straight sell, institutional, narrative, dialogue/monologue, picture caption,* and *device.*

In **straight-sell copy**, writers immediately explain or develop the headline and visual in a straightforward, factual presentation.

Writing Effective Copy [9–D]

- **Get to the main point—fast.**
- **Emphasize one major idea simply and clearly.**
- **Be single-minded.** Don't try to do too much. If you chase more than one rabbit at a time, you'll catch none.
- **Position the product clearly.**
- **Keep the brand name up front and reinforce it.**
- **Write with the consumer's ultimate benefit in mind.**
- **Write short sentences.** Use easy, familiar words and themes people understand.
- **Don't waste words.** Say what you have to say—nothing more, nothing less. Don't pad, but don't skimp.
- **Avoid bragging and boasting.** Write from the reader's point of view, not your own. Avoid "we," "us," and "our."
- **Avoid clichés.** They're crutches; learn to get along without them. Bright, surprising words and phrases perk up readers and keep them reading.
- **Write with flair.** Drum up excitement. Make sure your own enthusiasm comes through in the copy.

- **Use vivid language.** Use lots of verbs and adverbs.
- **Stick to the present tense, active voice.** It's crisper. Avoid the past tense and passive voice. Exceptions should be deliberate, for special effect.
- **Use personal pronouns.** Remember, you're talking to just one person, so talk as you would to a friend. Use "you" and "your" whenever appropriate.
- **Use contractions.** They're fast, personal, natural. People talk in contractions (listen to yourself).
- **Don't overpunctuate.** It kills copy flow. Excessive commas are the chief culprits. Don't give readers any excuse to jump ship.
- **Read the copy aloud.** Hear how it sounds; catch errors. The written word is considerably different from the spoken word so listen to it.
- **Rewrite and write tight.** Edit mercilessly. Tell the whole story and no more. When you're finished, stop.

institutional copy
A type of body copy in which the advertiser tries to sell an idea or the merits of the organization or service rather than the sales features of a particular product.

lead-in paragraph
In print ads, a bridge between the headlines, the subheads, and the sales ideas presented in the text. It transfers the reader interest to product interest.

interior paragraphs
Text within the body copy of an ad where the credibility and desire steps of the message are presented.

narrative copy A type of body copy that tells a story. It sets up a problem and then creates a solution using the particular sales features of the product or service as the key to the solution.

dialogue/ monologue copy
A type of body copy in which the characters illustrated in the advertisement do the selling in their own words either through a quasi-testimonial technique or through a comic strip panel.

picture-caption copy A type of body copy in which the story is told through a series of illustrations and captions rather than through the use of a copy block alone.

device copy
Advertising copy that relies on wordplay, humor, poetry, rhymes, great exaggeration, gags, and other tricks or gimmicks.

The straight-sell approach appeals to the prospect's intelligence. Straight-sell copy is particularly good for high think-involvement products or products that are difficult to use. It's very effective for direct-mail advertising and for industrial or high-tech products. Advertisers use the straight-sell approach more than all other techniques combined.[29]

Advertisers use **institutional copy** to promote a philosophy or extol the merits of an organization rather than product features. Institutional copy is intended to lend warmth and credibility to the organization's image. Banks, insurance companies, public corporations, and large manufacturing firms use institutional copy in both print and electronic media. However, David Ogilvy warned against the "self-serving, flatulent pomposity" that characterizes the copy in many corporate ads.[30]

Copywriters use **narrative copy** to tell a story. Ideal for the creative writer, narrative copy sets up a situation and then resolves it at the last minute by having the product or service come to the rescue. Narrative copy offers good opportunities for emotional appeals. An insurance company, for example, might tell the poignant story of the man who died unexpectedly but, fortunately, had just renewed his policy.[31]

By using **dialogue/monologue copy**, the advertiser can add the believability that narrative copy sometimes lacks. The characters portrayed in a print ad do the selling in their own words. A caution: Poorly written dialogue copy can come off as dull or, even worse, hokey and unreal.

The selection of a body copy style can have a big impact on the effectiveness of an ad. The use of photos with picture-caption copy in this print ad from Rubbermaid (www.rubbermaid. com) does a good job communicating all of the benefits of its new premier containers.

Sometimes it's easier to tell a story with illustrations and captions. A photo with **picture-caption copy** is especially useful for products that have a number of different uses or come in a variety of styles or designs.

With any copy style, the copywriter may use some device copy to enhance attention, interest, and memorability. **Device copy** uses figures of speech (such as puns, alliteration, and rhymes) as well as humor and exaggeration. Verbal devices help people remember the brand and tend to affect attitudes favorably.[32]

Humor can be effective when the advertiser needs high memorability in a short time, wants to dispel preconceived negative images, or needs to create a distinct personality for an undifferentiated product. However, humor should always be used carefully and never be in questionable taste. Humor also grows old very quickly; the same joke is not funny for long. Therefore, a variety of executions should be created to keep the idea fresh. Some researchers believe humor distracts from the selling message and can even be detrimental when used for serious services like finance, insurance, and crematoriums.[33]

Formatting Body Copy The keys to good body copy are simplicity, order, credibility, and clarity. Or, as John O'Toole said, prose should be "written clearly, informatively, interestingly, powerfully, persuasively, dramatically, memorably, and with effortless grace. That's all."[34]

Four basic format elements are used to construct long copy ads: the *lead-in paragraph*, *interior paragraphs*, *trial close*, and *close*.

As John O'Toole said, prose should be "written clearly, informatively, interestingly, powerfully, persuasively, dramatically, memorably, and with effortless grace. That's all."

Lead-in paragraph. The **lead-in paragraph** is a bridge between the headline and the sales ideas presented in the text. The lead-in paragraph is part of the *interest* step. It must engage and convert a prospect's reading interest to product interest.

Interior paragraphs. The **interior paragraphs** of the body copy should develop *credibility* by providing proof for claims and promises and they should build *desire* by using language that stirs the imagination. Advertisers should support their product promises with data, testimonials, and warranties. Such proofs convince customers of the validity of the product, improve goodwill toward the advertiser, and stimulate sales.

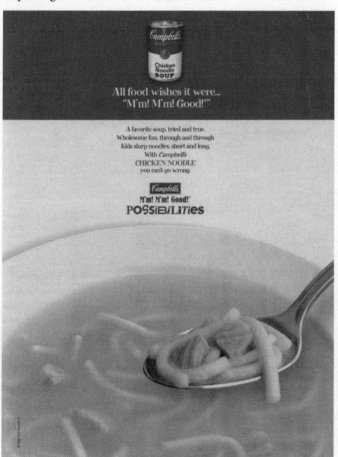

The slogan "M'm! M'm! Good!" has become synonymous with Campbell's soup (*www.campbells.com*). It would be surprising to find a Campbell's soup print ad without the familiar red and white Campbell's logo and the memorable "M'm! M'm! Good!" tagline.

Trial close. Interspersed in the interior paragraphs should be suggestions to *act* now. Good copy asks for the order more than once; mail-order ads ask several times. Consumers often make the buying decision without reading all the body copy. The **trial close** gives them the opportunity to make the buying decision early.

Close. The **close** is the real *action* step. A good close asks consumers to do something and tells them how. The close can be indirect or direct (a subtle suggestion or a direct command). A direct close seeks immediate response in the form of a purchase, a store or Web site visit, or a request for further information.

The close should simplify the audience's response, making it easy for them to order the merchandise, send for information, or visit a showroom or a Web site. A business reply card, a toll-free phone number, or a map may be included.

Of course, not all ads sell products or services. Advertisers may want to change attitudes, explain their viewpoints, or ask for someone's vote. By giving a Web address, the advertiser can offer additional information to those readers who are interested in learning more.

Slogans

Many **slogans** (also called **themelines** or **taglines**) begin as successful headlines, like AT&T's "Reach out and touch someone." Through continuous use, they become standard statements, not just in advertising but for salespeople and company employees.

Slogans have two basic purposes: to provide continuity to a series of ads in a campaign and to reduce an advertising message strategy to a brief, repeatable, and memorable positioning statement. Wheaties cereal, for example, positions itself as the "Breakfast of Champions." And ads for DeBeers still use the famous "Diamonds are forever" slogan.

Seals, Logos, and Signatures

A **seal** is awarded only when a product meets standards established by a particular organization, such as the Good Housekeeping Institute or Underwriters Laboratories. Because these organizations are recognized authorities, their seals provide an independent, valued endorsement for the advertiser's product.

Logotypes (logos) and **signatures** are special designs of the advertiser's company or product name. They appear in all company ads and, like trademarks, give the product individuality and provide quick recognition at the point of purchase.

check yourself ✓

1. What are the key format elements in a print ad?

2. What are some important types of headlines?

3. When would an advertiser use straight-sell copy rather than device copy?

LO3 Outline how great copy is created in electronic ads.

CREATING GREAT COPY IN ELECTRONIC MEDIA

For electronic media, the fundamental elements—the five steps of the creative pyramid—remain the primary guides, but the copywriting formats differ. Radio and television writers prepare *scripts* and *storyboards*.

Writing Radio Copy

A **script** resembles a two-column list. On the left side, speakers' names are arranged vertically, along with descriptions of any **sound effects** (abbreviated **SFX**) and music. The right column contains the dialogue, called the **audio.**

Copywriters first need to understand radio's strengths and weaknesses. Radio provides entertainment or news to listeners who are busy doing something else—driving, washing dishes, reading the paper, or even studying. To get attention, an advertising message must be catchy, interesting, and unforgettable. Radio listeners usually decide within five to eight seconds if they're going to listen. To attract and hold attention, radio copy must be intrusive.

Intrusive, yes; offensive, no. An insensitive choice of words, an overzealous effort to attract listeners with irritating everyday sounds (car horn, alarm clock, screeching tires), or characters that sound too exotic, odd, or dumb can result in listener resentment and lost sales. Tom Bodett's often-imitated ads for Motel 6 demonstrate the effectiveness of a personal, relaxed, and natural style.

One of the greatest challenges for radio copywriters is making the script fit the time slot. The delivery changes for different types of commercials, so writers must read the script out loud for timing. With electronic compression, recorded radio ads can now include 10 to 30 percent more copy than text read live. Still, the following is a good rule of thumb:

10 seconds: 20–25 words
20 seconds: 40–45 words
30 seconds: 60–70 words
60 seconds: 130–150 words[35]

Creating Effective Radio Commercials [9–E]

Writing for radio takes a sharp ear, empathy for the listener, and the ability to create pictures inside the consumer's head. These tips will help you create great radio spots.

- **Make the big idea crystal clear.** Concentrate on one main selling point. Radio is a good medium for building brand awareness, but not for making long lists of copy points or complex arguments.
- **Mention the advertiser's name early and often.** If the product or company name is tricky, consider spelling it out.
- **Take time to set the scene and establish the premise.** A 30-second commercial that nobody remembers is a waste of money. Fight for 60-second spots.
- **Use familiar sound effects.** Ice tinkling in a glass, birds chirping, or a door shutting can create a visual image. Music also works if its meaning is clear.

- **Paint pictures with your words.** Use descriptive language to make the ad more memorable.
- **Make every word count.** Use active voice and more verbs than adjectives. Be conversational. Use pronounceable words and short sentences.
- **Be outrageous.** The best comic commercials begin with a totally absurd premise from which all developments follow logically. But remember, if you can't write humor really well, go for drama.
- **Ask for the order.** Try to get listeners to take action.
- **Remember that radio is a local medium.** Adjust your commercials to the language of your listeners and the time of day they'll run.
- **Presentation counts a lot.** Even the best scripts look boring on paper. Acting, timing, vocal quirks, and sound effects bring them to life.

logotypes Special design of the advertiser's name (or product name) that appears in all advertisements. Also called a *signature cut*, it is like a trademark because it gives the advertiser individuality and provides quick recognition at the point of purchase.

signatures A product or company's primary graphic identity. A signature may be comprised of some combination of a graphic symbol, a logotype, and a slogan.

script Format for radio and television copywriting resembling a two-column list showing dialogue and/or visuals.

sound effects (SFX) Sounds other than music or dialogue used in radio and television.

audio The sound portion of a commercial. Also, the right side of a script for a television commercial, indicating spoken copy, sound effects, and music.

Radio writing has to be clearer than any other kind of copywriting.

Healthier America
Lost Campaign
Radio: 60
"Neighbor"
Expiration date: 2/23/05

SFX: Phone ringing

Bill:	Hello...?
George:	Hi, Bill? This is George Dewey from up the street.
Bill:	Hey, George. How ya doin?
George:	Good, good. Say, I noticed you've been walking to work these days instead of driving...and I, uh, don't quite know how to say this, but...but...
Bill:	But what?
George: *(stammering)*	But...But...Your butt, your buttocks, your butt—I think I found your butt on my front lawn. Have you recently lost it?
Bill:	As a matter of fact, I have, George *(pleased)*. It's about time someone noticed.
George: *(playful)*	Well, it was kinda hard to miss if you know what I mean......Anyways, would you like it back?
Bill:	Would I like it back? No, not really.
George:	So, it's okay if I throw it out?
Bill:	Sure, that's fine. Take it easy, George.

SFX: Phone ringing

Announcer:	Small step #8—Walk instead of driving whenever you can. It's just one of the many small steps you can take to help you become a healthier, well, you. Get started at www.smallstep.gov and take a small step to get healthy.
Legal:	A public service announcement brought to you by the U.S. Department of Health and Human Services and the Ad Council.

A radio script format resembles a two-column list, with speakers' names and sound effects on the left and the dialogue in a wider column on the right. This national public service announcement (PSA) was created by McCann-Erickson and is one of many in a campaign designed to inspire Americans to take small steps toward a healthier lifestyle.

Radio writing has to be clearer than any other kind of copywriting. For example, the listener can't refer back, as in print, to find an antecedent for a pronoun. Likewise, the English language is so full of homonyms (words that sound like other words) that one can easily confuse the meaning of a sentence ("who's who is whose").[36]

Writing Television Copy

Radio's basic two-column script format also works for television. But in a TV script, the left side is titled "Video" and the right side "Audio." The video column describes the visuals and production: camera angles, action, scenery, and stage directions. The audio column lists the spoken copy, sound effects, and music.

Broadcast commercials must be believable and relevant. Even zany commercials must exude quality in their creation and production to imply the product's quality. While the art director's work is very important, the copywriter typically sets the tone of the commercial, establishes the language that determines which visuals to use, and pinpoints when the visuals should appear.

To illustrate these principles, let's look at a particular commercial. Many people want smooth, soft skin and consider a patch of rough, flaky skin anywhere on their body a disappointment. If you were the copywriter for Lubriderm skin lotion, how would you approach this somewhat touchy, uncomfortable subject?

The creative staff of J. Walter Thompson crafted an artistic solution for Lubriderm. An alligator was the big idea. The gator's scaly sheath was a metaphor for rough, flaky skin. Its appearance ignited people's survival instincts; they paid attention, fast. A beautiful, sophisticated woman with smooth, feminine skin was seated in a lounge chair, completely unruffled by the passing gator. The swing of the animal's back and tail echoed the graceful curves of the two simple pieces of furniture on the set, and its slow stride kept the beat of a light jazz tune.

This commercial opened with an attention-getting big idea that was visually surprising, compelling, dramatic, and interesting. It was also a quasi-demonstration: we saw the alligator's scaly, prickly skin and the woman's confidence and willingness to touch the alligator as it passed by, which symbolized the confidence Lubriderm can bring.

This ad follows the creative pyramid. The alligator captures attention visually while the announcer's first words serve as an attention-getting headline: "A quick reminder." The ad commands us to listen and sets up the interest step that offers this claim: "Lubriderm restores lost moisture to heal your dry skin and protect it." Now for the credibility step: "Remember, the one created for dermatologists is the one that heals and protects." And then the desire step recaps the primary product benefit and adds a touch of humor: "See you later, alligator."

L04 Discuss the role of art in electronic ads.

THE ROLE OF ART IN RADIO AND TV ADVERTISING

According to *Advertising Age* columnist Bob Garfield, the best commercial of 1997 was for Esencial hand cream. The spot opens with a woman riding her bicycle to the persistent squeak of its unlubricated chain. She dismounts, opens a jar of Esencial, and rubs some of the cream onto the chain. Then she rides away—but the squeak is still there. Why? Because, as the voice-over points out, "Esencial moisturizes, but it has no grease."

No big production. No digital effects. No jingle. No celebrity. No big comedy payoff. Just a pure advertising idea: a problem/resolution spot where the brand pointedly cannot solve the problem. It's a vivid demonstration of brand nonattributes. Inspired. Cunning. Brilliant. A big idea.

Developing the Artistic Concept for Commercials

Creating the concept for a radio or TV commercial is similar to creating the concept for print ads. The first step is to determine the big idea. Then the art director and copywriter must decide what commercial format to use. Should a celebrity present the message? Or should the ad dramatize the product's benefits with a semifictional story? The next step is to write a script containing the necessary copy or dialogue plus a basic description of any music, sound effects, and/or camera views.

In both radio and TV, the art director assists the copywriter in script development. But in television, artistic development is much more extensive. Using the TV script, the art director creates a series of **storyboard roughs** to present the artistic approach, the action sequences, and the style of the commercial.

Good casting is critical. The most important consideration is relevance to the product; agencies don't use a comic to sell financial products—or cremation services. And in spite of Michael Jordan's success for Nike, Gatorade, and McDonald's, some experts don't believe in using celebrities. David Ogilvy, for example, thought viewers remember the celebrity more than the product.[37]

Formats for Radio and TV Commercials

Similar to print advertising, the format for a broadcast ad serves as a template for arranging message elements into a pattern. Once the art director and copywriter establish the big idea, they must determine the commercial's format.

Many radio and TV commercial styles have been successful. Here we consider eight common commercial formats that can be used in either radio or television: *straight announcement, presenter, testimonial, demonstration, musical, slice of life, lifestyle,* and *animation.*

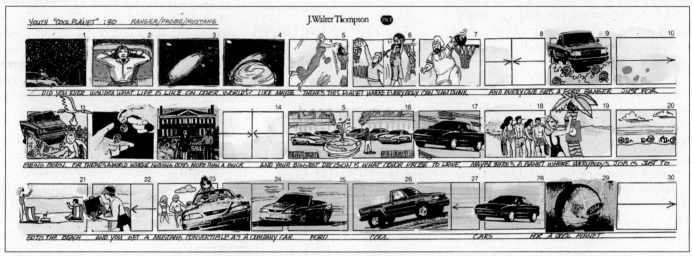

After the initial concepts for a television ad are finalized, creatives develop a storyboard rough composed of small sketches that depict the various scenes of the ad. The storyboard rough is used to present the creative concept to the account team and the client.

Straight Announcement

The oldest and simplest type of radio or TV commercial and probably the easiest to write is the **straight announcement**. One person, usually a radio or TV announcer, delivers the sales message. Music may play in the background. Straight announcements are popular because they are adaptable to almost any product or situation. In radio, a straight announcement can also be designed as an **integrated commercial**—that is, it can be woven into a show or tailored to the style of a given program.

For TV, an announcer may deliver the sales message **on camera** or off screen, as a **voice-over**, while a demonstration, slide, or

Creating Effective TV Commercials [9–F]

- **Begin at the finish.** Concentrate on the final impression the commercial will make.
- **Create an attention-getting opening.** An opening that is visually surprising or full of action, drama, humor, or human interest sets the context and allows a smooth transition to the rest of the commercial.
- **Use a situation that grows naturally out of the sales story.** Avoid distracting gimmicks. Make it easy for viewers to identify with the characters.
- **Characters are the living symbol of the product.** They should be appealing, believable, nondistracting, and most of all, relevant.
- **Keep it simple.** The sequence of ideas should be easy to follow. Keep the number of elements in the commercial to a bare minimum.

- **Write concise audio copy.** The video should carry most of the weight. Fewer than two words per second is effective for demonstrations. For a 60-second commercial, 101 to 110 words is most effective; more than 170 words is too talky.
- **Make demonstrations dramatic but believable.** They should always be true to life and avoid the appearance of camera tricks.
- **Let the words interpret the picture and prepare viewers for the next scene.** Use conversational language; avoid "ad talk," hype, and puffery.
- **Run scenes five or six seconds on average.** Rarely should a scene run less than three seconds. Offer a variety of movement-filled scenes without "jumping."
- **Keep the look of the video fresh and new.**

film shows on screen. If the script is well written and the announcer convincing, straight announcements can be very effective. Since they don't require elaborate production facilities, they save money, too.

Presenter The **presenter commercial** uses one person or character to present the product and carry the sales message. Some presenters are celebrities, such as Catherine Zeta-Jones for T-Mobile. Others may be experts, such as corporate officers (Lee Iacocca) or professionals (doctors), or they may be actors playing a role ("I'm a Mac. I'm a PC"). A *man-on-the-street* may interview real people and get them to share their thoughts about a client's products or services. And, of course, a presenter doesn't have to be a real person. Remember Tony the Tiger?

A **radio personality**, such as Rush Limbaugh or Howard Stern, may *ad lib* an ad message live in his or her own style. Done well, such commercials can be very successful, as evidenced by the initial success of Snapple. However, the advertiser surrenders control to the personality.

Testimonial The true **testimonial**—where a satisfied user tells how effective the product is—can be highly credible in both TV and radio advertising. Celebrities may gain attention, but they must be believable and not distract from the product. Actually, people from all walks of life endorse products, from known personalities to unknowns and nonprofessionals. Which type of person to use depends on the product and the strategy. Satisfied customers are the best sources for testimonials because their sincerity is usually persuasive. Ogilvy suggested shooting candid testimonials when the subjects don't know they're being filmed.[38] Of course, advertisers must be sure to get their permission before using the piece.

Demonstration Television is uniquely suited to visual demonstrations. And a **demonstration** convinces an audience better and faster than a spoken message. So don't say it, show it.[39] Naturally, it's easier to demonstrate the product on TV than on radio, but some advertisers have used the imaginative nature of radio to create humorous, tongue-in-cheek demonstrations.

Products may be demonstrated in use, in competition, or before and after. These techniques help viewers visualize how the product will perform for them.

> " In television, good casting is critical. The most important consideration is relevance to the product. "

Musical The **musical commercials**, or **jingles**, we hear on radio and TV are among the best—and worst—ad messages produced. Done well, they can bring enormous success, well beyond the average nonmusical commercial. Done poorly, they can waste the advertising budget and annoy audiences beyond belief.

Advertisers have three sources of music. They can buy the right to use a tune from the copyright owner, which is usually expensive. They can use a melody in the public domain, which is free. Or they can hire a composer to write an original song. Some original tunes, including Coke's famous "I'd like to teach the world to sing," have become hits.

Slice of Life (Problem Solution) A commercial that dramatizes a real-life situation is called **slice of life**. It usually starts with just plain folks, played by professional actors, discussing some problem or issue. Often the situation deals with a problem of a personal nature: bad breath, loose dentures, dandruff, body odor, or yellow laundry. A relative or a co-worker drops the hint, the product is tried, and the next scene shows the result—a happier, cleaner, more fragrant person off with a new date. The drama always concludes with a positive outcome. Such commercials can get attention and create interest, even though they are often irritating to viewers and hated by copywriters.

The key to effective slice-of-life commercials is simplicity. The ad should concentrate on one, compelling product benefit and make it memorable. Often a **mnemonic device** (a technique that helps you remember something) can dramatize the benefit and trigger instant recall. The Aflac duck immediately reminds viewers that Aflac (www.aflac.com) is there to help pay your bills if you get hurt and can't work.

Believability in slice-of-life commercials is difficult to achieve. People don't really talk about "the sophisticated taste of Taster's Choice," so the actors must be highly credible to pull it off. That's why most *local* advertisers don't use the slice-of-life technique. Creating that believability takes professional talent and a lot of money. In all cases, the story should be brand relevant and simply told.

Lifestyle To present the user rather than the product, advertisers may use the **lifestyle technique**. For example, Diesel

Ads that appeal to lifestyle present the type of user associated with the product, rather than the product itself. This ad for MasterCard is aimed at sports fans, and specifically Boston Red Sox fans, who are willing to do just about anything for their team.

VO: Red Sox World Series tickets
Baseball Enthusiast #1: Five hundred bucks.
Man Waiting in Line: I'd pay four grand.
Weightlifter: My car. My truck. My computer.
Girl #1: Two months' salary.
Weightlifter: . . . my entire savings account.

Man with Painted Face: Anything, anything.
Little Boy: My fish.
Young Woman: My dog.
Weightlifter: My girlfriend.

Fan at Ballpark: My first-born kid.
Girl #3: Really.
VO/Super: Seeing the Red Sox in the World Series: Priceless.

VO/Super: There are some things money can't buy.
VO/Super: For everything else there's MasterCard.
VO/Super: Devoted fan of the devoted fans.

> **Television is so visually powerful and expressive that the art director's role is particularly important.**

pitches its denim to urbanites by showing characters working and playing while wearing its latest line. Likewise, beer and soft-drink advertisers frequently target their messages to active, outdoorsy young people, focusing on who drinks the brand rather than on specific product advantages.

Animation Cartoons, puppet characters, and demonstrations with computer-generated graphics are **animation** techniques for communicating difficult messages and reaching specialized markets, such as children. The way aspirin or other medications affect the human system is difficult to explain. Animated pictures of headaches and stomachs can simplify the subject and make a benefit, demonstration clear and understandable.

Computer animation requires a great deal of faith on the part of advertisers. Since most of this very expensive work is done on the computer, there's nothing to see until the animation is well developed and a good bit of money has been spent (this is more fully discussed in Chapter 10).

Basic Mechanics of Storyboard Development

After the creative team selects the big idea and the format for a TV commercial, the art director and the writer develop the script. Television is so visually powerful and expressive that the art director's role is particularly important. Art directors must be able to work with a variety of professionals—producers, directors, lighting technicians, and set designers—to develop and produce a commercial successfully. Ad production is discussed in the next chapter.

Storyboard Design Once the basic script is completed, the art director must turn the video portion of the script into real images. This is done with a **storyboard**, a sheet preprinted with a series of 8 to 20 blank windows (frames) in the shape of TV screens. Below each frame is room to place the text of the commercial, including the sound effects and camera views. The storyboard works much like a comic strip.

Through a process similar to laying out a print ad (thumbnail, rough, comp) the artist carefully designs how each scene should appear, arranging actors, scenery, props, lighting, and camera angles to maximize impact, beauty, and mood. The storyboard helps the creatives visualize the commercial's tone and sequence of action, discover any conceptual weaknesses, and make presentations for final management approval. It also serves as a guide for filming.

Even when designed to the level of a comp, though, the storyboard is only an approximation of the final commercial. Actual production often results in many changes in lighting, camera angle, focal point, and emphasis. The camera sees many things that the artist couldn't visualize, and vice versa.

Animatic: The Video Comp To supplement the storyboard or pretest a concept, a commercial may be taped in rough form using amateur talent as actors. Or an **animatic** may be shot—a film strip of the sketches in the storyboard accompanied by the audio portion of the commercial synchronized on tape. A standard animatic costs more than $10,000 to produce, but computers are cutting costs dramatically. Avid Technologies, for example, developed a Mac-based editing system that lets the agency create moving pictures on the screen, lay sound behind them, and transfer the entire package onto videotape to send to the client. The system cuts production costs for testable material from about $10,000 to $1,000. This technology is being adopted by many agencies as they look for ways to better serve clients' creative needs for less money.

Upon approval of the storyboard and/or the animatic, the commercial is ready for production, a subject we cover in detail in Chapter 10.

Storyboard of "Power to Move" TV commercial

The storyboard is a visual representation of the ad, made up of sketches that indicate the art director's concept of the various scenes, camera angles, sound effects, and special effects to be used in the final production.

storyboard A sheet preprinted with a series of 8 to 20 blank frames in the shape of TV screens, which includes text of the commercial, sound effects, and camera views.

animatic A rough television commercial produced by photographing storyboard sketches on a film strip or video with the audio portion synchronized on tape. It is used primarily for testing purposes.

L05 Review the unique requirements in writing for the Web.

WRITING FOR THE WEB

The Internet is young and advertisers and agencies are still learning how best to use this exciting medium. This is to be expected. A similar learning period took place after the rapid spread of television in the 1950s. Agencies at first struggled to figure out how best to advertise in this new, thoroughly "modern" medium. The process took time. For proof, watch some commercials from the 1950s and consider how simplistic and ineffective they seem compared to those of the present. Fortunately, research is beginning to offer concrete suggestions that can help a designer create more effective Internet messages.

A designer should understand that the Internet, while it contains elements of both print and broadcast media, is a completely new medium that engages its users in a fundamentally different way. At the core of this engagement is *interactivity*. Smart companies realize that used effectively, the interactive nature of the Internet creates opportunities for a mutually satisfying dialogue between advertiser and consumer. Ultimately, that dialogue can help build brand loyalty and lead to a sale. Conversely, companies that use the Internet ineffectively (or ignore the medium altogether) may lose new customers or damage their relationships with existing ones. The stakes are obviously high.

Designers should also remember that Internet users are often important opinion leaders. For example, a satisfied visitor to Betty Crocker's Web site (http://www.bettycrocker.com) may e-mail several friends a recipe she found there. And, just as important, someone left dissatisfied by a company's messages or offerings can easily share that unhappiness with other people. Moreover, e-mail is not the only channel available to Web users. They can also share product-related opinions via message boards, a social network site, blogs, or even a YouTube video.

Of course, people differ in how likely they are to share their opinions with others. Research by Burson-Marsteller USA, a large New York public relations firm, suggests that there is a small but highly influential group of heavy Internet users who are especially likely to do so. The firm calls this group the e-fluentials. "An e-fluential is the rock that starts the ripple," said Chet Burchett, president and chief executive officer at Burson-Marsteller. "Each one communicates with an average of 14 people." E-fluentials can be reputation builders or busters.[40] Find out if you are an e-fluential at www.efluentials.com.

The most effective Web sites can be scanned quickly for useful information and are updated regularly with new content.

Company Web Sites Perhaps no consideration in design of a Web site is more important than understanding why people visit the site in the first place. Typically, a visitor to a product Web site arrives with a purpose. He or she may be seeking product information, such as how to operate the product safely or use it more effectively. Or the visitor may be looking for information about accessories, tips, coupons, or user groups.

Effectively designed Web sites help visitors find the information they need quickly and efficiently. For example, a visitor to the Betty Crocker site can easily locate where to go for recipes, meal ideas, coupons and promotions, and cookbooks. Information is easy to find because the layout of the site matches closely with the scanning pattern commonly observed among Web page readers: two quick horizontal scans across the top followed by a downward vertical scan. Think of a pattern that resembles an "F." Although the products and audience are very different, IBM's U.S. Web site is designed to accommodate the same scanning pattern (see http://www.ibm.com/us/) as are sites for Coke, Ford, Tide, and many other large advertisers. Each of these sites makes finding information simple and fast. Colors and photographs are carefully chosen to enhance the layout, attract Internet users, and guide their gaze through the page.

Banner Ads The purpose of a banner ad is to bring Internet users to a Web site other than the one they intended to visit. Once the dominant advertising approach, banner ads now compete with many other online forms, including video virals and paid search listings. Designers should keep in mind research findings that suggest effective banner ads are simple, focused, and clear about a product's benefit. Most effective banners make use of a striking image and emphasize a palette of rich, powerful colors.

Viral Ads The enormous popularity of video sites such as YouTube has inspired advertisers to place special video commercials on the Web. These are often called "viral" ads, because they rely on Internet users to spread messages to others. The design process for viral videos can have much in common with that for traditional commercials. But viral creators have a somewhat heavier burden because they must consistently entertain while informing about a product. The challenge is that viewers can't just like a viral; they have to love it. Otherwise they won't bother sharing it with others.

According to creatives at Crispin Porter + Bogusky, the talented Miami agency that created the "Subservient Chicken" Web site, the key to effectiveness is intrigue. "Interruption or disruption as the fundamental premise of marketing" doesn't work, according to CPB partner Jeff Hicks. "You have to create content that is interesting, useful or entertaining enough to invite (the consumer). Viral is the ultimate invitation." How does a creative create intrigue? A big idea is important (like a chicken that will

do anything it is asked to). The unexpected can also grab consumer interest. When Microsoft released its popular console game "Halo 2," it used an online marketing scheme that suggested villains were taking over a completely innocuous Web site, ilovebees.com.

check yourself ✓

1. What should a Web ad designer understand about the medium?

2. In what ways are Internet users different from users of traditional media?

CREATING ADS FOR INTERNATIONAL MARKETS

International advertisers have debated the transferability of campaigns for years. One side believes it's too expensive to create a unique campaign for each national group. They simply translate one overall campaign into each language. Another method is to think globally but act locally, creating ads that reflect the needs of different groups, but maintaining a consistent theme worldwide. Other advertisers believe the only way to ensure success is to create a special campaign for each market.

Citigroup uses a variation of this approach. With branches in 100 countries, the financial services giant adapts its ads and products to the needs of each market. For example, the large Indian population working abroad can open checking accounts in rupees instead of the local currency; family members back home can access the accounts via 250 Citibank ATMs in 28 cities in India, avoiding the steep fees usually associated with transferring money. Some advertisers find such solutions expensive and unnecessary. They run their ads in English worldwide, promoting their products generically rather than specifically. Advertisers must address their unique situations while paying careful attention to the economics of various promotional strategies.

Translating Copy

In international markets, a vital consideration for copywriters and creative directors is language. In Western Europe, people speak at least 15 different languages and more than twice as many dialects. A similar situation exists in Asia, Africa, and, to a lesser extent, South America.

Classic examples of mistranslations and faulty word choices abound in international advertising. A faulty Spanish translation for Perdue chickens reads "It takes a sexually excited man to make a chick affectionate" instead of "It takes a tough man to make a tender chicken."[41]

A poorly chosen or badly translated product name can undercut advertising credibility in foreign markets. A classic case was when Coke's product name was widely translated into Chinese characters that sounded like "Coca-Cola" but meant "bite the wax tadpole."[42]

People in the United States, Canada, England, Australia, and South Africa all speak English, but with wide variations in vocabulary, word usage, and syntax. Similarly, the French spoken in France, Canada, Vietnam, and Belgium may differ as much as the English spoken by a British aristocrat and a Tennessee mountaineer. Language variations exist even within countries. The Japanese use five lingual "gears," ranging from haughty to servile, depending on the speaker's and the listener's respective stations in life. Japanese translators must know when to change gears.

Advertisers should follow some basic rules in using translators:

- **The translator must be an effective copywriter.** In the United States and Canada, most people speak English, yet relatively

Global advertisers often use a single basic ad, translating it into the languages of the various countries where it will run.

few are good writers and even fewer are good copywriters. Too often advertisers simply let a translation service rewrite their ads in a foreign language. That's not good enough.

- **The translator must understand the product.** The translator must also know the product's features and its market. It is always better to use a translator who is a product or market specialist rather than a generalist.

- **Translators should translate into their native tongue.** Ideally, they should live in the country where the ad will appear. This way the advertiser can be sure the translator understands the country's social attitudes, culture, and idioms.

- **The advertiser should give the translator easily translatable English copy.** The double meanings and idiomatic expressions that make English such a rich language for advertising rarely translate well. They only make the translator's job more difficult.

There is no greater insult to a national market than to misuse its language. The translation must be accurate and punctuated properly, and it must also be good copy.

English is rapidly becoming a universal language for corporate ad campaigns directed to international businesspeople, and some firms print their instructional literature and brochures in English as well. But this approach can incite nationalistic feelings against the company. Worse yet, it automatically limits a product's use to people who understand technical English.[43]

Art Direction for International Markets

Philosophers often refer to the arts as a kind of international language whose nonverbal elements translate freely regardless of culture. A nice idea but, in advertising, not always an accurate one. People ascribe different meanings to color depending on their culture. When designing ads for use in other countries, the art director must be familiar with each country's artistic preferences and peculiarities.

Some consider color to indicate emotion: Someone "has the blues" or is "green with envy" (refer back to Commercial Break 8, "The Psychological Impact of Color").

An **icon**, a visual image representing some idea or thing, can have a meaning that cuts across national boundaries and reflects the tastes and attitudes of a group of cultures. An ad with a snake (an icon for the devil and eroticism in many Western cultures) could easily lose sales in North American markets. But in the Far East, where the snake represents renewal (by

When preparing an ad for the international market, the art director must be sure that the imagery and concepts will not be too foreign to the intended audience. This South African ad for Lego (www.lego.com) doesn't need long copy or a striking headline to make its point; the imagery of a Lego periscope peering up from a Lego ocean is enough to inspire building enthusiasts everywhere.

shedding its skin), the same visual might work as a dynamic expression of a product's staying power.

Similarly, a model considered attractive in one culture is not necessarily seen that way in another. Just as with copy translation, advertisers working in global markets must pretest art and design concepts with natives of each country. ■

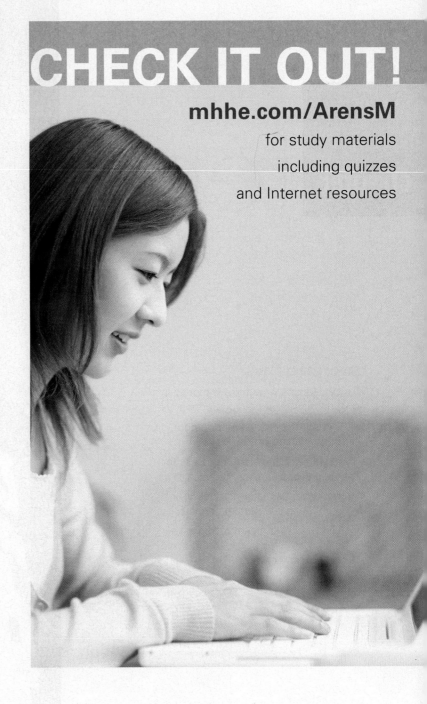

CHECK IT OUT!

mhhe.com/ArensM

for study materials

including quizzes

and Internet resources

chapter ten

LEARNING OBJECTIVES

LO1 Understand ways to save money in print and electronic production.

LO2 Explain the processes for producing print ads and brochures.

LO3 Explain the production process for radio ads.

LO4 Describe the major production techniques for TV commercials.

LO5 List ways that digital media save money as compared with print and electronic media.

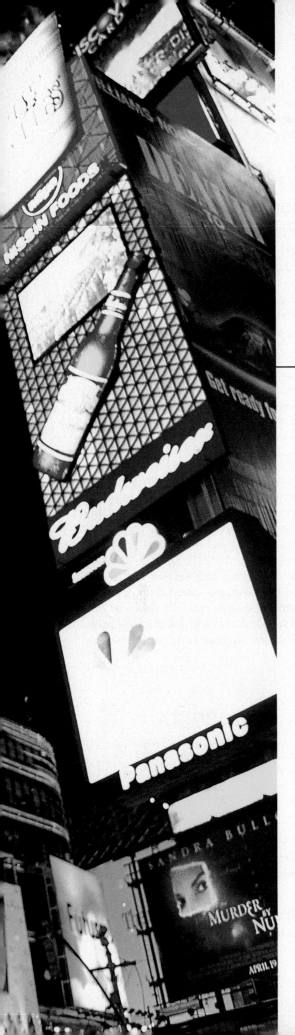

producing
ads

For Toyota, choosing an agency for a global campaign for Prius, its technologically superior hybrid car, was a monumental project. Hundreds of agencies would have loved to handle the account, but the competition was limited to the client's roster agencies, those firms that already worked for Toyota.

In offices around the world, teams of copywriters and creative directors produced and discarded countless concepts. Finally, each agency selected their best ideas. They presented their work to the client and then crossed their fingers. The winning agency would produce local and international print ads and create a global TV spot—one that would be translated into dozens of languages and aired all over the world.

Saatchi & Saatchi Los Angeles already handled U.S. advertising for Toyota. Naturally, the agency wanted the assign-

ment, but it wasn't a slam-dunk. It was up against some of the biggest agencies in the world and was even forced to compete with many of its own offices, some of which—London, Paris, New York— were famous for outstanding creativity.

It didn't hurt that the Prius was the kind of car the agency could really get behind. With little to no advertising, the previous limited-production model had already become the leader in its field. Equipped with Bluetooth technology, low emission rates, and fantastic fuel economy, this sleek hybrid was already a favorite among environmentally conscious consumers and the Hollywood set. Now that Toyota was rolling the car out globally, Saatchi knew that to win the campaign it would have to speak to a new segment of the market.

There were ample challenges. Saatchi wanted to create a campaign for the

continued on p. 254

THE ALL-NEW PRIUS.

HYBRID SYNERGY DRIVE

careful management is the key to success in producing advertising, we'll discuss some management issues before examining the production processes.

The Role of the Production Manager or Producer

All ads go through a highly complex process with many steps, including the reproduction of visuals in full color, the shooting and editing of scenes, the specification and placement of type, and the checking, approving, duplicating, and shipping of final art, negatives, tape, or film to communications media (newspapers, magazines, radio, TV stations, and Web publishers).

These tasks are usually the responsibility of a **print production manager** or, for electronic media, a **producer**. The job of this manager is to keep the project moving smoothly and within budget, while maintaining the required level of quality through every step of the production process.

Production managers and producers perform the four classic functions of management: *planning, organizing, directing,* and *controlling.* The Prius print producer at Saatchi was Johanna Leovey. Her job was to review the conceptual art and then *decide* which production process to use to fulfill each requirement. Next she *organized* the tasks and established priorities in order to meet the client's media schedule. She then *directed* the production staff in completing each section of the art. Finally, to perform the *control* function—essential for optimizing quality, economy, and speed—she carefully reviewed the work of each staffer and subcontractor and solicited feedback from her supervisor and the art director, to be sure they were in sync.

continued from p. 253

Prius that would appeal to a wide audience, regardless of national and cultural differences, but that would still be specific enough to truly speak to the buyer. L.A. creative directors Max Godsil and Doug Van Andel were assigned the project. They spent weeks reviewing the research and analyzing the markets. After many false starts, they hit upon a concept that was complex but friendly, futuristic but warm, and clean without being clinical.

Saatchi's senior creative director, Steve Rabosky, liked it. This, everyone felt, was the idea that would win the account, and they were right. Toyota Japan awarded the global introduction of the Prius to Saatchi & Saatchi Los Angeles.[1]

A few months later, when Toyota asked them to cut back on the advertising, they knew for certain that they had done something right. There simply weren't enough cars to meet the growing demand. In this chapter, we'll see what they did and study how they did it. ■

[Production managers and producers perform the four classic functions of management: *planning, organizing, directing,* and *controlling.*]

MANAGING ADVERTISING PRODUCTION

Experienced advertising people, including art directors, designers, and producers, know that ads go through many intricate technical stages from start to finish. They know it's the details that give an ad added impact and completeness. Since

Planning and Organizing An important management responsibility is the *allocation of time.* Across a variety of tasks, the production manager must anticipate where problems may occur.

Directing and Controlling Supervising the production staff and suppliers is another challenge. If artists fail to follow the art director's design correctly, they can kill an ad's power,

With great power comes great responsibility.
And now, vice versa.

While a national ad like this one for Toyota's Prius may require only 15 seconds to read, what most people don't realize is that, from initial concept to completion, an ad of this caliber may require a month, or even longer, to create. As ideas are born and discarded and then meticulously crafted into a finished work, an advertisement passes through many hands before it is finally ready to debut.

beauty, and effectiveness. Improper printing processes, papers, or inks can also weaken the impact of the image, increase costs, and even lead to time-consuming reprinting. Print production managers waste money (and sometimes lose their jobs) by forgetting to double-check the details of print production and the work of the production staff.

The producer also has to keep up with all the technological changes occurring in print and electronic production, including new forms of digital media. And because all ad agency employees now use computers, the manager must also understand how computers serve the production process and which software programs offer the best results.[2]

LO1 Understand ways to save money in print and electronic production.

Managing Production Costs

When Saatchi began working on the Prius campaign, it submitted an estimate for production costs, including computer artwork and subcontracted work such as photography, reproduction services, and delivery. When Johanna Leovey received the approved ad concepts a couple of weeks later, it was understood that she would make every effort to keep the actual costs below the estimate.

A good production manager continually monitors the time spent on a job and the charges submitted by outside suppliers so as to not exceed the budget.

Common Budget Busters
There are five problems that commonly break budgets. The most frequent cause of cost overruns is inadequate planning and lack of preparation. Another

culprit is production luxuries. When the creative director wants to reward the staff by taking everyone to lunch at the company's expense, the first question should be: Was money budgeted for this? The third budget buster is overtime: night and weekend work. Whenever possible, managers should develop alternative plans to avoid overtime hours. Special equipment for unusual production effects can also wreak havoc on budgets. It's often far more expensive to use an exotic computer gizmo than standard equipment. Finally, a complex hierarchy of decision makers, approvers, and lawyers can stall decision making, cause unproductive debate, and stop progress.

Some other budget issues are unique to each medium.

Managing the Cost of Print Production
The term **print production** refers to the systematic process an approved design goes through from concept to final publication in a printed medium such as magazines, newspapers, or collateral materials like brochures and direct-mail packages.

For print media, production managers must translate the rough or comprehensive design into a final assembly of black-and-white artwork called a *mechanical* or *pasteup*. Then, working with an engraver or printer, they make sure the mechanical is converted into an accurate set of negatives for the printer to use to make printing plates.

A big cost factor in the production of many print ads is the *engraver* that provides all the color separations, retouching, press proofs, and digital files. Paper costs affect budgets, too. When agencies place ads in print media, the cost of paper is included in the charge for the ad. But when an agency prints collateral materials such as data sheets, brochures, or packaging for a client, the cost of paper is noticeable.

For the Prius campaign, Saatchi assembled a teaser promo to send to car shows and dealers. Designed to create interest in the Prius before the rest of the promotional material came out, it was encased in an elegant, origami-style pocket made of translucent paper. Among other things, Saatchi included a small flyer printed on a textured paper embedded with seeds. The copy read: "Hybrid Synergy Drive: Sometimes the seeds of change are brilliantly designed as a car. Or in this case, a card." The recipient simply planted the piece of paper and could expect the seeds to grow.

print production manager Manager who oversees the entire production process, including reproduction of visuals in full color, shooting and editing of scenes, precise specification and placement of type, and the checking, approving, duplicating, and shipping of final art, negatives, tape, or film to the communication media.

producer For electronic media, the person responsible for keeping the project moving smoothly and under budget, while maintaining the required level of quality through every step of the production process.

print production The systematic process an approved design goes through from concept to final production in a printed medium, such as magazines, newspapers, or collateral materials.

Managing the Cost of Electronic Production The term **electronic production** refers to the process of converting a script or storyboard to a finished commercial for use on radio, TV, or digital media. While the process is similar to print production, the technical details and the costs are quite different. And the end result, rather than print film or negatives, may be audio- or videotape, film, or a digital format such as a DVD or Flash file.

Radio. Radio is the least expensive electronic medium to produce because it deals only with the dimension of sound. There's no need for hairstylists, makeup artists, lighting specialists, or cue-card holders. And commercials are duplicated on inexpensive audiotape.

The primary control factors in producing radio spots, therefore, are the costs of talent and music. Celebrity talent can be very

Television. In 2008, the average cost of producing a 30-second national television spot was $302,000.[3] Factors that increase TV production budgets include famous talent and directors, large casts, animation, special effects, use of both location and studio shooting for one commercial, expensive set decoration or construction, additional shooting days, and major script changes during a shoot.[4] Commercial producers have to be aware of all these factors and plan for them.

There is a belief in the industry that high-priced celebrity talent and extravagant effects get attention and increase memorability. That may not always be true. One study showed that advertising that features a brand differentiation message along with a demonstration of the product is actually more effective and costs on average 28 percent less to produce.[5]

Digital media. Digital media have increased the importance of the tasks performed by the agency producer and creative staff and made it critical for them to stay current with new technologies.

> "Digital media have increased the importance of the tasks performed by the agency producer and creative staff and made it critical for them to stay current with new technologies."

expensive. But even the cost of standard union talent, paid at **scale** (the regular charge agreed to in the union contract), can mount rapidly if there are multiple voices or if the commercial is aired in many markets or for an extended period of time. The advertiser, for example, may initially contract for a four-week or a thirteen-week run. If the commercial is extended beyond that time, the advertiser owes a **residual fee** to the talent.

Likewise, the cost of original music (composing, scoring, and orchestration) can range from very inexpensive to frightful, depending on the talent and scope of use. For this reason, many clients—especially small local and regional advertisers—prefer to use prerecorded **stock music** available for commercial use from a studio or radio station.

From airport check-in to grocery check-out, consumers are getting used to self-service touch screens and credit card readers on digital **kiosks**. Agencies are busy preparing digital presentations for kiosks, which can automatically present the customer with options to upgrade or add on to their orders: the self-service grocery checkstand asks if you need ice, and the kiosk at the airport may feature tickets to attractions in your destination city.[6]

For many digital ads, production managers may subcontract the work. Saatchi & Saatchi, for instance, has a special design and interactive media group.[7] The Prius campaign included many interactive components, including an in-depth look at the vehicle on the Toyota Web site (www.toyota.com/prius).

check yourself ✓

1. What are the five common budget busters every print production manager should be aware of?

2. What is the difference in the cost of paper for print ads versus collateral materials?

3. What is the least expensive electronic medium and why?

THE PRINT PRODUCTION PROCESS

Once Toyota's advertising managers approved the Prius ad concept, Johanna Leovey could give it her full attention. The process she used was the same as for any other print job, whether a brochure, a poster, or a direct-mail piece. Her goal is always the same—to produce the job as closely as possible to the concept intended by the creative team.

The **print production process** consists of four major phases: *preproduction, production, prepress,* and *printing and distribution.* For a simple model of this process, see Exhibit 10–1.

L02 Explain the processes for producing print ads and brochures.

The Preproduction Phase: Planning the Project

The first step, **preproduction**, begins when the creative department submits the approved creative concepts—rough or comprehensive layout and copy—to the production department. The production manager's first task is to communicate with the agency's traffic manager and log the project into the department's *traffic system.* Together they will open a **job jacket** for storing the various pieces of artwork and ideas that will be generated throughout the process, and then they will examine the general nature of the job and consider several questions pertinent to managing it efficiently. For example,

- What equipment is needed?

- How will we get it? (Will we have to lease another machine?)

- What materials are necessary? (If this is a packaging job, what material will we be printing on: tin, paper, cardboard?)

- What human resources are needed? (Do we need to hire freelancers like photographers or illustrators?)

- Will there be any special expenses? (Do we need to do location photography, for example, or use the specialized services of a food designer?)

- How many production artists will be needed? (Is the deadline so near that we'll have to call up the reserves?)

Once these general questions are answered, the production manager can look more closely at the specific needs of the project.

preproduction The period of time before the actual recording or shooting of a commercial—the planning phase in commercial production.

job jacket In the preproduction phase, a place to store the various pieces of artwork and ideas that will be generated throughout the process.

▼ **EXHIBIT 10–1** The print production process.

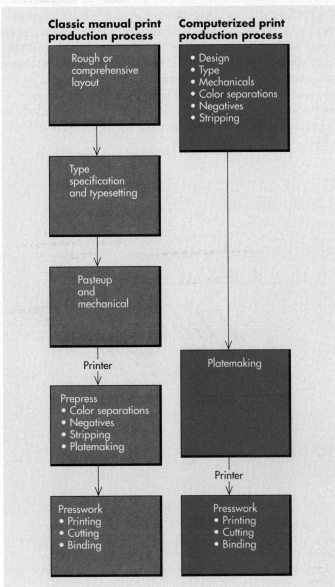

> # Four important criteria for selecting type are readability, appropriateness, harmony, and emphasis.

Working backward from publication **closing dates** (deadlines), the traffic and production managers decide when each step of the work must be finished. Deadlines can vary from hours to months. The manager tries to build extra time into each step because every word, art element, and aesthetic choice may need some last-minute change. The traffic manager's job is to make sure deadlines are not missed and that proper approvals are obtained in a timely fashion. The team at Saatchi & Saatchi was given a prototype of the Prius for a total of only five days. In this time they were required to photograph the vehicle for use in all of the print ads, collateral work, as well as several 15-second spots used in their prelaunch campaign.

Typography

Art directors select type styles to enhance the desired personality of the product and complement the tone of the ad. Typefaces affect an ad's appearance, design, and readability. Good type selection can create interest and attract readers.

It is imperative that production managers and graphic artists understand **typography**, the art of selecting and setting type. Four important criteria for selecting type are *readability, appropriateness, harmony or appearance,* and *emphasis.* Commercial Break 10, "The Characteristics of Type," describes these and other type-related topics.

To make their ads unique, some advertisers commission a new type design. Other companies tailor their typography to blend with the magazines or newspapers their advertising appears in. This gives the ad an editorial look and, the advertiser hopes, enhanced credibility. For consistency, Saatchi & Saatchi uses one type style in all Toyota ads.

Planning the Job

The purpose of the preproduction phase is planning thoroughly, which entails making a number of strategic choices before launching into full production. For example, since the art director's conceptual rough layouts are often made with marker colors that do not match printing inks, the production manager should consult with the art director to formally select a color palette, using a color guide such as the PANTONE® system.

For brochures, there is also the question of which printing process and which type of printing press to use for the job. This will affect the budget and dictate how art is to be prepared in the production and prepress phases.

Finally, the production manager must decide early which is most important for a project: *speed, quality,* or *economy.* Typically, the manager must sacrifice one in favor of the other two. The answer determines the production methods used and the

An advertisement's type style can play a significant role in reinforcing the brand's personality and setting the tone of the ad. In this ad for Singapore Airlines (www.singaporeair.com) the typeface effectively communicates luxury and integrates beautifully into the layout, while not sacrificing readability.

personnel employed. Once all these decisions are made, the manager can begin the production phase.

The Production Phase: Creating the Artwork

The **production phase** involves completing ancillary functions such as illustrations or photography, setting up the artwork and typesetting, and then melding all these components into a final form for the printer or publisher.

Creating the Visual

Almost every ad has a visual. The visual may be an illustration or a photograph or even a combination of the two. But where do these pictures come from?

When reviewing the layout with the art director, the decision will be made whether to use illustrations or photography and how to get the pictures the creatives envisioned. To save the client money, the art director or producer may choose to purchase pictures from a stock photography house for a licensing fee. The fee is based on the intended use and the duration of the campaign.

Most expensive is commissioning an illustrator to draw an original picture or hiring a photographer to go on location to shoot a specific visual, especially if it's out of town. For photography, there are several important considerations, including who to use. That depends on the style of photograph desired. Some photographers are well-versed in photojournalistic techniques. Others are especially good at shooting interiors. And some specialize in food or fashion photography.

Other considerations include special equipment, props, or sets that will be needed. In the case of the Prius ad, the creative team worked in a studio, photographing the car against a white backdrop. Later, they completed the image by adding other visuals and text.

Preparing Mechanicals

The **mechanical** is the camera-ready pasteup of the artwork. It includes type, photos, and line art, all attached to an art board. To create the mechanical for an ad, brochure, or package, the production artist begins by marking out a grid on which to lay the type and art. Artists do this with pagemaking computer software. The grid provides an underlying consistency to the spacing and design of the piece.

The production artist then specifies the style and size of the typefaces and inputs this information, along with the copy, into the computer. The type may be positioned electronically, or it

Producing Ads [10]

You probably think it is unrealistic to plan on producing a real ad for your client. After all, advertisers spend millions of dollars getting their ads produced for television. Even print and radio are expensive.

But you might think differently if you knew the costs were low. Even free. Which is not to say it will be easy. But if you want to take a stab at producing an attractive and effective ad, here are some tools that are low cost or free.

If you want to:

Do desktop publishing. Try Indesign alternative Scribus (http://www.scribus.net/). Price: free.

Work with and manipulate images. Try Photoshop alternative GIMP (http://www.gimp.org/). Price: free.

Create logos and simple designs. Try Raven (http://aviary.com/home). Price: free.

Create more complicated illustrations. Try Inkscape (http://www.inkscape.org/). Price: free.

Purchase an inexpensive and mobile video recorder. Try Flip Video (http://www.theflip.com/). Price: usually under $150.

Edit a video (and you're new at it). Try Windows MovieMaker (http://windowslive.com/Desktop/MovieMaker). Price: free.

Post videos online where the world can see them: Try YouTube (www.youtube.com). Price: free.

Build a Web site for your client (and you're new at it). Try Google Sites (http://sites.google.com/). Price: free.

Build a Web site for your client (and you really know what you're doing). Try Aptana (http://aptana.com/). Price: free.

Edit sound files: Try Audacity (www.audacity.sourceforge.net). Price: free.

Spice up your ads with royalty-free photos: Try www.freeedigitalphotos.net. All photographs are free for personal use.

leading The measurement of the space between separate lines of text (pronounced *ledding*).

kerning The measurement of the space between individual letters of text.

display type A style of typeface used in advertising that is larger and heavier than normal text type.

text type The smaller type used in the body copy of an advertisement.

serif The most popular type group that is distinguished by smaller lines or tails called serifs that finish the ends of the main character strokes and by variations in the thickness of the strokes.

Readability

The most important consideration in selecting a typeface is readability. As David Ogilvy said, good typography helps people read; bad typography prevents them from doing so. General factors that contribute to readability include the type's style, boldness, and size; the length of the line; and the spacing between words, lines, and paragraphs. An ad is meant to be read, and reduced readability kills interest. Difficult-to-read typefaces should be used infrequently and only to create special effects.

Large, bold, simply designed typefaces are the easiest to read. However, the amount of space in the ad and the amount of copy that must be written limit the use of these type forms. The length of the line of copy can also affect readability. Newspaper columns are usually less than two inches wide; magazine columns slightly wider. For readability, columns of copy should be less than three inches wide.

Spacing between lines also influences an ad's readability. This space allows for descenders (the part of the letter that extends downward, as in the letters j, g, p) and ascenders (the part of the letter that extends upward, as in the letters b, d, k). When this is the only space between lines, type is said to be "set solid." Sometimes an art director adds extra space between lines (called **leading**, pronounced "ledding") to give a more "airy" feeling to the copy.

Kerning (the space between letters) also affects appearance and readability. The narrower the kerning, the more type can fit into the available space. Narrow kerning is effective in headlines because people read large type faster when the letters are close together. But narrow kerning is hard to read if overdone, especially in smaller type sizes.

Appropriateness

A typeface must be appropriate to the product being advertised. Each typeface and size conveys a mood and feeling quite apart from the meanings of the words themselves. One typeface whispers "luxury," another screams "bargain!" A typeface that looks old-fashioned is probably inappropriate for a digital watch.

Harmony/Appearance

Advertising novices often mix too many typefaces, creating disharmony and clutter. Type should harmonize with the other elements of an ad, including the illustration and layout. Skilled artists often choose typefaces in the same family or faces that are closely related in appearance.

Emphasis

Contrast creates emphasis. Artists often use more than one type style or mix italic and roman, small and large type, lowercase and uppercase. But they must be careful not to emphasize every element or they won't emphasize any.

Classes of Type

Two classes of type are used in advertising.

Display type is larger and heavier than text type; useful in headlines, subheads, logos, and addresses, and for emphasis.

Text type is smaller and finer, used in body copy.

Type Groups

Because of its readability and warm personality, **serif** (roman) type is the most popular type group. It is distinguished by small lines or tails called serifs that finish the ends of the main strokes and by variations in the thickness of the strokes. It comes in a wide variety of designs and sizes. **Sans serif** (gothic) type is the second most popular type group; it is also referred to as block or contemporary. Characterized by lack of serifs (*sans* is French for *without*) and relatively uniform thickness of the strokes, it is not as readable as roman but is widely used because the simple, clean lines give a slick, modern appearance (see **a**).

Square serif type combines sans serif and serif typefaces. It has serifs, but letter strokes have uniform thickness.

Cursive or *script type* resembles handwriting; letters often connect and may convey a feeling of femininity, formality, classicism, or beauty. It is difficult to read and is

Roman type	Square serif type
Typography	Typography
Typography	
Typography	Script type
Typography	*Typography*
	Typography
Sans serif type	
Typography	Ornamental type
Typography	Typography
TYPOGRAPHY	Typography

(a)

used primarily in headlines, formal announcements, and cosmetics and fashion ads.

Ornamental type uses novel designs with a high level of embellishment and decorativeness. It adds a "special effects" quality but is often difficult to read.

Type Families

A **type family** is made up of related typefaces. The serif typeface used for the text of this book is called Garamond. Within a family, the basic design remains the same but varies in the proportion, weight, and slant of the characters. The type may be light, medium, bold, extra bold, condensed, extended, or italic. Variations enable the typographer to provide contrast and emphasis without changing the family (see **b**).

A **font** is a complete assortment of capitals, small capitals, lowercase letters, numerals, and punctuation marks for a particular typeface and size.

Garamond Book	Garamond Condensed Book
Garamond Book Italic	*Garamond Condensed Book Italic*
Garamond Bold	**Garamond Condensed Bold**
Garamond Bold Italic	***Garamond Condensed Bold Italic***
Garamond Light	Garamond Condensed Light
Garamond Light Italic	*Garamond Condensed Light Italic*
Garamond Ultra	**Garamond Condensed Ultra**
Garamond Ultra Italic	***Garamond Condensed Ultra Italic***

(b)

Measuring Type

Type characters have height, width, weight, and, for some ornamental typefaces, depth. They also come in shapes called a case.

Size is the height of a character (or letter) measured in **points** (72 points to the inch) from the bottom of the descenders to the top of the ascenders (see **c**).

The width of a letter, known as an em space, is usually based on the maximum width and proportions of the capital letter M for that particular typeface. The width of the letter N is called an en space.

Capital letters are uppercase, small letters lowercase (in the days of manual typesetting, the case containing the capital letters was stored above the one with the small letters). It's easiest to read a combination of uppercase and lowercase. Type may be set in all caps (for emphasis) or in commoncase (caps and small caps).

Applying the Breaks

Use the various figures and terms in this Commercial Break to answer the following:

1. Describe the class, group, family, and size of the type used in the title "Producing Ads," which appears on the second page of this chapter.
2. Do the same for the captions that appear in the exhibits in this book.

Text type	Display type
6 pt. Type size	16 pt. Type size
8 pt. Type size	18 pt. Type size
9 pt. Type size	20 pt. Type size
10 pt. Type size	24 pt. Type size
12 pt. Type size	30 pt. Type size
14 pt. Type size	36 pt. Type size

(c)

overlay On a pasteup, a piece of clear plastic containing a second image from which a second printing plate can be made for color printing.

halftone The process of converting continuous-tone artwork, such as a photograph, into a pattern of different size dots that simulate shades of gray. When printed, the dots merge to give an illusion of continuous tone to the naked eye.

prepress phase The process of converting page art and visuals into materials (generally film negatives and color separations) needed for printing.

stripping Assembling line and halftone negatives into one single negative, which is then used to produce a combination plate.

base art The first image on an artboard on which an overlay may be placed.

camera-ready art A finished ad that is ready for the printer's camera to shoot—to make negatives or plates—according to the publication's specifications.

line art Any artwork or type that is comprised of a solid color. There are no continuous tones—shades of gray or any other color.

continuous tones Normal photographic paper produces images in black and white with shades of gray in between.

may be output onto paper and glued onto an artboard within the image area.

When an additional color is to be printed, a second artboard marked to the same dimensions is used for the second image. The second image may be glued onto a clear plastic **overlay** that lies on top of the first image (called the **base art**). The production artist places cross-marks in the corners of the base art and then superimposes cross-marks on the transparent overlay precisely over those on the base art. This registers the exact position of the two layers of art in relation to one another.

The art elements must be properly positioned in the artwork (whether mechanical or computer generated) because the printer needs to have layers of art that can be reproduced individually. The total image is then constructed as each layer is printed over the previous one. Because the printer must photograph each layer to make separate plates, this is called **camera-ready art**.

Camera-Ready Art and Halftones
Production art for the printing process is like an on/off switch: Where the art is

black, ink will stick; where the art is white, ink won't stick. The production artist adheres to this printing principle by using *line art* and *halftones*.

Line art. Any artwork or type that is comprised of a solid color, such as black, is called **line art**. There are no shades of gray or shades of any other color.

Halftones. Most photographs and some drawings contain images with **continuous tones**, such as shades of gray. However, printing presses cannot print gray—just black or white. Continuous-tone artwork must therefore be broken up into dots, by shooting it through a *halftone screen*. The combination of dots, when printed, produces a **halftone**, an optical illusion of shading, as in a photo. In the dark areas of the image, large dots bump into each other and make the paper appear nearly black. In the gray areas, smaller black dots allow more of the white paper to show through. The human eye perceives the dots as gradations of tone.

The fineness of the halftone screen determines the quality of the illusion. Glossy magazine ads are printed with halftone screens as fine as 200 lines per inch (lpi), while newspaper photos appear very coarse at 80 to 100 lpi. Coarser screens are used to print on coarse, ink-absorbent paper (like newsprint) because the ink spreads when it hits the paper and fills in the white areas. The dots in a coarse screen can be seen quite easily with the naked eye.

The artist's final step is to mark any halftones and line art for size and indicate where they should be placed. The artist simply

A halftone screen breaks up continuous-tone artwork into tiny dots. The combination of printed dots produces an optical illusion of shading, as in a photograph. The color dots show the separation for the color photo above. The other set of dots shows the range that would appear in a black-and-white photo.

sticks a photocopy of the visual to the artboard in its exact location with the letters FPO (for position only) written across the image. That way the printer doesn't think this is the actual final art.

The Prepress Phase: Stripping, Negs, and Plates

When Saatchi & Saatchi completed all the production for the Prius ad on its computers, the next step was to get the finished artwork ready for the press.

In the **prepress phase**, the printer makes plates from the mechanical. The elements of the ad are converted into film negatives, which are mounted together in perfect registration—through a process known as **stripping**—onto opaque plastic sheets called **flats**. A completed flat is a mask that allows light to pass through only where lines and dots are to appear on the plate. The flat is pressed against the printing plate, and ultraviolet light exposes the plate's photosensitive emulsion. Once exposed, the emulsion is developed, etching the plate in the process. This leaves some areas of the plate capable of holding ink and others unable to do so. Once dry, the plates are "hung" on the press, ready for printing.

New digital solutions allow printers to go directly from "computer to plate," eliminating labor-intensive, complex, and costly steps required in the conventional prepress process.

Printing in Color

A printing plate can print only one color at a time. An advertiser who wants to print an ad or a brochure in blue, green, and black needs three different plates, and the job is referred to as a three-color job. To print in full color, a **four-color process** is used. This process can simulate nearly all colors by combining the four primary colors: *process blue* (cyan), *process yellow*, *process magenta*, and *black* (which provides greater detail and density as well

as shades of gray). In the parlance of the trade, this is also called **CYMK printing**, the K standing for black. To print in full color, therefore, the printer prepares four printing plates—one for each process color plus black.

Designs that don't need full color are printed in blended inks rather than process colors. To print a brochure in black and burgundy, it's cheaper to use only those two ink colors.

A PANTONE® color, one of a spectrum of colors that makes up the **PANTONE Matching System® (PMS)**, is a single ink premixed according to a formula and given a specific color number. The PANTONE swatch book features more than 1,000 colors in solid and screened blocks printed on different paper finishes.[8]

Four-Color Separations

Four separate halftone negatives are needed to make a set of four-color plates: one each for cyan, yellow, magenta, and black (See Exhibit 10–2). Each of the resulting negatives appears in black and white, and the set is called the **color separation**. In printing, the process color inks are translucent, so two or three overlapping colors create another color. For example, red is reproduced by overlapping yellow and magenta dots. Color inkjet computer printers produce color images in much the same way using four ink cartridges.

Electronic scanning systems can produce four-color separations and screens in minutes instead of the hours or days previously needed for camera work and hand etching.

Regardless of the separation method used, when properly printed, tiny clusters of halftone dots in various colors, sizes, and shapes give the eye the illusion of seeing the colors of the original photograph or painting.

The Duplication and Distribution Phase: Printing, Binding, and Shipping

The last phase of the print production process involves the actual printing, proofing, and finishing steps of drying, cutting, binding, and shipping.

Several printing processes are available—letterpress, offset, rotogravure, flexography—the choice largely dependent on the type of surface being printed, the quality required, and the size of the job. However, all of the processes involve applying ink to a plate and then transferring the inked impression to the paper (or some other surface).

The Press Run When paper, plates, and ink are ready, the press is run briefly to check the image's alignment on the paper. In multicolored printing, proper alignment of all the colors is critical. When the initial proofs show good alignment, the presses are started again and gradually sped up to maximum output.

Finishing Once all the pieces are printed, the ink must dry. Excess paper is cut away using huge cutting machines. Depending on the nature of the job, the pieces may be delivered to special subcontractors who emboss or die-cut or perform other special techniques to enhance the final printed piece. The final stop may be the bindery for folding and stapling.

(a)

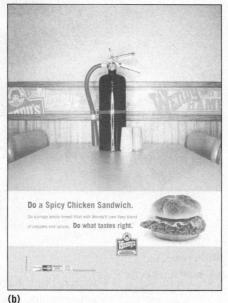

(b)

▼ **EXHIBIT 10–2** Four-color ads are created by combining translucent inks from four printing plates. Here we show the separation of four-color artwork into its (a) yellow, (b) magenta, and (c) cyan components. When these three process colors are combined with (d) the fourth color (black) on the printing press, the resulting ad will closely resemble (e) the original artwork.

(c)

(d)

(e)

QUALITY CONTROL IN PRINT PRODUCTION

At various stages of the print production process, the production manager verifies the quality. Artwork for a newspaper or magazine ad, for example, must be camera-ready. Many agencies now just send a disk, and the publisher converts the computer image to negatives. Magazines provide specific instructions and measurements for each ad size they offer.

Finally, the production manager must check all proofs for errors and obtain approvals from agency and client executives before releasing ads to publications or artwork to printers. Proofing is a time-consuming task made more so by the fact that not everyone is available when the work is ready for approval.

For the production process to run smoothly, everyone concerned must understand the procedure. The later in the process errors are discovered, the more expensive they are to fix. [9]

Production Phase Quality Issues

The task of quality control really begins in the production phase. Proofs of the production art, with all its type and images, are carefully inspected for misspellings, mismeasured lines, improperly sized images, misplaced cropmarks, or a myriad of other errors that could lead to a problem later.

Prepress Quality Issues

The slightest flaw in the final printed piece can have serious repercussions. The production manager must check and double-check, even triple-check, the film negatives before they're sent off to a magazine. An analog or digital proof of the negatives should be carefully checked and sent with the negatives.

What to Look For in a Proof
When checking proofs, production managers and art directors look for any scratches, minute holes or dots, blemishes, or unevenness of ink coverage. Using a *loupe* (magnifying glass), they inspect the dot pattern in halftones to make sure the registration of color is perfectly tight. Then they check *traps* and *bleeds*.

Designers often plan for typesetting to *overprint* (print on top of) the background color with black ink. But when colored type is printed over a different background color, the background color must let white show to avoid distorting the true color of the colored type. This **reverse knockout** requires careful trapping.

A **trap** is where the edge of one color slightly overlaps its neighbor to make sure the white paper underneath doesn't show through (see Exhibit 10–3).

For full-color ads, it's often wise to print text in black ink. When ads or brochures are reprinted, advertisers often make type changes. If all the text is black, the advertiser needs only to change the black negative and plate. If the text is any other color, all the negatives, stripping, and plating will have to be changed.

Finally, designers also need to consider **bleeds**—colors, type, or visuals that run all the way to the edge of the page. Production artists must set up their artwork for at least a quarter inch of extra color *outside* the image area to accommodate variations in the printing and cutting processes.

---

reverse knockout Area within a field of printed color on a page that is free of ink and allows the paper's surface to show.

trap Where, in the printing process, one color overlays the edge of another to keep the paper from showing through.

bleeds Colors, type, or visuals that run all the way to the edge of the page.

> For the production process to run smoothly, everyone concerned must understand the procedure. The later errors are discovered, the more expensive they are to fix.

---

check yourself ✓

1. What is the primary role of the print production manager?

2. What does the traffic manager do and why is it such an important position?

3. What are the phases in print production?

▼**EXHIBIT 10–3** Black ink can overprint a background color (far left). However, art or text printed in a color other than black should have no background color underneath. For example, if a green letter "a" appears on an orange field, a white reverse knockout will keep the green from being affected by the orange (second from left). If the green letter and the reverse knockout aren't properly aligned or the green letter is smaller than the white knockout, the letters will not trap, and white paper will show between the two colors (far right).

Letter overprints background   Reverse knockout   Proper trap   Improper trap

LO3   Explain the production process for radio ads.

THE RADIO COMMERCIAL PRODUCTION PROCESS

Radio commercials, called **spots**, are among the quickest, simplest, and least expensive ads to produce. In fact, many radio stations provide production services free to local advertisers.

Some spots are delivered live by the announcer, in which case the station gets a script or highlight sheet and any recorded music to be used. The material must be accurately timed. A live commercial script should run about 130 to 150 words per minute so the announcer can speak at a normal, conversational pace. The best way to do this is to use a popular DJ and let him or her improvise. It's a lot more entertaining and links the DJ's credibility to the product.[10]

The disadvantages of live commercials are that announcers may be inconsistent in their delivery, and sound effects are quite limited. Uniform delivery requires a recorded commercial. The process of producing a recorded commercial includes *preproduction, production,* and *postproduction* (or finishing) phases (see Exhibit 10–4).

▼**EXHIBIT 10–4** Radio commercials have three production phases. The preproduction and finishing phases are usually the most complex. Preproduction and postproduction editing and mixing typically require far more time than the actual recording session.

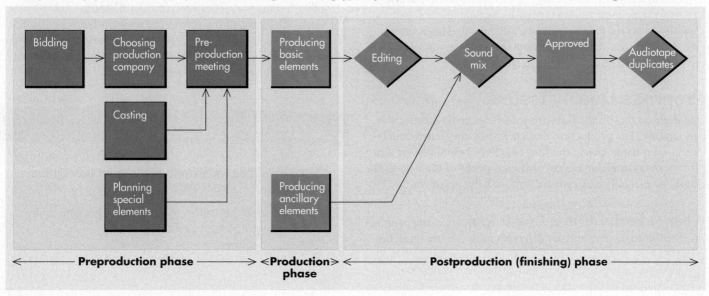

←——— **Preproduction phase** ———→ ←**Production phase**→ ←——— **Postproduction (finishing) phase** ———→

spots Another name for radio commercials.

director The director supervises preproduction, production, and postproduction of radio and television commercials.

session The time when the recording and mixing of a radio commercial takes place.

control room In a recording studio, the place where the producer, director, and sound engineer sit, monitoring and controlling all the sounds generated in the sound studio.

Preproduction

In the preproduction phase, the advertiser and agency perform a variety of tasks that allow production to run smoothly, on time, and within budget. The agency assigns a radio producer from its staff or hires a freelance producer. Based on the script, the producer selects a studio and a director, determines what talent will be needed, estimates costs, and prepares a budget for the advertiser's approval.

To control the production process and get the finest sound reproduction, most ad agencies use independent recording stu-

Production: Cutting the Spot

All of the elements to be used in the commercial—voices, music, sound effects—come together and are recorded at a **session**. Depending on the nature of the spot, a session can last from a half-hour to more than a day. Since studios charge by the hour, preproduction rehearsals are important.

The Sound Studio At the session, the voice and music talent perform in a studio, which has sound-dampening wall surfaces, a carpeted floor, microphones, a window to a control

> [Radio spots are among the quickest, simplest, and least expensive ads to produce.]

dios. The best audio studios have experienced sound directors and technicians, close ties to well-known talent, and the latest recording equipment.

During the preproduction phase, the producer (or a casting director) searches for the right talent. The advertiser and the agency consider several factors before arriving at a decision: the person's tone of voice, vocal acting skills and creativity, intelligence, style of thinking, and reputation.

If the script calls for music, the producer decides whether to use prerecorded music or hire a composer and/or arranger. Any needed sound effects can be created or, most often, collected from prerecorded sources. All these decisions, of course, affect the budget, but they also have a dramatic impact on the effectiveness of the spots.

Once the talent is hired and music prepared, the **director** supervises rehearsals until everything is ready for recording.

room, and wall plugs for connecting equipment and instruments to the control room.

Standard items in the sound studio are microphones, headphones, and speakers. Announcers and singers wear headphones to hear instructions from the director in the control room or to monitor prerecorded instrumental tracks as they sing (keeping the music track from being recorded onto the voice track).

Studio technicians and engineers carefully select and position the microphones to capture the full spectrum of sounds. The studio may have a separate sound booth (a small windowed room or partitioned area) to isolate drums or louder backup talent so the sound technicians can better balance the collection of sounds.

The Control Room The agency producer, director, and sound engineer (and often the client and account executive) sit in the **control room**, where they can monitor all the sounds generated in the sound studio. The control room is separated from the studio by a thick glass window

audio console (board) In a sound studio control room, the board that channels sound to the appropriate recording devices and that blends both live and prerecorded sounds for immediate or delayed broadcast.

postproduction phase The finishing phase in commercial production—the period after recording and shooting when a radio or TV commercial is edited and sweetened with music and sound effects.

check yourself ✓

1. What is a session?
2. What is a control room and what is it used for?

A sophisticated audio console manipulates sound electronically, making sounds sharper or fuzzier, with more echo, or more treble or bass. Its multitrack mixing and sound enhancement capabilities are most useful during postproduction.

and soundproofed walls, so the people monitoring the session can hear the sounds on quality speakers and discuss the various takes.

The director and sound engineer work at an **audio console** (also called a **board**), the central "switchboard" for controlling the sounds and channeling them to the appropriate recording devices. As they monitor the sounds coming from the studio, they keep the pitch and loudness within acceptable levels for broadcast.

The board also serves as a sound mixer, blending both live and prerecorded sounds for immediate or delayed broadcast.

Postproduction: Finishing the Spot

After the commercial is recorded a number of times, a selection is made from the best takes. The sound engineer usually records music, sound effects, and vocals separately and then mixes and sweetens them during the **postproduction phase** (or finishing phase). The final recording is referred to as the **master**.

From the master tape, the engineer makes duplicates called **dubs**, records them onto quarter-inch magnetic tape, and sends them to radio stations for broadcast.

L04 Describe the major production techniques for TV commercials.

THE TELEVISION COMMERCIAL PRODUCTION PROCESS

While Johanna Leovey was working on the Prius print ads, another team across the office was working on the television commercials. The creatives had come up with a great concept for the Prius, and it was right on the money strategically, but it would have to be produced exceedingly well to communicate the idea credibly and resonate with the company's diverse audiences. That meant bringing in one of the agency's top TV producers, and Richard Bendetti was selected to do the job.

The commercial to be produced is portrayed by the storyboard in Chapter 9 (page 246). The spot features cars, buses, and people hurrying along the sidewalk. However, instead of moving forward, the tires on the vehicles simply go round and round, and the people on the street appear to be walking in place. This happens in various locations, urban and rural, all over the world. Suddenly, the Prius emerges—the only forward-moving motion in the shot.

The Role of the Commercial Producer

Students of advertising need to know basic TV production concepts to understand how commercials are made, why production is so expensive, and what methods they can use to cut costs without sacrificing quality or effectiveness.

As with radio, the process of producing a TV commercial always involves three stages, as shown in Exhibit 10–5:

1. *Preproduction:* all the work prior to the actual day of filming.

2. *Production:* the actual day (or days) the commercial is filmed or videotaped.

3. *Postproduction (or finishing):* all the work done after shooting to edit and finish the commercial.

master The final recording of a radio commercial, with all the music, sound, and vocals mixed, from which dubs are recorded and sent to radio stations for broadcast.

dubs Duplicates of radio commercials made from the master tape and sent to stations for broadcast.

live action The basic production technique in television that portrays real people and settings, as opposed to animation.

animation The use of cartoons, puppet characters, or demonstrations of inanimate characters that come to life in television commercials; often used for communicating difficult messages or for reaching specialized markets, such as children.

▼**EXHIBIT 10–5** The production processes for film and video are very similar to those for radio until the sound-mixing stage. Computerized editing speeds up the finishing phase for video.

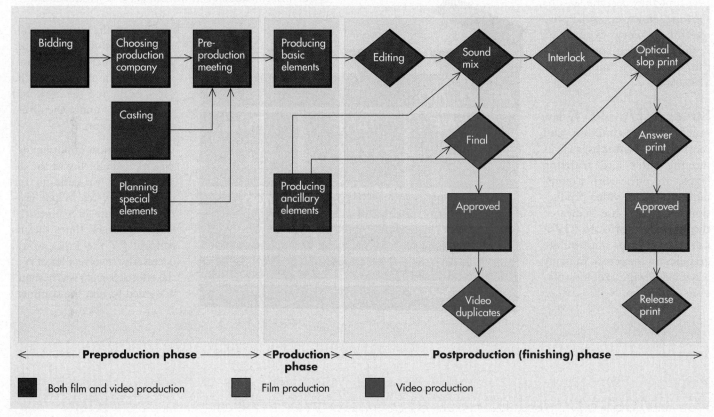

The Preproduction Phase

Good planning before production saves money. That's the purpose of the preproduction phase. The first thing the producer must do, therefore, is study the script and storyboard and analyze the production techniques that will be called for in the commercial. Three major categories of production techniques are used today: *live action, animation,* and *special effects.*

Live Action To portray people and things in lifelike, everyday situations, like typical slice-of-life TV commercials, advertisers use the **live action** technique.

If a commercial calls for live action, the producer decides whether the action will be staged indoors in a studio, outside on a studio lot, or on location away from the studio. Will it be taped or filmed? All these factors influence what equipment and personnel are required, what permissions are needed, what talent can be used, and, of course, what the commercial costs.

Working with the creative team, Richard Bendetti concurred that shooting on location was crucial to the Prius spot, which meant finding several locations around the world. This meant coordinating with foreign officials to get the necessary permits, police security, and environmental clearances. This created a bit of a problem in Japan, where the government doesn't allow traffic flow to be impeded at major intersections.

Animation Animation—cartoons, dancing puppets, and demonstrations in which inanimate objects come to life—can

SPECIAL EFFECTS SHOULD NEVER DISTRACT FROM THE PRODUCT—OR THE STRATEGIC MESSAGE.

effectively communicate difficult messages or reach special markets such as children.

Traditional animation techniques include *cartoons, photo animation, stop-motion photography,* and *video animation.* Cartoons often score the highest viewer interest and the longest life, so over time they cost the least per showing. However, initial production is very expensive. A fully animated commercial can easily cost more than $200,000.[11]

Special Effects Today, much video animation and most **special effects**, such as moving titles and whirling logos, are done with a computer. All major video production companies use dedicated **digital video effects (DVE)** units that can manipulate graphics on the screen in many ways: fades, wipes, zooms, rotations, and so on.

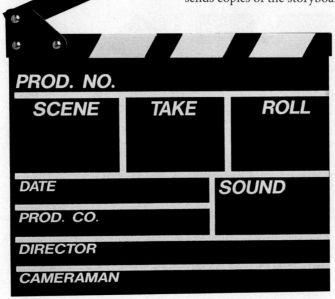

Planning Production Commercials are created by a team that includes a producer, writer, art director, director, and sometimes a musical composer and choreographer. The agency producer is responsible for completing the job on schedule and within budget. The producer usually sends copies of the storyboard to three studios for competitive bids. When the studio is chosen, the producer and casting director select the cast and hire the announcer. Next the set is built, and the crew and cast rehearse under the director's supervision.

One of the most important decisions is the hiring of the director. Such was certainly the case for the Prius. When Saatchi was looking for a director, it was told several times that its concept for the Prius would necessarily involve a lot of special effects. Saatchi was hesitant; it wanted to film the commer-

> ## Most special effects are done with a computer. Video production companies use digital video effects units to manipulate screen graphics.

However, these techniques should never distract from the product—or the strategic message. Further, more than one fantasy or **mnemonic device** (Energizer Bunny or Jolly Green Giant) might confuse audiences. David Ogilvy suggested that, to make the strongest impression on the viewer, fantasies should relate to the product's claims and be repeated heavily.[12]

cial with as little special effects as possible. Tarsem Singh was an obvious choice as the director. Not only did Tarsem seem excited by the Prius concept, but he agreed that the ad should be shot in the most natural way possible.

During the preproduction period meetings take place among the director, the agency producer, the account representative,

SFX: Music throughout
(Aerial shot of barn roof as surrounding countryside blows in the wind.)
VO (MAYA ANGELOU): The truth does not stand still for a moment.

(A tornado approaches. High winds blow against a wheelbarrow and pick up telephone and utility poles.)
It twists and turns, picks up your opinions, and sets them down a thousand miles away.

(The twister hits and the barn breaks up into splinters of debris that mix with typed letters.)

(The letters fall from the grip of the tornado, neatly into place as part of *The New York Times* newspaper text.)
When was the last time something you read moved you?

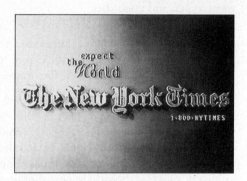

(SUPER: *The New York Times* logo.)
The New York Times.

Special effects play a major role here in grabbing the viewer's attention and adding drama to the message. The metaphor of a tornado combined with simple, yet sophisticated copy distinguish this thoughtful spot for The New York Times.

the writer, the art director, the commercial director, possibly the advertiser, and anyone else important to the production. This is where they iron out any last-minute problems and make final decisions about the scenes, the actors, and the announcer. They should review everything—music, sets, action, lighting, camera angles. A finished 60-second film commercial takes only 90 feet of film, but the shooting may require 3,000 to 5,000 feet of film. And unlike video, film can't be used again.

The soundtrack may be recorded before, during, or after actual production. Recording sound in advance ensures that the commercial will be neither too long nor too short; it also helps when the subject has to move or dance to a specific music theme or rhythm.

Production: The Shoot

The actual shooting day (or days) can be very long and tedious. It may take several hours just to light the set to the director's liking. The Prius spot, for instance, took six full days to shoot—in five different locales in four countries—over the course of a two-week period.

Quiet on the Set: Sound Procedures for recording and controlling music and sound effects are similar to those used in radio. Microphones capture sound; recorders transfer the sound and store it on a medium like magnetic tape. Then, with the use of a multichannel control board, a sound engineer manipulates sounds for effect and records them onto film, video, disk, or a playback system synchronized with film.

studio lot Outdoor space at a film studio, shielded from undesirable noises. It provides large spaces, scenery, and natural lighting, without the added cost and logistics of location shooting.

location Shooting away from the studio. Location shooting adds realism but can also be a technical and logistical nightmare, often adding cost and many other potential problems.

talent The actors in commercials.

postproduction phase The finishing phase in commercial production—the period after recording and shooting when a radio or TV commercial is edited and sweetened with music and sound effects.

Lights Light establishes a visual mood. Intense light from a single source gives a harsh appearance and may be used to create anxiety in the viewer. By using filters, warmer lights, diffusion screens, and reflectors, the cinematographer can create a more consistent, softer illumination—and a more romantic mood. The director works with the art director, the cinematographer, and the lighting engineer to choose the most appropriate placement, types, and intensities.

Camera Professional film cameras used for making TV commercials shoot 16 millimeter (mm), 35 mm, and 75 mm film, the diagonal measurement of a single film frame.

Producers of local TV commercials used to shoot with the grainier but less expensive 16 mm film; national spots were shot on 35 mm for extra quality and precision; and 75 mm film provides the highest-quality image. While film is still widely used for national spots because of the atmosphere it brings to an image, most local spots are now shot on video.

Unlike film cameras, studio video cameras are tied to a control room by electronic cables. In the control room, multiple video screens and sound channels are wired to a control panel. Working at the control panel, the director can switch from one camera to another and simultaneously set the input and output levels of sound and visuals. Control panels also have DVE units for creating text or visual effects on screen.

Action: Staging and Talent Staging for a commercial may be done in the isolation of a studio, outside on a studio lot, or on location. The studio offers the most control.

Most film and video studios have heavy soundproofing to eliminate outside noises such as sirens and low-flying aircraft. The studios are lightproof, which allows for complete lighting control. Special equipment is easier to use in the controlled environment of a studio. But studio lighting can make a scene appear artificial.

For scenes requiring large amounts of space, historic or unique architecture, scenery, and the full effect of outdoor lighting, the **studio lot** offers the best control. The lot is outside acreage shielded from stray, off-site sounds. The lot is convenient to the studio's carpentry shop, and sets can be left standing until all shootings and retakes are completed.

Different types of lighting can enhance a scene and create special moods. Here, strong keylights light up the actors. A fainter light casts a window-shaped pattern onto the background. The effect light above enhances the reflected glow of the candle on the table top. To bystanders the scene appears very bright, but when the camera's aperture is set properly, the film sees a darker, more shadowy play of lights and darks.

In any commercial production, it's typical to have many more people behind the camera than in front of it. In addition to the director and assistant director, other important players behind the scenes may include a sound editor, lighting technicians, electricians, and grips (skilled workers who set up and adjust the equipment).

Although it adds realism, **location** shooting is often a technical and logistical nightmare. Every location has natural and manufactured features that create obstacles. Natural lighting creates bright highlights that contrast with harsh shadows. Large reflective screens and high-intensity lights are required to brighten up shadows for a more even-toned exposure. Energy sources for lighting and equipment may be insufficient, requiring long cables and mobile generators. But because sets don't have to be built, location shooting can be good for some low-budget or short lead-time commercials. However, natural events such as rain and fog can cause costly interruptions and serious delays.

Whether at the studio or on location, most scenes require several takes for the **talent** (actors) to get them right. Lighting may need readjusting as unexpected shadows pop up. Each scene may be shot from two or three different angles: one to establish the characters, one to show only the speaker, and one to show the listener's reaction.

Scenes aren't necessarily shot in order. Those with no synchronized sound are usually shot last since they don't require the full crew.

A long time may be needed between scenes to move the camera, reset the lights, reposition the talent, and pick up the action, sound, and look to match the other scenes. Each action must match what comes before and after. Commercials with disconcerting jumps destroy credibility.

Once all the scenes are "in the can," the commercial enters the postproduction, or finishing, phase.

Postproduction

In the **postproduction phase**, the film editor, sound mixer, and director actually put the commercial together.

In postproduction, the director and editor can save time and money by using computerized video and sound editing equipment for the assembly of the final product. At this stage, the director and editor will select and splice scenes into their respective order, removing all the unneeded footage. Next, they add off-camera special effects, like supers, and incorporate any necessary music or voice-overs.

supers Words superimposed on the picture in a television commercial.

work print The first visual portion of a filmed commercial assembled without the extra effects or dissolves, titles, or supers. At this time, scenes may be substituted, music and sound effects added, or other changes made.

mixed interlock The edited version of a filmed television commercial mixed with the finished sound track. Used for initial review and approval prior to being duplicated for airing.

answer print The final print of a film commercial, along with all the required optical effects and titles, used for review and approval before duplicating.

With computer and video technology, editors can convert the film to tape and add effects such as wipes and dissolves electronically. Although a director will spend many hours editing a commercial shot on video, it will still be considerably less than what would be needed for film editing.

Even so, many professionals prefer the beauty of images captured on film. The visual portion of the commercial appears on one piece of celluloid (film) without the effects of dissolves, titles, or **supers** (words superimposed on the picture). The sound portion is assembled on another piece of celluloid. This is the **work print** stage (also called the *rough cut* or *interlock*).

External sound is recorded next. The sound engineer records the musicians and singers, as well as the announcer's voice-over narrative. Prerecorded stock music may be bought and integrated into the commercial. The mixing also includes any sound effects, such as doorbells ringing or doors slamming.

Once sound editing is complete, the celluloid with the finished sound is combined with the almost-completed visual celluloid, yielding the **mixed interlock**. The addition of optical effects and titles results in the **answer print**. This is the final commercial. If it is approved, **dupes** (duplicate copies) are made for delivery to the networks or TV stations.

check yourself ✓

1. What three stages are involved in producing radio and TV spots?

2. What does a commercial producer do?

3. Who are the key individuals involved in the television commercial production process?

LO5 List ways the digital media save money as compared with print and electronic media.

PRODUCING ADVERTISING FOR DIGITAL MEDIA

Digital media are channels of communication that join multimedia formats with the electronic system capabilities of modern telecommunications, television, and computer technologies.

The three categories of places where we experience digital media are based on audience size: *mass audience, private audience,* and *personal audience venues.*

The Academy Awards show is a good example of a **mass audience venue**. With hundreds of people in the live audience and millions more watching at home, the multimedia presentation has a huge reach. Multimedia is also used in major sporting events, the Olympics opening ceremonies, political conventions, and other mass audience events.

Many digital media events are in **private audience venues**, though some of these may be quite large. A major marketer's national sales meeting, large corporate conferences, educational conferences, and training seminars all use computer-driven multimedia presentations, utilizing software programs to inform, persuade, remind, and entertain people.

The **personal audience venue** involves one person sitting in front of a personal computer receiving multimedia information off the Internet from an online service, or from software bought in a computer store.

The Role of Digital Media in Advertising

As an important tool for IMC, digital media give marketers new ways to reach prospects and begin a relationship—or improve their relationship with current customers.

In some cases, the medium itself is the ad, as in the case of a multimedia sales presentation or a dedicated kiosk offering information about a company's wares. In Internet advertising,

[Ads developed for digital media are virtually free of restrictions associated with time or space costs in traditional media.]

The emergence of digital media requires the development of an entirely new set of skills to produce ads. Art directors and designers must understand how to integrate print and video into a single medium, and they must also comprehend the features and limitations of the computer software used to produce such work.

the advertiser sets up a Web page, or places a banner ad on another company's Web page. Digital media also include many types of social media such as Facebook and YouTube. New software programs such as Flash and Quicktime make it easy to include video and audio.

For the agency producer, this presents exciting challenges and opportunities. The possibilities are endless. The challenge will be to keep current with the available technology and to learn how best to use technology to serve client needs.

The People Who Produce Digital Media Advertising

The ranks of production managers and producers are already swelling as media vehicles multiply.[13] New titles appearing on agency rosters: multimedia producers, directors, and technicians; interactive planners and writers; computer programmers and system designers; kiosk media buyers; and so on. At Saatchi & Saatchi, Nathan Hackstock was the creative director for integrated marketing. He and his staff of art directors, copywriters,

Nike exemplifies great digital media advertising, combining superb production and interactivity.

and producers, who specialize in creating interactive ads for Saatchi's clients, helped move toyota.com from the seventh most visited automotive Web site to number one. Outside the agencies are a host of new suppliers: interactive software developers, digital media-buying services, and so on.

The Production Process

The digital media production process is a hybrid of all the other processes we've discussed. That's because some digital media are akin to print and outdoor media (computer billboards and Web pages), while others are more closely associated with TV and radio.

Regardless of the medium, the production manager or producer goes through a planned sequence of activities: preproduction, production, and postproduction. Preproduction includes the planning, costing, and hiring activities. The production stage is when the artwork is created, the video and audio recorded, or the computer program developed. Postproduction includes the editing, duplicating, and distribution activities. The difference for digital media is in the details of activities in the production and postproduction stages.

How Digital Media Differ from Print and Electronic Media

Production costs for digital media can be quite expensive, depending on the advertiser's objectives. For example, a top-quality digital film for the Web can cost just as much, or

even more, than a 30-second commercial. For example, several years ago BMW developed a series of eight short Web films starring actor Clive Owen and featuring a roster of high-priced directors and talent (including Madonna, Ray Liotta, Gary Oldman, and Dennis Haysbert). The production budget for the spots was extremely expensive, for even a large advertiser like BMW.

But BMW could afford the high production costs because it cost the company next to nothing to use the Web to reach its intended audience. This is an important digital media advantage: advertisers enjoy big savings against costs associated with traditional media space or time. It costs a national advertiser hundreds of thousands of dollars each time a spot runs on a highly rated network show. By contrast, placing the ad on the Web has very little cost associated with it. And while the intrusiveness of television or print guarantees a large audience, digital ads can find their own viewers. BMW's short films, watched only on the Web, were seen over 11 million times in a four-month period.

Ads developed for digital media are also virtually unrestricted by space or time limits. The Carousel spot that was presented in the opening of Chapter 9 comes in at 2 minutes and 19 seconds. This is prohibitively long for a TV commercial, but poses no special problem for a digital ad. In a similar vein, the costs of a full-page newspaper or magazine ad are much more expensive than are those of a digital print ad or information at a Web site. Compared with traditional media, digital advertisers can provide prospects with more information and do so at a much lower price. ■

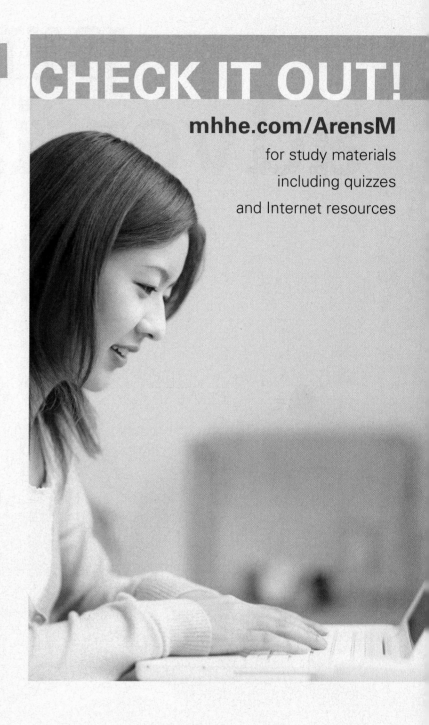

CHECK IT OUT!

mhhe.com/ArensM

for study materials

including quizzes

and Internet resources

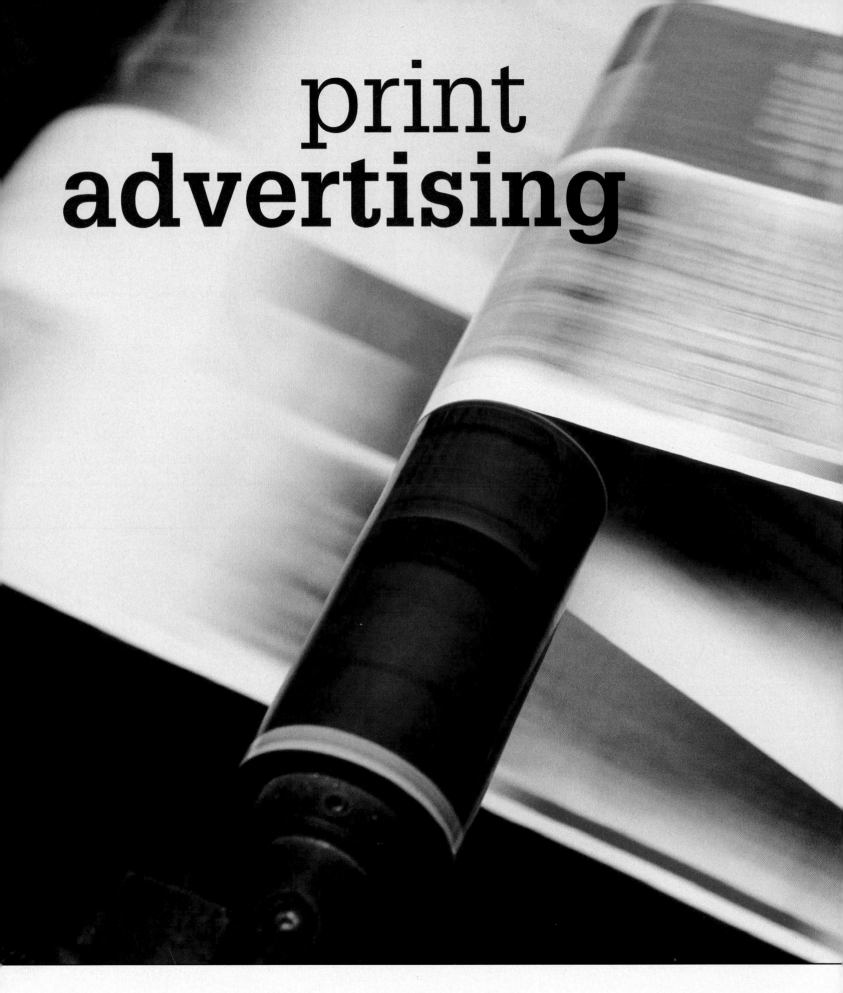

print
advertising

The majority of advertising directs its viewers to do something—buy a product, believe in a brand, desire a certain lifestyle. So *demarketing*, which tries to persuade audiences not to adopt certain behaviors, often sticks out like a sore thumb. And convincing teens—a rather independent-minded demographic—that something many of their friends are doing is not cool, is a huge challenge.

Such was the situation for the American Legacy Foundation, an organization created by the Master Settlement Agreement (MSA) signed by the big four tobacco companies: Philip Morris (Altria), Lorillard, R. J. Reynolds, and Brown & Williamson. American Legacy is responsible for using the money from a court settlement between the companies and state attorneys general to generate a demarketing campaign against tobacco products aimed at teenagers.[1]

The timing for such a campaign was ripe: following a decades-long reversal, teen smoking took a sharp rise in the 1990s. The number of younger teens smoking had increased by almost half, and smoking among high school seniors was up by about one-third.[2] Antismoking advocates were well aware that a major campaign was needed to shed some light on the facts about teen smoking.

Enter Miami-based agency Crispin Porter + Bogusky (CP + B). In 1997, the agency created the **truth**® campaign as part of a statewide antismoking initiative in Florida. And when the American Legacy Foundation began to receive funds from the settlement agreement with tobacco companies in 1999, it turned to CP+B to flesh out the campaign on a national scale.

continued on p. 280

LEARNING OBJECTIVES

LO1 Explain the advantages and disadvantages of magazine advertising.

LO2 Discuss how magazine circulation is measured and rates are set.

LO3 Explain the advantages and disadvantages of newspaper advertising.

LO4 Describe the major types of newspapers and newspaper advertising.

LO5 Discuss the various ways newspapers charge for advertising.

LO6 Explain the unique roles played by directory and Yellow Pages advertising.

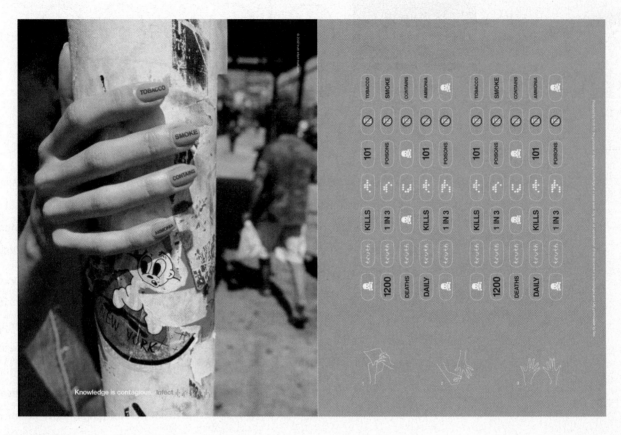

continued from p. 279

To get a better understanding of why teens smoke and what sorts of antismoking messages would appeal to them, CP+B staffers hit the streets at night and talked to teens. Learning that conventional scare tactics only made teens want to smoke more, the agency came to believe that it had to adopt the same tactics as its opponent in order to succeed. Acknowledging that cigarette brands mesh well with teens' desire to express themselves, their allegiance to brands, and their willingness to take risks, creative director Alex Bogusky created an anti-brand named **truth**® to capture teens' attention and sway them from smoking.[3]

In early 2000, the American Legacy Foundation launched **truth**®, which quickly became the largest national youth-focused anti-tobacco education campaign ever. Instead of trying to scare kids straight, the spots presented the absurdities behind the marketing tactics of what they called "Big Tobacco" with an infectious energy and let teens make up their own minds about the tobacco companies.

Was Alex Bogusky right—could speaking to teens using "the **truth**®" really make a difference? It seems so. Monitoring the Future, a comprehensive substance abuse survey, cited the **truth**® campaign in explaining a sharp decline in cigarette smoking among eighth, tenth, and twelfth graders. From 2000 to 2002, the number of high school cigarette smokers dropped by more than 1 million.[4]

The **truth**® Web site quotes some similarly impressive statistics: 75 percent of 12- to 17-year-olds in the United States—a total of 21 million teens—can accurately describe one or more of the **truth**® ads. An even greater number of teens said that the **truth**® ad they saw was convincing. And a slightly smaller number reported that the **truth**® ad gave them good reasons not to smoke.[5]

"Despite a decline in funding, **truth**® continues to successfully share with American youth the facts about tobacco and the ways the tobacco industry markets its products towards them," said Dr. Cheryl Healton, president and CEO of the American Legacy Foundation. "More than 1,200 Americans die every day from tobacco-related diseases, from cancers and heart disease to emphysema and stroke. By educating young people, **truth**® hopes to bring that sad and tragic statistic to an end."[6]

SELECTING MEDIA

Selecting the most appropriate media mix for an advertising campaign requires two distinct skills: understanding the unique characteristics of the various media alternatives and determining which medium will most efficiently and effectively reach the campaign's target audience.

These chapters in Part 5 will discuss the unique elements of the most common media classes. Then, in Chapter 15, we will examine how media planners and buyers decide which media to use, when to use them, and how to purchase them. In that chapter, we will also discuss audience measurements. For now, it will help if you have a basic understanding of two key terms: *reach*—the number of different people exposed, at least once, to a medium during a given period of time; and *frequency*—the average number of times those people are exposed to that medium during that period of time.

Understanding the characteristics of media options is important not only to media planners and buyers; account managers, planners, and creatives must also have an appreciation for the strengths and weaknesses of each medium so they can develop strategies and executions that will take full advantage of their alternatives.

PRINT MEDIA

Print advertising certainly includes magazines and newspapers, but it could include any message that is produced on printed surfaces, such as brochures, directories, mail, posters, and outdoor boards. All print advertising has several unique elements in common. Compared to television or radio, print advertising has more permanence. Since it stays around for awhile, it may be read more than once or passed along to other readers. People also tend to spend more time with print advertising, so it provides an opportunity to present more detailed information and longer explanations.

Obviously, print advertising can be an important ingredient in the **media mix**, the combination of media types that work together to most effectively deliver an advertiser's message. In this chapter, we'll examine the characteristics of magazines and newspapers. Other forms of print media will be discussed in Chapters 13 and 14.

LO1 Explain the advantages and disadvantages of magazine advertising.

USING MAGAZINES IN THE MEDIA MIX

Advertisers use magazines in their media mix for many reasons. That's why it's the second-largest medium (after television) in terms of advertising revenue, receiving 20.1 percent of the dollars spent by advertisers in the United States.[7] First and foremost, magazines allow an advertiser to reach a particular target audience with a high-quality presentation. The American Legacy Foundation is just one of the many leading advertisers that use magazines as an important element of their creative mix. (Exhibit 11–1 lists the top U.S. magazine advertisers.)

media mix
The combination of media types that work together to most effectively deliver an advertiser's message.

The Pros and Cons of Magazine Advertising

Magazines offer a wide variety of benefits to advertisers. The **truth**® campaign benefited greatly from the outstanding color reproduction available only from magazines. Further, by running in culture magazines such as *Vibe* and *Vogue Teen*, read by teens of different lifestyles and ages, the American Legacy Foundation was able to precisely target its audience. Magazines offer a host of other features too: flexible design options, prestige, authority, believability, and long shelf life. Magazines may sit on a coffee table for months and be reread many times. People can read a magazine ad at their leisure; they can pore over the details of a photograph; and they can study carefully the information presented in the copy. This makes it an ideal medium for high-involvement think and feel products.

However, like every medium, magazines also have a number of drawbacks (see My Ad Campaign 11–A, "The Pros and Cons of Magazine Advertising"). They are expensive (on a cost-per-reader basis), especially for color ads. And since they typically come out only monthly, or weekly at best, it's difficult to reach a large audience quickly or frequently. For these reasons, many advertisers use magazines in combination with other media—such as newspapers, which we'll discuss later in this chapter (see Commercial Break 11–A, "Magazines and the Media Mix").

▼ **EXHIBIT 11–1** Top 10 Magazine Advertisers in the United States, 2009

Rank	Advertiser	Magazine Ad Spending ($ millions)
1	Procter & Gamble Co.	$949,073
2	L'Oréal SA	382,165
3	Johnson & Johnson	311,019
4	Kraft Foods Inc.	289,840
5	Unilever	268,892
6	General Motors Corp.	265,023
7	Pfizer Inc.	259,122
8	Time Warner Inc.	221,902
9	Merck & Co. Inc.	206,391
10	Clorox Co.	175,771

Source: PIB, data as of January 8, 2010, © Magazine Publishers of America, http://www.magazine.org/ADVERTISING/HANDBOOK/Top_50_ADV_2009.aspx.

Special Possibilities with Magazines

Media planners and buyers need to be aware of the many creative possibilities magazines offer advertisers through various technical or mechanical features. These include bleed pages, cover positions, inserts and gatefolds, and special sizes, such as junior pages and island halves.

When the dark or colored background of the ad extends to the edge of the page (like the **truth®** ad at the beginning of this chapter), it is said to **bleed** off the page. Most magazines offer bleed pages, but they charge 10 to 15 percent more for them. The advantages of bleeds include greater flexibility in expressing the advertising idea, a slightly larger printing area, and more dramatic impact.

If a company plans to advertise in a particular magazine consistently, it may seek a highly desirable **cover position**. Few publishers sell ads on the front cover, commonly called the *first cover*. They do however sell the inside front, inside back, and outside back covers (the *second, third,* and *fourth covers,* respectively), usually at a substantial premium.

A less expensive way to use magazine space is to place the ad in unusual places on the page or dramatically across spreads. A **junior unit** is a large ad (60 percent of the page) placed in the middle of a page and surrounded with editorial matter. Similar to junior units are **island halves**, surrounded by

The Pros and Cons of Magazine Advertising [11–A]

The Pros
- **Flexibility** in readership and advertising. Magazines cover the full range of prospects; they have a wide choice of regional and national coverage and a variety of lengths, approaches, and editorial tones.
- **Color** gives readers visual pleasure, and color reproduction is best in slick magazines. Color enhances image and identifies the package. In short, it sells.
- **Authority and believability** enhance the commercial message. TV, radio, and newspapers offer lots of information but lack the depth needed for readers to gain knowledge or meaning; magazines often offer all three.
- **Permanence,** or long shelf life, gives the reader time to appraise ads in detail, allowing a more complete education/sales message and the opportunity to communicate the total corporate personality.
- **Prestige** for products advertised in upscale or specialty magazines such as *Architectural Digest, Connoisseur,* and *Town and Country.*
- **Audience selectivity** is more efficient in magazines than any other medium except direct mail. The predictable, specialized editorial environment selects the audience and enables advertisers to pinpoint their sales campaigns. Examples: golfers (*Golf Digest*), businesspeople (*BusinessWeek*), 20-something males (*Details*), or teenage girls (*Seventeen*).
- **Cost efficiency** because wasted circulation is minimized. Print networks give advertisers reduced prices for advertising in two or more network publications.
- **Selling power** of magazines is proven, and results are usually measurable.
- **Reader loyalty** that sometimes borders on fanaticism.
- **Extensive pass-along readership.** Many people may read the magazine after the initial purchaser.
- **Merchandising assistance.** Advertisers can generate reprints and merchandising materials that help them get more mileage out of their ad campaigns.

The Cons
- **Lack of immediacy** that advertisers can get with newspapers or radio.
- **Shallow geographic coverage.** They don't offer the national reach of broadcast media.
- **Inability to deliver mass audiences at a low price.** Magazines are very costly for reaching broad masses of people.
- **Inability to deliver high frequency.** Since most magazines come out only monthly or weekly, the advertiser can build frequency faster than reach by adding numerous small-audience magazines to the schedule.
- **Long lead time** for ad insertion, sometimes two to three months.
- **Heavy advertising competition.** The largest-circulation magazines have 52 percent advertising to 48 percent editorial content.
- **High cost per thousand.** Average black-and-white cost per thousand (CPM) in national consumer magazines is high; some trade publications with highly selective audiences have a CPM over $50 for a black-and-white page.
- **Declining circulations,** especially in single-copy sales, is an industrywide trend that limits an advertiser's reach.

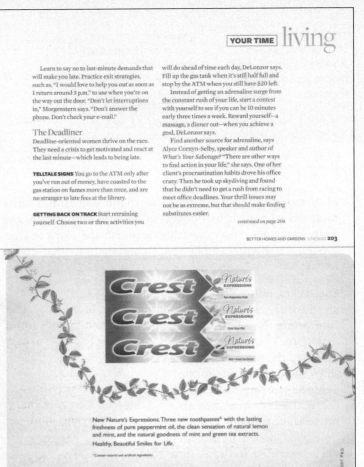

The opportunity to be creative is not limited to copywriters and art directors. Media planners and buyers can increase an ad's impact by exploring creative media buys. Crest toothpaste has made an impact greater than that which would be achieved by a full-page ad by purchasing staggered horizontal half-pages and developing an advertisement to effectively utilize that space.

> Print advertising is an ideal medium for high-involvement products.

Magazines and the Media Mix [11–A]

Read the My Ad Campaign 11–A, "The Pros and Cons of Magazine Advertising," and see if you can apply that information to the following situation:

You manage an elegant French restaurant in Los Angeles that is known for its intimate setting, excellent service, and a lovely outdoor garden patio. You decide to build the business by promoting the special ambience your restaurant offers. To enhance the sense of romance, you plan to give away a long-stem rose and a glass of champagne with each entrée. Your clientele consists primarily of wealthy, educated business leaders and celebrities. However, a growing segment of your customers are tourists and middle-class couples out for a special evening.

Applying the Breaks

1. Are magazines the best way to advertise this special? If not, explain why. If so, explain why and include which specific magazines would be best.

2. How can magazine advertising help you build the restaurant's image?

even more editorial matter. The island sometimes costs more than a regular half-page, but because it dominates the page, many advertisers consider it worth the extra charge. Exhibit 11–2 shows other space combinations that create impact.

Sometimes, rather than buying a standard page, an advertiser uses an **insert**. The advertiser prints the ad on high-quality paper stock to add weight and drama to the message, and then ships the finished ads to the publisher for insertion into the magazine at a special price. Another option is multiple-page inserts. Calvin Klein once promoted its jeans in a 116-page insert in *Vanity Fair*. The insert reportedly cost more than $1 million, but the news reports about it in major daily newspapers gave the campaign enormous publicity value.

A **gatefold** is an insert whose paper is so wide that the extreme left and right sides have to be folded into the center to match the size of the other pages. When the reader opens the magazine, the folded page swings out like a gate to present the ad. Not all magazines provide gatefolds, and they are always sold at a substantial premium. Commercial Break 11–B discusses other innovations in magazine advertising.

HOW MAGAZINES ARE CATEGORIZED

In the jargon of the trade, magazines are called *books*, and media planners and buyers commonly categorize them by content, geography, and size.

Content One of the most dramatic developments in publishing is the emergence of magazines with special content, which has given many of them good prospects for long-term growth. The broadest classifications of content are *consumer magazines, farm magazines,* and *business magazines.* Each may be broken down into hundreds of categories.

- **Consumer magazines**, purchased for entertainment, information, or both, are edited for consumers who buy products for their own personal consumption: *Time,*

▼ **EXHIBIT 11–2** An ad's position on the page influences its effectiveness. The size and shape of the ad often determine where it will fall on the page. These eight two-page spreads show most of the positions a fractional ad can take.

Facing horizontal half-pages to dominate a spread

Vertical halves across the gutter with the same objective

Checkerboard facing a half-page ad

Staggered horizontal half-pages

Outside halves of a spread

Checkerboard (multiple small space units on a single page)

Staircase units and double staircases on facing pages

Island spread

Innovations in Magazine Advertising [11–B]

Magazines work closely with advertisers to develop new technologies for presenting ideas and products. From these efforts have come such innovations as fragrance strips, color strips, pop-up ads, and 3-D ads.

Fragrance strips are a great favorite with perfume advertisers. With the Scentstrip, readers sample a scent by opening a sealed insert tucked into a magazine. Despite some consumer complaints, Scentstrips have proved incredibly popular. Fragrances are useful for other products as well. For example, a Rolls-Royce ad in *Architectural Digest* carried a Scentstrip bearing the essence of leather. For a St. Mungo's (London's largest homeless charity) ad, Saatchi & Saatchi played on consumers' expectations that Scentstrips accompany only ads for luxury goods. The urine-scented ad drove shocked readers to St. Mungo's Web site, where they could make a donation. The campaign won a Bronze Lion at Cannes.

Cosmetics manufacturers insert **color strip** samples of eye shadow, blush, lipstick, and other makeup that readers can try immediately. Color strips are expensive to produce, but many advertisers think they're worth it.

Another costly innovation is the **pop-up ad**. Corporate advertisers such as Honeywell and TransAmerica were among the first to try this eye-catching approach. Product ads, such as a pop-up for the Dodge Dakota, followed.

Other intriguing approaches include **3-D ads** (complete with 3-D glasses), product samples (facial tissues and paper towels), and unusual shapes and sizes for preprinted inserts. An ad for Sara Lee cheesecake used a single heavy-stock page with what appeared to be a bite taken out of a life-size cheesecake slice. A half-page insert for Gleem toothpaste featured a metallic graphic of a mirror with the slogan "Check your mirror."

Researchers are probing the possibilities of holograms and ads that talk when readers pass a device across the page. Already ads can sing—liquor companies included microchips that played Christmas carols in their December magazine ads, and ads for a cigarette brand played "Happy Birthday" on the brand's 75th anniversary.

Recently, Global Commerce Group invented the Web Decoder, a

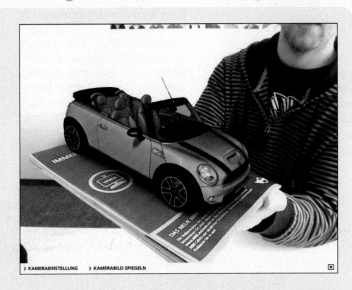

transparent device made of clear polyester Mylar. The recipient is invited to interact with an image on a Web site. When the piece is positioned over the designated image, a hidden word, icon, or phrase is revealed. Advertisers can tailor the Web Decoder to their specific promotional needs, from cents-off coupons to instant-winner prizes.

And in early 2008 the final "sense" barrier was broken when Welch's sponsored a "Peel 'n Taste" flavor strip that appeared in *People* magazine. Now homemakers, the target of the ad, could actually taste the concord grape flavor of Welch's Grape Juice.

The ad above uses a technology called Augmented Reality to display a 3-D model of a MINI convertible simply by holding the ad up to your computer's webcam. The image of the model turns as you pivot the ad.

Such innovative approaches not only attract readers' attention but also involve them in the experience by appealing to more than just the visual sense.

Applying the Breaks
What products besides cars could Augmented Reality be used to advertise?

farm publications

Magazines directed to farmers and their families or to companies that manufacture or sell agricultural equipment, supplies, and services.

business magazines

The largest category of magazines, which target business readers and include *trade publications* for retailers, wholesalers, and other distributors; *industrial magazines* for businesspeople involved in manufacturing and services; and *professional journals* for lawyers, physicians, architects, and other professionals.

Sports Illustrated, Glamour, Good Housekeeping. One would expect to see the **truth**® anti-tobacco ads in consumer magazines.

- **Farm publications** are directed to farmers and their families or to companies that manufacture or sell agricultural equipment, supplies, and services: *Farm Journal, Progressive Farmer, Prairie Farmer, Successful Farming.*

- **Business magazines**, by far the largest category, target business readers. They include *trade publications* for retailers, wholesalers, and other distributors (*Progressive Grocer, Bakery News*); *business* and *industrial magazines* for businesspeople involved in manufacturing and services (*Electronic Design,*

American Banker); and *professional journals* for lawyers, physicians, architects, and other professionals (*Archives of Ophthalmology*).

Geography A magazine may also be classified as *local, regional,* or *national.* Today, most major U.S. cities have a **local city magazine**: *San Diego Magazine, New York, Los Angeles, Chicago, Palm Springs Life.* Their readership is usually upscale business and professional people interested in local arts, fashion, and business.

Regional publications are targeted to a specific area of the country, such as the West or the South: *Sunset, Southern Living.* National magazines sometimes provide special market runs for specific geographic regions. *Time, Newsweek, Woman's Day,* and *Sports Illustrated* allow advertisers to buy a single major market. Exhibit 11–3 shows the 10 major geographic editions of *Reader's Digest.* This is important for local or regional advertisers who want the benefit of advertising in larger, more well-known publications while staying geographically relevant to the audience that may be reading the magazine.

National magazines range from those with enormous circulations, such as *TV Guide,* to small, lesser-known national

▼**EXHIBIT 11–3** Advertisers benefit from selecting regional editions similar to the 10 geographic editions of *Reader's Digest* shown on the map. With regional binding and mailing, advertisers can buy ad space for only the areas of distribution they need.

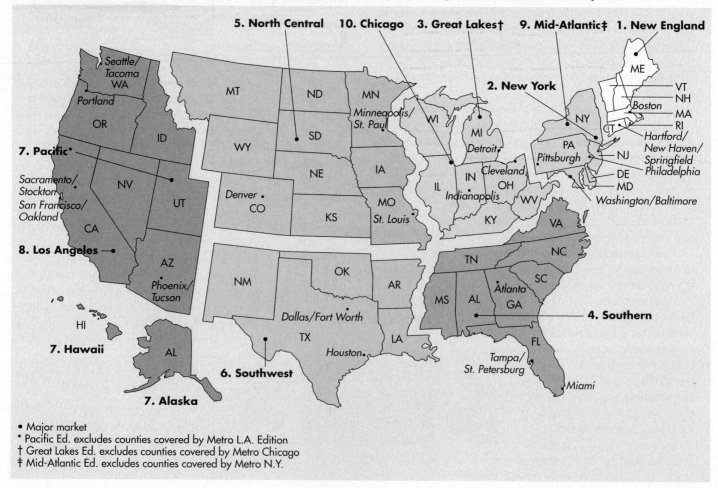

- Major market
- * Pacific Ed. excludes counties covered by Metro L.A. Edition
- † Great Lakes Ed. excludes counties covered by Metro Chicago
- ‡ Mid-Atlantic Ed. excludes counties covered by Metro N.Y.

magazines, such as *Nature* and *Volleyball Monthly*. The largest circulation magazine in the United States today is *AARP The Magazine*, distributed to the 24 million–member households of the American Association of Retired Persons.

Size

It doesn't take a genius to figure out that magazines come in different shapes and sizes, but it might take one to figure out how to get one ad to run in different size magazines and still look the same. Magazine sizes run the gamut, which can make production standardization a nightmare. The most common magazine sizes follow:

Size Classification	Magazine	Approximate Size of Full-Page Ad
Large	*Spin, Interview*	4 col. × 170 lines (9½ × 11⅓ inches)
Flat	*Time, Newsweek*	3 col. × 140 lines (7 × 10 inches)
Standard	*National Geographic*	2 col. × 119 lines (6 × 8½ inches)
Small or pocket	*Reader's Digest, Jet*	2 col. × 91 lines (4½ × 6½ inches)

check yourself ✓

1. Why do you think media planners and buyers need to be aware of the many creative possibilities offered by magazines?

2. If you were the media planner, what magazines would you consider for the **truth®** anti-tobacco print campaign?

L02 Discuss how magazine circulation is measured and rates are set.

BUYING MAGAZINE SPACE

When analyzing a media vehicle, media planners and buyers consider readership, cost, mechanical requirements, and ad closing dates (deadlines). To buy effectively, they must thoroughly understand the magazine's circulation and rate-card information.

Magazines that cater to specific geographic areas are considered local or regional publications. Sunset *magazine focuses its distribution in 13 western states, offering its readers information relevant to western climates, lifestyles, architecture, and food preferences. Marketers can target even more precisely by advertising in* Sunset's *regional or metro editions.*

Understanding Magazine Circulation

The first step in analyzing a publication's potential effectiveness is to assess its audience. The buyer studies circulation statistics, primary and secondary readership, subscription and vendor sales, and any special merchandising services the magazine offers.

Guaranteed versus Delivered Circulation A magazine's rates are largely based on its circulation. The **rate base** is the circulation figure on which the publisher bases its rates. It is generally equivalent to the **guaranteed circulation**, the minimum number of copies the publisher expects to

circulation audit
Thorough analysis of circulation procedures, distribution outlets, and other distribution factors by a company such as the Audit Bureau of Circulations (ABC).

horizontal publications Business publications targeted at people with particular job functions that cut across industry lines, such as *Purchasing* magazine.

paid-circulation
The total number of copies of an average issue of a newspaper or magazine that are distributed through subscriptions and newsstand sales.

Audit Bureau of Circulations (ABC)
An organization supported by advertising agencies, advertisers, and publishers that verifies circulation and other marketing data on newspapers and magazines for the benefit of its members.

primary circulation
The number of people who receive a publication, whether through direct purchase or subscription.

secondary (pass-along) readership
The number of people who read a publication in addition to the primary purchasers.

vertical publication
Business publications aimed at people in a specific industry; for example, *Restaurants & Institutions*.

circulate. This assures advertisers they will reach a certain number of people. If the publisher does not deliver its guaranteed figure, it must provide a refund. For that reason, guaranteed circulation figures are often stated safely below the average actual circulation.

Media buyers expect publications to verify their circulation figures. Publishers pay thousands of dollars each year for a **circulation audit**—a thorough analysis of the circulation procedures, outlets of distribution, readers, and other factors—by companies such as the **Audit Bureau of Circulations (ABC)**. Circulation actually gets overstated more often than people think. As many as 30 percent of consumer magazines audited by the ABC each year don't meet the circulation levels they guarantee to advertisers.[8]

Primary and Secondary Readership
Primary circulation represents the number of people who buy the publication, either by subscription or at the newsstand. **Secondary** (or **pass-along**) **readership**, which is an estimate determined by market research of how many people read a single issue of a publication, is very important to magazines. Some have more than six readers per copy. Multiplying the average pass-along readership by, say, a million subscribers can give a magazine a substantial audience beyond its primary readers.

Vertical and Horizontal Publications
There are two readership classifications of business publications: *vertical* and *horizontal*. A **vertical publication** covers a specific industry in all its aspects. For example, Cahners Publishing produces *Restaurants & Institutions* strictly for restaurateurs and food-service operators. The magazine's editorial content includes everything from news of the restaurant industry to institutional-size recipes.

Horizontal publications, in contrast, deal with a particular job function across a variety of industries. Readers of *Purchasing* work in purchasing management in many different industries. Horizontal trade publications are very effective advertising vehicles because they usually offer excellent reach and they tend to be well read.[9]

Subscription and Vendor Sales
Media buyers also want to know a magazine's ratio of subscriptions to newsstand sales. Today, subscriptions account for the majority of magazine sales. Newsstands (which include bookstore chains) are still a

major outlet for single-copy sales, but no outlet can handle more than a fraction of the many magazines available.

From the advertiser's point of view, newsstand sales are impressive because they indicate that the purchaser really wants the magazine and is not merely subscribing out of habit. However, according to the Magazine Publishers Association, single-copy sales accounted for only 10.4 percent of total magazine sales in 2009.[10]

Paid and Controlled Circulation Business publications may be distributed on either a *paid-circulation* or

Advertising Age is a good example of a vertical publication. The magazine is geared toward a variety of issues specific to the advertising industry. Unlike horizontal publications, which focus on a single job function across various industries, Ad Age *is read by people in a wide range of functions throughout the advertising industry.*

controlled-circulation basis. A paid basis means the recipient must pay the subscription price to receive the magazine. *BusinessWeek* is a **paid-circulation** business magazine.

In **controlled circulation**, the publisher mails the magazine free to individuals who the publisher thinks can influence the purchase of advertised products. For example, individuals responsible for packaging their company's products can receive a free subscription to *Packaging Digest* magazine. To qualify for the subscription list, people must indicate in writing a desire to receive it and must give their professional designation or occupation. Dues-paying members of organizations often get free subscriptions. For example, members of the National Association for Female Executives receive free copies of *Executive Female*.

Publishers of paid-circulation magazines say subscribers who pay are more likely to read a publication than those who receive it free. But controlled-circulation magazines can reach good prospects for the goods and services they advertise.

crease the effectiveness of its ads.[11] Magazines offer great potential for relationship marketing since they already have a relationship with their subscribers.

Reading Rate Cards

Magazine rate cards follow a fairly standard format. This helps advertisers determine costs, discounts, mechanical requirements, closing dates, special editions, and additional costs for features like color, inserts, bleed pages, split runs, or preferred positions.

Three dates affect magazine purchases. The **cover date** is the date printed on the cover. The **on-sale date** is the date the magazine is actually issued. And the **closing date** is the date all ad material must be in the publisher's hands for a specific issue. Lead time may be as much as three months.

Rates As we will discuss in Chapter 15, one way to compare magazines is to look at how much it costs to reach a thousand

> ## Newsstand sales are impressive because they indicate that the purchaser really wants the magazine.

Merchandising Services: Added Value Magazines, and newspapers too, often provide liberal added-value services to their regular advertisers, such as:

- Special, free promotions to retail stores.
- Marketing services to help readers find local outlets.
- Response cards that allow readers to request brochures and catalogs.
- Help handling sales force, broker, wholesaler, and retailer meetings.
- Advance copies for the trade.
- Marketing research into brand preferences, consumer attitudes, and market conditions.

If a publication's basic characteristics—editorial, circulation, and readership—are strong, these additional services can in-

people based on the magazine's rates for a one-time, full-page ad. You compute the **cost per thousand (CPM)** by dividing the full-page rate by the number of thousands of subscribers:

$$\frac{\text{Page rate}}{(\text{Circulation} \div 1,000)} = \text{CPM}$$

If the magazine's black-and-white page rate is $10,000, and the publication has a circulation of 500,000, then:

$$\frac{\$10,000}{(500,000 \div 1,000)} = \frac{\$10,000}{500} = \$20 \text{ CPM}$$

Consider this comparison. In 2010, the page rate for a full-color, one-page ad in *Car & Driver* was $187,269 on a rate base of 1,300,000; *Road & Track* offered the same ad for $109,373 on a rate base of 700,000. Which was the better buy on a CPM basis?[12]

Advertising rates

Full run and regional editions

	FULL RUN	PACIFIC NORTHWEST	NORTHERN CALIFORNIA	SOUTHERN CALIFORNIA
Rate base	1,250,000	270,000	350,000	315,000
4-COLOR				
Full page	$106,190	$39,700	$48,020	$48,090
⅔ page	$80,160	$29,980	$36,250	$36,300
½ page	$64,180	$24,000	$29,020	$29,050
⅓ page	$46,490	$17,390	$21,030	$21,060
BLACK-AND-WHITE				
Full page	$76,510	$28,560	$34,550	$34,590
⅔ page	$57,760	$21,570	$26,080	$26,110
½ page	$46,240	$17,260	$20,880	$20,900
⅓ page	$33,500	$12,510	$15,130	$15,150
COVERS				
4th cover	$138,040			
3rd cover	$116,810			
2nd cover	$127,420			

These rates and all advertising transactions are subject to the 2010 Advertising terms and conditions of Sunset Publishing Corporation.

2010 Publishing calendar

ISSUE	NATIONAL SPACE CLOSE, MATERIALS DUE	REGIONAL SPACE CLOSE, MATERIALS DUE	ON SALE
January	November 2	October 26	December 18
February	December 1	November 24	January 22
March	January 4	December 28	February 19
April	February 1	January 25	March 19
May	March 1	February 22	April 23
*Summer Trips**	March 11		May 7
June	April 1	March 25	May 21
July	May 3	April 26	June 18
August	June 1	May 26	July 23
September	July 1	June 24	August 20
*Weekend Trips**	July 7		September 3
October	August 2	July 26	September 24
November	September 1	August 25	October 22
December	October 1	September 24	November 19

*Special Interest Publication: All ad space available

Regional advertising coverage

PACIFIC NORTHWEST edition includes Alaska, British Columbia, Idaho, Oregon, and Washington.

NORTHERN CALIFORNIA edition extends from the Oregon border south to the counties of Fresno, Inyo, Kings, Mono, Monterey, and Tulare. Includes all of Nevada except Clark County.

SOUTHERN CALIFORNIA edition includes Imperial, Kern, Los Angeles, Orange, Riverside, San Bernardino, San Diego, San Luis Obispo, Santa Barbara, and Ventura counties, and Hawaii.

FULL RUN edition includes circulation in all 13 Western states, as well as national circulation.

This partial rate card for Sunset Magazine *(www.sunset.com) shows the closing and on-sale dates for each issue. Notice the special pricing for black-and-white ads, cover positions, and regional editions. Other options, discounts, and requirements are described on the complete rate card.*

▼ **EXHIBIT 11–4** Circulation and advertising costs for the 5 highest circulation U.S. consumer magazines (2010).

Magazine	Total Paid Circulation	Page Cost for a Four-Color Ad	CPM (cost per thousand)
AARP, The Magazine	24,371,637	$532,600	$21.85
AARP Bulletin	24,042,603	532,600	22.15
Better Homes & Gardens	7,621,786	468,200	61.43
Reader's Digest	7,114,955	241,800	33.98
Good Housekeeping	4,652,904	344,475	74.03

Exhibit 11–4 lists the circulations, color page rates, and CPMs for the five highest circulation consumer magazines.

Discounts Magazines and newspapers often give discounts. **Frequency discounts** are based on the number of ad insertions, usually within a year; **volume discounts** are based on the total amount of space bought during a specific period. Most magazines also offer *cash discounts* (usually 2 percent) to advertisers who pay right away, and some offer discounts on the purchase of four or more consecutive pages in a single issue. In fact, many magazine publishers now negotiate their rates. According to Harold Shain, executive VP/publisher of *Newsweek*, "Every piece of business is negotiated."[13]

Premium Rates Magazines charge extra for special features. Color printing normally costs 25 to 60 percent more than black and white. Bleed pages can add as much as 20 percent to regular rates, although the typical increase is about 15 percent.

Second and third cover rates (the inside covers) typically cost less than the fourth (back) cover. For example, in 2010 *Good Housekeeping* charged $344,475 for a normal color page and $430,585 and $413,370 for the second and third covers, respectively, but it charged $492,585 for the fourth cover.[14]

Magazines charge different rates for ads in geographic or demographic issues. **Geographic editions** target geographic markets; **demographic editions** reach readers

who share a demographic trait, such as age, income level, or professional status. *Newsweek* offers one-page, four-color ads in its Dallas edition for $18,150 (circulation only 25,000). For full-page, four-color ads, advertisers in *Newsweek Woman* pay $66,000 (circulation 600,000 female subscribers). To run the same ad nationally, advertisers pay $165,000 (circulation 1.5 million).[15]

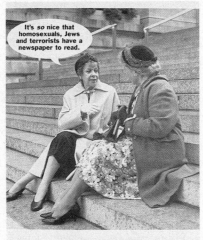

It's *so* nice that homosexuals, Jews and terrorists have a newspaper to read.

the village **VOICE**
NOT AMERICA'S FAVORITE PAPER

Newspapers are an important medium in the media mix, second only to television in advertising volume, but costing much less. This ad for the Village Voice *(www. villagevoice.com) shows how a niche business can use newspaper advertising to expand sales. Mimicking the freewheeling tone of the newspaper, the advertiser targeted those who already read the* Village Voice *but were not subscribers.*

USING NEWSPAPERS IN THE MEDIA MIX

When a small, alternative newspaper in Manhattan asked one of the newest and hottest creative shops in the city for help in promoting subscriptions, it had no idea what the little agency with the funny name, Mad Dogs & Englishmen, would do for it.

The *Village Voice* newspaper had always knocked the Establishment with its radical coverage of social issues, politics, media, and culture. So perhaps it shouldn't have come as a surprise when the Mad Dogs took the newspaper's own prose style and turned it around in a series of impertinent, self-mocking ads.

"Hell, I wouldn't have my home contaminated with a subscription to your elitist rag if you were giving away five-speed blenders," rants one ad in the series. "You people think New York is the friggin' center of the world." But then a second paragraph offers a dramatic alternative: "YES, I want to buy a year's subscription to the *Village Voice*," along with a coupon.

Selecting the medium was easy. Because most people who would be interested in a subscription are *Village Voice* readers, the campaign ran in the paper itself. It proved to be a wise choice. In the first year of the campaign, the *Voice* saw a 30 percent increase in its subscriber base, surpassing all expectations.[16]

Who Uses Newspapers?

Newspapers are now the third-largest medium (after television and magazines) in terms of advertising volume, receiving 17.7 percent of the dollars spent by advertisers in the United States.[17]

Consider these important facts:

- Approximately half of all adults (nearly 100 million) read a daily newspaper. Just over half (55.4 percent) read the Sunday edition.[18]

- The main news is the most widely read section among adult daily newspaper readers at 87 percent.[19]

- In 2008, there were 1,408 daily newspapers in the United States, with a total circulation of 48.6 million, off 6.2 percent over the past five years. The same year, the nation's 902 Sunday newspapers had a circulation of 49.1 million.[20]

- In May 2010, more than 123 million individuals viewed newspaper Web sites. They viewed an average of 43 pages per person.[21]

- Spending on print newspaper advertising in 2009 totaled $24.8 billion, a decline of 45 percent in only six years. However, ad spending on newspaper Web sites has grown to $2.7 billion, up 125 percent in the same period.[22]

www.naa.org

Although the newspaper is the major community-serving medium for both news and advertising, more and more national advertisers are shifting to radio and television. As a result, radio and TV carry most of the national advertising in the United States, while 84 percent of newspaper advertising revenue comes from local advertising. As Exhibit 11–5 shows, retail, cellular phone, and cable companies are the primary advertisers in newspapers.

LO3 Explain the advantages and disadvantages of newspaper advertising.

The Pros and Cons of Newspaper Advertising

The *Village Voice* promotion shows how small businesses with even smaller budgets can benefit from creative newspaper advertising. Print ads in general and newspapers in particular provide a unique, flexible medium for advertisers to express their creativity—especially with businesses that rely on local customers.

Newspapers offer advertisers many advantages. One of the most important is timeliness; an ad can appear very quickly, sometimes in just one day. Newspapers also offer geographic targeting, a broad range of markets, reasonable cost, and more. But newspapers suffer from lack of selectivity, poor production quality, and clutter. And readers criticize them for lack of depth and follow-up on important issues.[23]

Use the My Ad Campaign 11–B, "The Pros and Cons of Newspaper Advertising," to answer the questions in Commercial Break 11–C, "Newspapers and the Media Mix."

check yourself ✓

1. Why do you suspect spending on print newspaper advertising is declining so dramatically? Where is that ad money going?

▼ **EXHIBIT 11–5** Top 10 newspaper advertisers in the United States (2008).

Rank	Advertiser	Newspaper Ad Spending in 2008 ($ in millions)
1	Verizon Communications	$686.7
2	Macy's	609.7
3	Sprint Nextel Corp.	460.6
4	AT&T	328.3
5	Time Warner	311.6
6	Fry's Electronics	229.3
7	Procter & Gamble	213.7
8	Sears Holding Co.	200.7
9	General Electric	200.7
10	Walt Disney	185.2

daily newspaper
Often called *dailies*, these newspapers are published at least five times a week, in either morning or evening editions.

weekly newspapers
Newspapers that are published once a week and characteristically serve readers in small urban or suburban areas or farm communities with an emphasis on local news and advertising.

standard-size newspaper The standard newspaper size, measures approximately 22 inches deep and 13 inches wide and is divided into six columns.

tabloid newspaper
A newspaper generally about half the size of standard-sized newspaper; it is usually about 14 inches deep and 11 inches wide.

LO4 Describe the major types of newspapers and newspaper advertising.

How Newspapers Are Categorized

Newspapers can be classified by frequency of *delivery, physical size,* or *type of audience.*

Frequency of Delivery A **daily newspaper** is published as either a morning or evening edition at least five times a week, Monday through Friday. Of the 1,408 dailies in the United States, 546 are evening papers and 872 are morning papers. (The total exceeds 1,408 because 10 "all day" newspapers print both morning and evening editions.)[24] Morning editions

tend to have broader geographic circulation and a larger male readership; evening editions are read more by women.

With their emphasis on local news and advertising, **weekly newspapers** characteristically serve small urban or suburban residential areas and farm communities. They are now the fastest-growing class of newspapers. A weekly newspaper's cost per thousand is usually higher than a daily paper's, but a weekly has a longer life and often has more readers per copy.

Physical Size There are two basic newspaper formats, standard size and tabloid. The **standard-size newspaper** is about 22 inches deep and 13 inches wide and is divided into six columns. The **tabloid newspaper** is generally about 14 inches deep and 11 inches wide. National tabloid newspapers such as the *National Enquirer* and the *Star* use sensational stories to fight for single-copy sales. Other tabloids, such as the *New York Daily News,* emphasize straight news and features.

The Pros and Cons of Newspaper Advertising [11–B]

The Pros
- **Mass medium** penetrating every segment of society. Most consumers read the newspaper.
- **Local medium** with broad reach. Covers a specific geographic area that comprises both a market and a community of people sharing common concerns and interest.
- **Comprehensive in scope,** covering an extraordinary variety of topics and interests.
- **Geographic selectivity** is possible with zoned editions for specific neighborhoods or communities.
- **Timeliness.** Papers primarily cover today's news and are read in one day.
- **Credibility.** Studies show that newspaper ads rank highest in believability. TV commercials are a distant second.
- **Selective attention** from the relatively small number of active prospects who, on any given day, are interested in what the advertiser is trying to tell them or sell them.
- **Creative flexibility.** An ad's physical size and shape can be varied to give the degree of dominance or repetition that suits the advertiser's purpose. The advertiser can use black and white, color, Sunday magazines, or custom inserts.

- **An active medium** rather than a passive one. Readers turn the pages, clip and save, write in the margins, and sort through the contents.
- **A permanent record,** in contrast to the ephemeral nature of radio and TV.
- **Reasonable cost.**

The Cons
- **Lack of selectivity** of specific socioeconomic groups. Most newspapers reach broad, diverse groups of readers, which may not match the advertiser's objectives.
- **Short life span.** Unless readers clip and save the ad or coupon, it may be lost forever.
- **Low production quality.** Coarse newsprint generally produces a less impressive image than the slick, smooth paper stock of magazines, and some newspapers can't print color.
- **Clutter.** Each ad competes with editorial content and with all the other ads on the same page or spread.
- **Lack of control** over where the ad will appear unless the advertiser pays extra for a preferred position.
- **Overlapping circulation.** Some people read more than one newspaper. Advertisers may be paying for readers they already reached in a different paper.

standard advertising unit (SAU) A system of standardized newspaper advertisement sizes that can be accepted by all standard-sized newspapers without consideration of their precise format or page size. This system allows advertisers to prepare one advertisement in a particular size or SAU and place it in various newspapers regardless of their format.

column inch The basic unit by which publishers bill for advertising. It is one vertical inch of a column. Today, most newspapers—and virtually all dailies—have converted to the SAU system. An SAU column inch is 2¹⁄₁₆ inches wide by 1 inch deep.

Newspapers used to offer about 400 different ad sizes. But in 1984, the industry introduced the **standard advertising unit (SAU)** system, which standardized the newspaper column width, page sizes, and ad sizes. An SAU **column inch** is 2¹⁄₁₆ inches wide by 1 inch deep. There are now 56 standard ad sizes for standard papers and 32 for tabloids. Virtually all dailies converted to the SAU system and so did most weeklies.

Type of Audience

Some dailies and weeklies serve special-interest audiences, a fact not lost on advertisers. They generally contain advertising oriented to their special audiences, and they may have unique advertising regulations.

Some serve specific ethnic markets. Today, more than 200 dailies and weeklies are oriented to the African American community. Others serve foreign-language groups. In the United States newspapers are printed in 43 languages other than English.

Specialized newspapers also serve business and financial audiences. *The Wall Street Journal,* the leading national business and financial daily, enjoys a circulation of over 2 million readers and is now the largest weekday newspaper in the United States. *The New York Times* has the largest Sunday circulation. Other papers cater to fraternal, labor union, or professional organizations, religious groups, or hobbyists.

Other Types of Newspapers

The United States has 902 Sunday newspapers, mostly Sunday editions of daily papers, with a combined circulation of more than 49 million.[25] Sunday newspapers generally combine standard news coverage with special functions like these:

- Increased volume of classified ads.

- Greater advertising and news volume.

- In-depth coverage of business, sports, real estate, literature and the arts, entertainment, and travel.

- Review and analysis of the past week's events.

- Expanded editorial and opinion sections.

Most Sunday newspapers also feature a **Sunday supplement** magazine. Some publish their own supplements, such as the *Los Angeles Magazine* of the *Los Angeles Times.* Other papers subscribe to syndicated supplements; *Parade* magazine has a readership of more than 72 million readers every week.[26]

Printed on heavier, coated paper stock, Sunday supplements are more conducive to color printing than newsprint, making them attractive to national advertisers who want better reproduction quality.

Another type of newspaper, the independent shopping guide or free community newspaper, offers advertisers local saturation. Sometimes called *pennysavers,* these **shoppers** offer free distribution and extensive advertising pages targeted at essentially the same audience as weekly newspapers—urban and suburban community readers. Readership is often high, and the publishers use hand delivery or direct mail to achieve maximum saturation.

North Americans also read national newspapers, including the *Globe and Mail* in Canada, *USA Today,* and the *Christian Science Monitor.* With a circulation of 1.8 million, *USA Today* easily surpasses *The New York Times* (951,063) in national distribution. Both papers trail *The Wall Street Journal* with a circulation of 2.09 million.[27]

Newspapers and the Media Mix [11–C]

Study My Ad Campaign 11–B, "The Pros and Cons of Newspaper Advertising," and see if you can apply that information to the following situation:

You're the product manager for a major brand of bar soap and you wish to go nationwide with an ad featuring a coupon.

Applying the Breaks

1. Which newspaper would be best?
   a. A weekly.   b. A daily.
2. If you use a daily, in what section of the paper do you want your ad to appear?
3. If you decided to run a coupon in the Sunday paper, which of the following would you choose and why?
   a. *Parade* magazine.
   b. Color coupon insert.
   c. Display ad.

A creative solution to promote an everyday activity—grocery shopping—is a perfect concept for a full-color newspaper ad, as in this example by Publix Supermarkets (www.publix.com).

Types of Newspaper Advertising

The major classifications of newspaper advertising are display, classified, public notices, and preprinted inserts.

Display Advertising

Display advertising includes copy, illustrations or photos, headlines, coupons, and other visual components—such as the ads for the *Village Voice* discussed earlier. Display ads vary in size and appear in all sections of the newspaper except the first page of major sections, the editorial page, the obituary page, and the classified advertising section.

One common variation of the display ad, the **reading notice** (or **advertorial**), looks like editorial matter and sometimes costs more than normal display advertising. To prevent readers from mistaking it for editorial matter, the word *advertisement* appears at the top.

As we discussed in Chapter 3, retailers often run newspaper ads through **cooperative** (or **co-op**) **advertising** programs sponsored by the manufacturers whose products they sell. The manufacturer pays fully or partially to create and run the ad, which features the manufacturer's product and logo along with the local retailer's name and address.

Classified Advertising

Classified ads provide a community marketplace for goods, services, and opportunities of every type, from real estate and new-car sales to employment and business opportunities. A newspaper's profitability often relies heavily on a large and healthy classified section. However, newspapers have been hit hard by the migration of classified ads to Web sites like Craigslist and Monster.com.

Classified rates are typically based on how many lines the ad occupies and how many times the ad runs. Some newspapers accept **classified display ads**, which run in the classified section of the newspaper but feature larger type and/or photos, art borders, and sometimes even color.

Public Notices

For a nominal fee, newspapers carry legal **public notices** of changes in business and personal relationships, public governmental reports, notices by private citizens and organizations, and financial reports. These ads follow a preset format.

> Newspapers have been hit hard by the migration of classified ads to Web sites.

Preprinted Inserts Like magazines, newspapers carry **preprinted inserts**. The advertiser prints the inserts and delivers them to the newspaper plant for insertion into a specific edition. Insert sizes range from a typical newspaper page to a double postcard; formats include catalogs, brochures, mail-back devices, and perforated coupons.

Some large metropolitan dailies allow advertisers to limit their inserts to specific circulation zones. A retail advertiser that wants to reach only those shoppers in its immediate trading area can place an insert in the local-zone editions. Retail stores, car dealers, and large national advertisers are among those who find it less costly to distribute their circulars this way compared to mailing them or delivering them door to door.

An increasingly popular ad delivery method is a small sticker on the main section of the newspaper. It is removable and can double as a coupon. Newspapers charge about $50 per thousand stickers applied. Guests at upscale Omni hotels found scented stickers on the front pages of their copies of *USA Today*. A blackberry aroma suggested that guests start the day with a cup of Starbucks "paired with a fresh muffin."[28]

Preprinted inserts give advertisers control over the quality of their catalogs and brochures. Newspapers distribute these inserts at a lower cost than mailing or door-to-door delivery.

L05   Discuss the various ways newspapers charge for advertising.

HOW ADVERTISERS BUY NEWSPAPER SPACE

To get the most from the advertising budget, the media planner and buyer must know the characteristics of a newspaper's readership: the median age, sex, occupation, income, educational level, as well as buying habits of the typical reader.

Understanding Readership and Circulation

Readership information is available from various sources, such as Simmons Market Research Bureau (SMRB) and Scarborough Research Corp. Most large papers also provide extensive data on their readers.

In single-newspaper cities, reader demographics typically reflect a cross section of the general population. In cities with two or more newspapers, however, these characteristics may vary widely. The *Los Angeles Times* is directed to a broad cross section of the community while *La Opinion* targets Los Angeles's large Hispanic population.

Rate Cards Like the magazine rate card, the newspaper **rate card** lists advertising rates, mechanical and copy requirements, deadlines, and other information. Because rates vary greatly, advertisers should calculate which papers deliver the most readers and the best demographics for their money.

Local versus National Rates Most newspapers charge local and national advertisers at different rates. The **national rate** averages 75 percent higher, but some papers charge as much as 254 percent more.[29] Newspapers attribute

The newspaper rate card for the Maine Times Record is similar to that for magazines. It shows the variety of ad units available and lists their costs.

higher rates to the added costs of serving national advertisers. For instance, an ad agency usually places national advertising and receives a 15 percent commission from the paper. If the advertising comes from another city or state, then additional costs, such as long-distance telephone calls, are also involved.

But many national advertisers reject the high rates and take their business elsewhere. Only 6.1 percent of national ad money now goes to newspapers.[30] In response to declining national advertising revenue, newspapers are experimenting with simplified billing systems and discount rates for their national clients.

Flat Rates and Discount Rates

Many national papers charge **flat rates**, which means they allow no discounts; a few newspapers offer a single flat rate to both national and local advertisers.

Newspapers that offer volume discounts have an **open rate** (their highest rate for a one-time insertion) and **contract rates**, whereby local advertisers can obtain discounts of up to 70 percent

ethical issues

What's at Stake with Sweepstakes?

Many of us have probably received an envelope in the mail with the phrase "You Are a Winner!" or something similar, plastered in large, bold type. And perhaps, for a split second you believed that you had won the $100,000 prize. Then you discovered otherwise. Perhaps you were misled into believing that purchasing magazine subscriptions would increase your chances of winning.

Until recently, this is how many sweepstakes were pitched to consumers. According to the Direct Marketing Association, sweepstakes are by definition, "an advertising or promotional device by which items of value (prizes) are awarded to participating consumers by chance, with no purchase or 'entry fee' required in order to win." However, by entering a sweepstakes you are volunteering your name and address to be put on lists for acquisition by other direct marketers. In turn you are offered a chance to win what seems like easy money. For years it was difficult for recipients to tell whether or not they had a winning entry. With statements claiming "You are a winner" and simulated checks, the line separating promotion and deception became very thin.

All of this changed in 2000. Following investigations of sweepstakes firms in more than 40 states, three of the biggest sweeps marketers—Publisher's Clearing House (PCH), Time Inc., and U.S. Sales Corp.—were each brought to court by numerous state regulators, alleging that the marketing giants conducted deceptive sweepstakes promotions. In California alone, state officials claimed that 5,000 consumers spent more than $2,500 each a year in unnecessary magazine subscriptions through PCH because they believed that it improved their odds of winning. Accusations were similar for all three companies, and each defended their marketing practices claiming they always believed their mailings were clear. One PCH spokesman stated that 98 percent of the consumers who purchased magazines through their promotions were spending less than $300 a year. However, because litigation in so many states—47 in Time Inc.'s case—would have been too costly, each company decided to settle and agreed to reform its practices. Combined, the three marketers refunded more than $50 million in fines and restitution to state regulators and consumers who had purchased unnecessary magazines.

The reforms agreed to by these companies were in accord with the Deceptive Mail Prevention and Enforcement Act that became effective in April 2000. The act changed how direct-mail sweepstakes are presented and packaged. Some of the most significant changes included abandoning any "winner" proclamations unless the recipient had truly won a prize, and displaying a "fact box" that "clearly and conspicuously" explained all the terms and rules of the sweepstakes, including the odds of winning. Each mailing is also required to include the statements "No purchase is necessary to enter" and "A purchase does not improve your chances of winning" in boldfaced, capital letters in the mailing, in the rules, and on the order/entry form itself. In addition, each company is required to include a statement providing an address or toll-free number where recipients can either write or call to have their name and address removed from the mailing list.

Does this mean an end to sweepstakes? Probably not, since many people seem to jump at the chance to strike it rich for the cost of a stamp.

How much harm, if any, are sweepstakes really causing? Isn't part of promotion getting consumers to believe that they want what is being advertised? Without question, the ethical issues involved are complicated, but at least now you won't have to read the fine print to get the whole story.

Questions

1. Are sweepstakes companies really at fault for misleading their consumers? Why or why not?
2. Do you believe it is ethical for sweepstakes to "disguise" their promotions for the purpose of advertising?

by signing a contract for frequent or bulk space purchases. **Bulk discounts** offer advertisers decreasing rates as they use more inches. Advertisers earn **frequency discounts** by running a given ad repeatedly in a specific time period. Similarly, advertisers can sometimes get **earned rates**, a discount applied retroactively as the volume of advertising increases through the year.

Short Rate

An advertiser who contracts to buy a specific amount of space during a one-year period at a discount and then fails to fulfill the promise is charged a **short rate**, which is the difference between the contracted rate and the earned rate for the actual inches run. Conversely, an advertiser who buys more inches than contracted may be entitled to a rebate or credit.

Combination Rates

Combination rates are often available for placing a given ad in (1) morning and evening editions of the same newspaper; (2) two or more newspapers owned by the same publisher; and (3) in some cases, two or more newspapers affiliated in a syndicate or newspaper group.

Run of Paper versus Preferred Position

Run-of-paper (ROP) advertising rates entitle a newspaper to place a given ad on any newspaper page or in any position it desires. Although the advertiser has no control over where the ad appears in the paper, most newspapers try to place an ad in the position the advertiser requests.

Color Advertising

Color advertising is available in many newspapers on an ROP basis. Because of their high-speed presses and porous paper stock, newspapers are not noted for high-quality color printing. The cost of a color ad is usually based on the black-and-white rate plus an extra charge for each additional color.

Split Runs

Many newspapers (and magazines) offer **split runs** so that advertisers can test the *pulling power* of different ads. The advertiser runs two ads of identical size, but different content, for the same product on the same day in different press runs. The idea is to eliminate as many variables as possible. By measuring responses to the two ads, the advertiser is able to compare and contrast the effectiveness of each. For this service, newspapers typically charge extra and set a minimum space requirement.

Co-ops and Networks

As an aid to national advertisers, the NAB created the Newspaper Co-op Network (NCN). Salespeople from participating newspapers helped national advertisers line up retailers for dealer-listing

> ## Split runs allow advertisers to test the pulling power of different ads.

An advertiser can ensure a choice position for an ad by paying a higher **preferred-position rate**. A tire manufacturer, for example, may pay the preferred rate to ensure a position in the sports section.

There are also preferred positions on a given page. The preferred position near the top of a page or at the top of a column next to reading matter is called **full position**. It's usually surrounded by reading matter and may cost the advertiser 25 to 50 percent more than ROP rates.

ads. The advertiser would produce the ad and include a blank space for each paper to insert local retailers' names. The system also helped manufacturers manage local advertising tie-ins to national campaigns and themes. Before the development of NCN, national advertisers had to place ads and recruit local dealers individually.

In 1992, the Newspaper Advertising Bureau merged with the American Newspaper Publishers Association and five other marketing associations to form the **Newspaper Association of America (NAA)**, which continued to simplify national

Co-ops and networks help simplify the ad buying process for advertisers by consolidating the purchasing paperwork and requirements for publications in a single location. This example of an insertion order for Supra Media is typical of what these contracts look like. Important information such as run date, size, and identifying captions is included.

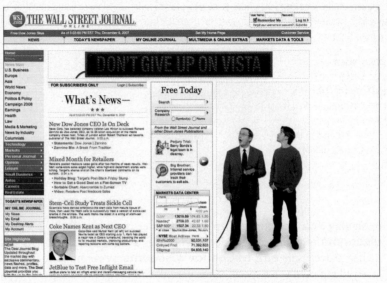

Most newspapers and magazines have established Web sites which mirror their printed publications. Though traffic to these sites has increased dramatically, publishers have not yet succeeded in generating sufficient online ad revenue to offset the declines they have experienced in traditional media.

newspaper ad buys. In 1994, the NAA launched a *one-order, one-bill system* for national advertising, called the Newspaper National Network. Advertisers can make multimarket newspaper buys by placing one order and paying one bill, instead of having to contact—and pay—each paper individually.[31]

Chrysler was the first marketer to use the new network, placing ads for its national minivan sale in 75 newspapers in March 1994.[32] The Newspaper National Network offers advertisers competitive CPM pricing and guaranteed positioning, in addition to its one-order, one-bill appeal.[33] It also allows smaller papers to participate in national advertising.[34]

Insertion Orders and Tearsheets

When advertisers place an ad, they submit an **insertion order** to the newspaper stating the date(s) on which the ad is to run, its size, the desired position, the rate, and the type of artwork accompanying the order.

When a newspaper creates ad copy and art, it gives the advertiser

a **proof copy** to check. In contrast, most national advertising arrives at the newspaper *camera ready*, either in the form of a photo print or an electronic file via e-mail. To verify that the ad ran, the newspaper tears out the page on which the ad appeared and sends it to the agency or advertiser. Today, most **tearsheets** for national advertisers are handled through a private central office, the Advertising Checking Bureau.

When a tearsheet arrives, the advertiser examines it to make sure the ad ran according to instructions: in the right section and page position, and with quality reproduction. If the ad did not run per instructions, the agency or advertiser is usually due an adjustment, a discount, or even a free rerun.

PRINT MEDIA AND NEW TECHNOLOGIES

With computers came revolutionary media options, such as the Internet and DVDs, challenging both traditional print media and advertisers to adapt. Newspapers and magazines are rushing to make alliances with cable, regional telephone, and online companies to get a toehold in the interactive information market.

By now, virtually all metropolitan news organizations and national magazines have established an online presence. News organizations are information-rich, and much of the specialized information they don't run in the paper or the magazine fits perfectly with the online world's narrower interests. They are still, however, trying to figure out how to incorporate advertising into their new ventures. Most ads are still simply banners, but customers who are interested can click on the banners for more in-depth information. This becomes a value-added service for the print

my ad campaign

medium's advertising customers. George Gilder, media expert and author, believes that the newspaper industry is in a particularly advantageous position, because "the convergence of text and video will cause a revolution in advertising, with targeted

Planning and Evaluating Print Media [11–C]

At this point in your project you should have decided whether or not to use print (magazine and newspaper) as a communication vehicle. The next step is deciding which of the thousands of options makes the most sense for your client's brand.

The beauty of media planning and buying is that you have a blank slate from which to build your plan. As you start to build your plan, however, you need to consider what you are working toward. By answering a set of simple questions you can build the foundation of your recommendation. You should approach planning print media in the same way you would approach planning the brand strategy:

- Who do you want to reach?
- Why use print?
- What are the brand objectives?
- Where do you want to place your advertising to best achieve your objectives?
- How should you execute your plan?

When you have answered these questions, it is time to analyze and evaluate your opportunities and develop your plan.

Selecting publications requires both critical thinking and hard and fast numbers. For instance monthly magazines can take up to 12 weeks to gain full readership (called to "cume" their audience). This can obviously be an issue if your communication objectives are centered on building reach quickly. On the other hand, weekly magazines cume their audience in approximately one to two weeks, making them great to generate reach around key events. Lastly, the number of insertions by title also depends on your strategy. If you are telling a sequenced story through three ads, then you need to plan for three insertions in each publication (pub). This will obviously be expensive and likely will reduce the number of pubs on the plan, ultimately limiting your reach.

The great thing about print advertising is that it offers a large number of opportunities for brands to engage consumers in niche environments, thereby limiting brand wastage. However, not all brands want or need such niche vehicles, and lucky for those brands there are more mass-oriented publications too:

Targeted	Mass Books
Golf	People
Field and Stream	TV Guide
Baby Talk	Parade
Ski	National Enquirer
Martha Stewart Living	Reader's Digest

Some of you will be focusing on large national advertisers and can utilize nearly all types of print options. But what opportunities exist for the local advertiser? First, newspapers are typically a staple of any large local advertiser. Second, most of the print publications that we have discussed thus far will allow you to layer in demogeographical targeting to help fine-tune your plan. Take this into account as you build your plan. It doesn't make sense to advertise in a national pub if your client is only located in the southeastern United States.

See Ad Campaigns 11–A and 11–B for checklists of the pros and cons of magazine and newspaper advertising.

As you can see, common sense plays a major role in planning print campaigns, especially for large advertisers. But for other brands, advertising in print is a bit more difficult because the names of the targeted publications don't just roll off the tongue like Sports Illustrated or People. To plan for those campaigns, most advertisers use syndicated research such as Media Mark's MRI product. This is a piece of planning software that indexes, through surveys, people's readership of tens of thousands of different publications. So when Microsoft wants to reach IT decision makers in the enterprise (in companies with over 100 employees), MRI tells the media planner that she can find a high composition (concentration of overall readership) of that target in publications like eWeek, InformationWeek, and Baseline magazine.

While we detail a number of tools in this chapter, for the large majority of projects access to these tools will be limited. Therefore, think about the medium in terms of the mindset of the readers when you place an ad in front of them. The closer you can get that mindset to match the category, industry, or association of your brand's product, the better off you are.

messages leading consumers step-by-step to a transaction."[35]

We'll deal with these issues in greater depth in Chapter 13.

check yourself ✓

1. If you were running an ad selling big screen televisions, would you pay a premium for the ad to appear in a specific section of the newspaper? What section would be best?

2. Imagine you are reading a newspaper online. What advertising might appeal to you and possibly get you to purchase something on the spot?

LO6 Explain the unique roles played by directory and Yellow Pages advertising.

DIRECTORIES AND YELLOW PAGES

Directories represent a unique form of print advertising. A **directory** is an alphabetical or subject listing containing names, descriptions, and contact information for persons or organizations. Directories share print advertising's long shelf life and its ability to target a specific audience. They serve their consumers as a valuable reference, containing information that readers actually seek out when they need it. If you want to find out who does what in a particular product or service category, directories provide a listing for those companies that offer that product or service. For most businesses, there is little question whether they need to advertise in directories. Rather, they must decide in how many directories to advertise and how best to use them to serve their purposes.

Thousands of directories are published each year by phone companies, trade associations, industrial groups, and others. They mainly serve as locators, buying guides, and mailing lists, but they also carry advertising aimed at specialized fields. The Yellow Pages is by far the most frequently used directory.

Approximately 87 percent of the U.S. population used the printed Yellow Pages in 2007. That represented 13.4 billion references. Internet Yellow Pages searches are growing, reaching 3.8 billion in that same year.[36] These electronic directories provide photos, maps, and links to additional resources such as coupons or special promotions. Unlike the traditional Yellow Pages, the Internet versions can be routinely changed to provide updated information.

In Yellow Pages ads, content is most important. The ad should tell people how to make the purchase, not why. As with most advertising media, the larger the ad, the more attention it attracts.[37] Most businesses find that advertising in the Yellow Pages is very expensive, but many of them would no longer be in business without it.

Unlike other forms of print advertising, Yellow Pages advertising is typically sold on an annual basis. A basic one-line listing usually comes with business telephone service. A business can upgrade that listing and purchase a variety of ad sizes, ranging from setting a listing in boldface type to a large full-page advertisement. Some businesses add color to emphasize a logo, graphic, or line of type. The cost for advertising in the Yellow Pages, obviously, depends upon the amount of space, as well as the circulation size of the book. A large metropolitan Yellow Pages book commands a much higher rate per ad than does a small-town book, for instance.

The United States has about 6,000 local telephone directories with a combined circulation of 350 million. Since deregulation of the phone industry and the 1984 breakup of AT&T, the Yellow Pages business has boomed, with ad revenues reaching over $16.5 billion in 2009.[38] In fact, the Yellow Pages is now the fourth-largest medium, ahead of Internet, magazines, and outdoor. As a result of consolidation, the four largest publishers by 2009 accounted for 73 percent of the industry's revenues. Competition is possible because the Yellow Pages name is not trademarked. Hundreds of independent publishers produce Yellow Pages directories, and market share for these companies is steadily increasing.

Stiff competition has forced phone and directory companies to differentiate their Yellow Pages with more user-friendly directories containing supplemental general-interest information, such as local maps and information on parks, events, community services, transportation, coupons, and shopping. Some phone directories offer free interactive voice services *(audiotext)* that link the telephone with a host computer to allow the easy retrieval of helpful information.

[Many businesses would no longer be in business without Yellow Pages advertising.]

In addition, highly specialized directories aim at particular audiences, such as the Chinese-language Yellow Pages in San Francisco and the *Paginas Amarillas* in the border states.

Yellow Pages are often the sole advertising medium for local businesses, and nearly 85 percent of Yellow Pages revenue is derived from local advertisers.[39] But Yellow Pages directories can be an important medium for national advertisers, too. For example, U-Haul spends more than $20 million a year on Yellow Pages ads.

A growing number of publishers now offer a "ride-along" program that lets regional and national marketers deliver advertising, coupons and product samples along with the white and Yellow Pages directories. The ride-along program reaches about 75 percent of the top 300 markets, resulting in a potential audience of 60 million households.[40] ■

check yourself ✓

1. What businesses likely rely on Yellow Pages advertising for survival?

2. What advantages do online Yellow Pages offer over the printed version?

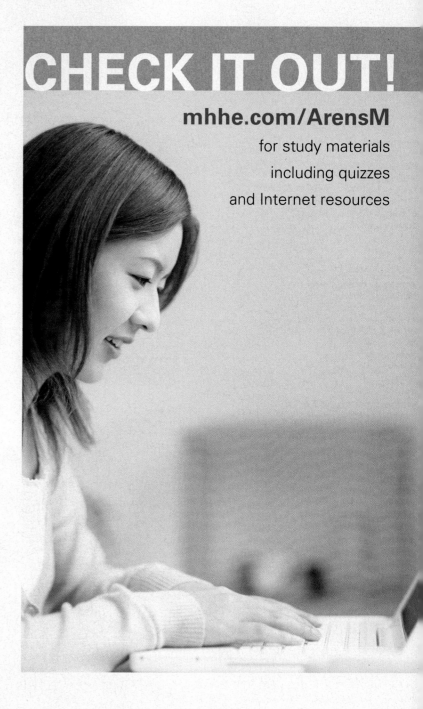

CHECK IT OUT!

mhhe.com/ArensM

for study materials

including quizzes

and Internet resources

electronic media:
television and radio

I n early 2009 the economy had been depressed for nearly four months and consumer confidence was at an all-time low. Most car companies were pulling back their ad spending in hopes the saved dollars could afford them a longer runway during the unsettling times. However, a few companies saw this as an opportunity, a chance to take on the historically aggressive-spending U.S. automakers and the highly popular Japanese automakers. One of these companies was Hyundai Motor America, a company that just 10 years prior was not a real contender in the consumer mind. Because of durability and reliability issues, Hyundai sales plummeted in the United States in the mid- to late-nineties. Rather than abandoning the American market, Hyundai chose to invest heavily in new product designs and improvements in overall quality and reliability. However, just making the product better wasn't going to win over a now jaded consumer. Studies done at the time suggested that quality had in fact improved but that public perceptions had changed very little.

The automaker had to take action, and it did. In 1999 Hyundai shocked the automotive world by offering an unprecedented, 10-year, 100,000 mile warranty. Rightly dubbed "America's Best," this warranty, *continued on p. 306*

continued on p. 306

LEARNING OBJECTIVES

LO1 Describe the advantages and disadvantages of broadcast television as an advertising medium.

LO2 Discuss the various options for advertising on television.

LO3 Explain how to measure television audiences and select the best programs to buy.

LO4 Describe the advantages and disadvantages of radio as an advertising medium.

LO5 Explain the options for advertising on radio and how radio audiences are measured.

continued from p. 305

the Hyundai Advantage, covered all major components such as the engine and transmission, for the entire fleet. "We thought an improved warranty would make a statement about our quality and get us on more people's shopping lists," Finbarr O'Neill, chief executive of Hyundai Motor America, said in an interview.[1]

Fast forward to late 2008 and another brilliant first for Hyundai Motor executives. Their launch pad was Super Bowl XLIII, the number one most-watched game of all time with 98.7 million viewers.[2] Teamed with Goodby, Silverstein and Partners, they planned a three-tier onslaught. First they unveiled the brand-new 2010 Hyundai Genesis Coupe. Next up was a brilliant ad showing fictitious executives from Lexus and BMW yelling angrily in their native tongues, with the only understandable word being "HYUNDAI," in response to the 2009 Genesis Sedan being selected North American Car of the Year by JD Powers and Associates. Jeff Bridges reads the tagline: "Win one little award and suddenly everyone gets your name right. Hyundai, like Sunday."

But they didn't stop there. Hyundai realized that in these troubling times the last thing that anyone wants, after losing a job, is facing creditors. Therefore, most consumers were not buying new, or even used, cars. Hyundai's idea was simple—let's take away the risk. So the Hyundai Assurance program was born. If you lose your income after you buy a Hyundai, the company will allow you to return the car and be released from all final payments.

The advertising promoting this program clearly worked. Year over year sales for February 2009 were down 1.5 percent; however, when the industry as a whole was down 37 percent that number looked pretty good, especially when it represented a 25 percent increase in sales volume from the prior month.[3]

For the second time in 10 years Hyundai had come through with a consumer-centered idea that changed the industry. For the second time in 10 years the little Korean car company that had been the brunt of many jokes was again turning heads. And for the first time it was seeing success in the midst of chaos.

So much emphasis these days is put on the medium of choice rather than the ideas that shape promotions. Regardless of how Hyundai decided to distribute this message—and mind you they chose television, the largest stage in the world—the assurance program idea took center stage. Hyundai was first to market, establish a competitive advantage, and chose to see the economic situation as an opportunity. There is a valuable lesson in that. ■

LO1 Describe the advantages and disadvantages of broadcast television as an advertising medium.

THE MEDIUM OF TELEVISION

Back in 1950, U.S. advertisers spent $171 million, or about 3 percent of total U.S. advertising volume, on the new medium of television. It didn't take long, though, for the nation's advertisers to discover the

The growth in cable and satellite TV systems has dramatically increased the number of channels available to viewers. This has given consumers almost unlimited program alternatives, making it easier for advertisers to reach a more selective audience.

power of this new vehicle to reach mass audiences quickly and frequently. TV also offered unique creative opportunities to imbue their brands with personality and image like never before. In 2008, over $65 billion was spent on TV advertising, accounting for more than 45 percent of all U.S. ad spending.[4] Exhibit 12–1 lists the top network television advertisers in the United States and their annual expenditures.

Today, the medium of television is available to advertisers in two principal forms: broadcast and cable. **Broadcast TV** reaches its audience by transmitting electromagnetic waves through the air across some geographic territory. **Cable TV** reaches its audience through wires, which may be strung from telephone poles or laid underground, or via satellite signals.

Broadcast TV

Until the advent of the Internet, broadcast television grew faster than any other advertising medium in history. As both a news and entertainment medium, it caught people's fancy very quickly. From its beginnings after World War II, broadcast TV rapidly emerged as the only medium that offered sight, sound, and motion. People could stay home and still go to the movies. As TV's legions of viewers grew, the big national brand advertisers quickly discovered they could use the medium very efficiently to expand distribution across the country and sell products like never before. Not only that, the medium was ideal for building an image for their brands—even better than magazines, which had previously been the image-building medium of choice. It didn't take long for marketers to switch their budgets from radio, newspapers, and magazines.

The United States now has 1,379 commercial TV stations.[5] Stations in the United States operate as independents unless they are affiliated with one of the national networks (ABC, NBC, CBS, Fox, CW). Both network affiliates and independent stations may subscribe to nationally syndicated programs as well as originate their own programming. However, increasing competition from cable TV is taking viewers from the national network programs. To compensate, some networks are investing in cable TV systems or starting their own. For example, NBC (which is owned by GE) started CNBC and MSNBC, and ABC (which is owned by Disney) owns a piece of ESPN, Lifetime, A&E, and other cable channels.

EXHIBIT 12–1 Top 10 network TV advertisers in the United States (2008).

Rank	Advertiser	Network TV Ad Spending 2008 ($ in millions)
1	Procter & Gamble	$1,078.1
2	AT&T	817.4
3	General Motors	737.9
4	Ford Motor Co.	553.0
5	Johnson & Johnson	536.8
6	Verizon Communications	496.7
7	Toyota Motor Corp.	424.7
8	GlaxoSmithKline	418.6
9	Time Warner	414.5
10	PepsiCo	360.6

Cable TV

For more than 30 years, broadcast TV, especially network TV, was the dominant entertainment medium for most Americans. Today, other electronic media have dramatically changed that dominance. Chief among the challengers is cable television.

Cable TV has been around since the late 1940s. Initially, it carried television signals by wire to areas with poor reception such as mountainous regions. But in the 1970s, the advent of satellite TV signals, the proliferation of channels, and the introduction of uncut first-run movies via premium cable channels such as Home Box Office (HBO) and Showtime made cable TV more attractive to all viewers, even people in urban areas.

At first, many subscribers valued cable simply for the full array of regional channels and access to premium services such as HBO. But once this novelty wore off, subscribers wanted more. A variety of advertiser-supported cable networks soon appeared with specialized programming in arts, history, sports, news, cooking, and comedy, along with diversified pay services and many more local shows. All of this attracted more and more subscribers—and consequently drew viewers away from the big broadcast networks.

In the last three decades, cable's growth has been extraordinary. In 1975, only 13 percent of TV households in the United States had cable. By 2010, cable (wired and satellite) reached more than 91 percent of all TV households.[6] The share of households reached by wired cable peaked in 2001 and has been declining ever since, with all the growth coming from direct broadcast satellite, such as Dish Network and DirecTV.[7] Although cable subscribers may receive more than 160 channels, most households only watch 15 to 20 channels.[8]

Most channels are privately owned and operated. These include local network affiliates and independents, cable networks, superstations, local cable system channels, and community access channels. The cable fees represent about one-third of cable TV revenues; advertising makes up the remainder. Networks such as CNN, USA, the Discovery Channel, Arts & Entertainment, Lifetime, Comedy Central, and Spike TV now compete for advertisers' dollars, each selling its own niche audience.[9] For an additional price, subscribers can receive premium services such as HBO, Showtime, and Cinemax and see special events such as first-run films, championship boxing matches, and baseball and football games through pay-per-view subscriptions.

There are now some 97 ad-supported national cable networks in the United States and a growing number of regional networks.[10] Exhibit 12–2 lists the most widely carried ones. There are also a handful of *superstations* (such as TBS

EXHIBIT 12–2 Major cable TV networks.

Network	Number of Subscribers	Program Type
ABC Family	96.8	Family/youth
CNN	98.6	News/information/business/financial/health
Comedy Central	96.6	Comedy/entertainment
Discovery Channel	98.3	Biography/history/wildlife/science
ESPN	97.7	Sports
ESPN2	97.3	Sports
Fox News	94.8	News/information/business
Lifetime Television	97.6	Comedy/drama/movies/women's interest/reality
MTV	97.0	Music/entertainment/reality
Nickolodeon	98.1	Animation/family/youth
TBS	98.6	Comedy/family/movies/sports/reality
TLC	97.4	Information/education
Turner Network Television	97.7	Drama/movies/mysteries/sports
The Weather Channel	98.3	Weather/news/science
USA Network	97.9	Drama/family/movies/sports

Atlanta) and local, over-the-air TV stations whose signals are delivered via satellite to cable systems across the country and that carry some national advertising.

DTV

On June 12, 2009, as mandated by Congress, the United States made the switch to digital television (DTV). DTV sends and receives moving images and sound by digital signals ("0"s and "1"s) rather than the analog signals (waveforms).

Digital TV has many benefits. As stated on the Web site http://www.dtv.gov, consumers will benefit because digital broadcasting allows stations to offer improved picture and sound quality, and digital is much more efficient than analog. For example, rather than being limited to providing one analog program, a broadcaster is able to offer a super sharp "high definition" (HD) digital program or multiple "standard definition" (SD) digital programs simultaneously through a process

Planning and Buying TV and Radio [12–A]

Media planners use a variety of syndicated and proprietary research tools to plan and buy both TV and radio ads. Primarily these tools help identify the larger concentrations (composition) of a target audience in specific programming, and the cost associated with those audiences. The complexity of TV and radio arises from the need to build plans that cost-efficiently reach a target audience with an effective frequency. The currency for these two media is a ratings point, which represents 1 percent of the target audience a media buyer is trying to reach. Both TV and radio, therefore, are bought based on demographics. So when certain prime time shows have a rating of 14 for A25–49, it means that a particular program reaches 14 percent of all adults between the ages of 25 and 49. A buyer's cost per point (CPP) is her way of determining a vehicle's (program's) efficiency in delivering her target audience. As this chapter will explain, ratings points are additive. Therefore two spots on shows with 14 targeted ratings points means that the advertiser has purchased 28 gross ratings points or GRPs.

Most of you will not have access to the types of tools that help you plan and optimize broadcast media plans, so your focus should be on the merits of each of these media in achieving your marketing and advertising objectives and how they match your overall media strategies. First we will discuss the advantages and nonmonetary value of TV and then of radio.

Television

TV is still the largest mass medium; 114 million homes in America have at least one TV set. However, it is becoming a fragmented marketplace. In fact, the average home receives over 118 different channels. While the average viewer only watches 15 channels on a regular basis, those channels may not be the same 15 channels as the ones his neighbor watches, making the media planner's job that much more difficult in building mass audiences.

Besides the large audiences, the other core benefit of TV is that it builds awareness relatively quickly. If you are launching a new product or trying to gain a high level of awareness in a relatively short period of time, TV is your medium. While TV will take up a large portion of your budget, its dynamic nature, the ability to include sight, sound, and motion in the advertisement, makes it a great story-telling medium.

Lastly, TV is still the best medium to generate excitement around a brand, whether that is with internal constituents (employees) or external audiences. As proclaimed by Marshall McLuhan in his book, *Understanding Media: The Extensions of Man*, the medium is the message, and no medium, to date, gives people the same perception of legitimacy as a well-produced TV advertisement.

Radio

Like TV, radio is a broadcast medium, but its ability to generate mass awareness immediately is different. The radio formats appeal to more specific targets, giving it less spillover than TV, which can be both good and bad—good in that your audience is the only one that hears the message, bad in that an advertiser may not extend out of its target market and hit markets it wasn't aware would be receptive to its message.

So why do advertisers use radio? One reason is that radio is much more efficient than TV; CPPs are sometimes 1/10 that of TV. Radio also is much less expensive to produce; in fact typically all you need is copy and talent, making the lead time to go live with radio as short as one to two weeks. It also happens to be more promotional in nature—stations typically have a loyal audience following and advertisers can usually be a part of any local station events and get the station personalities to endorse the brand. Testimonials, and especially personality testimonials, can be very valuable to advertisers that are looking to build legitimacy in themselves or their product.

So while you think about what your TV and radio ads will do for your brand(s), it is important to reflect on what part of the objectives and strategies each will fulfill and how they might work in concert with each other. Think of starting a new advertising campaign with TV messages and the support of radio. The TV will generate awareness and legitimacy immediately, and the radio will allow you to get out of the higher cost media quickly while allowing for long-term continuity of messaging at a more efficient rate.

called "multicasting." Multicasting allows broadcast stations to offer several channels of digital programming at the same time, using the same amount of spectrum required for one analog program. This means more programming choices for viewers. Further, DTV can provide interactive video and data services that are not possible with analog technology.

TV Audience Trends

As a way to reach a mass audience, no other medium today has the unique creative abilities of television: the combination of sight, sound, and motion; the opportunity to demonstrate the product; the potential to use special effects; the empathy of the viewer; and the believability for viewers of seeing it happen right before their eyes (see My Ad Campaign 12–B, "The Pros and Cons of Broadcast TV Advertising"). As Exhibit 12–3 shows, over half of adult viewers

my ad campaign

The Pros and Cons of Broadcast TV Advertising [12–B]

The Pros

Contemporary broadcast television offers advertisers many advantages over competing media.

- **Mass coverage.** A full 98 percent of all U.S. homes have a TV (most have more than one), and viewing time for the average household increased from about five hours a day in 1960 to over eight hours in 2009.
- **Relatively low cost.** Despite the often huge initial outlays for commercial production and advertising time, TV's equally huge audiences bring the cost per exposure down to $2 to $10 per thousand viewers.
- **Some selectivity.** Television audiences vary a great deal depending on the time of day, day of the week, and nature of the programming. Advertising messages can be presented when potential customers are watching, and advertisers can reach select geographic audiences by buying local and regional markets.
- **Impact.** Television offers a kind of immediacy that other forms of advertising cannot achieve, displaying and demonstrating the product with sound, motion, and full color right before the customer's eyes.
- **Creativity.** The various facets of the TV commercial—sight, sound, motion, and color—permit infinite original and imaginative appeals.
- **Prestige.** Because the public considers TV the most authoritative and influential medium, it offers advertisers a prestigious image. Hallmark, Xerox, Coca-Cola, and IBM increase their prestige by regularly sponsoring cultural programs on network TV.
- **Social dominance.** In North America, most people under age 35 grew up with TV as a window to their social environment. They continue to be stirred by TV screenings of the Olympics, space travel, assassinations, wars, and political scandals around the world.

The Cons

Sometimes broadcast TV just doesn't "fit" the creative mix because of cost, lack of audience selectivity, inherent brevity, or the clutter of competitive messages.

- **High production cost.** One of broadcast TV's greatest handicaps is the high cost of producing quality commercials. Depending on the creative approach, the cost of filming a national commercial today may run from $200,000 to more than $1 million.
- **High airtime cost.** The average cost of a prime-time network commercial ranges from $200,000 to $400,000. A single 30-second commercial for a top-rated show in prime time may cost over $500,000 and in special attractions like the Super Bowl cost over $2 million. The cost of wide coverage, even at low rates, prices small and medium-size advertisers out of the market.
- **Limited selectivity.** Broadcast TV is not cost-effective for advertisers seeking a very specific, small audience. And it is losing some of its selectivity because of changing audience trends. More women are working outside the home or watching cable TV, hurting advertisers on network soap operas.
- **Brevity.** Studies show that most TV viewers can't remember the product or company in the most recent TV ad they watched—even if it was within the last five minutes. Recall improves with the length of the commercial; people remember 60-second spots better than 30-second spots.
- **Clutter.** TV advertising is usually surrounded by station breaks, credits, and public service announcements, as well as six or seven other spots. All these messages compete for attention, so viewers become annoyed and confused and often misidentify the product.
- **Zipping and zapping.** DVR users who skip through commercials when replaying recorded programs are zipping; remote-control users who change channels at the beginning of a commercial break are zapping.

believe TV is the most authoritative advertising source, compared to only 21.7 percent for newspapers, 12.3 percent for magazines, 10.4 percent for radio, and 6.4 percent for the Internet. Television was also rated as the most influential, persuasive, and exciting medium.[11]

The heaviest viewers of broadcast TV are middle-income, high school–educated individuals and their families, so most programming is directed at this group. People with considerably higher incomes and more education typically make use of a more diverse range of media and entertainment options.

In the United States, nearly every home has a television set. The average adult viewer watches TV more than five hours per day. The average child age two to eleven watches about 3.5 hours per day. Older Americans (age 65+) watch nearly seven hours per day.[12]

Cable in North American homes has significantly altered TV viewing patterns and the use of other media. Households with cable spend less time watching broadcast TV. They also spend less time listening to the radio, reading, or going to the movies. Cable seems to reach an audience that is difficult to get to in any other way. As a result of this audience fragmentation, advertising on broadcast networks has become less cost effective. DVD rentals have also increased dramatically, drawing more viewers away from advertiser-supported TV, both broadcast and cable (which is why ads now appear on DVDs).

National advertisers have been using cable since the late 1970s and cable advertising revenues have grown steadily, reaching nearly $19 billion in 2008.[13] One reason is that cable's upscale audience buys proportionately more goods and services than noncable subscribers (see Exhibit 12–4). Procter & Gamble traditionally spends the most on network cable. However, local retailers also find local cable a good place to advertise.

Nielsen studies indicate that the average U.S. household receives 118.6 TV channels. A larger number of channels, however, doesn't translate into more TV viewing. The Nielsen data indicate that the more channels a household has, the lower the percentage of channels watched. Households with the most channels (more than 150) tuned in to only 16 channels.[14]

While there is no doubt that the media play an ever-expanding role in our daily lives, there is a finite limit to the number of advertising exposures people can absorb. When that limit is reached, any new media will simply be fighting for market share. This is the reason for the increasing fragmentation of the audience and the precipitous decline in the huge share of audience once held by the broadcast networks. This is also why media buyers and planners are growing in importance as advertisers search for the elusive audience and fight for their share of that audience in an overcrowded media environment.

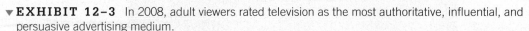

▼EXHIBIT 12–3 In 2008, adult viewers rated television as the most authoritative, influential, and persuasive advertising medium.

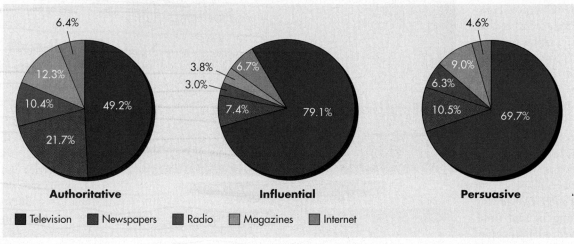

| Authoritative | Influential | Persuasive |

■ Television ■ Newspapers ■ Radio ■ Magazines ■ Internet

Source: From Television Bureau of Advertising and Nielsen Media Research. Reprinted with permission of Television Bureau of Advertising.

Cable versus Noncable Household Characteristics			
Upscale Profiles	Cable HH vs. U.S. Average (Index)	Noncable HH vs. U.S. Average (Index)	% Advantage Cable HH
Occupation: Professional	108	88	+23%
Education: Graduated college+	110	85	+29%
Occupation: Management/financial	105	93	+13%
Household income: $75,000+	112	80	+40%
Value of home: $500,000+	109	87	+25%
Downscale Profiles	Cable HH vs. U.S. Average (Index)	Noncable HH vs. U.S. Average (Index)	% Advantage Cable HH
Education: Did not graduate HS	86	122	−30%
Employment: Not working	99	101	−2%
Occupation: Construction/maintenance	87	120	−17%
Household Income: <$20,000	87	121	−28%
Value of Home: <$60,000	83	127	−35%

Source: Used by permission of Cable TV Advertising Bureau.

The Impact of Technology

What if you could effortlessly record the entire season of your favorite show, pause a live broadcast while you answer the phone, and automatically skip every commercial? That's all possible today with the use of the **digital video recorder (DVR)**. Introduced in 1999 under the TiVo and ReplayTV brands, DVRs could have a profound effect on the way we watch television and the way sponsors advertise. In response, several TV networks are beginning to offer some of their hit shows, commercial free, in a fee-based, video-on-demand format.

However, nobody expects the demise of the television commercial. Without commercials, there would be far less money to produce TV shows. Instead, it is expected that advertisers will find new ways to deliver their messages. As of 2009, about 34 percent of TV households owned a DVR.[15] Even though roughly 25 percent of television viewers watch time-shifted TV, they still spend over 95 percent of their TV viewing hours watching in real time. Similarly, over 40 percent of viewers have watched video on the Internet, but that activity represents less than 2 percent of their television viewing time.[16]

Nevertheless, advertisers are scrambling to innovate and adapt to the new medium, which compels them to reach consumers with advertising vehicles other than the traditional 30-second commercial. In particular, television advertisers are working to increase program sponsorship and product placement and to make commercials more engaging and relevant. Forrester Research asked television advertising executives how they might cope in a DVR-saturated environment. We are already seeing evidence of several of the approaches in Exhibit 12–5.

The Use of Television in IMC

Television today is very versatile. For many years it was strictly a mass medium, used to great advantage by the manufacturers of mass consumption goods: toiletries and cosmetics, food, appliances, and cars (see Exhibit 12–6). But today, thanks to the narrowcasting ability of cable TV, television can also be a highly selective niche medium.

▼ EXHIBIT 12–5 Responses of 55 national advertisers when asked "If large numbers of consumers could skip commercials while watching television, which of the following forms of advertising would you spend more on?"

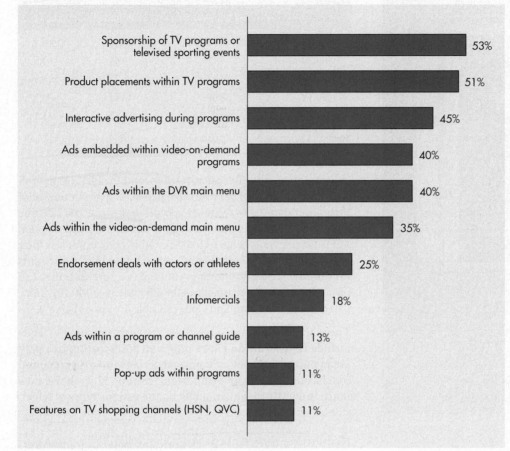

Category	%
Sponsorship of TV programs or televised sporting events	53%
Product placements within TV programs	51%
Interactive advertising during programs	45%
Ads embedded within video-on-demand programs	40%
Ads within the DVR main menu	40%
Ads within the video-on-demand main menu	35%
Endorsement deals with actors or athletes	25%
Infomercials	18%
Ads within a program or channel guide	13%
Pop-up ads within programs	11%
Features on TV shopping channels (HSN, QVC)	11%

It's not unusual, for instance, to see ads for special feed for thoroughbreds and show horses on ESPN's *Grand Prix of Jumping*. And thanks to local cable, TV is now affordable for even small local advertisers. This makes it a very viable option for use in an IMC program.

While single programs don't deliver the mass audience they once did, television is still the most cost-effective way to deliver certain kinds of messages to large, well-defined audiences. When it comes to awareness and image advertising, for instance, television has no rival. The same is true for brand reinforcement messages.[17]

Through its unique ability to deliver a creative big idea, television can

> " When it comes to awareness and image advertising, television has no rival. "

▼ EXHIBIT 12–6 Top 10 cable network advertisers (2008).

Rank	Advertiser	Cable TV Spending (in millions)
1	Procter & Gamble	$886.2
2	Time Warner	276.3
3	Johnson & Johnson	215.9
4	General Motors Corp.	210.6
5	General Mills	208.3
6	Walt Disney Co.	201.0
7	Sprint Nextel	195.4
8	AT&T	185.3
9	Kraft Foods	183.5
10	Berkshire Hathaway	182.8

impart *brand meaning* (the symbolism or personality of the brand) to either attract people to the brand or reinforce their current relationship with it. Television is also a good leverage tool. That is, an advertiser might take advantage of the relatively low CPM of television to reach out to many prospects. Prospects can identify themselves by responding to the commercial, and then the advertiser can follow up with less expensive, one-to-one or addressable media.[18]

What's important to remember in all this is that the high visibility of TV forces the sponsor to create ads that people find interesting and that consistently reinforce the brand's strategic position (remember our definition of great advertising). The brands that succeed are the ones that are the most popular. And "ad liking" has a lot to do with brand popularity.

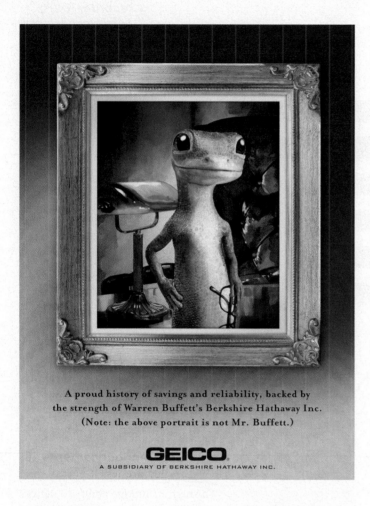

A proud history of savings and reliability, backed by the strength of Warren Buffett's Berkshire Hathaway Inc.

(Note: the above portrait is not Mr. Buffett.)

GEICO
A SUBSIDIARY OF BERKSHIRE HATHAWAY INC.

check yourself ✓

1. What are some ways advertisers are innovating to adapt to the expanded use of digital video recorders?

2. Why has cable television been a good thing for local advertisers and those selling specialty products?

LO2 Discuss the various options for advertising in television.

Types of TV Advertising

Advertisers use different strategies to buy time on broadcast and cable television. The major broadcast networks offer a variety of *programs* that appeal to different audiences. So the advertiser buys ads based on the viewing audience of each program. A national advertiser that wants to reach a broad cross section of women ages 25 to 45, for example, might find *Desperate Housewives* an efficient buy at a cost of $228,851 for a 30-second commercial.

▼**EXHIBIT 12-7**   Where does all the money go? Measured TV spending in billions of dollars (2008).

	2007 Ad Spending ($ billions)	2008 Ad Spending ($ billions)	Percent Change
Network TV	25.42	26.71	+5.1
Syndicated TV	4.17	4.44	+6.5
Spot TV	16.82	15.15	−9.9
Cable TV	18.02	18.83	+4.5
Total	**64.43**	**65.13**	**+1.1**

Source: http://adage.com/images/random/datacenter/2009/spendtrends09.pdf and http://adage.com/images/random/datacenter/2008/spendtrends08.pdf.

When buying cable TV, an advertiser can buy ads over the full schedule of a channel because cable networks typically aim all of their programming to relatively specific *audiences*. The Lifetime and Family channels heavily weigh programs toward women; MTV targets viewers ages 16 to 25. Cable companies sell their network channels in bundles at a discount and offer discounts for *run-of-schedule* positioning—multiple ad purchases they can place throughout a channel's daily schedule (see My Ad Campaign 12–C, "The Pros and Cons of Cable TV Advertising").

There are various ways advertisers can buy time on TV. They include sponsoring an entire program, participating in a program, purchasing spot announcements between programs, and purchasing spots from syndicators. Exhibit 12–7 shows how much money is spent nationally on the various types of television advertising.

Network Advertising   Historically, major U.S. advertisers purchased airtime from one of the national broadcast **networks**. Cable has slowly eroded the networks' audiences. At one time the big three (ABC, CBS, and NBC) had more than 90 percent of the prime-time audience. In the 2003–2004 season, ad-supported cable networks pulled ahead of the U.S. broadcast networks in prime time for the first time in the history of U.S. television, pulling in 44 percent of the audience, compared to 41 percent for the broadcast networks and 15 percent who were watching other television outlets, such as HBO and PBS. And the cable networks haven't looked back, more recently reporting a share in excess of 54 percent.[19]

Networks offer large advertisers convenience and efficiency because they broadcast messages simultaneously across many affiliate stations throughout the country. Broadcast networks tend to reach masses of American consumers representing a cross section of the population, while cable networks tend to reach more selective niches.

An advertiser who underwrites the cost of a program is engaging in **sponsorship**. In a sole sponsorship, the advertiser is responsible for both the program content and the total cost of production. Sponsorship is so costly that single sponsorships are usually limited to specials. Companies that sponsor programs (AT&T, Xerox, and Hallmark, for example) gain two important advantages. First, the public more readily identifies with the product(s)

networks Any of the national television or radio broadcasting chains or companies such as ABC, CBS, NBC, or Fox. Networks offer the large advertiser convenience and efficiency because the message can be broadcast simultaneously throughout the country.

sponsorship The presentation of a radio or TV program, or an event, or even a Web site by a sole advertiser. The advertiser is often responsible for the program content and the cost of production as well as the advertising. This is generally so costly that single sponsorships are usually limited to TV specials.

participation Several advertisers share the sponsorship of a television program. A "participating" advertiser has no control of the program content. Partnership commitment is usually limited to a relatively short period.

spot announcements An individual commercial message run between two programs but having no relationship to either. Spots may be sold nationally or locally. They must be purchased by contacting individual stations directly.

due to the prestige of sponsoring first-rate entertainment. Second, the sponsor controls the placement and content of its commercials. The commercials can be fit to the program and run any length the sponsor desires so long as they remain within network or station regulations.

Sponsorship offers many opportunities. When the popular drama series *24* started its second season, the first episode was presented commercial-free, thanks to a full sponsorship by Ford Motor Company. The episode also featured numerous Ford vehicles in the show. To save money and reduce risks, many advertisers cosponsor programs, sponsoring on alternate weeks or dividing the program into segments. NFL games, for instance, are always sold as multiple sponsorships.

> **Local businesses are frequently seen on spot schedules.**

my ad campaign

Most network TV advertising is sold on a **participation** basis, with several advertisers buying 30- or 60-second segments within a program. This enables them to spread their budgets and avoid long-term commitments to any one program. It also lets smaller advertisers buy a limited amount of time and still get the nationwide coverage they need.

Network advertising also has several disadvantages: lack of flexibility, long lead times, inconvenient restrictions, and forced adherence to network standards and practices, not to mention high prices. Costs can run as high as $623,000 for a spot on *American Idol* (see Exhibit 12–8). For this reason, most advertisers decide to buy *spot announcements*.

Spot Announcements Spot announcements run in clusters between programs. They are less expensive and

The Pros and Cons of Cable TV Advertising [12–C]

The Pros

- **Selectivity.** Cable offers specialized programming aimed at particular types of viewers. Narrowcasting allows advertisers to choose programming with the viewer demographics that best match their target customers.
- **Audience demographics.** Cable subscribers are younger, better educated, and more affluent, have higher-level jobs, live in larger households, and are more likely to try new products and buy more high-ticket items, such as cars, appliances, and high-tech equipment.
- **Low cost.** Many small companies get TV's immediacy and impact without the enormous expenditures of broadcast TV. Cable advertising can sometimes cost as little as radio. Many national advertisers find sponsorship attractive, since an entire cable series can cost less to produce than a single broadcast TV commercial.
- **Flexibility.** Broadcast TV commercials need to be short because of the high costs of production and airtime, but cable ads can run up to two minutes and, in the case of infomercials, much longer. They can also be tailored to fit the programming environment.

- **Testability.** Cable is a good place to experiment, testing both new products and various advertising approaches: ad frequency, copy impact, and different media mixes.

The Cons

Like every medium, cable TV has its drawbacks.

- **Limited reach.** Only about 10 percent of households don't have cable. This was cable's main weakness in the past, but it is less so today.
- **Fragmentation.** With more than 50 channels at their disposal, cable viewers do not watch any one channel in enormous numbers. To reach the majority of the cable audience in a particular market, ads must run on many stations.
- **Quality.** Cable, particularly local cable, sometimes has poorer production quality and less desirable programming than broadcast TV.
- **Zipping and zapping.** Cable TV has some of the same drawbacks as broadcast TV, such as zipping and zapping.

▼**EXHIBIT 12–8** Advertising cost per 30-second spot on the 10 most expensive shows (2009 season, upfront prices).

Rank	Show and Network	Price
1	*American Idol* (Fox)	$623,000
2	*24* (Fox)	366,000
3	*Desperate Housewives* (ABC)	251,000
4	*Grey's Anatomy* (ABC)	224,000
5	*Two and a Half Men* (CBS)	227,000
6	*Dancing with the Stars: Results* (ABC)	205,000
7	*Survivor: Gabon* (CBS)	204,000
8	*Dancing with the Stars* (ABC)	196,000
9	*Heroes* (NBC)	194,000
10	*Brothers and Sisters* (ABC)	195,000

Source: http://blogs.tampabay.com/media/2009/04/american-idol-24-desperate-housewives-among-tvs-biggest-moneymakers.html.

more flexible than network advertising because they can be concentrated in specific regions of the country. Therefore, local businesses are frequently seen on spot schedules. An advertiser with a small budget or limited distribution may use spots to introduce a new product into one area at a time. Or an advertiser can vary its message for different markets to suit promotional needs.[20]

Spots may run 10, 15, 30, or 60 seconds and be sold nationally or locally. Spot advertising is more difficult to buy than network advertising because it involves contacting each station directly. The national rep system, in which individuals act as sales and service representatives for a number of stations, alleviates this problem.

Meanwhile, a number of large cable rep firms are also working to make the purchase of spot cable more convenient for national advertisers through technology that interconnects various cable companies in a region.[21]

Spot advertising is available only at network station breaks and when network advertisers have not purchased all of the available time, so spot ads may get lost in the clutter—which is why they tend to have less viewers and a smaller piece of the ad spending pie.

Syndication
As audiences fragment, syndicated programs become an increasingly popular adjunct or alterna-

tive to network advertising. In a little over 10 years, the syndication industry has grown from almost nothing into a $2.3 billion advertising medium.[22]

Syndication is the sale of programs on a station-by-station, market-by-market basis. In other words, a producer (for example, Warner Bros. or Disney) deals directly with stations, often through a distribution company, rather than going through the networks (see Exhibit 12–9). This efficient "direct-from-the-factory" approach gives local TV stations more programming control and greater profits. It also gives advertisers access to **inventory** (commercial time) that they might not get on network programs—often at better prices.[23] Syndication has become the largest source of programming in the United States.

Television syndication comes in three forms: off-network, first-run, and barter. In **off-network syndication**, former popular network programs (reruns) are sold to individual stations for rebroadcast. Examples include *Seinfeld* and *Friends*.

▼**EXHIBIT 12–9** TV network and syndication distribution.
a. The networks are essentially middlemen.
b. Syndication is often a more efficient way of financing and distributing programs, as the networks are cut out of the transaction.

a. Network

b. Syndication

Infomercials provide a unique opportunity for advertisers like Total Gym to demonstrate their products and generate immediate results.

First-run syndication involves original shows, like *Oprah, Inside Edition,* and *Judge Judy,* which are produced specifically for the syndication market. One of the fastest-growing trends in television is **barter syndication** (also called *advertiser-supported syndication*). These are off-network or first-run programs offered by producers to local stations free or for a reduced rate, but with some of the ad space (usually more than half) presold to national advertisers. *Wheel of Fortune, Jeopardy,* and *30 Rock* are some of the most popular examples.[24]

Syndication is a popular tool for many national advertisers. It enables them to associate with popular programs and reach some otherwise difficult to reach audiences at a lower cost per viewer than network shows. However, syndicated shows tend to be more cluttered with advertising and may not air in all markets or at consistent times.

Program-Length Ads (PLAs) In the fall of 1992, independent presidential candidate Ross Perot sat in front of a TV camera for 30 minutes with homemade flip charts and a down-home pitch for the White House and drew 20 million viewers. A month later, he pulled a respectable 19 percent of the vote.

Perot made advertising history by catapulting the **program-length advertisement (PLA)**, or **infomercial**, into the limelight. He also proved what companies that produce and sell infomercials have been saying for years: Long-form advertising can communicate a message in a way other forms can't.[25] As a result, *Advertising Age* named Perot its adman of the year.

Infomercials aren't new, but their respectability is. Before Perot, most PLA users were off–Madison Avenue marketers of hand mixers, juicers, and car waxes. Today, major marketers such as P&G, Microsoft, and Pfizer have ventured into the infomercial arena.[26] And now even networks air some of these ads, which were once relegated to independents and cable channels.[27]

Video Alternatives to TV Commercials

The thirty-second commercial faces an ever-growing list of competitors for advertising dollars, not only from traditional rivals such as print and radio, but from video alternatives. Some of these, such as Web-based programming, we discuss more fully in Chapter 13. But here we present some non-Web based advertising alternatives that either resemble or take the place of TV commercials.

TV Product Placements TV **product placements** occur when advertisers showcase their brands within television programming rather than commercials. Most people who've watched the popular show *American Idol* can't help but notice the prominent Coke cups placed in front of the judges. An entire episode of the ABC comedy *Modern Family* revolved around the Apple iPad. While these are some of the most obvious examples of product placements, advertisers such as Snapple *(Celebrity Apprentice)*, Nissan *(Heroes)*, and Ford *(24)* have invested heavily in product placements. Viewers may not even be aware just how frequently product placements appear on television. Exhibit 12–10 demonstrates just how common product placement has become.

The value of product placements can be difficult to quantify, at least in comparison to traditional advertising. One firm estimated that $4.5 billion was spent on U.S. placements in 2005, a sizable sum. Year-to-year growth in product placements was 39 percent in 2008 according to Nielsen, a growth rate that is far higher than that for traditional commercials.[28]

Product placement, where brands are woven into the content of shows, is turning up in more TV shows and movies as advertisers seek new ways to get their products noticed. Fox Television's American Idol *judges are always seen with their Coca-Cola cups prominently displayed.*

Top 10 Brands with TV Product Placement Jan. 1 to Nov. 29, 2009			Top 10 Shows with Product Placement Jan. 1 to Nov. 29, 2009		
Brand	**Category**	**Total # Occurrences**	**Program**	**Network**	**Total # Occurrences**
AT&T	Telecom	422	The Jay Leno Show	NBC	1,015
Coca-Cola	Soft Drinks	319	The Biggest Loser	NBC	704
Apple	Computer Systems	271	American Idol	Fox	553
Ford	Autos	251	Extreme Makeover: Home Edition	ABC	483
24 Hour Fitness	Fitness Centers	249	The Celebrity Apprentice	NBC	428
Nike	Apparel/Shoes	247	America's Next Top Model	CW	380
Dell	Computer Systems	207	Dancing with the Stars	ABC	331
Chevrolet	Autos	199	The Amazing Race 14	CBS	270
Star Trac	Exercise Equipment	156	The Amazing Race 15	CBS	195
Dolby	Business Services	138	Gossip Girl	CW	192

Source: The Nielsen Company. Retrieved from: http://adage.com/print?article_id=141214, December 28, 2009.

Product placement is also common in films. The prominence of the Wonder bread logo in the movie Talladega Nights: The Ballad of Ricky Bobby *will ensure that viewers remember the brand even if they forget the movie.*

Product placements offer advertisers several important benefits relative to traditional commercials. First, advertisers are increasingly concerned that many viewers avoid watching commercials. Research does suggest that in households with digital video recorders, many programs are recorded and watched after they are broadcast. People who watch a recorded show often skip through commercial messages. By placing a brand within the show, advertisers can minimize the impact of commercial avoidance. Second, having brands appear within programming offers advertisers the chance to link their products with popular characters. For example, *24* viewers don't just see the Ford Expedition, they see it being driven by Jack Bauer as he pursues the bad guys. Third, the use of product placements helps advertisers avoid the credibility issues that surround commercials. Viewers know that commercials, as sponsored messages, represent the biased viewpoint of the adver-

tiser. But brand appearances in programming may help advertisers do an "end around" such credibility problems.

Film Product Placements Marketers can also take advantage of product placements in feature films. While product placements are often thought of as a television phenomenon, the practice has a long history in film. The James Bond movie *Goldfinger* created worldwide attention for Aston Martin cars (at a cost to Ford Motor of $35 million) and most people know that Reese's Pieces candy sales surged after an appearance in the film *ET*. The

This gasoline pump from Austin, Texas–based Dresser Wayne offers Internet news headlines, traffic information, weather reports, and customized promotions on its 15-inch touchscreen. Consumers have the option to print coupons for special offers, such as a discount on a cup of coffee or an oil change. Local businesses can purchase advertising on the video screen, generating additional revenue for the fuel retailer. This WiFi- and Bluetooth-capable pump will also sell you music, which can be downloaded to your cell phone or automobile's entertainment system.

practice continues today. More recently, the 2008 movie, *Sex and the City* appealed to its target audience with a long list of products: Skyy Vodka, Apple Macbook, and Mercedes Benz, to name a few.[29] Clearly, product placements are here to stay. Hopefully, television shows will not start looking like 60-minute commercials.

Commercials at Service Stations

Prefilm commercials capitalize on an obvious reality: Filmgoers don't have much to do while they wait for the movie to start so perhaps they will find watching entertaining commercials preferable to doing nothing. This same logic lies behind the emerging practice of showing ads on service station gas pumps. The appeal for advertisers who purchase time on Gas Station TV (www.gstv.com) is that the audience is "basically tethered at the pump for an average of four to four-and-a-half minutes," according to GSTV CEO David Leider.[30] His company offers national and local advertisers the chance to present standard-length commercials with ad costs that are comparable to spot cable. Early national sponsors include Chevrolet, Pepsi, Allstate, Goodyear, and Walmart.

check yourself ✓

1. Why is syndication a popular tool for many national advertisers?

2. What are the possible benefits of product placement versus traditional commercials?

L03 Explain how to measure television audiences and select the best programs to buy.

TV AUDIENCE MEASUREMENT

Efficient advertisers study the audiences of various programs and analyze their impact and cost effectiveness against other media vehicles. To do this, they must understand the techniques and terminology used in television audience measurement.

Rating Services

The companies that measure the program audiences of TV and radio stations for advertisers and broadcasters are called **rating services**. These firms pick a representative sample of the market and furnish data on the number and characteristics of the viewers or listeners. Companies subscribe to a service and use it as a basis for planning, buying, or selling media advertising.

In the United States, Nielsen Media Research is the major rating service for television. Its flagship service, the Nielsen Television Index (NTI), uses a national sample of households equipped with

---

rating services These services measure the program audiences of TV and radio stations for advertisers and broadcasters by picking a representative sample of the market and furnishing data on the size and characteristics of the viewers or listeners.

sweeps The four, month-long periods each year when rating services measure all TV markets for station viewing habits and demographic information for the purpose of setting advertising rates. Sweep months are February, May, July, and November.

---

meters to develop audience estimates for all national TV programming. The meters are hooked up to TV sets in 25,000 homes across the country and continuously measure the channels to which each set is tuned. People meters go a step further in 25 major markets and gather information about who is watching in addition to the channel tuned.

At the local level, Nielsen surveys 1.6 million households. Household members record their viewing habits in diaries. Four times each year, during the **sweeps** month-long rating periods, Nielsen collects and processes the data. This information is used by networks and local stations to determine how much they can charge for advertising on their shows. (See Commercial Break 12–A.)

Many advertisers and broadcasters maintain that Nielsen's reports are unstable and inaccurate.[31] Nielsen's biggest problem may be the low cooperation rate among viewers who are supposed to fill out diaries. In addition, some networks and local affiliates use elaborate schemes to improve their ratings during sweeps periods, making the results not necessarily representative of the balance of the year. These issues are critical to the networks and advertisers alike, since Nielsen's numbers determine the fate of billions of dollars' worth of programming and advertising every year.

For demographic studies of TV audiences, advertisers also use the Simmons Market Research Bureau and Mediamark Research. These companies perform extensive surveys of the U.S. marketplace and publish their findings on consumer lifestyles, product usage, and media habits. Advertisers use the results for strategic planning purposes.

Cable Ratings

Reliable information on the audiences for cable programs is even harder to gather. Traditional techniques often rely on too small a sample to be statistically significant, so major cable programming services provide their own reports of audience viewership by show. Interpreting cable ratings is a confusing process, since the media planner has to integrate so much information from so many different sources. Some companies are trying to remedy the situation. ADcom Information Services, for example, is a ratings service that installs in-home recording devices to provide more reliable information. One test with Continental Cablevision in Jacksonville, Florida, confirmed that Nielsen had been underreporting cable TV audiences—in some cases dramatically.[32] Nielsen, meanwhile, has introduced its own cable TV ratings service but has been criticized for using older broadcast reporting technology.[33] This controversy is destined to rage for some time.

Defining Television Markets

Television rating services define unique geographic television markets to minimize the confusion of overlapping TV signals. The Nielsen station index uses the term **designated market areas (DMAs)** for geographic areas (cities, counties) in which the local TV stations attract the most viewing. For example, the DMA for Columbus, Georgia (see Exhibit 12–11), is the 17 counties in which the local area TV stations are the most watched.

Dayparts

Advertisers must decide when to air commercials and on which programs. Programs continue to run or are canceled depending on their ratings (percentage of the population watching). Ratings also vary with the time of day a program runs. Television time is divided into dayparts roughly as follows:

Early morning:	6:00–9:00 a.m.	(Eastern and Pacific)
Daytime:	9:00 a.m.–4:30 p.m.	
Early fringe:	4:30–7:30 p.m.	
Prime access:	7:30–8:00 p.m.	
Prime time:	8:00–11:00 p.m.	
Late news:	11:00–11:30 p.m.	
Late night:	11:30 p.m.–2:00 a.m.	

Advertising to Children: Child's Play?

Kids make up a considerable consumer group whose number and purchasing power are growing. In 1999, children ages four to twelve took in $31.3 billion in income from allowances, jobs, and gifts, and spent 92 percent of it, says James MacNeal, a market researcher who specializes in the children's market. Today, children are influencing the family's buying behavior for everything from cars to orange juice—up to $500 billion a year. Whether they're spending their own money or asking their parents to spend theirs, marketing to kids is big business and it's only getting bigger.

The benefits of reaching children are great. If won over now, they tend to be loyal customers into adulthood. Besides selling to children, advertisers also sell through children. Some companies believe they can sell more by appealing to children's preferences than to those of adults. The minivan was created because children demanded more room, says Mr. MacNeal. When kids decided the vehicle was "uncool," their opinions helped to develop the SUV. Saturday morning cartoons are the traditional vehicle for ads promoting cereals, candy, and toys. But parents are asked to buy particular brands of vacuum cleaners and other household goods because their kids saw them advertised on TV. Marketers rely on kids' "pester power" to get their products sold.

The dangers of marketing to kids from an ethical perspective are fairly clear: Children are the "vulnerable" market. They are less experienced. Their concepts of self, time, and money are immature. As a result, they know very little about their own desires, needs, and preferences—or how to use economic resources rationally to satisfy them. It is likely that child-oriented advertising can lead to false beliefs or highly improbable product expectations. Telling children about a product and accurately describing that product is probably ethical. Convincing them that they must have a toy to be popular with their friends is probably not. Nothing is likely to enrage parents and society-at-large more than the prospect of marketers manipulating and taking advantage of children.

Cereal is better if a fun character is selling it; so are beer and cigarettes as the Budweiser frogs and lizards and Joe Camel proved. In the U.K., there is criticism over the use of TV characters such as the Simpsons and Teletubbies, as well as the Spice Girls, to sell snack foods high in fat, sugar, and salt. The junk food firms face a crackdown on the hard sell of products that can make children overweight and unhealthy.

Both critics and defenders agree that advertisers should not intentionally deceive children. Federal legislation has been introduced that would reimpose the 1974 guidelines limiting advertising on children's programs. These guidelines deal with truth and accuracy.

The mood in several European countries is to tighten up children-and-advertising guidelines. Sweden has some of the strictest controls in Europe on children and advertising, banning all television advertisements aimed at children under 12. This ban includes advertisements on toys, foods, sweets, drinks, and any products that might appeal to preteens.

In the United States, the Children's Advertising Review Unit (CARU) of the Council of Better Business Bureaus (BBB) promotes responsible children's advertising and responds to public concerns. The basic activity of CARU is the review and evaluation of child-directed advertising to help avoid deceptive messages. When children's advertising is found to be misleading, inaccurate, or inconsistent with its guidelines, CARU seeks changes through the voluntary cooperation of advertisers. The BBB Web site at www.bbbsilicon.org/guidelinechild.html discusses CARU's guidelines.

Questions

1. Do bans on marketing to children compromise a basic freedom of choice and speech? Whose responsibility is it to make sure children are not inappropriately influenced by advertising? Their parents? The government? Advertisers? How far should advertisers have to go to ensure that children are not misled by their ads?

2. Study the CARU guidelines and then watch the advertising on a children's network or Saturday morning television. How well do you feel the advertisers are adhering to those guidelines?

For four decades, the life and death of network TV programs have been in the hands of the Nielsen families, households chosen with the aid of national census and other data to reflect the country's demographics. Originally there were two measuring types: those who kept diaries and those who had a black box attached to their TV sets. Someone in each of 2,400 diary homes kept a written record of which shows each person watched during the week. In the 1,700 black box households, an audiometer attached to the TV kept track of when the set was on and what channel it was tuned to. Nielsen Media Research paid these families for the permission to gather data from their viewing patterns. The information is used to compute its Nielsen Television Index (NTI), the sole source of national TV ratings.

But that method of determining national ratings has been replaced by the more accurate people meter (see illustration), an electronic device that automatically records a household's TV viewing. The people meter records the channels watched, the number of minutes of viewing, and who in the household is watching. Each person must punch in and punch out on a keypad. The microwave-based people meter keeps track of second-by-second viewing choices of up to eight household members and relays the data to a central computer, which tabulates the data overnight.

The original people meter was developed by AGB Research, a British company. AGB found clients in ad agencies, cable networks, and syndicators—all of whom believed NTI overreported broadcast network shows and underreported other types. However, Nielsen developed its own people meter, and AGB abandoned the U.S. market.

Unfortunately, Nielsen's people meter had its share of problems. At one point, Nielsen's numbers showed that millions of people suddenly stopped watching TV. The networks hit the roof, but Nielsen officials defended their system. The networks gave advertisers $150 million worth of free time, since they hadn't met rating guarantees, and decided to use eight-year trends for rating guarantees instead of just the current year's ratings. And critics are still convinced that people meter numbers are flawed.

Nielsen's competitor Arbitron is developing a passive people meter whose portable technology can register TV viewing and radio listening anywhere respondents are using them, even out of home. The new Portable People Meter (PPM) is pager-sized and would be worn by each panelist. The meter works by detecting identification codes that can be implanted in any form of audio transmission. Respondents are not required to do anything except wear the device, which will eliminate problems with panelist participation incumbent in the current people meter system.

Nielsen joined with Arbitron in its initial U.S. test of the Portable People Meter in Philadelphia in fall 2000. The Portable People Meter has already been tested successfully in the United Kingdom. Currently, Arbitron, like Nielsen, is using meters and diaries to collect TV and radio ratings.

Nielsen conducts its survey sweeps four times a year in major market areas and publishes sweeps books that are the basis for network and local station ad rates. With the advent of the passive people meter, advertisers may once again believe in the ratings they're paying for.

An interesting development in audience measurement is the single-source data made available by supermarket scanners. Once information on a family's viewing habits has been gathered, its packaged-goods purchases are measured. The implications are monumental for marketing and media planners. The leaders in single-source measurement today are Information Resources, Inc. (IRI), with its BehaviorScan service, and Nielsen, with its Home Scan service.

Applying the Breaks

1. Would you be willing to be in a Nielsen household? How would you feel about having your media and shopping habits tracked and analyzed? Is it an invasion of your privacy?
2. Does it sound to you like the rating data are reliable? If you were a network executive would you be willing to pay for it?

Source: From Billboard/Howard Appelbaum Publisher.

prime time Highest level of TV viewing (8 p.m. to 11 p.m.)

audience share The percentage of homes with TV sets in use (HUT) tuned to a specific program.

total audience The total number of homes reached by some portion of a TV program. This figure is normally broken down to determine the distribution of audience into demographic categories.

audience composition The distribution of an audience into demographic or other categories.

gross rating points (GRPs) The total audience delivery or weight of a specific media schedule. One rating point equals 1 percent of a particular market's population.

cost per rating point (CPP) A computation used by media buyers to determine which broadcast programs are the most efficient in relation to the target audience. The CPP is determined by dividing the cost of the show by the show's expected rating.

cost per thousand (CPM) A common term describing the cost of reaching 1,000 people in a medium's audience. It is used by media planners to compare the cost of various media vehicles.

daypart mix A media scheduling strategy based on a specific combination of broadcast time segments.

TV households (TVHH) The number of households in a market area that own television sets.

households using TV (HUT) The percentage of homes in a given area that have one or more TV sets turned on at any particular time. If 1,000 TV sets are in the survey and 500 are turned on, the HUT figure is 50 percent.

program rating The percentage of TV households in an area that are tuned into a specific program.

▼ **EXHIBIT 12–11** This map of the area surrounding Columbus, Georgia, shows media planners which counties are included in the designated market area (DMA) and will be reached by advertising placed on the local television stations. Columbus, Georgia, is the 125th largest DMA in the United States and contains over 200,000 TV households.

Columbus, GA Audience Figures

- DMA Market Size: #125
- Total DMA TV Households: 207,820
- Total DMA Persons 18+: 388,000
- Total DMA Adults 25-54: 214,000
- Total DMA Working Women: 92,000
- % of Cable in DMA Households: 76%

Local TV Stations

WTVM ABC - Columbus (Muscogee) Georgia
WRBL CBS - Columbus (Muscogee) Georgia
WCGT Ind. - Columbus (Muscogee) Georgia
WMCF TBN - Opelika (Lee) Alabama
WJSP/WGTV PBS - Columbus (Muscogee) Georgia
WLGA UPN - Opelika (Lee) Alabama
WCAG UATV - Lagrange (Troupe) Georgia
WLTZ NBC - Columbus (Muscogee) Georgia
WGIQ/WBIQ PBS - Louisville (Barbour) Alabama
WXTX FOX - Columbus (Muscogee) Georgia
WLGA UPN - Opelika (Lee) Alabama

Viewing is highest during **prime time** (8 to 11 p.m. Eastern and Pacific Time; 7 to 10 p.m. Central and Mountain Time). Late fringe ranks fairly high in most markets among adults, and daytime and early fringe tend to be viewed most heavily by women. To reach the greatest percentage of the advertiser's target audience with optimal frequency, the media planner determines a **daypart mix** based on TV usage levels reported by the rating services.

Audience Measurements

Rating services and media planners use many terms to define a station's audience, penetration, and efficiency. **TV households (TVHH)** refers to the number of households that own television sets. The number of TVHH in a particular market gives an advertiser a sense of the market's size. Likewise, the number of TVHH tuned in to a particular program helps the advertiser estimate the program's popularity and how many people a commercial is likely to reach.

The percentage of homes in a given area that have one or more TV sets turned on at any particular time is expressed as **households using TV (HUT)**. If there are 1,000 TV sets in the survey area and 500 are turned on, HUT is 50 percent (500/1,000).

The **program rating** refers to the percentage of TV households in an area that are tuned in to a specific program. The rating is computed as follows:

$$\text{Rating} = \frac{\text{TVHH tuned to a specific program}}{\text{Total TVHH in area}}$$

Networks want high ratings because they measure a show's popularity. More popular shows can command higher advertising rates.

The percentage of homes with sets in use (HUT) tuned to a specific program is called the **audience share**.

$$\text{Share} = \frac{\text{TVHH tuned to a specific program}}{\text{HH with a TV turned on}}$$

A program with only 500 viewers can have a 50 percent share if only 1,000 sets are turned on. *Ratings,* in contrast, measure the audience as a percentage of all TVHH in the area, whether the TV sets are on or off.

The actual number of homes reached by some portion of a program is called **total audience.** This figure is normally broken down into demographic categories to determine **audience composition**.

Gross Rating Points

In television, **gross rating points (GRPs)** are the total rating points achieved by a particular media schedule over a specific period. For example, a weekly schedule of five commercials on programs with an average household rating of 20 would yield 100 GRPs.

GRPs allow advertisers to draw conclusions about the different markets available for a client's ads by providing a comparable measure of advertising weight. However, GRPs do not reflect a market's size. For example, while campaigns in Knoxville and Charlotte might have the same GRPs, they would differ significantly in the number of homes reached.

	TV Homes (000s)	Average Cost Per Spot	Average Rating	Avg. Homes Reached (000)	Number of Spots	GRPs
Knoxville	1,002	$1,500	15	150	5	75
Charlotte	638	1,250	15	96	5	75

To better determine the relative value of television advertising markets, other measures are used, such as cost per rating point (CPP) and cost per thousand (CPM). These and other media terms will be described here and in Chapter 15.

BUYING TELEVISION TIME

The process of buying TV time can be lengthy and, depending on the number of stations in the buy, quite involved. The procedures are so complex that most large advertisers use ad agencies or media-buying services. Buying services have gained in popularity because they charge less and can save advertisers money by negotiating for desirable time slots at reduced rates. Local advertisers typically rely on station reps to help determine the best buys for their money.

Selecting Programs for Buys

Media buyers select the most efficient programs in relation to the target audience using the **cost per rating point (CPP)** and the **cost per thousand (CPM)** for each program:

$$\text{CPP} = \frac{\text{Cost}}{\text{Rating}}$$

$$\text{CPM} = \frac{\text{Cost}}{\text{Thousands of people}}$$

For example, assume *CSI* has a rating of 25, reaches 200,000 people in the primary target audience, and costs $2,000 for a 30-second spot on station WALB-TV in Albany, Georgia. Then,

$$\text{CPP} = \frac{\$2,000}{25} = \$80$$

$$\text{CPM} = \frac{\$2,000}{(200,000 \div 1,000)} = \$10$$

By calculating CPP, the media buyer can compare the cost of a rating point (reaching 1 percent of TVHH) from one program or network to another. That's good information for beginning negotiations. But rating points relate to the whole market. The real important figure is the cost of reaching 1,000 prospects in

Chart 1: Best Programs for Memphis, TN

Program	Rating	Cost	Spots	GRP
Family Matters (early evening daily, rerun, 30/70 adults to kids)	15	$34,000	32	____
Saturday morning cartoons (kids ages 2–12)	____	34,000	30	300.0
Major League Baseball game (weekends, mostly adults)	7.8	34,000	29	____
After-school special (kids ages 7–13, afternoon, daily)	____	34,000	27	205.0

Chart 2

City	TV Homes (000s)	Average Cost per Spot	Average Rating	GRP
Memphis	1,002	$1,500	15	____
Charlotte	638	1,250	15	____
Knoxville	847	____	____	____

Frequency: 5 spots

"You're Out" baseball mitts have expanded to television. As the marketing director, you choose to examine the gross rating points (GRPs) for placing your advertising. You have an idea of the days and times you want the ads to be placed. Chart 1 indicates the best programs for Memphis, Tennessee, and relevant planning data your assistant has gathered according to your preferences. Due to time constraints the chart is incomplete, but enough data are available for you to finish the chart.

Chart 1 shows the marketing figures for a single city, but now you decide to determine which of the three major cities in Tennessee will serve "You're Out" baseball mitts the best. Your assistant didn't quite finish Chart 2, but with the help of Chart 1 you can complete the needed calculations.

Applying the Breaks

1. Using the formulas in the text as a guide, complete Chart 1.
2. Assuming your budget is $68,000, use Chart 1 to decide which programs would be most effective for reaching children. Explain your selection.
3. Using Chart 1, complete the "per spot" and "rating" figures in Chart 2. Next, calculate how many GRPs each city will deliver if you buy five spots of advertising.
4. Using the completed Chart 2, calculate for each city the number of household impressions.
5. Knowing that you are running five spots, find the CPP and CPM for all three cities.
6. Based on the completed Chart 2, what city is ideal for "You're Out" baseball mitts?

your target market. That's why the CPM should be calculated against the size of your target audience, not the whole market. The lower the cost per 1,000 people in your target audience, the more efficient the show is at reaching your real prospects.

To get the best buys within the available budget, then, the media buyer substitutes stronger programs for less efficient ones.

Negotiating Prices

TV stations and cable companies publish rate cards to sell their airtime. However, since TV audiences are estimated at best, television reps will always negotiate prices.

The media buyer contacts the rep and explains what efficiency the advertiser needs in terms of CPM to make the buy. The buyer has numerous ways to negotiate lower rates: work out a package deal, accept *run-of-schedule positioning* (the station chooses when to run the commercials), or take advantage of preemption rates. A **preemption rate** is lower because the advertiser agrees to be "bumped" (preempted) if another advertiser pays the higher, nonpreemption rate.

After the advertising airs, the station returns a signed and notarized **affidavit of performance** to the advertiser or agency, specifying when the spots aired and what makegoods are available. **Makegoods** refer to free advertising time an advertiser receives to compensate for spots the station missed or ran incorrectly or because the program's ratings were substantially lower than guaranteed.[34]

check yourself ✓

1. What are some of the criticisms of ratings services?

2. What is the difference between *program rating* and *audience share*?

LO4 Describe the advantages and disadvantages of radio as an advertising medium.

THE MEDIUM OF RADIO

Radio is a personal, one-on-one medium; people tend to listen alone. And radio is mobile. It can entertain people who are driving, walking, at home, or away from home. This makes it a particularly strong way to reach people who commute by car; almost half of radio listening takes place in a car.

Radio is also adaptable to moods. In the morning, people may want to hear the news, upbeat music, or interesting chatter; in the afternoon, they may want to unwind with classical or easy-listening music.

Who Uses Radio?

In an average week, 93 percent of the U.S. population listens to radio; in an average day, over 71 percent. The average American listens to the radio more than two hours every weekday and four hours on the weekend. Radio is also cost-effective. In the last decade, the CPM for radio advertising has risen less than for any other major medium and substantially less than the consumer price index.[35] As a result, radio's advertising revenues have grown steadily.

More national advertisers are discovering radio's audience potential. Back when it was still a little company in Queens, New York, and strapped for money, Snapple Natural Beverages decided to use radio. It put its entire ad budget into a year-long schedule with a young, relatively unknown radio show host named Howard Stern. Snapple liked the way he delivered its spots as a live reader.

A few years later, Snapple began receiving letters and phone calls from people in the Midwest and West, where it didn't even have distribution. It seems that nationally syndicated talk show host Rush Limbaugh, on a restricted-calorie diet, had been giving enthusiastic on-air endorsements for Snapple Diet Iced Tea. The firm moved quickly to sign him as a paid endorser. What it learned was the power of radio, especially when combined with a popular radio personality. This combination doubled Snapple's sales every year for five years, propelled it into national distribution, and turned it into a major national advertiser, spending more than $30 million every year advertising in more than 100 U.S. radio markets.[36]

> While television tends to be a passive medium, radio actively involves people.

Although about 26 percent of the total time consumers spend with media is spent listening to the radio, spending on radio advertising only accounts for about 7.2 percent of all ad spending.[37] Clearly, although it is much cheaper to produce than television advertising, radio advertising is underrepresented and has room to grow. In the first quarter of 2010, however, revenue for radio grew 7.4 percent, more than any other medium except television.[38] As demonstrated in Exhibit 12–12, the largest national radio advertisers come from retail, automotive, telecommunications, and insurance industries.

The Use of Radio in IMC

While television tends to be a passive medium that people simply watch, radio actively involves people. They listen intently to their favorite personalities; they call in to make requests, participate during a contest, or contribute to a discussion; they use their ears and imaginations to fill in what they cannot see.

With radio, national companies can tie in to a local market and target the specific demographic group they want to reach. Most important, radio enables advertisers to maintain strategic consistency and stretch their media dollars through **imagery transfer**. Research shows that when advertisers run a schedule on TV and then convert

▼ **EXHIBIT 12–12** Radio's Top 10 National Network & Spot Advertisers: Brands (2009).

Rank	Brand	Total Radio Spending ($ millions)
1	Home Depot	79.6
2	GEICO	65.9
3	Verizon Wireless	55.7
4	Safeway	43.7
5	Walmart	30.5
6	General Motors	28.2
7	AutoZone	24.5
8	Comcast Cable	23.2
9	Verizon Communications	23.2
10	Kohl's	22.6

Source: Kantar Media Ad Spender Online, Copyright 2010. These figures may not be reproduced in any manner without express consent of Kantar Media. Retrieved from http://www.rab.com/public/marketingGuide/rabRmg.html.

the audio portion to radio commercials, fully 75 percent of consumers replay the TV spot in their minds when they hear the radio spot.[39] That extends the life and builds the impact of a TV campaign at greatly reduced cost.[40] In an IMC campaign, where message consistency is a primary objective, this is a very important feature of radio.

Local retailers like the medium for the same reasons. Also, they can tailor it to their needs. It offers defined audiences; its recall characteristics are similar to those of TV; and retailers can establish an identity by creating their own ads. Finally, since radio is so mobile, retailers can reach prospects just before they purchase. Hence, recent years have seen major spending increases by local grocery stores, car dealers, banks, and home-improvement, furniture, and apparel stores.[41]

Radio Programming and Audiences

Radio stations plan their programming carefully to reach specific audiences and to capture as many listeners as possible. The larger the audience, the more a station can charge for commercial time. Therefore, extensive planning and research go into radio programming and program changes. Stations can use tried-and-true formats, subscribe to network or syndicated programming, or

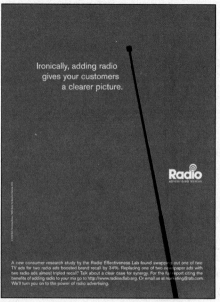

Ironically, adding radio gives your customers a clearer picture.

Radio is an important component of the media mix. It offers tremendous reach, attention, imagery, and selectivity, at a relatively low cost. In this ad, the Radio Advertising Bureau (www.rab. com) is publicizing the results of a research study that suggests advertisers can improve brand recall by replacing some of their TV and newspaper ads with radio spots (www.radioadlab.org).

devise unique approaches. Programming choices are greatly influenced by whether a station is on the AM or FM band. FM has much better sound fidelity, fewer commercial interruptions, and more varied programming.

To counteract FM's inroads, many AM stations switched to programs that don't rely on sound quality, such as news, talk, and sports. Some stations are experimenting with all comedy, midday game shows with audience participation, or formats geared to specific regions. AM stations are also trying to win back music listeners by improving their sound quality and offering stereo broadcasting.

When buying radio time, advertisers usually buy the station's *format,* not its programs. Most stations adopt one of the dozen or so standard **programming formats**: contemporary hit radio, adult contemporary, country, rock, easy listening, news/talk, and so on, as shown in Exhibit 12–13. Each format tends to appeal to specific demographic groups. The most common format is country music, which appeals to a broad cross section of Americans from 25 to 54 years old, but more adults listen to news/talk than any other format.

Contemporary hit radio (CHR) appeals to teenagers and women under 30. It provides a constant flow of top 40 hits,

▼**EXHIBIT 12–13** Radio's most popular formats. Graph shows number of radio stations for each format.

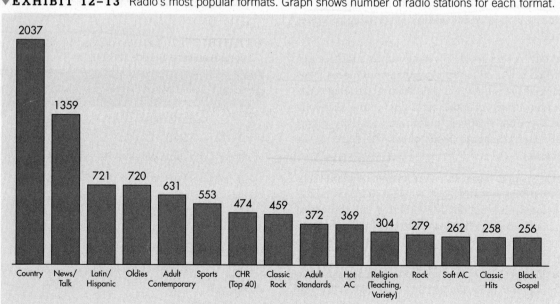

Source: Data provided with permission from the M Street Database. Copyright © 2008.

usually with minimal intrusion by disc jockeys. Another popular format, adult contemporary (or "easy oldies"), is often advertised as "light rock, less talk." This format aims at the desirable target group of working women between 25 and 54. The news/talk, easy-listening, and nostalgia formats tend to have high listenership among men and women over 35.[42]

A major trend in radio today is the resurgence of radio networks, which offer services and programs that complement a station's local programming. A station might subscribe to ABC Radio's daily Paul Harvey news and commentary, CBS's weekly *House of Blues Radio Hour,* EIB's Rush Limbaugh, and Westwood One's *Larry King Show.*

There are now over 20 national radio networks, including the multiple "mininetworks" of ABC, CBS, Westwood One, and Unistar (see Exhibit 12–14), and numerous syndicators offer programs from live rock concerts to public-affairs discussions. To stand out, 80 percent of licensed radio stations are opting for syndicated and network offerings.[43] As more stations carry these programs and more listeners tune in, national advertisers find them increasingly attractive.

Satellite Radio and Portable Music Devices

A challenge to "terrestrial" radio has been mounted by networks that transmit signals nationwide via satellite. Until 2008, **satellite radio** had been a two-player competition between first-out-of-the-block XM and its chief rival, Sirius. In July of that year, the two companies merged to become Sirius XM Radio. The combined networks have continued to add a sizable number of subscribers, reaching nearly 19 million in early 2010.

In order to receive satellite radio, an audience member must pay a monthly subscription fee and invest in a receiver capable of receiving the networks' signals. Sirius XM has attempted to convince people that radio is worth paying for by offering two important benefits not available to terrestrial radio listeners: a large number of program choices (dozens of stations and a variety of music and nonmusic formats) and exclusive programming, such as Howard Stern, Oprah Winfrey, and Martha Stewart.

How significant is satellite radio as an alternative to terrestrial radio? It is difficult at present to be sure. While Sirius XM has successfully leveraged exclusive talent and programming (NBA, NFL, and NASCAR) to attract subscribers, it took the company until 2010 to finally turn a small profit after nearly going bankrupt in 2009. The financial difficulties stem from the expense associated with high-priced talent, such as Stern, and the costs associated with attracting new subscribers. But there are bright signs as well. Increasing auto sales suggest promise for growth in the subscriber

programming formats The genre of music or other programming style that characterizes and differentiates radio stations from each other (i.e., contemporary hit radio, country, rock, etc.).

satellite radio A proprietary, subscription-based method of broadcasting digital audio programs via satellite.

▼ **EXHIBIT 12–14** The radio mininetworks provide various types of programming including news, talk, and sports. Each network targets a specific demographic group such as Adults 25–54 (CBS) or Men 18 years and older (ESPN).

ABC Radio Networks			Westwood One Radio Networks		
Network	**Target Demo**	**Affiliates**	**Network**	**Target Demo**	**Affiliates**
Prime	A 25–54	2,566	Westwood One Mutual	A 25–54	1,385
Platinum	A 25–54	2,566	Westwood One NBC	A 25–54	1,338
Galaxy	A 12+	1,030	Westwood One Source	A 12–34	115
Genesis	A 12–34	317	Westwood One Programming	A 12–54	3,600
Excel	A 18–49	111	Westwood One Play by Play Sports	A 18+	1,192
ESPN	M 18+	231	Westwood One Talk	A 25–54	1,236
ABC Special Programming	A 12+	3,829			

CBS Radio Networks			Unistar Radio Networks		
Network	**Target Demo**	**Affiliates**	**Network**	**Target Demo**	**Affiliates**
CBS Radio Network	A 25–54	470	Super	A 25–54	1,256
CBS Spectrum	A 25–54	570	Power	A 18–49	218
CBS Radio Sports	A 25–54	300	CNN+	A 25–54	1,248
CBS Radio Programs	A 18–54	126	CNBC Business Radio	A 25–54	72
CBS Hispanic Radio Network	A 25–54	39	Unistar Weekly Music/ Personality Programs	A 12–49	1,700

Source: Data provided with permission from the M Street Database. Copyright © 2008.

network radio Provides national and regional advertisers with simple administration and low effective net cost per station.

total audience plan (TAP) A radio advertising package rate that guarantees a certain percentage of spots in the better dayparts.

spot radio National advertisers' purchase of airtime on individual stations. Buying spot radio affords advertisers great flexibility in their choice of markets, stations, airtime, and copy.

local time Radio spots purchased by a local advertiser.

drive times The morning and afternoon hours when the number of radio listeners is the highest. Coinciding with rush hour, drive times are usually Monday through Friday at 6–10 a.m. and 3–7 p.m.

run-of-station (ROS) Leaving placement of radio spots up to the station in order to achieve a lower ad rate.

base. And the addition of exclusive programming has attracted big advertisers, including Acuvue, Dove, General Electric, Iams, JCPenney, SlimFast, Splenda, Target, and War-

ners TrueFit.[44] The merger also increased the size of the audience for advertisers and reduced the need to compete for content. At this point, it appears that satellite radio will remain a player.

Another challenge to radio is the explosion of iPods and other music players, now also being integrated into cell phones. Over 200 million iPods had been sold worldwide as of 2010 and roughly half of the recent model cell phones can play music. This will have the greatest impact on young (age 12–24) listeners who already listen to radio 20 percent less than the national average. And the trends suggest they are listening to radio less every year.[45]

check yourself ✓

1. What characteristics of radio make it such an "active" and "personal" medium?

2. How does *imagery transfer* work?

L05 Explain the options for advertising on radio and how radio audiences are measured.

BUYING RADIO TIME

Advertisers need a basic knowledge of the medium to buy radio time effectively: the types of radio advertising available for commercial use, a basic understanding of radio terminology, and how radio audiences are measured.

Types of Radio Advertising

An advertiser may purchase network, spot, or local radio time. Advertisers like the size of the audience, selectivity, and cost efficiency of radio (see My Ad Campaign 12–D, "The Pros and Cons of Radio Advertising").

Networks Advertisers may use one of the national radio networks to carry their messages to the entire national market simultaneously via stations that subscribe to the network's programs. In addition, more than 100 regional radio networks in the United States operate with information oriented toward specific geographic markets. **Network radio** provides national and regional advertisers with simple administration and low effective net cost per station.

Spot Radio **Spot radio** affords national advertisers great flexibility in their choice of markets, stations, airtime, and copy. They can put commercials on the air quickly—some stations require as little as 20 minutes' lead time—and advertisers can build local acceptance by using local personalities.

Local Radio **Local time** denotes radio spots purchased by a local advertiser or agency. Radio advertising can be either live or taped. Most radio stations use recorded shows with live news in between. Likewise, nearly all radio commercials are prerecorded to reduce costs and maintain broadcast quality.

Radio Terminology

For the most part, the terminology used for radio is the same as for other media, but some terms are unique to radio. The most common of these are the concepts of dayparts, average quarter-hour audiences, and cumes (cumulative audiences).

Dayparts The radio day is divided into five dayparts:

6 a.m.–10 a.m.	Morning drive
10 a.m.– 3 p.m.	Daytime
3 p.m.– 7 p.m.	Afternoon (or evening) drive
7 p.m.–midnight	Nighttime
Midnight–6 a.m.	All night

Rating services measure audiences for only the first four dayparts because all-night listening is very limited and not highly competitive. Heaviest radio use occurs during **drive times** (6–10 a.m. and 3–7 p.m.) during the week (Monday through Friday), when many listeners are commuting to or from work or school.

Radio stations base their rates on the time of day the advertiser wants commercials aired, but the rates are negotiable according to supply and demand at any given time. To obtain the lowest rate, an advertiser orders spots on a **run-of-station (ROS)** basis, similar to ROP in newspaper advertising. However, this leaves total control of spot placement up to the station. So most stations offer a **total audience plan (TAP)** package rate, which guarantees a certain percentage of spots in the better dayparts if the advertiser buys a package of time.

TWELVE HOURS WITH THE ROLLING STONES
SPECIAL. SATURDAY, JULY THE 22ᴺᴰ, FROM 12 AM TO 12 PM. RADIO SAIGON. FM 100.1

Radio stations that choose to accept programming from external sources, like the Westwood One Radio Network (www.westwoodone.com), can increase their market share during instances of special programming. Westwood One is well known for bringing high-quality recordings of top-name concerts, such as The Rolling Stones, to radio stations that might not otherwise be able to acquire such programming.

average quarter-hour audience (AQH persons)
A radio term referring to the average number of people who are listening to a specific station for at least 5 minutes during a 15-minute period of any given daypart.

Average Quarter-Hour Audience Average quarter-hour audience (AQH persons) identifies the average number of people listening to a specific station for at least 5 minutes during an average 15-minute period of any given daypart. For example, station KKDA in Dallas/Fort Worth, Texas, has an average quarter-hour afternoon drive listenership of 33,800, meaning that any day, during an average 15-minute period between 3 and 7 p.m., about 33,800 people ages 12 and older are tuned in for at least 5 minutes.

The Pros and Cons of Radio Advertising [12–D]

The Pros
The principal advantages of radio are high reach and frequency, selectivity, and cost efficiency.

- **Reach and frequency.** Radio offers an excellent combination of reach and frequency. The average adult listens more than three hours a day, radio builds a large audience quickly, and a normal advertising schedule easily allows repeated impact on the listener.
- **Selectivity.** Specialized radio formats, with prescribed audiences and coverage areas, enable advertisers to select the market they want to reach: a specific sex, age group, ethnic or religious background, income group, employment category, educational level, or special interest.
- **Cost efficiency.** Radio offers its reach, frequency, and selectivity at one of the lowest costs per thousand, and radio production is inexpensive. National spots can be produced for about one-tenth the cost of a TV commercial. And local stations often produce local spots for free.
- **Other advantages.** Radio also offers timeliness, immediacy, local relevance, and creative flexibility.

The Cons
In spite of these advantages, radio has limitations: It's an aural medium only, its audience is highly segmented, the advertiser's commercials are short-lived and often only half-heard, and each ad must compete with the clutter of other advertising.

- **Limitations of sound.** Radio is heard but not seen, a drawback if the product must be seen to be understood. Some agencies think radio restricts their creative options.
- **Segmented audiences.** If a large number of radio stations compete for the same audience, advertisers who want to blanket the market have to buy at multiple stations, which may not be cost-effective.
- **Short-lived and half-heard commercials.** Radio commercials are fleeting. They can't be kept like a newspaper or a magazine ad. Radio must compete with other activities for attention, and it doesn't always succeed.
- **Clutter.** Stations with the greatest appeal for advertisers have more commercials. Advertisers must produce a commercial that stands out from the rest.

average quarter-hour rating The average quarter-hour persons estimate expressed as a percentage of the total market population.

average quarter-hour share The radio station's audience (AQH persons) expressed as a percentage of the total radio listening audience in the area.

gross impressions The number of people in the audience multiplied by the number of times an advertisement is delivered to that audience.

gross rating points Gross impressions expressed as a percentage of a particular market's population.

cume persons The total number of different people listening to a radio station for at least one 15-minute segment over the course of a given week, day, or daypart.

cume rating The estimated number of cume persons expressed as a percentage of the total market population.

Because advertisers typically buy radio spots according to station format rather than by specific program, the AQH is typically a strong indicator of the most opportune time to run ads. Commercial ads, like this humorous spot from Hooked on Phonics.com (www.hop. com), are frequently aired during dayparts with high listenership, such as drive times. This works especially well for Hooked on Phonics.com, whose listener base—parents of younger children—are very likely to be in the car with their children at this time.

(DAD READING TO DAUGHTER)

DAD: OK, honey. One story, then it's bedtime . . .

LITTLE GIRL: OK, Daddy!

DAD: Once upon a time, there was the Letter A. But A couldn't find any other letters to play with . . .

LITTLE GIRL: Ohhh . . . that's so sad!

DAD: Wait, it gets better . . .

So A called a meeting. There, he met Letter B, who thought they should merge . . .

LITTLE GIRL (LAUGHING): Daddy, you're silly!

DAD: I know. Then, they did a leveraged buyout for letters C through L . . .

LITTLE GIRL: Really? . . .

DAD: And offered stock options for M through Z . . .

LITTLE GIRL: What's that? . . .

DAD: And they all lived happily ever after! . . .

LITTLE GIRL: Yayyyy!

SEGUE TO ANNOUNCER VOICEOVER OVER DISTINCTIVE NEEDLEDROP MUSIC. If you're a parent, you don't have to invent stories to get your kids to love reading. Just go to the best place in cyberspace for help . . . the Hooked on Phonics Web site. Visit us today at A-B-C-D-E-F-G dot-com. Take the FREE personalized reading assessment to find out how to help your child become a more confident reader.

So for all this—and much, much more—log onto Hooked on Phonics at the most memorable Web address anywhere: A-B-C-D-E-F-G dot-com. (Musical logo played under VO.)

NEEDLEDROP MUSIC OUT.

The Reports That Make or Break Radio Stations [12–C]

Media buyers use the data from three major audience rating services to determine which programs and stations will deliver the greatest number of target listeners.

Arbitron

The Arbitron rating service chooses a group of representative listeners in each of 257 cities and gives them a diary for tracking the time they spend listening to radio. Listeners return the diaries to Arbitron at the end of each week for tabulation, and Arbitron compiles the results into a quarterly report.

The Arbitron Book, available on Arbitron's Web site (www.arbitron.com), reports the number of listeners to particular stations and shows their ages, sexes, and preferred listening times. Radio stations are major clients, but some ad agencies and radio sales reps also subscribe.

Arbitron recently deployed the Portable People Meter in the top 50 radio markets (see Commercial Break 12–A), enabling the electronic measurement of radio audiences.

Birch Research

Birch Research uses phone surveys rather than diaries to obtain listener data. Interviewers talk to representative listeners in 130 major radio markets. Results are published monthly and summarized quarterly. Birch also offers Birchscan, a monthly computerized report.

RADAR

RADAR (Radio's All-Dimension Audience Research) also rates network radio programs based on phone interviews with listeners. Each listener is called daily for a week and asked about listening habits from the day before until that moment. RADAR conducts research year-round and publishes results annually in *Radio Usage* and *Network Radio Audiences*. A number of specialized reports are also available.

Applying the Breaks

1. What are the advantages and disadvantages of these radio audience measurement methods?
2. Which audience measurement method, diary or phone interview, is best? Why?

The **average quarter-hour rating** expresses the AQH persons as a percentage of the population. Since KKDA is located in an area of 3,072,727 people, its average quarter-hour persons could be expressed as an average quarter-hour *rating* of 1.1:

$$\frac{\text{AQH persons}}{\text{Population}} \times 100 = \text{AQH rating}$$

$$\frac{33,800}{3,072,727} \times 100 = 1.1\%$$

The same idea can be expressed in terms of **average quarter-hour share**: the station's audience (AQH persons) expressed as a percentage of the total radio listening audience in the area. For example, if the total average quarter-hour persons for all stations during the afternoon drive is 676,000, then radio station KKDA's average quarter-hour afternoon drive share is 5 percent:

$$\frac{\text{AQH persons of a station}}{\text{AQH persons of all stations}} \times 100 = \text{AQH share}$$

$$\frac{33,800}{676,000} \times 100 = 5\%$$

The **gross impressions** are arrived at by multiplying the station's audience (AQH persons) by the number of times a message is delivered to that audience. For example, if an advertiser runs 24 spots on KKDA during the afternoon drive, then 811,200 gross impressions will be delivered:

$$\frac{\text{AQH}}{\text{persons}} \times \frac{\text{Number}}{\text{of spots}} = \text{Gross impressions}$$

$$33,800 \times 24 = 811,200$$

The **gross rating points** of a radio schedule are the sum of all ratings points delivered by that schedule, or the gross impressions expressed as a percentage of the population being measured:

$$\frac{\text{Gross impressions}}{\text{Population}} \times 100 = \text{GRPs}$$

$$\frac{811,200}{3,072,727} \times 100 = 26.4$$

or

$$\text{AQH rating} \times \text{Number of spots} = \text{GRPs}$$

$$1.1 \times 24 = 26.4$$

Cume Estimates **Cume persons** is the total number of *different* people who listen to a radio station for at least five minutes in a quarter-hour within a reported daypart (also called *unduplicated audience* or *reach*).

In the example above, our schedule on station KKDA generated 811,200 gross impressions, but that does not mean that 811,200 different people heard our commercials. Many people heard the commercials three, four, or five times. By measuring the number of different people who listened to KKDA, rating services provide the *reach potential* of our radio schedule, which in this case was estimated to be 167,800.

The **cume rating** is the cume persons expressed as a percentage of the population being measured. For example,

$$\frac{167,800 \times 100}{3,072,727} = 5.5\%$$

This means that 5.5 percent of the Dallas/Fort Worth population listened to KKDA at least once during the afternoon drive. The average listener heard our commercial 4.8 times, but we'll learn how to calculate that in Chapter 15. ∎

check yourself ✓

1. Why would a radio advertiser be willing to pay a premium for one specific daypart over another?

2. What is the difference between a radio advertisement schedule's *GRP* and *cume rating*?

chapter thirteen

digital interactive media

When Electronic Arts brought out its ground-breaking game *Mercenaries 2,* there was never any question as to whether it would promote the game using social media. After all, when you make a living providing the ultimate interactive gaming experience, social media are just an extension of what you do best.

Social media have infiltrated the average American's life. Almost 99.5 million people accessed Youtube.com and 151 million U.S. people accessed Facebook in October 2010. Those two numbers rank 5th and 4th, respectively, in U.S. Web traffic. Social media are a staple in the fabric of every American's life and have revolutionized the way we connect and communicate.

Social media have also changed the way advertisers communicate, interact, and engage with audiences. Never before have marketers been able to really "hear" what their consumers are saying about a product. The ability of savvy marketers to quickly take stock of a product's viability, or even find problems, is unprecedented. Blogs, microblogs, and social networks allow consumers to express their opinions and experiences for anyone willing to listen. In fact certain big brands have set up shop inside of social media as a customer service tool.

Electronic Arts (EA) has understood the power of social media for years; it was one of the first advertisers to have a Myspace page, created for its *Burnout 3* title back in 2004. Since then, EA has developed blogs, microblogs, fan pages, company or channel pages, and more in an effort to participate in a conversation with fans—understanding their likes, dislikes, and overall product suggestions, good and bad.

The *Mercenaries 2* ad was a natural descendant of how the game plays; it included a brash over-the-top first-person shooter set in Venezuela and an ominous soundtrack. Ad agency Draftfcb West tapped Wojahn Bros. Music to create the track. As one blogger put it: "The

continued on p. 334

LEARNING OBJECTIVES

LO1 Discuss the various types of digital interactive media.

LO2 Describe who uses the Internet and how they use it.

LO3 Explain how time and space on the Internet are bought.

LO4 Discuss the types of Internet advertising.

LO5 Detail the problems with the Internet as an advertising medium and suggest ways to use it in IMC.

continued from p. 333

music selection is uniquely awesome. We're so used to seeing combat games being dressed up with special effects and a dark soundtrack that this one immediately stands out . . . *High School Musical s*tyle."

And then it happened—one person saw the ad, went looking for it on Youtube.com and sent it to all his friends. Then another person reposted the ad in his "channel," as did more and more, until suddenly the new *Mercenaries 2* ad had been viewed over 500,000 times in less than two days. With over 30 response videos and 2,000 comments, it quickly vaulted into the top 20 most discussed, most commented upon, and top-rated video game videos of all time on Youtube.

Users began posting videos of how to play the music behind the song. And then it really happened. An outpouring of love for the song manifested itself into a petition for a full-length version. And EA was listening. Within a few short days another video was released, this one a 2-minute 59-second behind-the-scenes making of the ad, and attached was the full-length version of the song.

Social networking site Facebook allows Web users to join networks organized by their school, city, or shared interest. Founded in 2004, the site has surged in popularity, attracting 124 million unique users worldwide in May 2008.

The song became so popular that it made its way onto radio, a Monday Night Football game, ringtones and iTunes, and ultimately into hip hop fame when Cam'Ron used the clip with his song *Owe Me.*

Everywhere the song went, the title of *Theme Song for the New* Mercenaries 2 *Game* also went, a true media extension.

Since the launch of the campaign, the *Mercenaries 2* ads have garnered well over 3.4 million views on Youtube.com alone, with pages and pages of comments.

So while advertisers are trying to figure out how to be effective in the "new" environment of social media, they might want to check with EA. Social media are where EA reaches its customers. And EA customers wouldn't have it any other way. ■

LO1 Discuss the various types of digital interactive media.

DIGITAL INTERACTIVE MEDIA

Advertising-related technologies never stop evolving. They've already given us the personal computer, the mobile phone, the Internet, high-definition TV, digital media players, blue-ray, IPTV, VOIP, and iPads—and the software to make it all simple enough for anybody to use.

These are not just advertising media. In many cases, they represent completely new ways of living and doing business. For example, a typical teen watching a high school basketball game won't just use his phone to place a call. He'll use it to snap a picture of the star player's Nike shoes, send the photo over Gmail to his Dad (asking for his own pair), post it at Facebook, and Twitter his friends to seek their opinions about the shoes. All of this will be accomplished in a minute or two. While e-mailing, Facebooking, and Twittering, the teen will be exposed to several marketing messages, some of which can easily identify his general location and interests. And he will leave a trail of activities for other marketers to ponder.

Digital media are truly revolutionary in their effect on our daily lives, and it's a revolution for marketers, too. As the nation's biggest advertisers realized that digital media offer wonderful opportunities for achieving real, bottom-line results, they started increasing their spending dramatically. In light of this change, the Internet research company eMarketer reports that online ad spending will reach $25 billion in 2010. That is an increase from 2009 of 10.8 percent.[1]

In addition to this phenomenal growth, by offering true interactivity, online media enable businesses and other organizations to develop and nurture relationships with their customers and other stakeholders on a global scale at very efficient cost.

The new interactive media include the Internet and all its associated online services, digital catalogs and magazines, mobile phones, and interactive television. Most prominent is the Internet, so that is our focus in this chapter. The Internet continues to surge in importance as a mass forum for advertising as well as other communications (see Exhibit 13–1). In recognition of this explosive growth, we need to understand what the medium is, how it is organized, how people get to it, and how advertisers buy it and use it in their marketing plans.

The Internet

The Internet has come a long way from its simple roots. While some people assume it is very new, in fact it has been around for close to 40 years.

The **Internet** is a global network of computers that communicate with one another through **protocols**, which are common rules for linking and sharing information. The Internet began in the early 1960s as a result of the Defense Department's Advanced Research Projects Agency (ARPA) plan to create a network that could survive a cold war attack. ARPAnet had little commercial value; its primary users were governmental organizations and research universities, and the Internet of today is a far different medium. However, ARPAnet was important because its structure, a **distributed network**, was revolutionary. Traditionally, media content has been delivered through **centralized networks**, in which a hub, such as a TV station, a

▼ **EXHIBIT 13–1** U.S. online advertising spending growth, 2002–2011 (% increase/decrease vs. prior year).

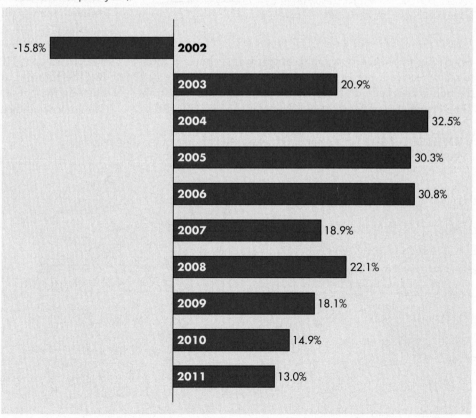

Year	Value
2002	-15.8%
2003	20.9%
2004	32.5%
2005	30.3%
2006	30.8%
2007	18.9%
2008	22.1%
2009	18.1%
2010	14.9%
2011	13.0%

Social media such as MySpace allow users to share personal profiles,
blogs, music, pictures, and video.

newspaper publisher, or a cable company, distributes content
to many receivers (see Exhibit 13–2). In a centralized system, if
the hub is knocked out, receivers are left without information.
But a distributed network is one characterized by many differ-

▼ **EXHIBIT 13–2** In a centralized network, a hub distributes content to many
receivers. A distributed network has many different hubs and links.

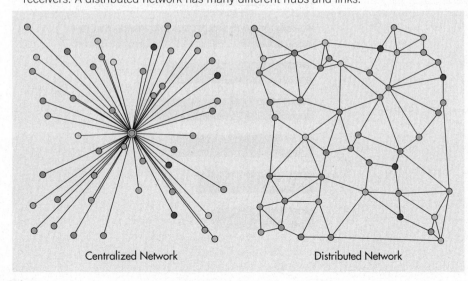

Centralized Network   Distributed Network

ent hubs and links, which allows continuous communication
even if some connections stop working. And, importantly, no
single participant controls the content.

There are at least two other important distinctions between
the Internet and traditional media. The first is the cost of
time and/or space. In traditional media, time (on TV or radio) and space (in print) are precious and limited resources.
Network TV commercials average 30 seconds, which is a very
small window, and that window is expensive, averaging in
the hundreds of thousands of dollars. In contrast, space on
the Internet is vast and inexpensive. Web sites can store as
much information as a company wishes. For consumers who
require lots of facts before they make a decision to buy, this is
a real plus.

The second distinction between traditional media and the Internet concerns the relationship between those who create
content and those who consume it. Traditional media were
content creators while audiences were content consumers. As
an example, NBC develops and schedules a show and, if you
enjoy it, you sit down on a certain night at the same time each
week to watch it. NBC is the creator and you are the consumer.
But the Internet, from its beginnings, has been *interactive,*
blurring the line between content providers and consumers.
The Internet audience doesn't just consume online content; it
interacts with it and helps to create it.

The Web

In the early 1980s, the National Science
Foundation expanded ARPAnet by supporting a fast data network that linked information centers across the United States.
At the same time, online content providers
such as AOL and CompuServe built an Internet audience by providing news, information, and e-mail services to subscribers.

Throughout the 1990s, the number of people using the Web doubled each year. Fueling the medium's growth were the
increasing popularity and affordability of
personal computers and modems, which
allowed computers to tap into the Internet
via an ordinary phone line. The 1990s was
also the decade in which people began

going online to access a particular part of the Internet known as the **Web**. The Web, as its name implies, was a distributed network of content providers and users, communicating through a protocol known as **HTML**, or HyperText Markup Language. HTML allowed for the relatively easy creation of Web pages that can be easily linked to all kinds of content, including other **Web pages** or sites (and, later, photographs, movies, databases, audio files, and such). Viewing Web pages was made easy by the development of **Web browsers**, software that interpreted HTML.

Today, the Internet is a global medium. People around the world use it to read news, research products, stay in touch with friends, and share information. They do so using high-speed broadband access, which makes it easy to watch videos, listen to audio programming, and download large files.

This new medium has proven highly popular. The Web exploded from about 50 sites in 1993 to over 206 billion as of June 2010.[2]

Web Portals and Popular Web Sites

Many of the Web sites that attract the largest audiences each day are known as portals. A **portal** is a site that provides an array of content

customers, but to sell directly without the expense of brick and mortar stores.

Google and Internet Search

Most people looking to find information on the Web use a **search engine**. Search engines are sites that allow people to type a word or phrase into a text box and then quickly find information.

Google is, at present, the most popular destination on the Web, reaching an astonishing 40 percent of all Web users each day.[4]

The Rise of Social Media

In our chapter opener we talked about social media platforms such as Facebook, Youtube.com, MySpace, and Twitter. The importance of social media can be seen by the fact that Facebook is beginning to challenge Google as the most popular destination on the Web. But what are **social media**? OnlineMatters defines social media as "any form of online publication or presence

> [Making money at a portal involves attracting lots of people and keeping them around to see advertising. This revenue model is similar to that of "old media."]

and services so broad that (it is hoped) users spend a lot of time at the portal and very little time anywhere else. The reason that portals want to keep visitors for as long as possible is that doing so creates many opportunities for exposing visitors to ads or fee-based content. Thus, making money at a portal involves attracting lots of people and keeping them around so they can see advertising. You may be thinking that this revenue model seems similar to that of traditional media and, in fact, it is. The more people a portal attracts, the more it can charge for ads on popular pages. The big portals are some of the most famous names on the Web: AOL, MSN, and Yahoo! Yahoo! remains one of the most visited sites on the Web, reaching over a quarter of all Web users on a daily basis.[3]

Many traditional media companies have also found success on the Web. CBS, the Weather Channel, ESPN, CNN, and Fox all have top-visited Web sites. Other popular sites are maintained by companies, including Apple, Microsoft, AT&T, Target, and Adobe. For traditional media, the Web offers new ways to engage audiences. And for big companies, the Web provides the means to not only communicate with

that allows end users to engage in multi-directional conversations in or around the content on the Web site."[5] This definition suggests that social media come in many forms. Facebook is an example, but so are Flickr, an online photo-sharing site, HuffingtonPost, a site for left-leaning blogs, and even Google Earth, since users can post information and photos about different places. In fact, most mainstream Web sites have incorporated social media elements into their sites to gain more *stickiness,* an industry term that refers to the ability of a site to keep visitors coming back. More likely than not, you have either a MySpace or a Facebook profile, or both. These sites are popular for their ability to connect individuals in a manner that has never been seen before. Social media replicate the real world without its geographical barriers. Until recently, if you wanted to socialize with individuals who had similar likes and dislikes you would form clubs or outings, such as a book club. However, you were limited to people who resided in your general vicinity, which restricted the size of the club. Social media break down those barriers and allow people to "meet" virtually to discuss and share their interests with each other.

> SOCIAL MEDIA GO BEYOND PROMOTION BECAUSE COMPANIES MUST LISTEN AS MUCH AS THEY SPEAK. BUT FOR ALL OF THE DIFFICULTIES, MARKETERS GAIN ONE ENORMOUS BENEFIT: THEY ARE PUT BACK IN TOUCH WITH THEIR CUSTOMERS.

Craigslist provides Internet users a free marketplace to buy and sell products. The rapid growth and dramatic success of such sites has come at the expense of newspaper classified sections.

MySpace, Facebook, and now Twitter have revolutionized the way we communicate with each other, allowing one person to share anything that interests them, with his or her entire friends list, whether that be related to work, politics, leisure, family, shopping, product use, or other.

Unfortunately for marketers, harnessing social media as an advertising medium is not as cut and dry as it is for other forms of media. In fact most best practices suggest that a brand first listen to what is being said, rather than jump right in to the social conversation. For marketers unused to a two-way exchange of information social media can be daunting.

One of the many attributes of social media is openness. When someone posts to Facebook, comments on another's blog, or bookmarks a page using De.lic.ious, that information is open for anyone to see. A host of tools collects all of this information using keywords. Companies like Nielsen's Buzzmetrics or JD Powers's Umbria Communications help marketers aggregate all the information being posted about their brands or products to understand the general consensus, negative or positive. Companies like Electronic Arts (as mentioned in the opening chapter vignette), Coca-Cola, Virgin America, and Procter & Gamble all have a social media component for each and every brand or product they market.

Smart marketers understand that social media foster interactions that go beyond promotion or advertising. In social media, companies must listen as much as they speak. Responsiveness is as important a skill as persuasiveness. But for all of the difficulties posed by social media, one important benefit for marketers stands out: social media put companies back in touch with their customers. And that can be a very good thing.

Other Interactive Media

In addition to the Internet, advertisers now also use other new media vehicles, such as DVDs, kiosks, and interactive TV. While they are not major media forms, they do warrant some brief discussion.

DVD and Blue-Ray Catalogs and Magazines
Virtually every new personal computer today comes equipped with **DVD**, or its successor, Blue-ray, capabilities. The benefit of this technology is storage space; a high concentration of data, combined with full-motion video and high-quality audio, can be stored on one inexpensive disk.

Interactive TV
Imagine you're watching *American Idol* and a spot for State Farm Insurance appears. You remember you're not happy with your current insurance carrier. You pick up your remote control and click it on a box in the corner of the screen: "For more information." A menu appears. You click on "Auto insurance," and a multimedia presentation begins. At various prompts, you click your remote to get more information. At the end you request the location of a State Farm agent. The directions print out on a PC printer attached to your TV. Then it's back to *American Idol*.

DVDs Digital Video Discs that have a large amount of storage space. DVDs can hold movies, music, and many other things that can be played on a DVD player or a computer.

interactive TV A personal audience venue where people can personally guide TV programming through a remote control box while watching TV.

Although this rosy scenario fills the dreams of many advertisers, the reality is not nearly so encouraging. **Interactive TV** is powered by digital video recorders (DVRs, sometimes also called *personal video recorders*). In 2003, interactive TV, provided by companies such as TiVo and DirecTV, reached 3.2 million U.S. households. TiVo subscribers take full advantage of their commercial-skipping powers, zooming past three-quarters of advertisements in programs they have recorded.

Other forms of advertising, like TiVo's "Showcase" feature, allow subscribers to access entertaining, long-format ads. For the moment, however, because the percentage of interactive TV households remains so low, most advertisers are simply repackaging existing TV or Internet spots for the interactive TV format rather than investing in developing unique content.

Mobile Advertising

Apple's iPhone has revolutionized digital advertising in a way not seen since the introduction of the Web. Over 16 million of the devices were sold in 2009, and

some predict sales in 2010 (with the introduction of the iPhone 4) could reach 40 million.[6]

The iPhone has increased data plan usage, or non-voice related consumption over the carriers' networks. iPhone users are heavy users of video and mobile TV.[7] People use their phones to download applications and games, surf the Web, and send multimedia messages. The appeal to advertisers is that the phone is the only real portable and personally identifiable medium. And using a phone for shopping is not some far-off possibility. Large numbers of people already shop on the phone now.[8]

While it still constitutes less than 1 percent of all advertising globally, mobile ad spending increased 80 percent from 2008 to 2009.[9] The most common form of mobile advertising, banner advertising (also called WAP, Wireless Access Protocol, Banner), is very similar to online banner advertising. Banner advertising is standardized by the Mobile Marketing Association (MMA), which much like the Interactive Advertising Bureau (IAB) for online banner advertising, has guidelines and standards for mobile Web advertising (they can be found here: http://mmaglobal.com/policies/global-mobile-advertising-guidelines). Banner ads can also be placed into applications that have been downloaded to a user's phone and can be swapped as those applications reconnect with the network.

The other form of advertising and the one that represents the largest inventory is sponsored SMS (Short Message System). Mobile phone users usually refer to these as "text messages." One benefit to marketers who generate these ads is that the end-user need not own a smartphone. Almost any mobile device can receive texts. Companies like 4INFO, in the United States, offer news, horoscopes, and sports scores, among other things, for free to users via SMS, and

People access the Web from many sources besides computers. Smartphones like the iPhone are increasingly important to digital advertisers.

advertisers sponsor these messages. The carriers have set up very strict guidelines in the use of SMS and act as a gatekeeper for all messages that go over their networks in an effort to reduce SMS spam. A smartphone user can respond to an SMS ad, via a link, at a mobile Web page.

check yourself ✓

1. What are the major types of digital interactive media?

2. What are some of the opportunities marketers can take advantage of with digital interactive media?

3. What are some of the important marketing-related destinations on the Web?

LO2 Describe who uses the Internet and how they use it.

MEASURING THE INTERNET AUDIENCE

When marketers and the media first began trumpeting the marvels of the Internet, they quickly noted the potentially vast size of its user population. As Exhibit 13–3 shows, most Americans use the Internet. And around the world, the number of Internet users is approaching two billion.[10]

How People Access the Internet

While traditionally people think of accessing the Internet through a computer, the reality is that most people are accessing the Internet these days in a variety of ways with a variety of devices. The iPhone, Blackberry, and phones running Google's Android, have increased consumer awareness and demand for access to the Internet. Millions of users also access the Web via gaming systems, such as the Xbox, the Sony Playstation 3, and the Nintendo Wii.

This is all made possible through high-speed connections, both wired and wireless. According to one study, 91 percent of the 18-and-over online population has broadband Internet access, making it the main connection type to the Internet. **Broadband** connections are really just a description of the ability to transmit multiple signals simultaneously on one data line. For

▼**EXHIBIT 13–3** Percentage of demographic groups who use the Internet, according to a 2008 Pew Internet & American Life Project survey.

Use the Internet	
Total Adults	**74%**
Women	75
Men	73
Age	
18–29	87%
30–49	82
50–64	72
65+	41
Race/Ethnicity	
White, Non-Hispanic	77%
Black, Non-Hispanic	64
Hispanic	58
Geography	
Urban	71%
Suburban	74
Rural	63
Household Income	
Less than $30,000/yr	57%
$30,000–$49,999	77
$50,000–$74,999	90
$75,000 +	94
Educational Attainment	
Less than High School	35%
High School	67
Some College	85
College +	95

Source: Pew Internet & American Life Project, www.pewinternet.org. Reprinted with permission. N = 2,253 adults, 18 and older, including 502 cell phone interviews. Margin of error is ±2%.

consumers it means faster Internet surfing and faster data uploads and downloads.

Why is this important to advertisers? There are many reasons, but primarily because as consumers get more comfortable interacting with and seeking out rich content such as videos, they will become more likely to supplement their other media usage with the Internet.

How People Use the Internet

Some people believe that the first era of the Web has already passed, and that a new philosophy drives the activities of some companies. This philosophy has been dubbed Web 2.0 and represents the idea that the future of the Web is in companies that encourage user sharing and collaboration (see Exhibit 13–4). Wikipedia, the popular online encyclopedia, is often cited as a prime example of this new philosophy. Unlike most other encyclopedias, Wikipedia is not constructed from articles penned by authorities or experts. Instead, anyone can create an entry, which in turn can be edited by someone else. In this sense, the site represents the efforts of thousands of users, rather than hundreds of authorities. Other examples of this type of collaboration include Twitter, Digg, Del.icio.us, and Craigslist.

One of the unique features of the Internet is the relative ease in finding and accumulating data based on advertising efforts. In this section we will discuss how the technology allows us to better understand users and refine our advertising efforts not only from campaign to campaign, but also while a campaign is in market. We will reflect on the two phases of online advertising that utilize and generate the most data: planning and tracking. Lastly, we will look at the issues surrounding all these data and how the industry approaches standardization.

Media Planning Tools

Several companies specialize in delivering audited measurement of potential reach to help media planners choose the right vehicles based on their target audience. The two largest are Nielsen-Online and comScore. Both have a suite of tools that help define target market size, behavior, and composition relative to each major Web site on the Internet. They also provide

views into how other advertisers are using the Internet, thereby giving competitive insights into industry and category best practices.

These companies measure the activities of a set number of people or a panel of people and provide reports on their usage patterns across Web sites and Internet applications, such as iTunes.

The Internet is a great repository and showcase for advertising that appears in many media. Adforum is a place where you can view thousands of ads from the present and the past.

▼**EXHIBIT 13–4** Contenders for Web 2.0 activities, according to 2008 Pew Internet & American Life Project surveys. Some of these activities have been around for a long time, but might qualify as Web 2.0 because they provide opportunities for content creation and interaction.

Internet Users Who Have Done This	Activity
37%	Upload photos to a Web site so you can share them with others online.
32	Rate a product, service, or person using an online rating system.
27	Share files from your own computer with others online.
21	Share something online that you created yourself, such as your own artwork, photos, stories, or videos.
11	Take material found online—such as songs, text or images—and remix it into your own artistic creation.
14	Create or work on your own Web page.
13	Create or work on Web pages or blogs for others, including for friends, groups you belong to, or work.
16	Use online social or professional networking sites such as Friendster or LinkedIn.
12	Create or work on your own online journal or blog.

Source: Pew Internet & American Life Project, www.pewinternet.org. Reprinted with permission.

Nielsen randomly recruits individuals to download and utilize a *desktop meter* so all Internet activity on that computer is then tabulated, measured, and recorded. This process is very similar to one of the methods Nielsen utilizes to measure TV audiences. Using a limited sample size, Nielsen then projects these numbers to the rest of the Internet audience as averages. For instance, if a panel identifies that 50 percent of all men aged 18–34 go to ESPN.com daily, whereas on average most sites garner only 25 percent of the male panel audience, Nielsen will project those numbers to the rest of the Internet to arrive at an index of 200 for ESPN.com relative to the entire Internet traffic for men between the ages of 18 and 34. Media planners utilize these numbers to identify the highest

Internet Ratings: A Call for Standards [13]

With the increased popularity of the Internet as an advertising medium comes increased reliance on measurement. However, because of a lack of standards, many measurement methods are available and it can be challenging to make heads or tails of the various solutions.

Each measurement company has its own way of "counting" and measuring, but for the most part there are two main buckets of measurement. There are planning tools such as comScore and Nielsen//NetRatings and tracking tools such as Doubleclick, Omniture, and WebTrends. All of these companies help quantify Internet usage, but the main difference between the sets is that one is based on projected activity from samples of consumers and the others are census-based, where census means complete records of activity at a site or ad campaign level.

The panel-based, or sample, approach has to date been widely accepted in the planning community for the main reason that it offers demographic and targeting based information that is still considered unreliable from the census companies. However, both comScore and Nielsen have come under tremendous pressure to come up with a better solution as they have been highly scrutinized for undercounting by up to two to three times what most publishers count from their own server logs. In fact, in April 2007, the CEO of the Interactive Advertising Bureau (IAB) sent a scathing open letter to both companies complaining that they better get their acts together. The IAB is a standards bodies committee made up of over 375 leading interactive companies that actively engages in and supports the sale of online advertising. An excerpt from the letter:

Imagine my surprise when I came to the IAB and discovered that the main audience measurement companies are still relying on panels—a media-measurement technique invented for the radio industry exactly seven decades ago—to quantify the Internet . . . To persist in using panels that undercount or ignore the diverse populations that are the future of consumer marketing is to deny marketers the insights they need to build their businesses. And it

certainly appears to us as if they are being undercounted or disregarded, for our members' server logs continue to diverge starkly from your companies' sample-based assessments, by [two times to three times] magnitudes in some cases—far beyond any legitimate margin of sampling error.

However, everything isn't all peaches and cream on the census side either. In fact anyone can perform a basic search for Internet measurement information and find a number of blogs, articles, and press releases about the monumental discrepancies between all of the various census-based reporting tools, and there are many. The discrepancies stem from a multitude of reasons: different data collection methods, unique data models, untagged pages, blocking software, cookie issues, and many more reasons. In fact Google Analytics, Google's free-to-use Web site tracking tool, has pages on its help site about why Google AdWords's clicks don't match Google Analytics's page visits. So is there hope? Yes and it comes in two forms: Media Rating Council (MRC) and start–ups.

The MRC's number one objective is **To secure for the media industry and related users audience measurement services that are valid, reliable and effective**. Hallelujah . . . right? It is definitely a step in the right direction; however, since the MRC is only an organization that can tell you what you "should do" not what you "must do," it is up to the advertisers and publishers to come to resolution if the industry really wants to see a change happen.

Or, you rely on the start-ups to make a better black box. Companies like Alexa, Quantcast, and even Google AdPlanner are coming up with different, possibly more acceptable, ways to measure Internet usage. But as with all start-ups, they have yet to truly prove themselves. Their task is to engage with advertisers and publishers and reliably deliver numbers that both sides feel comfortable with.

Applying the Breaks
1. What are some of the problems of Internet audience measurement?
2. Do you think these problems can be fixed? How?

concentration, or **composition**, of the target they are trying to reach. However, because of lack of standardization many companies report many different numbers, and it is a media planner's job to make heads or tails of the data.

The Promise of Enhanced Tracking

Companies now have some of the most precise tracking and targeting tools ever. In fact, every time you access the Internet, some computer may be tracking where you go. How? **Cookies** are small text files stored on your computer when you visit certain Web sites. These cookies can keep track of whether a certain user has ever visited a specific site. This allows the Web site to give users different information depending on whether they are repeat visitors. Cookies also indicate the users' frequency of visits, the time of last visit, and the domain from which they are surfing. Additionally, cookies give marketers great insights into their campaigns on a daily basis, such as the number of times users call for an ad, time of day, type of browsers they use, whether or not they click, and so on.

Typical online marketers employ the services of **third-party ad servers**. Third-party ad servers deliver ads from one central source, or server, across multiple Web domains, allowing advertisers the ability to manage the rotation and distribution of their advertisements. The best-known companies are DoubleClick, now owned by Google, and Atlas DMT, now owned by Microsoft. These companies allow advertisers to

One reason media budgets are shifting to the Internet is that the medium offers a variety of ways to track interactions of consumers with ads. One company that helps provide such metrics is comScore (www.comscore.com).

monitor the performance of their buys on a daily basis all the way down to conversion or sales. By placing a line of code on the last page of the sales process, Double-Click and/or Atlas can match the user back to the last advertisement they saw, via the cookies placed on the user's computer, and credit that advertisement with the sale. This allows the agency to understand Internet metrics from advertising to sales in near real time. This hyper-accountability is what ultimately brought the online ad industry out of the dot-com crash of the early 2000s—marketers could justify their Web spending's impact on the company's bottom line.

More sophisticated technology provides marketers with additional details about the consumer. The computer first assigns each user an anonymous and encrypted identification number for tracking purposes. A user profile is then created with data on the content read, keywords used in search, time and day that a Web page was viewed, the frequency with which an ad is seen, the sequence of ads that are seen, the computer operating system of the user, the browser type, and the IP address. From these data, marketers can guess the user's ISP, telephone area code, and NAIC code. They might additionally match these data with demographic information gathered offline to create a clearer picture of consumer behavior than has ever been available.

However, **behavioral targeting**, this new ability to track people's behavior on the Internet, has stirred considerable debate. Although software developers claim that the users are tracked anonymously with encrypted identification numbers, privacy advocates believe the marketing method is too invasive.

Seeking Standardization

As much as Madison Avenue may want Web measurements to resemble traditional media measurements, the Internet cannot provide them. As we'll describe shortly, simply counting advertising impressions from a Web page is an impractical method of tabulation. However, the basic questions remain the same: Do people see our ads? Are they effective? Until fairly recently, when a task force of the Internet Advertising Bureau (IAB) provided some practical definitions, Internet audience measurement information lacked the standardization needed to be able to compare its advertising effectiveness to other media.

cookies Small pieces of information that get stored on your computer when you download certain Web sites. These cookies can keep track of whether a certain user has ever before visited a specific site. This allows the Web site to identify returning users and to customize the information based on past browsing or purchase behavior.

third-party ad servers A method of delivering ads from one central source, or server, across multiple Web domains, allowing advertisers the ability to manage the rotation and distribution of their advertisements.

behavioral targeting Ability to track people's behavior on the Internet.

ad impression
A possible exposure of the advertising message to one audience member.

click rate In Internet advertising, the number of "clicks" on an advertisement divided by the number of ad requests. A method by which marketers can measure the frequency with which users try to obtain additional information about a product by clicking on an advertisement. Also called *click-through rate*.

The most simple measurement, yet an area of great controversy, is the **ad impression**. The IAB originally defined an ad impression as "an opportunity to deliver an advertising element to a Web site visitor."[11] When a user loads a Web page with ads on it, the browser will pull the advertisement from its host ad server and bring it up as a banner, button, or interstitial. The number of ad requests received can then be translated into the familiar cost form. The problem with this definition, from the point of view of advertisers and agencies, is that the advertiser is not guaranteed that a user will ever see an ad. People often click away to some other site before the requested ad ever comes up. Under the original definition, an advertiser would be charged for an ad that never had the opportunity to be seen. The AAAA prefers to define an ad request as an ad that is actually delivered to users' screens. Only then do they truly have an opportunity to see the ad. The controversy created reporting differences between what Web publishers count and what the agencies count and are willing to pay for. Eventually the IAB and other Internet advertising groups agreed that an impression has to be counted on the client-side (the Web user's browser loads the ad) rather than the server side.[12]

A second measurement, unique to the Internet, is the **click rate** or *click-through rate*. A click occurs when a visitor moves the mouse's pointer to a Web link and clicks on the mouse button to get to another page. The click rate is the number of

It's Not Always Nice to Share

If you are using this text for a college course, the popular social networking application Facebook needs little introduction. You already know all about it.

Facebook has many users, over 200 million worldwide. But it is especially popular on college campuses in particular. This is due partially to its origins—while Facebook is now available to anyone over age 13, it was started with a focus on college students. In fact, when founder Mark Zuckerberg launched the site in 2004, it was open only to members of his school, Harvard College.

What makes Facebook so irresistible? Certainly highly addictive features, like the "Wall," where friends can post messages, "pokes," "status," and lots of space for posting pictures, are part of the appeal. Users of Facebook can stay in touch with lots of people, almost in real time. The site is so addictive, in fact, that universities have begun trying to find ways to limit access during class hours.

So Facebook is a Web site that is visited by young, influential, highly educated users who spend inordinate amounts of time at the site and are passionate about what they do there. Can you think of anyone who might be interested in that group?

Of course the answer is advertisers, and in fact, advertising has, from the beginning, been a part of Facebook. The costs of running and maintaining the site are defrayed by ads, which is why it is free for users.

Software giant Microsoft has an exclusive contract with Facebook to serve display ads. Microsoft sells space to advertisers, then pays Facebook for the opportunity to show ads on the site's pages. The particular ads that appear on a given page are determined by data collected by Microsoft. The goal is to place the right banner ad on the right page. As you know from this chapter, this is typical practice on the Internet, not only for Microsoft but for other large companies like Google and Yahoo!

But in November of 2007 Facebook launched a program that was anything but typical. "Beacon" was designed to let users share information about offsite activities, including purchases, with their friends. Here's how it worked, at least in theory. You join Facebook. Later you visit a different Web site, like that of movie ticket vendor Fandango. You buy a movie ticket. Just a short while later, your Facebook profile updates and tells your friends about the tickets you bought.

It was almost inevitable that Facebook would develop something like Beacon. That is because what excites advertisers about social networks like Facebook, even more than the desirable demographics, is the fact that people are busy influencing one another at the site. This is the real power of social networks, and the real draw for advertisers.

Recall our earlier discussion of Gladwell's *The Tipping Point*. Gladwell describes the power of a few influential people in starting social epidemics. Advertisers see Facebook as a place where influentials can share information about what they buy with many other people, potentially starting many such epidemics. This is why Zuckerberg has long claimed that Facebook would start an advertising "revolution." And not coincidentally, it is why some valued Facebook's worth to be in excess of $15 billion.

But from the start Beacon was flawed. For one thing, even though third-party sites were supposed to inform Facebook users about what would happen when they bought at the site, it appears that some did not. So a Facebook user who bought something at Overstock.com was supposedly never told that Overstock was a member of the Facebook advertising network and that his or her purchase would be shared with friends.

Second, users did not "opt in" to the program (sign up for it), they had to "opt out" (cancel it). That virtually guaranteed that a lot clicks on an ad divided by the number of ad impressions. In essence, marketers are measuring the frequency with which users try to obtain additional information about a product by clicking on an advertisement.

L03 Explain how time and space on the Internet is bought.

BUYING TIME AND SPACE ON THE INTERNET

Media planners cannot think of the Internet in mass media terms. Interactive media are *personal audience venues*. That means one on one. So cost per thousand, ratings points, and share of audience don't really mean the same things in the interactive world. With interactive media, advertisers aren't always building sales volume. They're building relationships, one customer at a time. And the care companies exercise in buying and developing their interactive programs and integrating them with their mass media programs will determine their overall success.

of people would be unaware of how much information they were sharing with others. Eventually this was changed so that users had to opt in, but not before significant damage to Facebook's credibility had occurred.

Even worse, a software engineer discovered that even if Facebook users explicitly indicated that they did not want to share information about purchases, Facebook collected the information anyway. This turned out to be a practice that directly contradicted its publicly stated policies.

In the end, Zuckerberg decided that Beacon had to be changed. This was prompted by the bad press the program had received, the cancellation of several large advertisers, including Vodafone, Virgin Media, and Prudential, and several user-based petitions, including one organized by Moveon.org.

The founder posted an apology to users at the Facebook blog on December 5, 2007. It read in part (go to http://blog.facebook.com/blog.php?post=7584397130 to read the entire apology):

About a month ago, we released a new feature called Beacon to try to help people share information with their friends about things they do on the web. We've made a lot of mistakes building this feature, but we've made even more with how we've handled them. . . . When we first thought of Beacon, our goal was to build a simple product to let people share information across sites with their friends. . . . But we missed the right balance. At first we tried to make it very lightweight so people wouldn't have to touch it for it to work. The problem with our initial approach of making it an opt-out system instead of opt-in was that if someone forgot to decline to share something, Beacon still went ahead and shared it with their friends. It took us too long after people started contacting us to change the product so that users had to explicitly approve what they wanted to share. . . . I'm not proud of the way we've handled this situation and I know we can do better. Thanks for taking the time to read this.

Zuckerberg was good to his word, and the program was changed. The modern incarnation of Beacon is far different from the version introduced in late 2007. For example, according to the Facebook site, "When [an advertiser sends information about a purchase] to Facebook, the user is immediately alerted . . . and will be alerted again when they sign into Facebook. The user must proactively consent to have [the information] from your Web site published." This, of course, is a far cry from how things started.

So, for Zuckerberg and many Facebook users, the Beacon experience was a hard lesson learned. To Zuckerberg's credit, he acted fast and apologized for his mistakes when it became clear that users would not tolerate Beacon's privacy settings. Facebook continues to be one of the most popular (and valuable) locations on the Web. And there is little doubt that advertisers will continue to search for ways to leverage the unique attributes of social networks for promoting their brands.

Questions

1. Why was Beacon created? Was it ethical to ask users to "opt out" rather than "opt in" to the program?

2. Think of a purchase you have recently made that you would not want shared with your friends. How would you feel about a site that did so without your explicit permission?

3. Did Facebook's missteps with Beacon amount to a poor business decision, or do you think that it rose to the level of being unethical?

Sources: Brad Stone, "Facebook Executive Discusses Beacon Brouhaha, "New York Times Bits, http://hits.blogs.nytin1es.cod2007/11/29/facebook-responds-to-beacon-brouha 11a/; CA Security Advisor Research Blog, "Facebook's Misrepresentation of Beacon's Threat to Privacy; Tracking Users Who Opt Out or Are Not Logged In," http://community. ca.com/blogs/securityadvisor/archive/2007/II/29/facebook-s-misrepresentation-of-beacon-s-theat-to-privacy-tacking-users-who-opt-out-or-are-not-logged-in.aspx; Juan Carlos Perez, "Facebook's Beacon More Intrusive than Previously Thought," *PCWorld*, http://www.pcworld.codarticle/id, 140182-c,onlineprivacy/article.html; "Facebook Beacon," http://www.facebook.com/business/?beacon; "Leading Websites Offer Facebook Beacon for Social Distribution," http://www.facebook.com./press/releases.php?p=9166.

Currently, the leading national advertisers spend a small piece of their marketing communications pie on interactive media—less than 7 percent of their budgets. However, it still is the fastest-growing segment. Exhibit 13–5 lists the top 10 Internet advertisers ranked by spending. The best marketers are testing extensively. That means being willing to lose money for a while, which is, of course, not exciting to most advertisers or agencies. Many direct marketers are investing heavily in online catalogs. The effort is clearly worth it. Amazon.com averages over $65 million in sales a day.[13]

Pricing Methods

Advertising space on the Internet can be purchased in several different ways, as we will discuss later in the chapter. The most common means is the banner ad, typically billed on a cost-per-thousand basis determined by the number of ads displayed. On most Web pages, the base banner rate pays for exposure on a rotating display that randomly selects which ads to show.

The real marketing power of the Internet, however, is the ability to specifically target an audience in a way that is virtually impossible in traditional media. In addition to general banners, media buyers may opt to purchase more selective space. For example, ads may be purchased in a portal's information categories and subcategories, such as finance, news, travel, or games.

Prices vary according to category and increase as the buyer targets a more selective audience. Costs are tiered according to thousands, hundreds of thousands, or even millions of page requests per month.

Another augmentation to the general banner purchase is the **keyword** purchase, available on major search engines. Advertisers may buy specific keywords that bring up their ads when a user's search request contains these words. Keywords may be purchased individually or in packages that factor in the information categories and subcategories of a search engine site. In the early days of the Internet, some "keyword entrepreneurs" purchased large numbers of keywords from the search engines. They were later able to license these words to third parties at a substantial profit. This model has since changed to a bidding model, effectively killing keyword "entrepreneurs." We will go into more depth on these issues later when we discuss Google's AdSense and AdWords programs.

Some publishers will charge their clients according to **click-throughs**—that is, when a user actually clicks on a banner ad to visit the advertiser's landing page. Although the CPM cost for simple impressions is considerably lower, this method is still unpopular with publishers. When an advertiser buys on a per-click basis, the publisher may expose many users to an advertiser's banner message without being able to charge for the service.

For advertisers involved in e-commerce, some publishers offer an **affiliate marketing program** whereby they charge a percentage of the transaction cost. For example, a site devoted to music reviews may have a banner link to an online music retailer. When consumers buy music from the retailer, the site publisher receives a percentage of the sale for showing the banner.

▼ **EXHIBIT 13–5** Top 10 U.S. Internet advertisers.

Rank	Company	Estimated Spending (millions)
1	Experian Group Limited	378.3
2	Verizon Communications, Inc.	240.9
3	AT&T Corp.	220.4
4	NexTag, Inc.	219.3
5	Netflix, Inc.	217.3
6	Scottrade, Inc.	188.7
7	Vonage Holdings Corp.	177.1
8	General Motors Corporation	176.1
9	InterActiveCorp	168.3
10	Ford Motor Company	125.2

Source: Nielsen AdRelevance, August 2009. Reprinted with permission.

The Cost of Targeting

The very selective nature of the Internet can, for additional cost, be combined with tracking technology to be discussed later. This makes for a very focused campaign. Companies such as Tacoda work behind the scenes to meet the advertiser's CPM guarantees by using software that directs specific ads to a highly selective audience. Because Tacoda technology "tags" users, it can build a consumer profile and show those ads that are likely to be of the greatest interest to that specific Web user.

But contrary to popular belief, consumer targeting on the Internet is very cost intensive. While it is true that millions of people do indeed scour the Net each day, it is still difficult to find and reach specific consumers. Thus, prices for precise Internet business-to-business targeting can eclipse even those of direct mail.

Stretching Out the Dollars

One of the problems facing most Internet marketers is how to get enough reach from their advertising. The enormous numbers of users who utilize the major search engines make these sites attractive for advertisers. However, Internet users surf millions of other Web pages each day, many of which are potential sites for effective ads. Contacting all of these sites and negotiating advertising contracts on each is impossible.

For this reason, most advertisers work through **ad networks**, which act as brokers for advertisers and Web sites. Ad networks pool hundreds or thousands of Web pages together and facilitate advertising across these pages. The advantage is that this allows advertisers to gain maximum exposure by covering even the smaller sites. The drawback is that such advertising is more difficult to monitor. Each site must be watched for traffic and content, which creates problems when trying to calculate costs. Exhibit 13–6 lists the largest ad networks in the United States.

ad networks The Internet equivalent of a media rep firm, *ad networks* act as brokers for advertisers and Web sites. They pool hundreds or even thousands of Web pages together and facilitate advertising across these pages, thereby allowing advertisers to gain maximum exposure by covering even the small sites.

Web site A collection of Web pages on the Web that are linked together and maintained by a company, organization, or individual.

check yourself ✓

1. Why are some of the best advertisers losing money with Internet advertising?

2. What are some important ways to purchase Internet ads?

▼**EXHIBIT 13–6** Companies can now take advantage of ad networks that reach a majority of Internet users over the course of a month. The 10 largest networks are listed here.

Top 10 U.S. Ad Networks by Unique Visitor, March 2009		
Rank	Ad Network	Unique Visitors (000)	Reach (%)

Rank	Ad Network	Unique Visitors (000)	Reach (%)
	Total	192,173	100
1	Platform-A	173,772	90
2	Yahoo Network	165,578	86
3	Google Ad Network	160,762	84
4	ValueClick Networks	156,662	82
5	Yahoo sites	146,059	76
6	Google	143,570	75
7	24/7 Real Media	141,728	74
8	Traffic Marketplace	141,078	73
9	Fox Audience Network	140,922	73
10	Tribal Fusion	137,627	72

Notes: Reach denotes the percentage of the total Internet population that viewed a particular entity at least once in August. The Platform A ad network is an aggregation of ad servers used by the following individual advertising network entities: Advertising.com, Tacoda, AOL, Quigo, and Userplan.

Source: comScore, 2009.

LO4 Know the types of Internet advertising.

TYPES OF INTERNET ADVERTISING

The nature of the Internet is a constant state of evolution. Therefore advertisers have new and interesting ways to reach target audiences that extend beyond the more standard ad placements (see Exhibit 13–7). We will discuss the less fluid advertising elements first and then look at the ways in which the medium is continuing to grow. In approaching this topic we will work our way back up the generic online "sales funnel." The Internet is truly unique as a medium in its ability to lead directly to sales so we will approach the section in that way, but beware of pigeonholing the Internet as a direct marketing medium. It has often been said that the accountability factor is not only the Internet's saving grace, it is also the bane of its existence.

Web Sites, Microsites, and Landing Pages

The technical definition of a **Web site** is a collection of Web pages, images, videos, or data assets that is hosted on one

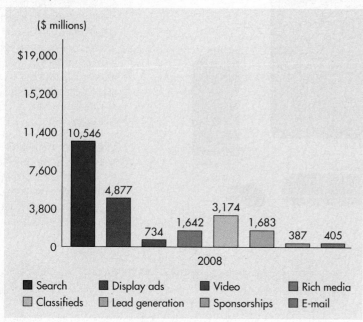

Source: Used by permission of eMarketer.com.

or more Web servers, usually accessible via the Internet. A corporate site is used to give background information about an organization, product, or service. A commerce site is used primarily to sell a product or service. Of course there is a fine line between these definitions; for companies like Amazon.com the corporate site is the commerce site and vice versa. Good marketers look at their Web site broadly. They understand that the Web site is an extension of the brand and that the Web site experience is synonymous with a brand experience. Knowing that not all corporate sites are quite up to snuff to deliver on this brand extension, many marketers use microsites and landing pages to deliver the desired experience.

A **microsite** is used as a supplement to a Web site. For advertisers it is typically singular in focus and delivers on the current advertising message. For instance, when Electronic Arts (EA) launched the *Return of the King* video game after the very popular movie trilogy *The Lord of the Rings,* it had Freestyle Interactive build a robust microsite that gave users cheats, codes, game screens, and exclusive videos and also gave users a chance to win a replica sword from the movie. The kicker was that to unlock the content, users actually had to go on an Internet-based scavenger hunt to find four pieces, or shards, of the sword. Each piece unlocked more content until the sword was "reforged" and the user could open the cheats and enter to win the replica sword. The microsite was able to identify how many pieces each user had found.

Any Web page can be a **landing page**—the term used to describe direct links to deeper areas of the Web site that advertising drives consumers to beyond the homepage. Typically advertisers use landing pages to give consumers a more relevant experience as it relates to the message from the advertising. For instance, if someone searches for "men's dress pants" on Google, Dockers wants to send them directly to the *men's apparel* section, and more specifically all the way to the pants page, rather than making the user click two or three more times just to find the relevant products. Advertisers use landing pages to streamline the selling or information-gathering process, as studies have found that people's attention spans are limited online. If they cannot find what they are looking for right away, they may be lost forever. Consumers are fickle and anything to help them on their online journey is typically a smart approach.

Search Engine Marketing

Most people looking to find information on the Web use a **search engine**. Search engines are Web sites that allow people to type a word or phrase into a text box and quickly receive a listing of information on a **search-results page**.

In the late 1990s, several companies competed to be the leading brand for searches. For now, there is a clear winner: Google (see Exhibit 13–8). Moreover, the story of how Google used a superior search capability to become one of the fastest-growing and most profitable companies in the world offers important lessons for advertising on the Internet.

When Google's creators, Sergey Brin and Larry Page, first met at Stanford, they did not know how search could be profitable. But at the time, profits were not their main interest. Brin and Page were interested in helping users find information and believed they had a better system for doing so.

The two created an algorithm, named *Pagerank,* that analyzed the links and relationships of Internet sites to come up with

▼ **EXHIBIT 13-8** Percentage of online searches by search engine used, April 2009.

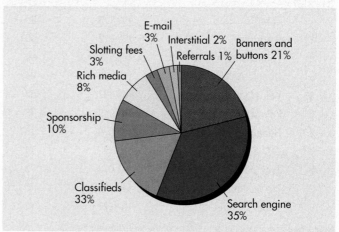

Source: ComScore Release April 2009, U.S. Search Engine Rankings, retrieved from http://www.comscore.com/Press_Events/Press_Releases/2009/5/comScore_Releases_April 2008_U.S._Search_Engine_Rankings. Reprinted with permission of ComScore.

rankings. When a keyword is entered in a search, Google looks for Web sites that mention the word. This is no different from what many of their early competitors did. But in addition, Google analyzes Web links in order to determine what sites are considered useful. Consider two sites that each use the term *marketing* five times. If a Web user used *marketing* as a search term, Google's search engine would locate both sites. But which site should be listed relatively high, where it will be viewed quickly, and which should be listed lower? This is where Pagerank comes in. Sites that other sites link to are assigned higher Pageranks and end up prominently in search results. For example, if 20 Web sites link to one of the two marketing sites and just one links to the other, the first site gets a more prominent listing. The algorithm also analyzes the *quality* of the links. Specifically, sites with especially popular or authoritative Web sites linking to them get higher Pageranks. The net result of this is a fast search engine that returns remarkably relevant search results.

the same time presenting an immediate opportunity to buy. For instance, if you are working for Dockers and you are targeting men seeking business attire, where do you spend your money? On a magazine ad that may or may not get in the hands of someone thinking about clothes or on an AdWords placement for the phrase *dress pants*?

Google's search results page is composed of two distinct areas: search results based on Pagerank, which are organic (unaffected by sponsorship), and **sponsored links**. Sponsored links have three important characteristics. First, advertisers do not pay for impressions, a common practice with banner ads. Instead, advertisers pay only when a user clicks on the link and visits the sponsor's site. This performance-based **pay-per-click** model has proven very attractive to advertisers. Second, the amount that an advertiser owes for each click is determined

> ## For advertisers, there is really no better place to put a message than search. No other environment allows them to gain insight into what consumers are thinking about.

Because the company created a better search engine, Google was able to attract growing numbers of Web users. However, throughout the 1990s it lacked a clear way to make money from search. Like many companies at the time, Google sustained itself on venture capital. After the dot-com bust of the early 2000s, Google investors encouraged Brin and Page to develop a revenue model. Their response was two advertising programs, AdWords and AdSense. It is difficult to overstate how successful these programs have been, because in a few short years Google has used them to create an annual revenue stream in excess of $23 billion dollars.[14]

AdWords

Do a search on Google and you will notice that search results are not the first thing you encounter on the results page. The first listings are in a light-blue shaded area that is described as "Sponsored Links." These sponsored links are not search results, but paid listings. For advertisers there is really no better place to put a message. There is no other environment that allows advertisers to gain such insight into what consumers are thinking while at

in an auction, where companies can bid for keywords. Higher bids generally lead to better listings, but don't guarantee them, because the ranking of sponsored listings is also determined by

Searching for marketing on Google produces a page that displays both sponsored links (which are created by AdWords) and search results (created by PageRank).

an ad's performance. Text ads that attract lots of clicks rise in the rankings, while links that are ignored fall. Third, Google benefits from the targeted nature of search. When people are hunting for a term like *marketing*, they often find that the sponsored links are as useful as the search results. Google estimates that almost 15 percent of searches result in click-throughs to sponsors, an astonishingly high *conversion rate* in comparison with other media, interactive or traditional. Google's model clearly emphasizes performance.

AdSense

Google's other major ad program is AdSense. Web sites that use AdSense set aside a portion of pages for Google text ads. The ads themselves are selected by Google software and inserted automatically, without any input from the Web site.

The revenue model for the AdSense program is very similar to AdWords. Advertisers pay Google only when Web users click the link and visit the sponsor sites. In this case, the owner of the site also gets revenue. For popular Web sites this can generate a great deal of revenue, and it is thus a powerful incentive for site owners to participate in the Google program.

Large Web sites, such as Microsoft or Yahoo! generally don't use programs such as AdSense, preferring to sell ad space themselves. But AdSense has helped thousands of small to midsized sites and blogs develop steady revenue streams. Tiny, targeted, and text-based ads have revolutionized the Web.

From an advertiser's perspective, search-based ad programs are beneficial only if the company has a Web site that converts visitors into customers. Businesses ranging from your local florist to global manufacturers are using the Internet to present multimedia content that includes catalogs, videos, games, and music. The key is making a sale, because the advertiser pays Google for sending the customer to its site.

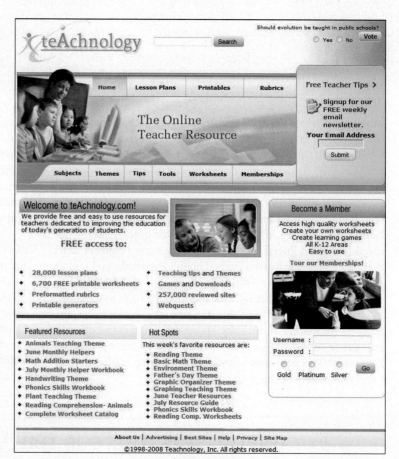

Nothing demonstrates the Web's power better than sites that offer the helping professions ways to improve their efforts. The site teAchnology is one such Web destination. Teachers can find thousands of lesson plans and worksheets, as well as teaching tips and themes. Revenue from advertising helps keep the site fresh and easy to use.

Banners and Buttons

Another type of Web advertising is the ad banner. A **banner** is a little billboard that spreads across the top or bottom of the Web page. When users click their mouse pointer on the banner, it sends them to the advertiser's site or a buffer page. The standard size for an ad banner is 468 pixels (picture elements) wide by 60 pixels high. That means that on a standard 8½- by 11-inch page, the banner would measure just over 4½ inches wide by 1/2 inch high.

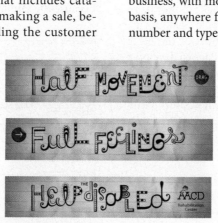

In the banner ad above, the user drags the top half of the text across the bottom, eventually revealing the message "Help the disabled." The ad won a Cannes Bronze Lion.

While banners are a common unit of Web advertising, the cost of a banner can range wildly—anywhere from free to thousands of dollars per month. Some standardization is taking place in the business, with most sites now charging, on a cost-per-thousand basis, anywhere from $0.25 to $100.00 CPM, depending on the number and type of visitors the site regularly receives.

In 2003, in response to many agency requests to simplify the ad buying process, the Interactive Advertising Bureau (IAB) introduced the Universal Ad Package, a suite of 16 standard ad sizes (including skyscrapers, rectangles, pop-ups, banners, and buttons) designed to improve the efficiency and ease of planning, buying, and creating online media.

Similar to banners are **buttons**, small versions of the banner that often look like an icon and usually provide a link to an advertiser's landing page, a marketing tool that leads people into the purchasing or relationship-building process. Because buttons take up less space than banners, they also cost less.

The advancements in Adobe's Flash have greatly enhanced the once-static banner and button ads. Full motion, animation, and user interaction, for example, are now commonplace. In fact, one of the greatest areas of recent growth has been **rich-media advertising**, which includes graphical animations and ads with audio and video elements that overlay or float over the page.

Some of the more common types of rich-media ads include animated banners, interstitials, and Superstitials. The **interstitial** is a catchall term for a variety of ads that play between pages on a Web site, popping up on the screen while the computer loads a Web site. All of their various formats tend to perform well in terms of click-through rates and brand recall—which is what the advertisers care about. The Superstitial is actually a trademark of Unicast, now owned by Viewpoint. The Superstitial makes use of a "polite download" technology to push ads into a Web browser's cache only when the computer's bandwidth is idle; the ads then play when the user requests a new Web page. With polite download technology, the ad avoids tying up bandwidth when the user needs it. The standard Superstitial ad is quite large and plays for a long period of time (up to 20 seconds). The size and playing time of this type of ad are similar to television ads, making them as rich as any experience available online.

Rich mail allows graphics, video, and audio to be included in e-mail. When you open up a rich e-mail, your e-mail client automatically calls up your Internet connection and launches an HTML page in your e-mail window. E-mail clients that are offline will invite you to click on the link when you have your Internet connection open again. If your e-mail client does not support graphics, you will receive the e-mail in text only.

Sponsorships and Added-Value Packages

A form of advertising on the Internet that is growing in popularity is the **sponsorship** of Web pages. Corporations sponsor entire sections of a publisher's Web page or sponsor single events for a limited period of time, usually calculated in months. In exchange for sponsorship support, companies are given extensive recognition on the site. Sometimes an added-value package is created by integrating the sponsor's brand with the publisher's content, as a sort of advertorial, or with banners and buttons on the page.

IBM has exclusively sponsored the Super Bowl Web page, at an estimated cost of $1 million for each event. Other forms of sponsorships have included Web serials, sites devoted to women's issues, contests, and giveaways.

Crispin Porter + Bogusky struck gold with its Web campaign for Virgin Atlantic Airways (www.virgin-atlantic.com), which won a Pencil (a prestigious ad award) at the One Show Awards. The lighthearted banners deliver the benefits of Virgin's services and keep to the brand's playful, cheeky tone.

> ## A KEY TO VIRAL MARKETING SUCCESS IS TO PRESENT AN OFFER WITH REAL VALUE—ONE THAT PEOPLE WILL SHARE WITH ONE ANOTHER.

Classified Ads

Another growing area for Internet advertisers, and an excellent opportunity for local advertisers, is the plethora of **classified ad Web sites**, like Craigslist. Many of these offer *free* classified advertising opportunities because they are typically supported by ad banners of other advertisers. In style, the classifieds are very similar to what we are all familiar with from newspapers.

E-Mail Advertising

According to *Forbes*'s "2009 Ad Effectivness Study," 74 percent of marketers send **e-mail advertising** to customers who have asked for it. Marketers have always known that direct-mail advertising is the most effective medium for generating inquiries and leads and for closing a sale. It's also been the most expensive medium on a cost-per-exposure basis. Now, thanks to the Internet, the power of direct mail is increased even more, and the cost is reduced dramatically.[15]

A word of caution, though: It's important to differentiate responsible e-mail advertising from **spam**, which is really just electronic junk mail. Spam generally refers to unsolicited, mass e-mail advertising for a product or service that is sent by an unknown entity to a purchased mailing list or newsgroup. Spammers face the wrath of frustrated customers, tired of having their inboxes filled with unwanted e-mails. Since January 2004, spammers also face litigation under the CAN-SPAM Act (Controlling the Assault of Non-Solicited Pornography and Marketing). Legitimate e-mail advertisers are required to (1) clearly mark the e-mail as advertising, (2) provide a valid reply-to e-mail address, and (3) allow recipients to opt out of future mailings. The first lawsuits under the act were filed in April 2004, against two companies that had sent nearly a million e-mails advertising bogus diet patches

and growth hormones. Lawsuits have also been filed against companies that sent e-mails that falsely appeared to come from recipients' friends[16] or with misleading subject lines.[17] With this in mind, wary marketers are focusing their e-mail efforts on **customer retention and relationship management (CRM)** rather than on prospecting.

One of the hottest trends on the Internet today actually started as an application of e-mail, but has been enhanced by social media. Thanks to *viral marketing,* Amazon.com, eBay, Blue Mountain Arts, and Hotmail all made it big on the Web, reaching unexpected heights in short time spans, most with surprisingly low marketing budgets.[18] **Viral marketing** is the Internet version of word-of-mouth advertising. The term was coined in 1997 by Steven Jurvetson and his partners at the venture capital firm Draper Fisher Jurvetson. They were describing free e-mail provider Hotmail's incredible growth to 12 million users in just 18 months through the use of a little message at the bottom of every e-mail. The message invited recipients to sign up for their own free Hotmail account.

Since that time, many other marketers have come up with ways to induce their satisfied customers to recommend their product or service to friends and family members. One of the keys to viral marketing success is to present an offer with real perceived value—one that people will want to share with one another. Audible, a Web site featuring digital audiobooks, for example, uses a referral program whereby members are rewarded with free books each time someone they refer to the site signs up and becomes a member. Since members enjoy the site so much, it's natural that they would want to share the pleasure with their friends and families. Another example is Blendtec's "Will it blend" series, which was started on Youtube.com (it can now be found at http://www.willitblend.com) and has brought a new consumer market to a blender company that formerly served industry.

classified ad Web sites Web sites that specialize in providing classified advertisements, often provided for free. Many classified ad Web sites are supported by ad banners of other advertisers.

e-mail advertising One of the fastest growing and most effective ways to provide direct mail.

spam Unsolicited, mass e-mail advertising for a product or service that is sent by an unknown entity to a purchased mailing list or newsgroup.

customer retention and relationship management (CRM) A promotional program that focuses on existing clients rather than prospecting for new clients.

viral marketing The Internet version of word-of-mouth advertising e-mail.

check yourself ✓

1. What are the major types of Internet advertising?

2. What is Google's AdWords program and how is it different from non-search digital advertising?

L05 Detail the problems with the Internet as an advertising medium and suggest ways to use it in IMC.

PROBLEMS WITH THE INTERNET AS AN ADVERTISING MEDIUM

The Internet, like any medium, has its drawbacks. It is not a mass medium in the traditional sense, and it may never offer mass-media effectiveness. Some marketers may decide it's too complex, too cumbersome, too cluttered, or not worth the time and effort.

It is not controlled by any single entity, so there may be no one to hold accountable. Security (for example, for credit card purchases) has improved, but it's still a problem for some. One potential problem with Internet advertising was summed up by Nielsen this way: "Ask a friend a simple question: 'What's your favorite online ad?'" The company's point was your friend probably couldn't think of ANY online ads.[19]

As this chapter has shown, the Internet now addresses consumers in so many forms that it is not possible to identify one set of strengths and weaknesses. Smart advertisers are availing themselves of multiple forms: Web sites, search advertising, and social media, to balance out weaknesses.

But whatever the form, any advertiser who commits to the Internet should be prepared to stay engaged with his or her target audiences. That engagement requires constant attention and time. While relationships can be automated at some Web sites, it is not possible, or desirable, in social media. The bottom line: the online marketer must be prepared to engage consumers on a daily basis.

USING THE INTERNET IN IMC

As we discussed in Chapter 7, one of the keys to successfully developing an integrated marketing communications program is to promote purposeful dialogue between the company and its stakeholders. That is what interactivity really means. And that is where the Internet offers its greatest potential.

For the first time, customers and other stakeholders can truly respond to a company's media communications in real time, using the same channel for feedback that the company used for promotion. This means that even if a customer finds herself accidentally at the company's Web site and, if something there strikes her fancy, she can commence a dialogue (relationship) with the company immediately. Of course, this also means that, if the Web site triggers her memory of a less-than-satisfactory experience with the company, she can use the same mechanism for complaining. But that's actually good, because a customer that complains usually cares. And a complaint gives the company the opportunity to correct the situation and set things right. It also gives the company information on how to improve. Sophisticated marketers cherish feedback.

While all of this is well and good, it also brings up a new problem for marketers today. In the good old days of simple mass-media advertising, manufacturers placed their ads on network TV and went on about their business. The retailers took care of customers, so the manufacturers didn't really have to be concerned about them. In the new age of integrated marketing communications, that is no longer the case. Yes, the retailer is still there. But today's consumer doesn't want to talk to the retailer. She's a pretty sophisticated person. She knows who makes the product and if she's got a complaint that's who she wants to talk to. So it's not good enough for companies to put up a pretty Web site and then walk away from it. It has to be staffed—daily—and it must be kept up to date—daily. But this is expensive—often requiring companies to double or triple their Internet budget with no increase in advertising exposure. So the decision to use the Internet for integration is a big one and cannot be taken lightly.

To refresh yourself about the savvy use of digital media in IMC, reread the Obama campaign opener from Chapter 1. Recall that the campaign spent the vast majority of its money on traditional (intrusive) media like television, not on digital interactive.

But it would be a mistake to confuse dollars spent with impact, because Obama used digital interactive and traditional media for different purposes. Traditional media were used to reach low-involvement voters who were relatively unengaged with the election, especially the new voters that would prove crucial to his eventual success.

Digital interactive media were used to connect with fans and supporters. The result was that many in these groups were

Using Facebook and Google [13]

It is actually amazingly easy to help your client begin advertising on two of the most popular sites on the Internet: Facebook and Google.

With Facebook visit: http://www.facebook.com/advertising. You or the client will need a Facebook account, of course. Once you are at the site, you can read some case studies about how Facebook advertising helped advertisers achieve their IMC objectives.

Facebook makes it fairly simple to begin a campaign. You begin by inputting a destination URL, which is where the Facebook ad will send a potential customer that clicks on your message. You will also give your ad a title (limited to 25 characters), body text, (135 characters), and an image.

Next you choose a target. In the United States, you can indicate whether your ad should be seen everywhere, or limited by state or city. You can also limit the ad to different age categories and just men or just women. You can even target people based on likes and interests, people who have different connections, or marital status and education.

You then give your campaign a name and set a budget. Your budget will limit how much the client will pay on a daily basis for click-throughs. Once the budget has been reached, the ad will not be shown to Facebook users.

The last bit of information you provide is the maximum you are willing to bid per click. Higher bids will be viewed more often, but can quickly eat up a daily budget.

Once the campaign starts, you have many tools available to track your results. Facebook reports the CTR (click-through rate, a measure of how often people exposed to your ad click on it), your CPM, the amount you've spent, the impressions you've generated, and even provides a helpful graph that can show clicks, CTR, or Impressions over a period of time.

Google AdWords has a similar, easy-to-use series of steps for placing ads that will appear during searches on the popular site (https://adwords.google.com). The company provides a wealth of helpful instructions about how to reach customers, understand costs, and benefit from AdWords success stories. As with Facebook, AdWords campaigns are based on a pay-for-performance model and it is easy to set daily budgets.

Google stresses the importance of the keywords that you choose for the campaign, because it is these words or phrases that determine which searches will present your ad to your target audience. Google suggests the following tips for choosing keywords:

1. **Choose your keywords carefully.** Make sure they're specific and directly relate to the theme of your ad and the page you are directing your customers to. Keywords of two or three words tend to work most effectively.
2. **Include relevant variations** of your best keywords, including singular and plural versions. If applicable, consider using colloquial terms, synonyms, and product or serial numbers.
3. **Be specific.** Keywords that are too broad or general will not reach users as effectively as keywords that are highly targeted.

Whether you choose to run a Facebook or Google campaign, or both, you'll be amazed how quick and easy it is to be up and running, and how many tools each company provides to help you track your success. If your Web site does its part by converting visitors into customers, you are on the way to using the Web as a profitable medium.

transformed into volunteers and donors, two vital resources for any campaign. Obama's fans wanted information about the candidate. Lots of information. And guided by the campaign's digital presence, they responded with time, effort, and cash. Political campaigns are not the same as brand campaigns. But the lessons from Obama's campaign about the value of digital interactive media have not been lost on the world's best marketers. ■

check yourself ✓

1. What are the potential problems facing advertisers who use digital media?

2. How can digital advertisements be used in IMC?

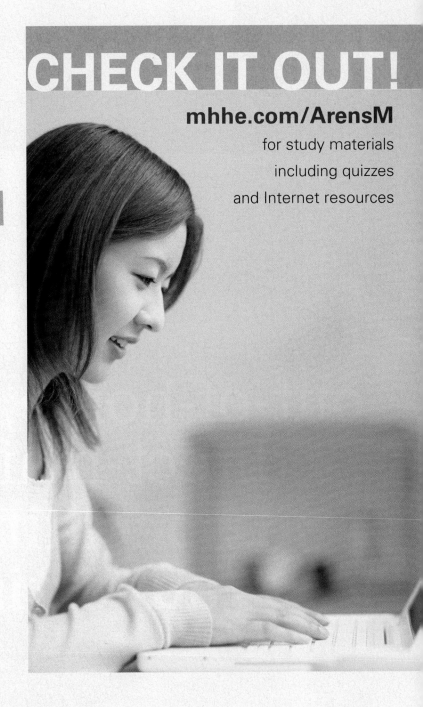

CHECK IT OUT!

mhhe.com/ArensM

for study materials

including quizzes

and Internet resources

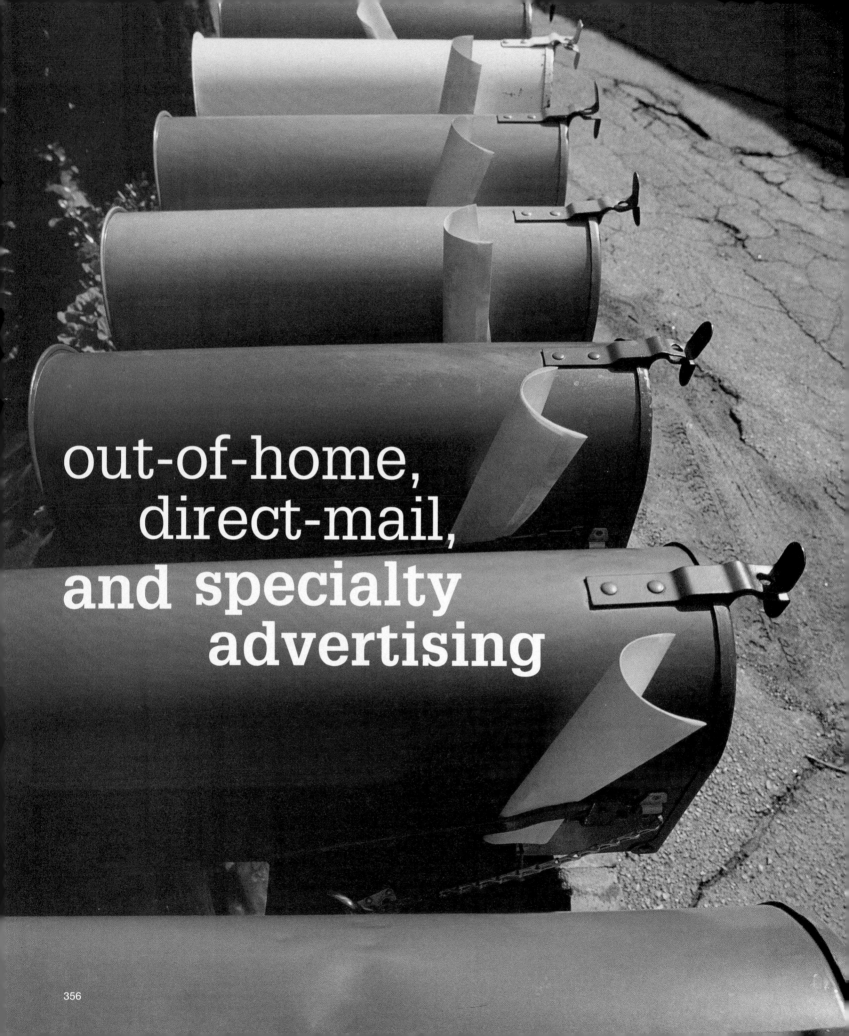

out-of-home,
direct-mail,
and specialty
advertising

fourteen

So what do you do if you are a local company and want to gain some visibility without spending hundreds of thousands of dollars on advertising? What about billboards? They communicate your message quickly, at a low cost per thousand, and they "hang" around for a long time. That was the conclusion reached in 2008 by James Ready and Leo Burnett Toronto.

For those of you who don't know James Ready, here is a quick lesson. James Ready is an Ontario micro-brewery and not a person. This brand of beer has been brewed since 1875 by the James Ready Brewing Company of Niagara Falls, Ontario, Canada.[1] It features jokes on the undersides of the bottle caps and prides itself on selling for "a buck" ($1). So when the Ontario province decided to raise taxes on alcoholic beverages, James Ready and Leo Burnett Toronto devised the "Share Our Billboard" campaign to help keep James Ready at a buck.[2]

James Ready fans were already accustomed to helping the brand maintain its low price by routinely sending back bottle caps and labels for reuse. So taking it a step further only helped aid the cult-like status the beer was achieving with its loyal audience. The idea was simple, but truly effective. The message was "Help Keep James Ready a Buck" by making an offer to share their billboard space. To enlist the community, Leo Burnett Toronto used a multimedia approach—out-of-home, newspaper, e-mails, Web banner ads, and newsletters. The campaign began with a series of classified ads that appeared in local newspapers directing people to www. jamesready.com where they could post their best offer (no money was actually accepted) and upload messages and photos to be included on the billboards.

Within a week, the Web site was flooded with requests to share the billboards, from band posters, to wedding

continued on p. 358

LEARNING OBJECTIVES

LO1 Discuss the various types of outdoor advertising and its pros and cons.

LO2 Describe how outdoor advertising is purchased.

LO3 Discuss the various types of transit advertising and its pros and cons.

LO4 Discuss the various types of direct-mail advertising and its pros and cons.

LO5 Describe the basic components of direct-mail advertising.

LO6 Explain the value of advertising specialties.

HELP KEEP JAMES READY A BUCK.
SHARE OUR BILLBOARD.
MAKE US AN OFFER AT JAMESREADY.COM

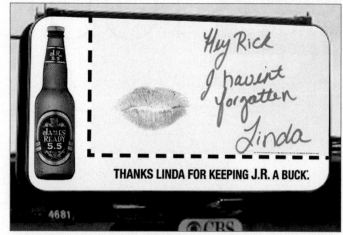

Hey Rick
I haven't forgotten
Linda

THANKS LINDA FOR KEEPING J.R. A BUCK.

Ready
to tie
the knot

THANKS TRACY & DEAN FOR KEEPING J.R. A BUCK.

All you need
is James

THANKS DAN FOR KEEPING J.R. A BUCK.

continued from p. 357

announcements, to photos demonstrating the people's love for the brand. And, as is true with any social endeavor, there was content that could never be put on a billboard. But most importantly, the 106 billboards around southern Ontario showcased people in their hometowns, making them instant celebrities and spokespeople for the beer. To see the pages upon pages of entries, go to www.jrbillboard.com. Under each customer photo, the copy read: "THANKS (your name here) FOR KEEPING J.R. A BUCK."[3]

The unspoken goal of advertising is to get people to talk about your brand.

Pick up any study about what influences people to purchase and by and large word of mouth is always the first answer. So advertising's main goal is to involve people in such a manner that they "pass it on." The James Ready campaign stayed true to the brand. You didn't see high-gloss photography or expensive TV commercials. And what's most remarkable is the amount of consumer participation from a social media campaign. This just goes to show that good campaigns leverage the medium of choice, and great campaigns have no media boundaries. Leo Burnett's Canadian president and CEO David Moore summarized it well: "I'm particularly proud of the simplicity of the idea—no high tech, no special effects, just pure creativity in one of the world's oldest mediums."[4]

The James Ready case study is an excellent example of how brands can engage with their consumers and establish lifelong loyalists, promote pass-along, and generally build a buzz around the brand with a single campaign. The work claimed victory and entered its second year, but not without taking home a few awards—a Gold Lion from Cannes, a Gold ANDY, and a Gold CLIO.

But how to maintain that buzz? James Ready and Leo Burnett Toronto did it in 2010 with another outdoor campaign. Recognizing the impact of the recession, James Ready invited consumers to "save money on necessities and spend it on James Ready Beer instead." The company partnered with local businesses to offer "JR-type deals for things JR drinkers need," like "two holes pierced for the price of one." By taking pictures of billboard coupons and showing them to the corresponding establishments, consumers "helped local establishments in tough times" and "saved money so they could spend it on more James Ready Beer."[5] Again, true to the brand. ∎

OUT-OF-HOME MEDIA

Media that reach prospects outside their homes—like outdoor advertising, bus and taxicab advertising, subway posters, and terminal advertising—are part of the broad category of **out-of-home media** (see Exhibits 14–1 and 14–2). Today, there are more than 40 different types of out-of-home media, generating $5.9 billion in revenues in 2009.[6] The most common is *on-premise signage,* which promotes goods and services or identifies a place of business, on the property where the sign is located.[7] The golden arches at McDonald's franchises are a good example. On-premise signage is important for helping us find a place of business, but it doesn't provide any kind of market coverage, and it isn't an organized medium like, for instance, the standardized outdoor advertising business.

In the past three chapters, we've looked at the traditional mass media forms as well as some of the interesting new media vehicles that have

burst upon the advertising scene in recent years. Now, to round out our discussion of advertising media, we'll present in this chapter some of the other vehicles that advertisers use today.

We'll start with the last major media category: the organized out-of-home media. These include standardized outdoor and transit advertising. We'll also briefly discuss some other out-of-home vehicles that are gaining in popularity: cinema advertising, ATMs, mobile billboards, and digital

▼**EXHIBIT 14–1** Spending in the five major out-of-home product categories (2009).

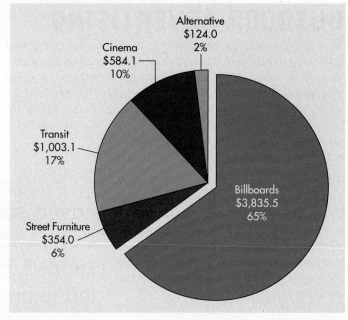

Note: Figures in millions.
Source: The Outdoor Advertising Association of America.

▼**EXHIBIT 14–2** Types of displays in each of the out-of-home product categories.

Number of Out of Home Displays (2009)			
Billboards	**Street Furniture**	**Transit**	**Alternative**
Bulletins 159,485 faces	**Bus Shelters** 43,995 displays	**Buses** 340,777 faces	**Cinema** **Arena & Stadiums**
Digital Billboards 1,800 faces	**Phone Kiosks** **Newsracks** **Urban Furniture**	**Airports** 68,560 faces	**Interior Place-Based** **Convenience Stores** **Video Networks**
Posters 165,528 faces	**Shopping Malls** 40,734 displays	**Subway & Rail** 219,645 faces	**Health Clubs** **Restaurants/Bars**
Junior Posters 33,158 faces		**Truckside/Mobile** 10,543 vehicles	**Exterior Place-Based** **Airborne**
Walls/Spectaculars 1,697 faces		**Taxis/ Wrapped Vehicles** 50,329 vehicles	**Marine** **Resorts & Leisure**

Source: OAAA.

signs and displays. Then we'll discuss direct-mail advertising, one of the most efficient, effective, economical and most widely used media today. And finally, we'll touch on specialty advertising, an important component of the very large promotional products industry.

LO1 Discuss the various types of outdoor advertising and its pros and cons.

OUTDOOR ADVERTISING

As a national and global medium, outdoor advertising has achieved great success. It was probably the first advertising medium ever used, dating back more than 5,000 years to when hieroglyphics on obelisks directed travelers. In the Middle Ages, bill posting was an accepted form of advertising in Europe. And in the nineteenth century, it evolved into a serious art form, thanks to the poster paintings of both Manet and Toulouse-Lautrec.[8]

Today, from Africa to Asia to Europe to South America, both local and global marketers use outdoor media for the same reasons as James Ready: to communicate a succinct message or image to a mass audience quickly and frequently at the lowest cost per thousand of any major medium.

> "Outdoor advertising is never turned off, zipped, zapped, put aside, or left unopened."

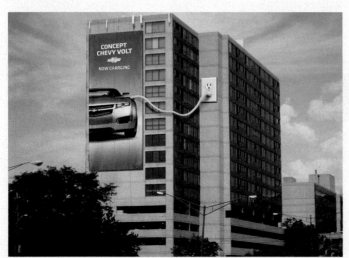

One of the most common forms of out-of-home advertising is the billboard. Compared to other major media, billboards offer the lowest cost per thousand. Chevy made clever use of this medium to demonstrate that its Volt runs on electricity.

In 2009, U.S. advertisers spent a total of $3.8 billion in outdoor advertising.[9] Outdoor's popularity is expected to continue as advertisers seek alternatives to the declining audiences and ad clutter of other mass media forms. Now that TV viewers can choose from hundreds of channels, it has become increasingly difficult for national advertisers to tell their story to mass audiences. But there's still one medium that can carry their message 24 hours a day, seven days a week, without interruption. It's never turned off, zipped, zapped, put aside, or left unopened. And it's big. That's outdoor. For that reason, some experts refer to billboards as the last mass medium.[10]

Outdoor advertising may be used for a variety of purposes. For example, nothing beats outdoor as a directional medium for motorists. It can reach a large percentage of a market, with high frequency, at a very reasonable cost. Of course, outdoor cannot communicate with the same depth as other media, but in an integrated marketing program, outdoor greatly enhances awareness of or reinforces the advertiser's core message.

Standardization of the Outdoor Advertising Business

Standardized **outdoor advertising** uses scientifically located structures to deliver an advertiser's message to markets around the world.

In the United States, there are approximately 450,000 outdoor ad structures owned and maintained by some 3,000 outdoor advertising companies, known as *plants*.[11] Plant operators find suitable locations (usually concentrated in commercial and business areas), lease or buy the property, acquire the necessary legal permits, erect the structures in conformance with local building codes, contract with advertisers for poster rentals, and post the panels or paint the bulletins. Plant operators also maintain the structures and keep the surrounding areas clean and attractive.

The plant operator may have its own art staff to supply creative services for local advertisers; ad agencies usually do the creative work for national advertisers. The biggest outdoor advertisers are telecommunications, restaurant, insurance, entertainment, and beverage companies (see Exhibit 14–3). Typically, the smaller the market, the larger the percentage of local advertisers. On average, 77.1 percent of billboard advertisers are locally owned businesses.[12]

Types of Outdoor Advertising

To buy outdoor advertising effectively, the media planner must understand its advantages and disadvantages and the types of structures available (see My Ad Campaign 14–A, "The Pros and Cons of Outdoor Advertising"). Standardized structures come in three basic forms: *bulletins, 30-sheet poster panels,* and *eight-sheet posters.* For extra impact, some companies may use the nonstandard *spectacular.*

Bulletins Where traffic is heavy and visibility is good, advertisers find that the largest **bulletin structures** work best, especially for long-term use. Bulletins measure 14 by 48 feet, plus any extensions, and may carry either painted or printed messages. They are created in sections in the plant's shop and then brought to the site, where they are assembled and hung on the billboard structure.

Painted displays are normally lighted and are repainted several times each year (color is very important for readability; see Commercial Break 14–A). Some bulletins are three-dimensional or embellished by extensions (or cutouts) that stretch beyond the frames of the structure. Variations include cutout letters, backlighting, moving messages, and electronic time and temperature units called *jump clocks*.

Painted bulletins are very costly, but some advertisers overcome this expense by rotating them to different choice locations in the market every 60 or 90 days. Over time, this gives the impression of wider coverage than the advertiser is

Rank	Advertiser	Outdoor Spending ($000)
1	Verizon	$79,667
2	McDonald's Restaurant	67,647
3	AT&T	42,725
4	GEICO	30,239
5	Warner Bros Pictures	29,385
6	Coca-Cola	28,010
7	Pepsi	25,250
8	State Farm	25,099
9	Apple	24,395
10	Metro PCS	22,340

The Pros and Cons of Outdoor Advertising [14–A]

The Pros

- **Accessibility.** Outdoor carries the message 24 hours per day and cannot be fast-forwarded, put aside, zapped, or turned off.
- **Reach.** For the same dollars, outdoor reaches over 86 percent compared with spot TV (76 percent), radio (72 percent), and newspaper (72 percent) of the same target audience in the same city. The audience is mostly young, educated, affluent, and mobile—an attractive target to many national advertisers.
- **Frequency.** Most people reached with outdoor advertising see it daily.
- **Geographic flexibility.** Outdoor advertisers can place their advertising where they want it nationally, regionally, or locally in more than 9,000 markets across North America.
- **Demographic flexibility.** Messages can be concentrated in areas frequented or traversed by young people, upper-income people, or people of specific ethnic backgrounds. With computerization, it's possible to characterize outdoor audiences by age, sex, income, and lifestyle down to the block level.
- **Cost.** Outdoor offers the lowest cost per exposure of any major advertising medium. Rates vary depending on market size and concentration, but the GRP system makes cost comparisons possible from market to market.
- **Impact.** Because advertisers can build up GRPs very fast, outdoor is the ideal medium for those with a short, simple message.
- **Creative flexibility.** Outdoor offers a large display and the spectacular features of lights, animation, and brilliant color. New fiber optics, giant video screens, and backlit display technologies offer even more creative options.
- **Location.** Outdoor can target consumers by activity, reaching shoppers on their way to the store, businesspeople on their way to work, or travelers on their way to the airport, thereby influencing consumers just before they make a purchase decision.

The Cons

- **Fleeting message.** Customers pass quickly, so outdoor advertising must be intrusive to be effective. The design and copy must tell a story briefly and crisply, and the words must sell.
- **Environmental influence.** Outdoor messages are influenced by their environment. Placement in a rundown area can detract from a product's image.
- **Audience measurement.** Audience demographics are difficult to measure. Not every passerby sees or reads the ad, so some media buyers distrust audience estimates.
- **Control.** Unlike print and broadcast ads, it's difficult to physically inspect each outdoor poster panel.
- **Planning and costs.** Outdoor messages usually require six to eight weeks of lead time for printing and posting. High initial preparation cost may discourage local use. And for national advertisers, buying outdoor is complex. As many as 30 companies may sell ad space in a single market.
- **Availability of locations.** Outdoor is so popular that demand for good locations now exceeds the supply.
- **Visual pollution.** Some people object to outdoor advertising as visual pollution. They may have a negative reaction to advertisers who use it.

Outdoor advertising is generally viewed from 100 to 500 feet away by people in motion. So it must be simple, brief, and easy to discern. Large illustrations, bold colors, simple backgrounds, clear product identification, and easy-to-read lettering are essential for consumer comprehension.

Type Weight and Spacing

The recommended maximum for outdoor copy is seven words. Very bold typefaces appear blurred and thin ones seem faded. Ornate typefaces are too complicated. Simple type is the most effective. Spacing between letters and words (kerning) should be increased to improve readability.

Color Contrast and Value

In outdoor advertising, a full range of colors can be vividly and faithfully reproduced. A huge poster or bulletin alive with brilliant reds, greens, yellows, and blues produces an effect unmatched by any other medium.

In choosing colors for outdoor, the designer should seek high contrast in both hue (the color itself, such as red, green, yellow) and value (the color's lightness or darkness) to make it more readable. Contrasting colors work well at outdoor-viewing distances; colors lacking contrast blend together and obscure the message.

The Color Wheel demonstrates the relationships between colors. Colors that are across from each other are complementary or opposites. These colors contrast with each other in the most extreme way possible. For example, green and red are opposite each other on the wheel and are therefore complementary colors. They contrast well in hues—but when their values are similar, they can create an annoying visual vibration. The same is true of a blue and orange combination.

Blue and green, and orange and red, are especially poor combinations to use because they are generally so similar in both hue and value.

Most readable	Least readable
Upper & Lower Case	ALL UPPER CASE
Regular Kerning	Tight Kerning
Bold Face	Light Face
Uniform Thicknesses	**Too Thick & Thin**

Yellow and violet (dissimilar in both hue and value) provide a strong, effective contrast for outdoor.

White goes well with any dark-value color, while black is good with colors of light value.

Applying the Breaks

Observe several examples of outdoor advertising and signs. Which ones are easy to read and which ones are not? What is it about the style or color of the text and graphics that causes this?

---

actually paying for. The dominating effect of bulletins frequently makes them well worth the extra cost—especially in small markets.

Poster Panels
A poster consists of blank panels with a standardized size and border. Its message is printed on large sheets of paper or vinyl and then mounted by hand on the panel. Poster sizes are referred to in terms of *sheets*. This term originated in the days when printing presses were much smaller and it required many sheets to cover a poster panel.

The **30-sheet poster panel** (*standard billboard*) is the most widely used form of outdoor advertising. It is far less costly per unit than the bulletin. The poster sheets are mounted on a board with a total surface of 12 by 25 feet and are usually changed every 30 days. The majority of them are illuminated.

Some local advertisers get high-quality outdoor advertising at reduced cost by using **stock posters**. These ready-made, 30-sheet posters are available in any quantity and often feature the work of first-class artists and lithographers. Local florists, dairies, banks, or bakeries simply place their name in the appropriate spot.

Eight-Sheet Posters
Manufacturers of grocery products, as well as many local advertisers, use smaller poster sizes. Called **eight-sheet posters** (or *junior panels*), these offer a 5- by 11-foot printing area on a panel surface 6 feet high by 12 feet wide.

30-sheet poster panel The basic outdoor advertising structure; it consists of blank panels with a standardized size and border. Its message is first printed on large sheets of paper and then mounted by hand on the panel.

stock posters A type of outdoor advertising consisting of ready-made 30-sheet posters, available in any quantity and often featuring the work of first-class artists and lithographers.

eight-sheet posters A smaller type of outdoor advertising, often used in urban areas, close to the point of purchase.

spectaculars Giant electronic signs that usually incorporate movement, color, and flashy graphics to grab the attention of viewers in high-traffic areas.

100 showing The basic unit of sale for billboards or posters is 100 gross rating points daily. One rating point equals 1 percent of a particular market's population.

Allstate provides an innovative example of why a driver might want to be in "good hands" with this outdoor spot showing a car seemingly teetering at the edge of a garage.

They are typically concentrated in urban areas, where they can reach pedestrian as well as vehicular traffic. Space costs roughly half that of a 30-sheet poster and production costs are significantly lower. They are an excellent medium for advertising close to the point of purchase.

Spectaculars

Times Square in New York is well known for its **spectaculars**—giant electronic signs that usually

Spectaculars are expensive, elaborate animated signs found primarily in the heart of large cities. They incorporate movement, color, and flashy graphics to grab attention in high-traffic areas.

incorporate movement, color, and flashy graphics to grab attention in high-traffic areas. Spectaculars are very expensive to produce and are found primarily in the world's largest cities, such as Tokyo, London, New York, Los Angeles, and, of course, Las Vegas. A variation on the spectacular is the *wall mural,* a painted or vinyl mural that might cover an entire building.

L02 Describe how outdoor advertising is purchased.

Buying Outdoor Advertising

Advertisers use outdoor advertising for a variety of purposes. For example, to introduce a new product or announce a change in package design, an advertiser might want to saturate the market rapidly. For a small portion of its total media budget, for example, Saturn was able to buy 400 billboards and dominate the outdoor medium in the important California market, contributing significantly to the success of the car's introduction.

The basic unit of sale for billboards, or posters, is *100 gross rating points daily,* or a **100 showing**. One rating point equals 1 percent of a particular market's population. Buying 100 gross rating points does not mean the message will appear on 100 posters or on 100 percent of the posters; it means the message will appear as many places as needed to provide a daily exposure *theoretically* equal to 100 percent of the market's total population.

global positioning systems (GPSs)
New satellite-based system whereby outdoor advertising companies give their customers the exact latitude and longitude of particular boards. Media buyers, equipped with sophisticated new software on their desktop computers, can then integrate this information with demographic market characteristics and traffic counts to determine the best locations for their boards without ever leaving the office.

For less saturation, a company can purchase 75, 50, or 25 gross rating points (GRPs), equivalent to 75 percent, 50 percent, or 25 percent of the market's population. For example, if a showing provides 750,000 total impression opportunities daily in a market with a population of 1 million, it delivers 75 GRPs (75 percent of the population) daily. Over a period of 30 days, the showing would earn 2,250 GRPs (30 days $\times$ 75 GRPs per day).

▼ **EXHIBIT 14–4**   Typical billboard locations in Baton Rouge that would achieve at least 100 GRPs daily when posted for 30 days. The red semicircles indicate which way the boards face.

Outdoor advertising doesn't consist of billboards only. Customers entering the parking lot to fetch their cars are met with this inventive ad for Fiat, which employs photographic adhesives to create a lifelike image. The copy reads, "If it always happens to your car, change for a Fiat." Can you imagine the effect this might have on a person whose car is in fact in need of work?

A showing, as indicated above, has historically been measured by a rudimentary equation that takes the number of people who pass by an out-of-home display as its measure of reach. This measurement is called Daily Estimated Circulation, or DEC. However, in 2009, the Outdoor Advertising Association of America (OAAA) and the Traffic Audit Bureau developed a new method of measuring out-of-home's true reach and frequency. Their new rating system is called Eyes On Impressions (EOI). EOI actually takes into account many factors other than the number of people that pass a display, such as size of the display, angle to the road, format, street type, distance from the road, and roadside position. This new rating system then calculates those factors into a formula that estimates the number of people that *actually* see the ad in a week. The main factor that differentiates DECs from EOIs is estimating how many *pass by* the ad on a daily basis versus estimating how many *see* the ad on a weekly

basis. The net effect is twofold, (1) out-of-home is now the only ad medium that tracks viewers of ads, rather than just the potential to see ads and (2) the frequency of out-of-home has been drastically reduced over a monthly period where the difference in reach is negligible.[13]

Location, Location, Location   As in real estate, location is everything in outdoor advertising. Advertisers that want more saturation can increase the number of posters or purchase better locations to achieve 200 or 300 GRPs per day. The map in Exhibit 14–4 shows the billboard locations in Baton Rouge, Louisiana, that together would total 100 or more GRPs per day. To achieve a 100 showing in Baton Rouge, Lamar Outdoor Advertising would place 30-sheet posters along all major traffic arteries, facing in both directions. Rates vary considerably from market to market due to variations in property prices, labor costs, and market size. As you would expect, Exhibit 14–5 shows that locations in larger markets with high traffic volume have higher rates. However, as a rule of thumb, a standard billboard costs around $600–$700 per month. At that rate, billboards still offer the lowest cost per thousand (an average of $2.26 for a 30-sheet poster) of any major mass medium.[14]

Location is everything in outdoor advertising.

Market	Adult Population	25 Daily GRPs		50 Daily GRPs		100 Daily GRPs		Average Cost per Billboard for 100 GRPs	100 GRP Daily CPM
		Number	Cost	Number	Cost	Number	Cost		
Bakersfield, CA	572,900	10	$10,470	20	$20,940	39	$40,833	$1,047	2.55
Baton Rouge, LA metro	405,500	10	8,200	20	15,960	39	28,665	735	2.52
Boise, ID	183,804	4	3,728	8	7,456	16	14,912	932	2.90
Buffalo Niagra, NY	885,000	26	22,620	52	43,264	103	77,353	751	3.12
Cincinnati, OH metro	1,186,800	24	17,520	48	35,040	95	69,350	730	2.09
Chicago, IL suburbs	1,180,200	20	15,000	40	39,000	80	48,000	600	1.45
Nashville, TN	844,000	11	8,250	21	14,700	41	24,600	600	1.04
Omaha, NE	575,000	9	5,418	17	9,979	33	17,985	545	1.12
Pittsburgh, PA metro	1,898,721	42	56,238	83	97,857	166	174,466	1,051	3.28
Tallahassee, FL	189,000	4	2,760	7	4,725	14	8,400	600	1.59

Note: Costs are for space only, based on a 4-week posting period; they do not include production. Rates are effective as of the date of publication and are subject to change.

Source: http://www.lamaroutdoor.com/index.html.

Technology in Outdoor Advertising

In the past it was always a problem for a media buyer in New York to adequately supervise the selection of outdoor boards in Peoria, Illinois. A buyer can't just jump on a plane and travel to all the cities where the client's boards are posted to verify the value of the locations. Fortunately, though, new technology has helped solve this dilemma and has thus made outdoor an even more attractive medium to national advertisers. Today, outdoor companies can use sophisticated **global positioning systems (GPSs)** to give the exact latitude and longitude of particular boards using satellite technology. Media buyers, equipped with sophisticated new software on their desktop computers, can then integrate this information with demographic market characteristics and traffic counts to determine the best locations for their boards.[15]

Many outdoor companies provide digitized videos of their locations so the buyer can see the actual boards and the environment in which they are located. Other developments include bar coding of materials so they can be tracked, posted, and authenticated, all by computer. Computerized painting on flexible vinyl guarantees a high-quality, high-resolution, faithful reproduction of the advertiser's message regardless of the market.[16]

Perhaps the most exciting development in outdoor advertising is the availability of digital billboards. Ads can be implemented the same day and updated quickly and easily, from hundreds of miles away, over the Internet. Digital billboards can rotate ads among various advertisers or move ads around town, changing them once every 6 to 8 seconds. A restaurant can feature breakfast specials in the morning and dinner specials in the evening. Law enforcement can display the image of a missing person or update emergency information in minutes. Production costs are reduced dramatically. Some digital billboards will even interact with passersby, responding to a friendly wave or communicating with consumers' cell phones. Presently, there are about 1,800 digital billboards in the United States, with several hundred being added each year at a cost of $200,000 to $300,000 each. Due to safety concerns, more than a dozen cities have banned digital billboards. Others have

Among the most important users of digital billboards are law enforcement agencies. The FBI uses digital billboards to track down wanted fugitives and crack difficult cases. To date, the FBI credits digital billboards with directly leading to more than 35 arrests. (Source: www.oaaa.org)

Does Spillover Need Mopping Up?

While numerous laws and self-regulatory efforts have banished products like tobacco and hard liquor from the airwaves, it is virtually impossible to keep minors from being exposed to such advertising due to the spillover nature of some media. The ethical issues involved with spillover media are complex, including the kind of advertising appeals used to target audiences.

Take outdoor advertising, for example. It is the most public mass medium. It cannot be turned off like television, radio, or the Internet, and it's displayed 24 hours a day for all to see—even children.

The trend in outdoor advertising today is toward eye-catching, sexually explicit ads, seen especially in densely populated urban areas. Most outdoor advertising regulations have focused on the location of billboards, not the content. The Outdoor Advertising Association of America's (OAAA) Code of Principles says that they "support the right to reject advertising that is misleading, offensive, or otherwise incompatible with community standards." But it is unknown how often this clause is invoked. Communities, therefore, have taken it upon themselves to regulate the placement and content of outdoor advertising, rather than relying on self-regulation by the advertising industry. In 1998, for example, the Los Angeles City Council passed an ordinance that prohibited alcoholic beverage advertising on virtually all publicly visible sites, even store windows. The OAAA and other local Los Angeles trade association members filed a federal civil rights action, claiming that the ordinance violates the right to free speech.

As technology advances, so do the venues for advertising. Advertisers have found ways to work around billboard restrictions. Taxicabs and buses have carried ads for years; however, now appearing on Boston cabs are electronic billboards that have the ability to change their message minute by minute—depending on a few desired variables. The full-color ads change depending on the time of day and location of the cab. Different neighborhoods will see different ads and, if appropriate, in different languages. The taxi's location is monitored by a GPS tracking system. This new technology is inexpensive for advertisers and may become a common feature on taxicabs across America. However, this raises legal and ethical questions. Should mobile billboards be subjected to the same restrictions as stationary billboards? Neighborhoods and schools may be protected from unwanted billboard advertising, but can concerned parents protect their children from advertising that travels on taxis?

Spillover also reaches children in other media vehicles besides out-of-home. The movies, for example, consistently show people smoking. And if the smoker is a celebrity, an impressionable child might interpret that as an endorsement. In a study conducted by Dartmouth Medical School, researchers concluded that actor endorsements of tobacco brands jumped tenfold in the 1990s. The study also found that 87 percent of popular movies contain tobacco use and about one-third display identifiable brand-name logos. Minors make up a large percentage of moviegoers and through movies they may be getting more exposure to smoking endorsements than in real life. Young people who look up to sport stars and movie celebrities may be vulnerable to intentional and unintentional endorsements. Benedict Carey of the *Los Angeles Times* calls today's movies "almost as smoke-laden as the stock car racing circuit."

Many people feel that ads are not to blame for the rise of teen sexual activity and tobacco and alcohol use. Others feel that advertisers have a greater responsibility to separate youth from the adult world of unhealthy and explicit activity. Regardless of who is right, advertisers, agencies, and media companies must be sensitive to public opinion and seek creative solutions to protect impressionable children. Otherwise, the industry will risk severe restriction and regulation for having failed to responsibly and conscientiously assert firm ethical standards itself.

Questions

1. Do you believe the goal of protecting children justifies banning the advertising of legal products or their glorification in movies? Which products specifically?
2. Should ads in spillover media be censored for sexually explicit content? If so, who should the censors be and what specifically should they prohibit?
3. What alternatives might be available to fight teenage smoking, drinking, and sexual promiscuity besides banning advertising for legal adult products?

placed a moratorium on them while the National Highway Safety Traffic Administration studies their possibly distracting effect on drivers.[17]

Exciting new technologies may change the future of how we "see" outdoor and other out-of-home ads. TeamOne recently launched a revolutionary campaign for Lexus that included a full-sized hologram of the new IS sedan. Using interactive kiosks located in Times Square and other prime U.S. locations, the display featured a hologram of the Lexus in motion and touch pads that allowed visitors to change the car's color and other features.[18] This opens up many thrilling possibilities for advertisers: Imagine a bulletin-size structure on the highway promoting the latest Batman film, with a larger-than-life superhero coming at you in 3-D.

Regulation of Outdoor Advertising

The Highway Beautification Act of 1965 controls outdoor advertising on U.S. interstate highways and other federally subsidized highways. It was enacted partly in response to consumer complaints that outdoor advertising was spoiling the environment. Over 700,000 billboards were removed by 1991, the year Congress banned the construction of new billboards on all scenic portions of interstate highways.[19] Since that time, the image of outdoor advertising has improved dramatically. Today, most people polled say they like billboards, believe they promote business, and find they provide useful travel information for drivers.[20]

Each state also regulates, administers, and enforces outdoor advertising permit programs through its department of transportation. Some states (Maine, Vermont, Hawaii, and Alaska) prohibit outdoor advertising altogether. Ironically, though, some of these states use outdoor advertising themselves in other states to promote tourism.

The Ethical Issue, "Does Spillover Need Mopping Up?" discusses some of the problems inherent in the very public nature of outdoor advertising and whether regulation will be needed here too.

check yourself ✓

1. What is unique about the Eyes On Impressions (EOI) out-of-home rating system?

2. What are the advantages of digital billboards?

L03 Discuss the various types of transit advertising and its pros and cons.

TRANSIT ADVERTISING

When Campbell Soup started advertising in 1910, the company spent its first $5,000 placing ads on one-third of the buses in New York City for one year. The ads were so successful that after only six months, Campbell enlarged the contract to include all surface vehicles in the city. People started buying more Campbell's soup and soon sales were up 100 percent. For the next 12 years, transit advertising was the only medium Campbell employed. Today, Campbell is still a major user of transit advertising.

Transit advertising is a category of out-of-home media that includes bus and taxicab advertising as well as posters on transit shelters, terminals, and subways. Although transit is not considered a major medium by most advertising practitioners, standardization, better research, more statistical data, and measured circulation have made transit advertising more attractive to national advertisers. National marketers of designer apparel and movies, for example, are two of the many categories of advertisers spending dramatically more in this medium, replacing the traditional transit advertising leaders such as petroleum products, financial services, and proprietary medicines.[21]

Transit advertising is a cost-effective way for marketers to reach a large audience of people. Buses and taxis provide high ad exposure by traversing the busiest streets of a city many times a day. A recent 1-800-Flowers.com campaign promoting the company's specialty bouquets featured ads on buses, on subway stations, and in other urban locations. The company's sales were seven times higher in markets where the outdoor campaign ran.[22]

Transit advertising is equally popular with local advertisers. Retailers can expand their reach inexpensively and often receive co-op support from national marketers, which thrive on the local exposure[23] (see My Ad Campaign 14–B, "The Pros and Cons of Transit Advertising").

Types of Transit Advertising

Transit advertising targets the millions of people who use commercial transportation (buses, subways, elevated trains, commuter trains, trolleys, and airlines), plus pedestrians and car passengers, with a variety of formats: transit shelters; station, platform, and terminal posters; inside cards and outside posters on buses; and taxi exteriors.

This clever transit ad makes it appear that the passenger is receiving an injection. The headline reads, "Doesn't hurt at all." It's promoting a competitively priced health insurance plan in Hong Kong.

transit shelter advertising A form of out-of-home media, where advertisers can buy space on bus shelters and on the backs of bus-stop seats.

taxicab exteriors In transit advertising, internally illuminated two-sided posters positioned on the roofs of taxis. Some advertising also appears on the doors or rear.

terminal posters One-sheet, two-sheet, and three-sheet posters in many bus, subway, and commuter train stations as well as in major train and airline terminals. They are usually custom designed and include such attention getters as floor displays, island showcases, illuminated signs, dioramas (three-dimensional scenes), and clocks with special lighting and moving messages.

inside card A transit advertisement, normally 11 by 28 inches, placed in a wall rack above the windows of a bus.

car-end posters Transit advertisements of varying sizes, positioned in the bulkhead.

outside posters The variety of transit advertisements appearing on the outside of buses, including king size, queen size, traveling display, rear of bus, and front of bus.

Transit Shelters In cities with mass-transit systems, advertisers can buy space on bus shelters and on the backs of bus-stop benches. **Transit shelter advertising** is a relatively new out-of-home form enjoying great success. It reaches virtually everyone who is outdoors: auto passengers, pedestrians, bus riders, motorcyclists, bicyclists, and more. It is extremely inexpensive and available in many communities that restrict billboard advertising in business or residential areas. In fact, shelter advertising is sometimes the only form of outdoor advertising permitted. It's also an excellent complement to outdoor posters and bulletins, enabling total market coverage in a comprehensive outdoor program.

my ad campaign

Terminal Posters In many bus, subway, and commuter train stations, space is sold for one-, two-, and three-sheet **terminal posters**.

Major train and airline terminals offer such special advertising forms as floor displays, island showcases, illuminated cards, dioramas (3-D scenes), and clocks with special lighting and moving messages.

In Paris, Nike made a splash at the French Open tennis tournament even though a competitor had locked up advertising rights within the stadium. Nike covered the city by buying space on some 2,500 buses during the tournament. As the coup de grace, it bought up every bit of signage space at the Porte d'Auteuil metro (subway) station close to the stadium and turned it into a Nike gallery of terminal posters featuring famous tennis players from around the world.[24]

Inside and Outside Cards and Posters The **inside card** is placed in a wall rack above the vehicle windows. Cost-conscious advertisers print both sides of the card so it can periodically be reversed to change the message, saving on paper and shipping charges. Inside **car-end posters** (in

The Pros and Cons of Transit Advertising [14–B]

The Pros

- **Long exposure.** The average transit ride is 25 minutes.
- **Repetitive value.** Many people take the same routes day after day.
- **Eagerly read messages.** Riders get bored, so readership is high and ad recall averages 55 percent.
- **Low cost.** Transit ads cost less than any other medium.
- **Creative flexibility.** Special constructions and color effects are available at relatively low cost.
- **Need satisfying.** Transit can target the needs of riders—with ads for cool drinks in summer, for example. Food ads do well as evening riders contemplate dinner.
- **Environmentally sensitive.** As social pressure to use public transportation increases, transit is well positioned as a medium of the future.

The Cons

- **Status.** Transit lacks the status of the major advertising media, like print and broadcast.
- **Crowded environment.** Rush-hour crowding limits the opportunity and ease of reading. The vehicle itself, if dirty, may tarnish the product's image.
- **Limited selectivity.** Transit reaches a nonselective audience, which may not meet the needs of some advertisers.
- **Clutter.** Cards are so numerous and look so similar they may be confusing or hard to remember.
- **Location.** With outlying shopping malls, fewer suburbanites make trips downtown.
- **Creative restrictions.** Although transit cards may carry longer messages than billboards, copy is still limited.

bulkhead positions) are usually larger than inside cards, but sizes vary. **Outside posters** are printed on high-grade cardboard and often varnished for weather resistance. The most widely used outside posters are on the side, rear, and front of a bus.

Advertisers may also buy space on **taxicab exteriors**, generally for periods of 30 days, to display internally illuminated, two-sided posters positioned on the roofs. Some advertising also appears on the doors or rear of taxicabs. In Southern California, advertisers can rent cards mounted on the tops of cabs that travel throughout Los Angeles, Orange, and San Diego counties, serving major airports and traveling the busiest freeways in the country. Costing an average of $100 to $200 per month per cab ($400 in New York City!), this is a very cost-effective way to reach the mobile public.

The New Orleans–based company Adfleet (www.adfleet.com) has even started selling advertising space on taxi hubcaps in more than 20 North American markets, which are fitted with a special disc that allows the advertisement to remain station-ary as the wheels turn. Adfleet, whose clients include Taco Bell, TNT, and Virgin Cola, charges $150 to $200 per cab for a four-week cycle.[25]

Buying Transit Advertising

The unit of purchase for transit advertising is a **showing**, also known as a *run* or *service*. A **full showing** (or *100 showing*) means that one card will appear in each vehicle in the system. Space may also be purchased as a *half* (50) or *quarter* (25) *showing*.

Rates are usually quoted for 30-day showings, with discounts for 3-, 6-, 9-, and 12-month contracts. Advertisers supply the cards at their own expense, but the transit company can help with design and production.

Cost depends on the length and saturation of the showing and the size of the space. Rates vary extensively, depending primarily on the size of the transit system. Advertisers get rates for specific markets from local transit companies.

> Transit shelter advertising reaches virtually everyone who is outdoors.

Unique and resourceful use of transit advertising is on display in this bus design from the National Geographic Channel. The clever illusion created by the opening and closing of the bus doors is a concept that was sure to get people talking.

Special Inside Buys In some cities, advertisers gain complete domination by buying the **basic bus**—all the inside space on a group of buses. For an extra charge, pads of business reply cards or coupons (called **take-ones**) can be affixed to interior ads for passengers to request more detailed information, send in application blanks, or receive some other benefit.

Special Outside Buys Some transit companies offer **bus-o-rama signs**, jumbo full-color transparencies backlighted by fluorescent tubes and running the length of the bus. A bus has two bus-o-rama positions, one on each side. A single advertiser

Any visitor to the Las Vegas Convention Center monorail station can't help but become totally immersed in the Coca-Cola brand. As corporate sponsor of this station, Coca-Cola has branded the floor, the train entry doors, and the escalator entry and has provided a convenient opportunity to purchase its products.

may also buy a **total bus**—all the exterior space, including the front, rear, sides, and top.

For years, New York subways have been running **brand trains**, which include all the subway cars in a particular corridor. However, with the July 2004 opening of its monorail system, the city of Las Vegas took the concept further. The glitz of the city's strip extends to its public transportation: Each of the nine monorail trains and seven stations has a corporate sponsor, and many feature elaborate immersive advertising themes. **Immersive advertising** describes the

three times that amount. Consider the deal that the city struck with Nextel, estimated at $50 million. The company signed on for a 12-year sponsorship of one train and the system's "crown jewel," the main station at the Las Vegas Convention Center, which more than 1 million annual visitors are expected to pass through each year.[26] A complete train wrap costs $15,000 per week, plus $45,000 to produce, install, and remove the wrap.

OTHER OUT-OF-HOME MEDIA

As mentioned earlier, there are many forms of out-of-home media. Some are so new that they are still unproven. However, several seem to be gaining in popularity, and they demonstrate how far advertisers will go to get their messages seen by the consuming public.

Cinema Advertising

There was a time not long ago when the only thing cinema audiences could watch before a feature film was a couple of coming attractions. In recent years marketers have leapt to fill in the empty time before a movie starts with advertisements. Advertising in movie theaters is a growing but controversial practice. **Cinema advertising** includes on-screen advertising, such as commercials airing in advance of movie previews and the feature presentation, as well as lobby-based videos, sampling, special events and concession-based promotions. Although some movie-going audiences resent watching ads, cinema advertising is becoming more and more attractive to marketers. "Unlike traditional media, we don't

> ## Any blank space is an invitation to advertise.

integration of advertising into the message delivery mechanism so effectively that the product is being promoted while the audience is being entertained. The result is that the prospect becomes totally immersed in the message and the brand.

Las Vegas city officials banked on the monorail system (www. lvmonorail.com), which is entirely funded by passenger fares instead of tax dollars, to generate at least $6.5 million annually in advertising revenue. However, with the help of ad agency Promethean Partners, ad revenues are now expected to be at least

have to fight for our audience's attention; they don't flip channels," says Bob Martin, president and chairman of the Cinema Advertising Council.[27] Cinema advertising grew to a $584 million industry in 2009, up 2 percent from 2008, an impressive gain compared to the steep drops in print and broadcast.

Cinema advertising offers some compelling advantages to marketers. Arbitron estimates that 81 percent of teens and 67 percent of young adults see a movie at least once a month. A full 25 percent of teens see 20 or more movies each year. Arbitron also reports that while those who go to movies, in comparison to non-moviegoers, are more likely to skip ads on TV, most don't mind ads in movies. Nonetheless, some movie theater chains prohibit on-screen advertising for fear of offending their audience.

ATMs

With so many thousands of money devices in service, it's only natural that the captive audience of ATMs be targeted for creative promotional tactics. Fleet Financial Group has capitalized on ATM technology by printing retailer coupons on the backs of receipts, the other piece of paper that customers receive from the machines. The coupons, which were initially redeemable at Bruegger's Bagels, Firestone, Great Cuts, Oil Doctor, and Pizza Hut, originated in Massachusetts and provided advertising that customers were likely to carry around in their wallets or cars.

One ATM innovation, developed by Electronic Data Systems Corp., puts full motion video ads on the machine's screen as customers wait for their transactions to be processed. The 15-second ads, which debuted in 7-Eleven stores in San Diego, replace the "Transaction being processed" or "Please wait" messages that appeared on the screen. The original ads promoted Fox Searchlight Pictures's films *The Ice Storm* and *The Full Monty*.

Other promotions run through ATM machines include a MasterCard International and Coca-Cola USA collaboration on the "Coca-Cola incredible summer," in which customers could win cash instantly by using a special disposable ATM card.

Mobile Billboards

The **mobile billboard**, a cross between traditional billboards and transit advertising, was conceived as advertising on the sides of tractor-trailer trucks. Today in some large cities, specially designed trucks carry long billboards up and down busy thoroughfares. Local routes for mobile ads are available on delivery trucks in several cities. And, of course, many of these mobile billboards are going digital. Speaking of digital, a San Francisco company called Smart Plate is developing a license plate that will display custom advertising messages if your car is halted for more than four seconds in traffic or at a red light. California is evaluating this idea as a way to generate revenue for the state. The plates could also be used to broadcast Amber Alerts or traffic information.[28]

Digital Signage

Digital signs display text and graphic messages much like the big screens in sports stadiums. The signs can transmit commercial messages to retail stores, where shoppers see them. The stores pay nothing for the signs and receive a percentage of the advertising revenue. In Montreal, Alstom (www.telecite.com) used its visual communication network (VCN) technology to install digital display panels on subway cars. Advertisers got a powerful, inexpensive, and flexible medium with a large, captive audience; the transit authority got a modern, self-financed emergency and public information system; and passengers got something to watch while they ride.[29] Digital signs can be updated easily or even automatically, based on store traffic, weather conditions, and so on. Some digital signs allow shoppers to interact directly with the information on the screen, using their cell phones.

Where will it end? It seems that any blank space is an invitation to advertise. Ads have appeared on bathroom stalls, urinal walls, sandy beaches, city sidewalks, airplane tray tables, manhole covers, football fields, and construction barriers. If consumers might see it, advertisers will try it out.

Clever out-of-home buys can give public exposure and cut through the advertising clutter in a spectacular way. Crispin Porter's ad campaign for the BMW Mini emphasized novel, creative, and inexpensive ways to reach the intended target audience. This lavatory ad represents yet another way audiences were exposed to unusual, humorous messages about the car.

digital signs Signs that display text and graphic messages similar to the big screens in sports stadiums. The signs can transmit commercial messages to retail stores, where shoppers see them. The stores pay nothing for the signs and receive a percentage of the advertising revenue.

direct-mail advertising All forms of advertising sent directly to prospective customers without using one of the commercial media forms.

dimensional direct mail Direct-mail advertising that utilizes three-dimensional shapes and unusual materials.

e-mail Electronic mail messages transmitted electronically between computers.

sales letters The most common form of direct mail. Sales letters may be typeset and printed, or computer generated.

postcards Cards sent by advertisers to announce sales, offer discounts, or otherwise generate consumer traffic.

check yourself ✓

1. How does the meaning of "100 showing" differ between outdoor advertising and transit advertising?

2. What creative application of digital signage would be effective on your college campus?

L04 Discuss the various types of direct-mail advertising and its pros and cons.

DIRECT-MAIL ADVERTISING: THE ADDRESSABLE MEDIUM

All forms of advertising sent directly to prospects through a government, private, or electronic mail delivery service are called **direct-mail advertising**. As we will discuss in Chapter 16, direct mail advertising is a form of direct-response advertising because a response is expected from the recipient directly to the advertiser. And it is a type of direct marketing since it is an addressable medium, the goal of which is to obtain a measurable purchase or donation. In dollars spent, direct mail is the second-ranked advertising medium today, surpassed only by television.

Both large and small companies use direct mail. New firms often use direct mail as their first advertising medium. The reason is clear: Of all media, direct-mail advertising offers the straightest line to the desired customer. And businesses don't need big budgets to advertise with direct mail. With a computer and desktop publishing software, a business can create a professional-looking mailer.

And some Web sites provide companies with tools to design a mailer, import a mailing list, and have the campaign printed and sent, all online.

Direct mail is used by for-profit businesses, charities, and political campaigns. Mailings are typically targeted to the advertiser's best prospects, selected based on where they live, demographic characteristics, past purchasing behavior, or interest they have expressed in certain product categories. Direct mail may also be targeted to businesses rather than individuals, in an effort to generate orders or leads for a sales force. Since direct-mail marketers don't want to waste money sending advertising to disinterested prospects, consumers can opt out by contacting the Direct Marketing Association's Mail Preference Service (www.dmachoice.org).

Many experts predicted that the combination of the recession, rising postage rates, and a growing preference among marketers for low-cost, digital communications would lead to a steep decline in the dollars spent on direct-mail advertising. But contrary to those predictions, spending on direct mail is expected to increase by more than $1 billion in 2010, according to an annual study from the Direct Marketing Association. The study predicts that this advertising medium will rise from the $44.4 billion spent in 2009 to $45.5 billion in 2010. The study also reports that direct mail (not including catalogs) continues to boast an impressive ROI, returning $15.22 for every dollar spent in 2009.[30]

Today's leading mail-order products include computers, electronics, and medical and office supplies, as well as other products and services listed in Exhibit 14–6.

Types of Direct-Mail Advertising

Direct-mail advertising comes in a variety of formats, from handwritten postcards to **dimensional direct mail**, utilizing three-dimensional shapes and unusual materials. The message can be one sentence or dozens of pages. And within each format—from tiny coupon to thick catalog or box—the creative options are infinite. In 2003, the United States Postal Service approved Customized Market-Mail (CMM), a new class of mail that gives

▼ **EXHIBIT 14–6** Top 10 catalog companies (2008).

Rank	Company	2008 Direct Sales (in millions)	Market Segment
1	Dell	$51,936	computers
2	Thermo Fisher Scientific	10,500	laboratory and research supplies
3	IBM	9,076*	Computer hardware, software, services
4	Staples	8,900	office supplies
5	CDW Corp.	8,100	computers
6	Henry Schein	6,400	dental, medical, and veterinary supplies
7	Wesco International	6,111	electrical and industrial maintenance supplies
8	United Stationers	4,987	office and facility supplies
9	OfficeMax	4,310	office supplies
10	Office Depot	4,146	office supplies

* estimated

Source: http://multichannelmerchant.com/2009MCM100.pdf.

direct-mail advertisers the opportunity to truly innovate. The new regulations allow for pieces of mail of almost any shape, within certain dimensions, to be sent without an envelope. No longer limited to rectangles, direct mail can now take more

Direct-mail advertising can be very targeted and personalized. This sales letter from Target provides helpful hints to new parents along with a promotion for Huggies diapers.

novel, eye-catching forms. From simple geometric shapes, like circles, to more curious and bizarre shapes, like Zambonis (used by First Tennessee Bank to promote a checking account associated with a local hockey team), CMM stands out in a sea of mail that might otherwise go directly into the trash.[31] In addition to the dimensional direct-mail category are the following:

E-mail, as mentioned in Chapter 13, is an important tool in direct marketing and is best used for customer retention and relationship management. It is most effective when the marketer first seeks *permission* to mail. In other words, advertisers should always give people the opportunity to opt in and to opt out of their e-mail programs. For new business acquisition, the best use is in a viral marketing campaign—otherwise it will probably be perceived as spam.

Sales letters, the most common direct-mail format, are often mailed with brochures, price lists, or reply cards and envelopes. **Postcards** are used to announce sales, offer discounts, or generate customer traffic. National postal services regulate formats and dimensions. Some advertisers use a double postcard, enabling them to send both an advertising message and a perforated reply card. To encourage response, some advertisers use **business reply mail** so the recipient can respond without paying postage. On receiving a response, the advertiser pays postage plus a handling fee of a few cents.

Folders and **brochures** are usually printed in multiple colors with photos or other illustrations on good paper stock. **Broadsides** are larger than folders and are sometimes used as window displays or wall posters in stores. They fold to a compact size to fit in a mailbag.

Self-mailers are any form of direct mail that can travel without an envelope. Usually folded and secured by a staple or seal, they have special blank spaces for the prospect's name and address.

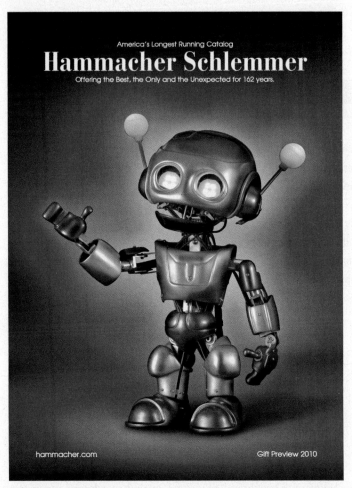

Mail-order catalogs are big business. They also help support retailers' stores and Web sites. Hammacher Schlemmer is America's longest running catalog. More than 30 million copies are mailed each year, generating an estimated 70 percent of the company's revenues, with the remainder coming from online sales and the retail location in New York City.

Statement stuffers are ads enclosed in monthly customer statements from department stores, banks, oil companies, and the like. To order, customers write in their credit card number and sign the reply card.

House organs are publications produced by associations or business organizations—for example, shareholder reports, newsletters, and dealer publications.

Catalogs are reference books that list, describe, and often picture the products sold by a manufacturer, wholesaler, or retailer. With more high-income families shopping at home, specialized catalogs have become very popular.

Some catalog retailers prosper with specialized approaches like lifestyle clothing (L.L. Bean, Anthropologie, Lands' End), electronic gadgets (Sharper Image), and gourmet foods (Dean & Deluca).

Catalogs are big business; approximately 13 billion catalogs are mailed each year. However, due largely to rising postage costs, that figure is down from 20 billion only four years earlier. Over 8,000 catalog companies disappeared during that time.[32] The catalog industry spent $15.1 billion producing and distributing catalogs to generate $110.5 billion in sales in 2009.[33] According to MediaMark, a respected consumer behavior research group, 49 percent of Americans shop from catalogs.[34]

To increase readership and stand out from the glut of other catalogs, some marketers have added editorial and slick photography, all designed to sell a certain image. Abercrombie & Fitch, for instance, launched its *A&F Quarterly* in 1997, to supplement the clothing line with advice on how to attain a "cool" lifestyle beyond what you wear. By selling the Abercrombie lifestyle, A&F hoped to bring more people into the stores. At the same time, though, A&F stirred up a lot of controversy by featuring nude and seminude models, often in suggestive poses. Under pressure, the magazine was pulled from stores in December 2003, but is expected to help A&F regain lost business with its return in 2010 at a cost of $10 per copy.[35]

Some catalogs, especially those sent by business-to-business marketers, are being converted to a DVD format. Catalog companies can significantly reduce printing and mailing costs, while being more environmentally friendly. Often a digital catalog is easier for users to search and it can be updated quickly and relatively inexpensively. Digital catalogs can also be enhanced with audio and video or linked to the Internet for more information or online ordering.

Using Direct Mail in the Media Mix

Direct mail is an efficient, effective, and economical medium for sales and business promotion (see My Ad Campaign 14–C, "The Pros and Cons of Direct-Mail Advertising"). That's why it's used by a wide variety of companies, charity and service organizations, and individuals. Direct mail can increase the effectiveness of ads in other media. For example, Publishers Clearinghouse typically uses TV spots to alert viewers to the impending arrival of its direct-mail sweepstakes promotions.

Direct mail has two main drawbacks: cost and the "junk mail" image, both of which are almost inescapable. No other medium (except personal selling and consumer targeting on the Internet) has such a high cost per thousand. For this reason, many small advertisers participate in cooperative (rather than solo) mailings with companies such as ADVO, which serves most major U.S. cities. ADVO mails an envelope containing a coupon for each participating company to targeted zip codes.

Some large advertisers don't send unsolicited mail. To locate prospects, they use other direct-response media such as advertising with toll-free "800" numbers or soliciting inquiries on the Internet. Then they use direct mail to respond to those inquiries. They save money by mailing only to qualified prospects, and by sending higher-quality materials, they build their image and improve their chances of establishing a worthwhile relationship.

statement stuffers Advertisements enclosed in the monthly customer statements mailed by department stores, banks, utilities, or oil companies.

house organs Internal and external publications produced by business organizations, including stockholder reports, newsletters, consumer magazines, and dealer publications. Most are produced by a company's advertising or public relations department or by its agency.

catalogs Reference books mailed to prospective customers that list, describe, and often picture the products sold by a manufacturer, wholesaler, jobber, or retailer.

check yourself ✓

1. Why is Customized Market-Mail (CMM) a benefit to direct-mail advertisers?

2. What are some ways that direct mail could be effectively used in conjunction with other elements of the media mix?

The Pros and Cons of Direct-Mail Advertising [14–C]

The Pros

- **Selectivity.** Direct mail helps advertisers communicate directly with the people most likely to buy. Computerized mailing lists group people by occupation, region or state, income, and other characteristics.
- **Intensive coverage and extensive reach.** Everyone has a mailbox. With direct mail, an advertiser can reach 100 percent of the homes in a given area.
- **Flexibility.** Direct-mail advertising can be uniquely creative, limited only by the advertiser's ingenuity and budget and postal regulations. Advertisers can produce direct-mail pieces fast and distribute them quickly.
- **Control.** Preprinted direct-mail pieces enable an advertiser to precisely control circulation and reproduction quality.
- **Personal impact.** Advertisers can personalize direct mail to the needs, wants, and whims of specific audiences without offending other prospects or customers.
- **Exclusivity.** There are no distractions from competitive ads (in solo mailings).
- **Response.** Direct mail achieves the highest response of any advertising medium. About 15 percent of the responses arrive within the first week, so the advertiser can quickly judge a campaign's success.
- **Testability.** Direct mail is good for testing prospect reactions to products, pricing, promotions, copy approaches, sales literature, and so on.

The Cons

- **High cost per exposure.** Direct mail has the highest cost per exposure of any major medium, about 14 times as much as most magazine and newspaper advertising.
- **Delivery problems.** The mass media offer precise delivery times, but the postal service makes no delivery commitments on third-class mail. And up to 10 percent of mailings may be undeliverable because people move.
- **Lack of content support.** Direct mail must capture and hold the reader's attention without the support of editorial or entertainment content.
- **Selectivity problems.** Effective direct mail depends on correctly identifying the target audience and obtaining a good list. Some groups of prospects, such as physicians, are so saturated with direct mail they ignore it.
- **Negative attitudes.** Many consumers think of direct mail as junk mail and automatically throw it away. This may also negatively impact the product's image.
- **Environmental concerns.** Some consumers see direct mail as landfill fodder. Some direct marketers (Eddie Bauer, L.L.Bean) print parts of their catalogs on recycled paper, and now new de-inking facilities will make more catalogs recyclable.
- **Antispam laws.** The CAN-SPAM Act and similar laws impose many requirements, making it more difficult for marketers to electronically send prospective clients unsolicited marketing materials.

LO5 Describe the basic components of direct-mail advertising.

Components of Direct-Mail Advertising

The three basic components of direct-mail advertising are the mailing list, the offer, and the creative package. Direct-mail experts say the mailing list is responsible for up to 60 percent of the success of a mailing. The offer is good for 25 percent of a mailing's success and the creative package is worth 15 percent. Many advertisers focus too much time and money developing the creative side of a mailing but give insufficient attention to the actual lists.

Acquiring Direct-Mail Lists
The heart of any direct-mail program is the mailing list. Each list actually defines a market segment. Direct-mail advertisers use three types of lists: *house*, *mail-response*, and *compiled*.

House lists. The company's database of current, recent, and long-past customers as well as identified prospects comprises the **house list** for direct-mail programs. Because customers are its most important asset, every company should focus sufficient resources on developing a rich database of customer and prospect information and profiles. There are several ways a company can build its own house list.

Consumer product companies like General Electric gather customer data by enclosing an owner registration form with their products. On the mail-in form, purchasers give their name, address, phone number, birth date, occupation, income range, home ownership status, and number of children. They also indicate their hobbies and interests (such as golf, foreign travel, photography, or bowling). Companies use this information for their own mailings and sell it to other direct-mail advertisers.

Mail-response lists. The advertiser's second most important prospects are people who respond to direct-mail pieces from other companies—especially those with

Typical listing from Direct Mail List Rates and Data, *published by Standard Rate & Data Service.*

complementary products or services. **Mail-response lists** are the house lists of other direct-mail advertisers, and they can be rented with a wide variety of demographic breakdowns.

Compiled lists. The most readily available lists are those that some entity compiles for a different reason and then rents or sells—for example, lists of car owners, new-home purchasers, business owners, and so on. **Compiled lists** typically offer the lowest response rate, so experts suggest using numerous sources, merging them on computer with mail-response and house lists, and then purging them of duplicate names.[36]

Direct-mail lists can be bought or rented. Purchased lists can be used without limit; rented lists may be used for a single mailing only. List owners plant decoy names in the list to be sure renters don't use it more than once.

Some list owners pay a **list broker** a commission (usually 20 percent) to handle the rental details. The advertiser, in turn, benefits from the broker's knowledge of list quality without having to pay more than the rental cost.

Lists can be tailored to reflect customer location (zip code); demographics such as age, income, and home ownership; or psychographic characteristics such as personality and lifestyle. The SRDS *Direct Mail List Rates and Data* comes in two volumes, *Consumer Lists* and *Business Lists,* and contains more than 60,000 list selections in hundreds of classifications.

Mailing list prices vary according to the accuracy and currency of the data. Rental rates average about $55 per thousand names but can be as little as $35 per thousand or as much as $400 per thousand. The more stringent the advertiser's selection criteria, the more expensive the list. An extra $10 per thousand is often well worth the savings in mailers and postage that would otherwise be wasted.

The average mailing list changes more than 40 percent a year as people relocate, change jobs, get married, or die. So mailing lists must be continually updated *(cleaned)* to be sure they're current and correct. Advertisers can also test the validity and accuracy of a given list. They rent or buy every *n*th name and send a mailer to that person. If the results are favorable, they purchase additional names, usually in lots of 1,000.

Developing the Offer
Every direct-mail package should contain an offer. The offer is the incentive or reward that motivates prospects to respond to a mailing, either with an order or with a request for more information. To be effective, an offer must be clear and specific, it must offer value to the potential customer, it must be believable, and it must be easy to acquire. The more difficult it is for prospects to respond to an offer, the lower the response rate will be. The direct-mail package should provide clear instructions, a conspicuous address (mailing and Internet), and a toll-free phone number.

The offer should promote a benefit that will address a prospect's needs. It should clearly explain why this mail is being sent to this prospect at this time. In other words, there should be a *call to action:* What does the advertiser want the recipient to do when he or she receives the mail? And finally, it should give the prospect a reason to act NOW.

Creating, Producing, and Distributing the Package
To create a direct-mail package, the advertiser may use in-house staff, an ad agency, or a freelance designer and writer. Some agencies specialize in direct mail (see Commercial Break 14–B, "Developing Effective Direct-Mail Packages").

The direct-mail piece normally goes through the same production process as any other print piece. The size and shape of the mailing package, as well as the type, illustrations, and colors, all affect printing costs. Special features such as simulated blue-ink signatures, cardboard pop-ups, and die-cutting (the cutting of paper stock into an unusual shape) add to the cost. But the larger the printing volume, or run, the lower the printing cost per unit.

Remaining production and handling tasks can be done by a local **letter shop** (or *mailing house*), or the advertiser can do them internally. On a cost-per-thousand basis, letter shops stuff and seal envelopes, affix labels, calculate postage, and sort, tie, and stack the mailers. Some shops also offer creative services. If the advertiser is using third-class bulk mail, the letter shop separates mailers by zip code and ties them into bundles to qualify for low bulk rates. Then the letter shop delivers the mailers to the post office.

Almost every business uses advertising specialties, and almost any specialty item can be imprinted with a company's advertising message and logo.

Distribution costs are based chiefly on the weight of the mailer and the delivery method. U.S. advertisers can use the U.S. Postal Service, air freight, or private delivery services like UPS and FedEx. The most common, the U.S. Postal Service, offers several types of delivery.

LO6 Explain the value of advertising specialties.

SPECIALTY ADVERTISING
The Promotional Products Association International (PPAI) defines an **advertising specialty** as a promotional product, usually imprinted with an advertiser's name, message, or logo, that is distributed free as part of a marketing communications program.[37] Specialty advertising is one component of the large promotional products industry, which also includes premiums, incentives, business gifts, awards, and commemoratives. Today, nearly every business uses advertising specialties of some sort. As many as 15,000 different specialty items, ranging from coffee mugs to ballpoint pens, key chains, and T-shirts, represent an annual volume of nearly $16 billion. The largest product category for promotional items is *wearables,* which include T-shirts, golf shirts, jackets, caps, hats, footwear, and the like, which make up over 31 percent of the total. Other popular categories include writing instruments (8.7 percent), bags (7.6 percent), calendars (7.1 percent), drinkware (6.8 percent), and desk and office accessories (5.2 percent).[38]

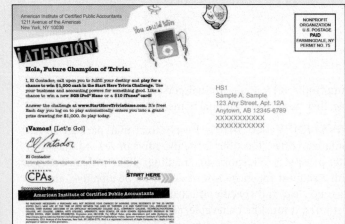

This colorful, attention-grabbing mail piece is meant to attract high school and college students who might be interested in accounting.

Good direct-mail campaigns help build relationships between advertisers and customers. As with an ad, the effectiveness of a direct-mail campaign relies heavily on both its message and its overall appearance.

Shaping the Message

When the AICPA (American Institute of Certified Public Accountants) wanted to present the cooler side of accounting to high school and college students, it contacted Wunderman. The AICPA had created a recruiting Web site called "Start Here. Go Places." which featured a trivia game. Wunderman's task was to get the students to the Web site where they would play the game and learn more about the accounting profession as a result. Lucky players of the game could win prizes like cash, iPods, and gift cards. Wunderman created the highly graphic, attention-getting postcard shown here, which was sent to targeted high school and college students.

To develop the message element in direct mail, experts suggest several techniques: stress the benefits; repeat your offer more than once; offer an incentive; offer a guarantee; don't be afraid of long copy; don't write copy that is over the reader's head; and give the customer more than one option for responding.

Integrating the Message with the Direct-Mail Pieces

Creating direct mail involves fitting the message with the key physical components of the direct-mail package. As discussed in Chapter 8, the five steps of the creative pyramid (attention, interest, credibility, desire, and action) may be guidelines for

forming the message. Next, this information must be incorporated into all the components of the direct-mail package.

The AICPA postcard attracts *attention* with its colorful and humorous graphics. The mismatched fonts and image of the Contador beckon the recipient to look further. The specifics within the postcard build *credibility* by providing data that the offer is real and important. The prizes offered further attract the target's *desire* to visit the site. What student could turn down a chance at winning cash or an iPod? The desired *action* (playing the game), is made easy by providing the Web address of the game on both the front and the back of the postcard.

Some Secrets of Direct Mail

Research has revealed countless direct-mail techniques that improve response rates: indent type and set it flush left with a ragged right edge; avoid printing in reverse type; list dollars saved in your offer rather than percentages; use the word *you* in the text; provide a reason for sale pricing (almost any will do); and do not paste labels over old addresses—print new materials.

Applying the Breaks

1. Locate a direct-mail package that has the four components common to most mailings and list how the elements of the creative pyramid are integrated throughout the components.

2. Review the copywriting in your direct-mail package and identify how many of the techniques mentioned in this Commercial Break are used or could be improved.

Advertising specialties are effective tools for improving people's perception and recollection of a business. They are often distributed in association with trade shows, public relations programs, employee events, new product introductions, or brand-building programs. Some specialty items may be kept for years and serve as continuous, friendly reminders of the advertiser's business. In fact, 58 percent of the recipients keep these gifts for at least a year. Companies often spend substantial sums for goodwill items to promote their businesses, and studies indicate that this investment pays off. Nearly 90 percent of recipients could recall the name of the advertiser on a promotional item they received in the past 24 months.[39]

An advertising specialty is different from a premium. **Premiums** are also promotional products; they are typically more valuable and usually bear no advertising message. However, to get a premium, recipients must buy a product, send in a coupon, witness a demonstration, or perform some other action advantageous to the advertiser. An advertising specialty, on the other hand, is always given free as a goodwill item.

Business-to-Business Specialties

In the business-to-business arena, companies use more structured specialty promotions to improve their goodwill standing over competitors. In one case, including an ad specialty with a thank-you letter improved customer attitude by 34 percent compared to sending a thank-you letter alone. At the same time, customers' general feelings about the company and its sales reps improved 52 percent.[40]

In one test, a group of Realtors received a $1.49 ballpoint pen imprinted with a mortgage company's name, a second group received a $10 sports bag (also imprinted), and a third group got nothing. In a follow-up questionnaire, Realtors who received nothing were least inclined to recommend the product, but both the sports bag and ballpoint groups responded equally positively. Evidently, gift recipients felt obliged to reciprocate, but the value of the gift was not crucial. So the $1.49 pen offered the better return on investment.

Inappropriate specialty items can backfire no matter what the cost. A recipient may perceive an overly expensive gift as a form of bribery, yet a cheap trinket could make a quality-conscious business look cheap. Finally, marketers should realize that the value and nature of gifts may raise ethical issues. ■

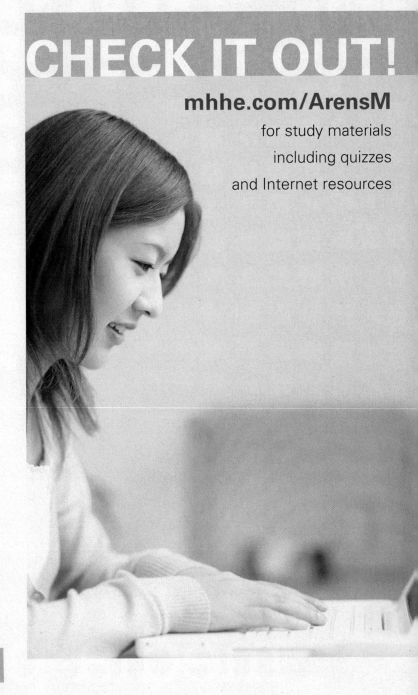

CHECK IT OUT!

mhhe.com/ArensM

for study materials
including quizzes
and Internet resources

check yourself ✓

1. What is the difference between an advertising specialty and a premium?

2. How might a business-to-business gift raise ethical issues?

media planning
and buying

People love the iPhone, or at least that is what the long lines and sold-out inventory of new iPhone3G's at Apple stores in July of 2008 would suggest.

It was not always so. When MIT asked people in 2004 to name the invention that you hate the most but can't live without, standing at the top of the list was the mobile phone, easily outscoring the alarm clock. Users doubtless liked that mobile phones helped for staying in touch with family, friends, customers, and coworkers. But back then the phones were not always easy to use. And they often weren't much fun either.

So in 2007, when CEO Steve Jobs announced that Apple had reinvented the phone, people took notice. For many,

continued on p. 382

LEARNING OBJECTIVES

LO1 Describe how media planning has changed over the past decades and what has caused these changes.

LO2 Discuss the important types of media objectives and identify the terms that define strategies for achieving these objectives.

LO3 Identify the factors that influence media strategy and tactics.

LO4 Describe different types of advertising schedules and the purpose for each.

LO5 Explain the role of the media buyer.

continued from p. 381

the marriage of mobile phone utility and Apple's skill at designing products with both beautiful form and function seemed irresistible. When it finally arrived, critics and consumers alike agreed that the original iPhone lived up to the hype.

Apple sold 4 million units in its first year. Not bad, considering the phone could only be used with one carrier (AT&T) and came with a $400 price tag.

But this was no ordinary mobile phone. Slim, futuristic, colorful, easy-to-use, the iPhone instantly became the one to beat in the "smart phone" category. Other phones might let users watch YouTube videos, read *The New York Times*, or listen to music, but the iPhone made it a snap. It was three devices in one: Phone + iPod + Internet device in a skinny little package. The entire surface was marred only by one small button. The beautiful screen was bigger, clearer, heck, just plain cooler than any competitor's. For millions of iPhone buyers, it was love at first sight.

The original iPhone's successor, the iPhone3G, offered consumers even more benefits, such as faster 3G-network technology and a

price tag just half that of the original iPhone. When it went on sale in July of 2008, Apple sold more than a million units in just the first three days. Analysts expect sales of 10 million units by the end of its first year. Consumers are very excited about the iPhone3G.

So are advertisers. But for them, it isn't the hardware that is so exciting. It's the software.

To see why this is so, do a thought experiment. Ask yourself, from an advertiser's perspective, what would the ideal medium look like? Several criteria come to mind. Lots of people should use the medium and they should spend a lot of time with it. And people should interact with the medium throughout the day, not just in the morning (as they do with newspapers) or evening (as they do with television). The ideal medium would allow people to use coupons (like newspapers) but also view video (like TV) and hear sound (like radio). The medium should be responsive and interactive, allowing consumers to find out more about an advertiser's product if they wish (like the Web). The medium should allow for advertising accountability, in other words, advertisers should be able to track what people are doing with their ads (like direct response advertising). Since we are just dreaming, why not add that the medium should be able to draw people a map from wherever they happen to be directly to the place where they can buy a product or use a service?

Sound like any medium you know? Actually, the only medium that can accomplish all of these things, at least for now, is the mobile phone.

Many people bring (and use) their phones in places they would never think to bring other media. For example, one survey suggests that most Americans consider it acceptable to use mobile phones in the supermarket and just under half think it is fine to use them while riding on public transportation. One out of five believes it is OK to use mobile phones in a restaurant. And nearly 4 out of 10 say it is acceptable to use the phone in the bathroom. The bottom line: Many people spend more time with their phones than with any other thing, person, or place.

And there are lots of mobile phones, an estimated 203 million in the United States alone. The people who own them also tend to be young, economically well-off, and tech savvy. In other words, just the kind of prospects that many advertisers are interested in reaching.

So the mobile phone may just be the perfect advertising medium. But until recently there haven't been many ways to advertise effectively on mobile phones because customers frankly are not interested in seeing ads when they make or receive a call. That is where "smart phones" like the iPhone3G come in. The 3G won't serve you ads when you are making calls (at least for now). But it will take advantage of all of the other things you like to do with an iPhone.

Like many smart phones, the 3G allows users to surf the Web. This capability immediately broadens the audience for ads delivered by big Web companies like Google, Yahoo, and Microsoft.

But the iPhone3G also affords advertisers the opportunity to serve ads to people when they are not surfing the Web. This is because the iPhone 2.0 operating system runs tiny applications, such as games, utilities, and custom content. Hundreds of companies have developed such programs, which Apple makes available for download at its iTunes store.

Ads that run within these applications can be pretty powerful. For example, iPhone apps can open the iTunes store, play audio,

launch a video, share a video with others, dial a phone number, or start a map application that displays retailers near the user's location. To cite just one example, a job search app built for Careerbuilder.com shows the user listings within close proximity to his or her location.

Almost overnight the iPhone3G is making the dream of effective mobile phone advertising a reality. Big advertisers like Universal Pictures, Ford, Land Rover, and Jaguar have all developed iPhone campaigns. And Web giants like Google, MySpace, and Facebook have rushed to introduce their own iPhone programs (even as Google quietly readies its own smart phone operating system, Android). New mobile advertising companies, like AdMob, have attracted clients such as AccuWeather, MovieTickets, and Electronic Arts. In just one month in 2008, AdMob served up nearly 52 million ads on the iPhone platform.

Despite the excitement, smart advertisers are thinking carefully before striking because, as *Advertising Age*'s Chad Currie puts it, software is the content. What he means is that iPhone content is controlled by the user. Advertisers can't force their way in, like TV commercials do. Instead, content is invited in by the user. So serving up boring, irrelevant ads won't work. "As with any branded content, if you bring value you will be welcomed," writes Currie. "If not, then you can wait for inventory to open up to sponsor someone else's killer app."

Top media planners want proof that iPhone ads are effective before they will recommend them to clients. So developers are introducing "app analytics" that will help planners track the size of the audience for different apps and determine what app features people use most.

It is still way too early to fully predict how all of this will play out. Sales of the 3G easily met Apple's expectations and the buzz about the new phone has to be the envy of every technology company. But some perspective is in order. Apple's mobile phone market share, even if it sells 14 million units by the end of the year, will still be just a fraction of the 3 billion phones in use worldwide. And, according to recent estimates, 4.5 billion people around the world still don't even have a cell phone. Of course, a lot of people might view that as more of an opportunity than a problem.

continued on p. 384

continued from p. 383

Greg Yardley, CEO of Pinch Media, acknowledges that "The Apple experience is so compelling and there's a real opportunity down the road for rich interactive advertising. But right now an ad agency has to ask itself, 'How many people am I really reaching here?'" Perhaps not many, just yet. But Steve Jobs has heard from naysayers before. Jobs, who has consistently proven one of the past several decades' greatest visionaries, has led Apple's successful attempts at revolutionizing the personal computer, the digital music player, and music retailing. Advertisers are increasingly betting he will do the same with mobile phones. ■

LO1 Describe how media planning has changed over the past decades and what has caused these changes.

MEDIA PLANNING: INTEGRATING SCIENCE WITH CREATIVITY IN ADVERTISING

The purpose of **media planning** is to conceive, analyze, and creatively select channels of communication that will direct advertising messages to the right people in the right place at the right time. The Media Edge believes that "anything you put your message on is media." That includes shopping bags, book covers, and parking meters. As a result, media planning today involves many decisions. For example,

- Where should we advertise? (In what countries, states, or parts of town?)
- Which media vehicles reach and engage our target markets?
- When during the year should we concentrate our advertising?
- How often should we run the advertising?
- What opportunities exist for integrating our advertising with other communication tools?

Some of these decisions require research and detailed mathematical analysis, aided by sophisticated computer software programs.

The Challenge

Historically, the people who plan and buy media have enjoyed relative anonymity compared to the "stars" in the creative and account service departments. Today the media planner's assignment is just as critical as the creative director's: One media planner can be responsible for millions of client dollars. The planner's work attests to an agency's strategic ability to negotiate the best prices and use effectively the incredible array of media choices.

Jack Klues, when he was the director of U.S. media services for Leo Burnett USA, said, "Our mission is to buy and plan media so effectively that our clients obtain an unfair advantage versus their competitors."[1]

Volkswagen's "Buy a New Beetle, get an iPod" promotion tapped into multiple forms of media—from TV ads to printed collateral to a Web presence—to make its message known. Arnold Worldwide won several awards for this campaign, which centered on a simple slogan, "Pods unite."

media planning
The process that directs
advertising messages to
the right people in the right
place at the right time.

▼**EXHIBIT 15–1** U.S. ad spending by medium (2009).

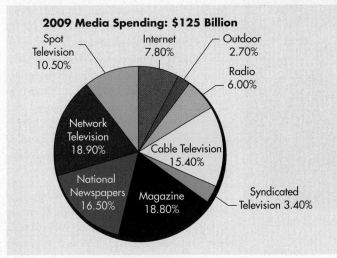

2009 Media Spending: $125 Billion

Spot Television 10.50%
Internet 7.80%
Outdoor 2.70%
Radio 6.00%
Network Television 18.90%
Cable Television 15.40%
National Newspapers 16.50%
Magazine 18.80%
Syndicated Television 3.40%

Source: *Advertising Age,* June 21, 2010, p. 10.

The media department gained new prominence in the 1990s when clients started taking an a la carte approach to agency services, and agencies began competing for media planning and buying assignments separately from the creative business.[2] By the early 2000s, media wins were big news: Universal McCann won the $150 million Nestlé account; Gillette awarded its $600 million media account to Mindshare; and Kraft consolidated its $800 million media business at Starcom MediaVest Group.[3]

With greater complexity, media decisions become more critical and clients more demanding. Advertisers want agencies to be more than efficient. They want accountability and information, particularly about media options. And they want creative buys.

What makes media planning today so much more complicated and challenging than it was just a few years ago?

Increasing Media Options There are many more media to choose from today, and each offers more choices. It wasn't long ago that major advertisers could ensure a big audience by simply advertising on TV. Not anymore. Today it's much more difficult to reach a big audience. As Stacey Lippman, director of corporate media at TBWA Chiat/Day, says, "There's too much to keep track of and too many things to explore."[4]

TV is now fragmented into network, syndicated, spot, and local television, as well as network and local cable. Specialized magazines now aim at every population and business segment. Even national magazines publish editions for particular regions or demographic groups. Finally, the incredible growth of the Internet has brought with it a host of new media options. But it has also added to the complexity of media work as planners face the challenge of staying current with the constantly expanding technology and mastering a whole new vocabulary.

Nontraditional media—from DVD and cinema advertising to product placement and even restrooms—also expand the menu of choices. In addition, many companies spend a considerable portion of their marketing budgets on specialized communications like direct marketing, sales promotion, public relations activities, and personal selling, topics we'll discuss in the next two chapters. In fact, these "below-the-line" (noncommissionable) activities are the fastest-growing segments at some of the large agency holding companies, like WPP and Interpublic.[5]

For companies practicing IMC, the "media menu" needs to include everything that carries a message to and/or from customers and other stakeholders. The proliferation of toll-free phone numbers, e-mail, and Web sites makes it easy and cost-effective to facilitate customer feedback. The result is that advertisers can be very creative in designing systems for both sending and receiving messages. That means that companies and agencies need to think in terms of message handling, being as responsible for receiving messages as for sending them. Mark Goldstein, the president of integrated marketing at Fallon Worldwide in Minneapolis, says, "Media is no longer planned and bought; instead it's created, aggregated, and partnered." Perhaps the media department of the future will be called the *connect department.*[6]

Increasing Fragmentation of the Audience Further evidence of the maturing marketplace is the fragmentation of the media audience. This also complicates the media planner's job. Readers and viewers have scattered across the new media options, selectively reading only parts of magazines or newspapers, watching only segments of programs, and listening to many different radio stations. This makes it very difficult to find the prospect. Consumers spend on average 3,530 hours with media—but an increasing proportion of that time is spent with less traditional media vehicles.[7]

Increasing Costs While there are more media choices, the number of messages that need to be communicated has also grown—so much so, in fact, that they have outstripped the ability of consumers to process them. People can cope with only so many messages, so media restrict the number of ads they sell. As a result, the costs are increasing for almost all media. In the last decade, the cost of exposing 1,000 people to each of the major media (cost per thousand) rose faster than inflation. Shows that can deliver a big audience are sold at a premium. To run a 30-second spot on *American Idol,* for instance, now costs over $750,000.[8] Rising costs make media planning more challenging than ever, especially for advertisers with small budgets. Clients want proof that planners are squeezing the most they can out of every media dollar.

Increasing Complexity in Media Buying and Selling As the process of buying media has become more complex, so has the process of selling media. In the battle for additional sales, many print and broadcast media companies developed "value-added" programs to provide extra benefits. Besides selling space or time, these companies now offer reprints, merchandising services, special sections, event sponsorships, and mailing lists. To get a bigger share of the advertiser's budget, larger media companies bundle the various stations, publications, or properties they own and offer them in integrated combinations as further incentives.

The Discovery Network, for example, which includes the Travel Channel, TLC, Animal Planet, Discovery, Discovery Health, and the Science Channel, offers its advertisers "multiplatform convergence content sponsorships." This means that each advertiser gets a major Internet/TV sponsorship with four or five commercials in a special-event Discovery show and Webcast. Specially created TV spots promote the program and the Webcast, as well as Discovery's Web site and the advertiser's Web site. Moreover, advertisers get additional off-air exposure in hundreds of Discovery Network retail stores nationwide, which also run in-store videos promoting the shows and the sponsors.[9]

The sports fan's perennial heckle, "Come on, ref, do you need glasses?" has finally been answered. Specsavers, a Scottish optical care provider and retailer, has begun to sponsor soccer referees. In addition to providing eye exams and optical eyewear for referees, the company outfits them and advertises in stadiums. The media mix for the campaign combined the clever sponsorship with point-of-sale advertising and newspaper-friendly press releases. As the 22 percent increase in sales shows, Specsavers has positioned itself squarely in Scottish men's field of vision.

Value-added packages often employ communications vehicles outside traditional media planning, such as public relations activities, sales promotions, and direct marketing. With BMW, for instance, *Yachting* magazine sponsors sailing weeks in various markets and displays the advertiser's cars on site. So people who can afford expensive sailboats are also exposed to the cars, to BMW signage, and to any premium giveaways the sponsors might offer.[10] Integrated events like these help advertisers build relationships with their customers and prospects, and that's a major goal today. But placing a value on these deals is difficult because the nonmedia elements are hard to quantify.

IMC and relationship marketing are creating a new breed of media planner: younger, computer-savvy, and schooled in new media. The good media specialist today is actually a real advertising generalist. Media professionals have finally come into their own.

Increasing Competition   The final element making media planning more challenging is the competitive environment, which in just a few years has completely changed the structure of the advertising business. In the 1990s, as clients sought greater efficiency with their media dollars, independent media buying services came into the fore, attracting some of the best and brightest talent in the business to compete with agencies

for what was once their private domain. Initially, the independents bought advertising at lower bulk rates and then sold it for a commission to advertisers or agencies lacking a fully staffed media department. As the media specialists grew, though, clients came to realize the virtues of scale, and financial clout emerged as a potent weapon in negotiating media buys.[11] By 2004, the independents handled 16.4 percent of all national media (advertising and marketing) accounts.[12]

In response, ad agencies unbundled their own media departments, setting them up as separate media specialist subsidiaries like The Media Edge. These companies could compete with the independents as well as with other agencies for media-only accounts. Over time, all these firms became quite expert at the media function. With the rapid increase in billings, they were able to pour a substantial amount of money into the development of new research tools, which was critical given the continued fragmentation of the mass media into smaller and smaller niches.

At this point, the big multinational advertisers realized that they could receive greater impact from their ad dollars by consolidating their media budgets within a single large shop. Procter & Gamble, for instance, pooled $1.2 billion at TeleVest. As the big media shops started winning the big accounts, the large agency holding companies went on an acquisition binge, buying up the largest of the independent media agencies and sometimes merging them with their own subsidiaries and then, as in the case of TME, relaunching them as global media firms. By 2000 the process had gone full circle. For the most part, the agencies were again back in control of the media budgets—albeit at arm's length.[13] And while the structure was different, so was the compensation. They were no longer getting 15 percent of the media budget. In fact, 2 to 3 percent was the norm. But the volume was so high that the business could still be quite profitable.[14]

The Role of Media in the Marketing Framework

As we've discussed, the key to successful advertising is proper planning. Thus, before media planning begins—indeed, before advertising is even considered—companies must first establish their overall marketing and advertising plans.

As we saw in Chapter 7, the top-down marketing plan defines the market need and the company's sales objectives and

Closed-Circuit Programming

Dan is a middle-aged man recovering at his local hospital from a recent stroke. Bedridden, he spends a lot of time watching TV. In a boredom-induced daze, he half-wittedly flips through the channels and stumbles across a show featuring a man in a blue plaid shirt sitting in a doctor's office. A voice chimes in: "Daniel Sorby had no idea that he had high cholesterol—until he suffered from a stroke." Immediately Dan's attention perks up.

For the next half-hour, a discussion ensues on the difference between "good" and "bad" cholesterol, revealing their potential role in heart attacks and strokes. The program ends. Then comes a short commercial break.

The spot is for Plavix—"a prescription pill that can help protect you from a heart attack or stroke if you've recently had one," says a friendly grandmother, as the camera rolls to pictures of her playing with her grandkids.

This scene is played out every day in more than 1,000 hospitals nationwide due to the introduction of the Patient Channel—a 24-hour network piped directly into patient and waiting rooms at no cost to the hospital or patient.

Founded in 2002 by General Electric Co., the Patient Channel is one of a growing number of closed-circuit programming channels providing news and educational programs to hospitals, schools, and fitness centers across the country. Yet it is not the programs that are making the national headlines. Rather, it is the advertising that pays for the service, such as the Plavix spot, which has stirred much recent debate.

Proponents for the network are principally the pharmaceutical companies that now have direct advertising access to over 22 million patients. Never before have the drug manufacturers been able to "directly associate their products with a particular condition within a hospital setting." By achieving such a full measure of direct-to-consumer advertising, the pharmaceuticals will likely generate enormous revenues on their new drugs.

Opponents of the network are led by a consumer advocacy group called Commercial Alert, which feels the Patient Channel's ads "pitch drugs at a time when [patients] are most worried about disease, in a way that carries the implicit authority and endorsement of the hospital and its doctors." Furthermore, the group feels the channel unfairly exploits a "captive audience at a time of maximum vulnerability and emotional distress."

Refuting such claims, proponents point to the educational content the network provides. Federal requirements state that hospitals must provide a certain amount of patient education. General Electric, the pharmaceutical advertisers, and some within the medical profession have argued that the channel helps hospitals address this patient education requirement while freeing up already overworked nurses.

Hospitals are not the only venues subject to closed-circuit TV programming. For over 17 years, Channel One has broadcast news and current events to American middle, junior, and high school classrooms. Each day, 6 million students view a 12-minute newscast featuring stories on breaking news events and teen topics, supported, of course, by advertising.

In the process, Channel One keeps teens aware of and involved in a multitude of issues by presenting them in a manner that can easily be absorbed and understood. Channel One also provides a Web site for teens to visit to learn more about the news, find out about the latest teen crazes, offer opinions, play games, take quizzes, and learn about the dangers of alcohol and drug abuse. Plus, for the 400,000 teachers that use Channel One in the classroom, ChannelOneTeacher.com provides ideas and lesson plans—everything they need to teach the news.

However, once again the advertisements have captured the controversial spotlight. As with the Patient Channel, the cost of providing the much-needed free TVs and DVDs to classrooms is offset by the ads that accompany the news segment—often for junk-food products. Some students and parents have raised their voices in an effort to remove the programs, stating that teens should not be the victims of deceptive advertising campaigns. One parent said he is opposed to Channel One because it creates a slippery slope that could open schools up to even more commercial interests. He said that he would hate to "live in a district where the kids run on the Pepsi track or work out in the Nike gym." The overall concern is that children of this age are highly impressionable, and that makes the junk-food advertisements seen on Channel One unethically exploitative.

In this debate, both the pros and cons seem to have good arguments, making it difficult to craft a policy that would resolve the issue entirely. The future of this medium will depend on how advertisers attempt to use it and how consumers in turn react, as closed-circuit programming becomes more prevalent in the years to come.

Questions

1. Is the value of the educational programming provided to hospitals and schools worth the price of the commercial messages that accompany it?
2. Do you feel it's unethical for advertisers to pitch products to patients and students in this fashion? Why?

details strategies for attaining those objectives. Exhibit 15–2 shows how objectives and strategies of a marketing plan result from the marketing situation (or SWOT) analysis, which defines the company's strengths and weaknesses and uncovers any marketplace opportunities and threats. The objectives and strategies of an advertising plan unfold from the marketing plan. But advertising objectives focus on communication goals.

The situation analysis
Purpose: To understand the marketing problem. The company and its competitors are analyzed on:
1. Internal strengths and weaknesses.
2. External opportunities and threats.

The marketing plan
Purpose: To plan activities that will solve one or more of the marketing problems.
Includes the determination of:
1. Marketing objectives.
2. Product and spending strategy.
3. Distribution strategy.
4. Which marketing mix to use.
5. Identification of "best" market segments.

The advertising plan
Purpose: To determine what to communicate through ads.
Includes the determination of:
1. How product can meet consumer needs.
2. How product will be positioned in ads.
3. Copy themes.
4. Specific objectives of each ad.
5. Number and sizes of ads.

Setting media objectives
Purpose: To translate marketing and advertising objectives and strategies into goals that media can accomplish.

Determining media strategy
Purpose: To translate media goals into general guidelines that will control the planner's selection and use of media. The best strategy alternatives should be selected.

Selecting broad media classes
Purpose: To determine which broad classes of media best fulfill the criteria. Involves comparison and selection of broad media classes: newspapers, magazines, radio, television, and others. Audience size is a major factor used in comparing the various media classes.

Selecting media within classes
Purpose: To compare and select the best media vehicles within broad classes, again using predetermined criteria. Involves making decisions about the following:
1. If magazines were recommended, then which magazines?
2. If television was recommended, then
   a. Broadcast or cable TV?
   b. Network or spot TV?
   c. If network, which program(s)?
   d. If spot, which markets?
3. If radio or newspapers were recommended, then
   a. Which markets shall be used?
   b. What criteria shall buyers use in making purchases in local media?

Media use decisions—broadcast
1. What kind of sponsorship (sole, shared participating, or other)?
2. What levels of reach and frequency will be required?
3. Scheduling: On which days and months are commercials to appear?
4. Placement of spots: In programs or between programs?

Media use decisions—print
1. Numbers of ads to appear and on which days and months.
2. Placement of ads: Any preferred position within media?
3. Special treatment: Gatefolds, bleeds, color, etc.
4. Desired reach or frequency levels.

Media use decisions—other media
1. Billboards:
   a. Location of markets and plan of distribution.
   b. Kinds of outdoor boards to be used.
2. Direct mail or other media: Decisions peculiar to those media.
3. Interactive media:
   a. Which kind of interactive media?
   b. How will responses be handled?

Media objectives and strategies flow from the advertising plan. They determine how the communications goals will be accomplished through the selection of media. The media department's job is to make sure the advertising message (developed by the creative department) gets to the correct target audience (established by the marketing managers and account executives) in an effective manner (as measured by the research department).

The Media Planning Framework

Development of a media plan proceeds in much the same way as marketing and advertising planning. First, review the marketing and advertising objectives and strategies and set relevant, measurable objectives that are both realistic and achievable by the media. Next, devise an ingenious strategy for achieving these objectives. Finally, develop the specific tactical details of media selection and scheduling.

check yourself ✓

1. What is meant by "increasing fragmentation of the audience" and why has that trend made a media planner's job more difficult?

2. What caused the unbundling of media departments? Did it benefit advertisers?

LO2 Discuss the important types of media objectives and identify the terms that define strategies for achieving these objectives.

DEFINING MEDIA OBJECTIVES

Media objectives translate the advertising strategy into goals that media can accomplish. Exhibit 15–3 shows general media objectives for a hypothetical new food product. They explain who the target audience is and why, where messages will be delivered and when, and how much advertising weight needs to be delivered over what period of time.

Media objectives have two major components: audience objectives and message-distribution objectives.

Audience Objectives

Audience objectives define the types of people the advertiser wants to reach. Media planners typically use geodemographic

classifications to define their target audiences. In Exhibit 15–3, for example, objectives 1 and 2 suggest that the target audience is food purchasers for large families who live in urban areas. This group might even be narrowed further according to specific income, educational, occupational, or social groupings—any of the segments we discussed in Chapter 4.

Media planners rely heavily on secondary research sources, such as Arbitron and Nielsen Media Research, which provide basic demographic characteristics of media audiences. Other sources, such as Simmons Market Research Bureau (SMRB) and Mediamark Research, Inc. (MRI), describe media audiences based on purchase tendencies. These syndicated reports give demographic profiles of heavy and light users of various products and help planners define the target audience. The reports also specify which TV programs or magazines heavy and light users watch and read, which helps planners select media with large audiences of heavy users. Planners can then select **media vehicles**—particular magazines or shows—according to how well they *deliver* the message to an audience that most closely resembles the desired target consumer.

Unfortunately, due to cost restraints, most media research is not as specific as marketers would really like. Most radio, TV, newspaper, and outdoor audience reports, for example, are

audience objectives Definitions of the specific types of people the advertiser wants to reach.

media vehicles Particular media programs or publications.

▼**EXHIBIT 15–3** How media objectives are expressed.

ACME **Advertising**

Client: Econo Foods

Product/Brand: Chirpee's Cheap Chips

Project: Media plan, first year introduction

Media Objectives

1. To target large families with emphasis on the family's food purchaser.

2. To concentrate the greatest weight of advertising in urban areas where prepared foods traditionally have greater sales and where new ideas normally gain quicker acceptance.

3. To provide extra weight during the introductory period and then continuity throughout the year with a fairly consistent level of advertising impressions.

4. To deliver advertising impressions to every region in relation to regional food store sales.

5. To use media that will reinforce the copy strategy's emphasis on convenience, ease of preparation, taste, and economy.

6. To attain the highest advertising frequency possible once the need for broad coverage and the demands of the copy platform have been met.

Media planners must be more creative than ever. Sometimes that means purchasing a product placement rather than a traditional ad.

limited to age and gender. So media planners often have to rely on judgment and experience to select the right vehicles.[15] This is especially problematic with new media such as the Internet where the media planner's experience may be limited.

Message-Distribution Objectives

Distribution objectives define where, when, and how often advertising should appear. Objectives 3 thru 6 from Exhibit 15–3 represent this type. To answer distribution objectives, a media planner must understand a number of terms, including *message weight, reach, frequency,* and *continuity.*

Audience Size and Message Weight Marketers are naturally interested in having their messages exposed to as many customers and prospects as they can afford. So they are also logically most interested in those vehicles that offer the

largest audiences.[16] The basic way to express audience size is simply to count the number of people in a vehicle's audience. This is what media research firms like Nielsen and Arbitron do for broadcast media, typically using a statistical sample to project the total audience size. For print media, firms like the Audit Bureau of Circulations verify a vehicle's subscribers and newstand sales (the **circulation**) and then multiply by the estimated number of **readers per copy (RPC)** to determine the total audience. RPC factors in the **pass-along rate**, the number of people who read a magazine or newspaper without actually buying it. For example, most households subscribe to a single issue of a newspaper, even though multiple individuals in each home read it.

Media planners often define media objectives by the schedule's **message weight**, the total size of the audience for a set of ads or an entire campaign, because it gives some indication of the exposure of the campaign in a given market. There are two ways to express message weight: *gross impressions* and *gross rating points.*

If planners know the audience size, they can easily calculate the number of advertising impressions in a media schedule. An **advertising impression** is a *possible* exposure of the advertising message to one audience member. It is sometimes referred to as an **opportunity to see (OTS)**. Why? Because when a newspaper or magazine is delivered or bought, that counts as an impression. It cannot be determined whether the individuals who received those vehicles actually saw any particular ad. By multiplying a vehicle's total audience size by the number of times an advertising message is delivered during the period, planners arrive at the **gross impressions**, or potential exposures, possible in that vehicle. Then, by summing the gross impressions for each medium used, they know the total gross impressions for the schedule (see Exhibit 15–4).

With large media schedules, though, gross impressions can run into the millions and become difficult to comprehend, so that's where the concept of ratings comes in. The **rating** is simply the percentage of homes exposed to an advertising medium.

▼**EXHIBIT 15–4** Gross impressions analysis for Alpha brand in the second quarter, 2011.

Media Vehicle	Target Audience*	Messages Used	Gross Impressions
TV–Ch. 6 News	140,000	15	2,100,000
Daily newspaper	250,000	7	1,750,000
Spot radio	10,000	55	550,000
Total gross impressions			4,400,000

*Average.

Percentages are not only simpler numbers to deal with; they are also more useful in making comparisons. One rating point is equal to 1 percent of a given population group. When we hear that a particular TV show garnered a 20 rating, it means 20 percent of the households with TV sets (expressed as **television households** or **TVHH**) were tuned in to that show. The higher a program's rating, the more people are watching.[17] This definition applies to many media forms, but it is most commonly used for radio and TV.

By adding the ratings of several media vehicles (as we did for gross impressions) we can determine the message weight of a given advertising schedule, only now it's expressed as **gross rating points (GRPs)** (see Exhibit 15–5). When we say a schedule delivered 440 GRPs, that means the impressions generated by our schedule equaled 440 percent of the target market population. For broadcast media, GRPs are often calculated for a week or a four-week period. In print media, they're calculated for the number of ads in a campaign. For outdoor advertising, they're calculated on the basis of daily exposure.

In the calculation of message weight, advertisers ignore the fact that there is overlap or duplication. As a result, certain individuals within the audience may see the message several times while others don't see it at all. So, while message weight gives an indication of audience size, it does not reveal much about who is in the audience or how often they are reached. This fact led to the development of other media objectives, including reach, frequency, and continuity.

Audience Accumulation and Reach
The term **reach** refers to the total number of *different* people exposed, at least once, to a medium during a given period of time, usually four weeks.[18] For example, if 40 percent of 100,000 people in a target market tune in to radio station WKKO at least once during a four-week period, the reach is 40,000 people. Reach should not be confused with the number of people who will actually be exposed to and consume the *advertising*, though. It is just the number of people who are exposed to the *vehicle* and therefore have an *opportunity* to see or hear the ad or commercial.

▼**EXHIBIT 15–5** Gross rating points analysis for Alpha brand in the second quarter, 2011.

Media Vehicle	Adult Rating*	Messages Used	Gross Rating Points
TV–Ch. 6 News	10	15	150
Daily newspaper	25	10	250
Spot radio	1	35	35
Total gross rating points			435

*Assumes market size of 1 million people.

An advertiser may accumulate reach in two ways: by using the same media vehicle repeatedly or by combining two or more media vehicles.[19] Naturally, as more media are used, some duplication occurs. Exhibit 15–6 is a statistical table that estimates how reach builds as additional media are added. To see how it works, locate the column for the first vehicle showing a reach of 60. Then locate the row for vehicle 2 showing a reach of 35. The number at their intersection is 74. But 35 added to 60 is 95. Why has reach only increased to 74? The answer is the two vehicles share some of their users. Only unduplicated users increase a campaign's reach. Duplicated users are useful, however, for another media objective that we turn to next: frequency.

Exposure Frequency
To express the number of times the same person or household has an opportunity to see a message—a radio spot, for example—in a specified time span, media people use the term *frequency*. Whereas reach measures the *breadth*, **frequency** measures the *intensity* of a media schedule, based on repeated exposures to the vehicle or the program. Frequency is important because repetition is the key to learning and memory.

Frequency is calculated as the *average* number of times individuals or homes are exposed to the vehicle during a specific period of time. For instance, suppose in our hypothetical 100,000-person market that 20,000 people tune in to WKKO and have three OTSs during a four-week period, and another 20,000 have five OTSs. To calculate the average frequency, divide the total number of exposures by the total reach:

$$\text{Average frequency} = \text{Total exposures} \div \text{Audience reach}$$
$$= [(20{,}000 \times 3) + (20{,}000 \times 5)] \div 40{,}000$$
$$= 160{,}000 \div 40{,}000$$
$$= 4.0$$

▼**EXHIBIT 15–6** Find the reach of the first vehicle on the horizontal axis. Find the reach of the second vehicle on the vertical axis. The point of intersection shows the combined reach of the two. The difference between the sums of the reach of each vehicle and the numbers in the table are due to audience duplication between the vehicles.

		Reach of First Vehicle													
		25	30	35	40	45	50	55	60	65	70	75	80	85	90	95
Reach of Second Vehicle	25	46	47	51	55	59	62	66	70	74	77	81	85	89	92	95
	30	—	51	54	58	61	65	68	72	75	79	82	86	90	93	95
	35	—	—	58	61	64	67	71	74	77	80	84	87	90	93	95
	40	—	—	—	64	67	70	73	76	79	82	85	88	91	94	95
	45	—	—	—	—	70	72	75	78	81	83	86	89	92	94	95
	50	—	—	—	—	—	75	77	80	82	85	87	90	92	95	95
	55	—	—	—	—	—	—	80	82	84	86	89	91	93	95	95
	60	—	—	—	—	—	—	—	84	86	88	90	92	94	95	95
	65	—	—	—	—	—	—	—	—	88	89	91	93	95	95	95
	70	—	—	—	—	—	—	—	—	—	91	92	94	95	95	95
	75	—	—	—	—	—	—	—	—	—	—	94	95	95	95	95
	80	—	—	—	—	—	—	—	—	—	—	—	95	95	95	95
	85	—	—	—	—	—	—	—	—	—	—	—	—	95	95	95
	90	—	—	—	—	—	—	—	—	—	—	—	—	—	95	95
	95	—	—	—	—	—	—	—	—	—	—	—	—	—	—	95

For the 40,000 listeners reached, the average frequency, or number of exposures, was four.

Once we understand reach and frequency, we have another, simple way to determine the message weight. To calculate gross rating points, just multiply a show's reach (expressed as a rating percentage) by the average frequency. In our radio example, 40 percent of the radio households (a 40 rating) had the opportunity to hear the commercial an average of four times during the four-week period:

$$\text{Reach} \times \text{Frequency} = \text{GRPs}$$
$$40 \times 4 = 160 \text{ GRPs}$$

Thus, the message weight of this radio campaign would be equal to 160 percent of the total market—or 160,000 gross impressions.

Continuity Media planners refer to the duration of an advertising message or campaign over a given period of time as **continuity**. Few companies spread their marketing efforts evenly throughout the year. They typically *heavy up* before prime selling seasons and slow down during the off-season. Likewise, to save money, a media planner for a new product might decide that after a heavy introductory period of, say, four weeks, a radio campaign needs to maintain *continuity* for an additional 16 weeks but on fewer stations. We'll discuss some common scheduling patterns in the section on media tactics.

While frequency is important to create memory, continuity is important to *sustain* it. Moreover, as people come into and out of the market for goods and services every day, continuity provides a means of having the message there when it's most needed. Ads that can be scheduled to hit targets when they are ready to make a purchase are more effective and require less frequency.[20]

Optimizing Reach, Frequency, and Continuity: The Art of Media Planning

Good media planning is both an art and a science. The media planner must get the most effective exposure on a limited budget. As Exhibit 15–7 shows, the objectives of reach, frequency,

▼**EXHIBIT 15–7** Reach, frequency, and continuity have an inverse relationship to one another. For instance, in the example below, an advertiser can reach 6,000 people once, 3,000 people approximately 5.5 times, or 1,000 people 9 times for the same budget. However, to achieve continuity over time, the advertiser might have to sacrifice some reach and/or frequency.

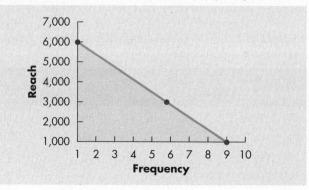

continuity The duration of an advertising message or campaign over a given period of time.

effective reach A term used to describe the quality of exposure. It measures the number or percentage of the audience who receive enough exposures for the message to truly be received.

effective frequency The average number of times a person must see or hear a message before it becomes effective.

wearout The point at which an advertising message has been seen or heard so often that it starts to irritate consumers and therefore loses its effectiveness.

advertising response curve A graphical representation of the relationship between advertising levels and sales results.

and continuity have inverse relationships to each other. To achieve greater reach on a limited budget, some frequency and/or continuity has to be sacrificed, and so on. Research shows that all three are critical. But since all budgets are limited, which is most critical? This has always been the subject of hot debate in advertising circles.

Effective Reach

One of the problems with reach is that, by itself, the measurement doesn't take into account the *effectiveness* of the exposures. Some people exposed to the vehicle still won't be aware of the message. So, on the surface, reach doesn't seem to be the best measure of media success. Media people use the term **effective reach** to describe the *quality* of exposure. It measures the percentage of the audience who receive enough exposures to truly notice the message. That brings us to effective frequency.

Effective Frequency

Similar to the concept of effective reach is **effective frequency**, defined as the average number of times a person must see or hear a message before it becomes effective. In theory, effective frequency falls somewhere between a minimum level that achieves message awareness and a maximum level that becomes overexposure, which leads to **wearout** (starts to irritate consumers).

The S-shaped **advertising response curve** in Exhibit 15–8 suggests that at a low frequency there is little response. This is because the intensity of advertising is below a threshold where most of the target audience would notice it. Once that threshold is crossed, there is a dramatic response to increasing levels of advertising. Eventually though, the target market becomes saturated

▼**EXHIBIT 15–8** The S-shaped response curve suggests that a minimum threshold (A) of advertising frequency must be crossed before a meaningful response is achieved. At some level of frequency, another threshold (B) is crossed and the response begins to level off or even decline due to overexposure.

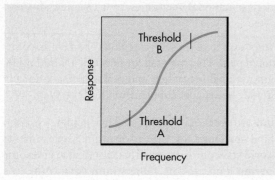

and, while advertising frequency continues to increase, the market response levels off or may even decline. The challenge to media planners is to determine the frequency of advertising that will exceed threshold A but remain below threshold B. To complicate matters further, different products or different advertising campaigns may generate different advertising response curves.

Following the publication of Michael Naples's classic book *Effective Frequency* in 1979, the industry fell in love with his claim that, in most cases, effective frequency could be achieved by an average frequency of three over a four-week period. Here was a nice, simple conclusion that all media planners could use.

However, this assumes that all exposures are equal. If that's the case, then where does advertising creativity come in? And what about the environment in which the advertising appears? Doesn't that have some effect on the quality of exposure? There is no simple solution to this problem.

Once the media objectives have been determined—that is, the optimum levels of message weight, reach, frequency, and continuity—the media planner can develop the strategy for achieving them.

check yourself ✓

1. What are the two types of media objectives? Give examples of each.

2. What is message weight?

3. How does the media planner optimize reach, frequency, and continuity?

4. How are GRPs and CPMs calculated?

L03 Identify the factors that influence media strategy and tactics.

DEVELOPING A MEDIA STRATEGY: THE MEDIA MIX

The media strategy describes how the advertiser will achieve the stated media objectives: which media will be used, where, how often, and when. Just as marketers determine marketing strategy by blending elements of the marketing mix, media planners can develop media strategies by blending the elements of the media mix.

Factors in the Media Strategy: The Five Ms

Many factors go into developing an effective media strategy. For simplicity and ease of memory, we have sorted them into five categories and given them the alliterative moniker of the **five Ms**: *markets, money, media, mechanics,* and *methodology.*

Markets refers to the various targets of a media plan: trade and consumer audiences; global, national, or regional audiences; ethnic and socioeconomic groups; or other stakeholders. In an integrated marketing communications plan, the media planner wants to understand the reasons and motivations for the prospect's purchase and usage patterns and then create a media plan based on those findings.[21]

Using intuition, experience, marketing savvy, and analytical skill, the media planner determines the second element, **money**—how much to budget and where to allocate it. How much for print media, how much in TV, how much to nontraditional or supplemental media, how much to each geographic area?

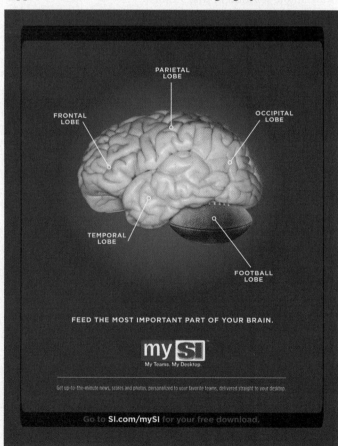

Market research helps advertisers understand their target audiences. The interactive nature of the Web allows Sports Illustrated to provide its users with personalized content. In turn, the magazine and its advertisers gain a richer understanding of SI's audience.

Media includes *all* communications vehicles available to a marketer—anything you can put your name on. This includes radio, TV, newspapers, magazines, outdoor, the Internet, and direct mail, plus sales promotion, direct marketing, public relations activities and publicity, special events, brochures, and even shopping bags. Good media planners champion the integration of all marketing communications to help achieve their companies' marketing and advertising objectives. They look at the media element both analytically and creatively.

The media planner also has to deal with the complex **mechanics** of advertising media and messages. Radio and TV commercials come in a variety of time units, and print ads are created in a variety of sizes and styles. The myriad media options now available offer exciting, creative ways to enhance consumer acceptance of the advertiser's message and offer the consumer a relevant purchase incentive.

The **methodology** element refers to the overall strategy of selecting and scheduling media vehicles to achieve the desired message weight, reach, frequency, and continuity objectives. It offers the opportunity for creativity in planning, negotiating, and buying.

Factors That Influence Media Strategy Decisions

Media decisions are greatly influenced by some factors over which the media planner has little or no control. These include the scope of the media plan, sales potential of different markets, competitive strategies and budget considerations, availability of different media vehicles, nature of the medium, mood of the message, message size and length, and buyer purchase patterns.

Scope of the Media Plan
The location and makeup of the target audience strongly influence the scope of the media plan, thereby affecting decisions regarding the market, the money, and the media elements.

Domestic markets. A media planner normally limits advertising to areas where the product is available. If a store serves only one town, or if a city has been chosen to test-market a new product, then the advertiser will use a *local* plan.

A *regional* plan may cover several adjoining metropolitan areas, an entire state or province, or several neighboring states. Regional plans typically employ a combination of local media, regional editions of national magazines, spot TV and radio, and the Internet.

Advertisers who want to reach several regions or an entire country use a *national* plan. This may call for network TV and radio, full-circulation national magazines and newspapers, nationally syndicated Sunday newspaper supplements, and the Web.

International markets. As we discussed in Chapter 3, foreign media can be a challenge for U.S. advertisers. Governments around the world still control many broadcast media, and some still do not permit commercials. Others limit advertising to a certain number of minutes per hour or per day.

markets Groups of potential customers who share a common interest, need, or desire; who can use the offered good or service to some advantage; and who can afford or are willing to pay the purchase price.

money In media planning, one of the five elements in the media mix.

media A plural form of *medium,* referring to communications vehicles paid to present an advertisement to their target audience.

mechanics One of the five Ms of the media mix; dealing creatively with the available advertising media options.

methodology The overall strategy of selecting and scheduling media vehicles to achieve the desired reach, frequency, and continuity objectives.

brand development index (BDI) The percentage of a brand's total sales in an area divided by the total population in the area; it indicates the sales potential of a particular brand in a specific market area.

In countries that do allow TV advertising, advertisers face other problems: how many people own TV sets, who they are, and what channels they receive. While this is not an issue in Europe and is becoming less so in Latin America, it is still a problem in many of the less developed nations.

Most marketers develop an international media plan by formulating individual national plans first. But it's not as simple as it sounds. Depending on the country, precise media information may not be available, circulation figures may not be audited, audience demographics may be sketchy, and even ad rates may be unreliable. Finally, the methodology used in media research may be considerably different from one market to another, making comparisons virtually impossible.

Because of the media variations from country to country, most international and global advertisers entrust national media plans to in-country foreign media specialists or the local foreign branches of global media agencies such as Starcom Mediavest, MindShare, OMD Worldwide, The Media Edge, or Carat, rather than risk faulty centralized media planning.[22]

Sales Potential of Different Markets

The market and money elements of the media mix also depend on the sales potential of each area. National advertisers use this factor to determine where to allocate their advertising dollars. Planners can determine an area's sales potential in several ways.

The brand development index. The **brand development index (BDI)** indicates the sales strength of a particular brand in a specific market area. It compares the percentage of the brand's total U.S. sales in an area to the percentage of the total U.S. population in that area. The larger the brand's sales relative to the area's percentage of U.S. population, the higher the BDI and the greater the brand's sales development. BDI is calculated as

$$\text{BDI} = \frac{\text{Percent of the brand's total U.S. sales in the area}}{\text{Percent of total U.S. population in the area}} \times 100$$

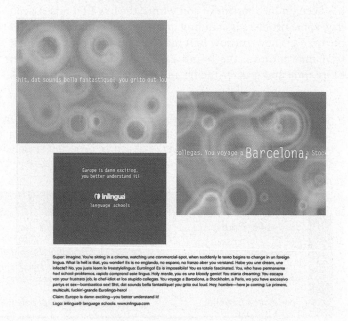

Reaching international markets presents unique challenges to advertisers. Inlingua Language Schools decided to embrace the diversity of Europe's languages in a TV spot that combines slang from all over the continent.

Suppose sales of a brand in Los Angeles are 1.58 percent of the brand's total U.S. sales and the population of Los Angeles is 2 percent of the U.S. total. The BDI for Los Angeles is

$$BDI = \frac{1.58}{2} \times 100 = 79$$

An index number of 100 means the brand's performance is in balance with the size of the area's population. A BDI index number below 100 indicates poor development of the brand in that market. Conversely, a BDI greater than 100 indicates better than average development.

The category development index. To determine the strength of the whole product category, media planners use the **category development index (CDI)**, which works on the same principle as the BDI and is calculated in much the same way:

$$BDI = \frac{\text{Percent of the product category's total U.S. sales in the area}}{\text{Percent of total U.S. population in the area}} \times 100$$

If category sales in Los Angeles are 4.92 percent of total U.S. category sales, the CDI in Los Angeles is

$$CDI = \frac{4.92}{2} \times 100 = 246$$

The combination of BDI and CDI can help the planner determine a media strategy for the market (see Exhibit 15–9). In our example, a low BDI (under 100) and a high CDI (over 100) in Los Angeles indicate that the product category offers great potential but the brand is not selling well (low market share). This may represent a problem or an opportunity. If the brand has been on the market for some time, the low BDI raises a red flag; some problem is standing in the way of brand sales. But if the brand is new, the low BDI may be a positive sign. The high CDI may indicate the brand can grow substantially, given more time and greater media and marketing support. At this point, the media planner should assess the company's share of voice (discussed in Chapter 7) and budget accordingly.

Competitive Strategies and Budget Considerations

Advertisers always consider what competitors are doing, particularly those that have larger advertising budgets. This affects the *media, mechanics,* and *methodology* elements of the media mix. Several services, like TNS Media Intelligence Ad-spender, detail competitive advertising expenditures in the different media. By knowing the size of competitors' budgets, the media they're using, the regionality or seasonality of their sales, and any new-product tests and introductions, advertisers can better plan a counterstrategy.

Again, the media planner should analyze the company's share of voice in the marketplace. If an advertiser's budget is much smaller than the competition's, the brand could get lost in the shuffle. While it sometimes makes sense to use media similar to the competition's if the target audiences are the same or if the competitors are not using their media effectively, advertisers should generally bypass media that competitors dominate and choose other media in which they can achieve a strong position.

When Anne Myers, media director of Palmer Jarvis DDB, Toronto, had to develop a media plan for Panasonic Canada's Power Activator batteries, she didn't have the budget of Energizer or Duracell to work with. So she didn't want to place her ads where theirs were. Myers and her team creatively fashioned a guerrilla media plan that targeted a cynical, hard-to-reach audience, 15- to 22-year-olds, right where they lived—in the clubs, on the street, and on the Internet. The campaign included posters in the dance clubs; sponsorship of popular DJs and VJs; free Power Activator T-shirts, hats, posters, and stickers; an eight-week run of television spots on popular music shows tied to a month-long cross-promotion with a new CD release; and a special contest run on a micro Web site that was linked to Panasonic's home page. The response was excellent: Sales were up 136 percent over the previous year, and the contest promotion generated more than 16,300 entries on the Web site with a click-through rate of 35 percent.[23]

▼ **EXHIBIT 15–9** Media buyers compare the brand development index with the category development index for their products to better understand which markets will respond best to advertising. Advertising can be expected to work well when BDI and CDI are both high, but probably not when both are low.

	Low BDI	High BDI
High CDI	Low market share *but* Good market potential	High market share *and* Good market potential
Low CDI	Low market share *and* Poor market potential	High market share *but* Poor market potential

Media Availability and Economics: The Global Marketer's Headache

North American advertisers are blessed—or cursed—with an incredible array of media choices, locally and nationally. Such is not always the case in other areas of the world, which is one reason their per capita advertising expenditures are so much lower than in the United States.

Every country has communications media, but they are not always available for commercial use (especially radio and television) and coverage may be limited. Lower literacy rates and education levels

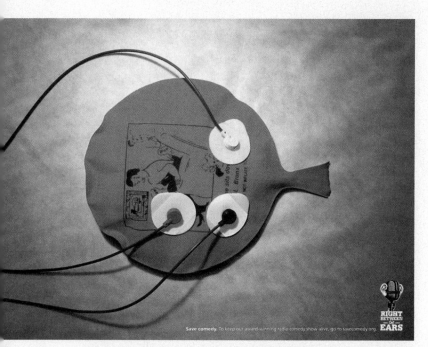

This ad by Bernstein-Rein Advertising for Right Between the Ears, a radio comedy show, is executed like a good joke: it's brief, to the point, and uses unexpected imagery to make a convincing statement. This print campaign was intended to influence readers to help keep the radio show on the air.

category development index (CDI) The percentage of a product category's total U.S. sales in an area divided by the percentage of total U.S. population in the area.

Nature of the Medium and Mood of the Message

An important influence on the *media* element of the mix is how well a medium works with the style or mood of the particular message.

Advertising messages differ in many ways. Some are simple messages: "Just do it" (Nike). Others make emotional or sensual appeals to people's needs and wants: "The great taste of fruit squared" (Jolly Rancher candies). Many advertisers use a reason-why approach to explain their product's advantages: "Twice the room. Twice the comfort. Twice the value. Embassy Suites. Twice the hotel."

Complex messages, such as ads announcing a new product or concept, require more space or time for explanation. Each circumstance affects the media selection as well as the *methodology* of the media mix.

A new or highly complex message may require greater frequency and exposure to be understood and remembered. A dogmatic message like Nike's may require a surge at the beginning, then low frequency and greater reach, plus continuity.

Once consumers understand reason-why messages, pulsing advertising exposures at irregular intervals is often sufficient. Emotionally oriented messages are usually more effective when spaced at regular intervals to create enduring feelings about the product. We discuss these scheduling methods further in the next section on media tactics.

Message Size, Length, and Position Considerations

The particular characteristics of different media affect the mechanics element of the media mix. For example, in print, a full-page ad attracts more attention than a quarter-page ad and a full-color ad more than a black-and-white one (see Exhibit 15–10).

Should a small advertiser run a full-page ad once a month or a quarter-page ad once a week? Is it better to use a few 60-second commercials or many 15- and 30-second ones? The planner has to consider the nature of the advertising message; some simply require more time and space to explain. Competitive activity often

in some countries restrict the coverage of print media. Where income levels are low, TV ownership is also low.

To reach lower-income markets, radio is often the medium of choice, as both Coke and Pepsi have demonstrated successfully for years. Auto manufacturers make good use of TV and magazine advertising to reach the upper class. And movie advertising can reach whole urban populations where TV ownership is low because motion picture attendance in such countries is very high.

Some companies are attempting to become true global marketers of their brands with centralized control of media and standardized creative. As a group, global media are growing, which is good news for global marketers.[24] However, there are still few true global media. So these major advertisers must continue to use local foreign media in the countries where they do business and localize their campaigns for language and cultural differences.

▼ **EXHIBIT 15–10** Effect of size and color on ad readership (total ads studied = 107,506).

a. Size—as size increases so does readership.

b. Size and color—advertising readership increases with size and the use of color.

dictates more message units. The product itself may demand the prestige of a full-page or full-color ad. However, it's often better to run small ads consistently rather than one large ad occasionally. Unfortunately, space and time units may be determined by someone other than the media planner—creative or account management, for example—in which case the planner's options are limited.

The position of an ad is another consideration. Preferred positions for magazine ads are front and back covers; for TV, sponsorship of prime-time shows. Special positions and sponsorships cost more, so the media planner must decide whether the increased audience is worth the higher costs.

As we can see, the nature of the creative work has the potential to greatly affect the media strategy. This means that media planners have to be flexible, since the initial media plan may well have been determined prior to beginning the creative work.

Buyer Purchase Patterns

Finally, the customer's product purchasing behavior affects every element of the media mix. The media planner must consider how, when, and where the product is typically purchased and repurchased. Products with short purchase cycles (convenience foods and paper towels) require more constant levels of advertising than products purchased infrequently (refrigerators and notebook computers).

Stating the Media Strategy

A written rationale for the media strategy is an integral part of any media plan. Without one, it's difficult for client and agency management to analyze the logic and consistency of the recommended media schedule.

Generally, the strategy statement begins with a brief definition of target audiences (the market element) and the priorities for weighting them. It explains the nature of the message and indicates which media types will be used and why (the media element). It outlines specific reach, frequency, and continuity goals and how they are to be achieved (the methodology element). It provides a budget for each medium (the money element), including the cost of production and any collateral materials. Finally, it states the intended size of message units, and any position or timing considerations (the mechanics element).

Once the strategy is delineated, the plan details the tactics to be employed, the subject of the next section.

check yourself ✓

1. What is BDI? What is CDI?

2. What is the "sweet spot" of the BDI/CDI index?

3. What factors influence media strategy decisions?

MEDIA TACTICS: SELECTING AND SCHEDULING MEDIA VEHICLES

Once the general media strategy is determined, the media planner can select and schedule particular media vehicles. The planner usually considers each medium's value on a set of specific criteria. Commercial Break 15 summarizes many of the media advantages discussed in Chapters 11–14.

Criteria for Selecting Individual Media Vehicles

In evaluating specific media vehicles, the planner considers several factors: overall campaign objectives and strategy; size and characteristics of each vehicle's audience; attention, exposure, and motivational value of each vehicle; and cost efficiency.

Overall Campaign Objectives and Strategy The media planner's first job is to review the nature of the product or service, the objectives and strategies, and the primary and secondary target markets and audiences. The characteristics of the product often suggest a suitable media choice. A product with a distinct personality or image, such as a fine perfume, might be advertised in media that reinforce this image. The media planner considers how consumers regard various magazines and TV programs—feminine or masculine, highbrow or lowbrow, serious or frivolous—and determines whether they're appropriate for the brand.

The content and editorial policy of the media vehicle and its compatibility with the product are important considerations. *Tennis* magazine is a poor vehicle for cigarette or alcohol ads even though its demographic profile and image might match the desired target audience.

Consumers choose a particular vehicle because they gain some "reward": self-improvement, financial advice, career guidance, or simply news and entertainment. Advertising is most effective when it positions a product as part of the solution that consumers seek. Otherwise, consumers may see it as an intrusion.[25]

If the marketing objective is to gain greater product distribution, the planner should select media that might also influence resellers. If the goal is to stimulate sales of a nationally distributed product in isolated markets, ads should be placed in local and regional media that penetrate those markets. Pricing strategy influences media choices too. A premium-priced product should use prestigious media to support its market image.

The language and imagery of this Godiva chocolate (www.godiva.com) ad exudes a sense of elegance that suits the audience of the medium selected. Godiva placed the ad in magazines such as Architectural Digest to reach a target audience of affluent, well-educated individuals. The photo, type, and layout elements reflect the nature of the magazine, the advertiser, and even the audience.

Characteristics of Media Audiences

An **audience** is the total number of people or households exposed to a vehicle. The planner needs to know how closely the vehicle's audience matches the profile of the target market and how interested prospective customers are in the publication or program. A product intended for a Latino audience, for example, would likely appear in specific media directed toward Hispanics. Simmons Market Research Bureau (SMRB) provides research data on age, income, occupational status, and other characteristics of magazine readers. Simmons also publishes demographic and psychographic data on product usage of consumers. Likewise, Nielsen provides audience statistics for television programs and Arbitron for radio stations.

The *content* of the vehicle usually determines the type of people in the audience. Some radio stations emphasize in-depth news or sports; others feature jazz, rock, or classical music. Each type of programming attracts a different audience.

Exposure, Attention, and Motivation Value of Media Vehicles

The media planner has to select media that will not only achieve the desired *exposure* to the target audience, but also attract *attention* and *motivate* people to act.

Exposure. As we discussed earlier, just because someone reads a particular magazine or watches a certain program doesn't mean he or she sees the ads. Some people read only one article, set the magazine aside, and never pick it up again. Many people change channels during commercial breaks or leave to get a snack. Comparing the **exposure value** of different vehicles,

exposure value
The value of a medium determined by how well it exposes an ad to the target audience.

Media Selection: Quick List of Advantages [15]

Medium	Advantages
Newspapers	Quick placement. Local targeting. Audience interest. Current.
Magazines	High-quality graphics/reproduction. Prestige factor. Color. Selective targeting.
TV	Combines sight, sound, movement. A single message. Demonstration. Social dominance.
Radio	Intimacy. Loyal following. Ability to change message quickly. Repetition and frequency.
Internet	Immediate response. Interactive. Highly selective targeting. Global. Fastest growing medium.
Direct mail	Measurable. Graphics, color. 3-D. Highly personal. Adaptable message length.
Outdoor/Transit	Local targeting. Graphics, color. Simple message. Larger than life. Repetition.

Applying the Breaks

What creative advantages can you add to the list? What are some drawbacks of the media listed here?

attention value
A consideration in selecting media based on the degree of attention paid to ads in particular media by those exposed to them.

motivation value
A consideration in selecting media based on the medium's ability to motivate people to act. Positive factors include prestige, good quality reproduction, timeliness, and editorial relevance.

cost per thousand
or **CPM** A common term describing the cost of reaching 1,000 people in a medium's audience.

cost efficiency
The cost of reaching the target audience through a particular medium as opposed to the cost of reaching the medium's total circulation.

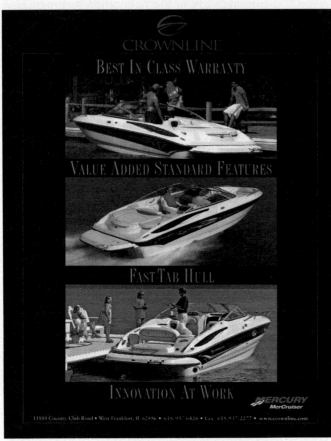

This ad for Crownline boats will get more exposure and receive more attention in Lakeland Boating *magazine than in a general-interest publication. Readers will have nautical activities on their minds and may be very motivated if they are actively seeking product information.*

therefore, is very difficult. Without statistics, media planners have to use their best judgment based on experience.

Five factors affect the probability of ad exposure:

1. The senses used to perceive messages (for example, scratch-and-sniff ads really improve the exposure value of magazines).

2. How much and what kind of attention the vehicle requires (higher involvement suggests greater ad exposure).

3. Whether the vehicle is an information source or a diversion (for example, radio news programs offer greater ad exposure than elevator music).

4. Whether the vehicle or program aims at a general or a specialized audience (exposure value will be higher with specialized audiences).

5. The intrusiveness of the ad in the vehicle (placement within broadcast programs gives greater exposure than placement between programs; ads placed next to editorial material get greater exposure than ads placed next to other print ads, larger ads attract more attention).

Attention. Degree of attention is another consideration. As we discussed in Chapter 5, consumers with no interest in motorcycles or cosmetics won't remember ads for those products. For a variety of reasons, they fail to penetrate the viewer's perceptual screens. But someone in the market for a new car tends to notice every car ad.

Exposure value relates only to the vehicle; **attention value** concerns the advertising message and copy, as well as the vehicle. Special-interest media, such as boating magazines, can offer good attention value to a marine product. But what kind of attention value can the daily newspaper offer such a product? Do sailors think about boats while reading the newspaper? Much research still needs to be done, but six factors are known to increase attention value:[26]

1. Audience involvement with editorial content or program material.

2. Specialization of audience interest or identification.

3. Number of competitive advertisers (the fewer, the better).

4. Audience familiarity with the advertiser's campaign.

5. Quality of advertising reproduction.

6. Timeliness of advertising exposure.

Motivation. These same factors affect a vehicle's **motivation value**, but in different ways. Familiarity with the advertiser's campaign may affect attention significantly but motivation very little. The attention factors of quality reproduction and timeliness can motivate someone, however.

Media planners analyze these values by assigning numerical ratings to their judgments of a vehicle's strengths and weaknesses. Then, using a weighting formula, they add them up. Planners use similar weighting methods to evaluate other factors, such as the relative importance of age versus income.

Cost Efficiency of Media Vehicles Finally, media planners analyze the cost efficiency of each vehicle. A common term used in media planning and buying is **cost per thousand**, or **CPM** (M is the Roman numeral for 1,000). If a daily newspaper has 300,000 subscribers and charges $5,000 for a full-page ad, the cost per thousand is the cost divided by the number of thousands of people

in the audience. Since there are 300 *thousand* subscribers, you divide $5,000 by 300:

$$\text{CPM} = \frac{\$5,000}{300,000 \div 1,000} = \frac{\$5,000}{300}$$

$$= \$16.67 \text{ per thousand}$$

However, media planners are more interested in **cost efficiency**—the cost of exposing the message to the *target audience* rather than to the total circulation. Let's say the target audience is males ages 18 to 49, and 40 percent of a magazine's subscriber base of 250,000 fits this category. If the magazine

Developing Media Objectives and Strategies [15]

Over the past 20 years the media landscape has changed dramatically, becoming much more fragmented and full of choice. This has elevated the complexity of the media planning role. In this part of your assignment you are nonetheless considering all types of media to help distribute your message. You will most likely be given a media budget and asked to formulate a plan of attack. To better support your choices it is imperative that you develop sound objectives and strategies.

In some cases, your professor may have given you a set of marketing objectives or your research on clients may have indicated their main goals for advertising. It is important to note here that marketing objectives do not equal media objectives. They do, however, help us shape our media objectives, which in turn help us develop sound media strategy.

Developing Media Objectives
The first place to start in developing media objectives is with the marketing objectives themselves. You should view media objectives as the goals that become the building blocks of the media plan and that ultimately help clients meet their marketing goals.

Here are some examples of marketing objectives, translated into media objectives:

Marketing Objectives	Media Objectives
• Increase awareness among target audience by 23 percent.	• Generate mass awareness among target audience.
• Steal 2 percent share of sales from competitors.	• Differentiate brand from competitors.
• Build customer database of 5,000 individuals.	• Generate leads/requests for more information.

While the media objectives seem very similar to marketing objectives, they are actually quite different. Media objectives

should focus on only what the media can achieve. Remember that the media plan is one of many components that go into building a successful promotional or communications plan and it has a distinct role, which is what you are trying to highlight in the objectives.

Developing Media Strategies
Media strategies are born out of the media objectives and describe a specific plan of action for achieving stated objectives. The strategy seeks to accomplish two things: setting the foundation for media ideas that help you meet the objective or goal and providing a position of advantage over your client's competitors.

The media strategy itself is built on key plan parameters on which the entire communications team has had input:
- Target audience
- Seasonality
- Geography
- Overall communication goals
- Budget
- Creative
- Competitive analysis

So how do media objectives translate into strategies? Let's look at the three we detailed earlier:

Media Objectives	Media Strategies
• Generate mass awareness among target audience.	• Use mass media (broadcast) to build reach against M18–34.
• Differentiate brand from competitors.	• Secure high-profile sponsorship with category exclusivity.
• Generate leads/requests for more information.	• Use interactive media to elicit registration.

charges $3,000 for a full-page ad, the **target CPM (TCPM)** is computed as follows:

$$\text{Target audience} = 0.40 \times 250{,}000 = 100{,}000$$

$$\text{TCPM} = \frac{\$3{,}000}{100{,}000 \div 1{,}000} = \$30 \text{ per thousand}$$

Buyer Purchase Patterns

Finally, the customer's product purchasing behavior affects every element of the media mix. The media planner must consider how, when, and where the product is typically purchased and repurchased. Products with short purchase cycles (convenience foods and paper towels) require more constant levels of advertising than products purchased infrequently (refrigerators and furniture).

Stating the Media Strategy

A written rationale for the media strategy is an integral part of any media plan. Without one, it's difficult for client and agency management to analyze the logic and consistency of the recommended media schedule.

The more costly (on an absolute basis) daily newspaper might turn out to be more cost efficient than the magazine if 60 percent of its readers (180,000) belong to the target audience:

$$\text{TCPM} = \frac{\$5{,}000}{180{,}000 \div 1{,}000}$$
$$= \$27.78 \text{ per thousand}$$

The media planner may also want to compare the **cost per point (CPP)** of different broadcast programs. This is done the same way as cost per thousand, except you divide the cost by the rating points instead of the gross impressions.

Comparing different vehicles by CPM or CPP is important but does not take into account each vehicle's other advantages and disadvantages. The media planner must evaluate all the criteria to determine

1. How much of each vehicle's audience matches the product's target audience.

2. How each vehicle satisfies the campaign's objectives and strategy.

3. How well each vehicle offers attention, exposure, and motivation.

The Synergy of Mixed Media

A combination of media is called a **mixed-media approach**. There are numerous reasons for using mixed media:

- To reach people who are unavailable through only one medium.

- To provide repeat exposure in a less expensive secondary medium after attaining optimum reach in the first.

- To use the intrinsic value of an additional medium to extend the creative effectiveness of the ad campaign (such as music on radio along with long copy in print media).

- To deliver coupons in print media when the primary vehicle is broadcast.

- To produce **synergy**, where the total effect is greater than the sum of its parts.

Television, for example, can be used to introduce a new product and give importance to the message. Magazine ads can then follow up for greater detail, image enhancement, longevity, and memory improvement.

A mixed-media campaign was effective for General Electric's lighting products. The promotion used a combination of network TV spots, print advertising, Sunday supplement inserts, in-store displays in more than 150,000 stores, and a highly creative publicity program. By using an integrated, mixed-media approach, the campaign produced "unprecedented" consumer awareness and dealer support. It achieved synergy.[27]

Methods for Scheduling Media

After selecting the appropriate media vehicles, the media planner decides how many space or time units to buy of each vehicle and schedules them for release over a period of time when consumers are most apt to be in the market for the product.

Continuous, Flighting, and Pulsing Schedules

To build continuity in a campaign, planners use three principal scheduling tactics: *continuous, flighting,* and *pulsing* (see Exhibit 15–11).

In a **continuous schedule**, advertising runs steadily and varies little over the campaign period. It's the best way to build continuity. Advertisers use this scheduling pattern for products consumers purchase regularly.

Flighting alternates periods of advertising with periods of no advertising. This intermittent schedule makes sense for products and services that experience large fluctuations in demand

flighting An intermittent media scheduling pattern in which periods of advertising are alternated with periods of no advertising at all.

pulsing Mixing continuity and flighting strategies in media scheduling.

bursting A media scheduling method for promoting high-ticket items that require careful consideration, such as running the same commercial every half-hour on the same network in prime time.

roadblocking Buying simultaneous airtime on all four television networks.

blinking A scheduling technique in which the advertiser floods the airwaves for one day on both cable and network channels to make it virtually impossible to miss the ads.

▼**EXHIBIT 15–11** Three ways to schedule the same number of total gross rating points: continuous, flighting, and pulsing.

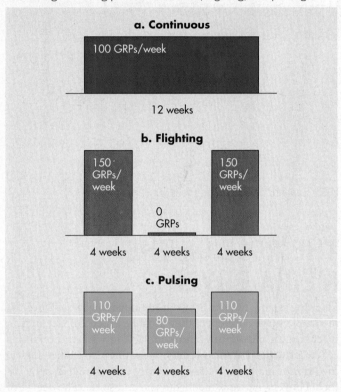

during prime time—can be effective. A variation is **road-blocking**, buying airtime on all three networks simultaneously. Chrysler used this technique to give viewers the impression that the advertiser was everywhere, even if the ad showed for only a few nights. Digital Equipment used a scheduling tactic called **blinking** to stretch its slim ad budget. To reach business executives, it flooded the airwaves on Sundays (on both cable and network TV channels) to make it virtually impossible to miss the ads.[28]

Once the scheduling criteria are determined, the media planner creates a flowchart of the plan. The flowchart is a graphic presentation of the total campaign to let the creative department, media department, account services, and the client see the pattern of media events that will occur throughout the campaign, usually one year (see Exhibit 15–12).

Computers in Media Selection and Scheduling

The last decade has seen a profusion of new desktop computer software to assist media planners. Computers perform the tedious computations for GRPs, CPMs, reach, frequency, and the like. They also save time and money. One agency found it could plan the entire TV, radio, and print co-op budgets for one of its largest clients in two days with only three people and one software package. Previously, that task required 70 staffers working manually for a week and a half.

throughout the year (tax services, lawn-care products, cold remedies). The advertiser might introduce the product with a four-week flight and then schedule three additional four-week flights to run during seasonal periods later in the year. Flighting is also often used by products and services to stretch limited budgets.

The third alternative, **pulsing**, mixes continuous and flighting strategies. The advertiser maintains a low level of advertising all year but uses periodic pulses to heavy up during peak selling periods. This strategy is appropriate for products like soft drinks, which are consumed all year but more heavily in the summer.

Additional Scheduling Patterns
For high-ticket items that require careful consideration, **bursting**—running the same commercial every half hour on the same network

▼**EXHIBIT 15–12** A media plan flowchart like this computerized printout of Telmar's FlowMaster gives a bird's-eye view of the major media purchases and where and when they will appear over a specified period of time.

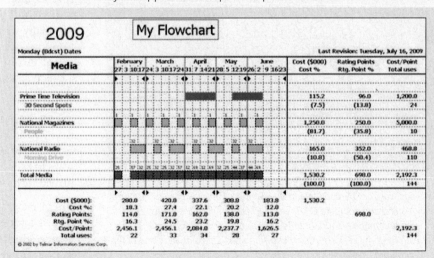

Established in 1968, Telmar (www.telmar.com) was the first independent supplier of computerized media planning systems. Today, it is the world's leading supplier of Windows and Internet-based media planning software and support services. More than 5,000 users in 85 countries use Telmar systems for media and marketing decision making.[29]

Telmar's software suite is designed to help media planners, buyers, research analysts, and sellers work more efficiently and to help them make better judgments in the evaluation or sales process. The software allows advertising executives to estimate the effectiveness of multifaceted marketing plans that use various combinations of media including print, broadcast, in-store, special promotions, special events, PR, and other "new media." Its flexibility permits the user to analyze the potential effectiveness of any and every marketing tool used to reach the consumer.

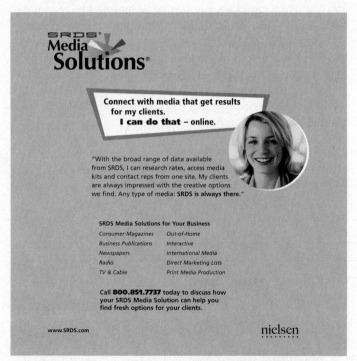

The advent of computer software has taken some of the more grueling, laborious work out of media planning. Planners can now crunch numbers, track results, and compute GRPs and CPMs right at their desktops. This saves an enormous amount of time and money. The SRDS Media Planning System (www.srds.com) shown here is an example of one of the many programs available.

Even with technology, though, it's still up to the media planner to know the product, the market, and the media, and to then make the call. Computers can't decide which medium or environment is best for the message. They can't evaluate the content of a magazine or the image of a TV program. They can't judge whether the numbers they're fed are valid or reliable, and they can't interpret the meaning of the results. What they can do is help the process along.

L05 Explain the role of the media buyer.

THE ROLE OF THE MEDIA BUYER

Planning is only the first stage in the media process. Once the media plans are developed, they must be executed. The person in charge of negotiating and contracting with the media is called a **media buyer**. Media buyers often specialize in one medium or another, so there are print media buyers, spot TV media buyers, network media buyers, and so on. The degree of specialization depends on the size of the advertiser or the agency. In small agencies, for example, media buyers do it all.

Media buying is a complicated process. Buyers must perform several functions in the process of converting a media plan into a successful buy. Placing an ad is not as easy as it may seem, especially when there are hundreds of television and radio stations, newspapers, and magazines around the country with different deadlines, different requirements, and different rates. The job can be very tedious and time-consuming.

Fortunately, media buyers now have a variety of software programs available to assist them. STRATA Marketing, Inc. (www.stratag.com), for example, has developed media buying software for each form of media. It offers media buyers various ways to keep track of orders, clients, and rate information, while providing a large variety of formats for generating reports.

These programs, and others similar in function, save media buyers a lot of time, thereby increasing productivity and efficiency. More time can be spent analyzing information, evaluating various vehicles, and exercising creativity.

The most successful media buyers have developed key skills in the following areas:

Knowing the marketplace. Media buyers have frequent contact with media representatives. As a result, they often gain insights about trends or opportunities. Some of the best media buys are the result of an alert buyer taking advantage of an opportunity or anticipating a problem.

Negotiating the buy. Media vehicles have published rate cards, but everything is negotiable. Media buyers can often bargain for special rates on volume buys, uncover last-minute deals, negotiate preferred positions, or garner promotional support.

Monitoring performance. The media buyer is responsible for ensuring that what was purchased was delivered. Did the advertising appear where and when it was scheduled? Was the size of the audience what was promised? If not, payments must be adjusted or *makegoods* must be negotiated. Whatever the outcome, the client expects to see a *post-buy report* on what audience was actually delivered. ■

check yourself ✓

1. How is a media buyer different from a media planner?

2. What are the important skills for a media buyer?

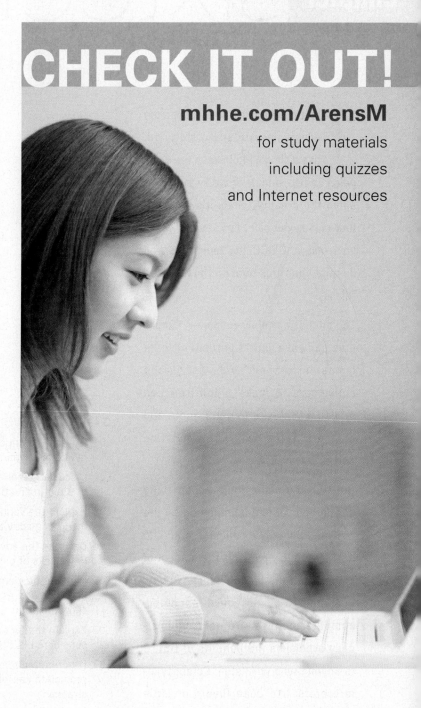

CHECK IT OUT!

mhhe.com/ArensM

for study materials

including quizzes

and Internet resources

The rules of using direct response advertising are straightforward: use a simple pitch, keep the campaign unified, and don't worry too much about the creative, since it's the offer that closes the sale. For several years now, insurer GEICO has done quite well despite ignoring two of those three rules.

The pitch is certainly simple—"15 minutes can save you 15 percent or more on car insurance." Ads encourage consumers to make a toll-free call or visit a Web site to get a quote and compare rates with their existing carrier.

But GEICO's campaigns are anything but unified. One, accompanied by the tag line "So easy a caveman could do it," humorously portrays the disgust of cavemen at the slogan's insensitivity. In another, a gentle, British-accented, computer-generated gecko whimsically proclaims the benefits of GEICO to anyone who will listen. Celebrity interpreters, like Joan Rivers or Little

continued on p. 408

LEARNING OBJECTIVES

LO1 Explain the importance of relationship marketing and IMC.

LO2 Discuss the benefits and challenges of direct marketing.

LO3 Explain the various types of direct marketing activities.

LO4 Describe the advantages and drawbacks of personal selling.

LO5 Identify the elements that must be considered in establishing a trade show program.

LO6 Explain the factors that must be considered in designing packaging.

LO7 Describe the roles that sales promotion can play in a marketing strategy.

IMC: direct marketing, personal selling, packaging, and sales promotion

continued from p. 406

Richard, sit next to customers and translate their experiences with GEICO. Still another ad parodies advertising itself by using spots that appear to be commercials for other products. We're also told to believe that if Elmer Fudd has trouble saying the letter "R," then GEICO's 15 percent savings claim must be true. And in yet another campaign, a stack of bills with googlie eyes represents the money you could be saving with GEICO.

Why so many different executions? Doesn't that just confuse consumers?

GEICO's approach is guided by a clear "share of voice" strategy (see Chapter 7). The company, which has a relatively small share (8%) of the insurance market behind giants like State Farm (18%) and Allstate (11%), spends more on advertising than any of its competitors, over $2 billion since 2001.[1] The investment has paid off—91 percent of shoppers recall being exposed to a GEICO message over the past year versus 80 percent and 78 percent for the brand's top competitors, respectively. Advertising has helped with the bottom line, too. GEICO is the fastest growing major auto insurer with an 8.9 percent growth in policies in 2008.[2]

So consumers are apparently not confused by all of the executions. In fact, the reason GEICO runs so many different campaigns simultaneously is that each is intended for a different audience.[3] As a large insurance company, GEICO sells policies to customers from many demographic and psychographic backgrounds. Knowing that one campaign will not be equally effective with everyone,

the company uses some of the spots, like the caveman, to appeal to younger audiences. Others, like the gecko, resonate more with older audiences.[4]

Committing a relatively large amount to advertising is also part of the company's overall IMC strategy, since GEICO relies on a much smaller sales force than its competitors. As we will see later in this chapter, personal selling is an effective but expensive way to market a product. Using a smaller sales force means lower costs, which GEICO passes along to customers. But it also means advertising must do much of the heavy lifting when it comes to reaching new customers. That can be a smart move, but only if the ads are effective.

Ted Ward is the VP of marketing at GEICO. When he started with the company in 1984 the ad division relied exclusively on direct-mail campaigns. He notes that "We have essentially a direct-to-consumer business model. We try to strip out costs to deliver the lowest price—it includes having very few agents in a process by having a superior technology model, which back in the '70s was direct mail; in the '80s and '90s, a telephone; and in the last 10 years, the online delivery of rates."[5]

GEICO's partner in creating the ads is the Martin Agency, headquartered in Richmond, Virginia. The agency and advertiser have an unusually long working relationship, almost 15 years. The value of a close and comfortable fit between advertiser and agency is reinforced in Ward's recall of how the gecko was born. "I was sitting around with . . . [an] art director at Martin, shooting the breeze after some focus groups and literally it was on a napkin and the rest just played out."[6]

Not that Ward was completely sold. "It was not my favorite campaign, personally" he recalls. "I quickly became much more fond of him as we sold more policies. I'm a big fan of anything that makes our phone ring or Web site click. He really has helped us brand-wise."[7]

The GEICO story suggests some important lessons. Direct response advertising should be focused, but it doesn't have to be boring. And GEICO's success reveals that an advertiser does not have to choose between generating an immediate response versus building brand equity. Great ads can do both. ■

LO1 Explain the importance of relationship marketing and IMC.

THE IMPORTANCE OF RELATIONSHIP MARKETING AND IMC

In Chapter 7, we pointed out that the key to building brand equity in the twenty-first century is the development of interdependent, mutually satisfying relationships with customers and other stakeholders. Further, to manage these relationships, companies need to consciously (and conscientiously) integrate their marketing communications activities with all their other company functions so that all the messages the marketplace receives about the company are consistent.

However, this is a lot easier said than done, since everything a company does (and doesn't do) sends a message. Seamless, consistent communication—from every corner of the company—is how a firm earns a good reputation. And that is the principal objective of IMC—integrated marketing communications—the process of building and reinforcing relationships by developing

I like drama on the big screen but not in my server room.

In the past, a large company could often muscle its way into significant market share. But with tighter budgets and more competitive markets, companies realize that even the most ordinary contact with the customer is a prime opportunity to build and maintain relationships. Companies like Dell (www.dell.com) that adopt such integrated strategies are much more likely to succeed in the long run.

and coordinating a strategic communications program through a variety of media or other contacts.

GEICO is a good example of how IMC works. To attract prospects and initiate the relationship-building process, GEICO integrates its advertising efforts with a host of other marketing communications tools—direct marketing, sales promotion, personal selling, and public relations activities. While the forms and styles of these messages may vary, all reinforce a consistent proposal—that GEICO can save you money on insurance.

A simple adage: Advertising can create an image, but a reputation must be earned. For GEICO, this means delivering on its low-rate promise.

While the integration of marketing with other company functions is beyond the scope of an advertising textbook, it is important for advertising people to understand how to integrate the various tools of marketing communications. As they plan a campaign, advertising practitioners need a basic understanding of what other communications tools are available to them and how they can best be used in the overall marketing communications mix. In this chapter, we will discuss the interactive, one-to-one communication tools of direct marketing and personal selling. We'll also look at packaging and sales promotion, which might be called "value-added" tools. In the next chapter, we'll address the "credibility" tools companies use to enhance their reputations. These include various public relations activities, sponsorships, and corporate advertising.

check yourself ✓

1. Make a list of the "tools" of marketing communications.

2. Why can't advertising create a reputation?

Direct marketing is an interactive system in which buyers and sellers participate in a dialogue. Its intent is to stimulate a response in the form of a request for information, an actual purchase, or a visit. This poster by Britain's National Society for the Prevention of Cruelty to Children (NSPCC) prompted calls from abused teenagers to jump 124 percent in just six weeks. The number of Web site visitors also increased, from 4,000 to more than 32,000.

LO2 Discuss the benefits and challenges of direct marketing.

UNDERSTANDING DIRECT MARKETING

There is a lot of confusion surrounding the term *direct marketing,* even among the experts.

Direct marketing is defined by the Direct Marketing Association (DMA) as "an interactive process of addressable communication that uses one or more advertising media to effect, at any location, a measurable sale, lead, retail purchase, or charitable donation, with this activity analyzed on a database for the development of ongoing mutually beneficial relationships between marketers and customers, prospects, or donors. Along with mass advertising, direct marketing allows organizations to

The famous gecko uses a softer, less edgy style to describe the benefits of saving on insurance by calling GEICO. That may explain the appeal of this campaign with older audiences.

inform potential customers, create brand awareness, or spur immediate purchase behavior. In addition, direct marketing enjoys certain advantages over mass advertising such as measurability, accountability, efficiency, and higher return on investment."[8]

There are several key characteristics of direct marketing within this definition. First and foremost, direct marketing is *interactive,* meaning buyers and sellers can exchange information with each other directly. GEICO can direct its message to prospective customers and those prospects can interact with GEICO by requesting rate quotes. Interactivity is so important that Joan Throckmorton, a prominent direct marketing consultant and writer, urged that the term direct marketing be dropped completely and replaced with *interactive marketing.*[9] Of course, this interaction can take place *at any location.* Customers may respond by telephone, via mail-in coupons, over the Internet, at a retail store, or even at a kiosk. GEICO processes the vast majority of its quote requests by phone and via the Web.

This DMA definition also refers to *addressable* communication, suggesting that marketers can identify those prospects, customers, or donors (by nonprofit organizations) most likely to be interested in their product or service. Addressability is the goal of **database marketing**—a form of direct marketing that uses a **database** of current and prospective customers to generate personalized communications. That, of course, leads to the possibility of the *ongoing mutually beneficial relationships* described above. So today, database marketing is a major component of many IMC programs.

Note that the definition of direct marketing refers to the use of *one or more advertising media.* Part of the confusion with the direct marketing name is its similarity to direct mail. But direct mail is just one of the many media that direct marketers use. In the GEICO story, for instance, we saw how the company used a mass media form—television—to elicit responses from people who might be interested in saving on insurance. GEICO uses other media as well, including radio and direct mail, to reach its target audience. In fact, experienced direct marketers have known for years that using more than one medium can be far more productive than using a single medium.[10]

As noted above, direct marketing works effectively "with mass advertising" to *inform, create awareness, and spur immediate purchase behavior.*

The final point in the definition distinguishes direct marketing from mass advertising in the areas of measurability, accountability, efficiency, and return on investment. The kind of advertising direct marketers use is called **direct-response advertising**. This is because direct marketing efforts are always aimed at stimulating some action or response on the part of the customer or prospect. It may be in the form of a request for information, a store visit, or an actual purchase. Because these responses can be *measured*, direct marketing is *accountable*. And that, more than any other reason, accounts for the tremendous growth of direct marketing in recent years. Managers like it because they can measure its *efficiency* and *return on investment*—what they got for their money.

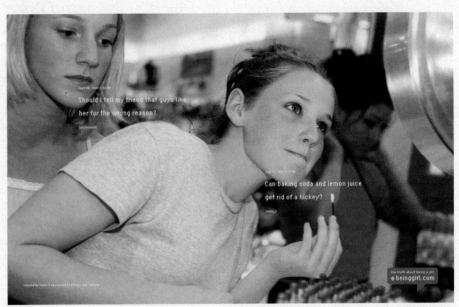

Web sites are an example of linkage media because they provide a way for consumers to hook up with companies. An integrated campaign of radio, print, e-mail, and pop-up ads for Procter & Gamble products like Tampax and Always instructed girls to visit www.beinggirl.com to register for a sweepstakes.

THE ROLE OF DIRECT MARKETING IN IMC

Today, sophisticated companies use the skills developed by direct marketers to establish, nourish, and maintain relationships, not just with customers, but with all stakeholders.

GEICO, for instance, uses TV advertising as one of its linkage media—media that help prospects and customers link up with a company—to inform prospects how to inquire about its products. Next, it uses these responses to build its database of names, addresses, and e-mail addresses. Then it uses the database to communicate with prospects, open a dialogue, and establish a relationship. It may send a mail piece with ordering information or direct people to its Web site to enable prospects to connect with GEICO directly.

The Evolution of Direct Marketing

Direct marketing is the oldest marketing method, and today it is growing incredibly fast, propelled by the major social and technological changes of recent decades. Over 50 percent of American women now work full- or part-time.[11] So while families have more income, they have less time to spend shopping, thus making the convenience of telephones and the Internet an important factor in direct marketing.

Rank	Agency	U.S. Revenue (millions)
1	Epsilon/Purple@Epsilon	$460.5
2	Rapp	364.5
3	DraftFCB	306.0
4	Wunderman	268.0
5	Aspen Marketing Services	212.6
6	Merkle	211.1
7	Harte-Hanks Direct	177.7
8	OgilvyOne Worldwide	115.8
9	Ketchum Directory Advertising	101.2
10	Digitas	94.3

Likewise, the expanding use of credit cards has revolutionized the way consumers buy goods and services. Electronic, cashless transactions make products easier and faster to purchase. And now, with advances in payment security, more and more people are shopping right from their computers.

Companies spent an estimated $149 billion on direct marketing in the United States in 2009. (Exhibit 16–1 shows the largest direct-response agencies in the United States.) Those expenditures generated $1.78 trillion in sales in 2009, or 8.3 percent of the total U.S. gross domestic product. Direct marketing–driven sales are forecast to grow by 3.5 percent in 2010, with above average growth in financial services and retail trade.[12]

Direct marketing advertising expenditures accounted for 54.3 percent of all advertising expenditures in 2009. Although direct mail and telemarketing are the most heavily used direct marketing methods, forecasters predict that over the next five years expenditures in Internet marketing and commercial e-mail will grow 18 percent.[13]

The boom in telecommunications and computer technology is spurring the growth of direct marketing worldwide. In the mid-1990s, for instance, European spending on direct marketing jumped by more than 23 percent to $46 billion. Today, Germany is by far the largest national market in Europe, spending more than $25 billion on direct marketing efforts annually. Britain comes in second at more than $17 billion, followed closely by France. Interestingly, outside the United States, Japan is by far the number-one market for direct marketing, with estimated annual spending close to $70 billion.[14]

Telephone companies worldwide provide toll-free numbers for customers to place orders or request information. Toll-free numbers give companies immediate, direct responses and help them collect information to create and refine their databases. GEICO relies heavily on a toll-free number to sell insurance.

Certain challenges in foreign markets have limited the growth of direct marketing efforts. There are, of course, a wide variety of legal and regulatory environments to contend with. Likewise, payment and postal systems in different countries vary considerably, as do conventions for addressing mail. And finally, cultural nuances and language can get in the way.

The Impact of Databases on Direct Marketing

Modern computer technology enables marketers to compile and analyze important customer information in unprecedented ways. Pitney Bowes, for instance, was the dominant company in the postal meter business. However, its growth rate and profitability were flattening. So the company used its database to identify its best customers, their value to the organization, and their needs and buying behavior. From this, Pitney Bowes created a **customer lifetime value (LTV)** model based on the customer's historical and potential worth. Computing and ranking the lifetime value of all of its 1.2 million customers showed that more than two-thirds of the customer base value resided in fewer than 10 percent of the customers. The company also found it had a major retention problem within its low-volume, low-cost accounts. Cancellation rates were running as high as 40 percent per year in some segments. This analysis led Pitney Bowes to develop a distinct direct marketing strategy for both its best and its worst customers. It began a sophisticated *loyalty program* for its best customers and a *retention program* for its problem accounts. By the end of the first year, the program had reduced attrition by 20 percent, and the reduction in cost of sales alone paid back the entire direct marketing investment.[15] In another situation, a company might determine from its LTV analysis that its best course of action is simply to drop the most unprofitable customers.

> "The company that understands its customers' needs and wants will create a sustainable competitive advantage."

Loyalty (or **continuity**) **programs** are designed to reward customers for their continued business. Most loyalty programs compensate consumers for frequent and continuous patronage. The frequent flyer club, introduced by American Airlines in 1981, is the model for today's continuity programs. Consumer purchases are tabulated on a company's database and discounts, free products, or services are awarded when specific levels are reached. The database can also provide the company with a demographic profile and purchase history for each customer.

The database is the key to direct marketing success, especially in an IMC program. It enables marketers to target, segment, and grade customers. It is the corporate memory of all important customer information: name and address, telephone number, e-mail address, source of inquiry, history of purchases, and so on. It should record every transaction across all points of contact with both channel members and customers. The company that understands its customers' needs and wants better than any of its competitors will create a sustainable competitive advantage.

The database also lets the company measure the efficiency of its direct-response advertising efforts to determine, for instance, which radio or TV commercials, or which mailing lists, perform the best.

The Importance of Direct Marketing to IMC

Perhaps the greatest reason for direct marketing's current growth is that marketers and agencies realize they can't do the job with just one medium anymore. As the mass audience fragmented and companies began to integrate their marketing communications, customer databases became key to retaining and growing customers.

Direct marketing is the best way to develop a good database. The database enables the marketer to build a relationship by learning about customers in-depth: their nuances, what and where they buy, what they're interested in, and what they need. With a database, companies can choose the prospects they can serve most effectively and profitably—the purpose of all marketing. "You don't want a relationship with every customer," says Philip Kotler. "In fact, there are some bad customers out there."[16] Retailer Best Buy uses direct mail to send sales promotions materials, but only to its best customers.[17]

People like to see themselves as unique, not part of some 100-million-member mass market. Through direct marketing, especially addressable electronic media, companies can send discrete messages to individual customers and prospects. With different types of sales promotion (discussed in the last part of this chapter), a company can encourage individuals, not masses, to respond and can develop a relationship with each person. By responding, the prospect self-selects, in effect giving the marketer permission to begin a relationship.[18] The direct marketing database, then, becomes the company's primary tool to initiate, build, cultivate, and measure the effectiveness of its loyalty efforts.[19]

By providing a tangible response, direct marketing offers accountability. Marketers can count the responses and determine the cost per response. They can also judge the effectiveness of the medium they're using and test different creative executions.

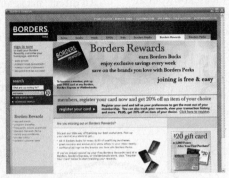

Computer databases have dramatically increased the effectiveness of customer loyalty programs. The Borders Rewards program (*www.bordersrewards.com*) keeps track of every purchase made by members at Borders, Borders Express, or Waldenbooks and issues Borders Bucks savings at specific spending levels. The Borders Rewards program also tracks member preferences and provides relevant e-mail offers and recommendations.

Direct marketing offers convenience to time-sensitive consumers, and it offers precision and flexibility to cost-sensitive marketers. For example, to reach small B2B markets, there is no more cost-effective method than the database-driven, direct-response media.

Also, the economics of direct marketing are becoming more favorable. It used to be easy for big companies to spend a few million dollars for prime-time network TV spots when everybody was home watching and the average cost was only a penny to 10 cents per person. But those days are over. Everybody's not home today. And if they are, they're watching 160 different channels or a DVD. They have a remote control to mute ads or a DVR to skip them. Further, network TV advertising is far more expensive than it used to be. Thus,

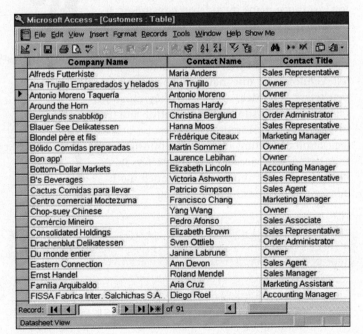

Database marketing was much more difficult before the development of personal computers because of the intense data management requirements. Today, with the low cost of personal computers, even the smallest companies can engage in complex database building and marketing strategies.

targeted, direct-response media (magazines, cable TV, direct mail, e-mail, kiosks) are more cost-competitive than ever before.

Finally, unlike the public mass media, direct-response media can be more private. A company can conduct a sales letter campaign without the competition ever knowing about it.

Drawbacks to Direct Marketing

At the same time, direct marketing still faces some challenges. In the past, direct marketers were sales oriented, not relationship oriented. This gave direct marketing a bad reputation in the minds of many consumers. Some people also enjoy the experience of visiting retail stores and shopping. They like to see and feel the goods personally, and they are hesitant to buy goods sight unseen. This is why the objective of many direct marketing campaigns is now to help drive traffic to retail locations.

Direct marketing efforts often have to stand on their own without the content support of the media that advertising enjoys. They don't always get the prestigious affiliation offered by some media. This makes it more difficult (and costly) to build an image for the product, something mass-media advertising is particularly good at.

Direct marketing also suffers from clutter. People are deluged with mail from commercial sponsors and drum-beating politicians. Cable channels are filled with infomercials for food processors. And telemarketing pitches for insurance plans intrude on consumers at home and at work.

Many consumers are also concerned with privacy. They don't like having their names sold by list vendors. At one national forum of direct marketers, attendees were told they must self-regulate, give consumers more control, and treat privacy like a customer service issue—or risk legislation restricting access to the information they desperately need.[20] Wise marketers have heeded these warnings and developed methods for responsible direct marketing.

check yourself ✓

1. What are the key characteristics that differentiate direct marketing from most other forms of marketing tools?

2. What role do databases play in direct marketing?

TYPES OF DIRECT MARKETING ACTIVITIES

All direct marketers face two basic strategy decisions: the extent to which they will use *direct sales* and the extent to which they will use *direct-response advertising*. They can use either or both.

Direct Sales

In a **direct-sales** strategy, marketers' representatives sell to customers directly, either at home or at work, rather than through a retail establishment or some other intermediary. Direct sales feature *personal* (face-to-face) *direct selling* or *telemarketing*.

Personal Direct Selling Professors Robert Peterson and Thomas Wotruba define **direct selling** as face-to-face selling away from a fixed retail location. In this sense, direct selling usually refers to a method of marketing consumer goods—everything from encyclopedias and insurance to cosmetics and nutritional products.[21] Companies such as Avon, Amway, Herbalife, Mary Kay Cosmetics, World Book, and Tupperware have achieved very high levels of success in direct sales. In personal direct selling, the representative introduces the product to the customer, convinces the customer of the product's value, and, if successful, completes the sale. There are two main forms of personal selling: person-to-person and group sales. In some *network marketing* (or multilevel marketing—MLM) organizations such as Amway, Nikken, and Shaklee, the direct salespeople are both distributors (sellers) and end users. They often do very little actual retailing of the products. Their primary effort is usually to recruit new distributors who will buy the products at wholesale and consume them personally. We will discuss personal selling more completely in the next section of this chapter.

Telemarketing As a method of direct sales, telemarketing has been used for decades, but the term is relatively new. **Telemarketing** includes selling and prospecting by telephone, answering phone inquiries, and providing sales-related services to callers. The information collected is also used to update the company's customer database. Telemarketing is the major source of income for some companies and organizations, such as nonprofit and charitable causes, political candidates, and home-study courses. In 2008, marketers spent 24 percent of all their direct marketing media expenditures, or an estimated $42.5 billion, on outbound telemarketing calls to both consumers and businesses.[22]

direct-sales Selling to customers directly, at home or at work, rather than through a retail establishment or other intermediary.

direct selling Face-to-face selling away from a fixed retail location. Usually refers to a method of marketing consumer goods—everything from encyclopedias and insurance to cosmetics and nutritional products.

telemarketing Selling products and services by using the telephone to contact prospective customers.

direct-response advertising An advertising message that asks the reader, listener, or viewer to provide feedback straight to the sender. It can take the form of direct mail, or it can use a wide range of other media, from matchbook covers or magazines to radio, TV, or billboards.

catalogs Reference books mailed to prospective customers that list, describe, and often picture the products sold by a manufacturer, wholesaler, jobber, or retailer.

Each year telemarketing generates an estimated $538 billion in sales in the United States. It is cited as the direct marketing medium of choice, providing elements of direct personal sales yet at a substantially lower cost. Telemarketing also integrates easily into database management campaigns for gathering new data and for utilizing the collected data.

The reasons for this are economics and consumers' acceptance of teleculture. First, telemarketing costs a lot less money than personal selling. In the insurance business, for example, the expense ratio for car and home insurance is currently running at 27 percent for all insurers. The most efficient insurers, like GEICO, employ high-tech database marketing techniques from phone centers and operate at around a 20 percent expense ratio.[23] That difference goes straight to the bottom line.

Telemarketing is the next best thing to a face-to-face, personal sales call. In the business-to-business arena, for example, good telemarketers can develop strong, lasting relationships with customers they have never met but with whom they speak every week. Stand Out Designs in San Diego employs highly skilled telemarketers who call on zoos, museums, and boutique retailers all across the country to get them to order and stock the company's unique line of silk-screened T-shirts. The telemarketers don't just take orders; they counsel the dealers with display and promotion suggestions, offer advertising tips, and arrange for special imprints on the shirts when appropriate.

When combined with other direct-response media, telemarketing becomes even more effective. For example, experience shows that when telemarketing is combined with direct mail, there is usually at least a 10 percent increase in responses—often a lot more.

Direct-Response Advertising

Advertising that asks the reader, viewer, or listener to provide feedback straight to the sender is called **direct-response advertising**. Any medium can be used for direct response, but the most common are direct mail, catalogs, magazines, television, and digital interactive media (e-mails and search engines).

Direct Mail Next to personal selling and telemarketing, direct mail is the most effective method for closing a sale or generating inquiries. It's very useful to direct marketers seeking an

> ## Good telemarketers can develop strong, lasting relationships with customers they have never met.

Second, people have come to accept the idea of shopping by phone. It's convenient, hassle-free, and inexpensive. In the United States, the toll-free telephone business is booming. In any given week, 30,000 to 50,000 toll-free numbers are added across North America. Heavy demand caused the pool of 800 numbers to run dry in 1996. Soon thereafter, concern grew that even the 888 numbers faced depletion, leading to limits on their allocation. Then 877 and 866 numbers were introduced, with other numbers to be added for toll-free use as needed.[24]

immediate response. While 35 percent of all direct marketing expenditures are allocated to direct mail, the largest portion, the trend is expected to be away from printed materials and toward digital media, like e-mail and mobile marketing.[25]

Catalog Sales The largest direct marketers are catalog companies and catalogs are still the most popular medium for multichannel marketers. **Catalogs** are expensive to produce and mail, but consumers like to hold them in their hands. They like to circle the products they like and tear out the pages. Print catalogs have advantages over other marketing tools in creating product awareness, acquiring customers, and building brand loyalty. Consumers commonly then turn to their computers or telephones to order, but they start by shopping the catalogs. We discussed the use of direct mail and catalogs in greater detail in Chapter 14.

Direct-Response Print Advertising

Newspaper ads and inserts featuring coupons or listing toll-free phone numbers can be very effective at stimulating customer responses. Today, the same is true with magazines. Moreover, in magazines, advertisers can devote most of the space to image-building, thus maximizing the medium's power. We discussed the use of print media in Chapter 11.

Direct-Response Broadcast Advertising

Direct marketers' use of TV and radio has increased dramatically in recent years. Total Gym, whose products are normally sold through health care and physical fitness professionals, worked with American Telecast to develop a 30-minute infomercial featuring TV star Chuck Norris and supermodel Christie Brinkley. The campaign exceeded their wildest expectations, producing more than $100 million in sales the first year and continuing to generate similar

Television is a powerful instrument for direct marketers like Home Shopping Network (www.hsn.com) because of its mass coverage and the ability to display and demostrate the product with sound and full color right before the customers' eyes. Bobbi Ray Carter, shown here, has long been one of HSN's most popular hosts.

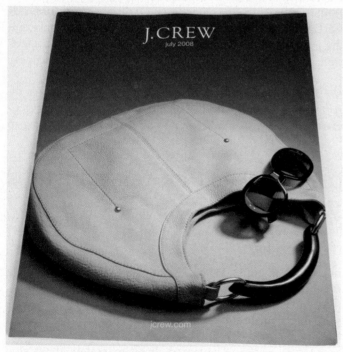

Catalog sales make up the largest portion of direct marketing. Catalogs, such as this one from J. Crew (www.jcrew.com), display a company's products and enable customers to order at their convenience via mail, phone, fax, or Internet. Victoria's Secret, L. L. Bean, and Lands' End are just a few of the multitude of consumer catalogs available today.

returns for the next four years.[26] As Exhibit 16–2 shows, relatively young and affluent people are watching infomercials and buying the advertised products.

For many years, radio commentator Paul Harvey was very successful pitching a wide variety of products to his loyal audience. Likewise, talk jocks Howard Stern and Rush Limbaugh made Snapple an overnight success by drinking the product and touting its good taste on the air. Still, until fairly recently, radio has rarely been the medium of choice for direct-response advertising. Radio industry executives now expect to see a dramatic increase in the number of direct-response ads on radio. We discussed radio, TV, and infomercials in Chapter 12.

▼ **EXHIBIT 16–2** Who watches (and buys from) infomercials.

	Total Viewers	Total Buyers
Primary gender	Female, 53.2%	Female, 51.7%
Mean age	41.2	45.9
Primary ethnicity	Caucasian	Caucasian
Primary employment	Full-time	Full-time
Marital status	Married, 49.3%	Married, 60.3%
Children present	Yes, 40.1%	Yes, 43.1%
Residence	Suburban	Suburban
Mean household income	$56,000	$55,000

The Internet's impact has been extraordinary. Consumers are free to make inquiries, book flights, find hotels, and access a vast amount of information at their leisure, often eliminating the need for person-to-person communication. Shown here are three competing companies that offer just those services: Orbitz (www.orbitz.com), Hotwire (www.hotwire.com), and Expedia (www.expedia.com).

Interactive Media Interactive media systems allow customers and prospects to control both the content and the pace of presentations and to order merchandise directly from the system. The most popular interactive media currently are online personal computers. Although still in the development stage, interactive TV may allow viewers to respond to questions during a commercial, giving advertisers a wealth of demographic information for future promotions. The use of the new digital interactive media was explored in depth in Chapter 13. Now let's take a brief look at the ultimate interactive communication tool, personal selling.

check yourself ✓

1. What is the key difference between direct sales and direct-response advertising?

2. Which of those strategies is more effective for closing a sale or generating inquiries and why do you think that's the case?

L04 Describe the advantages and drawbacks of personal selling.

PERSONAL SELLING: THE HUMAN MEDIUM

Personal selling is the best marketing communications tool for relationship building because the sales rep and the customer are face to face. It's the ultimate one-to-one medium. It's also the most expensive medium. For most companies, personal selling expenditures far exceed expenditures for advertising. And in many companies, the primary role of advertising is to lend support to the sales force either directly by producing leads or indirectly by creating a positive atmosphere for the sales call. That

is certainly true for all of the GEICO ads that direct audiences to the company's toll-free number.

Personal selling can be defined in a number of ways, depending on the orientation of the company using it. For our purposes we define **personal selling** as the *interpersonal communication* process by which a seller ascertains and then satisfies the needs of a buyer, to the mutual, long-term benefit of both parties.[27]

Thus, the task of personal selling is a lot more than just making a sale. The objective of personal selling should be to build a relationship, a partnership, that will provide long-term benefits to both buyer and seller (a win-win situation). The salesperson discovers the buyer's needs by helping the customer identify problems, offers information about potential solutions, assists the buyer in making decisions, and provides after-sale service to ensure long-term satisfaction. Influence and persuasion are only one part of selling. The major part is problem solving.

Types of Personal Selling

Everyone sells, at one time or another. Children sell lemonade, magazine subscriptions, and Girl Scout cookies. Students sell prom tickets, yearbook ads, and term papers. Doctors sell diets to unwilling patients. Lawyers sell pleas to skeptical juries. And cops sell traffic safety to nervous motorists.

The fact is that everything has to be sold, by someone to somebody. A retail clerk may sell you a cell phone. Behind that clerk is a virtual army of other salespeople who sold raw materials to the manufacturer, capital equipment for use in the manufacturing process, business services such as human resources and accounting, plant and office furniture, vehicles, advertising services, media space and time, and insurance. Then the manufacturer's salespeople sold the cell phone to a wholesaler who, of course, had to buy transportation services and warehousing from other salespeople. And then the wholesaler's sales reps sold the phone to the retail outlet where you bought it.

As this scenario shows, people in sales work for a wide variety of organizations and call on an equally wide variety of customers. They may call on other businesses to sell products or services used in the manufacture of other products. They may call on resellers—people who buy the product, add value, and resell it. Or they may sell to consumers, either in a retail store or, as we discussed earlier, in a direct selling situation away from a fixed retail location.

Because advertising is basically designed to support and reinforce a company's sales efforts, advertising people (whether in the company or at an agency) have to understand the selling environment their companies or clients deal in. Many companies have their advertising people make calls with the sales force for this very reason. The advertising person can experience firsthand what questions prospects ask, how customers view the company (and its competitors), how people use the company's product, and what information (in either an ad or a piece of sales material) might help the salesperson communicate better with the prospect.

Advantages of Personal Selling

The greatest strength of personal selling is its personal nature. Nothing is as persuasive as personal communication. A skilled salesperson can observe a prospect's body language and read between the lines to detect what's troubling the customer. The rep can ask questions and answer queries as they arise. The face-to-face situation facilitates instant feedback. And the rep has the flexibility to adjust the presentation, tailoring it specifically to the needs and interests of the particular prospect. Not only that, the salesperson can demonstrate the product live. And the rep can negotiate, finding those terms that best suit the buyer's needs.

Time is on the rep's side, too. The sale doesn't have to be made today. The relationship has to be established, though, and a human being is better at doing that than any nonpersonal medium.

One of the major jobs of personal selling is to gain distribution for new products—a task no other communications tool can do as well. In fact, in many trade and industrial situations, personal contact may be vital to closing the sale. This is also true for certain high-ticket or technical consumer products such as computers, health care, and estate planning. In these cases, personal selling is well worth its high cost— because it gets the job done.

Drawbacks of Personal Selling

Personal selling is very labor-intensive. That's why it's the most costly way to communicate with prospects. This is its single biggest weakness. The average business-

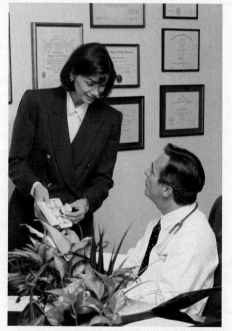

This pharmaceutical sales representative is engaging in missionary selling when she presents the benefits of her products to a doctor. The representative understands that the doctor will not place an order, but she is attempting to get the doctor to prescribe the pharmaceutical for his patients so her company will get an order from the patient's drugstore.

to-business sales call today costs in excess of $300. Not only that, it's very time-consuming. Because it is basically a one-on-one medium, there are few economies of scale.

This is why one important role of advertising is to reduce the cost of sales by communicating as much relevant information as possible about the company and its products to prospects and customers before the salesperson even calls. That information may be functional (specifically about the product) or symbolic (building image and credibility for the company).

Another drawback is the poor reputation of personal selling with many people. Decades of "suede shoe" salesmen employing high-pressure tactics have dishonored the profession. Thus the common jibe: "Would you buy a used car from that man?" Salespeople are frequently given fancier titles such as marketing associate, marketing representative, or account manager in an attempt to reduce guilt or the rejection associated with personal selling.[28]

There's an old saw about one bad apple ruining a barrel. Imagine spending millions of dollars on a nationwide advertising campaign to communicate your expertise and good customer service and then sending an unprofessional sales force out that is improperly groomed or, worse, ignorant of product features and benefits and lacking empathy for customer needs. Unfortunately, it happens all the time. The salesperson has incredible power to either make or break a delicate relationship. As a result, sophisticated firms go to great lengths to screen sales applicants to find the right personality attributes and then invest heavily in training. Of course, this goes both ways. A tasteless advertising campaign can hurt a company's national reputation more than one bad salesperson. As always, it's the responsibility of marketing management to ensure consistency among what the advertising presents, what the sales force promises, and what the company actually delivers.

The Role of Personal Selling in IMC

Salespeople are the company's communicators. In fact, to the customer who doesn't know anybody else at the company, the salesperson doesn't just represent the firm. He or she *is* the firm. The customer's impression of the salesperson, therefore, will frequently govern his or her

Personal selling is especially important in the high-end cosmetics industry. Two factors account for this. First, consumers expect and enjoy the assistance of a well-trained cosmetics salesperson. Second, the profit margins for cosmetics are high enough to support an expensive sales staff. But even here advertising still has an important role to play by providing consumers with information about cosmetics and creating strong brand images.

perception of the company. Again, this makes the sales rep a very important person.

In an integrated marketing communications program, personal selling can play a very important role. Salespeople provide four distinct communications functions: information gathering, information providing, order fulfillment, and relationship building. We'll discuss each of these briefly.

Gathering Information

Sales reps often serve as the eyes and ears of the company. Because they are out in the field talking to customers or attending trade shows, they have access to information and they can see trends. For example, salespeople provide information on who's new in the business, how customers are reacting to new products or styles, what the competition is doing, and where new sales opportunities might exist. Generally, information gathering by the sales force relates to three areas: prospecting; determining customer wants, needs, and abilities; and monitoring the competition.

Providing Information

Salespeople not only gather information; they deliver it. The stereotype (both negative and positive) of a good salesperson is someone who is a good talker, articulate and persuasive. In truth, a superior salesperson is a good listener first and a good talker second. Salespeople impart information both upstream and downstream within their organization. They deliver information to customers about the company and its

products, they recommend solutions to problems, and they use information to communicate value and to build relationships and trust.

Personal selling incorporates all three legs of the IMC integration triangle we learned about in Chapter 7—say → do → confirm—because what the sales rep says and does will either confirm or contradict the company's other messages. The rep's skill, therefore, will definitely color the relationship between the company and the customer. It's critically important that the salesperson's performance be consistent with the firm's positioning and reinforce its other marketing communications.

Fulfilling Orders

There comes a time in every relationship when someone has to make a commitment. Asking for that commitment can be very difficult if the preceding steps have not been handled well. The inevitable tasks of personal selling are to motivate the customer to action, close the sale, and then make sure the goods and services are delivered correctly.

An important part of personal selling is following up after the sale, making sure the goods or services are delivered in a timely fashion, and seeing to it that the customer is completely satisfied. This is a combination of the "do" and "confirm" steps, and it's critical to continued relationship building.

This is also where cross-functional management and open communication come back into play. If there is any kind of manufacturing glitch or delay in shipping, the salesperson needs to notify the customer immediately. But to do that, the salesperson must be informed. Similarly, goods need to be protected and shipped with care. Salespeople hate to receive calls from new customers saying their first shipment arrived with damaged goods. All employees, including those in the warehouse, need to understand the impact of their actions.

Likewise, if the company is advertising a certain model of a product and the salesperson closes the sale on the product, that model had better be in stock. Again, good internal communication is a key to good external relationships.

Nordstrom strives to provide exceptional service to its customers. An engaging and helpful Web site is part of that effort. So is the company's lenient returns policy and justifiably famous focus on consumer satisfaction.

Building Relationships

A company's sales staff should be the ultimate relationship marketers. People naturally want to buy from the salesperson they like and trust. Salespeople build relationships by paying attention to three simple things: keeping commitments, servicing their accounts, and solving problems. Interestingly, those are also probably the three basic requirements for any company's success.

Here again, advertising people can help. When a company advertises, it is making a commitment to its customers and prospects. It is very difficult for a salesperson to keep those commitments if the advertising has overpromised. So puffery should be avoided wherever possible, since by its very nature, it tends to overpromise.

Likewise, it's difficult for salespeople to adequately service their accounts if every time people call customer service they get a busy signal. This happened to the giant telephone utility U.S. West when it downsized and reengineered the company. It continued running ads touting its great service, but nobody could get through to them. Not smart. Advertising people have to know what's going on in the company, and sometimes they need to recommend that advertising be stopped.

Finally, advertising as well as salespeople should be concerned with solving problems. If the sales staff uncovers a problem that

Developing a Plans Book [16–A]

A plans book, quite simply, is the representation of all the hard work you have put in to develop the ideas for your project. For some of you this is an actual deliverable for the project; for the rest of you, it is good practice and good process management to develop a plans book to ensure that all of your thinking exists in one place.

Don't let the word *book* fool you—what we are talking about here is a binder or a set of binders that houses information relevant to your client's problem. Whether it is competitive news and information, industry news, research on target audiences, and/or SWOT analysis, this binder should comprise all of that organized information. The plans book is the foundation you will use to build the final presentation (we talk about the final presentation in Chapter 17), a concise explanation of how you will utilize the information in the plans book to put your campaign ideas into action.

Here is the information that should be represented in your plans book:

• Objectives
• Challenges
• SWOT analysis
• Target audience analysis
• Creative strategy
• Creative brief
• Creative concepts
• Media strategy and plan
• Evaluation or success metrics

Objectives

This is a statement or a set of statements that describes what you hope to achieve from advertising for your client's product. Some common goals are lifting awareness within a new audience, stealing share from competitors, or changing perceptions of consumers. It is better to stay focused and not try to do too much.

Challenges

Think about what you are trying to achieve and what barriers exist that make your work that much harder. If you are trying to lift sales for your client's products, one challenge may be that there is little to no awareness.

SWOT or Situation Analysis

Understanding the strengths, weaknesses, opportunities, and threats for your client's product(s) helps you focus on the appropriate strategy to market the brand. Along with target analysis the SWOT analysis should lead right into your strategy for marketing the product/brand.

Target Audience Analysis

Hopefully you have done a combination of primary research (interviews) and secondary research (syndicated or already done by a third party) to help understand what motivates your consumers to take action. Once you understand this, advertising becomes much easier; this section should highlight the research done and the insights from that work.

Creative Strategy

Your creative strategy is an overarching guide to how you will approach reaching your target with your client's message. All of your tactics should easily fall out of your strategy statement.

Creative Brief

This can be a single document or a set of documents, but either way it should be the parameters for all of your creative work. Look back to Chapter 8 for how to develop a brief.

Creative Concepts

The creative concept is a visual representation of your idea or set of ideas, complete with messaging and layouts.

Media Strategy and Plan

The media strategy should act as a framework for all of your tactical media ideas. The media plan itself is just a representation of the tactical ideas with timing included. (See Chapter 15 for an example of a media plan.)

Evaluation or Success Metrics

Of course all of your ideas will work, mainly due to the fact that you have done all of your homework, but what if one of them didn't . . . how would you know? This is where you detail how you plan to track and measure your campaign's effectiveness. This could be as simple as sales growth or more complex, like a pre/post attitudinal study.

customers frequently encounter, and the company's product can help solve that problem, then that should become the focus of some planned communications—advertising, publicity, or company-sponsored events.

L05 Identify the elements that must be considered in establishing a trade show program.

TRADE SHOWS

Trade shows provide an extraordinary opportunity for personal selling. A unique aspect of trade-show selling is that prospective clients and customers come to you; they already have a desire to learn about you and your product and the services you provide.

When establishing an exhibit booth program, managers must consider planning, budgeting, promotion, people, and productivity.[29]

Planning Planning pivots on four major areas: the budget, the image of the company or brand, the frequency of the shows, and the flexibility of the booth configuration.[30] In planning the actual exhibits or trade-show booths, advertisers need to consider numerous factors: size and location of the space; desired image or impression of the exhibit; complexities of shipping, installing, and dismantling; number of products to be displayed; need for storage and distribution of literature; use of preshow advertising and promotion; and the cost of all these factors.

Budgeting Trade shows are expensive, and costs have increased substantially in the last decade. A large company may spend $1 million or more on a booth for one trade show. With staffers' travel, living, and salary expenses and preshow promotion added to booth costs, the cost per visitor engaged rises to

trade shows Exhibitions where manufacturers, dealers, and buyers of an industry's products can get together for demonstrations and discussion; expose new products, literature, and samples to customers; and meet potential new dealers for their products.

booths At trade shows, a major factor in sales promotion plans. To stop traffic, it must be simple and attractive and have good lighting and a large visual.

exhibits A marketing or public relations approach that involves preparing displays that tell about an organization or its products; exhibits may be used at fairs, colleges and universities, or trade shows.

> ## Good internal communication is a key to good external relationships.

Every major industry sponsors annual **trade shows**—exhibitions where manufacturers, dealers, and buyers get together for demonstrations and discussions. More than 14,000 industrial, scientific, and medical shows are held in the United States each year, and many companies exhibit at more than one show. Trade shows are also very important for global marketers, because they may be the only place where an advertiser can meet the company's major international prospects at one time. Moreover, some of the world's largest trade shows are held overseas.

The construction of trade-show **booths** and **exhibits** has become a major factor in sales promotion plans. To stop traffic, a booth must be impactful and attractive and have good lighting and a large visual. It should also provide a comfortable atmosphere to promote conversation between salespeople and prospects. Many trade-show exhibitors use state-of-the-art technology, such as holograms, fiber optics, and interactive computer systems, to attract and hold the attention of visitors.

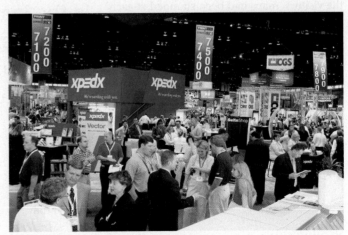

Trade shows are an important component in the marketing mix. They provide a unique opportunity for advertisers to meet with a large number of prospects. Over half of trade-show visitors make buying plans as a result of visiting a show.

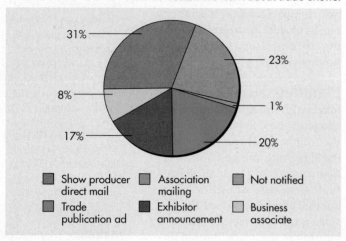

Legend:
- Show producer direct mail
- Trade publication ad
- Association mailing
- Exhibitor announcement
- Not notified
- Business associate

more than $195.[31] Despite the expense, trade shows can still be a cost-effective way to reach sales prospects, less expensive than a sales call.

Promotion To build traffic for a trade-show booth or exhibit, marketers send out personal invitations, conduct direct-mail campaigns, place ads in trade publications, issue news releases, and perform telemarketing. The pie chart in Exhibit 16–3 portrays how customers typically learn about the trade shows they attend.[32]

At the show itself, activities at the booth and promotional materials (handouts, brochures, giveaway specialty items, raffles) can stimulate customer interest and improve product exposure. 3M's Telcomm Products Division mailed 6,000 potential show attendees a Pony Express theme folder that invited them to pick up a trail map at the booth. The map guided the visitors (Pony Express riders) through a series of stations shared by seven product groups within the huge booth. Once the visitors' maps had been stamped at each station, they were given a "pay envelope" containing replicas of 1850 coins and vouchers redeemable for merchandise awards.[33]

People The company representatives staffing the booth personify the kind of service the customer can expect to receive. They should be articulate, people-oriented, enthusiastic, knowledgeable about the product, and empathetic listeners.[34]

The primary goal of a trade-show booth is to meet with qualified prospects face to face. Ideally, 80 percent of the salesperson's time should be spent listening and 20 percent talking.[35]

Productivity A company's trade-show effort may be wasted if prospects' names are not collected and organized properly. Each lead should be evaluated as to the prospect's readiness to receive another contact (A = now; B = 2 weeks; C = 6 months;

D = never).[36] The resulting lead list is the link to future sales and augments the company's prospect database. Follow-up contacts are key to extracting the maximum value from trade shows.

check yourself ✓

1. What makes a trade show a unique personal selling opportunity?

2. What trade show activity is critical to augmenting the company's prospect database?

LO6 Explain the factors that must be considered in designing packaging.

PRODUCT PACKAGING

In 2007, North American companies spent close to $121 billion on packaging.[37] Since upward of 70 percent of all buying decisions are made at the point of purchase, packages play a major role in both advertising and selling. The package is not only the last "ad" a consumer sees before purchasing the product, it is the only "ad" the consumer sees when using the product. So it is more than just another *planned message*. Packaging influences the *product message* as well, since (as we discussed in Chapter 7) it is often an intrinsic aspect of the basic product concept.

> The package is the last ad a consumer sees before purchasing the product.

Packaging encompasses the physical appearance of the container and includes design, color, shape, labeling, and materials. Packaging serves marketers in four major ways: protection, preservation, information, and promotion.[38] Although the protection and preservation aspects reduce the costly effects of damage, pilferage, and spoilage, the importance of packaging as an informational and promotional tool cannot be underestimated. An attractive package can create an immediate relationship with the customer, influence in-store shopping decisions, help set the product apart from competitors, and inform customers of the product's features and benefits.

Designers consider three factors: the package's stand-out appeal, how it communicates verbally and nonverbally, and the prestige or image desired.

Packaging design can be as important as advertising in building a product's brand image. Packaging establishes or reinforces the brand's personality at the point of sale. So if status is the goal, the package designer must consider what consumers regard as prestigious. This is especially important for so-called nonrational products—cosmetics and perfumes, sports accessories, confection gifts, and certain luxury products—in which fantasy, impulsiveness, or mystique may overrule rational choice.

To sell products off the shelf, packages may use shape, color, size, interesting visuals, or even texture to deliver a marketing message, give product information, and indicate application. After they are purchased, packages continue promoting the product in the home, reinforcing the brand's image, so they should open and close with minimal effort and be easy to handle.

Environmental Issues in Packaging

As manufacturers continue to produce environmentally safe packaging, the marketer's cost of materials rises. And what some consumers expect from *green packaging* is not necessarily what manufacturers traditionally offer or what marketing intermediaries prefer to use.[39]

With the public's growing concern for the environment, especially in international markets, recyclable tin-coated steel and aluminum packages are enjoying a resurgence in popularity. Because European countries are so densely populated, their regulations requiring environmentally friendly packaging are far more stringent than in North America. Marketers need to take this into consideration since such regulations add to the cost of doing business overseas.

Government Impact on Packaging

Government agencies also influence package design. The Food and Drug Administration (FDA), for example, and the Nutrition Labeling and Education Act of 1990 (which went into effect in 1994) imposed stricter labeling requirements for nutrition and health products. And sometimes a state's packaging requirements differ from the federal government's, adding even more complexity for manufacturers.

Package Manufacturing

Packages may come in many forms: wrappers, cartons, boxes, crates, cans, bottles, jars, tubes, barrels, drums, and pallets. And they may be constructed of many materials, from paper and steel ("tin" cans) to wood, glass, and burlap. Newer packaging materials include plastic-coated papers, ceramics, metal foils, and even straw. Improvements in packaging include amber-green glass bottles that protect the contents from light damage and heavy-duty, gray computer-disk jackets that

reflect heat and protect the disk. The plastic film pouch for food products has become a substitute for tin cans and is more flexible, light, and compact. For pharmaceutical products, consumers prefer plastic containers.[40]

The second phase of packaging, the *production process,* may require the use of many packaging specialists: experts in package engineering (box designers, packaging materials consultants, and specialists in equipment configuration); graphic artists (designers, production/computer artists, illustrators, and photographers); label producers (printers and label manufacturers); die-cutters for custom packages; and package warehousing companies (wholesalers of prefabricated packages and package manufacturers).

Ad agencies are not usually involved in packaging decisions. This is typically the realm of specialists. However, it's not uncommon for an agency to be consulted on the design of labels and packages, and some may even prepare the copy that goes on them. In an IMC program, the agency can be very helpful in coordinating this work with the overall theme of the ad campaign.

When Should a Package Be Changed?

There are many reasons to change a package: product alteration or improvement, substitution in packaging materials, competitive pressure, environmental concerns, changes in legislation, or the need to increase brand recognition.[41]

Advertisers spend millions researching and promoting new images. And packages have to reflect a contemporary brand image consistent with constantly changing consumer perceptions and desires. However, marketers should always exercise caution. Designers often change packaging very gradually to avoid confusing consumers.

Packaging is an extremely important medium since it typically serves as the last advertising a consumer sees before taking the product home. Plus, package design plays a major role in how the quality of the product is perceived. Good packaging can often make or break the deal for a consumer. How does the packaging for Gleukos Performance Punch help the product better appeal to consumers interested in fitness?

check yourself ✓

1. What are the four functions of packaging?

2. What role might advertising agencies play in packaging decisions?

THE ROLE OF SALES PROMOTION IN IMC

Imagine walking into the fresh-fruit section of your local grocery store, picking up a big, juicy mango, and discovering a sticker on it stating: "Now available in Snapple. Mango Madness." You turn around and suddenly notice that there, right next to the fresh-fruit bin, stands a big display of, you guessed it, Snapple Mango Madness.

It actually happened. New York agency Kirshenbaum, Bond & Partners launched Snapple's new Mango Madness drink nationally with stickers on 30 million pieces of fruit.[42] Talk about out-of-the-box thinking and creative media planning! Moreover, it was an outstanding example of how sales promotion can be perfectly integrated with a company's positioning, in this case Snapple's "100% natural" message strategy.

The term *sales promotion* is often misunderstood or confused with advertising or publicity. This may be because sales promotion activities often occur simultaneously and use both advertising and publicity as part of the process. In truth, though, it is a very specific marketing communications activity.

Sales promotion is a direct inducement that offers extra incentives anywhere along the marketing route to enhance or accelerate the product's movement from producer to consumer. Within this definition, there are three important elements to consider. Sales promotion

- May be used anywhere in the marketing channel: from manufacturer to wholesaler, wholesaler to dealer, dealer to customer, or manufacturer to customer.

- Normally involves a direct inducement (such as money, prizes, extra products, gifts, or specialized information) that provides extra incentives to buy now or buy more, visit a store, request literature, display a product, or take some other action.

- Is designed to change the timing of a purchase or to shift inventory to others in the channel.

Let's see how this definition applies to Snapple. In an interesting combination of both consumer advertising and *trade pro-*

Snapple's clever promotion of its Mango Madness flavor demonstrates an ingenious integration of sales promotion and product positioning. By placing a sticker ad on actual mangoes in the fresh-fruit section, Snapple reinforced its slogan of "100% natural" and grabbed the attention of customers not necessarily looking to buy the beverage. The marketing strategy was supported by placing bottles of Mango Madness in close proximity to the fruit.

motion (sales promotion aimed at members of the distribution channel), Snapple used the fresh mangoes as an unusual new advertising medium to introduce its Mango Madness to consumers and to stimulate initial demand for the drink. The magnitude of that media effort (30 million pieces of fruit) served as a huge incentive to retailers to grant Snapple extra floor space (very expensive real estate, by the way) to display Mango Madness right next to the fresh-fruit stand. The result: Snapple sold a lot more Mango Madness a lot faster, and for a lot less money, than it would have if it had just placed some expensive ads in consumer magazines or on TV. Moreover, by creatively integrating different forms of marketing communications, Snapple simultaneously bolstered its positioning strategy and enhanced its relationship with the retail trade—its primary customer.

Some marketers consider sales promotion supplementary to advertising and personal selling because it binds the two together, making both more effective. In reality, however, sales promotion is far more than supplementary. One study showed marketers spend 54 percent of their advertising/promotion budget on sales promotion compared to only 46 percent for advertising.[43] We'll see why shortly.

Sales promotion is expensive. But it's also effective. Unfortunately, it has serious drawbacks, which lead to furious battles in marketing circles between proponents of sales promotion and proponents of advertising. Each approach has an important role to play, but advertisers must consider the positives and negatives and get the balance right.

The Positive Effect of Sales Promotion on Brand Volume

Effective sales promotion accomplishes a number of things. First of all, it adds tangible, immediate, extra value to the brand. Snapple's creative media buy suddenly made Mango Madness more valuable to the retail trade. This induced retailers to stock up on the new product and display it prominently. Similarly, when McDonald's runs its Monopoly game, it's adding instant value to the products it sells. This is why we refer to sales promotion as the *value-added tool.*

Second, by adding immediate value, sales promotion *maximizes* sales volume. A short-term price cut or rebate, for instance, may be very effective at boosting sales. While advertising helps develop and reinforce a quality, differentiated brand reputation and build long-term market value, sales promotion helps build short-term *market volume.* To become a market leader, therefore, a brand needs both advertising and sales promotion.

Finally, when all brands appear to be equal, sales promotion can be more effective than advertising in motivating customers to try a new brand or to select one brand over another. It can also motivate some customers who might be unmoved by advertising efforts. And sales promotions often generate a more immediate, measurable payoff than traditional advertising campaigns. This is why we might also refer to sales promotion as the "sales accelerator."

The Negative Effect of Sales Promotion on Brand Value

Advertisers need to understand the negative effects of sales promotion, too. For instance, excessive sales promotion at the expense of advertising can reduce

sales promotion
A direct inducement offering extra incentives all along the marketing route— from manufacturers through distribution channels to customers— to accelerate the movement of the product from the producer to the customer.

> ## To become a market leader, a brand needs both advertising and sales promotion.

To succeed, sales promotions should be creative and hard to imitate. Kirshenbaum, Bond & Partners certainly demonstrated that with its Snapple labels. My Ad Campaign 16–B, "Creating Effective Sales Promotions," outlines some basic ideas to consider in designing promotions.

profitability. Some marketers believe a proper expenditure balance for consumer packaged-goods products is approximately 60 percent for trade and consumer promotion, 40 percent for advertising.

A high level of trade sales promotion relative to advertising and consumer sales promotion has a positive effect on short-term market share but may have a negative effect on brand attitudes and long-term market share. Without an effective advertising effort to emphasize brand image and quality, customers

Creating Effective Sales Promotions [16–B]

- **Set specific objectives.** Undisciplined, undirected creative work is a waste of time and resources.
- **Set a theme that is relevant.** Start with a strategy, preferably from a unified marketing or advertising plan. Stay on track.
- **Involve the trade.** Build relationships. Carrier Air Conditioning sponsored the Junior Olympics in key markets, sharing sponsorship with its dealer in each city.
- **Coordinate promotional efforts with other marketing plans.** Be sure to coordinate schedules and plans. A consumer promotion should occur simultaneously with a trade promotion; a free sample promotion should be timed to the introduction of a new line.
- **Know how basic promotion techniques work.** A price-off deal can't reverse a brand's downward sales trend.
- **Use simple, attention-getting copy.** Most promotions are built around a simple idea: "Save 75 cents." Emphasize the idea and don't try to be cute.
- **Use contemporary, easy-to-read graphics.** Don't expect to fit 500 words and 20 illustrations into a quarter-page freestanding insert.

- **Clearly communicate the concept.** Words and graphics must work together to get the message across.
- **Add advertising when you need measurable responses.** When part of a promotion, advertising directed at too broad an audience is usually wasted. However, trial-building promotions designed to attract new users, for example, can be helped by targeted advertising.
- **Reinforce the brand's advertising message.** Tie promotions to the brand's ad campaign.
- **Support the brand's positioning and image.** This is especially important for image-sensitive brands and categories, like family-oriented Kraft.
- **Know the media you work through.** Determine which media will work best. Should samples be distributed in stores, door to door, or through direct mail? Does the promotion need newspaper or magazine support?
- **Pretest promotions.** Pretesting doesn't have to be expensive. For packaged goods, small samplings in a few stores can reveal how to maximize coupon redemption rates by testing various values, creative approaches, and delivery methods.

push strategies
Marketing, advertising, and sales promotion activities aimed at getting products into the dealer pipeline and accelerating sales by offering inducements to dealers, retailers, and salespeople.

trade promotions
Promotion activities aimed at wholesalers and retailers to induce product purchase, display, and consumer sales promotion.

trade advertising
The advertising of goods and services to middlemen to stimulate wholesalers and retailers to buy goods for resale to their customers or for use in their own businesses.

pull strategies
Marketing, advertising, and sales promotion activities aimed at inducing trial purchase and repurchase by consumers.

consumer sales promotions
Promotions aimed at consumers to stimulate product interest, trial, or repurchase.

become deal-prone rather than brand loyal. And overemphasis on price (whether in advertising or sales promotion) eventually destroys brand equity.[44]

Another drawback of sales promotion is its high cost. One analysis showed that only 16 percent of sales promotions were profitable. In other words, many manufacturers spend more than $1 to generate an extra $1 of profits.[45]

Finally, overly aggressive sales promotion or advertising can draw competitors into a price war, which leads to reduced sales and profits for everyone.

Thus, if too much of the marketing mix is allocated to advertising, the brand may gain a high-quality, differentiated image but not enough volume to be a market leader. On the other hand, as Larry Light, McDonald's chief global marketing officer says, "Too much [sales] promotion, and the brand will have high volume but low profitability. Market leadership can be bought through bribes, but enduring profitable market leadership must be earned through building both brand value as well as volume."[46]

SALES PROMOTION STRATEGIES AND TACTICS

To move their products through the distribution channel from the point of manufacture to the point of consumption, marketers employ two types of strategies: push and pull. **Push strategies** are primarily designed to secure the cooperation of retailers. **Trade promotions**—sales promotions aimed at members of the distribution channel—are one of the principal tactics marketers use to push products through the distribution pipeline and gain shelf space. We'll discuss some of these tactics in the next section. Marketers may also use **trade advertising** (advertising in publications read by members of the trade) as a push tactic.

Pull strategies, on the other hand, are designed to attract customers and increase demand for the product (see Exhibit 16–4). Consumer advertising and **consumer sales promotions** are examples of pull strategies because they are designed to induce consumers to seek out or ask for the product, in effect pulling the product through the pipeline. Today, some national advertisers spend more dollars on trade sales promotions than on either consumer sales promotions or media advertising. But that is often the price they have to pay to gain and maintain distribution, without which they cannot make any sales.

Giving Brands a Push with Trade Promotions

In supermarkets today, shelf space and floor space are hard to come by. To maintain their own images, department stores set standards for manufacturers' displays. This means that retailers often won't use the special racks, sales aids, and promotional literature supplied by manufacturers.

These are minor problems; major ones have to do with control of the marketplace. **Trade concentration**—more

▼**EXHIBIT 16–4** Two marketing communications approaches.

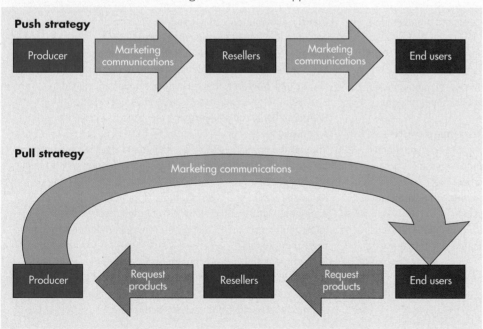

products going through fewer retailers—gives greater control to the retailers and less to the manufacturers. Increased competition for shelf space gives retailers even more power, enabling them to exact hefty deals and allowances. As a result, manufacturers of national brands often don't have enough money left to integrate consumer advertising or sales promotions.[47]

Despite these problems, many manufacturers still implement effective push strategies. And the smart ones safeguard enough money for consumer advertising. Trade tactics include slotting allowances, trade deals, display allowances, buyback allowances, advertising allowances, cooperative advertising and advertising materials, dealer premiums and contests, push money, and company conventions and dealer meetings.

Slotting Allowances

In response to the glut of new products, some retailers charge manufacturers **slotting allowances**—fees ranging from $15,000 to $40,000 or more for the privilege of obtaining shelf or floor space for a new product. The practice is controversial because some manufacturers think they're being forced to subsidize the retailer's cost of doing business. Smaller manufacturers complain that the allowances shut out all but the largest suppliers. The Federal Trade Commission and Small Business Administration are considering taking steps to limit the use of slotting allowances because they reduce competition.

Trade Deals

Manufacturers make **trade deals** with retailers by offering short-term discounts or other dollar inducements. To comply with the Robinson-Patman Act, trade deals must be offered proportionally to all dealers. Dealers usually pass the savings on to customers through short-term sale prices, or "specials."

Excessive trade deals threaten brand loyalty because they encourage customers to buy whatever brand is on sale. Furthermore, marketers who use trade discounts extensively find themselves in a vicious circle: If they cut back on the promotions, they may lose shelf space and then market share.

In addition, some retailers capitalize on trade discounts by engaging in forward buying and diverting. With **forward buying**, a retailer stocks up on a product when it is on discount and buys smaller amounts when it sells at regular price. **Diverting** means using the promotional discount to purchase large quantities of an item in one region, then shipping portions of the buy to areas where the discount isn't offered.

Display Allowances

More and more stores charge manufacturers **display allowances**—fees to make room for and set up displays. In-store displays include counter stands, floor stands, shelf signs, and special racks that give the retailer ready-made, professionally designed vehicles for selling more of the featured products.

Buyback Allowances

When introducing a new product, manufacturers sometimes

THE SECOND LINE THAT'S NO SECOND STRINGER.

It's your business, your time and your reputation. Choose a second line that will help you protect it. Payne offers a range of low-cost high quality heating and cooling options. Durable and dependable, we can help you increase your margins without increasing your maintenance costs. With easy-to-sell and easy-to-install products like our ENERGY STAR® labeled 12 SEER cooling and 90% heating systems, Payne can help you make the most of every opportunity.

A MEMBER OF THE UNITED TECHNOLOGIES CORPORATION FAMILY. STOCK SYMBOL: UTX.

www.payne.com

With the energy crisis here to stay, your customers are going to be looking for this symbol. Low-cost, high-efficiency Payne models can help you stay ahead of the game.
Energy Star and the Energy Star logo are registered U.S. marks.

PAYNE ®
HEATING & COOLING
RIGHT FOR YOU.

Trade promotions are business-to-business programs that are strategically aimed at increasing distribution. This ad for Payne Heating and Cooling (www.payne.com) aims to persuade buyers for HVAC companies to purchase and install Payne units for their customers.

Manufacturers like DeWalt often pay a display allowance for their in-store exhibits, banners, and shelf signs. These fees benefit retailers like Home Depot by compensating them for the space occupied by the displays. And the manufacturer benefits from the increased exposure.

offer retailers a **buyback allowance** for the old product that hasn't sold. To persuade retailers to take on their product line, some manufacturers even offer a buyback allowance for a competitor's leftover stock.

Advertising Allowances
Manufacturers often offer **advertising allowances** as either a percentage of purchases or a flat fee paid to the retailer. Advertising allowances are more common for consumer than industrial products. They are offered primarily by large companies, but some smaller firms give them to high-volume customers. The purpose of these allowances is to encourage retailers to advertise the manufacturer's products, but compliance is not always enforced.

Co-op Advertising and Advertising Materials
With **cooperative (co-op) advertising**, national manufacturers reimburse their dealers for advertising the manufacturer's products or logos in their trading area. The manufacturer usually pays 50 to 100 percent of the dealer's advertising costs based on a percentage of the dealer's sales. Special co-op deals are used to introduce new products, advertise certain lines, or combat competitors.

Unlike advertising allowances, co-op programs typically require the dealer to submit invoices and proof of the advertising

(*tearsheets* from the newspaper or affidavits of performance from radio or TV stations). Many manufacturers also give their dealers prepared advertising materials: ads, glossy photos, sample radio commercials, and so on. To control the image of their products, some advertisers insist that dealers use these materials to qualify for the co-op advertising money.

Dealer Premiums, Contests, and Push Money
To encourage retail dealers and salespeople to reach specific sales goals or push certain products, manufacturers may offer special prizes, gifts, or financial incentives. One inducement is cash payments made directly to the sales staff, called **push money (PM)**, or **spiffs**. For example, a shoe salesperson may suggest shoe polish or some other high-profit extra; for each item sold, the salesperson receives a 25- to 50-cent spiff. Some retailers believe that manufacturers' incentives are a potential source of conflict, causing salespeople to serve their own self-interests rather than the interests of their employers. Ethics can also be an issue when dealers and salespeople push certain products on consumers solely for their personal gain.

Company Conventions and Dealer Meetings
Most major manufacturers hold **company conventions** and **dealer meetings** to introduce new products, announce sales promotion programs, or show new advertising campaigns. They may also conduct sales and service training sessions. Meetings can be a dynamic sales promotion tool for the manufacturer.

Push strategies are virtually invisible to consumers. Yet successful inducements mean the product gets more shelf space, a special display, or extra interest and enthusiasm from salespeople. And extra sales interest can spell the difference between failure and success.

Using Consumer Promotions to Pull Brands Through
One reason for today's increased focus on consumer sales promotions is the change in TV viewing habits. With cable TV, DVRs, and DVDs, fewer people watch any one program. Advertising

audiences are more fragmented, and major manufacturers must turn to new methods to reach these moving targets.

Common consumer sales promotions include point-of-purchase materials, coupons, electronic coupons and convenience cards, cents-off promotions, refunds, rebates, premiums, sampling, combination offers, contests, and sweepstakes. A successful IMC campaign may integrate several of these techniques along with media advertising, product publicity, and direct marketing. Commercial Break 16 offers the opportunity to apply what you've learned about push and pull strategies to the marketing of textbooks.

Point-of-Purchase (P-O-P) Materials
Walk into any store and notice the number of display materials and advertising-like devices that are designed to build traffic, exhibit and advertise the product, and promote impulse buying. Collectively, these are all referred to as **point-of-purchase (P-O-P) materials**.

P-O-P works best when used with other forms of advertising. For example, by advertising its gum and candy, one marketer increased sales by about 150 percent. But when P-O-P was added to the same program, the purchase rate jumped 550 percent.[48]

In one poll, 56 percent of mass-merchandise shoppers and 62 percent of grocery shoppers said they noticed point-of-purchase materials. More than half reported noticing signs and displays, 18 percent remembered coupon dispensers, and 14 percent could recall samplings and demonstrations.[49]

Today's consumers make their decisions in the store 66 percent of the time and make unplanned (impulse) purchases 53 percent of the time, so P-O-P can often be the major factor in stimulating purchases.[50]

Consumer sales promotions expose potential customers to a product and induce them to seek it out. While trade promotions push products through distribution channels, consumer sales promotions are intended to pull the product through due to customer demand. This STK (www.stkusa.com) point-of-purchase display serves to incite interest in its durable truck bedliners.

company conventions
Meetings held by companies with their employees, sales representatives, and/or customers to announce new products, policies, and marketing programs.

dealer meetings
Meetings held by companies with their authorized brokers, distributors, and/or retailers to announce new products, policies, and marketing programs.

point-of-purchase (P-O-P) materials
Materials set up at a retail location to build traffic, advertise the product, and promote impulse buying.

P-O-P materials may also include window displays, counter displays, floor and wall racks to hold the merchandise, streamers, and posters. Often, the product's shipping cartons are designed to double as display units. A complete information center may

Applying Push/Pull Strategies to Sales Promotion [16]

Moving a product from the manufacturer to the consumer is not a simple task. Goods often have to go through four or five separate steps: from the manufacturer to an agent or broker, then to the wholesaler, to the retailer, and finally to the consumer. Communicating messages along this same path can also be torturous. Something's bound to get lost along the way. This is why push and pull promotions are so important.

By offering incentives in the form of money, prizes, trips, and promotional materials to "push" products into the distribution pipeline, the marketer can also obtain invaluable middleman assistance. Pushing is when a company uses any form of marketing communications (personal selling, advertising, or sales promotion) for the purpose of gaining shelf space and cooperation. Reversing the process, the company can also use consumer advertising or offer rebates, coupons, two-for-one deals, or some other incentive directly to the customer. By stimulating demand, that form of communication helps "pull" products through the pipeline.

Applying the Breaks
If you were working for McGraw-Hill/Irwin (the publisher of this textbook), how would you suggest using push and/or pull strategies to increase the sales of the company's textbooks? Which strategy do you think would be more effective?

even provide literature, samples, product photos, or an interactive computer in a kiosk.

The trend toward self-service retailing has increased the importance of P-O-P materials. With fewer and less knowledgeable salespeople available to help them, customers are forced to make purchasing decisions on their own. Eye-catching, informative displays can give them the nudge they need. Even in well-staffed stores, display materials can offer extra selling information and make the product stand out from the competition.

The proliferation of P-O-P displays has led retailers to be more discriminating in what they actually use. Most are beginning to insist on well-designed, attractive materials that will blend harmoniously with their store atmosphere.

The emphasis on P-O-P has led to a variety of new approaches, including ads on shopping carts and grocery aisle floors, on-shelf coupon dispensers, advertising jingles activated when in-store refrigerator doors are opened, and interactive computers for selecting everything from shoe styles to floor coverings. Digital technology has led to Hallmark Cards's Touch-Screen Greetings interactive kiosks, which print a customer's personal message onto any card.[51] To send it, look for one of the new Automated Postal Centers rolled out by the U.S. Postal Service. The kiosks allow customers to weigh materials to be mailed, buy postage, and look up zip codes.[52]

Coupons

A **coupon** is a certificate with a stated value presented to the retail store for a price reduction on a specified item. Marketers in the United States distributed more than 367 billion coupons in 2009— the highest in over 30 years—but only about 3.3 billion were ever redeemed.[53]

Coupons may be distributed in newspapers or magazines, door to door, on packages, in stores, by direct mail or online. Nearly 90 percent reach consumers through colorful preprinted newspaper

Most coupons reach consumers through newspaper freestanding inserts (FSIs), which have a higher redemption rate than regular newspaper or magazine coupons.

ads called **freestanding inserts (FSIs)**. FSIs have a higher redemption rate than regular newspaper and magazine coupons; coupons in or on packages have the highest redemption levels of all.[54] Online coupon distribution increased 92 percent in 2009 and redemption of those coupons was up over 360 percent (but still only represented 1.5 percent of all coupons redeemed.)[55]

Manufacturers lose hundreds of millions of dollars annually on fraudulent coupon submissions. Some coupons are counterfeited; others are submitted for products that were never purchased. To fight this problem, some companies have developed computerized systems to detect fraudulent submissions and charge them back to the retailers who made them.

Electronic Coupons and Convenience Cards

High-tech **electronic coupons** work like paper coupons in that they entitle the shopper to a discount, but their method of distribution is entirely different. Interactive touch-screen videos at the point of purchase and coupon printers at checkout counters generate instant discounts, rebates, and offers to try new brands. Electronic coupons are spreading quickly in the nation's supermarkets, though they still represent only a small percentage of the total coupons distributed annually.

Nonetheless, most of the nation's top brand marketers are involved with the Catalina Marketing Network. Catalina's system is installed in more than 24,000 stores across the country and records some 300 million transactions per week.[56]

Electronic couponing targets consumers with specific offers in ways that would not be possible with paper coupons. Many supermarket chains now issue customers **convenience cards** entitling them to discounts at the checkout counter. Consumers often provide detailed information about themselves when they apply for these cards. When customers use a card, a record of their purchases is sent to a database. The card saves customers the hassle of clipping paper coupons, it allows retailers to better understand their customers' purchasing behaviors, and it provides consumers with targeted offers.

Similar systems are used internationally. Catalina now has more than 8,000 store installations in the United Kingdom, France, Italy, Germany, and Japan.[57]

Cents-Off Promotions, Refunds, and Rebates
Cents-off promotions are short-term reductions in the price of a product in the form of cents-off packages, one-cent sales, free offers, and box top refunds. Some packages bear a special cents-off sticker, which the clerk removes and credits at the checkout counter.

Some companies offer *refunds* in the form of cash or coupons that can be applied to future purchases of the product. To obtain the refund, the consumer must mail in a proof of purchase, such as three box tops.

Rebates are larger cash refunds on items from cars to household appliances. Large rebates (like those given on cars) are handled by the seller. For small rebates (like those given for coffeemakers), the consumer sends in a certificate.

Research indicates that many people purchase a product because of an advertised rebate but never collect the rebate because of the inconvenience.[58] This is a phenomenon called **slippage**. Consumers Union estimates that 60 percent of all rebates go unfilled.[59]

Electronic coupon printers in grocery, drug, and general merchandise stores deliver coupons specific to each shopper's demographics and past purchase behavior.

Premiums
A **premium** is an item offered free or at a bargain price to encourage the consumer to buy an advertised product. Premiums affect purchase behavior the same way as rebates but tend to be more effective at getting consumers to buy a product they didn't really need (see Exhibit 16–5). Premiums are intended to improve the product's image, gain goodwill, broaden the customer base, and produce quick sales.

A premium should have strong appeal and value and should be useful or unusual. It may be included in the product's package (*in-pack premium*), on the package (*on-pack premium*), mailed free or for a nominal sum on receipt of proof of purchase (box top or label), or given with the product at the time of purchase. Cosmetics companies often hold department store promotions in which scarves, purses, and cosmetics samplers are given free or for a low price with a purchase.

The purchased cosmetics sampler is an example of a *self-liquidating* premium: The consumer pays enough so that the seller breaks even but doesn't make a profit. A variation is the *continuity premium,* given weekly to customers who frequent

▼**EXHIBIT 16–5** Next to coupons, premiums are one of the most effective sales promotion techniques for changing consumer behavior.

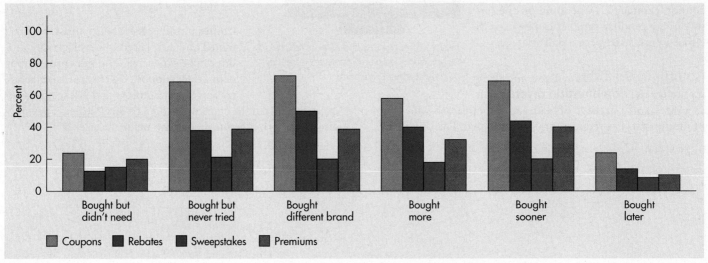

Legend: ■ Coupons ■ Rebates ■ Sweepstakes ■ Premiums

sampling Offering consumers a free trial of a product, hoping to convert them to habitual use.

sweepstakes A sales promotion activity in which prizes are offered based on a chance drawing of entrants' names.

game A sales promotion activity in which prizes are offered based on chance. A game is conducted over a longer period of time than a sweepstakes.

polybagging Samples that are delivered in plastic bags with the daily newspaper or a monthly magazine.

In-store sampling The handing out of free product samples to passing shoppers.

combination offers A sales promotion device in which two related products are packaged together at a special price, such as a razor and a package of blades.

contest A sales promotion device for creating consumer involvement in which prizes are offered based on the skill of the entrants.

the same store. With a minimum dollar purchase of other items, the customer receives a dish or book each week to complete a set.

Sampling

Sampling is the most costly of all sales promotions. It is also one of the most effective for new products, because it offers consumers a free trial in hopes of converting them to habitual use. Sampling should be supported by advertising and must involve a product available in small sizes and purchased frequently. Successful sampling depends heavily on the product's merits. It offers the greatest credibility and can turn a nonuser into a loyal customer instantly—if the product lives up to its promise.

Samples may be distributed by mail, door to door, via coupon advertising, or by a person in the store. They may be given free or for a small charge. Sometimes samples are distributed with related items, but this limits their distribution to those who buy the other product. In **polybagging**, samples are delivered in plastic bags with the daily newspaper or a monthly magazine. This enables distribution to targeted readers and lets publications give their subscribers added value at no cost.[60]

In-store sampling is very popular. Most in-store sampling programs are tied to a coupon campaign. Depending on the nature of the product, samples can be used as either a push strategy or a pull strategy.

Combination Offers

Food and drug marketers use **combination offers**, such as a razor and a package of blades or a toothbrush with a tube of toothpaste, at a reduced price for the two. For best results,

In-store sampling displays allow consumers to test products in an environment where they may be readily purchased.

the items should be related. Sometimes a combination offer introduces a new product by tying its purchase to an established product at a special price.

Contests and Sweepstakes

A **contest** offers prizes based on entrants' skill. A **sweepstakes** offers prizes based solely on a chance drawing of entrants' names. A **game** has the chance element of a sweepstakes but is conducted over a longer time (like bingo-type games designed to build store traffic). A game's big marketing advantage is that customers must make repeat visits to the dealer to continue playing.

Both contests and sweepstakes encourage consumption of the product by creating consumer involvement. These devices pull millions of entries. Usually contest entrants must send in some proof of purchase, such as a box top or label. For more expensive products, consumers may only have to visit the dealer or take a test drive to pick up an entry blank.

To encourage entries, sponsors try to keep their contests as simple as possible. The prize structure must be clearly stated and all the rules listed. Sweepstakes and games are now more popular than contests because they are much easier to enter and take less time. Sweepstakes require careful planning by the advertiser. Companies cannot require a purchase as a condition for entry or the sweepstakes becomes a lottery and therefore illegal. Marketers must obey all local and postal laws.

Contests and sweepstakes must be promoted and advertised to be successful, and this can be expensive. And sales promotions need dealer support. To ensure dealer cooperation, many contests and sweepstakes require the entrant to name the product's local dealer. They may also award prizes to the dealer who made the sale. ■

chapter seventeen

IMC: **public relations, sponsorship, and corporate advertising**

I f you are reading this book there is no doubt that you not only have heard of Facebook, MySpace, Twitter, and Youtube, chances are you are using them on a daily basis. In Chapter 13 we talked about how social media can give life to simple advertising campaigns, but it can also elevate or crush a company's brand. In this book we have detailed countless times how much the Internet has changed advertising, and we have even highlighted its effect on how brands communicate. One aspect of the Internet is again rapidly changing the way companies interact with their customers.

Social media has made possible connections that brands have only dreamed of in the past. For many years marketers sought ways to build deeper, long-lasting relationships with their customer base, and now it's as easy as being "fanned" or "followed." With this great ease also comes peril. As easy as it is to connect with your consumers, it is even easier for consumers to broadcast their ire toward a company. In a recent case, the makers of Motrin publicly apologized on their Web site for offending moms with an ad campaign. The ill feelings started when some influential mommy-bloggers reacted to a line of copy that depicted a mom carrying her baby in a baby sling as "wearing her baby." This simple statement sent shockwaves through the blogosphere and promoted a boycott of the pain reliever. This type of reaction frightens brand managers about social media. A consumer response that savvy public relations professionals could once handle now becomes their responsibility.

At the same time, though, only now can brands get instant feedback about how
continued on p. 436

LEARNING OBJECTIVES

LO1 Distinguish between advertising and public relations.

LO2 Describe the key tasks of public relations practitioners.

LO3 Explain the potential benefits and drawbacks of sponsorships in an IMC plan.

LO4 Discuss the functions of corporate advertising.

435

continued from p. 435

their communications are actually affecting their customer base. In years past it would have taken extensive testing, research, and media dollars to find out that your advertising didn't work or didn't resonate. And in most of those cases, why it didn't work could never be known. This instant-feedback mechanism is of course both good and bad, but it has made brands rethink how they approach customers, how they staff their marketing, PR and customer service departments, and how they handle employees who want to contribute to the social space.

By and large, today, each company has corporate guidelines on how to utilize social media and policies on employee involvement, including termination clauses around the type of content posted.

Companies like Dell and Starbucks have wholeheartedly embraced the social media space and have asked their customers to help them create more customer-centered companies. Dell employs a social/community team of 30 to 40 customer service experts, marketing professionals, and PR professionals. Comcast, in an effort to change customer perceptions, has dedicated a person to do nothing but manage Comcastcares on Twitter.com. This customer service expert answers people's questions—from queries about bills to technical questions, in 140 characters of text or less.

Social media have given rise to an ecosystem of companies that help marketers and advertisers understand what is being said about them. They have also created new jobs inside marketing departments and advertising agencies to help harness the power of the social Web. And it has helped consumers find companies that meet their requirements. Sites like Tripadvisor and Yelp help users find companies and/or services based on reviews and ratings. Both of these sites now also allow the companies to speak back to the reviewers. If you owned a hotel and someone posted a bad review about their stay, Tripadvisor (after you sign up as the hotel manager) will alert you of the posting and allow you to comment and engage in a dialogue on Tripadvisor.com. This helps companies quickly deal with issues before they become problems.

From public relations, to customer service, to marketing, and ultimately to promotion or advertising, social media give brands opportunities they have only previously wished for. As the adage goes, "be careful what you wish for"; sometimes such clarity can be daunting. But if leveraged appropriately, the positives of social media far outweigh the negatives as an ongoing part of the marketing and advertising mix. ■

LO1 Distinguish between advertising and public relations.

THE ROLE OF PUBLIC RELATIONS

The primary role of public relations is to manage a company's reputation and help build public support for its activities. Today's business environment has become so competitive that public approval can no longer be assumed; it must be earned continuously.[1]

public relations (PR) The management function that focuses on the relationships and communications that individuals and organizations have with other groups (called *publics*) for the purpose of creating mutual goodwill.

publics In PR terminology, employees, customers, stockholders, competitors, suppliers, or the general population of customers are all considered among an organization's publics.

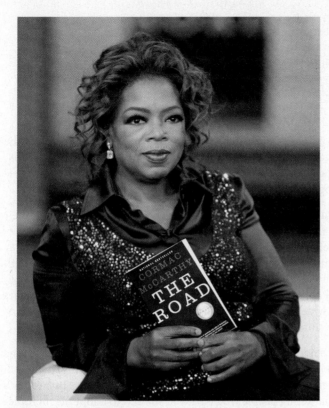

Oprah Winfrey's influence with her millions of regular viewers is undeniable. For example, the host's decision to include a new title in her book club inevitably results in a surge of sales. Oprah possesses the characteristics that every marketer desires in a persuasive source: she is credible (trustworthy and an expert) and she is attractive.

The term *public relations* is widely misunderstood and misused. Part of the confusion is due to the fact that public relations covers a very broad area. Depending on the context and one's point of view, it can be a concept, a profession, a management function, or a practice. For our purposes, we define **public relations (PR)** as the management function that focuses on the relationships and communications that individuals and organizations have with other groups for the purpose of creating mutual goodwill.

As we've already discussed, every company, organization, or government body has relationships with groups of people who are affected by what it does or says. They may be employees, customers, stockholders, competitors, suppliers, legislators, or the community in which the organization resides. Marketing professionals refer to these people as *stakeholders* because they all have some vested interest in the company's actions. In PR terminology, each of these groups is considered one of the organization's **publics**, and the goal of PR is to develop and maintain goodwill with most, if not all, of its publics. Failure to do so may mean loss of customers and revenues, time lost dealing with complaints or lawsuits, and loss of respect (which weakens the organization's brand equity as well

as its ability to secure financing, make sales, and expand).

A company's publics change constantly. After being acquired by Unilever, Ben & Jerry's Homemade Ice Cream encountered previously silent publics. Criticism of the company appears to have increased after the acquisition. The Center for Science in the Public Interest (CSPI) accused Ben & Jerry's of misleading the public by claiming that some of its products were "all-natural" when they in fact contained hydrogenated oils and artificial flavors. CSPI called upon the FDA to take action against the company.[2] Ben & Jerry's hedged response was that the term "all-natural" had various definitions in the food industry, but that it would work with natural food organizations on the issue.[3] In 2003, the company voluntarily recalled pints of its Karamel Sutra ice cream that contained peanuts not mentioned on the label. After receiving one illness complaint about this common food allergen, the recall went forward, with CEO Yves Couette stating that "Our primary concern is always for the health and safety of our consumers."[4]

Because of the powerful effect of public opinion, companies and organizations must consider the breadth of the impact of their actions. This is especially true in times of crisis, emergency, or disaster. But it also holds true for major policy decisions: changes in management or pricing, labor negotiations, the introduction of new products, or changes in distribution methods. Each decision affects different groups in different ways. Effective public relations can channel groups' opinions toward mutual understanding and positive outcomes.

> While PR offers greater credibility, advertising offers precision and control.

In short, the goals of public relations are to improve public opinion, build goodwill, and establish and maintain a satisfactory reputation for the organization. PR efforts may rally public support, obtain public understanding, or simply respond to inquiries. Well-executed public relations is an ongoing process that molds good long-term relationships and plays an important role in relationship marketing and integrated communications.[5]

The Difference between Advertising and Public Relations

Since they both use the media to create awareness or to influence markets or publics, advertising and public relations are similar—but they're not the same. Advertising reaches its audience through media the advertiser pays for. It appears just as the advertiser designed it, with the advertiser's bias built in. Knowing this, the public views ads with some skepticism or ignores them outright. So, in an integrated marketing communications program, advertising is rarely the best vehicle for building credibility.

Many public relations communications, like publicity, are not openly sponsored or paid for. People receive these communications in the form of news articles, editorial interviews, or feature stories after the messages have been reviewed and edited—filtered—by the media. Since the public thinks such messages are coming from the media rather than a company, it trusts them more readily. For building credibility, therefore, public relations is usually the better approach.

However, while advertising is carefully placed to gain particular reach and frequency objectives, PR is less precise. Public relations objectives are not as easy to quantify. In fact, the results gained from public relations activities depend greatly on the experience and skill of the people executing them and the relationship they have with the press. But PR can go only so far. Editors won't run the same story over and over. An ad's memorability, however, comes from repetition. While PR activities may offer greater credibility, advertising offers precision and control.

Advertising and PR in the Eyes of Practitioners

Another major difference between public relations and advertising is the orientation of professional practitioners. Advertising professionals see *marketing* as the umbrella process

companies use to determine what products and services the market needs and how to distribute and sell them. To advertising professionals, advertising and public relations are marketing tools used to promote sales.

Public relations professionals take a different view. With their background often in journalism rather than marketing, they believe *public relations* should be the umbrella process. They think companies should use PR to maintain relationships with all publics, including consumers. As *Inside PR* magazine says, "Public relations is a management discipline that encompasses a wide range of activities, from *marketing and advertising* to investor relations and government affairs."[6]

To date, though, few companies are structured with a public relations orientation; most are still marketing oriented, perhaps due to marketing's bottom-line focus. But today's marketing people would be well advised to adopt the multiple-stakeholder approach and relationship consciousness that PR people bring to the table. Moreover, in times of crisis, the candid, open-information orientation of PR is invariably the better perspective to adopt. Fortunately, with the growing interest in relationship marketing, two-way interactivity, and IMC, companies are finally beginning to embrace a public relations philosophy. Exhibit 17–1 shows some of the PR industry's largest firms.

When PR activities are used for marketing purposes, the term **marketing public relations (MPR)** is often used. In support of marketing, public relations activities can raise awareness, inform and educate, improve understanding, build trust, make friends, give people reasons or permission to buy, and create a climate of consumer acceptance—usually better than advertising.[7] Marketing strategists Al and Laura Ries believe the best way to build a brand is through publicity—a PR activity. They cite numerous examples of leading companies that achieved their cachet with relatively little advertising but extensive publicity: Starbucks, The Body Shop, and Walmart, to name a few.[8]

In an integrated marketing communications program, advertising and MPR need to be closely coordinated. Many ad agencies now have PR departments for this very purpose. And many companies now have communications departments that manage both advertising and PR.

▼**EXHIBIT 17–1** 2009 Worldwide Fees of Independent Public Relations Firms with Major U.S. Operations.

Rank	Firm	Net Fees ($000)	Employees
1.	Edelman, New York	$440,110	3,143
2.	Apco Worldwide, Wash., DC	100,300	507
3.	Ruder Finn Group, New York	89,175	564
4.	Text 100 Global PR, San Francisco	48,600	454
5.	Schwartz Communications, Waltham, MA	24,905	177
6.	ICR, Westport, CT	22,011	88
7.	Regan Communications Group, Boston	19,859	45
8.	Gibbs & Soell, New York	16,888	94
9.	Allison & Partners, San Francisco	14,662	80
10.	Cooney/Waters Group, New York	12,344	38

Copyright © 1998–2010 J.R. O'Dwyer Company, Inc.

L02 Describe the key tasks of public relations practitioners.

THE PUBLIC RELATIONS JOB

The public relations job comprises a variety of activities, from crisis communications to fundraising. And PR practitioners use many tools besides press conferences and news releases.

PR Planning and Research

The first function of a PR practitioner is to plan and execute the public relations program. Part of this task may be integrated with the company's marketing efforts (for instance, product publicity), but the PR person typically takes a broader view. He or she must prepare an overall public relations program for the whole organization.

Because public opinion is so important, the PR person must constantly monitor, measure, and analyze changes in attitudes among a variety of publics. A common form of public relations research is **opinion sampling** using techniques discussed in Chapter 6: shopping center or phone interviews, focus groups, analysis of incoming mail, and field reports. Some advertisers set up toll-free phone lines and invite consumer feedback.

The PR practitioner analyzes the organization's relationships with its publics; evaluates people's attitudes and opinions toward the organization; assesses how company policies and actions relate to different publics; determines PR objectives and strategies; develops and implements a mix of

PR activities, integrating them whenever possible with the firm's other communications; and solicits feedback to evaluate effectiveness.

Reputation Management

One of the principal tasks of public relations is to manage the standing of the firm with various publics. **Reputation management** is the name of this long-term strategic process.[9] PR practitioners employ a number of strategies and tactics to help them manage their firm's or client's reputation, including publicity and press agentry, crisis communications management, and community involvement.

Publicity and Press Agentry Many public relations professionals focus primarily on generating news and placing it in the media for their companies or clients. A major activity of public relations, **publicity** is the generation of news about a person, product, or service that appears in print or electronic

SACRAMENTO BUSINESS JOURNAL | JANUARY 4, 2008

sacramento.bizjournals.com

Coffee roaster gets buzz with cash infusion

Woodland company has a patented method to make lower-acid coffee

MARK ANDERSON | STAFF WRITER

A Woodland coffee company with a low-acid product got a jolt of $700,000 from a Bay Area investment group.

Puroast Coffee Co. Inc. closed a second-stage seed round of funding from Keiretsu Forum, an angel investment group.

The money will be used to expand production and marketing of Puroast, an organic coffee with half the acid of regular coffee, Puroast spokeswoman Jessica Rea said. The coffee purchased with "fair trade" practices, which guarantee a living wage to the small farmers who grow it.

The company raised equity and debt financing, and it has options for additional financing in the first quarter of the year.

Kerry Sachs, Puroast's founder and chief executive, is an agricultural engineer. He used South American methods to roast coffee beans that produce a coffee with half the acid of regular roasts. The method is patented and considered by the company to be proprietary, Rea said.

Roasters take acute care in regulating the temperature during the roasting process, which uses wood chips. The roasting is done in Woodland, and the coffee is distributed across the country. So far, the West Coast is its largest market, but East Coast states are also catching on, Rea said.

Puroast's claims of low acid were corroborated by research done at the University of California Davis, she said.

Puroast's investors think there is a

bright future for the beverage company. In 2006, Americans spent almost $1 billion for over-the-counter antacids, and they paid more than $13 billion on prescribed medications for digestive acid problems.

"Puroast had all the attributes of a great investment opportunity for Keiretsu Forum members with its well-defined market, solid management team and sales in a number of supermarket chains," said Barry Hotchkies, Keiretsu due-diligence team leader. He and another forum member took seats on Puroast's advisory board.

Puroast is selling its coffee at locations including Ralph's, Kroger's, Albertson's, Sweet Bay and Save Mart stores.

Keiretsu is a structured group of investors who work together to perform due diligence on investment decisions and then decide individually whether to invest.

In the Puroast deal, four West Coast chapters decided to make the investment. The accredited private-equity investors include individual angel investors,

Puroast Coffee Co. Inc. received $700,000 in funding from investors for its low-acid coffee.

PHOTO COURTESY OF PUROAST COFFEE CO. INC.

venture capital companies and corporate and institutional investors.

The forum was founded in the East Bay, and it has a worldwide network of people looking at deals, doing due diligence and making investments.

There are Northern California chapters in San Francisco, East Bay, Silicon Valley and North Bay. There are also four chapters in Southern California, two chapters in Washington state, and one each in Idaho, Colorado, Beijing, London and Barcelona.

manderson@bizjournals.com | 916-558-7874

A company will often use publicity to enhance or defend their firm's reputation. Here, the Puroast Coffee Company (www.puroast.com) used the press to announce its receipt of $700,000 in venture funding from Keiretsu Forum (www.k4forum.com), an investment group. This publicity will help to promote Puroast to grocery retailers and the general public and Keiretsu to other companies that might need venture funding.

media. Companies employ this activity either for marketing purposes or to enhance the firm's reputation.

Some people think of publicity as "free" because the media don't charge to run it (they also don't guarantee they'll use it). This is a misconception, though. Someone still gets paid to write the release and coordinate with the press. However, as a marketing communications vehicle, publicity often offers a considerably greater return on money invested than other communications activities. A large ad campaign might require an investment of 5 to 20 percent of sales; a major publicity program, only 1 to 2 percent.

To attract media attention, publicity must be *newsworthy*. Typical publicity opportunities include new-product introductions, awards, company sales and earnings, major new contracts, mergers, retirements, and speeches by company executives. Sometimes publicity is unfavorable and accrues unintentionally, such as when peanuts were found in Ben & Jerry's ice cream. And since publicity can originate from any source, it may be difficult—or impossible—to control. In IMC terms, unintentional publicity is an *unplanned message*.

The planning and staging of events to generate publicity is called **press agentry**. Press agentry helps to bring attention to new products or services or to portray their organizations favorably. For print media, the publicity person deals with editors and feature writers. For broadcast media, he or she deals with program directors, assignment editors, or news editors. Successful PR practitioners develop and maintain close, cordial relations with their editorial contacts. An MPR professional practicing IMC sees the press as an important *public,* and writers and editors as important *stakeholders*.

Crisis Communications Management

One of the most important public relations tasks for any corporation is **crisis management**. Brand value can be quickly destroyed if "damage control" is not swift and thorough. For example, Martha Stewart's profitable marketing persona quickly became a liability in 2002, when her involvement in an

insider-trading scheme surfaced. (She was later tried and sentenced to a prison term.) Even though her company, Martha Stewart Living Omnimedia, immediately took steps to distance itself from its founder's legal troubles by removing her name from some products and publications, its stock value and revenues both dropped by more than 30 percent between 2003 and 2004.[10]

But the classic case of exemplary crisis communications management was Johnson & Johnson's handling of a product-tampering episode in 1982. Several people died when a criminal laced bottles of J&J's Extra-Strength Tylenol with cyanide on retail shelves. The moment they received the news, management strategists at J&J and McNeil Products (the J&J subsidiary that markets Tylenol) formulated three stages of action:

1. Identify the problem and take immediate corrective action. J&J strategists got information from the police, FBI, FDA, and press; identified the geographic area affected; corrected rumors; and immediately withdrew the product from the marketplace.

2. Actively cooperate with authorities in the investigation. Johnson & Johnson was proactive. It helped the FBI and other law enforcement agencies generate leads and investigate security at its plants, and it offered a $100,000 reward.

3. Quickly rebuild the Tylenol name and capsule line, including Regular Strength capsules, which were recalled, too. Although J&J believed the poisoning had taken place at the retail end of the chain, it first made sure that the tampering hadn't occurred at McNeil. The company's two capsule production lines were shut down, and dog teams were brought in to search for cyanide.

The insatiable appetite of the news media plus a flood of inquiries from anxious consumers put J&J's PR people under enormous pressure. All communications between the media and the company were channeled through the corporate communications department. All customer, trade, and government communications were coordinated within the company. This way, J&J maintained open, clear, consistent, legal, and credible communications and avoided rumors, political backbiting, and corporate defensiveness.

In the first 48 hours after the news broke, phone calls to Johnson & Johnson and McNeil were nonstop. In the basement at McNeil, a bank of phones usually used for sales was staffed by employees who were briefed on what to say, what not to say, and where to refer tough questions.

At the same time, management and employees had to be informed, authorities contacted, and many others notified. J&J and McNeil public relations managers and staff had to plan, coordinate, and supervise this enormous task.

As infrequent as disasters are, there is no more important activity for PR professionals and public information officers than crisis communications management—especially those in highly sensitive fields such as airlines, government agencies, the military, law enforcement, chemical and oil companies, and public utilities.

Since the Tylenol incident, many companies in normally nonsensitive industries have prepared crisis management plans. The manner in which a company handles communications

The social mission sections of Ben & Jerry's country-specific Web sites reflect both global concerns and local initiatives. Each site shows the company's support for world peace, hormone-free dairy products, and blood donation drives. In Spain, the company also sponsors a homeless shelter for the mentally ill and a group that fights pet abandonment. The Ben & Jerry's Web site for Sweden links to a Swedish organization devoted to child welfare in Benin, West Africa.

> " There is no more important activity for PR professionals than crisis communications management. "

during emergencies or catastrophes will determine to a great extent how the public responds to the news. When corporations have no plans for coping with a crisis, the resulting press coverage can be disastrous. Experts on crisis management encourage all companies to follow J&J's example by being open and candid. Withholding information or evading questions inevitably backfires, as many politicians have learned.

Attitudes toward a former crisis can soften over time. Ben & Jerry's offered a quick, apologetic, and sincere response when traces of nuts were found in pints of ice cream that did not have warning labels. In 2004, after the negative press and consumer skepticism had calmed somewhat, a tongue-in-cheek Ben & Jerry's poster appeared in London tube cars, "warning" consumers that some ice cream flavors "May Contain Nuts: Lots of Them."

Community Involvement The goal of **community involvement** is to develop a dialogue between the company and the community.[11] This is best done by having company

officers, management, and employees contribute to the community's social and economic development. Every community offers opportunities for corporate involvement: civic and youth groups, charitable fundraising drives, cultural or recreational activities, and so on. A company should ideally adopt one program relevant to its expertise and focus its *mission marketing* activities. The PR department may help set up such programs and publicize them to the community (see Commercial Break 17–A).

Other Public Relations Activities

In addition to planning and reputation management, public relations professionals are often involved in activities such as public affairs and lobbying, speechwriting, fundraising and membership drives, creation of publications, and special-events management.

Public Affairs and Lobbying Organizations often need to deal with elected officials, regulatory and legislative bodies,

Since its introduction in the mid-1980s, environmental advertising has become a significant aspect of marketing. Advertisers saw the consumer desire for environmentally safe products and tried to meet the demand as quickly as possible. Many advertisers embraced genuine concern for the environment. But it didn't take long for consumers to catch on to the fact that some companies were making false claims, using such vague terms as *environmentally friendly* and *green*.

In a short time, consumers grew wary of the environmental appeal and advertisers reacted by reducing its emphasis. To avoid future trouble, many companies waited for state and federal governments to define terms and provide legal guidelines. Over the past decade, the Federal Trade Commission (FTC) has established rules and guidelines, while several states have adopted a set of laws setting definitions for terms like *ozone friendly, biodegradable,* and *recycled.* In 1995, California's Truth in Environmental Advertising law was enacted. It was shortly repealed and introduced again in 1997 without success.

Presently, there are no federal laws governing what a seller can say about a product. The FTC, in cooperation with the Environmental Protection Agency (EPA), has developed new guidelines for advertisers, to ensure that their environmental marketing claims do not mislead consumers. These Guidelines for the Use of Environmental Advertising Claims carry no force of law and compliance is voluntary.

Several companies and organizations act as intermediaries between advertisers and consumers regarding environmental claims. Scientific Certification Systems (SCS) (www.scscertified.com), for instance, verifies claims of recycled content in products. It uses an environmental report card, which measures a product's total environmental impact.

Green Seal (www.greenseal.org), an independent, nonprofit organization, promotes the manufacture and sale of environmentally responsible consumer products. It awards a Green Seal of Approval to products that cause less harm to the environment than other similar products. Founded in 1994, Green Seal "focuses on the measure of environmental damage that scientists have found to be most important in certain product categories," says Norman Dean, president.

Today's new marketing sensitivity toward the environment and social consciousness focuses on consumer purchasing behavior. Seventy-nine percent of Americans consider themselves environmentalists, 83 percent say they have changed their shopping habits to help protect the environment, and 67 percent say they would be willing to pay 5 to 10 percent more for environmentally friendly products. The data, however, are contradicted by more recent studies that reveal that people in America do not actually buy the products they claim to prefer. Even though studies show a high concern for the environment, the public lacks a behavior consistent with such concerns. Researchers believe that this attitude–behavior gap exists when the competitive advantage of green products is overcome by factors of price, quality, and convenience.

But in an increasingly competitive marketplace, firms must ultimately benefit from their green actions. A new environmental management tool called SPINE was developed to help industries achieve environmental recognition. SPINE makes it possible for customers to verify marketers' environmental claims by following a product's manufacturing process through every step.

Even with organizations such as Scientific Certification Systems and Green Seal, and reference tools such as SPINE, it is still a major challenge to get businesses and consumers to understand the value of green advertising, especially when no stringent regulations are in effect. Today, the consumer can only speculate how "environmentally friendly" a company actually is. Thinking about the future, either through regulation or voluntary action, companies will have to provide consumers with more information about the environmental friendliness of their products so customers decide for themselves how well a product suits their needs.

Applying the Breaks

1. Imagine you are marketing a new product that sells for $1.25 and is environmentally safe. Would you spend thousands of dollars for a Green Seal on your impulse product if research indicates that consumers are ambivalent toward such environmentally safe goods? Explain.

2. Imagine that you just made manufacturing changes to your product so that it is now easily recyclable. How would you publicize these changes?

and various community groups—the realm of **public affairs**. Public affairs usually requires a specialist. Many experts think PR and public affairs should become more integrated to combine the skills and policy expertise of the specialist with the PR person's media and community relations savvy.

Lobbying refers to informing government officials and persuading them to support or thwart administrative action or legislation in the interests of some client. Every organization is affected by the government, so lobbying is big business.

Speechwriting Because company officials often have to speak at stockholder meetings, conferences, or conventions, PR practitioners often engage in **speechwriting**. They are also frequently responsible for making all the arrangements for

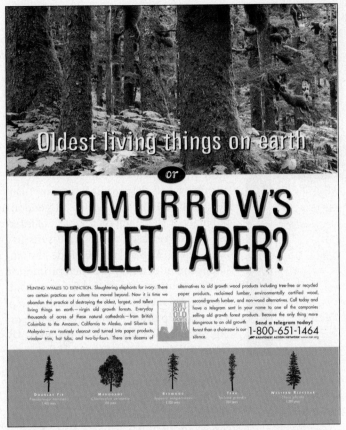

To meet demanding operating budgets, nonprofit organizations often devote a significant portion of their advertising to raising funds. The Rainforest Action Network (www.ran.org) ran this ad to create awareness of the destruction of virgin old-growth forests.

speaking opportunities and developing answers for questions company representatives are likely to be asked. Since public relations people may sometimes represent their employers at special events, press conferences, and interviews, they too should be articulate public speakers.

participation. In the process, the company PR people may work closely with the advertising department or agency to create ads promoting the particular cause or to publicize the company's involvement with the cause in product ads.

Publications Public relations people prepare many of a company's communications materials: news releases and media kits; booklets, leaflets, pamphlets, brochures, manuals, and books; letters, inserts, and enclosures; annual reports; posters, bulletin boards, and exhibits; audiovisual materials; and position papers. Here again, they may work with the advertising department or the agency to produce these materials. The advertising people need to keep the company's overall positioning strategy in mind while trying to help accomplish the particular PR objectives.

Social Media As with all areas of advertising, the Internet has transformed the way we approach business and our communication to consumers. However, for PR the world seems to be flipped upside down. With the advent of social media and the rise in popularity of blogging and tweeting, staying on top of who is writing about what is a full-time job. It used to be that a PR professional would have to know a score of people from each industry; nowadays that number is exponentially bigger. However,

> [With the advent of social media, staying on top of who is writing about what is a full-time job.]

Fundraising and Membership Drives A public relations person may be responsible for soliciting money for a nonprofit organization or for a cause the company deems worthwhile, such as the United Way or a political action committee (PAC).

Charitable organizations, labor unions, professional societies, trade associations, and other groups rely on membership fees or contributions. The PR specialist must communicate to potential contributors or members the goals of the organization and may integrate promotional tie-ins to publicize the drive or encourage

with the bad comes the good, and the clarity that comes from social media allows PR professionals to stay on top of any trends and deal with them before they become brand epidemics. With a good social media strategy, PR professionals can help get influential people to showcase their client's products as they launch, keeping early adopters and loyalists abreast of new developments before the advertising hits.

Corporate Blogs Maintaining and managing a **corporate blog** can help address important concerns, introduce

Public Relations Tools

The communications tools at the PR person's disposal vary widely, from news releases and photos to audiovisual materials and even advertising. We'll discuss some of the more common ones briefly.

new products or services, and maintain a dialogue between a company and its publics. My Ad Campaign 17–A, "Corporate Blogging," provides some guidelines for using this public relations activity.

Special-Events Management

The sponsorship and management of special events is a rapidly growing field. In fact, it has become such an important topic that we devote the next major section of this chapter to it, following our discussion of PR tools.

Zappos has built its company using social media. Employees are encouraged to use Twitter, Facebook, and Youtube. Here is its company blog written by a large collection of employees.

News Releases and Press Kits

A **news release** (or **press release**), the most widely used PR tool, consists of one or more typed sheets of information (usually 8½ by 11 inches) issued to generate publicity or shed light on a subject of interest. News releases cover time-sensitive hard news. Topics may include the announcement of a new product, promotion of an executive, an unusual contest, landing of a major contract, or establishment of a scholarship fund. For pointers in preparing releases, see My Ad Campaign 17–B, "How to Write a News Release."

A **press kit** (or **media kit**) supports the publicity of special events such as press conferences, grand openings, and trade shows. It includes a basic fact sheet of

Corporate Blogging [17–A]

As mentioned in the chapter opening vignette, most corporations have guidelines for blogging. Here is a set of marketing-related guidelines that every corporation should think about if they intend on using blogging for a marketing tool.

• **Know the environment.** What are people saying about you and your products? Venture out into the Web and see what happens when you type your company name into Google or visit popular blogs that deal with your company's product category.

• **Determine what you hope to accomplish.** What is your purpose? Why have you started the blog? To address rumors? Share company news? Inform customers about new products? Develop a corporate personality? Having clear objectives will make decisions about what and when to blog much easier.

• **Practice, practice, practice.** Do a trial run. Blogging is time-consuming, sometimes difficult, and a different kind of activity for many organizations. Smart companies generate initial blog posts internally until it is clear that the tactic will be useful and rewarding.

• **Remember that it's a two-way street.** Learn to share control. Blogs without comments have minimal value, but with comments comes criticism. Smart companies value input from critics at their blogs because it offers them an opportunity to respond and educate.

• **Live up to the commitment.** Attention to blogs withers if postings aren't regular.

• **Offer value.** Providing information that publics can't find elsewhere gives people a reason to visit your blog or subscribe to feeds.

• **Ask if you have readers.** Is your public suitable for blogging? Not every market contains people who read blogs. If yours doesn't, you're wasting time and resources. Search for other blogs related to your industry or product and locate secondary information on your target market's use of the Web to find out whether your blog might make a difference.

• **Avoid hype and puffery.** The online community has a different personality than that of people who rely on traditional media. Web users are suspicious of hype and can be critical when they sense they are being preached to or misled.

• **Monitor the one place everyone visits**—its name is Wikipedia. If your company or product is mentioned there it is important to monitor, and occasionally correct, what is posted.

• **Use blogging as one piece of the puzzle.** Blogging can be an effective way to reach and respond to your publics. But it is rarely a stand-alone tactic. Smart companies make it a part of their overall IMC and public relations plans.

information about the event, a program or schedule of activities, and a list of the participants and their biographical data. The kit also contains a news story about the event for the broadcast media, news and feature stories for the print media, and any pertinent photos and brochures.

Photos Photos of events, products in use, new equipment, or newly promoted executives can lend credence or interest to a dull news story. In fact, a photo tells the story faster. Photos should be high quality and need little or no explanation. Typed captions should describe the photo and accurately identify the people shown.

my ad campaign

Feature Articles Many publications, especially trade journals, run **feature articles** (soft news) about companies, products, or services. They may be written by a PR person, the publication's staff, or a third party (such as a freelance business writer). As an

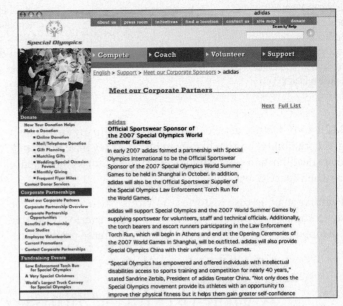

This electronic press release announced the role adidas played as the official sportswear sponsor of the Special Olympics. adidas hoped to receive favorable publicity for their role in this event.

How to Write a News Release [17–B]

The Role of the News Release

The news release is an effective tool for publicizing information for several reasons. It helps to protect the publicist and the client from being misquoted. It permanently records the preferred word usage, specific terms, key phrasing, and unique details.

Its standardized format also speeds up the process. It eliminates debate over how to format the information, highlights the data most needed by the recipient (contact person's name and telephone, date, etc.), and spells out the source and topic of the story.

The news release also simplifies dissemination by providing a form that is easily reproduced and transferred (e-mail, fax, postal mail, etc.) and by ensuring that all recipients receive the same message.

Preparing the News Release

The news release follows a format generally accepted throughout the news industry.

- **Double-space the text and use wide margins.**
- **At the top of the page (left or right side) place the name and phone number of your contact person.** If your page is not pre-printed with your company's name and address, add it below the contact person. Finally, write FOR IMMEDIATE RELEASE or TO BE RELEASED AFTER [date].
- **Write a headline that signals the key fact or issue of the story.** For example, TECHCO PRESIDENT SPEAKS TO BAY CITY LIONS CLUB THURSDAY.
- **Place the most important information first.** The editors may shorten your news release by cutting from the bottom.
- **Lead sentence.** The lead sentence is the most important. Keep it focused strictly on who, what, where, when, why, and how. For example, "Techco President Ralph J. Talk will address the Bay City Lions Club at 8 p.m., Thursday, September 16, 2004."
- **Body text.** Add directly related support information. "Mr. Talk's speech will be 'Technology in Albania.' Mr. Talk served five years as assistant to the president of the Albania Travel Association."
- **Final text.** Fill in background details. "Mr. Talk was born on April 30, 1956, and is married to Alice Johnson of Bay City. They have two children. Mr. Talk is a board member of the Bay City Little League."
- **Keep the text as factual, direct, and short as possible.**
- **Carefully proof your copy.**

Etiquette

- **Don't call to see whether the editor received your release.** Editors don't like to be pressured. Don't ask for tearsheets. An editor has little time to send you a copy. Don't promise you'll advertise if the item is published; the editor will be offended at the suggestion that news can be bought. If the article is run, send a thank-you letter to the editor.

Mailing List

- **Prepare a list of local publications.** You may want to group them so that you mail out appropriate news releases to publications that are likely to use that type of information. Refrain from sending mass mailings. Update your list regularly, because editors change and offices move.
- **Ascertain in advance if the editors on your list prefer to have news releases sent by e-mail or postal mail.**

MPR tool, feature articles can give the company or product great credibility. Editors like them because they have no immediate deadline and can be published at the editor's convenience or when space is available.

Features may be case histories, how-to's (such as how to use the company's product), problem-solving scenarios (how one customer uses the company's product to increase production), or state-of-the-art technology updates. Other formats include roundups of what's happening in a specific industry and editorials (such as a speech or essay by a company executive on a current issue).

Printed Materials

Printed materials are the most popular tools used by public relations professionals.[12] They may be

> A well-produced house organ can do a great deal to motivate employees and appeal to customers.

House organs may be sent to customers to promote goodwill, increase sales, or influence public opinion. SMUD, a Sacramento, California, energy provider, encloses this two-page newsletter in its monthly mailings. It provides public interest stories, important news, and energy-saving ideas in an appealing and easy-to-read format.

brochures or pamphlets about the company or its products, letters to customers, inserts or enclosures that accompany monthly statements, the annual report to stockholders, other reports, or house organs.

A **house organ** is a publication about happenings and policies at the company. An internal house organ is for employees only. External house publications go to company-connected people (customers, stockholders, suppliers, and dealers) or to the general public. They may take the form of a newsletter, tabloid-size newspaper, magazine, or even a periodic **e-zine** (a magazine published online or sent by e-mail). Their purpose is to promote goodwill, increase sales, or influence public opinion. A well-produced house organ can do a great deal to motivate employees and appeal to customers. However, writing, printing, and distributing can be expensive—and very time-consuming.

Posters, Exhibits, and Bulletin Boards

Posters can be used internally to stress safety, security, reduction of waste, and courtesy. Externally, they can impart product information, corporate philosophy, or other news of interest to consumers.

Companies use **exhibits** to describe the organization's history, present new products, show how products are made, or explain future plans. Exhibits are often prepared for local fairs, colleges and universities, and trade shows.

Internally, the public relations staff often uses **bulletin boards** to announce new equipment, new products, meetings, promotions, construction plans, and recreation news to employees. Many companies now maintain an **intranet** site where they can post their internal bulletin boards.

Audiovisual Materials Slides, films, filmstrips, CDs, and videocassettes are all forms of **audiovisual materials** and may be used for training, sales, or public relations. Considered a form of *corporate advertising,* nontheatrical or sponsored films (developed for public relations reasons) are often furnished without charge to movie theaters, organizations, and special groups, particularly schools and colleges. Classic examples include *Why Man Creates,* produced for Kaiser Aluminum, and Mobil Oil's *A Fable,* starring the famous French mime Marcel Marceau.

Many PR departments provide **video news releases (VNRs)**—news or feature stories prepared by a company and offered free to TV stations, which may use the whole video or just segments. Video news releases are somewhat controversial. Critics see them as subtle commercials or even propaganda and object when stations run the stories without disclosing that they came from a public relations firm, not the station's news staff.

check yourself ✓

1. What tools does an organization have to determine how it is viewed by its publics?

2. In what ways has social media affected the PR professional's job?

LO3 Explain the potential benefits and drawbacks of sponsorships in an IMC plan.

SPONSORSHIPS AND EVENTS

In 1984, the owner of a large bicycle shop in the upper Midwest sent some of his mechanics to a local bicycle race sponsored by a national charity. At the time, his store was doing about $200,000 per year in retail sales, and he wanted to help out the charity while finding out what the racers thought of his and his competitors' businesses.

An unexpected benefit of the company's presence at the race was that participants started showing up in his store. Encouraged by these results, the company now supports more than 100 bicycle events each year and sends staff members to dozens of such events. It has hired a full-time representative to coordinate company involvement in special bicycle events that have the potential of increasing its exposure and business revenue.

In 20 years, the company has gone from a low-key presence at bicycling events, donating a few water bottles embossed with the company's name, to large-scale sponsorship, participating in event registration, providing event participants with workshops on bicycle maintenance, and offering in-store discounts to event participants. Within a week of one event, 30 participants had visited his store. Even better news for the company was that nearly half of the more than 5,000 riders reported purchasing goods from it.

By 1996, the company had revenues of $3 million. The owner attributes much of his success to his sponsorship of bicycle events. In his words, "I support them, and they support us."[13]

The Growth of Sponsorship

Advertising and public relations people get involved in sponsoring many kinds of special events. In fact, sponsorship may be the fastest-growing form of marketing today. It actually embraces two disciplines: sales promotion and public relations. Some sponsorships are designed to create publicity, others to improve public relations through personal contact and affiliation with a worthy cause, and others to immediately improve the sales and bottom line.

A **sponsorship** is a cash or in-kind fee paid to a property (which may be a sports, entertainment, or nonprofit event or organization) in return for access to the exploitable commercial potential associated with that property.[14] In other words, just as advertisers pay a fee to sponsor a program on radio or TV, they may also sign on to sponsor a bike race, an art show or chamber music festival, a fair or exhibition, or the Olympics. The sponsorship fee may be paid in cash or **in kind** (that is, through a donation of goods and services). For instance, if a local TV station signs on as a sponsor of a 10K run, it will typically pay for some part of its sponsorship by providing advertising time for the event.

Cause marketing, a related strategy, is a partnership between a for-profit company and a nonprofit organization, which increases the company's sales while raising money and visibility for the organization's cause. Typically, a portion of the proceeds from the sale of certain products is donated to the cause. For example, Yoplait yogurt's 11th *Save Lids to Save Lives* campaign urged consumers to buy pink-lidded cups of yogurt and mail the lids back. For each lid mailed in, Yoplait donated ten cents to the Susan G. Komen Foundation, up to $1.5 million per year, more than $22 million to date.

While the sponsored event or organization may be nonprofit, sponsorship is not the same as philanthropy. **Philanthropy** is support of a cause without any commercial incentive. Sponsorship is used to achieve commercial objectives. According to *IEG Sponsorship Report*, global spending on partnerships grew 2.1 percent to $44 billion in 2009. For 2010, a 4.5 percent growth is expected in worldwide sponsorship to $46 billion. The largest gains will come from Africa and South America, in part due to activity and interest surrounding South Africa's hosting the 2010 FIFA World Cup. Spending on sponsorships by North American companies in 2009 was $16.5 billion, down for the first time ever from the prior year. However, the 0.6 percent decline was significantly less than the 7.8 percent drop in total North American media spending. The industry forecasts a 3.4 percent increase in sponsorship spending in North America in 2010, projecting the total amount spent to be over $17 billion.[15]

The reasons for the historical pattern of sponsorship growth relate to the economics of marketing we discussed earlier: the escalating costs of traditional advertising media, the fragmentation of media audiences, the growing diversity in leisure activities, and the desire to reach targeted groups of people economically. Initial growth probably came from the tobacco and alcohol companies, which many governments banned from broadcast advertising. Legislation in the United

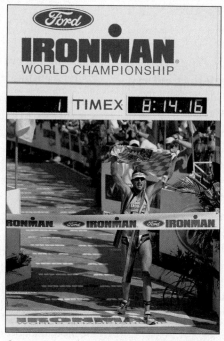

Companies sponsor events or organizations by providing money or other resources that are of value to the sponsored event. This is usually in return for advertising space at the event or as part of the publicity of the event. Ford (www. ford.com) is in its sixth year as the title sponsor of the Ford Ironman Triathlon events (www. ironman.com).

Kingdom, Canada, and the United States threatens to end tobacco sponsorships altogether, but their success at sponsoring sports and other events has shown the way for mainstream advertisers, who are rapidly picking up the slack.

Today, there is greater media coverage of sponsored events—everything from beach volleyball to Texas hold 'em poker to Xtreme games to cultural events. This provides a highly desirable venue for advertisers seeking young, upwardly mobile, educated consumers. Likewise, for transnational marketers, there is growing interest in global events such as World Cup soccer, the Olympics, and the America's Cup yacht race. The international soccer tournament generated $1.6 billion in sponsorship revenue during the 2007–2010 period, up from $584 million between 1999 and 2002. Adidas, Coca-Cola, Emirates Airlines, Hyundai/Kia, Sony, and Visa each paid an estimated annual fee of between $24 million and $44 million for global rights to a broad array of FIFA activities, including World Cup.[16]

Benefits of Sponsorship

In the past, for marketers with limited media alternatives (such as tobacco and alcohol companies), sponsorship simply offered a means of communicating with customers and prospects. Today, the many benefits of sponsorship are well documented and more far-reaching.

Certainly one benefit of sponsorship is that the public approves of it. One study by Roper Starch Worldwide reported that 80 percent of Americans believe corporate sponsorship is an important source of money for professional sports. This is a far higher approval rating than most companies would get for their advertising programs.

More than almost any other marketing communications tool, sponsorships and events have the ability to involve customers, prospects, and other stakeholders. Events are also highly self-selective of their target audience. So marketers that define their audiences tightly can select just those sponsorships that offer the closest fit. A significant benefit is the opportunity to enhance the company's public image or merchandise its positioning through affiliation with an appropriate event. Of course, marketers that sponsor an event simply because it has a large audience are misusing this tool.[17]

Unlike advertising, sponsorships and events can provide face-to-face access to current and potential customers. Depending on the venue, this access can be relatively clean and uncluttered by competition. Sponsoring a seminar, for instance, creates an opportunity for both customer education and brand involvement. In some cases, it even enables product demonstrations and the opportunity to give a personal sales pitch to multiple prospects at a time when they are open to new information.[18] This is especially good for business-to-business marketers.

Also important, but often overlooked, is the effect sponsorship can have on employees. Affiliating with a dynamic event can really boost the morale and pride of the troops in the trenches. And many companies offer attendance at the event (Super Bowl, Olympics, etc.) as an incentive to their sales staff.[19]

Some marketers have discovered that sponsorships can rapidly convert fan loyalty into sales. For example, 74 percent of stock-car racing fans report that they often buy products they see promoted at the racetrack. This is also true for other sports: 58 percent for baseball, 52 percent for tennis, and 47 percent for golf. Finally, sponsorships can be very cost-efficient, providing significant media exposure at a comparatively low cost.

cause marketing
A promotion in which a portion of the proceeds from certain for-profit products are donated to a nonprofit cause. The goal is usually to increase sales for the products while raising money and visibility for the cause.

philanthropy
Support for a cause without any commercial incentive.

The Client Presentation [17–C]

For most of you, the culmination of your project will be a presentation to the class or client that will be judged by the teacher, a group of peers, or local marketing and advertising executives. This presentation is by far the most important aspect of selling your ideas to the "client." It is not always the best idea that wins, and a great presentation can make a bad idea look great.

By now you have spent hours belaboring the who, what, when, and where of your advertising campaign, and now you need to explain why. You should think of your presentation as a Cliff Notes version of your thinking. While going through the process of developing a campaign, it is likely that you did not work sequentially—in fact most advertising processes are done in parallel—but your presentation should illustrate the linear path of thinking that netted your results.

Most advertising presentations utilize PowerPoint, but if you have the resources and the gumption, think about different ways to illustrate your thinking and your ideas. Remember that the more creative your approach, the more (virtual) points you'll receive, assuming of course that the creativity doesn't get in the way of coherent thoughts.

Follow this basic outline and focus on how each section transitions from one to the other:

• Goals and/or objectives of the campaign—What is the campaign trying to achieve?
• Target audience analysis—Who are we planning on speaking to and why?
• SWOT analysis—What are the strengths of the brand, the weaknesses, the opportunities, and the impending threats that factor into our decision-making process?

• Strategic insight(s)—Based on everything above, how are you going to solve the business challenge at hand?
• Creative presentation—Ideas, ideas, ideas. And don't forget to explain why these ideas will help achieve the goals/objectives.
• Media presentation—Where will these ads be placed, and what target and strategy insights led you to choose those vehicles?

The main objective of the presentation is to communicate, in a concise and succinct manner, your ideas, both strategic and tactical. One of the biggest misconceptions is that the strategy should be an ah-ha moment. In truth the strategy should feel more like a statement of the obvious because all of your research has led you down a certain path. If you explain the path appropriately you will receive the proverbial head-nods on the strategy slides. Where the whiz-bang should come in is how you tactically execute the strategy in its creative and placement (media) form.

Be sure to include everyone on your team in the presentation. This will be difficult as some people are better presenters than others, but that's okay because if the ideas and thinking are good they will break through.

Lastly, if you are doing a PowerPoint, hand out copies of the presentation (in color) so the "clients" can follow along and take notes. Props and gadgets are great to use too, so long as they don't distract from the presentation. When Foote, Cone and Belding was pitching kibu.com (a teen girl site) in 2000, it turned one of its conference rooms into a girl's bedroom, setting the mood and ambience for the presentation. It helped the firm win the pitch, because elements of the room were used to highlight the insights into the mindset of the site's main user, a teen girl.

> # COMPANIES DON'T HAVE TO BE BIG MULTINATIONALS TO REAP RICH REWARDS FROM SPONSORSHIPS.

▼ **EXHIBIT 17–2** Top U.S. Sponsors.

Amount	Company	2009 Rank	2008 Rank
$330M–$335M	PepsiCo, Inc.	1	1
$240M–$245M	The Coca-Cola Co.	2	2
$235M–$240M	Nike, Inc.	3	5
$205M–$210M	Anheuser-Busch Cos.	4	4
$180M–$185M	General Motors Corp.	5	3
$175M–$180M	AT&T Inc.	6	6
$150M–$155M	MillerCoors LLC	7	8
$140M–$145M	Toyota Motor Sales U.S.A., Inc.	8	7
$125M–$130M	Ford Motor Co.	9	9
$120M–$125M	Adidas North America, Inc.	10	10

Source: "Who Spent What In '09: IEG's Top Sponsors List," *IEG Sponsorship Report*, April 26, 2010.

on sports events. This includes everything from the Olympics to NASCAR racing to professional athletic leagues. And as we saw from the bicycle shop story, companies don't have to be big multinationals to reap rich rewards from sponsorships—if they do it properly. But without a concerted effort to tie an event to other marketing communications activities like a currently running ad campaign, the money spent on sponsorships can be wasted.[24]

Controversy often swirls around big sports sponsorships. The most controversial practice is **ambush marketing**, a promotional strategy nonsponsors use to capitalize on the popularity or prestige of an event or property by giving the false impression that they are sponsors. Ambush

Anheuser-Busch has been the top U.S. sponsorship spender for the past two years. Other top sponsors are listed in Exhibit 17–2.[20]

Drawbacks of Sponsorship

Like all marketing communications tools, sponsorship has some drawbacks. First, it can be very costly, especially when the event is solely sponsored. For this reason, most companies participate in co-sponsored events, which spreads the cost among several participants.

The problem with co-sponsored events is clutter. Some events have so many sponsors that getting one marketer's message through is extremely difficult. Look again at stock-car racing. How many logos do those cars sport?

Finally, evaluating the effectiveness of a particular sponsorship can be tricky at best—especially since it rarely happens in a vacuum. The problem is in separating the effects of a sponsorship from the effects of other concurrent marketing activities. We'll deal with these issues shortly.

Types of Sponsorship

While there are many, many avenues and events available for sponsorship, IEG Inc. groups most of them into six categories: sports; entertainment, tours, and attractions; causes; the arts; festivals, fairs, and annual events; and associations and membership organizations (see Exhibit 17–3).[21]

Sports Marketing North American corporations spent an estimated $11.3 billion in 2009 on sports marketing sponsorships, as reported by the IEG Sponsorship Report.[22] The most popular of these are motorsports and golf.[23] In fact, the vast majority of sponsorship money, approximately 68 percent, is spent

▼ **EXHIBIT 17–3** Annual sponsorship spending in North America (2009) ($ billions).

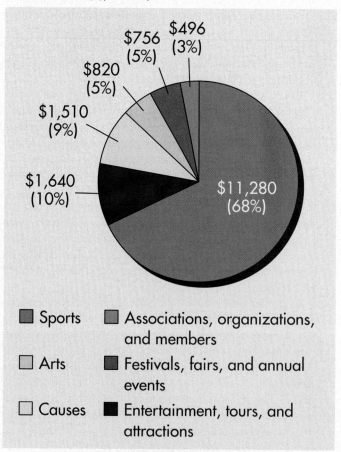

- ■ Sports
- ■ Associations, organizations, and members
- □ Arts
- ■ Festivals, fairs, and annual events
- □ Causes
- ■ Entertainment, tours, and attractions

Source: Annual Sponsorship Forecast, IEG, LLC, Reprinted with permission.

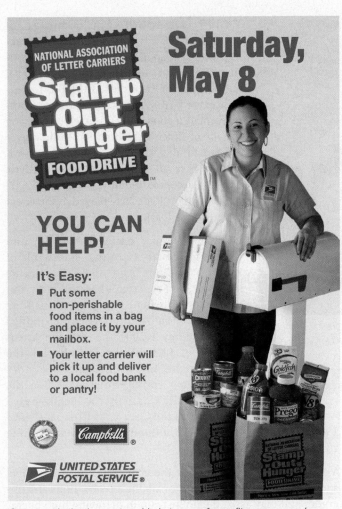

Cause marketing is a partnership between a for-profit company and a nonprofit organization. In this ad, Campbell promotes its connection to the National Association of Letter Carriers (www.nalc.org) annual food drive. Campbell is supporting this initiative by donating one can of soup to Feeding America for each Facebook fan that joins the fight against hunger. The company also sponsors, along with the U.S. Postal Service, a reminder postcard being mailed to more than 120 million homes the week of the drive. Now in its 18th year, Stamp Out Hunger (www.stampouthunger.info) has collected nearly one billion pounds of food, including a record-setting total of 73.4 million pounds in 2009.

marketing techniques, like buying up all the billboard space around an athletic stadium, are often employed by the competitors of the property's official sponsor. Budweiser was the official beer of the 2010 FIFA World Cup South Africa and the only beer company permitted to advertise within the stadium grounds. However, 36 women attended the Denmark vs. Netherlands match wearing orange minidresses that were provided by Dutch beer brewer, Bavaria. They were ejected from the game. Ironically, the women received a lot of media coverage, informing the world that beautiful girls like Dutch soccer and Dutch beer. Bavaria's UK marketing manager Sean Durkan said "Brand awareness has definitely increased. There's a lot more activity on Twitter and social media."[25]

One of the reasons this works is because people are often confused about who the official sponsors actually are—again, the problem is clutter. Just because a company advertises on the Olympic broadcast, for instance, does not mean it is an official sponsor. Ambush marketers take advantage of this.[26]

Entertainment
After sports marketing, the largest area of sponsorship is entertainment, which includes things like concert tours, attractions, and theme parks. For instance, numerous attractions at Disneyland and Disney World are sponsored by major corporations such as GE, AT&T, ARCO, Kodak, and Carnation. In 2009, U.S. companies spent an estimated $1.6 billion on this category.

Brands even sponsor entire tours. The Vans 2006 Warped Tour (subtitled "Presented by Cingular Wireless and Samsung Mobile") has a rotating lineup of 50 bands, with multiple stages and compounds sponsored by other companies, like Eastpak. Booths and tents at the festival provide ample targeted-marketing opportunities for co-sponsors like Wells Fargo, MySpace.com, and Vagrant Records. The "Girlz Garage" offers fashion and makeup, and the PlayStation tent offers the latest games for the PSP.[27]

Causes
Sponsorship of charity events and educational institutions is a tried-and-true PR activity that often fits with the IMC strategy of mission marketing. A number of large corporations (including Chevrolet, AT&T, American Airlines, Pepsi, and Kodak) co-sponsored the Live Aid concerts, for instance. In 2009, marketers spent an estimated $1.51 billion in cause-related sponsorships. Cause marketing will be the fastest growing category of sponsorship spending in 2010, predicts the IEG Sponsorship Report, rising 6.1 percent to $1.61 billion.

A vice president for corporate relations refers to mission marketing activities as "enlightened self-interest." People appreciate the fact that businesses do not really get anything tangible out of them to put in the bank.[28]

Arts
Symphony orchestras, chamber music groups, art museums, and theater companies are always in desperate need of funding. In 2009, sponsors spent an estimated $820 million to support the arts—one of the least funded of the major sponsorship categories. What this means is that this is still a relatively untapped area, and it provides outstanding sponsorship and underwriting opportunities for both national and local firms interested in audiences on the highest end of the income scale.

Festivals, Fairs, and Annual Events
In 1997, IEG surveyed 1,000 members of the International Association of

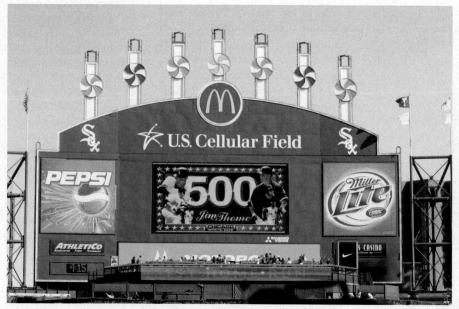

A hot form of sponsorship today is venue marketing, in which corporations pay money to associate their name with a sports arena, theater, or civic center. Often, these companies will invest money in repairs or improvements to existing facilities. In 2003, U.S. Cellular (www.uscellular.com) agreed to pay the Chicago White Sox $68 million over 20 years. In return, the new Comiskey Park was renamed U.S. Cellular Field. Approximately $48 million in renovations were made for the 2003 and 2004 baseball seasons.

Venue Marketing Finally, an area not covered by IEG's report is **venue marketing**, a form of sponsorship that links a sponsor to a physical site such as a stadium, arena, auditorium, or racetrack. In 2000, for instance, the Great American Insurance Company made a good name for itself by offering the city of Cincinnati about $75 million over 30 years for the naming rights to the soon-to-be-built baseball stadium on the Ohio River. The city accepted the offer, and since 2003 the Cincinnati Reds have played at the Great American Ballpark.[29]

Likewise, Denver has Coors Field, and Charlotte, North Carolina, has Bank of America Stadium. And AT&T has put its name on San Francisco's baseball park. But what happens when sponsors with naming rights become a liability? When Enron filed for bankruptcy in 2001, the Houston Astros shelled out $2.1 million to buy back the naming rights to Enron Field. The story had a happy ending however, when the Minute Maid Company, a locally-based subsidiary of the Coca-Cola Company since 1960, paid an estimated $170 million for a 28-year naming rights deal in 2002.

Venue marketing is changing the economics of professional sports. Sponsorships help pay for stadium renovations and upgrades and may assist the home team in defraying high operational costs. Many teams keep the money from their stadium luxury suites, stadium advertising, naming rights, and food and beverage concessions. Under the new economic rules, big stadium revenues are essential to signing big-name players and staying competitive.[30]

Fairs and Expositions. The findings revealed a very healthy, growing environment. The average yearly sponsorship increased a whopping 20 percent over the previous four years, with the biggest growth (30 percent) occurring between 1996 and 1997. Moreover, renewal rates averaged 88 percent! By 2009, sponsorship revenue increased to an estimated $756 million.

One of the largest annual events in the state of Michigan is the National Cherry Festival in Traverse City. Held every year around the Fourth of July, it boasts an impressive lineup of events and promotional activities that drive both attendance and sponsor visibility. Events include band parades, races, concerts, tournaments, an antiques show, an air show, Native American exhibits, and much more. Among the official sponsors are Pepsi, Ford, Toyota, Intel, BankOne, and Sony.

Associations and Membership Organizations

This sponsorship category was added by IEG in 2004. These sponsorships were previously considered a part of festivals, fairs, and annual events because most associations sponsored annual conventions. But that is no longer the case, as sponsors are now more likely to sign year-round partnerships with trade groups, professional membership organizations, and other associations. Those sponsors spent an estimated $496 million in this category in 2009.

Methods of Sponsorship

Companies interested in sponsorship have two choices: buy into an existing event or create their own. Event marketing specialist Paul Stanley predicts that many corporate event sponsorships will become "sponsownerships," where the sponsor owns and controls the entire event. This would allow more control and would likely be more cost-effective. It would also help the company achieve its marketing objectives.[31]

For most companies, though, it's easier to buy into an existing event, either as the sole sponsor (the Buick Invitational) or as one of many co-sponsors. What's most important is to get a good fit between the sponsor and

venue marketing
A form of sponsorship that links a sponsor to a physical site such as a stadium, arena, auditorium, or racetrack.

the event. Nabisco's Cornnuts brand, for instance, teamed up with the Aggressive Skaters Association (ASA) to sponsor the ASA Pro Tour and Amateur Circuits and to use the ASA World Champion female skater Fabiola da Silva as the product's spokesperson. According to Rich Bratman, president of the ASA, he chose Cornnuts because "the brand management and promotions team at Cornnuts really understands how important it is to reach teens in a credible way and is committed to supporting the skating lifestyle."

In his book *Aftermarketing,* Terry Vavra suggests several guidelines for selecting the right sponsorship opportunity or event. See My Ad Campaign 17–D, "How to Select Events for Sponsorship."

Measuring Sponsorship Results

One of the problems with event sponsorship (as with public relations activities in general) has historically been how to evaluate results. Experts suggest there are really only three ways to do this:

1. Measure changes in awareness or image through pre- and postsponsorship research surveys.

2. Measure spending equivalencies between free media exposure and comparable advertising space or time.

3. Measure changes in sales revenue with a tracking device such as coupons.

Unfortunately, none of these methods covers all the reasons for sponsoring. For example, how do you measure the effect on employee morale? What if the sponsorship is aimed at rewarding current customers or enhancing relationships within the trade? These are important possible objectives, but they are very difficult to measure.

Still, most companies are very concerned about the bottom line and look for a substantial return on investment for their sponsorship dollars. Delta Airlines, for example, is said to require $12 in new revenue for every dollar it spends on sponsorship—a ratio the airline claims to have achieved during its Olympic sponsorship.[32]

IEG suggests the following pointers for measuring the value of event sponsorships:[33]

- Have clear goals and narrowly defined objectives.

- Set a measurable goal.

- Measure against a benchmark.

- Do not change other marketing variables during the sponsorship.

- Incorporate an evaluation program into the overall sponsorship and associated marketing program.

- At the outset establish a budget for measuring results.

check yourself ✓

1. Why is sponsorship such a popular and growing strategy for marketers?

2. How can a company determine if a sponsorship has been effective?

my ad campaign

How to Select Events for Sponsorship [17–D]

- Can the sponsorship be an exclusive one?
- The demographics of the mass media audience and event participants should match, as closely as possible, the demographics of the target consumer.
- The event should in some way demonstrate, evoke, or represent a key attribute of the product or service (for example, a luxury product sponsoring a thoroughbred racing event—"the sport of kings").
- The value to the sponsored event of the company's association should be no greater than the benefit to the company from the

- additional mass media exposure from the sponsorship. (This has to do with who is leveraging whom.)
- The participation should promise sufficient (and appropriate) mass media exposure to offset any costs associated with the sponsorship.
- The association of the product with the event should ideally offer or suggest a meaningful sales campaign or theme to be run concurrently with sponsorship.
- Did the company initiate the negotiation or was the company solicited by the event promoters?
- How much financial support is required?

LO4   Discuss the functions of corporate advertising.

CORPORATE ADVERTISING

When a company wants to communicate a PR message and control its content, it may use a form of *corporate advertising*. In an integrated marketing communications program, corporate advertising can set the tone for all of a company's public communications. **Corporate advertising** covers the broad area of nonproduct advertising, including public relations advertising, institutional advertising, corporate identity advertising, and recruitment advertising.

Public Relations Advertising

To direct a controlled public relations message to one of its important publics, a company uses **public relations advertising**. PR ads may be used to improve the company's relations with labor, government, customers, suppliers, and even voters.

When companies sponsor art events, programs on public television, or charitable activities, they frequently place public relations ads in other media to promote the programs and their sponsorship, enhance their community citizenship, and create public goodwill. If the public relations people don't have advertising experience, they will typically turn to the firm's advertising department or agency for help.

Corporate/Institutional Advertising

In recent years, the term *corporate advertising* has come to denote a particular type of nonproduct advertising aimed at increasing awareness of the company and enhancing its image. The traditional term for this is **institutional advertising**. These ad campaigns may serve a variety of purposes: to report company accomplishments, position the company competitively in the market, reflect a change in corporate personality, shore up stock prices, improve employee morale, or avoid communications problems with agents, dealers, suppliers, or customers.

Historically, companies and even professional ad people have questioned, or misunderstood, the effectiveness of corporate advertising. Retailers in particular cling to the idea that institutional advertising, although attractive and nice, "doesn't

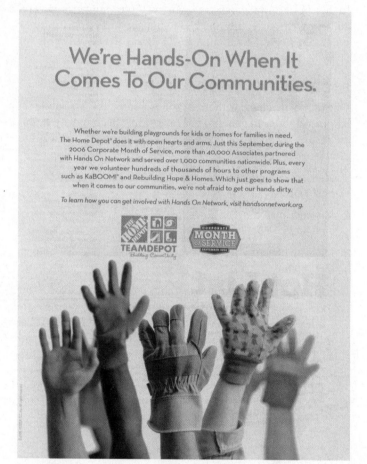

The Home Depot (www.homedepot.com) uses public relations advertising to inform consumers of its efforts to improve the communities it serves. During its annual Corporate Month of Service, Home Depot employees partner with nonprofit organizations, such as Hands On Network (www.handsonnetwork.org), to build playgrounds, refurbish schools, landscape parks, and restore housing. This advertising serves to acknowledge the efforts of Home Depot employees, as well as to let the public know that The Home Depot is a good corporate citizen.

make the cash register ring." A series of marketing research studies, however, offered dramatic evidence to the contrary. Companies using corporate advertising registered significantly better awareness, familiarity, and an overall better impression than those using only product advertising. Five corporate advertisers in the study drew higher ratings in every one of 16 characteristics measured, including being known

David Ogilvy on Corporate Advertising [17-B]

David Ogilvy, the late founder and former creative director of Ogilvy & Mather, worked with Shell, Sears, IBM, International Paper, Merrill Lynch, General Dynamics, Standard Oil of New Jersey, and other successful corporations.

According to Ogilvy, big corporations are increasingly under attack from consumer groups, environmentalists, governments, and antitrust prosecutors who try their cases in the newspapers. If a corporation does not take the time to cultivate its reputation, it loses by default.

"If it were possible, it would be better for corporations to rely on public relations (that is, favorable news stories and editorials) rather than paid advertising. But the media are too niggardly about disseminating favorable information about corporations. That is why an increasing number of public relations directors have come to use paid advertising as their main channel of communication. It is the only one they can control with respect to content, with respect to timing, and with respect to noise level. And it is the only one which enables them to select their own battleground," he said.

"So I guess that corporate advertising is here to stay. Why is most of it a flop?"

First, because corporations don't define the purpose of their corporate campaigns.

Second, because they don't measure the results. In a survey conducted by *The Gallagher Report,* only one in four U.S. corporate advertisers said it measured changes in attitude brought about by its corporate campaigns. "The majority fly blind," said Ogilvy.

Third, because so little is known about what works and what doesn't work. The marketing departments and their agencies know what works in brand advertising, but when it comes to corporate advertising they are amateurs.

Fourth, very few advertising agencies know much about corporate advertising. It is only a small part of their business. "Their creative people know how to write chewing-gum jingles for kids and how to sell beer to blue-collar workers. But corporate advertising requires copywriters who are at home in the world of big business. There aren't many of them," believed Ogilvy.

"I am appalled by the humbug in corporate advertising. The pomposity. The vague generalities and the fatuous platitudes. Corporate advertising should not insult the intelligence of the public."

Unlike product advertising, Ogilvy said, a corporate campaign is the voice of the chief executive and his or her board of directors. It should not be delegated.

What can good corporate advertising hope to achieve? Ogilvy thought at least one of four objectives:

1. **It can build awareness of the company.** Opinion Research Corp. states, "The invisibility and remoteness of most companies is the main handicap. People who feel they know a company well are five times more likely to have a highly favorable opinion of the company than those who have little familiarity."

2. **Corporate advertising can make a good impression on the financial community,** enabling you to raise capital at lower cost—and make more acquisitions.

3. **It can motivate your present employees and attract better recruits.** "Good public relations begins at home," Ogilvy said. "If your employees understand your policies and feel proud of your company, they will be your best ambassadors."

4. **Corporate advertising can influence public opinion on specific issues.** Abraham Lincoln said, "With public opinion against it, nothing can succeed. With public opinion on its side, nothing can fail."

"Stop and go is the typical pattern of corporate advertising. What a waste of money. It takes years for corporate advertising to do a job. It doesn't work overnight. Only a few companies have kept it going long enough to achieve measurable results," Ogilvy concluded.

Applying the Breaks

Find and discuss a corporate ad that demonstrates what Ogilvy referred to as the humbug in corporate advertising: the pomposity, vague generalities, and fatuous platitudes.

---

for quality products, having competent management, and paying higher dividends.[34] Ironically, the companies in the study that did no corporate advertising spent far more in total advertising for their products than the corporate advertisers did. Yet, despite the higher expenditures, they scored significantly lower across the board.

David Ogilvy, the late founder and creative head of Ogilvy & Mather, was an outspoken advocate of corporate advertising, but he was appalled by some corporate ads. For more on Ogilvy's views, see Commercial Break 17–B.

Responding to such criticisms and to marketplace forces, corporations now design their corporate advertising to achieve specific objectives: develop awareness of the company and its activities, attract investors, improve a tarnished image, attract quality employees, tie together a diverse product line, or take a stand on important public issues. The primary media used for corporate advertising are consumer business magazines and network TV.

A variation on corporate advertising is **advocacy advertising**. Companies use it to communicate their views on issues

> [Companies using corporate advertising registered an overall better impression than those using only product advertising.]

that affect their business, to promote their philosophy, or to make a political or social statement. Such ads are frequently referred to as **advertorials** since they are basically editorials paid for by an advertiser.

Corporate advertising can also build a foundation for future sales, traditionally the realm of product advertising. Many advertisers use **umbrella advertising** campaigns to simultaneously communicate messages about their products and their company.

While corporate advertising is an excellent vehicle for promoting the company's desired image, it cannot succeed if the image doesn't fit. If a big national bank, for example, tried to project a homey, small-town image, it would not be very credible.

Corporate Identity Advertising

Companies take pride in their logos and corporate signatures. The graphic designs that identify corporate names and products are valuable assets, and companies take great pains to pro-

tect their individuality and ownership. How does a company increase consumer awareness or enhance its image? What does a company do when it changes its name, logos, or trademarks, as when it merges with another company? This is the job of **corporate identity advertising**.

Familiar corporate name changes include the switch from Datsun to Nissan, the change from Consolidated Foods to Sara Lee Corp., and the rebranding of Philip Morris to Altria.

Recruitment Advertising

Companies use **recruitment advertising** to attract new employees. Most recruitment advertising appears in the classified help-wanted sections of daily newspapers or, increasingly more frequently, on the Internet and is placed by the human resources department rather than the advertising department. But many ad agencies now employ recruitment specialists, and some agencies even specialize in recruitment advertising. ■

check yourself ✓

1. How would you respond to a company that told you "institutional advertising doesn't make the cash register ring"?

2. Why does David Ogilvy believe that most corporate advertising is a flop?

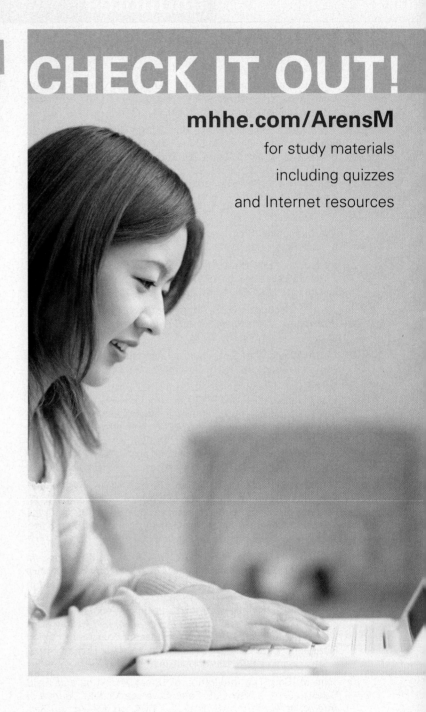

CHECK IT OUT!

mhhe.com/ArensM

for study materials

including quizzes

and Internet resources

endnotes

CHAPTER 1

1. Dana Blanton, "Fox News Poll: Obama Trails Clinton in 2008 Dem Primary," retrieved March 19, 2009, from http://www.foxnews.com/story/0,2933,235197,00.html.

2. Jon Swaine, "Barack Obama: How 2006 poll predicted McCain would win landslide against him," **The Daily Telegraph,** November, 2008, retrieved March 20, 2009, at http://www.telegraph.co.uk/news/newstopics/uselection2008/3384103/Barack-Obama-How-2006-poll-predicted-McCain-would-win-landslide-against-him.html.

3. http://www.cnn.com/ELECTION/2008/map/ad.spending/.

4. The Intangibles Blog, retrieved March 20, 2009, from http://intangibles.typepad.com.

5. Ryan Lizza, "How Obama Won," *The New Yorker,* November 17, 2008, retrieved March 19, 2009, from http://www.newyorker.com/reporting/2008/11/17/081117fa_fact_lizza?currentPage=all.

6. John McDonough, "FCB: From One-Man Fiefdom to Global Powerhouse," *Advertising Age,* Commemorative Section: "FCB at 120," December 13, 1993, p. F4.

7. "AMA Adopts New Definition of Marketing," (retrieved from www.marketingpower.com, December 19, 2005).

8. Quoted in "The Chronicle of Coca-Cola: Birth of a Refreshing Idea," retrieved July 19, 2006, from www2.coca-cola.com/heritage/chronicle_birth_refreshing_idea.html; Coca-Cola Heritage Timeline, retrieved July 19, 2006, from http://heritage.coca-cola.com; Barbara Mikkelson, "Design Err Shape," *Urban Legends Reference Pages: Coca-Cola,* posted May 2, 1999, retrieved July 17, 2006, from www.snopes.com/cokelore/bottle.asp.

9. "The Chronicle of Coca-Cola," op. cit.; Jack Hayes, "Dr. John S. Pemberton (inventor of Coca-Cola)," *Nation's Restaurant News,* February 1996, pp. 120–21, retrieved July 19, 2006, from the Library of Congress American Memory Project, http://rs6.loc.gov/ammem/ccmphtml/colainvnt.html.

10. Frederick Allen, *Secret Formula: How Brilliant Marketing and Relentless Salesmanship Made Coca-Cola the Best-Known Product in the World* (New York: HarperCollins, 1994), cited in Eleanor Jones and Florian Ritzmann, "Coca-Cola Goes to War: Coca-Cola at Home," http://xroads.virginia.edu/~class/coke/coke.html; Pat Watters, *Coca-Cola: An Illustrated History* (New York: Doubleday, 1978), cited in Eleanor Jones and Florian Ritzmann, "Coca-Cola Goes to War: Coca-Cola at Home," http://xroads.virginia.edu/~class/coke/coke.html.

11. John M. Coe, The Integration of Direct Marketing and Field Sales to Form a New B2B Sales Coverage Model." *Journal of Interactive Marketing* 18, issue 2, 2004, pp. 62–74; Jill Serjeant, "American Idol" Ratings Down, but Ad Sales Seem Up," *Reuters,* Los Angeles, May 4, 2010, www.reuters.com/article/idUSTRE64300F20100504.

12. Some material in this section has been adapted from Hugh M. Cannon, Course Packet for Advertising Management, Fall 1996, Wayne State University.

13. William O'Barr, address to the Council on Advertising History, Duke University, March 12, 1993, reported in *Advertising in America: Using Its Past, Enriching Its Future* (Washington, DC: Center for Advertising History of the National Museum of American History, 1994), p. 6.

14. Leonard L. Bartlett, "Three Giants—Leo Burnett, David Ogilvy, William Bernbach: An Exploration of the Impact of the Founders' Written Communications on the Destinies of Their Advertising Agencies," paper presented to the annual meeting of the Association for Education in Journalism and Mass Communication, Kansas City, August 13, 1993.

15. Schwarz, "A Brief History of Ad Time."

16. Cannon, Course Packet for Advertising Management.

17. Warren Berger, "Chaos on Madison Avenue," *Los Angeles Times Magazine,* June 5, 1994, p. 14.

18. William F. Arens and Jack J. Whidden, "La Publicité aux Etats-Unis: Les Symptômes et les Stratégies d'une Industrie Surpeuplée," *L'Industrie de la Publicité au Québec* (Montreal: Le Publicité Club de Montréal, 1992), pp. 383–84.

19. Berger, "Chaos on Madison Avenue," pp. 12, 14.

20. Bob Coen, "Bob Coen's Insider's Report," December 2002, McCann-Erickson WorldGroup, www.universalmccann.com/overview.html.

21. Judann Pollock, "Marketing Put on Hold," *Advertising Age,* September 17, 2001, pp. 1, 25.

22. Coen, "Bob Coen's Insider's Report."

23. "100 Leading Advertisers," *Advertising Age,* June 26, 2006.

24. Tom Cuniff, "The Second Creative Revolution," *Advertising Age,* December 6, 1993, p. 22.

25. John McManus, "Cable Proves It's Media's Live Wire," *Advertising Age,* November 26, 1990, p. S6; "Media & Measurement Technologies (Part 1)," *Direct Marketing,* March 1991, pp. 21–27, 79.

26. Tobi Elkin, "Analysts Predict iTV Growth in 2002," December 10, 2001, www.adage.com.

27. Clinton Wilder, "Interactive Ads," *Information Week,* October 3, 1994, p. 25.

28. Tom Cuniff, "The Second Creative Revolution," *Advertising Age,* December 6, 1993, p. 22.

29. Brad Lynch, address to the Council on Advertising History, Duke University, March 12, 1993, reported in *Advertising in America: Using Its Past, Enriching Its Future* (Washington, DC: Center for Advertising History of the National Museum of American History, 1994), p. 3.

CHAPTER 2

1. Jagdish Agrawal and Wagner A. Kamakura, "The Economic Worth of Celebrity Endorsers," *Journal of Marketing,* vol. 59 (2005), pp. 56–63.

2. Jeremy Mullen, "Reducing the Risk of Vick-timization," *Advertising Age,* July 23, 2007 (retrieved from http://web.ebscohost.com.lp.hscl.ufl.edu/ehost/detail?vid=4&hid=109&sid=4dc8792cc1b3-4c6d-9798-4d64035c4755%40sessionmgr108).

3. John O'Toole, *The Trouble with Advertising* (New York: Times Books, 1985), pp. 7–14.

4. Marcel Bleustein-Blanchet, *La Rage de Convaincre* (Paris: Editions Robert Laffont, 1970), p. 25.

5. Ernest Dichter, *Handbook of Consumer Motivations* (New York: McGraw-Hill, 1964), pp. 6, 422–31.

6. Richard E. Kihlstrom and Michael H. Riordan, "Advertising as a Signal," *Journal of Political Economy,* June 1984, pp. 427–50.

7. Ivan Preston, *The Tangled Web They Weave* (Madison: University of Wisconsin Press, 1994), pp. 94–95.

8. Fabiana Giacomotti, "European Marketers Keep Up Ad Budgets," *Adweek,* January 24, 1994, pp. 16–17.

9. Ivan Preston, "A New Conception of Deceptiveness," paper presented to the Advertising Division of the Association for Education in Journalism and Mass Communication, August 12, 1993.

10. "Pizza Hut Files Suit against Pizza Rival," *Advertising Age,* August 13, 1998; "Papa John's Ordered to Move 'Better' Slogan," *Advertising Age,* January 5, 2000 (retrieved from http://adage.com).

11. Stuart C. Rogers, "Subliminal Advertising: Grand Scam of the 20th Century," paper presented to the Annual Conference of the American Academy of Advertising, April 10, 1994.

12. Ibid.; Martha Rogers and Kirk H. Smith, "Public Perceptions of Subliminal Advertising," *Journal of Advertising Research,* March/April 1993, p. 10.

13. Andrew Jaffe, "Advertiser, Regulate Thyself," *Adweek,* August 2, 1993, p. 38.

14. Ibid.

15. Preston, *The Tangled Web They Weave,* p. 164.

16. Kevin Downey, "TV Ad Clutter Worsens, and Buyers Grouse," *Media Life Magazine,* February 15, 2002 (retrieved from www.medialifemagazine.com).

17. Steve McClellan, "Nielsen: Ad Clutter Spikes," *Adweek,* October 31, 2005 (retrieved from http://www.mediaweek.com/mw/news/recent_display.jsp?vnu_content_id=1001392205).

18. "The Public and Broadcasting," *FCC Mass Media Bureau,* June 1999 (retrieved from www.fcc.gov/mb/audio/includes/45-public_and_broadcasting.htm).

19. Shelly Garcia, "What's Wrong with Being Politically Correct?" *Adweek,* November 15, 1993, p. 62.

20. Adrienne Ward, "What Role Do Ads Play in Racial Tension?" *Advertising Age,* August 10, 1992, pp. 1, 35.

21. U.S. Census Bureau, *Statistical Abstract of the United States,* 2007 (retrieved from www.census.gov).

22. John B. Ford and Michael S. LaTour, "Differing Reactions to Female Role Portrayals in Advertising," *Journal of Advertising Research,* September/October 1993, pp. 43–52.

23. Michael L. Klassen, Cynthia R. Jasper, and Anne M. Schwartz, "Men and Women: Images of Their Relationships in Magazine Advertisements," *Journal of Advertising Research,* March/April 1993, pp. 30–39.

24. "Revealing Abercrombie Catalog Sparks a Boycott," *The Cincinnati Enquirer,* June 26, 2001 (retrieved from www.enquirer.com/editions/2001/06/26/tem_revealing.htm).

25. Matt Warren, "Are You Ready for This?" *The Scotsman,* Edinburgh (UK), October 6, 2000, p. 9 (retrieved from Lexis-Nexis Academic Universe).

26. Caity Olson, "Ad Boycott Concern Is Real," *Advertising Age,* June 13, 1994, p. 3.

27. Caity Olson, "Ad Boycott Concern Is Real," *Advertising Age,* June 13, 1994, p. 3.

28. Preston, "A New Conception of Deceptiveness."

29. Robert W. McChesney, *Corporate Media and the Threat to Democracy* (New York: Seven Stories Press, 1997), p. 23.

30. Preston, *The Tangled Web They Weave,* pp. 94, 127–31.

31. James R. Maxeiner, "United States," in Maxeiner and Schotthoffer, eds., *Advertising Law in Europe and North America,* p. 321; see also *Virginia State Board of Pharmacy v. Virginia Citizens Consumer Council,* 425 U.S. 748 (1976).

32. See *Central Hudson Gas & Electric Corp. v. Public Service Commission of New York,* 447 U.S. 557 (1980).

33. Kartik Pashupati, "The Camel Controversy: Same Beast, Different Viewpoints," paper presented to the annual conference of the Association for Education in Journalism and Mass Communication, Kansas City, MO, August 11, 1993; Maxeiner, "United States," pp. 321–22.

34. Steven W. Colford, "Big Win for Commercial Speech," *Advertising Age,* March 29, 1993, pp. 1, 47.

35. Joy Johnson Wilson, "Summary of the Attorneys General Master Tobacco Settlement Agreement," March 1999 (retrieved on April 1, 2009 at http://academic.udayton.edu/health/syllabi/tobacco/summary.htm).

36. "Self-Regulatory Guidelines for Children's Advertising," The Children's Advertising Review Unit (CARU), Copyright 2000 Council of Better Business Bureaus (retrieved from http://216.46.241.4/advertising/caruguid.asp); "CARU Issues Breakthrough Advertising Guidelines to Protect Children on the Internet," Better Business Bureau Press Release, April 21, 1997 (retrieved from www.caru.org/guidelines/index.asp).

37. "A Spoonful of Sugar: Television Food Advertising Aimed at Children: An International Comparative Survey," *Consumers International.*

38. "Online Privacy—It's Time for Rules in Wonderland," *BusinessWeek,* March 20, 2000, p. 85.

39. Elinor Mills, "Don't Like Targeted Ads? Opt Out, Says Online Ad Group," News Blog, cnet news, February 24, 2008 (retrieved on September 11, 2009, from http://news.cnet.com/8301-10784 3-9877604-7.html ?tag=mncol;txt).

40. Mark Sakalosky, "DoubleClick's Double Edge," ClickZ, September 3, 2002 (retrieved September 11, 2009, at http://www.clickz.com/1455141).

41. "Opinion Surveys: What Consumers Have to Say about Information Privacy," Testimony of Lee Rainie, Director, Pew Internet & American Life Project to the Subcommittee on Commerce, Trade, and Consumer Protection, House Committee on Energy and Commerce, May 8, 2001 (retrieved on September 11, 2009, from http://www.pewinternet.org).

42. Interactive Advertising Bureau Europe, "Manage Cookies: What Can I Do to Manage Cookies on My Computer?" (retrieved on September 11, 2009, from http://www.allaboutcookies.org/manage-cookies/).

43. "Online Privacy—It's Time for Rules in Wonderland."

44. www.ftc.gov/os/2000/07/onlineprofiling.htm.

45. Federal Trade Commission, "Vision, Mission, and Goals," 1997.

46. Minette E. Drumwright, "Ethical Issues in Advertising and Sales Promotion," in N. Craig Smith and John A. Quelch, eds., *Ethics in Marketing* (Burr Ridge, IL: Richard D. Irwin, 1993), p. 610.

47. Ann Carrns, "FTC Settles with Office Depot, Buy.com, Value America over 'Low Cost' PC Ads," *The Wall Street Journal,* June 30, 2000, p. B4.

48. Dean Keith Fueroghne, *But the People in Legal Said . . .* (Burr Ridge, IL: Professional Publishing, 1989), p. 14.

49. Christy Fisher, "How Congress Broke Unfair Ad Impasse," *Advertising Age,* August 22, 1994, p. 34.

50. "Editorial: A Fair FTC Pact?" *Advertising Age,* March 21, 1994, p. 22.

51. "Arizona Trade Association Agrees to Settle FTC Charges. It Urged Members to Restrain Competitive Advertising," FTC News Release, February 25, 1994 (retrieved from www.ftc.gov/opa/predawn/F95/azautodealers.htm).

52. "Comparative Advertising," *ADLAW,* copyright 2000 Hall Dickler Kent Goldstein & Wood (retrieved from www.adlaw.com/rc/handbk/rf_comparative.html).

53. "Crackdown on Testimonials," *The Wall Street Journal,* July 13, 1993, p. B7.

54. Drumwright, "Ethical Issues in Advertising and Sales Promotion," pp. 615–16.

55. Ira Teinowitz, "Doan's Decision Sets Precedent for Corrective Ads," *Advertising Age,* September 4, 2000, p. 57.

56. www.census.gov and www.fda.gov.

57. www.fda.gov.

58. "The Growing Brouhaha over Drug Advertisements," *The New York Times,* May 14, 1989, p. F8.

59. "FDA to Review Standards for All Direct-to-Consumer Rx Drug Promotion," FDA news release, August 8, 1997.

60. Jean Grow, "'Your Life Is Waiting!': Symbolic Meanings in Direct-to-Consumer Antidepressant Advertising," *Journal of Communication Inquiry,* April 2006, pp. 163–88.

61. "FDA Seeks Rx for Drug Ads; New Policy Delays Process," *Newsday* (Nassau and Suffolk edition), December 5, 2002.

62. Steven W. Colford, "Labels Lose the Fat," *Advertising Age,* June 10, 1991, pp. 3, 54; Steven W. Colford and Julie Liesse, "FDA Label Plans under Attack," *Advertising Age,* February 24, 1992, pp. 1, 50; John E. Calfee, "FDA's Ugly Package: Proposed Label Rules Call for Vast Changes," *Advertising Age,* March 16, 1992, p. 25; Pauline M. Ippolito and Alan D. Mathios, "New Food Labeling Regulations and the Flow of Nutrition Information to Consumers," *Journal of Public Policy & Marketing,* Fall 1993, pp. 188–205.

63. John Carey, "The FDA Is Swinging a Sufficiently Large Two-by-Four," *BusinessWeek,* May 27, 1991, p. 44; Steven W. Colford, "FDA Getting Tougher: Seizure of Citrus Hill Is Signal to Marketers," *Advertising Age,* April 29, 1991, pp. 1, 53.

64. Joe Mandese, "Regulation," *Advertising Age,* November 30, 1992, p. 23.

65. *U.S. Constitution,* Article 1, Section 8.

66. U.S. Copyright Office, Library of Congress, 1997.

67. Wayne E. Green, "Lawyers Give Deceptive Trade-Statutes New Day in Court, Wider Interpretations," *The Wall Street Journal,* January 24, 1990, p. B1.

68. Howard Schlossberg, "Marketers Say State Laws Hurt Their 'Green' Efforts," *Marketing News,* November 11, 1991, pp. 8–9.

69. "Closet Factory to Pay Penalty for Misleading Advertising," Orange County District Attorney press release, June 24, 2002.

70. Felix H. Kent, "Control of Ads by Private Sector," *New York Law Journal,* December 27, 1985; reprinted in Kent and Stone, eds., *Legal and Business Aspects of the Advertising Industry,* 1986, pp. 20–79.

71. "NAD Pilots Successful Resolution Between Neil Cooper and Avirex," Better Business Bureau News Release, August 11, 2000 (retrieved from www.nadreview.org/casereports.asp).

72. Public Relations Department, KLBJ, Austin, TX, 1991.

73. Public Relations Department, KDWB, Minneapolis/St. Paul, MN, 1991.

74. Public Relations Department, KSDO, San Diego, CA, 1991.

75. Kevin Goldman, "From Witches to Anorexics, Critical Eyes Scrutinize Ads for Political Correctness," *The Wall Street Journal,* May 19, 1994, p. B1.

76. Garcia, "What's Wrong with Being Politically Correct?" p. 62.

77. James Maxeiner and Peter Schotthoffer, eds., *Advertising Law in Europe and North America* (Deventer, The Netherlands: Kluwer Law and Taxation Publishers, 1992), p. v; Rein Rijkens, *European Advertising Strategies* (London: Cassell, 1992), pp. 201–2.

78. Keith Boyfield, "Business Europe: When Advertising Is against the Law," *The Wall Street Journal,* European edition, March 6, 2000, p. 11 (retrieved from Lexis-Nexis Academic Universe).

79. Peter Schotthoffer, "European Community," in Maxeiner and Schotthoffer, eds., *Advertising Law in Europe and North America,* p. 89.

80. Jaffe, "Advertiser, Regulate Thyself," p. 38.

81. Federal Trade Commission, 1991.

CHAPTER 3

1. www.rubios.com.

2. Henry A. Laskey, J. A. F. Nicholls, and Sydney Roslow, "The Enigma of Cooperative Advertising," *Journal of Business and Industrial Marketing,* vol. 8, no. 2 (1993), pp. 70–79.

3. Riccardo A. Davis, "Retailers Open Doors Wide for Co-op," *Advertising Age,* August 1, 1994, p. 30.

4. Jack Neff, "Walmart Ups the Ante with Brand Co-op Ads—in More Ways than One," *Advertising Age,* November 30, 2009, p. 4:23.

5. Sam Black, "General Mills Hikes Ad Spending," *Minneapolis/St. Paul Business Journal,* Friday, January 22, 2010 (retrieved from http://twincities.bizjournals.com/twincities/stories/2010/01/25/story4.html?b=1264395600^2763871).

6. *Standard Directory of Advertisers* (New Providence, NJ: National Register Publishing Company, 2000), p. 616.

7. Reuters, "Financials: The Procter & Gamble Company (PG)," (retrieved at http://www.reuters.com/finance/stocks/financialHighlights?symbol=PG).

8. "Global Marketers 2009," *Advertising Age* (retrieved at http://adage.com/globalmarketers09/).

9. E. Jerome McCarthy and William D. Perreault Jr., *Basic Marketing,* 11th ed. (Burr Ridge, IL: Richard D. Irwin, 1993), p. 593.

10. Peter S. Goodman, "For U.S. firms, foreign sales cushion domestic slowdown," *The New York Times,* Monday, November 19, 2007 (retrieved at http://www.nytimes.com/2007/11/19/business/worldbusiness/19iht-global.4.8395022.html).

11. Eric N. Berkowitz, Roger A. Kerin, Steven W. Hartley, and William Rudelius, *Marketing,* 3rd ed. (Burr Ridge, IL: Richard D. Irwin, 1992), p. 609.

12. "McDonald's prepares to roll out first global advertising," Brand Republic, September 3, 2002 (retrieved at http://www.brandrepublic.com/News/188915/McDonalds-prepares-roll-first-global-advertising/).

13. "Global Marketers 2009."

14. Jim Patterson, "Viewpoint: Global Communication Requires a Global Understanding," *Adweek,* October 31, 1994, p. 46; "Efficacy of Global Ad Prospects Is Questioned in Firm's Survey," *The Wall Street Journal,* September 13, 1984, p. 29.

15. "Global Advertising: Consumers Trust Real Friends and Virtual Strangers the Most," Nielsen Wire, July 7, 2009 (retrieved at http://blog.nielsen.com/nielsenwire/).

16. Amy Dockser Markus, "Advertising Breezes along the Nile River with Signs for Sale," *The Wall Street Journal,* July 18, 1997, p. A1.

17. Frederick R. Gamble, *What Advertising Agencies Are—What They Do and How They Do It,* 7th ed. (New York: American Association of Advertising Agencies, 1970), p. 4.

18. http://www.redbooks.com/.

19. Melanie Wells, "The Interactive Edge—Part II: Desperately Seeking the Super Highway," *Advertising Age,* August 22, 1994, pp. 14–19.

20. Jennifer Gilbert, "Gotham Gathers Interactive under Hinkaty," *Advertising Age,* July 31, 2000, p. 42 (retrieved from http://webgate.sdsu.edu).

21. *Standard Directory of Advertisers,* pp. 245–46.

22. www.im-na.com.

23. http://adage.com/digitalfamilytrees09/agency_companies.

24. "Readings in Account Planning," Hart Weichselbaum (Ed.), Copy Workshop, 2008.

25. William F. Arens and Jack J. Whidden, "La Publicité aux Etats-Unis: Les Symptômes et les Stratégies d'une Industrie Surpleuplée," *L'Industrie de la Publicité au Québec* (Montreal: Le Publicité-Club de Montréal, 1992), pp. 383–84.

26. Jean Marie Dru, "Viewpoint," Advertising Age, January 25, 2010 (retrieved at http://adage.com/columns/article?article_id=141641).

27. Andrew Jaffe, "Has Leo Burnett Come to the End of the 'Free Overservice' Era?" *Adweek,* December 6, 1993, p. 46; Melanie Wells and Laurel Wentz, "Coke Trims Commissions," *Advertising Age,* January 31, 1994, p. 2.

28. John Micklethwait, "Cut the Ribbon," *The Economist,* June 9, 1990, pp. S16–S17; Tom Eisenhart, "Guaranteed Results' Plan May Suit Business Marketers," *Business Marketing,* July 1990, p. 32; Jim Kirk, "Miller Sets Free Rates," *Adweek,* January 24, 1994, p. 4.

29. James R. Willis, Jr., "Winning New Business: An Analysis of Advertising Agency Activities," *Journal of Advertising Research,* September/October 1992, pp. 10–16.

30. Andrew Jaffe, "The Fine Art of Keeping Clients Happy While Chasing New Business," *Adweek,* May 9, 1994, p. 38.

31. Melanie Wells, "Courtship by Consultant," *Advertising Age,* January 31, 1994, pp. 10–11; "Accounts on the Move," *Advertising Age,* June 2, 1997 (retrieved from http://adage.com); "H&R Block Review Down to 3," *Advertising Age,* May 17, 2000 (retrieved from Daily Deadline, http://adage.com); "Monster, L.L. Bean Open Account Review," *Advertising Age,* July 12, 2000 (retrieved from Daily Deadline, http://adage.com); "Deutsch Tunes in $70 mil DirecTV Account," *Advertising Age,* August 18, 2000 (retrieved from Daily Deadline, http://adage.com).

32. Thorolf Helgesen, "Advertising Awards and Advertising Agency Performance," *Journal of Advertising Research,* July/August 1994, pp. 43–53.

33. Paul C. Katz, "Getting the Most of Your Advertising Dollars: How to Select and Evaluate an Ad Agency," *Bottomline,* March 1987, pp. 35–38.

34. Steven Raye, "Agencies, Clients: It's Mutual Contribution for Mutual Gain," *Brandweek,* September 12, 1994, p. 20; Ed Moser, "Inside Information," *Adweek,* January 24, 1994, p. 22;

35. Mat Toor, "Fear and Favour in Adland," *Marketing* (UK), November 15, 1990, pp. 30–32.

36. Paul C. N. Mitchell, Harold Cataquet, and Stephen Hague, "Establishing the Causes of Disaffection in Agency-Client Relations," *Journal of Advertising Research,* March/April 1992, pp. 41–48.

37. Isabelle T. D. Szmigin, "Managing Quality in Business-to-Business Services," *European Journal of Marketing,* vol. 27, no. 1 (1993), pp. 5–21.

38. Ron Jackson, "If You Hire a Vendor, You Get a Vendor Mindset," *Marketing News,* April 25, 1991, pp. 13–14.

39. Steven A. Meyerowitz, "Ad Agency Conflicts: The Law and Common Sense," *Business Marketing,* June 1987, p. 16.

40. Andrew Jaffe, "For Agencies, Conflict Taboo Seems Strong as Ever," *Adweek,* January 24, 1994, p. 46.

41. Betsy Sharkey, "New Suit," *Adweek,* June 20, 1994, p. 20.

42. Pat Fallon and Fred Senn, "Juicing the Orange," Harvard Business Books, 2006.

CHAPTER 4

1. Ed Garsten, "Establishing Brand Identity Gets Tougher as Competition Grows," *Detroit News,* January 6, 2003.

2. Alice Z. Cuneo, "Youth Target Warms to Scion," *Advertising Age,* July 21, 2003.

3. Fara Warner, "Learning How to Speak to Gen Y," *Fastcompany.com,* December 19, 2007.

4. Mark Cina, "Toyota Uses Unique Marketing Strategy for Scion," *Popular Mechanics,* July 2002.

5. Alice Z. Cuneo, "Attik Came Through," *Advertising Age,* July 21, 2003.

6. Matt Nauman, "Big Year For Toyota," *Mercury News,* January 27, 2006.

7. E. Jerome McCarthy and William D. Perreault Jr., *Basic Marketing: A Global-Managerial Approach,* 11th ed. (Burr Ridge, IL: Richard D. Irwin, 1993), pp. 5–6; Eric N. Berkowitz, Roger A. Kerin, Steven W. Hartley, and William Rudelius, *Marketing,* 3rd ed. (Burr Ridge, IL: Richard D. Irwin, 1992), p. 27.

8. Chart #649, U.S. Census Bureau, *Statistical Abstract of the United States: 2004–2005,* 124th ed. (Washington, DC: U.S. Department of Commerce, 2005).

9. S. Kent Stephan and Barry L. Tannenholz, "The Real Reason for Brand Switching," *Advertising Age,* June 13, 1994, p. 31; "Six Categories That Hold Elusive Consumers," *Advertising Age,* June 20, 1994, p. 32.

10. Quoted in Al Stewart, "Edgy Ads, Burgers Drive CKE," *Orange County Business Journal* 27, no. 30 (July 26, 2004): 5.

11. Nancy Ten Kate, "Squeaky Clean Teens," *American Demographics,* January 1995.

12. "Weather or Not to Sell," *Personal Selling Power,* September 1994, p. 79.

13. Leon E. Wynter, "Business and Race: JCPenney Launches Diahann Carroll Line," *The Wall Street Journal,* July 2, 1997, p. B1.

14. Marc Graser, "Toyota Hits Touch Points as It Hawks Yaris to Youth," *Advertising Age,* May 1, 2006 (retrieved from www.adage.com/article.php?article_id=108881, August 9, 2006).

15. Jean Halliday, "Smashing Home Appliances to Promote Ford's Fusion," *Advertising Age,* January 11, 2006 (retrieved from www.adage.com/article.php?article_id=48044, August 9, 2006).

16. Eric Schlosser, "Meat & Potatoes," *Rolling Stone* 800 (November 26, 1998); accessed November 9, 2004, via EBSCO.

17. Eric Schlosser, "The True Cost of America's Diet," *Rolling Stone* 794 (September 3, 1998); accessed November 9, 2004, via EBSCO.

18. Kathleen Barnes, "Changing Demographics: Middle Class," *Advertising Age International,* October 17, 1994, pp. 1–11, 1–16.

19. Zhao Yung, "Olympics Fuel Ad-Spending Surge in China," CRIEnglish.com, February 2, 2008.

20. Henry Assael and David F. Poltrack, "Can Demographic Profiles of Heavy Users Serve as a Surrogate for Purchase Behavior in Selecting TV Programs?" *Journal of Advertising Research,* January/February 1994, p. 11.

21. Emanuel H. Demby, "Psychographics Revisited: The Birth of a Technique," *Marketing Research: A Magazine of Management & Applications,* Spring 1994, pp. 26–29.

22. SRI Consulting Business Intelligence, "Welcome to VALS" (www.sric-bi.com/vals).

23. Ibid.

24. Ibid.

25. Malcolm Gladwell, *The Tipping Point: How Little Things Can Make a Big Difference* (New York: Little, Brown, and Company, 2002).

26. Lewis C. Winters, "International Psychographics," *Marketing Research: A Magazine of Management & Application,* September 1992, pp. 48–49.

27. James Hutton, "A Theoretical Framework for the Study of Brand Equity and a Test of Brand Sensitivity in an Organizational Buying Context," dissertation, University of Texas, Austin, 1993.

28. William D. Perreault Jr. and E. Jerome McCarthy, *Basic Marketing,* 12th ed. (Burr Ridge, IL: Irwin, 1996), p. 261.

29. *New Data for a New Economy,* U.S. Bureau of the Census, Economic Classification Policy Committee (Washington, DC: U.S. Department of Commerce, 1998).

30. U.S. Bureau of the Census, *Statistical Abstract of the United States: 1999,* 119th ed. (Washington, DC: U.S. Department of Commerce, 1999), pp. 741–42, 744.

31. Michael Schrage, "Think Big," *Adweek,* October 11, 1993, p. 25.

32. Perreault and McCarthy, *Basic Marketing,* pp. 48–49, 91–112.

33. Walter van Waterschoot and Christophe Van den Bulte, "The 4P Classification of the Marketing Mix Revisited," *Journal of Marketing,* October 1992, pp. 83–93.

34. The now widely popularized conceptual model of the 4Ps was developed by E. J. McCarthy, *Basic Marketing* (Homewood, IL: Richard D. Irwin, 1960); the usage of the marketing mix derived from Neil H. Borden, "The Concept of the Marketing Mix," *Journal of Advertising Research,* June 1964, p. 27.

35. Perreault and McCarthy, *Basic Marketing,* pp. 310–21.

36. Agam Shah, "Global computer usage, cell phone ownership jump," InfoWorld, October 5, 2007 (retrieved from www.infoworld.com/t/hardware/global-computer-usage-cell-phone-ownership-jump-956, June 11, 2010).

37. "Use of Cellular Phones Trends Upward, Survey Shows," press release, Decision Analyst, Inc., July 24, 1998; Matthew Klein, "More Callers Unleashed," *Forecast,* September 1998 (www.demographics.com).

38. Brian Wansink, "Making Old Brands New," *American Demographics,* December 1997 (www.demographics.com).

39. Adrienne Ward Fawcett, "In Glut of New Products, 'Different' Becomes Key," *Advertising Age,* December 13, 1993, p. 28.

40. "Popularity of Private Label Not Likely to Diminish," Progressive Grocer, May 19, 2010 (retrieved from www.progressivegrocer.com/progressivegrocer/content_display/features/center-store/e3iadc5fec7986db245aa6ed32fc196d18d, June 11, 2010).

41. "On the Pavement, 'Corporate Graffiti' to Sell Fruit Juice," *The New York Times,* May 19, 2002.

42. Alan Wolf, "TWICE/Campaigners Poll Shows Shoppers Choose Brand Over Price," *Twice: This Week in Consumer Electronics,* December 5, 2005, p. 18.

43. "The Best Global Brands; BusinessWeek and Interbrand Tell You What They're Worth," *BusinessWeek Special Report,* August 5, 2002 (retrieved from www.businessweek.com).

44. C. Manly Molpus, "Brands Follow New Shopping Patterns," *Advertising Age,* February 14, 1994, p. 22.

45. Stephan and Tannenholz, "The Real Reason for Brand Switching," p. 31.

46. Annetta Miller, "The Millenial Mind-Set," *American Demographics,* January 1999 (www.demographics.com/publications/AD/99_ad/9901_ad/ad990102a.htm).

47. Andrew Jaffe, "A Compass Point Out of Dead Calm: 'Brand Stewardship,'" *Adweek,* February 7, 1994, p. 38.

48. Perreault and McCarthy, *Basic Marketing,* p. 16.

49. "The ABCs of Franchising," International Franchising Association (retrieved from www.franchisingworld.com).

50. van Waterschoot and Van den Bulte, "The 4P Classification of the Marketing Mix Revisited," p. 89.

51. www.subway.com/subwayroot/index.aspx.

CHAPTER 5

1. Top 100 Ad Campaigns. Retrieved on August 16, 2010, at http://adage.com/century/campaigns.html.

2. Scott MacKenzie, R. J. Lutz, and G. Belch, 1986, "The Role of Attitude toward the Ad as a Mediator of Advertising Effectiveness: A Test of Competing Explanations," *Journal of Marketing Research* 23, 1986, pp. 130–143.

3. Steven P. Brown and D. M. Stayman, 1992, "Antecedents and Consequences of Attitude toward the Ad: A Meta-analysis," *Journal of Consumer Research* 19, pp. 34–51.

4. 11 Obscure Taco Bell Trivia Facts, retrieved on August 16, 2010, at http://www.11points.com/Food-Drink/11_Obscure_Taco_Bell_Trivia_Facts.

5. Alka Selzer Commercial Spicy Meatball, World News, Retrieved at http://wn.com/Alka_Seltzer_Commercial_Spicy_Meatball.

6. Noah J. Goldstein, S. J. Martin, and R. B. Cialdini, *Yes! 50 Scientifically Proven Ways to Be Persuasive,* (New York: Free Press, 2008).

7. Communication process adapted from J. Paul Peter and Jerry C. Olsen, *Understanding Consumer Behavior* (Burr Ridge, IL: Richard D. Irwin, 1994), p. 184.

8. Martin Ryder, "Semiotics: Language and Culture," *Encyclopedia of Science, Technology, and Ethics* (Macmillan Reference USA, July, 2005).

9. William O. Bearden, Thomas N. Ingram, and Raymond W. LaForge, *Marketing Principles and Perspectives,* 2nd ed. (Burr Ridge, IL: Irwin/McGraw-Hill, 1997) p. 99.

10. S. Kent Stephan and Barry L. Tannenholz, "The Real Reason for Brand Switching," *Advertising Age,* June 13, 1994, p. 31.

11. "Ad Nauseum," *Advertising Age,* July 10, 2000.

12. Kellaris, Cox, and Cox, "The Effect of Background Music on Ad Processing," *The Journal of Marketing,* October 1993, p. 123.

13. Michael J. McCarthy, "Mind Probe—What Makes an Ad Memorable? Recent Brain Research Yields Surprising Answers," *The Wall Street Journal,* March 22, 1991, p. B3.

14. Jack Trout, *The New Positioning* (New York: McGraw Hill, 1996), pp. 9–16.

15. Stephan and Tannenholz, "The Real Reason for Brand Switching."

16. J. Paul Peter and Jerry C. Olson, *Consumer Behavior and Marketing Strategy,* 4th ed. (Burr Ridge, IL: Richard D. Irwin, 1996), p. 554.

17. R. E. Petty, J. T. Cacioppo, and D. Schumann, "Central and Peripheral Routes to Advertising Effectiveness: The Moderating Role of Involvement," *Journal of Consumer Research,* vol. 10, no. 2 (1983), pp. 135–46.

18. This section and the model are adapted from Peter and Olson, *Consumer Behavior and Marketing Strategy,* pp. 554–55.

19. Ibid., pp. 556–57.

20. Yumiko Ono, "Overcoming the Stigma of Dishwashers in Japan," *The Wall Street Journal,* May 19, 2000, p. B2.

21. Karen A. Machleit, Chris T. Allen, and Thomas J. Madden, "The Mature Brand and Brand Interest: An Alternative Consequence of Ad-Evoked Affect," *Journal of Marketing,* October 1993, pp. 72–82.

22. Ibid.

23. Peter and Olson, *Consumer Behavior and Marketing Strategy,* p. 513.

24. Ken Dychtwald and Greg Gable, "Portrait of a Changing Consumer," *Business Horizons,* January/February 1990, pp. 62–74; Larry Light, "Trust Marketing: The Brand Relationship Marketing Mandate for the 90s," address to the American Association of Advertising Agencies annual meeting, Laguna Niguel, CA, April 23, 1993.

25. Colin McDonald, "Point of View: The Key Is to Understand Consumer Response," *Journal of Advertising Research,* September/October 1993, pp. 63–69.

26. McCarthy and Perreault, *Basic Marketing,* p. 204.

27. Vanessa O'Connell, "Nabisco Portrays Cookies as Boost to Women's Self-Esteem," *The Wall Street Journal,* July 10, 1998, p. B7.

28. John R. Rossiter and Larry Percy, *Advertising Communications and Promotion Management,* 2nd ed. (New York: McGraw-Hill, 1997), pp. 120–22.

29. Ibid., p. 121.

30. Ken Bryson and Lynne M. Casper, "Current Population Reports, Household and Family Characteristics: March 1997 and March 1998," U.S. Bureau of the Census; Laura Zinn, "Move Over, Boomers, the Busters Are Here—And They're Angry," *Business-Week,* December 14, 1992, pp. 74–82; Katy Kelly and Linda Kulman, "Kid Power," *U.S. News & World Report,* September 13, 2004, pp. 46–50, 52; *U.S. Census Bureau News,* September 12, 2007.

31. "The Worth of the Cool: Asking Teenagers to Identify the Coolest Brands," *Adweek,* May 9, 1994, p. 18.

32. Greg Farrell, "Star Search," *Adweek,* December 6, 1993, p. 26.

33. Jonah Freedman, "The 2007 Fortunate 50," http://sportsillustrated.cnn.com/more/specials/fortunate50/2007/.

34. McCarthy and Perreault, *Basic Marketing,* p. 131; Peter and Olson, *Consumer Behavior and Marketing Strategy,* p. 368.

35. Carolyn A. Lin, "Cultural Differences in Message Strategies: A Comparison between American and Japanese TV Commercials," *Journal of Advertising Research,* July/August 1993, pp. 40–48.

36. Ibid.

37. Peter and Olson, *Consumer Behavior and Marketing Strategy,* p. 413.

38. U.S. Census Bureau, *Statistical Abstract of the United States: 2007* (Washington, DC: U.S. Department of Commerce, 2006), Tables 15 and 16.

39. www.adage.com.

40. Rebecca Purto, "Global Psychographics," *American Demographics,* December 1990, p. 8.

41. The classic studies on cognitive dissonance were initiated by Leon Festinger, *A Theory of Cognitive Dissonance* (Evanston, IL: Row, Peterson, 1957), p. 83; for more recent views, see Hugh Murray, "Advertising's Effect on Sales—Proven or Just Assumed?" *International Journal of Advertising* (UK), vol. 5, no. 1 (1986), pp. 15–36; Delbert Hawkins, Roger Best, and Kenneth Coney, *Consumer Behavior;* 7th ed. (Burr Ridge, IL: McGraw-Hill/Irwin, 1998), pp. 609–10; Ronald E. Milliman and Phillip J. Decker, "The Use of Post-Purchase Communication to Reduce Dissonance and Improve Direct Marketing Effectiveness," *Journal of Business Communication,* Spring 1990, pp. 159–70.

42. Larry Light, "Advertising's Role in Building Brand Equity," speech to annual meeting of the American Association of Advertising Agencies, April 21, 1993.

43. Johan C. Yssel and Mark W. Walchle, "Using the FCB Grid to Write Advertising Strategy," paper presented to the Annual Conference of the Association for Education in Journalism and Mass Communication, 1992.

44. Chung K. Kim and Kenneth R. Lord, "A New FCB Grid and Its Strategic Implications for Advertising," in *Proceedings of the Annual Conference of the Administrative Sciences Association of Canada (Marketing),* Tony Schellinck, ed. (Niagara Falls, Ontario: Administrative Sciences Association of Canada, 1991), pp. 51–60.

CHAPTER 6

1. Pat Fallon and Fred Senn, *Juicing the Orange: How to Turn Creativity into a Powerful Business Advantage* (Boston: Harvard Business School Press, 2006).

2. Ibid.

3. Jon Steel, *Truth, Lies and Advertising: The Art of Account Planning* (New York: Wiley, 1998), p. 5.

4. Ibid., p. 37.

5. Ibid., p. 53.

6. Anthony Crupi, TargetCast: Price of Network:30 Slides 10% in Q1, Mediaweek, June 8, 2010 (retrieved from http://www.mediaweek.com on 6/12/2010).

7. 2010 U.S. National Edition Rates, *Time Magazine,* http://www.timemediakit.com.

8. Rilee-Kelley interview.

9. Jerry W. Thomas, "Media Advertising Is an Unfulfilled Promise," *Marketing News,* September 23, 1996, p. 28.

10. Ibid.

11. Kathryn Kranhold, "Agencies Boost Research to Spot Consumer Views," *The Asian Wall Street Journal,* March 10, 2000, p. 6.

12. Story adapted from "Cheese, Please!" *American Demographics.* March 2000, pp. S6–S8. (Copyright Primedia Intertec March 2000).

13. Ibid.

14. Pat Sloan, "DDB Boosts Planning by Hiring Brit Expert," *Advertising Age,* September 21, 1992, pp. 3, 53.

15. Perreault and McCarthy, *Basic Marketing,* p. 153.

16. Paul Conner, "Defining the 'Decision Purpose' of Research," *Marketing News,* September 23, 1996, p. 18.

17. Michael L. Garee and Thomas R. Schori, "Focus Groups Illuminate Quantitative Research," *Marketing News,* September 23, 1996, p. 41.

18. Robert West, Schering Canada, personal interview, May 17, 1993.

19. William Weylock, "Focus: Hocus Pocus?" *Marketing Tools,* July/ August 1994, pp. 12–16; Thomas L. Greenbaum, "Focus Groups Can Play a Part in Evaluating Ad Copy," *Marketing News,* September 13, 1993, pp. 24–25.

20. Pat Sloan and Julie Liesse, "New Agency Weapon to Win Clients: Research," *Advertising Age,* August 30, 1993, p. 37.

21. Ethnographic Research, Inc., www.ethnographic-research.com.

22. http://en-us.nielsen.com/tab/product_families/nielsen_homescan.

23. Jack Honomichl, "The Honomichl 50," *Marketing News,* June 10, 2002, p. H2; Don E. Schultz, Stanley I. Tannenbaum, and Robert F. Lauterborn, *Integrated Marketing Communications: Putting It Together and Making It Work* (Lincolnwood, IL: NTC Business Books, 1993), pp. 149–50.

24. Leah Rickard, "Helping Put Data in Focus," *Advertising Age,* July 11, 1994, p. 18.

25. http://en-us.nielsen.com/tab/product_families/iag.

26. Pamela L. Alreck and Robert B. Settle, *The Survey Research Handbook,* 2nd ed. (Burr Ridge, IL: Richard D. Irwin, 1995), pp. 56–59.

27. Pamela L. Alreck and Robert B. Settle, *The Survey Research Handbook,* 2nd ed. (Burr Ridge, IL: Richard D. Irwin, 1995), pp. 56–59.

28. Perreault and McCarthy, *Basic Marketing,* p. 173.

29. Alreck and Settle, *The Survey Research Handbook,* pp. 88–90.

30. MINITAB software for IBM-PC, for Microsoft Windows, and for academic use in an inexpensive student edition through Addison-Wesley Publishing Co., Reading, MA.

31. George S. Fabian, panelist, "Globalization: Challenges for Marketing and Research," *Marketing Review,* February 1993, p. 23.

32. Maureen R. Marston, panelist, "Globalization: Challenges for Marketing and Research," pp. 20–21.

33. Michael Brizz, "How to Learn What Japanese Buyers Really Want," *Business Marketing,* January 1987, p. 72.

34. Thomas L. Greenbaum, "Understanding Focus Group Research Abroad," *Marketing News,* June 3, 1996, pp. H14, H36.

35. Deborah Szynal, "Big Bytes," *Marketing News,* March 18, 2002, p. 3.

CHAPTER 7

1. Updated promo sheet and letter from BBDO-NY (1995).

2. Theresa Howard, "Brand Builders: Being True to Dew," *Brandweek,* April 24, 2000, p. 28.

3. Ibid., p. 30.

4. Christopher Lawton, "PepsiCo's Mountain Dew Backs Film," *The Wall Street Journal,* September 12, 2005, p. B4.

5. Chad Terhune, "U.S. Soda Volume Fizzles after Years of Growth," *The Wall Street Journal,* March 9, 2006, p. A13; Chad Terhune, "Pepsi Marketer's Quest: Find Fizz amid Flatness," *The Wall Street Journal,* June 14, 2006.

6. William O. Bearden, Thomas N. Ingram, and Raymond W. LaForge, *Marketing Principles & Perspectives,* 2nd ed. (Burr Ridge, IL: Richard D. Irwin, 1998), pp. 75–76.

7. Natalie Zmuda, "Why Mountain Dew Let Skater Dudes Take Control of Its Marketing," *Advertising Age,* February 22, 2010 (retrieved at http://adage.com/digitalalist10/article?article_id=142201).

8. "Market Analysis—Defining the Market," Tutor2u, (retrieved from www.tutor2u.net/business/marketing, February 26, 2003).

9. Sergio Zyman, *The End of Marketing As We Know It* (New York: HarperBusiness, 1999).

10. Kate MacArthur and Hillary Chura, "Urban Youth," *Advertising Age,* September 4, 2000, pp. 16–17.

11. Private interview with Scott Moffitt, Director of Marketing, Pepsi-Cola Company, December 2000.

12. Automation Marketing Strategies, "The Art of Market Positioning," *Strategic Advantage Newsletter,* January 2000 (retrieved from www.automationmarketing.com, February 2003).

13. Ernest Martin, "Target Marketing: Summary and Unit Learning Outcomes," Course Syllabus CADV 213 (retrieved from www.campbell.edu/faculty/martine/index.htm, February 26, 2003).

14. Raju Narisetti, "Xerox Aims to Imprint High-Tech Image," *The Wall Street Journal,* October 6, 1998, p. B8.

15. Farrell, "Dew Poses Real Pepsi Challenge to Coke," *USA Today,* 2000, p. B2.

16. Adapted from Al Ries and Jack Trout, *Bottom-Up Marketing* (New York: McGraw-Hill, 1989), p. 8.

17. Frederick E. Webster, Jr., "Executing the New Marketing Concept," *Marketing Management* 3, no. 1 (1994), pp. 8–16.

18. Philip Kotler and Gary Armstrong, *Principles of Marketing* (Englewood Cliffs, NJ: Prentice Hall, 1994), p. 560; Don E. Schultz, Stanley I. Tannenbaum, and Robert F. Lauterborn, *Integrated Marketing Communications: Putting It Together & Making It Work* (Lincolnwood, IL: NTC Business Books, 1993), p. 52.

19. Frederick E. Webster, Jr., "Defining the New Marketing Concept (Part I)," *Marketing Management* 2, no. 4 (1994), pp. 22–31.

20. Frederick E. Webster, Jr., "The Changing Role of Marketing in the Corporation," *Journal of Marketing,* October 1992, pp. 1–17, 22–31.

21. Ibid.

22. Ibid.

23. Kotler and Armstrong, *Principles of Marketing,* p. 559.

24. Ibid., p. 560.

25. Stan Rapp and Thomas L. Collins, "Nestlè Banks on Databases," *Advertising Age,* October 25, 1993, pp. 16, S–7.

26. Denison Hatch, "The Media Mix: How to Reach the Right Person with the Right Message in the Right Environment," *Target Marketing,* July 1994, pp. 8–10; and Kenneth Wylie, "Direct Response: Database Development Shows Strong Growth as Shops Gain 16.9% in U.S.," *Advertising Age,* July 12, 1993, p. S8.

27. Gary Levin, "Wunderman: 'Personalized' Marketing Will Gain Dominance," *Advertising Age,* October 25, 1993, p. S1.

28. Kotler and Armstrong, *Principles of Marketing,* p. 560.

29. Glen Nowak and Joseph Phelps, "Conceptualizing the Integrated Marketing Communications Phenomenon: An Examination of Its Impact on Advertising Practices and Its Implications for Advertising Research," *Journal of Current Issues and Research in Advertising,* Spring 1994, pp. 49–66.

30. Thomas R. Duncan and Sandra E. Moriarty, *Driving Brand Value: Using Integrated Marketing to Manage Stakeholder Relationships* (New York: McGraw-Hill, 1997), p. 42.

31. Adapted from Kotler and Armstrong, *Principles of Marketing,* pp. 560–61.

32. Arthur M. Hughes, "Can This Relationship Work?" *Marketing Tools,* July/August 1994, p. 4.

33. Hillary Chura and Kate MacArthur, "Flat Colas Anxiously Watch Gen Yers Switch," *Advertising Age,* September 25, 2000; and Howard, "Brand Builders," p. 30.

34. Kotler and Armstrong, *Principles of Marketing,* p. 561.

35. Schultz, Tannenbaum, and Lauterborn, *Integrated Marketing Communications,* p. 52.

36. Regis McKenna, "Marketing Is Everything," *Harvard Business Review,* January/February 1991, p. 65.

37. Tom Duncan, "Integrated Marketing? It's Synergy," *Advertising Age,* March 8, 1993, p. 22.

38. Glen J. Nowak and Joseph Phelps, (1994) "Conceptualizing the Integrated Marketing Communications' Phenomenon: An Examination of Its Impact on Advertising Practices and Its Implications for Advertising Research," *Journal of Current Issues & Research in Advertising,* vol. 26(1), pp. 49–66.

39. Karlene Lukovitz, "Get Ready for One-on-One Marketing," *Folio: The Magazine for Magazine Management,* October 1, 1991, pp. 64–70.

40. Don E. Schultz, "Four Basic Rules Lay Groundwork for Integration," *Marketing News,* August 16, 1993, p. 5.

41. William F. Arens and Jack J. Whidden, "La Publicité aux Etats-Unis, 1992; Les Symptomes et les Stratégies d'une Industrie Surpeuplée," *L'industrie de la Publicité au Québec 1991–1992* (Montreal: Le Publicité-Club de Montréal, October 1992), pp. 365–99.

42. Regis McKenna, "Marketing in an Age of Diversity," *Harvard Business Review,* September/October 1988, p. 88; Schultz, Tannenbaum, and Lauterborn, *Integrated Marketing Communications,* p. 21.

43. Duncan and Moriarty, *Driving Brand Value,* pp. 78–90.

44. Ibid., p. 90.

45. Adapted from Tom Duncan, "A Macro Model of Integrated Marketing Communication," paper presented to the annual conference of the American Academy of Advertising, Norfolk, VA, March 23–24, 1995, pp. 7–10.

46. Don E. Schultz, "The Next Step in IMC?" *Marketing News,* August 15, 1994, pp. 8–9.

47. Rapp and Collins, "Nestlé Banks on Databases," pp. 16, S7.

48. Don E. Schultz, "Trying to Determine ROI for IMC," *Marketing News,* January 3, 1994, p. 18; Don E. Schultz, "Spreadsheet Approach to Measuring ROI for IMC," *Marketing News,* February 28, 1994, p. 12; and Matthew P. Gonring, "Putting Integrated Marketing Communications to Work Today," *Public Relations Quarterly,* Fall 1994, p. 45.

49. Don E. Schultz, "Integration Helps You Plan Communications from Outside-In," *Marketing News,* March 15, 1993, p. 12.

50. McKenna, "Marketing Is Everything."

51. Schultz, Tannenbaum, and Lauterborn, *Integrated Marketing Communications,* pp. 55–58.

52. Wayne Henderson, "The IMC Scale: A Tool for Evaluating IMC Usage," *Integrated Marketing Communications Research Journal,* vol. 3, no. 1 (Spring 1997), pp. 11–17.

53. Ibid; Cyndee Miller, "Everyone Loves 'IMC,' but...," *Marketing News,* August 16, 1993, pp. 1, 6.

54. Don E. Schultz and Paul Wang, "Real World Results," *Marketing Tools,* premier issue, May 1994, pp. 40–47.

55. Ibid.

56. Don E. Schultz, "Integrated Marketing Communications: A Competitive Weapon in Today's Marketplace," *Marketing Review,* July 1993, pp. 10–11, 29.

57. Gregg Ambach and Mike Hess, "Measuring Long-Term Effects in Marketing," *Marketing Research: A Magazine of Management and Applications,* American Marketing Association, Summer 2000, pp. 23–30.

58. Robert D. Buzzell and Frederick D. Wiersema, "Successful Share-Building Strategies," *Harvard Business Review,* January/February 1981, p. 135; Siva K. Balasubramanian and V. Kumar, "Analyzing Variations in Advertising and Promotional Expenditures: Key Correlated in Consumer, Industrial, and Service Markets," *Journal of Marketing,* April 1990, pp. 57–68.

59. Bernard Ryan Jr., *Advertising in a Recession: The Best Defense Is a Good Offense* (New York: American Association of Advertising Agencies, 1991), pp. 13–29; Priscilla C. Brown, "Surviving with a Splash," *Business Marketing,* January 1991, p. 14; Edmund O. Lawler, "A Window of Opportunity," *Business Marketing,* January 1991, p. 16; Rebecca Colwell Quarles, "Marketing Research Turns Recession into Business Opportunity," *Marketing News,* January 7, 1991, pp. 27, 29.

60. Fabiana Giacomotti, "European Marketers Keep Up Ad Budgets," *Adweek,* January 24, 1994, pp. 16–17.

61. Leo Bogart, *Strategy in Advertising,* 2nd ed. (Chicago: Crain Books, 1984), pp. 45–47.

62. John Philip Jones, "Ad Spending: Maintaining Market Share," *Harvard Business Review,* January/February 1990, pp. 38–42; James C. Schroer, "Ad Spending: Growing Market Share," *Harvard Business Review,* January/February 1990, pp. 44–49.

63. Peter Breen, "Seeds of Change," Promo Sourcebook Supplement, Copyright 2000, INTERTEC, p. 18 (retrieved from www.lexisnexis.com).

CHAPTER 8

1. "Target through the Years," (retrieved at http://sites.target.com/site/en/company/page.jsp?contentId=WCMP04-031697).

2. Jeffrey Arlen, "Why Is Target So Cool?" DSN Retailing Today, April 2, 2001 (retrieved at http://findarticles.com/p/articles/mi_m0FNP/is_7_40/ai_73181652/).

3. Deborah Belgum, "Mossimo and Cherokee in Battle over Finder's Fees," Los Angeles Business Journal, Monday, July 15, 2002 (retrieved at http://www.allbusiness.com/north-america/united-states-california-metro-areas/252558-1.html).

4. Adapted from Bruce Bendinger, *The Copy Workshop Workbook* (Chicago: The Copy Workshop, 2002), pp. 128–47.

5. Nancy A. Mitchell, Diane M. Badzinski, and Donna R. Pawlowski, "The Use of Metaphors as Vivid Stimuli to Enhance Comprehension and Recall of Print Advertisements," in Karen

Whitehill King, ed., *Proceedings of the 1994 Conference of the American Academy of Advertising* (Athens, GA: Henry W. Grady College of Journalism and Mass Communication, the University of Georgia, 1994), p. 199.

6. Ibid.

7. Sandra Moriarty and Shay Sayre, "An Interpretive Study of Visual Cues in Advertising," paper presented to the annual convention of the Association for Education in Journalism and Mass Communication, Montreal, August 1992, p. 5.

8. Hank Seiden, *Advertising Pure and Simple* (New York: AMACOM, 1990), pp. 23–240.

9. Nancy A. Mitchell, Diane M. Badzinski, and Donna R. Pawlowski, "The Use of Metaphors as Vivid Stimuli to Enhance Comprehension and Recall of Print Advertisements," in Karen Whitehill King, ed., *Proceedings of the 1994 Conference of the American Academy of Advertising* (Athens, GA: Henry W. Grady College of Journalism and Mass Communication, the University of Georgia, 1994), p. 199.

10. Ibid.

11. Sal Randazzo, *The Mythmakers: How Advertisers Apply the Power of Classic Myths and Symbols to Create Modern Day Legends* (Chicago: Probus Publishing, 1995), pp. 28–51.

12. Barry A. Hollander, "Infomation Graphics and the Bandwagon Effect: Does the Visual Display of Opinion Aid in Persuasion?" paper presented to the annual convention of the Association for Education in Journalism and Mass Communication, Montreal, August 1992, p. 21.

13. Kevin Goldman, "Nike, H-P Gamble on New Sales Pitches," *The Wall Street Journal,* April 8, 1994, p. B8.

14. Allen F. Harrison and Robert M. Bramson, *The Art of Thinking* (New York: Berkley Books, 1984), pp. 26, 34, 181.

15. Ibid.

16. Roger von Oech, *A Kick in the Seat of the Pants* (New York: HarperPerennial, 1986), p. 12.

17. John O'Toole, *The Trouble with Advertising,* 2nd ed. (New York: Random House, 1985), p. 132; Fred Danzig, "The Big Idea," *Advertising Age,* November 9, 1988, pp. 16, 138–40.

18. O'Toole, *The Trouble with Advertising,* pp. 132–33.

19. Adapted with permission from von Oech, *A Kick in the Seat of the Pants,* pp. 55–87.

20. Bob Garfield, "Lovestruck Praying Mantis Is Hooked on Fila," *Advertising Age,* February 13, 1995, p. 3.

21. William D. Perreault Jr. and E. Jerome McCarthy, *Basic Marketing,* 17th ed. (Burr Ridge, IL: Richard D. Irwin, 2008).

22. Adapted with permission from von Oech, *A Kick in the Seat of the Pants,* pp. 89–111.

23. Bendinger, *The Copy Workshop Workbook,* pp. 170–74.

24. David Ogilvy, *Ogilvy on Advertising* (New York: Random House, 1985), pp. 17–18.

CHAPTER 9

1. Laurel Wenz, "TV Is Snubbed as Philips, Tribal DDB Win Film Grand Prix, June 27, 2009, http://adage.com/cannes09/article?article_id=137629.

2. Ibid.

3. Ed White, "Stink's Adam Berg Takes Us Behind Philips 'Carousel,'" Boards, http://www.boardsmag.community/blogs/behindthescenes/index.php?p=29.

4. Ibid.

5. Laurel Wentz, "Cannes Swept by PR, Integrated, Internet Winners," June 29, 2009, http://adage.com/cannes09/article?article_id=137630.

6. Sue Chastain, ed., "Types of Graphics Software," About.com (http://graphicssoft.about.com/od/findsoftware/a/pagelayout.htm).

7. "What Types of Ads Are Most Helpful," Search Engine Land (retrieved at http://searchengineland.com/what-ads-types-are-most-helpful-search-ads-follow-newspapers-tv-21913).

8. A. Jerome Jeweler and Bonnie L. Drewniany, *Creative Strategy in Advertising* (Belmont, CA: Wadsworth Publishing, 1998), p. 139.

9. Roy Paul Nelson, *The Design of Advertising* (Dubuque, IA: Brown & Benchmark, 1994), p. 107; J. Douglas Johnson, *Advertising Today* (Chicago: Science Research Associates, 1978).

10. John O'Toole, *The Trouble with Advertising,* 2nd ed. (New York: Random House, 1985), p. 149.

11. Axel Andersson and Denison Hatch, "How to Create Headlines That Get Results," *Target Marketing,* March 1994, pp. 28–35.

12. Murray Raphel and Neil Raphel, "A New Look at Newspaper Ads," *Progressive Grocer,* November 1993, pp. 13–14; David Ogilvy, *Ogilvy on Advertising* (New York: Random House, 1985), pp. 88–89.

13. Philip Ward Burton, *Advertising Copywriting,* 6th ed. (Lincolnwood, IL: NTC Business Books, 1991), pp. 65–66, 70.

14. Nelson, *The Design of Advertising,* p. 91.

15. Jeweler and Drewniany, *Creative Strategy in Advertising,* p. 115; Burton, *Advertising Copywriting,* p. 188; Julia M. Collins, "Image and Advertising," *Harvard Business Review,* January/February 1989, pp. 93–97.

16. Neil Raphel and Murray Raphel, "Rules to Advertise By," *Progressive Grocer,* December 1993, pp. 13–14; Murray Raphel, "How to Get Ahead in Direct Mail," *Direct Marketing,* January 1990, pp. 30–32, 52.

17. Ogilvy, *Ogilvy on Advertising,* p. 71.

18. Raphel and Raphel, "A New Look at Newspaper Ads," pp. 13–14.

19. James H. Leigh, "The Use of Figures of Speech in Print Ad Headlines," *Journal of Advertising Research,* June 1994, pp. 17–33.

20. Ogilvy, *Ogilvy on Advertising,* pp. 10–11.

21. Andersson and Hatch, "How to Create Headlines That Get Results," pp. 28–35.

22. Burton, *Advertising Copywriting,* p. 54; Arthur J. Kover and William J. James, "When Do Advertising 'Power Words' Work? An Examination of Congruence and Satiation," *Journal of Advertising Research,* July/August 1993, pp. 32–38.

23. Burton, *Advertising Copywriting,* p. 58.

24. Raphel and Raphel, "A New Look at Newspaper Ads," pp. 13–14.

25. Burton, *Advertising Copywriting,* p. 54.

26. Burton, *Advertising Copywriting,* p. 12.

27. Raphel and Raphel, "Rules to Advertise By," pp. 13–14.

28. Bendinger, *The Copy Workshop Workbook,* p. 192.

29. Burton, *Advertising Copywriting,* p. 74.

30. Ogilvy, *Ogilvy on Advertising,* p. 119.

31. Burton, *Advertising Copywriting,* p. 79.

32. Leigh, "The Use of Figures of Speech in Print Ad Headlines," pp. 17–33.

33. Burton, *Advertising Copywriting,* p. 90; Marjorie Zieff-Finn, "It's No Laughing Matter," *Direct Marketing,* September 1992, pp. 38–40.

34. O'Toole, *The Trouble with Advertising,* p. 149.

35. Levinson, *Guerrilla Advertising,* p. 203; Burton, *Advertising Copywriting,* pp. 221–22.

36. Herschell Gordon Lewis, "Radio Copywriting—Not as Easy as You May Think," *Direct Marketing,* July 1992, pp. 17–18.

37. Ogilvy, *Ogilvy on Advertising,* p. 109.

38. Ibid., pp. 103–13.

39. Bendinger, *The Copy Workshop Workbook,* p. 284.

40. "Corporate Advertising Study," Burson-Marsteller, October 13, 2003, www.efluentials.com/documents/pr_101303.pdf.

41. Richard N. Weltz, "How Do You Say, 'Ooops.'"

42. Lennie Copeland, "Foreign Markets: Not for the Amateur," *Business Marketing,* July 1984, pp. 112–18.

43. John Freiralds, "Navigating the Minefields of Multilingual Marketing," *Pharmaceutical Executive,* September 1994, pp. 74–78.

CHAPTER 10

1. Saatchi & Saatchi Los Angeles and Toyota Motor Sales, personal correspondence and interviews, January 2001.

2. Personal interview, Lorraine Alper Kramer, Saatchi & Saatchi Los Angeles, January 2001.

3. "2008 Executive Summary of the 4A's Television Production Cost Survey," Retrieved at http://www.aaaa.org/news/bulletins/Documents/2008TVPCSExecSumcosts.pdf.

4. Kenneth Roman and Jane Maas, *How to Advertise* (New York: St. Martin's Press, 1992), pp. 26–28; Miner Raymond, "How to Cut Commercial Production Costs without Anyone Knowing You've Done It," *Sales & Marketing Management in Canada,* December 1987, pp. 20–22; "Marketing Guide 19: Advertising Production," *Marketing* (UK), February 7, 1991, pp. 21–24.

5. Cleveland Horton, "Spots: Cheaper Is More Effective," *Advertising Age,* July 4, 1994, p. 6.

6. "Button Pushers: Ordering Kiosks Boost Sales and Speed of Service but Don't Necessarily Cut Labor Costs," *Chain Leader* 9, no. 1 (January 2004), p. 54 (retrieved from www.lexisnexis.com, August 26, 2004).

7. Personal interview, Dean Van Eimeren, Saatchi & Saatchi Los Angeles, January 2001.

8. PANTONE® is a registered trademark of PANTONE, Inc.

9. Kathleen Lewis, "Printing: Teach Your Boss a Lesson," *In-House Graphics,* February 1990, p. 89.

10. Jonathan Bond and Richard Kirshenbaum, *Under the Radar: Talking to Today's Cynical Consumer* (New York: John Wiley & Sons, 1998), p. 154.

11. Adapted from Greg Hofman, "Splash Graphics That Say 'Gotcha,'" *Step-by-Step Graphics,* May/June 1991, p. 40.

12. David Ogilvy, *Ogilvy on Advertising* (New York: Random House, 1985), pp. 113–16.

13. Tom Cuniff, "The Second Creative Revolution," *Advertising Age,* December 6, 1993, p. 22.

CHAPTER 11

1. The Citizens' Commission to Protect the Truth Web site (retrieved from www.protectthetruth.org/commission.htm, September 12, 2006).

2. Joe Serwach, "Teen Smoking Rates Continue to Decline," *The University Record Online,* January 9, 2006 (retrieved from www.umich.edu/~urecord/0506/Jan09_06/10.shtml, September 12, 2006).

3. Warren Berger, "Dare-Devils: The Ad World's Most Buzzed-About Agency Is Miami's Crispin Porter + Bogusky," CNN.com, April 1, 2004 (retrieved from http://money.cnn.com/magazines/business2/business2_archive/2004/04/01/366192/index.htm, September 12, 2006).

4. The Citizens' Commission to Protect the Truth Web site (retrieved from www.protectthetruth.org/commission.htm, September 12, 2006).

5. "Truth Campaign," The Citizens' Commission to Protect the Truth Web site (retrieved from www.protectthetruth.org/truthcampaign.htm, September 12, 2006).

6. "New Truth Campaign Uses Giant Arrows to Get Straight to the Point about Tobacco," Arnold Worldwide Web site (retrieved from www.arnoldworldwide.com/content.cfm?page=108&id=158, September 12, 2006).

7. TNS Media Intelligence, June 22, 2009 (retrieved from http://adage.com/images/random/datacenter/2009/spendtrends09.pdf).

8. Patrick M. Reilly and Ernest Beck, "Publishers Often Pad Circulation Figures," *The Wall Street Journal,* September 30, 1997, p. B12.

9. Shu-Fen Li, John C. Schweitzer, and Benjamin J. Bates, "Effectiveness of Trade Magazine Advertising," paper presented to the annual conference of the Association for Education in Journalism and Mass Communication, Montreal, Quebec, August 1992.

10. *The Magazine Handbook,* Magazine Publishers Association, 2004/05, www.magazine.org/cocontent/Files/MPA_handbook_04.pdf.

11. Gene Willhoft, "Is 'Added Value' Valuable?" *Advertising Age,* March 1, 1993, p. 18.

12. Answers: *Car & Driver* is $144.05 CPM, *Car & Driver* media kit; *Road & Track* is $156.25 CPM, *Road & Track* media kit (www.hfmus.com).

13. Lisa I. Fried, "New Rules Liven Up the Rate-Card Game," *Advertising Age,* October 24, 1994, p. S8.

14. www.ghmediakit.com.

15. www.newsweekmediakit.com.

16. Joyce Rutter Kaye, *Print Casebooks 10/The Best in Advertising,* 1994–95 ed. (Rockville, MD: RC Publications, 1994), pp. 63–65; Tony Case, "Getting Personal," *Editor & Publisher,* February 1, 1992, pp. 16, 31; Ann Cooper, "Creatives: Magazines—Believers in the Power of Print," *Adweek* (Eastern ed.), April 12, 1993, pp. 34–39.

17. TNS Media Intelligence, June 22, 2009 (retrieved from http://adage.com/images/random/datacenter/2009/spendtrends09.pdf).

18. www.naa.org.

19. ibid.

20. ibid.

21. The New York Times Ranks as Top Online Newspaper According to May 2010 U.S. comScore Media Metrix Data, *PR Newswire,* June 16, 2010 (retrieved from http://www.prnewswire.com/news-releases/the-new-york-times-ranks-as-top-online-newspaper-according-to-may-2010-us-comscore-media-metrix-data-96487229.html, on June 17, 2010).

22. www.naa.org.

23. Ronald Redfern, "What Readers Want from Newspapers," *Advertising Age,* January 23, 1995, p. 25.

24. www.naa.org.

25. ibid.

26. "Parade Media Solutions," *Parade* Web site (retrieved from http://mediakit.parade.com/parade/mediasolutions.html, on June 17, 2010).

27. U.S. newspaper circulation drops 8.7%, *USA Today*, Apr 26, 2010 (retrieved from http://content.usatoday.com/communities/ondeadline/post/2010/04/us-newspaper-circulation-drops-87/1, on June 17, 2010).

28. "Joint Promotion Adds Stickers to Sweet Smell of Marketing," Stuart Elliott, *The New York Times,* April 2, 2007 (retrieved from http://www.nytimes.com/2007/04/02/business/media/02adcol.html?_r=1&ref=media, on June 17, 2010).

29. *Newspaper Rate Differentials* (New York: American Association of Advertising Agencies, 1990); Christy Fisher, "NAA Readies National Ad-Buy Plan," *Advertising Age,* March 1, 1993, p. 12.

30. *The Source: Newspapers by the Numbers,* Newspaper Association of America (retrieved from www.naa.org/thesource, September 1, 2006).

31. John Flinn, "State of the National Buy," *Adweek,* June 26, 1995, p. 56.

32. Christy Fisher, "Chrysler's One-Stop Ad Buys Boost Ailing Newspapers," *Advertising Age,* March 7, 1994, p. 49.

33. Dorothy Giobbe, "One Order/One Bill System Gets a Dress Rehearsal," *Editor & Publisher,* March 12, 1994, pp. 26, 46.

34. Fisher, "Chrysler's One-Stop Ad Buys Boost Ailing Newspapers," p. 49; Ibid.

35. Stephen Barr, "Moving Ahead," *Adweek,* January 31, 1994, p. 26.

36. New Research Shows Overall Yellow Pages Usage Growing—17.2 Billion Searches in 2007, Yellow Pages Association, Feb 26, 2008 (retrieved from http://www.marketwire.com/press-release/New-Research-Shows-Overall-Yellow-Pages-Usage-Growing-172-Billion-Searches-in-2007-825649.htm, on June 17, 2010).

37. *Yellow Pages Industry Facts Booklet,* 1994–95 edition (Troy, MI: Yellow Pages Publishers Association, 1994), p. 32.

38. www.simbainformation.com.

39. Bradley Johnson, "Yellow-Pages Deals Red Hot as Telecom Industry Regroups," *Advertising Age,* January 6, 2003 (retrieved from www.proquest.com, May 12, 2003).

40. Randall Crosby, "Is Ride-Along the Right Track?" *Link,* February 1995, pp. 17–23.

CHAPTER 12

1. Michelle Krebs, "To Counter Stigma, Hyundai Bolsters Warranty," *The New York Times,* November 8, 1998 (retrieved from http://www.nytimes.com/1998/11/08/automobiles/to-counter-stigma-hyundai-bolsters-warranty.html, June 1, 2009).

2. Associated Press, "Updated Ratings Make Super Bowl XLIII the Most-Watched Ever," *USA Today,* February 4, 2009 (retrieved from http://www.usatoday.com/sports/football/nfl/2009-02-04-ratings_N.htm, June 1, 2009).

3. Hyundai Motor America Reports February 2009 Sales, Press Release, March 3, 2009 (retrieved from http://www.marketwatch.com/story/hyundai-motor-america-reportsfebruary-2009?dist=msr_2).

4. "100 Leading National Advertisers 2009, U.S. Ad Spend Trends: 2008," *Advertising Age,* June 22, 2009 (retrieved from http://adage.com/images/random/datacenter/2009/spendtrends09.pdf, June 22, 2010).

5. "Media Trends Track, TV Basics: Number of Commercial TV Stations," Television Bureau of Advertising, Inc. Source: Television & Cable Factbook. http://www.tvb.org/rcentral/mediatrendstrack/tvbasics/28_CommercialTVStations.asp.

6. "30.3% of American TV Households Now Subscribe to Alternate Delivery, An All-Time High." Source: Nielsen Media Research/NSI, May 2010 (retrieved from http://www.tvb.org/selling/competitive_landscape/case_against_cable/cl_ads_satellite_cable.asp, June 22, 2010).

7. "TV Basics: Commercial Television Stations," Television Bureau of Advertising, Inc. (retrieved from www.tvb.org, June 1, 2009).

8. ibid.

9. "TV Basics: Channels—Receivable vs. Viewed," Television Bureau of Advertising, Inc. (retrieved from www.tvb.org, August 26, 2004).

10. "Top 20 Cable Programs and Networks—2008 Estimate," (retrieved from www.neta.com/statistic/statistic/Top20Networks.aspx).

11. "2008 Media Comparisons Study," Television Bureau of Advertising, Inc. (retrieved from www.tvb.org, June 1, 2009).

12. "Television, Internet and Mobile Usage in the U.S., A2/M2 Three Screen Report, 4th Quarter 2008," The Nielsen Company (retrieved from http://i.cdn.turner.com/cnn/2009/images/02/24/screen.press.b.pdf, June 22, 2010).

13. "Local Cable Ad Revenues on the Rise," December 10, 2004 (retrieved from www.reclaimthemedia.org, November 15, 2005).

14. "U.S. Digital Cable TV Advertising Analysis & Forecast 2006–2009," Multimedia Research Group, June 2006, http://www.researchandmarkets.com/reportinfo.asp?report_id=339668 (accessed August 1, 2007).

15. "U.S. DVR Forecast, 2009 To 2014," James L. McQuivey, Ph.D., Forrester Research (retrieved from http://www.forrester.com/rb/Research/us_dvr_forecast,_2009_to_2014/q/id/53802/t/2, June 22, 2010).

16. "Television, Internet and Mobile Usage in the U.S., A2/M2 Three Screen Report, 4th Quarter 2008," The Nielsen Company (retrieved from http://i.cdn.turner.com/cnn/2009/images/02/24/screen.press.b.pdf, June 22, 2010).

17. Thomas R. Duncan and Sandra E. Moriarty, *Driving Brand Value: Using Integrated Marketing to Manage Stakeholder Relationships* (New York: McGraw-Hill, 1997), pp. 101–2.

18. Ibid.

19. George Winslow, "Reaching Out," http://www.worldscreen.com/featuresarchive.php?filename=0105cover.htm (accessed August 1, 2007).

20. Kathy Haley, "Spot TV Is Power Tool," *The Power of Spot TV,* supplement to *Advertising Age,* September 29, 1993, p. T3.

21. Michael Burgi, "Welcome to the 500 Club," *Adweek,* September 13, 1993, p. 45; Christopher Stern, "Advertisers Hear Promise of Smooth Spot Cable Buys," *Broadcasting & Cable,* April 26, 1993, pp. 56, 58.

22. "TV Syndication Upfront Dollars Up 15% to $2.3B," John Consoli, The Wrap News Inc., June 17, 2010, retrieved from http://www.thewrap.com/television/column-post/tv-syndication-upfront-dollars-15-23b-18476, June 22, 2010).

23. "What Is Syndication?" *1994 Guide to Advertiser-Supported Syndication,* supplement to *Advertising Age* (New York: Advertiser Syndicated Television Association, 1994), p. A6; David Tobenkin, "Action Escalates for Syndicators," *Broadcasting & Cable,* August 29, 1994, pp. 29–35.

24. "Syndication Showcase," *Broadcasting & Cable,* January 24, 1994, pp. 82–86.

25. Kathy Haley, "The Infomercial Begins a New Era as a Marketing Tool for Top Brands," *Advertising Age,* January 25, 1993, p. M3.

26. "Success in sports helps infomercials shed inferiority complex," *Sports Business Journal,* June 19, 2006, (retrieved from http://www.sportsbusinessjournal.com/article/50997, June 22, 2010).

27. Kevin Goldman, "CBS to Push Videotaping of Infomercials," *The Wall Street Journal,* November 15, 1993, p. B7.

28. "Nielsen: Product Placement on the Rise on Broadcast TV," John Eggerton, *Broadcasting & Cable*, 5/5/2008 (retrieved from http://www.broadcastingcable.com/article/113587-Nielsen_Product_Placement_On_The_Rise_On_Broadcast_TV.php, June 22, 2010).

29. "Sex, the City & All That Merchandise," *Media Money,* Julia Boorstin, June 1, 2010 (retrieved from http://www.cnbc.com/id/37398822/ on June 22, 2010).

30. Thom Forbes. "Gas Pump TV, With Ads, Offers Captive Audience," MediaPost News, June 6, 2006.

31. Bill Carter, "Television: A Monopoly Once More, Nielsen Is Still Unloved," *The New York Times,* September 7, 1992, p. 19; Jim Cooper, "Arbitron Exit Sparks Concern about Lack of Competition," *Broadcasting & Cable,* October 25, 1993, p. 45.

32. Will Workman, "ADcom's Cable Meter: A Revolution in the Making," *Cable World,* March 17, 1997 (www.mediacentral.com).

33. Ibid.

34. Kevin Goldman, "CBS Pays Price for Losing Bet on Ratings," *The Wall Street Journal,* November 30, 1993, p. B4; Kevin Goldman, "CBS Again Must Offer Make-Good Ads," *The Wall Street Journal,* October 27, 1994, p. B6; Kevin Goldman, "'Scarlett' Make-Goods," *The Wall Street Journal,* November 21, 1994, p. B8.

35. "Radio Is Cost-Effective," *1997 Radio Marketing Guide & Fact Book for Advertisers.*

36. "Radio's Personalities Help Find Snapple's Sales Targets," *The Power of Radio,* special advertising supplement to *Advertising Age,* October 18, 1993, p. R3.

37. *2006 Marketing Guide and Fact Book,* Radio Advertising Bureau (retrieved from www.rab.com).

38. "TNS Media Intelligence Reports U.S. Advertising Expenditures Increased 4.1 Percent in 2006," March 13, 2007, www.tns-mi.com/news/03132007.htm (accessed August 1, 2007).

39. "Media Comparisons," *1997 Radio Marketing Guide and Fact Book for Advertisers;* Imagery Transfer Study (New York: Network Radio Association, 1993).

40. Ibid.; *Media Facts: The Complete Guide to Maximizing Your Advertising* (New York: Radio Advertising Bureau, 1994), pp. 8–9.

41. "Maximize Your Marketing Message with Radio," *1997 Radio Marketing Guide and Fact Book for Advertisers; Radio Marketing Guide and Factbook for Advertisers: 1993–1994,* pp. 29–33.

42. "There's a Radio Format for Everybody," *1997 Radio Marketing Guide and Fact Book for Advertisers.*

43. Network Radio: *Targeting the National Consumer,* supplement to *Advertising Age,* September 6, 1993, pp. R2, R4; *Marketer's Guide to Media,* Fall/Winter 1992–93, pp. 69–70.

44. Meredith Deliso, "Oprah Delivers for XM Satellite," *Advertising Age,* September 25, 2006.

45. "iPods Shock Radio Jocks," February 16, 2005, http://newsosaur.blogspot.com (accessed August 1, 2007).

CHAPTER 13

1. eMarketer Digital Intelligence, "Double digit bounce back for Online Ad Spending," May 17, 2010, retrieved at http://www.emarketer.com/Article.aspx?R=1007702.

2. Netcraft, "June 2010 Web Server Survey," retrieved at http://news.netcraft.com/archives/2010/06/16/june-2010-web-server-survey.html.

3. Alexa, "Yahoo.com," retrieved June 27, 2010, at http://www.alexa.com/siteinfo/yahoo.com.

4. Alexa, "Google.com," retrieved June 27, 2010, at http://www.alexa.com/siteinfo/google.com.

5. OnlineMatters.com, "Glossary of Online Marketing Terms," retrieved at http://www.onlinematters.com/glossary.htm.

6. Fortune, "Rumor: 40-45 million iPhones in 2010," December 23, 2009, retrieved at http://tech.fortune.cnn.com/2009/12/23/rumor-40-45-million-iphones-in-2010/.

7. Steve Miller and Mike Beirne, "The iPhone Effect," Brandweek, April 28, 2008 (retrieved from http://www.adweek.com/aw/content_display/news/agency/e3ibef1ad200773laba65le-6216ba3b6267).

8. eMarketer Digital Intelligence, "Mobile Shopping Doubles in 2010," June 3, 2010, retrieved at http://www2.emarketer.com/Article.aspx?R=1007734.

9. Buzzcity, "Mobile Advertising Continues Strong Growth," Buzzcity, July 22, 2009 (retrieved from http://www.mobile-tech-today.com/story.xhtml?story_id=67945&full_skip=1).

10. Miniwatts Marketing Group, "Internet Usage Statistics," retrieved at http://www.internetworldstats.com/stats.htm.

11. IAB, "Ad Impression Measurement Guidelines," retrieved June 27, 2010, at http://www.iab.net/iab_products_and_industry_services/1421/1443/1455.

12. IAB, "Leading Global Advertising Industry Organizations Endorse Interactive Advertising Campaign Measurement Guidelines," retrieved June 27, 2010, at http://www.iab.net/about_the_iab/recent_press_releases/press_release_archive/press_release/4682.

13. Yahoo! Finance, "Amazon.com," retrieved June 24, 2010, at http://finance.yahoo.com/q/is?annual&s=amzn.

14. http://investor.google.com/financial/tables.html.

15. Samantha Yaffe, "Are Marketers Undervaluing the Internet?" *Strategy,* March 8, 2004, p. 1, retrieved September 3, 2004, at www.global.lexisnexis.com/us.

16. Wendy Davis, "Judge Brings Reunion.com and Spam Suit Together Again," Online Media Daily, April 12, 2010, retrieved at http://www.mediapost.com/publications/?fa=Articles.showArticle&art_aid=125938.

17. Matt Hines, "ISP hammers Bob Vila Site with Spam Suit," CNET News, March 5, 2004, retrieved at http://news.cnet.com/2100-1024-5170631.html.

18. Amanda Beeler, "Word-of-Mouth Pitches Mutate into New Forms on the Internet," *Advertising Age,* April 2000 (retrieved January 2001 from www.adage.com).

19. John Burbank, "What to Do About Web Advertising's Total Lack of Recall," January 5, 2009, retrieved at http://blog.nielsen.com/nielsenwire/online_mobile/what-to-do-about-web-advertisings-total-lack-of-recall/.

CHAPTER 14

1. "James Ready Beer—Share Our Billboard Campaign," March 4, 2010, *AdDude's Insights* (retrieved from http://lifson.com/?tag=james-ready-beer, June 26, 2010).

2. James Ready (Beer), Wikipedia.org, retrieved from http://en.wikipedia.org/wiki/James_Ready_(beer).

3. "James Ready—Share Our Billboard Campaign," Case Study, Adforum.com, retrieved from http://www.adforum.com/adfolio/reel_detail.asp?page=1&ID=34444670&TDI=Vdnpg80Qj8.

4. "Leo Burnett, James Ready Win Top International Outdoor Honour," Jeromy Lloyd, April 21, 2009, *Marketing* (retrieved from http://www.marketingmag.ca/english/news/agency/article.jsp?content=20090421_145348_6236, June 26, 2010),

5. "James Ready: Billboard Coupon," *Creativity* (retrieved from http://creativityonline.com/work/james-ready-billboard-coupon/19864, June 26, 2010).

6. "Outdoor Pie Chart," Outdoor Advertising Association of America (retrieved from http://www.oaaa.org/marketingresources/revenue/outdoorpiechart.aspx, June 26, 2010).

7. "Introduce Yourself to Outdoor Advertising," Outdoor Advertising Association of America, Inc. (retrieved from www.oaaa.org, October 8, 2004).

8. *Billboard Basics* (New York: Outdoor Advertising Association of America, 1994), p. 5.

9. "Outdoor Pie Chart," Outdoor Advertising Association of America.

10. Mary Jo Haskey, "The Last Mass Medium," *Mediaweek,* December 6, 1993, p. 17.

11. Ibid., pp. 11, 21; Kevin Goldman, "Billboards Gain Respect as Spending Increases," *The Wall Street Journal,* June 27, 1994, p. B5.

12. "Digital Technology Is Changing the Delivery of Information," Outdoor Advertising Association of America, Inc. (retrieved from http://www.oaaa.org/legislativeandregulatory/digital/aboutdigitalbillboardtechnology.aspx, on June 26, 2010).

13. TAB Eyes On—Out-Of-Home Media Measurement The Basics 2009 (retrieved from http://www.eyesonrating.com).

14. "CPM Comparisons for Major Media," Outdoor Advertising Association of America.

15. "Technology Standards," Outdoor Advertising Association of America, 1997 (www.oaaa.org/Tech).

16. Ibid.

17. "More Cities Ban Digital Billboards," Larry Copeland, *USA Today,* March 24, 2010 (retrieved from http://www.usatoday.com/news/nation/2010-03-22-visual-soup_N.htm, on June 26, 2010).

18. Karl Greenberg, "Lexus Accelerates into All Venues in Push for Revamped IS Sedan," *Brandweek,* August 31, 2005 (retrieved from http://www.brandweek.com/bw/news/autos/article_display.jsp?vnu_content_id=1001052022, September 8, 2006).

19. Cyndee Miller, "Outdoor Advertising Weathers Repeated Attempts to Kill It," *Marketing News,* March 16, 1992, pp. 1, 9; *Billboard Basics,* pp. 15–16.

20. "Surveys Show Americans Like Their Billboards," Outdoor Advertising Association of America, 1997 (www.oaaa.org).

21. Riccardo A. Davis, "Apparel, Movies Orchestrate an Outdoor Rebirth," *Advertising Age,* November 22, 1993, p. S1.

22. Riccardo A. Davis, "Retailers Open Doors Wide for Co-op," *Advertising Age,* August 1, 1994, p. 30. Melissa Korn, "Bricks Rivaling Clicks in Ad Spending," *Financial Times,* July 21, 2006 (retrieved from http://search.ft.com/searchArticle?queryText=1-800-flowers&y=4&javascriptEnabled=true&id=060721008312&x=8, September 9, 2006); "Outdoor Grows Online Sales: 1-800-Flowers.com Sales 7 Times Greater in Outdoor Markets," CBS Outdoor, retrieved from www.cbsoutdoor.com/news.php, September 12, 2006).

23. "Advertising That Imitates Art," *Adweek,* June 20, 1994, p. 18.

24. Larry Dobrow, "If the Cap Fits . . .," Mediapost.com, April 2006 (retrieved from http://publications.mediapost.com/index.cfm?fuseaction=Articles.showArticle&art_aid=40183, September 15, 2006).

25. Fara Warner, "DKNY Takes Upscale Ads Underground," *The Wall Street Journal,* October 6, 1994, p. B4; "Nextel, Las Vegas Link Brands in Monorail Deal," *Los Angeles Times,* November 17, 2003 (retrieved from www.lvmonorail.com/about_01_news_detail.asp, September 9, 2004).

26. Shahna Mahmud, "Cinema Ad Revenue up 15 Percent," *Adweek,* October 15, 2007.

27. "Why Digital License Plates Are a Great Idea," Chris Matyszczyk, cnet news, June 21, 2010 (retrieved from http://news.cnet.com/8301-17852_3-20008394-71.html, on June 26, 2010).

28. James Ferrier, "Spotlight on Technology—Telecite," *Advertising Age,* November 22, 1993, p. SS10.

29. "Mail Spend to Rise," *Darrell Dawsey,* January 7, 2010, https://www.delivermagazine.com/themagazine/2010/01/07/mail-spend-to-rise/.

30. Andrew K. Macris.

31. Lost in the Mail, Matthew Philips, *Newsweek,* March 30, 2010, http://www.newsweek.com/2010/03/29/lost-in-the-mail.html.

32. The High Costs of Catalog Retailing, *Adweek,* March 31, 2010, http://www.adweek.com/aw/content_display/news/client/e3id9db7bed8e9402cb0776f810c4fb9280.

33. Catalog Merchandise Marketing, Lindsay Richardson, http://www.catalogs.com/info/b2b/catalogmerchandise.html.

34. http://en.wikipedia.org/wiki/A%26F_Quarterly.

35. Robert H. Halowell III, "The Selling Points of Direct Mail," *Trusts & Estates,* December 1994, pp. 39–41.

36. "Promotional Products Fact Sheet," Promotional Products Association International, Irving, TX, 1995.

37. PPAI 2010 Promotional Products Fact Sheet, http://www.ppa.org/NR/rdonlyres/35235FB0-A367-4498-B0AF-EE88085C3A60B/0/PPAIProProFactSheet.pdf.

38. Ibid.

39. *How Specialty Advertising Affects Goodwill* (Irving, TX: Specialty Advertising Association International, 1993).

40. Avraham Shama and Jack K. Thompson, "Promotion Gifts: Help or Hindrance?" *Mortgage Banking,* February 1989, pp. 49–51.

CHAPTER 15

1. Julie Liesse, "Inside Burnett's Vaunted Buying Machine," *Advertising Age,* July 25, 1994, p. S6.

2. Yumiko Ono, "Cordiant Puts Hamilton in Key U.S. Post," *Advertising Age,* July 18, 1997, p. B2.

3. Stephanie Thompson, "Universal McCann Gets $150 Million Nestlé Account," AdAge.com, April 12, 2002; Richard Linnett and Jack Neff, "Mindshare Wins $600 Million Gillette Media Account," AdAge.com, September 26, 2002 (retrieved from www.adage.com).

4. Jon Lafayette, "Agency Media Staffs Gain Clout," *Advertising Age,* March 4, 1991, p. 12; Peter J. Danaher and Roland T. Rust, "Determining the Optimal Level of Media Spending," *Journal of Advertising Research,* January/February 1994, p. 28.

5. "Business: Hi Ho, Hi Ho, Down the Data Mine We Go," *The Economist,* August 23, 1997, pp. 47–48.

6. Tom Duncan and Sandra Moriarty, *Driving Brand Value* (New York: McGraw-Hill, 1997), p. 100.

7. Veronis Suhler Stevenson, 16th Annual Communications Industry Forecast, August 5, 2002 (retrieved from www.veronissuhler.com).

8. "Fox Breaks Prime-Time Pricing Record," September 12, 2005 (retrieved from www.adweek.com).

9. Wayne Friedman, "Discovery Pitches Ad Convergence," *Advertising Age,* March 2000 (retrieved from www.adage.com, December 2000).

10. Dorothy Giobbe, "Newspapers Urged to Be More Creative," *Editor & Publisher,* July 2, 1994, p. 38.

11. Christina Merrill, "Media Rising," *Adweek,* November 9, 1998 (retrieved from http://members.adweek.com/archive).

12. R. Craig Endicott and Kenneth Wylie, "Special Report: Agency Report," *Advertising Age,* May 2, 2005, p. S–1 and p. S–12.

13. Winston Fletcher, "Independents May Have Had Their Day: Media Buying Is Returning to the Full-Service Fold, but This Time Only at Arm's Length," *Financial Times,* July 27, 1999, p. 15.

14. Christina Merrill, "Media Agencies: What's in a Name? Lots."

15. Adapted from Donald W. Jugenheimer, Arnold M. Barban, and Peter B. Turk, *Advertising Media: Strategy and Tactics* (Dubuque, IA: Brown & Benchmark, 1992), p. 131.

16. Ibid., pp. 131–33.

17. Jim Surmanek, *Introduction to Advertising Media: Research, Planning, and Buying* (Chicago: NTC Business Books, 1993), p. 54.

18. Adapted from Surmanek, *Introduction to Advertising Media,* p. 106.

19. Jugenheimer, Barban, and Turk, *Advertising Media: Strategy and Tactics,* p. 135.

20. Joe Mandese, "Revisiting Ad Reach, Frequency," *Advertising Age,* November 27, 1995, p. 46.

21. Schultz, Tannenbaum, and Lauterborn, *Integrated Marketing Communications: Putting It Together & Making It Work,* pp. 116–22, 132–33; Julie Liesse, "Buying by the Numbers? Hardly," *Advertising Age,* July 25, 1994, p. S16.

22. Rein Rijkens, *European Advertising Strategies* (London: Cassell, 1992), pp. 86–87.

23. Special Report: Best Media Plan Competition, "Guerrilla Tactics Get Panasonic Noticed," *Strategy* (Canada), March 27, 2000, p. BMP10.

24. Todd Pruzan, "Global Media: Distribution Slows, but Rates Climb," *Advertising Age International,* January 16, 1995, p. I19.

25. Neil Kelliher, "Magazine Media Planning for 'Effectiveness': Getting the People Back into the Process," *Journal of Consumer Marketing,* Summer 1990, pp. 47–55.

26. Kenneth Longman, *Advertising* (New York: Harcourt Brace Jovanovich, 1971), pp. 211–12.

27. "The Power of Partnership," *NBC Marketing Supplement, Advertising Age,* November 16, 1992, p. 13.

28. Kevin Goldman, "Digital Warms Couch Potatoes with Only-on-Sunday TV Ads," *The Wall Street Journal,* November 22, 1994, p. B8.

29. Telmar Web site, July 2004 (www.telmar.com).

CHAPTER 16

1. Andrew Bary, "No. 4 Progressive Closes In on Auto-Insurance Leaders," *The Wall Street Journal* (retrieved from http://online.wsj.com/article/SB125763204384036233.html, on June 28, 2010).

2. www.geico.com/about/corporate/at-a-glance.

3. Maya Frazier, "GEICO's $500 M Outlay Pays off, "*Advertising Age,* July 9, 2007.

4. "Little Lizard Says Ello to a New Inflection," *Harford Courant,* February 22, 2006.

5. Mya Frazier, "GEICO Ad Chief Builds Insurer into Master of Marketing," *Advertising Age,* June 19, 2006.

6. Ibid.

7. Theresa Howard, "Gecko Wasn't First Choice for GEICO," *USA Today,* July 16, 2006 (http://www.usatoday.com/money/advertising/adtrack 2006-07-16-geico_x.htm).

8. What Is the Direct Marketing Association? (http://www.the-dma.org/aboutdma/whatisthedma.shtml).

9. Joan Throckmorton, "We Are Interactive—Repeat—We Are Interactive," *Direct,* November 1997.

10. Bob Stone, *Successful Direct Marketing Methods,* 4th ed. (Chicago: NTC Business Books, 1988), p. 3.

11. www.dol.gov.

12. www.the-dma.org.

13. "U.S. Direct Marketing Today: Economic Impact 2005," DMA/Global Insight (www.the-dma.org/research/economicimpact2005ExecSummary.pdf).

14. "Economic Impact: U.S. Direct Marketing Today Executive Summary; International Direct Marketing Expenditures in All Markets (Ranked by Level of 2001 Forecast)" (retrieved from www.the-dma.org).

15. Peppers and Rogers Group, Marketing 1 to 1 (www.m1to1.com/success_stories).

16. Thomas E. Caruso, "Kotler: Future Marketers Will Focus on Customer Data Base to Compete Globally," *Marketing News,* June 8, 1992, pp. 21–22.

17. Tom Van Riper, "The Why of Best Buy," (retrieved from www.forbes.com/business/2008/04/02/retail-best-buy-bizcommerce-cx_tvr_0402 retail.html, April 2, 2008).

18. Seth Godin, "GUEST COLUMNIST: Permission Key to Successful Marketing," *Advertising Age,* November 1997 (http://adage.com).

19. Poulos, "Customer Loyalty and the Marketing Database," pp. 32–35.

20. Mollie Neal, "Marketers Looking Ahead in Chicago," *Direct Marketing,* March 1993, pp. 9–11.

21. Robert A. Peterson and Thomas R. Wotruba, "What Is Direct Selling?—Definition, Perspectives, and Research Agenda," *Journal of Personal Selling and Sales Management,* 16, no. 4 (Fall 1996), pp. 1–16.

22. "DM Advertising Expenditures Compared to Total U.S. Advertising Expenditures, 2008," Direct Marketing Association, 2008 (retrieved from http://www.marketingcharts.com/direct/direct-marketing-to-account-for-53-of-us-ad-spend-in-2009-6939/).

23. Cyndee Miller, "Telemarketing Cited as Chief Form of Direct Marketing," *Marketing News,* p. 6.

24. "Brief History of Toll-Free Numbers" (retrieved from www.tollfreenumbers.com, August 7, 2004).

25. "New Media/Web 2.0, E-Mail Gaining Response Results (and Budgets): DMA Report," Brendan B. Read, March 12, 2009 (retrieved from http://www.fundraisingsuccessmag.com/article/new-mediaweb-20-e-mail-gaining-response-results-and-budgets-dma-report-404370/1).

26. Personal Interview with Tom Campanaro, President, Total Gym Inc., December 2000.

27. Adapted from Barton A. Weitz, Stephen B. Castleberry, and John F. Tanner Jr., *Selling: Building Partnerships* (Burr Ridge, IL: Richard D. Irwin, Inc., 1992), p. 5.

28. Edwin Klewer, Robert Shaffer, and Bonnie Binnig, "Sales Is an Investment, Attrition an Expense," *Journal of Health Care Marketing,* September 1995, p. 12.

29. Susan A. Friedmann, *Exhibiting at Trade Shows* (Menlo Park, CA: Crisp Publications, 1992), p. V.

30. Ibid., p. 16.

31. Quoted in "Customized MarketMail Testimonials: The Krispy Kreme Doughnut Company" (retrieved from www.usps.com/customizedmarketmail/testimonials.htm, September 1, 2004).

32. Friedmann, *Exhibiting at Trade Shows,* p. 24.

33. Ibid., pp. 34–39.

34. Ibid., p. 44.

35. Ibid., pp. 70–71.

36. Ibid., p. 90.

37. "Market Statistics—America," Packaging-Gateway.com (retrieved from www.packaginggateway.com/market_statistics_americas.asp#3, April 18, 2008).

38. W. Wossen Kassaye and Dharmendra Verma, "Balancing Traditional Packaging Functions with the New 'Green' Packaging Concerns," *SAM Advanced Management Journal,* Autumn 1992, pp. 15–23.

39. Ibid.

40. Chris Baum, "10th Annual Packaging Consumer Survey 1994: Consumers Want It All—And Now," *Packaging,* August 1994, pp. 40–43.

41. Kassaye and Verma, "Balancing Traditional Packaging Functions with the New 'Green' Packaging Concerns."

42. "Excerpt: Under the Radar," *Brandweek,* December 8, 1997 (http://members.adweek.com/archive/adweek/current/brandweek).

43. Peter Breen, "Seeds of Change," *Promo Sourcebook Supplement,* October 2000, p. 18.

44. Larry Light, "Trustmarketing: The Brand Relationship Marketing Mandate for the 90s," address to American Association of Advertising Agencies annual meeting, Laguna Niguel, CA, April 23, 1993.

45. Magid M. Abraham and Leonard M. Lodish, "Getting the Most Out of Advertising and Promotion," *Harvard Business Review,* May/June 1990, p. 51.

46. Light, "Trustmarketing."

47. Larry Light, "At the Center of It All Is the Brand," *Advertising Age,* March 29, 1993, p. 22.

48. *The Point of Purchase Advertising Industry Fact Book* (Washington, DC: POPAI, 1997), p. 51.

49. Kelly Shermach, "Study: Most Shoppers Notice P-O-P Material," *Marketing News,* January 1995, p. 27.

50. *The Point of Purchase Advertising Industry Fact Book,* p. 39.

51. Kelly Shermach, "Great Strides Made in P-O-P Technology," *Marketing News,* January 2, 1995, pp. 8–9.

52. Angela Lawson, "The End of the Line," June 18, 2004 (retrieved from www.kioskmarketplace.com, August 8, 2004).

53. Betsy Spethman, "Clipping Slows," www.promomagazine.com, April 1, 2006.

54. The 16th Annual Survey of Promotional Practices, Donnelley Marketing Inc., 1994.

55. "Coupon Trend Reports," Santella & Associates (retrieved from http://www.santella.com/Trends.htm).

56. http://www.catalinamarketing.com/company/FAQs.html.

57. Ibid.

58. Stephanie Moore, "Rebate Madness: How to Defend Yourself against Ruthless Rebate Scams" (retrieved from www.consumeraffairs.com, August 8, 2004).

59. *Washington Post,* Tuesday, February 1, 2005; Page C10, washingtonpost.com, www.washingtonpost.com/wp-dyn/articles/A52798-2005Jan31.html.

60. Lorraine Calvacca, "Polybagging Products to Pick Up Customers," *Folio: The Magazine for Magazine Management,* January 1993, p. 26.

CHAPTER 17

1. Jim Osborne, "Getting Full Value from Public Relations," *Public Relations Journal,* October/November 1994, p. 64.

2. CSPI Newsroom, "Ben & Jerry's Fudging the Truth, Says CSPI: Nothing 'All-Natural' about Ingredients," July 30, 2002 (retrieved from www.cspinet.org/new/200207301.html, August 8, 2004).

3. Ben & Jerry's Homemade, Inc., press release, "Ben & Jerry's Response to CSPI Concerns," July 31, 2002 (retrieved from www.benjerry.com, August 8, 2004).

4. Ben & Jerry's Homemade, Inc., press release, "Ben & Jerry's Voluntarily Initiates the Recall of Pints of Karamel Sutra Ice Cream with Code 02/14/04," March 28, 2003 (retrieved from www.benjerry.com, August 8, 2004).

5. Sandra Moriarty, "PR and IMC: The Benefits of Integration," *Public Relations Quarterly,* Fall 1994, pp. 38–44.

6. Publisher's Statement, *Inside PR,* March 1993, p. 3.

7. Thomas L. Harris, "PR Gets Personal," *Direct Marketing,* April 1994, pp. 29–32.

8. Al Ries and Laura Ries, *The 22 Immutable Laws of Branding* (New York: HarperCollins, 1998), pp. 25–31.

9. Bill Patterson, "Crisis Impact on Reputation Management," *Public Relations Journal,* November 1993, p. 48.

10. Ben White, "Stewart's Legal Problems Hurt Firm," *Washington Post,* August 4, 2004, p. E01 (retrieved from www.washingtonpost.com/wp-dyn/articles/A38202-2004Aug3.html).

11. Dennis L. Wilcox, *Public Relations Strategies and Tactics* (New York: HarperCollins, 1994), p. 381.

12. "What's Your Best Marketing Tool?" *Public Relations Journal,* February 1994, p. 12.

13. Adapted from Stephanie Gruner, "Event Marketing: Making the Most of Sponsorship Dollars," *Inc.,* August 1996, p. 88.

14. IEG FAQ:"What Is Sponsorship?" IEG Network 1998 (www.sponsorship.com).

15. "Sponsorship Spending Recedes for First Time; Better Days Seen Ahead," (http://www.sponsorship.com/IEGInsights/Forecast—Recession-Slams-Brakes-On-Sponsorship-Sp.aspx).

16. "FIFA Secures $1.6 Billion in World Cup Sponsorship Revenue," June 3, 2010 (http://www.sponsorship.com/news—information/news/2010/06-june/fifa-secures-$1-6-billion-in-world-cup-sponsorship.aspx).

17. Thomas R. Duncan and Sandra E. Moriarty, *Driving Brand Value: Using Integrated Marketing to Manage Stakeholder Relationships* (New York: McGraw-Hill, 1997), p. 203.

18. Ibid.; Terry G. Vavra, *Aftermarketing: How to Keep Customers for Life Through Relationship Marketing* (Burr Ridge, IL: Irwin Professional Publishing, 1992), p. 190.

19. Vavra, *Aftermarketing,* p. 192.

20. IEG Sponsorship Report (www.sponsorship.com).

21. "Sponsorship Spending to See Biggest Rise in Five Years," IEG Sponsorship Report, December 27, 2004 (www.sponsorship.com).

22. *IEG's 25th Annual Sponsorship Report* (retrieved from http://www.sponsorship.com).

23. David Sweet, "Everything Is for Sale in the World of Sports," January 24, 2008 (retrieved from www.msnbc.com).

23. "Where the Dollars Go," IEG Sponsorship Report 2003 (www.sponsorship.com/learn/wheredollarsgo.asp).

24. Junu Bryan Kim, "Most Sponsorships Waste Money: Exec," *Advertising Age,* June 21, 1993, pp. S2, S4.

25. "Bavaria Beer website traffic rockets after World Cup stunt," June 18, 2010 (http://www.marketingmagazine.co.uk/news/1010738/Bavaria-Beer-website-traffic-rockets-World-Cup-stunt/).

26. Lesa Ukman, "Assertions," IEG Sponsorship Report, February 23, 1998 (www.sponsorship.com).

27. Vans Warped Tour '06 (http://www.warpedtour.com/).

28. Wilcox, *Public Relations Strategies and Tactics,* p. 384.

29. Cliff Peale, "Great American to Name Ballpark," *Cincinnati Enquirer,* July 1, 2000.

30. John Karolefski, "The Sport of Naming," Brand Channel.com, May 13, 2002 (www.brandchannel.com).

31. Paul Stanley, "Sponsownership: Sponsorships Will Become Standard for Events," *Potentials in Marketing,* June 1990, p. 64.

32. Lesa Ukman, "Assertions," IEG Sponsorship Report, January 26, 1998 (www.sponsorship.com).

33. Vavra, *Aftermarketing,* p. 191.

34. "Corporate Advertising/Phase II, An Expanded Study of Corporate Advertising Effectiveness," conducted for *Time* magazine by Yankelovich, Skelly & White, undated.

index

Note: page numbers with n indicate note.